# JOURNAL FOR THE STUDY OF THE NEW TESTAMENT SUPPLEMENT SERIES

## 62

*Executive Editor*
David Hill

JSOT Press
Sheffield

# John
## the Baptizer
## and Prophet

### A Socio-Historical Study

### Robert L. Webb

Journal for the Study of the New Testament
Supplement Series 62

Copyright © 1991 Sheffield Academic Press

Published by JSOT Press
JSOT Press is an imprint of
Sheffield Academic Press Ltd
The University of Sheffield
343 Fulwood Road
Sheffield S10 3BP
England

Printed on acid-free paper in Great Britain
by
Billing & Sons Ltd
Worcester

British Library Cataloguing in Publication Data

Webb, Robert L.
    John the Baptizer and Prophet: A Socio-Historical Study.
    —(JSNT supplements. ISSN 0143-5108; 62)
    I. Title   II. Series
    232.94

ISBN 1-85075-316-4

# CONTENTS

# PREFACE

This work began as a seed sown by Dr Tom Wright who, over several pots of tea at an annual meeting of the Society of Biblical Literature, planted within me an interest in recent developments in historical-Jesus research. But it was in the Department of Biblical Studies at the University of Sheffield that this seed germinated and grew. It was pruned and given shape under the watchful care of the Department's professors and lecturers, and it was strengthened by critical examination in the weekly Staff and Post-Graduate Seminar. It finally came to full maturity as a PhD thesis submitted to the University in 1990, of which this work is a minor revision.

In bringing this work to its present state numerous people have provided invaluable assistance and stimulation. My supervisors, Dr David Hill and Dr Philip Davies, and more recently Dr Loveday Alexander, have guided and encouraged me along the way. Dr Hill read my work with meticulous care and contributed immeasurably to its substance and clarity. Though he retired from his post at the University, he continued to provide me with invaluable supervision and assistance. Dr Davies challenged me to look at my data in new ways and to think creatively, and he introduced me to the fascinating field of Qumran studies. Dr Alexander stepped into the breach when Dr Hill retired and assisted in the final shaping of the thesis.

Good friends stood with me when the struggles of research seemed too great. By being there and listening, or joining me in a run or a game of squash, they encouraged me to persevere. Particularly helpful in this regard were Dr Gavin McGrath, Mr Peter Gosnell, Ms Nancy Calvert and Dr Mark Brett. They knew the same struggles of thesis research and so could truly empathize with me. As well, Dr Tom Wright and Dr Mark Brett read my thesis carefully and made many valuable suggestions. My mother, Mrs Doreen Webb, also read it in its entirety; she was the most careful proofreader I had. I wish to thank my good friend, Mr Rick Wiebe, who read this work at its proof stage and also indexed it for me. I appreciate the meticulous care he takes in what seems a thankless task, but one which all students and scholars truly appreciate. This book is better and clearer as a result of all their help.

Tyndale House Research Council assisted me financially for two years. This help from them I greatly appreciated. They also provided a wider context in which to meet other students and to develop new friends as well as a quiet place to study. I also wish to thank the Tom Lane Home Group for their Christian fellowship; they accepted a foreign student and his family into their midst, welcoming us and making us feel at home with them. Special thanks must also be expressed to Miss Marjorie Nunn and Miss Connie Reville, whose constant support and care for each of us made our four years in Sheffield much brighter.

But it is to my family that I owe a debt which I could never repay. My parents, Dr Bud Webb and Mrs Doreen Webb, steadfastly strengthened me with their prayers and encouragement. My two sons, James and Joshua, showed understanding beyond their years as their Dad wrote 'another book' stuck away in his 'shoebox' study. They helped my sense of balance by dragging me out to play twenty-one with our new basketball. Finally, for Pat, my wife, I have the deepest appreciation of all. She has been a shining light in my times of darkness and a source of inspiration in my times of discouragement. 'She is worth far more than rubies.' I wish to dedicate this book to Pat, James and Joshua as a small token of my gratitude to them for their support.

As a note of interest, the thesis was completed the weekend on which St John the Baptist Day fell, June 24, 1990.

Robert L. Webb
St Andrews, Scotland
June 10, 1991

# ABBREVIATIONS

| | |
|---|---|
| AB | Anchor Bible |
| *AbrN* | *Abr-Nahrain* |
| AGJU | Arbeiten zur Geschichte des antiken Judentums und des Urchristentums |
| *AJT* | *American Journal of Theology* |
| ALGHJ | Arbeiten zur Literatur und Geschichte des hellenistischen Judentums |
| *AmerAnth* | *American Anthropologist* |
| *ANRW* | *Aufstieg und Niedergang der römischen Welt* |
| ANTJ | Arbeiten zum Neuen Testament und Judentum |
| *APOT* | R.H. Charles (ed.), *Apocrypha and Pseudepigrapha of the Old Testament* |
| *ASTI* | *Annual of the Swedish Theological Institute* |
| ATANT | Abhandlungen zur Theologie des Alten und Neuen Testaments |
| *AusBR* | *Australian Biblical Review* |
| *BA* | *Biblical Archaeologist* |
| BAGD | W. Bauer, W.F. Arndt, F.W. Gingrich and F.W. Danker, *A Greek-English Lexicon of the New Testament and Other Early Christian Literature* |
| *BASOR* | *Bulletin of the Americal Schools of Oriental Research* |
| BASORSup | Bulletin of the Americal Schools of Oriental Research Supplement Series |
| BBB | Bonner biblische Beiträge |
| BDB | F. Brown, S.R. Driver and C.A. Briggs, *A Hebrew and English Lexicon of the Old Textament* |
| BDF | F. Blass, A. Debrunner and R.W. Funk, *A Greek Grammar of the New Testament and Other Early Christian Literature* |
| BETL | Bibliotheca ephemeridum theologicarum lovaniensium |
| *BHS* | *Biblia hebraica stuttgartensia* |
| *Bib* | *Biblica* |
| BibOr | Biblica et orientalia |
| *BJRL* | *Bulletin of the John Rylands University Library of Manchester* |
| BJS | Brown Judaic Studies |
| *BK* | *Bibel und Kirche* |
| BNTC | Black's New Testament Commentaries |

| | |
|---|---|
| *BR* | *Biblical Research* |
| BSt | Biblische Studien |
| *BZ* | *Biblische Zeitschrift* |
| BZAW | Beihefte zur Zeitschrift für die alttestamentliche Wissenschaft |
| BZNW | Beihefte zur Zeitschrift für die neutestamentliche Wissenschaft |
| *CBQ* | *Catholic Biblical Quarterly* |
| CBQMS | Catholic Biblical Quarterly Monograph Series |
| CCWJCW | Cambridge Commentaries on Writings of the Jewish and Christian World 200 BC to AD 200 |
| CGTC | Cambridge Greek Testament Commentary |
| CNT | Commentaire du Nouveau Testament |
| ConBNT | Coniectanea biblica, New Testament |
| *ConNT* | *Coniectanea neotestamentica* |
| CRINT | Compendia rerum iudaicarum ad novum testamentum |
| CSCT | Columbia Studies in the Classical Tradition |
| *CurTM* | *Currents in Theology and Mission* |
| DBSup | Dictionnaire de la Bible, Supplément |
| EKKNT | Evangelisch-katholischer Kommentar zum Neuen Testament |
| *EncJud* | *Encyclopaedia Judaica* (1971) |
| *ETR* | *Etudes théologiques et religieuses* |
| *EvQ* | *Evangelical Quarterly* |
| *ExpTim* | *Expository Times* |
| FFNT | Foundations and Facets: New Testament |
| *FoiVie* | *Foi et Vie* |
| FOTL | The Forms of the Old Testament Literature |
| FRLANT | Forschungen zur Religion und Literatur des Alten und Neuen Testaments |
| GNS | Good News Studies |
| *GTJ* | *Grace Theological Journal* |
| HAR | Hebrew Annual Review |
| *HDB* | J. Hastings (ed.), *A Dictionary of the Bible* |
| HDR | Harvard Dissertations in Religion |
| *HeyJ* | *Heythrop Journal* |
| *HibJ* | *Hibbert Journal* |
| HSM | Harvard Semitic Monographs |
| HTKNT | Herders theologischer Kommentar zum Neuen Testament |
| *HTR* | *Harvard Theological Review* |
| *HUCA* | *Hebrew Union College Annual* |
| ICC | International Critical Commentary |
| *IDB* | G.A. Buttrick (ed.), *Interpreter's Dictionary of the Bible* |

| | |
|---|---|
| *IDBSup* | *Interpreter's Dictionary of the Bible,* Supplementary Volume |
| *Int* | *Interpretation* |
| *ISBE* | G.W. Bromiley (ed.), *The International Standard Bible Encyclopedia,* rev. edn |
| *ITQ* | *Irish Theological Quarterly* |
| *JBL* | *Journal of Biblical Literature* |
| *JewEnc* | *The Jewish Encyclopedia* |
| *JJS* | *Journal of Jewish Studies* |
| *JNES* | *Journal of Near Eastern Studies* |
| *JQR* | *Jewish Quarterly Review* |
| *JR* | *Journal of Religion* |
| *JSJ* | *Journal for the Study of Judaism in the Persian, Hellenistic and Roman Period* |
| *JSNT* | *Journal for the Study of the New Testament* |
| JSNTSup | Journal for the Study of the New Testament Supplement Series |
| *JSOT* | *Journal for the Study of the Old Testament* |
| JSOTSup | Journal for the Study of the Old Testament Supplement Series |
| *JSP* | *Journal for the Study of the Pseudepigrapha* |
| JSPSup | Journal for the Study of the Pseudepigrapha Supplement Series |
| *JSS* | *Journal of Semitic Studies* |
| *JTS* | *Journal of Theological Studies* |
| KAT | Kommentar zum Alten Testament |
| LCL | Loeb Classical Library |
| LSJ | H.G. Liddell, R. Scott and H.S. Jones, *A Greek-English Lexicon* |
| MeyerK | H.A.W. Meyer, Kritisch-exegetischer Kommentar über das Neue Testament |
| MM | J.H. Moulton and G. Milligan, *The Vocabulary of the Greek Testament Illustrated from the Papyri and Other Non-Literary Sources* |
| *NASB* | *New Americal Standard Bible* |
| NCB | New Century Bible |
| *Neot* | *Neotestamentica* |
| NHS | Nag Hammadi Studies |
| NICNT | New International Commentary on the New Testament |
| NICOT | New International Commentary on the Old Testament |
| *NIDNTT* | C. Brown (ed.), *The New International Dictionary of New Testament Theology* |
| NIGTC | New International Greek Testament Commentary |
| *NorTT* | *Norsk Teologisk Tidsskrift* |

| | |
|---|---|
| *NovT* | *Novum Testamentum* |
| NovTSup | Novum Testamentum Supplements |
| *NRSV* | *New Revised Standard Version* |
| NTAbh | Neutestamentliche Abhandlungen |
| NTL | New Testament Library |
| *NTS* | *New Testament Studies* |
| NTTS | New Testament Tools and Studies |
| *Numen* | *Numen: International Review for the History of Religions* |
| NumenSup | Numen Supplements |
| *OrChr* | *Orien christianus* |
| OTG | Old Testament Guides |
| OTL | Old Testament Library |
| *OTP* | J.H. Charlesworth (ed.), *The Old Testament Pseudepigrapha* |
| *OTS* | *Oudtestamentische Studiën* |
| *PEQ* | *Palestine Exploration Quarterly* |
| PVTG | Pseudepigrapha Veteris Testamenti graece |
| *RB* | *Revue biblique* |
| *REJ* | *Revue des études juives* |
| *Rel* | *Religion* |
| *ResQ* | *Restoration Quarterly* |
| *RevExp* | *Review and Expositor* |
| *RevQ* | *Revue de Qumran* |
| *RGG* | *Religion in Geschichte und Gegenwart* |
| *RL* | *Religion in Life* |
| *RSV* | *Revised Standard Version* |
| *RTR* | *Reformed Theological Review* |
| SB | Sources bibliques |
| SBLDS | Society of Biblical Literature Dissertation Series |
| SBLMS | Society of Biblical Literature Monograph Series |
| SBLSBS | Society of Biblical Literature Sources for Biblical Study |
| SBLSCS | Society of Biblical Literature Septuagint and Cognate Studies |
| SBLSP | Society of Biblical Literature Seminar Papers |
| SBLTT | Society of Biblical Literature Texts and Translations |
| SBT | Studies in Biblical Theology |
| *Scr* | *Scripture* |
| *SE* | *Studia Evangelica I, II, III* ( = TU 73 [1959], 87 [1964], 88 [1964], etc.) |
| *Sem* | *Semitica* |
| SJ | Studia judaica |
| SJLA | Studies in Judaism in Late Antiquity |
| *SJT* | *Scottish Journal of Theology* |

| | |
|---|---|
| SNTSMS | Society of New Testament Studies Monograph Series |
| SNTU | Studien zum Neuen Testament und seiner Umwelt |
| *ST* | *Studia theologica* |
| *StBibTh* | *Studia Biblica et Theologica* |
| STDJ | Studies on the Texts of the Desert of Judah |
| Str-B | H.L. Strack and P. Billerbeck, *Kommentar zum Neuen Testament aus Talmud und Midrasch* |
| SVTP | Studia in Veteris Testamenti pseudepigrapha |
| TBü | Theologische Bücherei |
| *TDNT* | G. Kittel and G. Friedrich (eds.), *Theological Dictionary of the new Testament* |
| *TDOT* | G.J. Botterweck and H. Ringgren (eds.), *Theological Dictionary of the Old Testament* |
| *ThVia* | *Theologica Viatorum* |
| *TLZ* | *Theologischer Literaturzeitung* |
| *TRu* | *Theologische Rundschau* |
| TU | Texte und Untersuchungen |
| *TWOT* | R.L. Harris, G.L. Archer and B.K. Waltke (eds.), *Theological Wordbook of the Old Testament* |
| *TynBul* | *Tyndale Bulletin* |
| *TZ* | *Theologische Zeitschrift* |
| *USQR* | *Union Seminary Quarterly Review* |
| *VC* | *Vigiliae christianae* |
| *VT* | *Vetus Testamentum* |
| VTSup | Vetus Testamentum Supplements |
| WBC | Word Biblical Commentary |
| WUNT | Wissenschaftliche Untersuchungen zum Neuen Testament |
| *ZAW* | *Zeitschrift für die alttestamentliche Wissenschaft* |
| *ZNW* | *Zeitschrift für die neutestamentliche Wissenschaft* |
| *ZRGG* | *Zeitschrift für Religions- und Geistesgeschichte* |
| *ZTK* | *Zeitschrift für Theologie und Kirche* |

Abbreviations of ancient literature should be self-evident. References to biblical works is according to the versification in English translations. If the versification in the MT or LXX is different, I only make reference to the different versification when making an explicit reference to the foreign language of the text involved. In these cases the alternate versification is placed in parentheses and identified as either MT or LXX.

All secondary sources are cited in the footnotes by the author's name and a convenient short title. A second reference to the same work in the same footnote is by the author's name alone. Full titles and other bibliographic information are provided in the Bibliography.

Chapter 1

# INTRODUCTION

## 1.1 *Background and Orientation*

This book owes its origin to the fact that I have been captivated by the enigmatic figure of the historical Jesus and fascinated by the ongoing attempts of biblical scholars to understand him. One of the more secure and widely accepted historical 'facts' about Jesus is his relationship with a figure usually called John the Baptist. Indeed, each of the four canonical Gospels begins its narrative of the public ministry of Jesus with a description of John the Baptist as the forerunner and baptizer of Jesus. Were it not for this portrayal of John, he would probably have remained a minor character mentioned in Josephus' *Antiquities* and have been the subject of a footnote or two in academic writing. Instead, because of the Evangelists' use of John in their narratives, he has assumed much greater importance; nevertheless, he has remained largely in the shadow of Jesus. The investigation of Jesus' relationship with John must be left for another time. Our concern in this book is with John the Baptist himself—the quest for the 'historical John' as it were—but it is helpful to begin by placing this concern in the larger context of historical-Jesus research, for it is in this context that John is usually discussed.

In recent times the scholarly field of Jesus research has burgeoned into a popular and productive endeavour. That it has achieved this status again is quite remarkable. With his classic work, *Von Reimarus zu Wrede*, which in translation is known by its more descriptive title, *The Quest of the Historical Jesus*, Albert Schweitzer sounded the death knell in 1906 of what became known as the 'Old Quest'. In the succeeding decades the historical judgment of Rudolf Bultmann was highly influential:

> I do indeed think that we can know almost nothing concerning the life and personality of Jesus, since the early Christian sources show no interest in either, are moreover fragmentary and often legendary; and other sources about Jesus do not exist.[1]

Bultmann's perspective was also to influence the study of NT theology. He began his *Theology of the New Testament* with this well-known statement:

The *message of Jesus* is a presupposition for the theology of the New Testament rather than a part of that theology itself. . . Thus, theological thinking—the theology of the New Testament—begins with the *kerygma* of the earliest Church and not before.[2]

Students of Bultmann however became dissatisfied with the theological consequences of his position. In 1953, Ernst Käsemann delivered the lecture which has since been recognized to herald the beginning of the 'New Quest' for the historical Jesus.[3] However, this New Quest was not without its limitations and concern for the study of the historical Jesus declined.[4]

In the last decade, as mentioned above, scholars have developed a renewed interest in historical-Jesus study. To distinguish this from the Old and New Quests, this renewed interest has been described by N.T. Wright as a 'Third Quest', and by James H. Charlesworth as 'Jesus Research'.[5] Such interest is not coordinated, nor is it the product of a particular theological perspective. In fact, those engaged exhibit a wide diversity of theological persuasions. Yet it might be said that two factors are common to these scholars. In the first place, they possess the conviction that certain things about Jesus may actually be known within the bounds of historical probability. Secondly, they hold to the perspective that Jesus must be understood within the context of the social, cultural and political dynamics of first-century Judaism. E.P. Sanders, one of the scholars who contributed to this research with a major work, *Jesus and Judaism*, expresses this conviction and perspective quite succinctly when describing the renewed interest in historical-Jesus study:

> The dominant view today seems to be that we can know pretty well what Jesus was out to accomplish, that we can know a lot about what he said, and that those two things make sense within the world of first-century Judaism.[6]

A number of methodological features also characterize at least some if not all of this research. First of all, there is an increased sensitivity to the social setting of persons and groups within Palestine. A growing

1   Bultmann, *Jesus*, 8.
2   Bultmann, *Theology*, 1.3, his emphasis.
3   Käsemann, 'Historischen Jesus', 125-53; in translation as 'Historical Jesus', 15-47. Cf. Robinson, 'New Quest', 9-125.
4   For criticism from one perspective, see Meyer, *Aims of Jesus*, 48-59, and from quite a different one, see Harvey and Ogden, 'New Quest?' 197-242.
5   Neill and Wright, *Interpretation*, 379; Charlesworth, *Jesus Within Judaism*, 1; Charlesworth objects to the use of the terms 'search' or 'quest'.
6   Sanders, *Jesus and Judaism*, 2. Examples of recent major works that exemplify this renewed interest include (in chronological order): Vermes, *Jesus the Jew*; Meyer, *Aims of Jesus*; Riches, *Transformation of Judaism*; Harvey, *Constraints of History*; Borg, *Conflict, Holiness and Politics*; Sanders, *Jesus and Judaism*; Horsley, *Spiral of Violence*; Borg, *New Vision*; Charlesworth, *Jesus within Judaism*.

realization of the social and religious complexity of Judaism contributes to this sensitivity, as does a greater appreciation of the contributions which may be made by related disciplines such as sociology and cultural anthropology.[7]

Secondly, this research lacks an explicit theological agenda (especially in contrast with the 'New Quest'). This is not only supported by the fact that those involved are drawn from a wide theological spectrum, but also by this very claim sometimes actually being made.[8] Lack of an *explicit* theological *agenda*, however, does not signify a rejection of *implicit* theological *interest*, or insensitivity to the theological implications of such research.[9] Rather, the intent is first of all to answer historical questions rather than theological ones.

Thirdly, from this last statement arises the observation that much of this historical-Jesus study utilizes historical methodology—the historical questions are answered on historical grounds. Due to the incompleteness of the available historical data and the interpretive nature of historical knowledge, historical reconstruction of the past involves the construction of hypotheses based upon probabilities.[10]

Fourthly, there has been developing within scholarly circles a realization that in the Second Temple period we cannot talk about 'normative Judaism'. At least two factors have contributed to this growing realization. First, a reconstruction of normative Judaism is heavily dependent upon the rabbinic literature, and there has been a greater appreciation of the problems with a wholesale reading of its data back into the first century. Yes, this literature may be relevant, but it must be used more critically than it has in the past. Also, we are now more aware of a large quantity of primary literature which is in fact from a pre-70 CE context and which may be profitably used to ascertain more adequately the diverse nature of first-century Judaism. This literature includes the Qumran scrolls as well as the increased number of extra-canonical Jewish texts from the Second Temple period.[11]

7  E.g. Horsley, *Spiral of Violence*; Borg, *New Vision*. The realization of this complexity within Second Temple Judaism is linked with a rejection of the concept of 'normative' Judaism in a pre-70 CE context; cf. the fourth point below.
8  E.g. Sanders, *Jesus and Judaism*, 2, 9.
9  In contrast to the quote above from Bultmann concerning the place of the historical Jesus in NT theology, compare this more recent statement by Goppelt (*Theology*, 1.6-7): 'Of primary importance for the Gospel tradition is the integration of the earthly ministry of Jesus and the kerygma so that the former becomes the supportive base for the latter. This "recollection" about Jesus remains, especially in the large Gospels, the primary intention. . . The interpretive explication of the Easter kerygma constituted the root of New Testament theology. Its base, however, was the recounting of the earthly ministry of Jesus. If we desire to represent New Testament theology in keeping with its intrinsic structure, then we must begin with the question of the earthly Jesus.' Thus, the subtitle to the first volume of Goppelt's NT theology is

Finally, this new interest in historical-Jesus studies exhibits an increasing emphasis upon Jesus' *actions*. At least one reason for this emphasis is a recognition that much of past Jesus research has focused upon the authenticity of Jesus' *sayings*. While not incorrect in itself, the impression is sometimes given that these words were spoken in a vacuum—as if they were contained in a paper read and discussed in an ancient graduate seminar in theology. However, examination of the historical Jesus needs to inquire, for example, concerning what was going on when Jesus healed, taught, or ate with 'sinners'. This is necessary for understanding these actions which are important for interpreting a historical figure and which also provide the social and historical context in which Jesus spoke.[12]

My work arises out of a fascination with this latest trend in Jesus research. In my preliminary investigations I sought for a starting point which was suitable both logically and methodologically. Sanders' book *Jesus and Judaism* had only been available for a year when I began my research, and its approach had a definite impact in shaping my thinking. He lists what he considers to be 'almost indisputable facts' concerning the life of Jesus:

1. Jesus was baptized by John the Baptist.
2. Jesus was a Galilean who preached and healed.
3. Jesus called disciples and spoke of there being twelve.
4. Jesus confined his activity to Israel.
5. Jesus engaged in a controversy about the temple.
6. Jesus was crucified outside Jerusalem by the Roman authorities.[13]

Of these facts he chooses Jesus' controversy about the temple as the starting point of his investigations, the results of which prove impressively fruitful. He places Jesus within the context of Jewish restoration eschatology, observing that 'the line from John the Baptist to Paul and the other early apostles is the line of Jewish eschatology, and it would be misleading to move the centre of our investigation off that line'. He states elsewhere that 'Jesus began his public work, as far as we have any

---

*The Ministry of Jesus in its Theological Significance.*
10  Sanders, *Jesus and Judaism*, 2-3; Neill and Wright, *Interpretation*, 398-400.
11  Cf. Charlesworth's discussion in *Jesus Within Judaism*.
12  Sanders, *Jesus and Judaism*, 3-18; Harvey, *Constraints*, 6-9; Borg, *New Vision*, 14-17. For further descriptions of these recent developments in Jesus research see Hollenbach, 'Recent Historical Jesus Studies', 61-78; Neill and Wright, *Interpretation*, 379-403; Charlesworth, *Jesus Within Judaism*, 1-29, 187-207, 223-43.
13  Sanders, *Jesus and Judaism*, 11. He lists two further 'facts', but these relate to the early Christian movement. The first is that 'after his death Jesus' followers continued as an identifiable movement', and the second fact is that 'at least some Jews persecuted at least parts of the new movement . . . , and it appears that this persecution endured at least to a time near the end of Paul's career. . .' Cf. the similar list in Harvey, *Constraints*, 6.

information at all about it, in close connection with John the Baptist, probably as a disciple'.[14] If some relationship with John the Baptist is the beginning point of Jesus' ministry, and Jesus' ministry continued in a 'line' from John, then the relationship between Jesus and John merits more careful investigation. Questions which deserve examination include: Was Jesus actually a disciple of John, and if so, what did this involve? Did Jesus participate in John's ministry? To what extent was Jesus' ministry a continuation of John's ministry, a development of it, a rejection of it, or a combination of these? What influences did John possibly have upon Jesus' ministry? To what extent did the people and the religious authorities perceive a relationship between Jesus' ministry and that of John? Before such questions can even be considered, a careful examination of John the Baptist would be required. Initially my plan for this work was to provide a historical analysis of John the Baptist as a preliminary stage to examining questions such as these. However, it soon became apparent that such a plan was too extensive. An investigation of even certain elements of John's ministry proved to be a task requiring more work than initially thought. Therefore, the relationship between John and Jesus has been set aside in order to focus exclusively upon an investigation of John's ministry.

Yet it may be asked why a fresh study of John the Baptist is required. Perhaps the easiest way to answer this question is by the simple observation that, generally speaking, the 'quest' for the historical John the Baptist has to a great extent followed the parallel quest for the historical Jesus. As the most recent stage of Jesus research represents a definite advance over the Old and New Quests, so the approaches and methods of this Jesus research may be profitably applied to research on John the Baptist. Before specifying these approaches as they apply to this work and John the Baptist research, the parallel relationship between the Quests for the historical Jesus and research on John should be established.

In the period during which scholars engaged in the Quests for the historical Jesus the approaches and methodologies which were applied to the quest for Jesus were also applied to John. In fact, much of the scholarly research on John the Baptist is found within larger works on Jesus. Thus, as the Gospels were subjected to historical criticism in the quest for Jesus, the figure of John was also subjected to similar criticism. For example, as the beginning of the Old Quest for the historical Jesus may be traced to Hermann Samuel Reimarus (first published in 1778), so also may the 'quest' for the historical John the Baptist. Reimarus argued that John and Jesus worked together to build each other up in the eyes of

14  Sanders, *Jesus and Judaism*, 8, 91.

the people. Their intention was essentially political. They sought to arouse the hopes of the people to expect deliverance from Rome by their support of the messianic King. John's role in this plot was to lay the groundwork for this expectation by his preaching, and to proclaim Jesus to be this Messiah at his baptism. Thus Reimarus interprets John as a political revolutionary.[15]

On the other hand, as pietistic lives of Jesus multiplied, they of course would include a section on John as well. Furthermore, because John was recognized as a saint, and for centuries had been a model for Christian monasticism,[16] pietistic lives of John were written as well.[17] Yet critical historical studies which focused upon John the Baptist were also produced. The most recent of these include Carl H. Kraeling, *John the Baptist* (1951), Charles H.H. Scobie, *John the Baptist* (1964), Jürgen Becker, *Johannes der Täufer und Jesus von Nazareth* (1972), and Josef Ernst, *Johannes der Täufer: Interpretation, Geschichte, Wirkungsgeschichte* (1989).

In 1911, Martin Dibelius, one of the fathers of form criticism, actually applied some of his insights to pericopae concerning John the Baptist in *Die urchristliche Überlieferung von Johannes dem Täufer* prior to publishing his classic study *Die Formgeschichte des Evangeliums*. He admits, however, that his work is not a historical investigation of John the Baptist: 'Eine Geschichte des Täufers und seiner Taufe ist noch nicht geschrieben; ich kann nur die literarhistorische Vorarbeit dazu liefern'.[18] It is, as the title indicates, an analysis of the early Christian traditions concerning John. Later historical works built on Dibelius' ground-breaking study.[19]

With the rise of redaction criticism in the 1950s even more significant contributions were made to the study of the NT pericopae concerning

---

15 Reimarus, *Fragments*, 135-50 (Part 2, §1-8). Reimarus, who lived from 1694 to 1768, never published his privately held views on religion which were contained in his personal manuscript *Apologie oder Schutzschrift für die vernünftigen Verehrer Gottes*. The entire work has never been published, but between 1774 and 1778 G.E. Lessing published seven excerpts as the *Wolfenbüttel Fragments* from Reimarus' *Apologie*, the last of which was 'On the Intention of Jesus and His Disciples'. It is this last fragment which is most well known, and the one referred to here.
  A fascinating play published in 1642 by G. Buchanan utilizes the story of John the Baptist as a political commentary upon English history of the day: *Tyrannicall-Government Anatomized: Or, a Discourse Concerning Evil Councellors: Being the Life and Death of John the Baptist*. It is available in the University of Sheffield's Rare Book Room.
16 Lupieri, 'John the Baptist: The First Monk', 11-23.
17 E.g. Meyer, *John the Baptist*; Darton, *John the Baptist*. See the representative list in Wink, 'John the Baptist', 24-25.
18 Dibelius, *Johannes dem Täufer*, iii.
19 Cf. the admission by Kraeling, *John the Baptist*, x-xii.

John the Baptist. Both the ground-breaking work of Willi Marxsen on Mark's Gospel and that of Hans Conzelmann on Luke include a redactional analysis of how John the Baptist functions in those Gospels.[20] Other short studies were also made of these pericopae, but the classic redactional analysis remains that by Walter Wink, *John the Baptist in the Gospel Tradition*.[21] He analyses the role of John in each of the four Gospels as well as in Q, and then concludes that, contrary to what is customarily attributed to the NT's use of Baptist traditions, the figure of John was *not* used primarily as polemic and apologetic against later disciples of John (in fact that tendency is only evident in John's Gospel). Rather, they preserved carefully circumscribed Baptist traditions which appreciate John's kerygmatic role as 'the beginning of the gospel of Jesus Christ'; a role which may be traced back to Jesus' own view of John.[22]

The most recent development within Gospel studies relevant to this survey is the application of emphases and approaches associated with the latest resurgence of Jesus research which was discussed above. One example is Paul W. Hollenbach's 1979 article 'Social Aspects of John the Baptizer's Preaching Mission in the Context of Palestinian Judaism'.[23] Hollenbach's contribution demonstrates a sensitivity to the social context out of which John arose, as well as the social situations of the audiences to which he addressed himself. Another example is Richard A. Horsley's 1985 examination of prophets and prophetic movements in first-century Palestine. He provides a social typology of prophets (as distinct from other social forms or movements such as banditry or messianic movements) whose ministries functioned chiefly among the common people. Horsley identifies two types of prophets, and of these he understands John the Baptist to be a lone 'oracular prophet' rather than a prophet leading a movement. He discusses the social and ideological contours of these types.[24]

20  Marxsen, *Mark the Evangelist*, 30-53; Conzelmann, *Theology of St Luke*, 18-27.
21  This volume forms only part of a larger work submitted as a ThD dissertation to Union Theological Seminary in 1963: 'John the Baptist and the Gospel'. The unpublished portions consist of a survey of past contributions to the quest for the historical John and an examination of the hypothesis of a relationship between John and the Qumran community. Wink's redaction-critical analysis was published in full.
22  Wink, *John the Baptist*, 111-15. More recent works include Lupieri, *Giovanni Battista*, (1988); Ernst, *Johannes der Täufer*, (1989), but these do not supersede Wink's work. Of course, other recent articles make further contributions to specific pericopae concerning John, or the portrayal of John in a particular Gospel. Unfortunately, von Dobbeler's recent work (*Das Gericht und das Erbarmen Gottes*, 1988) came to my attention too late for me to use.
      Helpful surveys of research may be found in Reumann, 'Historical Baptist', 181-99; Wink, 'John the Baptist', 4-74; von Dobbeler, 15-31.
23  Cf. his discussion of the relationship between John and Jesus in 'Conversion of Jesus', 196-219.
24  Horsley, 'Popular Prophets', 435-63; cf. Horsley, 'Popular Prophetic Movements', 3-

The orientation of these most recent studies of John the Baptist within the larger context of recent historical-Jesus research indicates that the time is ripe for a more extensive analysis of John the Baptist employing the insights and emphases being developed in recent Jesus research.

## 1.2 *Parameters and Approach*

In this work we examine the two central elements of John the Baptist's ministry which are defined by his roles of baptizer and prophet. This examination is made within the social, cultural and historical context of late Second Temple Judaism in order to determine the significance of these two elements within this context. Thus, this work is *not* a study of *all* data concerning John the Baptist; rather, it focuses on his baptismal and prophetic ministry. John's identity as a baptizer and a prophet were chosen because they best circumscribe the public roles he played in the eyes of his audience (in a way similar to recent emphasis in historical-Jesus research on Jesus' characteristic actions).

Our examination is also limited to the period *prior* to John's baptism of Jesus. Such a limitation helps us to focus upon John within his Jewish environment without being sidetracked by the complex issues involved in describing the relationship between John and Jesus. However, the arrest and execution of John will also be examined even though it falls outside this chronological parameter, for it is relevant to our concerns and is not connected with John's relationship with Jesus. According to these parameters, certain pericopae and issues may be eliminated from discussion. For example, the infancy narratives concerning John in Luke 1–2 are largely (though not entirely) irrelevant. Furthermore, NT pericopae concerned with the relationship between John and Jesus will not be employed. These pericopae are not ignored altogether; rather, they are only referred to when they contribute data concerning John's ministry itself (e.g. Mt. 11.2-6 = Lk. 7.18-23).

In one sense then, the 'thesis statement' of this work is that John's public roles of baptizer and prophet are best understood within the socio-historical context of late Second Temple Judaism. However, one might notice that this statement does not make explicit what we are setting out 'to prove'. The reason for this may be traced to the approach taken in this work. We are engaged here in an inductive investigation of John as baptizer and prophet within his Jewish context, rather than a deductive argument designed to establish certain points about John. This work certainly does produce conclusions concerning John which have greater or lesser historical probability, but the presentation of the

27; Horsley and Hanson, *Bandits*, 175-81. Cf. the discussion in §9.2.2, 9.3.3.

evidence by which we arrive at those conclusions precludes making a simple thesis statement at this point.

This work consists of three Parts. In Part I we examine the traditions concerning John the Baptist contained in our sources, both non-Christian and Christian, in order to understand how they portray the figure of John and to determine to what extent these sources may be used in a historical investigation. Chapter 2 focuses upon the tradition concerning John in Josephus' *Antiquities of the Jews* and other non-Christian literature, and Chapter 3 examines the portrayal of John in the early Christian Gospels, both canonical and extra-canonical.

In Parts II and III we examine John's ministry as defined by the roles of baptizer and prophet respectively. The approach in each case is to present an analysis of the data relevant to the particular subject drawn from the literature of the OT and Second Temple period. This establishes the social, cultural and historical context. Then the relevant pericopae concerning John are examined to determine their historical reliability. The historically reliable material is studied in light of the already analysed context in order to determine the significance of John's ministry within that context.

Part II applies this approach to John's public role as baptizer. In Chapter 4 we examine the evidence for the use of ablutions in the OT and Second Temple Jewish literature, and in Chapter 5 we do the same with respect to the Qumran literature. Then, in light of these two chapters, we consider the administration and functions of John's baptism in Chapter 6.

Part III focuses on John as prophet and applies this same approach to this role from two points of view. Since John's prophetic announcement emphasized an expected figure of judgment and restoration, Chapter 7 surveys the various expected figures of judgment and restoration in the OT and Second Temple Jewish literature. Chapter 8 applies this survey to John's announcement, discussing the identity and activities of John's expected figure as well as John's perception of the coming judgment and restoration. The other point of view from which to consider John's prophetic role is a comparison between John and other prophetic figures also found in Palestine in the late Second Temple period. These prophetic figures are surveyed in Chapter 9 and analysed according to an appropriate typology. Chapter 10 considers John's place in this typology and compares his ministry with the ministries of other prophetic figures within his category. Chapter 11 concludes the work by noting some of the contributions made by our study and suggesting possible areas of further research.

Three comments need to be made concerning this approach. First of all, the logical development of this work moves from that which is most distinctive to that which is more common. We consider first that area in which John could be considered most distinctive: his baptism. Then we proceed to John's announcement of an expected figure, an area in which John may be different but less distinctive. Finally we turn to the realm in which John had the most in common with others around him: he was one of a number of other prophetic figures.

Secondly, since the focus of this work is upon placing John within his social, cultural and historical context, most discussion concerns the presentation and analysis of the primary literature of that context, the OT and Second Temple Jewish literature. As a consequence, the discussion of the pericopae containing traditions concerning John does not interact with all the secondary literature concerning John. To do so is almost becoming impossible in the field of NT studies. In any case, due to the contextual focus of this work, not all secondary literature concerning John is strictly relevant to our interests here.

Thirdly, this inductive approach presents in each case the range of options in the Judaism of John's day before discussing the particular significance of John within that range. This approach helps us appreciate where John is to be located within the matrix created by the analysis of the social, cultural and historical context; unfortunately, it also contributes significantly to the length of this work. However, the advantages of being aware of the range of possibilities within John's context outweigh, I hope, the disadvantages of length.

# PART I

# THE TRADITIONS CONCERNING JOHN

Chapter 2

# THE TRADITIONS CONCERNING JOHN THE BAPTIST IN JOSEPHUS' *ANTIQUITIES OF THE JEWS* AND OTHER NON-CHRISTIAN LITERATURE

## 2.1 *Introduction*

Historical research on John the Baptist often concentrates on the data within the NT, and only cursory consideration is given to the other major historical source, the *Antiquities of the Jews* by Flavius Josephus.[1] For historical investigations like the one in which we are engaged, *Antiquities* is an equally valid, and valuable, source. Therefore, in an attempt to correct this imbalance, I begin this survey of traditions concerning John the Baptist with Josephus' reference to him in *Ant.* 18.116-19. The purpose of this chapter is four-fold: (1) to observe what Josephus says about John and how he is portrayed in the text; (2) to examine the question of the authenticity of this particular text; (3) to evaluate the general reliability of this text as a source for historical data concerning John; and (4) to consider whether or not traditions concerning John in other ancient, non-Christian literature could contribute further data to our investigation.

## 2.2 *The Portrayal of John the Baptist in* Ant. *18.116-19*

### 2.2.1 *The Text and Context of* Ant. *18.116-19*
Josephus' writing style betrays an attempt to imitate classical Greek style (especially Thucydides)[2] which leads him to use numerous participial and infinitival constructions as well as genitive absolutes. This style produces rather long and involved sentences. The following is the text of *Ant.* 18.116-19 and my own, rather literal, translation.[3]

---

1 For example, Ernst (*Johannes der Täufer*, 252), in his otherwise valuable work, states concerning Josephus' description of John the Baptist: 'Josephus bietet keine neuen Informationen, die äußeren Fakten stimmen mit dem Evangelium in den Grundzügen überein'. Consequently, other than in his brief survey of *Ant.* 18.116-19, references to this text are found only six times in the index to his work of over 400 pages.

2 Rajak, *Josephus*, 233-36.

3 I use parentheses (( )) to sort out Josephus' complicated sentences with their subordinate clauses, and square brackets ([ ]) to indicate my own additions to the text which clarify Josephus' meaning. The text reproduced here is from the LCL, edited

116Τισὶ δὲ τῶν Ἰουδαίων ἐδόκει ὀλωλέναι τὸν Ἡρώδου στρατὸν ὑπὸ τοῦ
θεοῦ καὶ μάλα δικαίως τιννυμένου κατὰ ποινὴν Ἰωάννου τοῦ
ἐπικαλουμένου βαπτιστοῦ. 117κτείνει γὰρ δὴ τοῦτον Ἡρώδης ἀγαθὸν
ἄνδρα καὶ τοῖς Ἰουδαίοις κελεύοντα ἀρετὴν ἐπασκοῦσιν καὶ τὰ πρὸς
ἀλλήλους δικαιοσύνῃ καὶ πρὸς τὸν θεὸν εὐσεβείᾳ χρωμένοις βαπτισμῷ
συνιέναι· οὕτω γὰρ δὴ καὶ τὴν βάπτισιν ἀποδεκτὴν αὐτῷ φανεῖσθαι μὴ
ἐπί τινων ἁμαρτάδων παραιτήσει χρωμένων, ἀλλ᾽ ἐφ᾽ ἁγνείᾳ τοῦ
σώματος, ἅτε δὴ καὶ τῆς ψυχῆς δικαιοσύνῃ προεκκεκαθαρμένης. 118καὶ
τῶν ἄλλων συστρεφομένων, καὶ γὰρ ἤρθησαν ἐπὶ πλεῖστον τῇ ἀκροάσει
τῶν λόγων, δείσας Ἡρώδης τὸ ἐπὶ τοσόνδε πιθανὸν αὐτοῦ τοῖς
ἀνθρώποις μὴ ἐπὶ στάσει τινὶ φέροι, πάντα γὰρ ἐῴκεσαν συμβουλῇ τῇ
ἐκείνου πράξοντες, πολὺ κρεῖττον ἡγεῖται πρίν τι νεώτερον ἐξ αὐτοῦ
γενέσθαι προλαβὼν ἀνελεῖν τοῦ μεταβολῆς γενομένης [μὴ] εἰς
πράγματα ἐμπεσὼν μετανοεῖν. 119καὶ ὁ μὲν ὑποψίᾳ τῇ Ἡρώδου δέσμιος
εἰς τὸν Μαχαιροῦντα πεμφθεὶς τὸ προειρημένον φρούριον ταύτῃ
κτίννυται. τοῖς δὲ Ἰουδαίοις δόξα ἐπὶ τιμωρίᾳ τῇ ἐκείνου τὸν ὄλεθρον
ἐπὶ τῷ στρατεύματι γενέσθαι τοῦ θεοῦ κακῶσαι Ἡρώδην θέλοντος.

116But to some of the Jews it seemed that Herod's army had been
destroyed by God, who was exacting vengeance (most certainly justly) as
satisfaction for John who was called Baptist. 117For Herod indeed put him
to death, who was a good man and one who commanded the Jews to practise virtue and act with justice toward one another and with piety toward
God, and [so] to gather together by baptism. For [John's view was that] in
this way baptism certainly would appear acceptable to him [i.e. God] if
[they] used [it] not for seeking pardon of certain sins but for purification of
the body, because the soul had already been cleansed before by righteousness. 118And when others gathered together [around John] (for they
were also excited to the utmost by listening to [his] teachings), Herod,
because he feared that his great persuasiveness with the people might lead
to some kind of strife (for they seemed as if they would do everything which
he counselled), thought it more preferable, before anything radically
innovative happened as a result of him, to execute [John], taking action
first, rather than when the upheaval happened to perceive too late, having
already fallen into trouble. 119Because of the suspicion of Herod, he [i.e.
John], after being sent bound to Machaerus (the fortress mentioned
before), was executed there. But the opinion of the Jews [was] that the
destruction of the army happened for vengeance of him [i.e. John] because
God willed to afflict Herod.

In Book 18 of *Antiquities*, prior to this account concerning John the
Baptist, Josephus narrates certain events in the political history of Judea,
Galilee and certain neighbouring nations, focusing particularly upon persons and events which caused unrest among the Jewish populace. His
accounts include Judas the Gaulanite and Saddok the Pharisee leading a
rebellion against the registration of property (18.1-9); the 'fourth
philosophy' of the Jews, begun by Judas the Galilean, refusing to submit
to Rome (18.23-25);[4] Samaritans scattering bones in the temple, defiling

by Feldman, *Josephus*, 9.80-84.
4   The description of the first three Jewish philosophies, Pharisees, Sadducees and
    Essenes, in 18.11-22 are given by Josephus as a backdrop against which he introduces
    this fourth philosophy; cf. *Ant.* 18.10.

it (18.29-30); Herod Antipas building Tiberias on a graveyard to which the Jews objected because it caused uncleanness (18.36-38); the people protesting against Pilate's introduction of the emperor's images into Jerusalem (18.55-59); the people objecting to Pilate's use of temple revenue to build an aqueduct for Jerusalem (18.60-62); Pilate crucifying Jesus (18.63-64),[5] and ruthlessly putting down a movement led by a Samaritan (18.85-87) for which he is relieved of his post (18.88-89).[6]

It is interesting to observe that several of these narratives have one of two related themes underlying them. The first theme is that the Jewish protests could be perceived as legitimate actions, especially in light of the people's heritage. The Jewish populace were responding to actions by the rulers which offended their Jewish sensitivities. The other theme is that sometimes these protests were repressed by ruthless and excessive action taken by those in authority.[7]

The immediately preceding context of our text describes the quarrel which arose between Aretas IV, king of Nabatea, and Herod Antipas, tetrarch of Galilee and Perea. Antipas had married the daughter of Aretas, a union which had provided a long period of peace and stability between these two regions. However, Antipas fell in love with Herodias, who was at that time the wife of his half-brother Herod.[8] Herodias agreed to marry Antipas after he had divorced his first wife. His wife, hearing of this plan, immediately returned to her father, Aretas IV, and informed him of Antipas' plan. Thus the peace between these two regions was broken. Border disputes led to a full-scale battle between the two, with Antipas' army being decisively defeated. As an aside, Josephus comments on this defeat in the passage in which we are interested by explaining how some Jews interpreted it: it was divine vengeance for Antipas' execution of John the Baptist.

From this survey we can observe several ways in which the account concerning John the Baptist fits into the larger context. First of all, it is

---

5  The problems with the authenticity of the *Testimonium Flavianum* are not relevant here. For discussion and references to other literature, see Schürer, *History*, 1.428-30; Feldman, *Josephus and Modern Scholarship*, 679-703; Feldman, '*Testimonium Flavianum*', 179-99.

6  Similar themes of unrest, civil war and conflict are also described in this section with respect to other nations. These include: the Parthians (18.39-52, 96-105); Commagene (18.53-54); in Rome priests of Isis trick Paulina into sexual relations with Mundus (18.65-80); in Rome four Jews are caught embezzling, causing the Jews to be expelled from the city (18.81-84); and then the conflict between Herod Antipas and Aretas IV, king of Nabatea (18.109-15).

7  Cf. Rajak's discussion (*Josephus*, 65-77) of 'Josephus' account of the breakdown of consensus', and Horsley's description (*Spiral of Violence*, 28-58) of 'the spiral of violence in Jewish Palestine'.

8  The dispute over the identity of this Herod as Philip according the NT is not relevant here; cf. §10.6.1.

further evidence of unrest among the Jewish populace of Palestine. Secondly, it provides a popular Jewish explanation for the military defeat of Herod Antipas at the hands of Aretas. Thirdly, it serves as another example of excessive action taken by a person ruling on behalf of Rome.

### 2.2.2 The Description of John in Ant. 18.116-19

Josephus, after describing Herod Antipas' defeat by Aretas, refers in 18.116 to a popular Jewish opinion concerning the cause of that defeat. Ultimately, the cause was divine: God was 'exacting vengeance' upon Herod for his unjust treatment of John. Josephus states that this view was taken by 'some of the Jews', but evidently he holds to a similar opinion on the matter, as indicated by the parenthetical comment inserted into the explanation, 'most certainly justly' (καὶ μάλα δικαίως).[9]

Two interesting points arise in 18.116. First of all, John the Baptist continued to be remembered by the Jewish people. The defeat of Antipas' army took place a number of years after his execution of John, yet after that defeat certain Jews linked the two events together. This implies that John was both a well-known and well-respected person among his people. Secondly, Josephus identifies John as the one 'who was called Baptist' (τοῦ ἐπικαλουμένου βαπτιστοῦ). The use of this nickname by Josephus provides a parallel to the usage in the synoptic Gospels (cf. §6.2).

In 18.117 Josephus evaluates John and summarizes his message and his understanding of baptism. Josephus considers John to be 'a good man' (ἀγαθὸν ἄνδρα),[10] which strengthens the above observation that Josephus was in agreement concerning the divine cause of Herod's defeat. Josephus' agreement with popular opinion is probably a major factor influencing the way he has sympathetically portrayed John.

According to Josephus, the first element in John's message was an ethical demand 'to practise virtue and act with justice toward one another and with piety toward God'. The terminology used to describe the content of John's ethics reflects categories which would be more understandable to Josephus' Greco-Roman audience than those which

---

9 Elsewhere Josephus describes events and explains them as the consequence of divine vengeance, implying that this is his own opinion. For example, Josephus comments in *Ant.* 17.60 that the death of Pheroras 'proved to be the beginning of Antipater's misfortunes even though he had sailed for Rome, for God was punishing him for the murder of his brothers. I shall relate the whole story of this in order that it may be an example and warning to mankind to practise virtue in all circumstances.' See also his discussion in *Ant.* 18.127-29. Cf. Rivkin, 'Locating John the Baptizer', 78-79.

10 Eisler's emendation (*Messiah Jesus*, 221-27) to ἄγριον ἄνδρα ('wild man') is quite speculative. It is based only on the Slavonic version, and finds no support in other manuscripts. Feldman (*Josephus*, 9.81) considers this emendation to be reckless. For discussion of the issues related to the Slavonic text, see §2.5.

may have been actually used by John.[11] Perhaps John's ethical imperative could best be summarized as a call to a righteous lifestyle, which is
suggested by his own summarizing reference to 'righteousness' at the end
of 18.117. The other element in John's message was a call 'to gather
together by baptism' (cf. §6.4.5). By introducing John's baptismal practice, Josephus has informed his readers why he was nicknamed 'the Baptist'. Josephus has not merely stated that John *practised* a type of baptism, but that his baptism was part of the message John *proclaimed*.
John's call for the Jews to be baptized flowed out of the ethical imperative he preached.

Josephus states that John's baptism is acceptable to God when used
'not for seeking pardon of certain sins but for purification of the body'.
The reason given is that 'the soul had already been cleansed before by
righteousness'. As an explanation in the context of John's ministry, this
righteousness most probably refers back to the earlier description of
John's ethical demand to practise virtue, justice and piety. This reason
explains that the 'pardon of certain sins' has already been accomplished
by responding to John's ethical imperative. While using different concepts, the phrases 'pardon for certain sins' and 'the soul had already been
cleansed' refer to essentially the same thing, though from two different
points of view: pardoning of sin and cleansing from sin's uncleanness.
Thus, according to Josephus, the essence of John's message was an ethical call to practise a righteous lifestyle which would cleanse the soul by
receiving pardon for sins, and then to perform a baptism which would
purify the body (cf. §6.2.1, 6.4.2, 6.4.3). The response to John's ethical
demand appears to be a condition for John's baptism. We should
observe that, while Josephus is explaining John's baptism, it is not clear
whether this explanation is *actually* from John's point of view or that of
Josephus.[12]

---

11 Ernst (*Johannes der Täufer*, 254) states that Josephus describes John as 'ein hel-
lenistischer Moralist. . .' Cf. the same practice in the terminology and manner with
which Josephus describes different Jewish parties in 18.11-22 (cf. *War* 2.119-66): the
Pharisees, Sadducees and Essenes are 'philosophies' ($\phi\iota\lambda o\sigma o\phi\iota\alpha\iota$, 18.111) and differ
over issues such as 'fate' ($\epsilon i\mu\alpha\rho\mu\acute{\epsilon}\nu\eta$); these are hardly categories characteristic of
Palestinian Judaism! The terminology used by Josephus may be more appropriate to
describing Judaism as understood in the Hellenistic diaspora. For example, see
Philo's description (*Spec. Leg.* 2.63) of the two main principles of Jewish ethics as
taught in the diaspora synagogue: 'one of duty to God as shewn by piety and holiness,
one of duty to men as shewn by humanity and justice ($\tau\acute{o}$ $\tau\epsilon$ $\pi\rho\grave{o}\varsigma$ $\theta\epsilon\grave{o}\nu$ $\delta\iota$'
$\epsilon\dot{\upsilon}\sigma\epsilon\beta\epsilon\acute{\iota}\alpha\varsigma$ $\kappa\alpha\grave{\iota}$ $\dot{o}\sigma\iota\acute{o}\tau\eta\tau o\varsigma$ $\kappa\alpha\grave{\iota}$ $\tau\grave{o}$ $\pi\rho\grave{o}\varsigma$ $\dot{\alpha}\nu\theta\rho\acute{\omega}\pi o\upsilon\varsigma$ $\delta\iota\grave{\alpha}$ $\phi\iota\lambda\alpha\nu\theta\rho\omega\pi\acute{\iota}\alpha\varsigma$ $\kappa\alpha\grave{\iota}$
$\delta\iota\kappa\alpha\iota o\sigma\acute{\upsilon}\nu\eta\varsigma$). Observe in this example the use of terminology similar to that used by
Josephus to describe John. For further discussion of ethical concepts in the diaspora,
see Collins, *Between Athens and Jerusalem*, 137-74. For a description of the different
Gentile philosophical schools in the Greco-Roman period which discussed ethics in
similar terms, see Meeks, *Moral World*, 40-64. For a discussion of the audience for
Josephus' writings, see Rajak, *Josephus*, 223-29.

In 18.118 Josephus describes John's audience and his effect upon them, as well as the resultant effect which this had upon Herod Antipas. John's audience is ambiguously identified in this section as 'others' (τῶν ἄλλων),[13] which suggests an alteration or expansion beyond the audience identified in 18.117 as 'the Jews'. As well, in 18.118 John appears to have an increased impact on his audience as suggested by Josephus in statements such as 'they were excited even to the utmost . . . his great persuasiveness with the people . . . they seemed as if they would do everything which he counselled. . .' What produced such a powerful response is mentioned simply as '[his] teachings'.

The precise identity of these 'others' is difficult to establish with certainty because Josephus gives no further details. However, a couple of observations may be made about them. First of all, 'others' stands in contrast to 'the Jews' of 18.117. This does not mean, however, that they are necessarily Gentiles, because the contrast may not be simply with Jews *per se*, but with Jews who were following John's message. In this view the 'others' would simply be a wider audience of Jews. But on the other hand, there is nothing in the context to suggest that they could not be Gentiles. The location of John's ministry suggests that he could have contact with Gentiles who travelled the trade routes coming from the East, as well as with Gentiles living in the region of the Trans-Jordan. It is not necessary to choose between these two possibilities, for the main point is probably not the ethnic makeup of the audience but the expansion of that audience, and this may well have included Gentiles as well as Jews.

The phrase '[his] teachings' is most naturally understood to refer to the message of John as described by Josephus in 18.117. This seemingly simple and unthreatening message does not appear at first glance to be one which would excite people to such an extent and cause Herod to fear strife. However, the socio-political implications of John's message could certainly produce such excitement, especially in light of the inseparable

12   The infinitive construction with φανεῖσθαι continues the indirect discourse from κελεύοντα, and thus Josephus is implying that the explanation is from John's point of view; cf. §6.2.1.
      Lichtenberger ('John the Baptist') argues that Josephus portrays John as an Essene, but this is not clear, for the portrayal is not distinctively Essene, and Josephus does not use the label for John even though he had a positive view of John (as he also had for the Essenes). For further discussion of Josephus' intent, see Nodet, 'Jésus et Jean-Baptiste selon Josèphe', 497-524.
13   This has sometimes been considered to be a textual error. While most manuscripts have ἄλλων, one (A) has corrected this to λαῶν, and the Latin version has *perplurima multitudo*. Conjectural emendations include ἀνθρώπων and πολλῶν. However, such conjectures are unnecessary because the text makes good sense as it stands. For these variants see Niese, *Iosephi*, 4.162; Feldman, *Josephus*, 9.82.

link between the socio-political ideals and the religio-ethical ideals which formed the heritage of the Jewish people as the chosen, covenant people of God. But the socio-political realities for the common people in Palestine of John's day stood in stark contrast to those ideals. To those who perceived themselves to be powerless and unjustly treated, John's ethical demand could imply a radical change in the socio-political *status quo*, producing a society in which John's ethical demand could be lived out: a society manifesting 'justice toward one another'. That same ethical demand would be perceived as a threat to the *status quo* of those who held the power in the current imperialist regime. Furthermore, John's message called his audience 'to gather together by baptism', and the gathering together of discontented, excited people is usually perceived as a threat by governments (ancient as well as modern).[14]

Thus, the combination of the socio-political implications of John's message with the excited response of large crowds was probably a threat to Antipas. The object of his fear was not John but the social and political consequences of a popular movement putting into practice the implications of his message. This understanding of the implications of John's message is confirmed by Josephus' explanation: Antipas decided to act 'before anything radically innovative (νεώτερον) happened as a result of him'. The word νεώτερος signifies that which is newer or innovative, and carries with it the idea of practical socio-political change or revolution.[15] To communicate the idea of being both new and revolutionary, νεώτερος is translated here as 'radically innovative'.

The implications of John's message and the enthusiastic response by the people caused Herod Antipas to be afraid. Josephus states that Antipas was afraid of στάσις caused by radical innovation (νεώτερος). The word στάσις may be used either of rebellion against the imperialist authority[16] or of civil strife between internal groups.[17] Tessa Rajak has shown that στάσις is an important word for Josephus' analysis of the causes of the Jewish War and is used most often to refer to civil strife between factions.[18] However, in the context of 18.118 it is unclear which is meant because either is possible, though the implications of John's message would most probably lead to a στάσις which was rebellion against an imperialist authority or its representatives. But even the possibility of such a στάσις could in turn lead to the στάσις of internal civil

---

14  Cf. *Ant.* 15.366; cf. the discussion in §10.3, 10.6.1.
15  LSJ, 1172-73; e.g. *Ant.* 15.165; 19.91; 20.106. With this significance the term is often used negatively by those supporting the *status quo* which is being challenged by that which is 'radically innovative'.
16  E.g. *Ant.* 18.62: the Jews protest at Pilate's use of temple funds to build the Jerusalem aqueduct.
17  E.g. *Ant.* 18.8: the strife existing between Jewish factions.
18  Rajak, *Josephus*, 10, 91-96.

strife. I therefore translate the word στάσις simply as 'strife'. In either case, Herod Antipas feared the rise of some form of socio-political unrest.[19] To what extent John intended his 'radically innovative' message to produce 'strife' is unclear, but according to Josephus it was clearly perceived this way by Antipas (cf. §10.6.1).

While several elements of this passage remain ambiguous, some things have become clear. An emphasis on the practical implications of his message produced an excited response by a larger audience than John had had earlier. These practical implications were viewed by Herod to be a threat to the socio-political *status quo* and to have the potential of causing strife. Thus, Antipas perceived John as a real threat and decided to remove him before the threat became a reality.

In 18.119 Josephus recounts Herod arresting and executing John in response to the perceived threat of John, and he repeats the Jewish interpretation of the destruction of Herod's army as divine retribution for this deed. The only point which needs to be observed in this text is that Machaerus is identified as the location of John's execution. This was a fortification east of the Dead Sea in the region of Perea. It had been refortified by Herod the Great who then used it as one of his residences. The region, along with Machaerus, passed into the control of Herod Antipas upon the death of his father.

We may conclude that Josephus chose briefly to describe John because his story serves as another example of the unrest in Palestine prior to the first Jewish War. The narrative also summarizes the popular explanation for the defeat of Herod Antipas by Aretas: it was divine vengeance for Antipas' unjust treatment of John—an opinion with which Josephus agrees. He has portrayed John as a preacher with an ethical imperative, which he described in Hellenistic terms. John is also portrayed as proclaiming and practising a baptism which purifies the body. Josephus describes the excitement caused by John's teaching which led Herod Antipas to consider him to be a threat to the socio-political *status quo*. By portraying John this way, Josephus almost gives the impression, when interpreted through Greco-Roman eyes (i.e. his readership), that John is a victim of circumstances beyond his control, an unfortunate, innocent martyr who simply wished the people to 'be good' and 'purify their bodies'. Yet, when the same text is read through the eyes of the first-century Palestinian common people, the implications of this portrayal of John and his message become more serious, suggesting that Antipas' fear that John's ministry might lead to something 'radically

---

19  In this instance both these alternatives may be combined, because Jews would perceive such στάσις as a rebellion against the *foreign* authority of Rome, but Rome, who ruled over Palestine, would perceive such στάσις as *domestic* or civil strife.

innovative' is not entirely unfounded. These are issues to which we
return later in this investigation (§8.5, 10).

### 2.3 *The Authenticity of* Ant. *18.116-19*

The authenticity of Josephus' narrative concerning John the Baptist has
often been critically examined. While a few have rejected it as a Christian interpolation, most scholars have accepted it. There are at least
three arguments which could be raised against its authenticity.

First of all, it could be objected that Josephus had more important
concerns and events about which to write than a minor Jewish figure
such as John. But, because John was a person of Christian interest, it
would be quite natural for Christian scribes to interpolate a reference to
him. However, such an objection misunderstands both Josephus and
John. Josephus' history was specifically focused on his own people, the
Jews, and attempted to present them as an ancient and honourable
people. As a Jew, John had evidently been a well-known figure, and he
could have been known by Josephus and used by him to promote his purposes. We have seen in our survey that this text concerning John fits the
context admirably and is consistent with the larger themes Josephus was
developing. A reference to John by Josephus would, therefore, be most
natural.

A second argument is that the nouns used for 'baptism' in this text
(βαπτισμός and βάπτισις, *Ant.* 18.117) are not found elsewhere in the
Josephan corpus, which may suggest that this vocabulary is foreign to
Josephus and is evidence of interpolation. However, we may object that
using a word only once does not mean it is foreign to an author.
Josephus uses many words only once; this hardly means that each of the
texts in which they appear is interpolated. As well, Josephus is knowl-
edgeable concerning the βαπτ- word group, for he uses the verbs
βαπτίζω 13 times and βάπτω three times.[20] He uses no other nouns for
'baptism' than those used here, which is quite strange if this text is a
Christian interpolation. He never uses the noun βάπτισμα, which is the
usual Christian noun for baptism (both John's baptism and Christian
baptism), and we would expect that term here if this text was a Christian
interpolation.[21] Therefore, the use of this vocabulary is hardly evidence
for Christian interpolation.

---

20  Βαπτίζω: *War* 1.437; 2.476; 2.556; 3.368; 3.423; 3.525; 3.527; 4.137; *Ant.* 4.81; 9.212;
    10.169; 15.55; *Life* 15; βάπτω: *War* 1.490; 4.563; *Ant.* 3.102.
21  Furthermore, Josephus' word βάπτισις is never used in the NT or early Christian lit-
    erature.  The other noun he uses, βαπτισμός, is only used for washing dishes (Mk
    7.4), or ritual washings (Heb. 6.2; 9.10). The only place it is used for Christian bap-
    tism is Col. 2.12, where it is textually uncertain. BAGD, 132; Oepke, 'βάπτω', 1.545.

Emil Schürer raises the objection that 'suspicion is aroused by the favourable verdict on John. . .' But he responds to his own objection by stating that 'it should be borne in mind that as an ascetic and moral preacher, he might have been viewed sympathetically by Josephus'.[22] If Josephus had portrayed John, incorporating eschatological and messianic elements such as are utilized by the Gospels, then a negative verdict by Josephus would be expected. But, since Josephus portrays John in terms quite acceptable to his Greco-Roman audience, his favourable verdict is not out of line.

On the other hand, there are several good reasons for accepting the authenticity of this passage. First of all, the text is found in all extant manuscripts of *Antiquities*.[23] Secondly, the vocabulary and style are consistent with Josephan usage, which would not necessarily be the case if the passage was interpolated. This argument is strengthened when we observe in the passage unusual terminology which is also used elsewhere in *Antiquities* (thus showing it to be Josephan vocabulary), but which would not be expected of a Christian interpolator. For example, for 'sin' in this passage Josephus uses the Ionic form ἁμαρτάς rather than ἁμαρτία;[24] this Ionic form is also found in *Ant.* 18.350 and seven times in *Ant.* 3, but not in the NT or other early Christian literature.[25] As another example, I have already pointed out above that the nouns used for 'baptism' in this text are different from those normally used for either John's baptism or Christian baptism.[26]

Thirdly, if this passage was a Christian interpolation, then we would expect an account which would more closely conform to the NT traditions about John. This expectation is reasonable because the probable purpose of such a Christian interpolation would be to confirm the NT account. However, there are a number of significant differences between the Josephan account and the NT. Some of these include the description of John's message, the explanation of John's baptism, and the reason for his arrest and execution. But the most significant difference is the silence of this text on the relationship between John the Baptist and Jesus.[27]

---

22  Schürer, *History*, 1.346 n. 24.
23  Niese, *Iosephi*, 4.161-62.
24  LSJ, 77.
25  BAGD, 42-43. Thackeray (*Josephus*, 132-33) uses this to argue that 'this passage betrays the unmistakable marks of the hack employed for this portion of the Antiquities' (132). Others have denied the hypothesis of the Thucydidean hack, but this denial does not negate the force of this argument for the text's authenticity. See especially the detailed analysis in Shutt, *Josephus*, 59-75. See also Feldman, *Josephus and Modern Scholarship*, 674-75; Rajak, *Josephus*, 233-36.
26  For other examples, see Thackeray, *Josephus*, 132-33.
27  Abrahams (*Pharisaism and the Gospels*, 1.31) states: 'Much more significant is the silence of Josephus as to any connection between John and Jesus. This, of itself, is

Finally, Origen, who wrote before the middle of the third century, provides external attestation for this passage by making reference to it in *Cels.* 1.47: 'For Josephus in the eighteenth book of the Jewish Antiquities bears witness that John was a baptist and promised purification to people who were baptized'. Origen also refers to Josephus elswhere, in 1.16, 2.13, and 4.11. The importance of this citation for the authenticity of this passage is strengthened by observing that Origen's text of Josephus' *Antiquities* appears to be one which contains less Christian interpolation elsewhere, for he states in this same passage (*Cels.* 1.47) that Josephus did not believe in Jesus as Christ. This statement is not supported by the extant text of Josephus (*Ant.* 18.63-64) which contains clear evidence of Christian interpolation concerning Jesus in the famous *Testimonium Flavianum*.

In light of these considerations it is reasonable to conclude that the passage in which Josephus describes John the Baptist (*Ant.* 18.116-19) may be accepted as authentic.[28]

## 2.4 *Josephus as a Historian*

While Josephus' historical works were rejected by his fellow Jews, the Christian church held them in high regard, both using them and preserving them for posterity. Jerome, for example, considered Josephus to be *Graecus Livius* ('the Greek Livy', *Ep. Eust.* 22.35). But, with the rise of modern, critical historiography, Josephus has not fared as well. He has been criticized for abusing his sources, being prejudiced in his viewpoint and propagandist in his presentation. Such criticism, by focusing on the weaknesses of Josephus as a historian, fails to view him in his own context and to recognize his strengths.

Josephus must be understood within the context of history-writing in the Greco-Roman period. Recent studies have examined just this element of Josephus' works. Particularly helpful in this regard is the recent work by Shaye J.D. Cohen, who explains the use of sources by Greco-Roman historians:

> An author was expected to take some liberties with his source. He could freely invent details to increase the color and dramatic interest of the account. He was expected to recast the narrative, to place his own stamp upon it, to use the material for his own purposes, to create something new. But on the whole he was faithful to the content and sequence of the original... But the ground rules were accepted: too close adherence to the

almost enough to authenticate the passage.'

28  Recent studies concur with this conclusion; e.g. Scobie, *John the Baptist*, 17-22; Schürer, *History*, 346 n. 24; Nodet, 'Jésus et Jean-Baptiste', 322-31; Ernst, *Johannes der Täufer*, 253-57.

source raised the spectre of plagiarism or, at least, of unprofessionalism.[29]

Josephus' style and use of his sources demonstrates his adherence to this Greco-Roman tradition of historiography.[30] It is against this contemporary background that he must be evaluated with respect to both his strengths and weaknesses. Cohen concludes his study of Josephus by observing that

> with the revision of language some revision of content is inevitable. Details are added, omitted, or changed, not always with reason. Although his fondness for the dramatic, pathetic, erotic, and the exaggerated, is evident throughout, as a rule Josephus remains fairly close to his original. Even when he modifies the source to suit a certain aim he still reproduces the essence of the story. Most important, he does not engage in the free invention of episodes. . .
>
> Regarding the sequence of his source Josephus is even more faithful. The most common reason for rearrangement is the desire for a thematic narrative. . .
>
> In all these points Josephus followed standard Greek practice.[31]

Cohen's conclusion also points out Josephus' weaknesses. His narratives are sometimes confused and contradictory, and he uses terminology loosely. Furthermore, his writings demonstrate strong motives for writing. He is an apologist for the Jews and Judaism, but he also writes in an attempt to justify his own actions during the Jewish War.[32]

By appreciating the historiographic environment in which Josephus wrote and recognizing both his strengths and his weaknesses, we may reasonably conclude that Josephus may be employed as a historical source, but with caution. Care must be exercised in discerning his use of Greek history-writing style and his apologetic concerns.[33]

We may now apply these general observations concerning Josephus' method of history-writing to his passage on John the Baptist. We

---

29  Cohen, *Josephus*, 31. See also Cadbury, 'Traditions of Writing History', 2.7-15.

30  Cohen, *Josephus*, 24-66; Attridge, *Biblical History*, 38-41; Downing, 'Josephus' Antiquities', 46-65; Varneda, *Historical Method*, 242-79; cf. Bilde (*Josephus*, 200-206) who considers Josephus to be employing both Jewish and Greco-Roman historiographic methods.

31  Cohen, *Josephus*, 233.

32  Cohen, *Josephus*, 232-42. Cf. Attridge, *Biblical History*, 29-70.

33  For further discussion evaluating Josephus as a historian, see Niese, 'Josephus', 7.576-77; Thackeray, *Josephus*, 1-22; Moore, *Judaism*, 1.208-10; Momigliano, 'Josephus as a Source', 10.884-87; Shutt, *Josephus*, 117-27; Williamson, *Josephus*, 274-97; Guignebert, *Jewish World*, 15-19; Hughes 'Value of Josephus', 179-83; Zeitlin 'Jewish Historiography', 178-214; Schalit, 'Josephus', 10.254-63; Schürer *History*, 1.43-63; Rhoads, *Israel in Revolution*, 11-14; Cohen, 'Masada', 385-405; Broshi, 'Credibility of Josephus', 379-84; Rajak, *Josephus*, 4-7, 197-201; Feldman, 'Josephus Revisited', 788-857; Moehring, 'Josephus ben Matthia', 864-944; Attridge, 'Josephus and His Works', 185-232; Attridge, 'Jewish Historiography', 311-43; Bilde, *Josephus*, 173-206.

observed above that his account concerning John fits into the larger context in several ways: (1) it is further evidence of unrest among the Jewish populace of Palestine; (2) it provides a popular Jewish explanation for the military defeat of Herod Antipas at the hands of Aretas; and (3) it serves as another example of excessive action taken by a person ruling a portion of the Jewish populace (cf. §2.2.1). These concerns demonstrate why Josephus portrayed John sympathetically and Antipas unsympathetically. They also suggest that Josephus has shaped his presentation of John, particularly in what he included and excluded in describing John's preaching and activities. But the actual preaching and activities of John are tangential to his concerns—nothing in the context suggests that Josephus had a particular axe to grind concerning John himself. Therefore, on the one hand, we may take the description of John to be a relatively objective account by Josephus within the parameters of Greco-Roman historiography. But on the other hand, Josephus' perspective is responsible for what has been included in the passage, and perhaps the way in which it has been described. This becomes clearer when we turn to examine the somewhat different portrayal of John in the Gospels.

## 2.5 *The Traditions Concerning John the Baptist in the Slavonic Josephus*

In the first part of this century the Slavonic text of Josephus was first translated into European languages.[34] Then, in 1929 and 1930 Robert Eisler published the two volumes of his controversial work, based on this Slavonic text, which was translated in 1931 in the abridged form: *The Messiah Jesus and John the Baptist according to Flavius Josephus' Recently Discovered 'Capture of Jerusalem' and Other Jewish and Christian Sources.* His central thesis was that Josephus originally wrote *The Jewish War* in Aramaic, and this text contained passages on John the Baptist and Jesus, but when the Greek version was written, these passages were deleted. Some of the additions in the Slavonic version are derived from this Aramaic original, and so provide important historical evidence for understanding John and Jesus in political terms as revolutionaries against Rome.[35] Eisler's work created a storm of controversy and much has been written in response. For our purposes here, I need only summarize problems with the authenticity of these additions.

---

34  Berendts and Grass, *Flavius Josephus: Vom Jüdischen Kriege Buch I–IV, nach der slavischen Übersetzung deutsch herausgegeben und mit dem griechischen Text verglichen*; Istrin, *La prise de Jérusalem de Josèphe le Juif*; a critical edition was prepared by N.A. Mescerskij, *Istorija iudeskoij vojny Josifa Flavija* [= History of the War of the Jews of Flavius Josephus in Old Russian], as cited by Feldman, 'Josephus Revisited', 772.

35  Eisler, *Messiah Jesus*, 22-220. An English translation of some of these extra passages is provided in Thackeray, *Josephus*, 3.635-60.

The language and style show evidence of compilation in the Byzantine period. The contents of at least some additions reveal the hand of a Christian author who uses phraseology which would be totally inconsistent with a Jewish writer. Furthermore, the anti-Roman bias of the added texts is quite inconsistent with Josephus' attitude of admiration for the Romans. The additions contain serious historical errors, some of which are in stark contradiction to the authentic portions of Josephus. Finally, the additions reveal the use of sources which include the NT, Hegesippus, Josippon, the early Christian writers and Christian apocryphal literature.[36]

In light of these arguments one must conclude that the additions to the Slavonic Josephus are inauthentic, late additions, and, therefore, they are of no value for historically reconstructing the lives of John the Baptist and Jesus.[37]

### 2.6  The Traditions Concerning John the Baptist in the Mandaean Literature

Mandaeism is a syncretistic Gnostic religion which still survives primarily in Iraq, but in Iran as well.[38] Among their religious books is the Sidrā d'Yahyā or *Book of John* (Yahyā is the Arabic form for 'John', and Yōhānā is the Mandaean form). This *Book of John* contains several passages describing the life and teaching of John the Baptist.[39] It has been argued that the Mandaean literature contains evidence for pre-Christian Gnosticism which entered Christianity through John. The influence of this pre-Christian Gnosticism has been perceived, by those who hold to this theory, in the Christian use of the redemption myth and in the ideas and terminology found especially in the fourth Gospel (e.g. dualism).[40]

36  The major works discussing these and other criticisms are Zeitlin, *Josephus on Jesus*; Creed 'Slavonic Version of Josephus' History', 279-319; Jack, *Historic Christ*. For other and more specialized discussions, see the works cited by Feldman, 'Josephus Revisited', 771-74, and Feldman, *Josephus and Modern Scholarship*, 48-56.

37  It should however be noted that Brandon (*Fall of Jerusalem*, 114-25) has since argued for the authenticity of the Slavonic Josephus; see also his *Jesus and the Zealots*, 364-368. However, he does not seem to have adequately answered the objections against its authenticity. Cf. Montefiore, 'Josephus and the New Testament', 318; Dunkerley, 'Riddles of Josephus', 127-34.

38  For a description see Yamauchi, 'Mandaeism', 563, and the literature cited there.

39  For a translation of those portions of the *Book of John* which concern John the Baptist, see Mead, *Gnostic John the Baptizer*, 35-70. Yōhānā appears only once in another Mandaean document, the *Ginza* ('Treasury') 2.1.151-52, for which see Scobie, *John the Baptist*, 25-26.

40  For support, see Bultmann, *John*, 7-9; Robinson, 'Johannine Trajectory', 261-66; Thomas, *Mouvement Baptiste*, 186-267; cf. the literature cited by Dodd, *Interpretation*, 115-30; Scobie, *John the Baptist*, 23-31; Yamauchi, *Pre-Christian Gnosticism*, 117-42.

While these theories are ingenious, the concrete evidence to support them is lacking. With respect to the references to John the Baptist, the compilation of the material probably took place in the 8th century CE, after the Islamic conquest of the area.[41] The traditions found in the Mandaean literature appear to be dependent upon NT traditions, but they also incorporate legendary material about John and teachings by John which support the developed Gnostic themes of their own religion. The most probable explanation of the presence of these Baptist traditions in the Mandaean literature is that, at the time of the Islamic conquest, when these traditions were evidently compiled, other faiths were tolerated by the Islamic masters only if they had a holy book and a prophet (like Islam). The incorporation into their religion of NT traditions concerning John the Baptist met their need for a prophet (they considered Jesus to be a false prophet). Therefore, while the incorporation of Baptist traditions into the Mandaean literature provides data for a historical study of Mandaeism, it provides no reliable historical data concerning John the Baptist himself.[42]

### 2.7 Conclusion

Josephus incorporated a brief description of John the Baptist into his history of the socio-political situation in Palestine leading up to the first Jewish War. It suited his purposes to provide a sympathetic picture of him, his ministry and his execution. Josephus portrayed John as a moral preacher and a baptizer. He called the people to a righteous lifestyle and to practise baptism for purifying the body. His teachings aroused the people to fever pitch, causing Herod Antipas to fear John's ministry would lead to strife, and so he had John imprisoned and executed.

This passage is an authentic text written by Josephus, and has been composed within the parameters of Greco-Roman historiography. Keeping in mind the limitations of both the text and Josephus' history-writing, this passage may be used as a source for historical data in our investigation of John the Baptist. The traditions concerning John found in the Slavonic Josephus and the Mandaean literature, however, contribute no further data relevant for our investigation.

---

41  One example of evidence for this judgment is that in the *Book of John* the name for John alternates between the Arabic form, Yaḥyā, and the Mandaean form, Yōhānā. Mead, *Gnostic John the Baptizer*, 31; Dodd, *Interpretation*, 124; Yamauchi, *Pre-Christian Gnosticism*, 124.

42  For more extensive criticisms, see Dodd, *Interpretation*, 115-30; Scobie, *John the Baptist*, 23-31; Yamauchi, *Pre-Christian Gnosticism*, 117-42, 163-69.

Chapter 3

# THE TRADITIONS CONCERNING JOHN THE BAPTIST
# IN EARLY CHRISTIAN GOSPELS

## 3.1 *Introduction*

As well as Josephus' reference to John the Baptist in his *Antiquities*, traditions concerning John are also found in early Christian literature, especially Gospels. Since the contribution I wish to make is primarily historical, it is not necessary to engage in a *detailed* redaction-critical analysis of the *all* these traditions. Such an analysis has already been done admirably by Walter Wink, and I am dependent upon him and others for the survey which follows.[1] The purpose of this chapter is: (1) to survey the material in the Gospels concerning John; (2) to observe how each Evangelist has portrayed John by shaping this material; and (3) to come to some general conclusions concerning the possibility of using this material as data in a historical investigation concerning John.

In this work I assume a two-source hypothesis for the synoptic Gospels. I am aware of the problems with this hypothesis and of other hypotheses which have been offered, but the explanation that Matthew and Luke used Mark and Q in addition to their own special traditions still appears to be the best explanation of the data, and it continues to find considerable scholarly support.[2]

## 3.2 *The Portrayal of John the Baptist in Q*

Six pericopae in Q contain traditions concerning John the Baptist.[3]

---

1 Wink, *John the Baptist*. Other studies upon which I am also dependent are referred to in the discussion of each Gospel. Detailed analysis of the pericopae relevant to this study is reserved for later chapters.
2 Farmer has led the attack on the two-source hypothesis and argued extensively for a return to the Griesbach hypothesis (Mark's Gospel is dependent on Matthew and Luke; cf. Farmer, *Synoptic Problem*). For a recent criticism of Farmer and a defence of Markan priority see Tuckett, *Griesbach Hypothesis*. Helpful surveys of the issues are Fitzmyer, 'Priority of Mark', 1.131-70; Styler, 'Priority of Mark', 223-32; Stein, *Synoptic Problem*, 29-157. Recently, major articles which have argued both for and against both Markan priority and the existence of Q have been brought together in a valuable collection by Bellinzoni, *Two-Source Hypothesis*.
3 Since the evidence for Q consists primarily in the evidence for a source common to Matthew and Luke, but not Mark, it is logically possible that Q consists of disparate traditions which Matthew and Luke both use, but they do not form a single document

These may be summarized as follows:[4]

| Subject | Luke | Matthew |
|---|---|---|
| 1. John preaches repentance and imminent judgment | 3.7-9 | 3.7-10 |
| 2. John announces a coming figure | 3.16-17 | 3.11-12 |
| 3. John questions Jesus' identity | 7.18-23 | 11.2-6 |
| 4. Jesus witnesses concerning John | 7.24-28 | 11.7-11 |
| 5. Jesus describes responses to John and himself | 7.31-35 | 11.16-19 |
| 6. Jesus relates John to the Law and Prophets and to the kingdom | 16.16 | 11.12-13 |

These six pericopae focus on two main subjects. Two pericopae, Q 3.7-9 and 3.16-17 (cf. 7.18-20), are concerned with John's proclamation, while the rest, Q 7.18-23; 7.24-28; 7.31-35 and 16.16, focus upon Jesus' view of John and his ministry.[5] In Q 7.18-23 these two concerns overlap: John

or source (e.g. Dibelius, *Tradition*, 233-35; Ellis, *Luke*, 21-24). However, others have argued (e.g. Crossan, *Cross that Spoke*, xii) that Q is a single document because the Q pericopae (1) bear common traits of orality (so Havener, *Q*, 29-45); (2) reveal a generic integrity (so Robinson, 'LOGOI SOPHON', 71-113); and (3) manifest a theological unity (so Jacobson, 'Literary Unity of Q', 365-89). This latter position has the support of most scholars engaged in Q research and appears more probable than the former position. Therefore, I analyse Q for its portrayal of John based on the reasonable hypothesis that Q was a single document with a reasonably unified point of view; cf. other studies of Q's theology cited below.

Q texts are cited here following the convention of the SBL Q Seminar; that is, by their Lukan position (e.g. Q 3.16 = Mt. 3.11 = Lk. 3.16). Kloppenborg (*Formation*, xvii) correctly notes that this method of citation 'in no way is meant to suggest that the Lucan working or location is necessarily that of Q'.

Other studies of John the Baptist in Q include Lohmeyer, *Johannes der Täufer*, 17-20; Manson, *Sayings*, 39-71; Wink, *John the Baptist*, 18-26; Hoffmann, *Logienquelle*, 15-79, 190-233; Bammel, 'The Baptist', 99-101; Laufen, *Doppelüberlieferungen*, 93-125; Edwards, *Theology of Q*, 55, 80-82, 94-99; Kloppenborg, *Formation*, 102-21; Havener, *Q*, 62-67; Sato, *Q und Prophetie*, 125-29, 208-12; Ernst, *Johannes der Täufer*, 39-80.

4   It is possible that portions of Mt. 3.1-6 = Lk. 3.1-4 (cf. Mk 1.2-6) might have been originally in Q, providing an introduction to the ministry of John the Baptist. But the evidence is not overwhelming and reconstruction of such an introduction in Q is problematic. Therefore, I discuss this pericope when examining the synoptic Gospels. See Kloppenborg (*Q Parallels*, 4-7) for discussion and further references. Similarly, whether or not Q originally contained an account of Jesus' baptism is difficult to determine. Kloppenborg (*Formation*, 84-85) notes that, while such an account may seem appropriate, the linguistic data are not compelling, and Q focuses upon John's proclamation and prophetic status rather than his baptismal ministry. But see Havener (*Q*, 64) who follows Polag (*Christologie*, 151-54; cited by Havener, 64 n. 49) in including Jesus' baptism in Q. See Kloppenborg (*Q Parallels*, 14-17) for discussion and further references.

5   For a similar division of the Q material concerning John the Baptist see for example Wink, *John the Baptist*, 18; Ernst, *Johannes der Täufer*, 39-40.

Edwards (*Theology of Q*, xiii, 97) evidently considers Lk. 7.29-30 to parallel Mt. 21.31b-32 and thus to form part of Q, but, as Fitzmyer states (*Luke*, 1.671), 'the formulation is so different that it is difficult to think that we are dealing with a "Q" parallel'. Similarly, Kloppenborg (*Formation*, 74) does not include this material in Q.

asks whether or not Jesus is to be identified with John's expected figure, and in response Jesus explains how he perceives his own ministry in relation to John's expectation.

This Q material begins in 3.7-9 with John, in prophetic style, denouncing his audience[6] and calling them to 'bear fruits in keeping with repentance'. They must do so because reliance upon their ethnic lineage as 'children of Abraham' is false security, and because the coming wrath is imminent in its execution. The next pericope (3.16-17) continues this thrust concerning judgment, but its orientation is different because the focus is upon the agents involved in the divine program and their respective roles. John is the agent who calls his audience to repentance (as in 3.7-9) and baptizes them in water, but the arrival of an agent mightier than John is imminent. This expected figure will have a greater ministry of baptizing with the Holy Spirit[7] and fire, cleansing the threshing floor, gathering the wheat and burning the chaff. John's prophetic proclamation and announcement introduces the eschatological crisis by presenting to his audience (and the audience of Q[8]) the radical demand of God in the face of imminent eschatological events.[9]

In Q (as we are able to reconstruct it) these sayings of John are followed by the narrative of Jesus' temptation (Q 4.1-13),[10] and then statements of his teachings recorded in the Sermon on the Mount/Plain (Q 6.20b-49) and his miracle of healing the centurion's son (Q 7.1-10). John then appears again on the scene, but now he is in prison. Through his disciples, John asks Jesus whether he is the one John announced: 'Are you the one who is coming, or shall we look for someone else?' Jesus responds by pointing to his performing healing miracles and announcing good news to the poor, both in terms reminiscent of Isa. 61.1 (Q 7.18-23). The order of Q's pericopae and the inclusion of this narrative clearly indicate that they function to identify Jesus as the expected figure John proclaimed. Jesus is the one who resolves the eschatological crisis introduced in John's proclamation.

6  For a discussion of this pericope's original audience, cf. §6.2.3.
7  When referring to the Christian presentation of John, I use the capitalized form of this expression, 'Holy Spirit' because the Evangelists evidently equated this aspect of John's announcement with Christian teaching concerning the Holy Spirit. This is in distinction to the possible use of the same expression by John whose use of it would not have had the same significance. So to refer to John's use of the same phrase I use the lower case: 'holy spirit'. Cf. §8.2.1, 8.4.1.
8  Ernst (*Johannes der Täufer*, 79) states that 'die Predigtsammlung Mt. 3,7-10.11f. par hält nicht nur die Erinnerung an den Gerichtsboten am Jordan wach, sie ruft die Hörer hier und jetzt in die Entscheidung'.
9  Wink, *John the Baptist*, 18.
10  On the possibility that Q may have originally contained a reference to Jesus' baptism by John see the above relevant note in this section.

Following his response to the delegation of John's disciples, Jesus turns to the crowds and eulogizes John (Q 7.24-28): he not only confirms his prophetic status but also identifies John with the eschatological messenger of Yahweh by citing Mal. 3.1, thus implicitly perceiving John as Elijah-*redivivus*.[11] So, Jesus concludes, no human being is greater than John. This high estimation of John is tempered by the qualifying statement: 'but the one who is lesser in the kingdom of God is greater than he [i.e. John]'.[12]

In the next Q pericope (Q 7.31-35) Jesus, after eulogizing John, condemns the people for rejecting John's ministry as demonic due to his ascetic lifestyle, as well as rejecting his own ministry as excessive because he ate and drank with society's marginalized members. While contrasting the styles of their ministries, Jesus places them both on an equal footing, and asserts that the outcome of their ministries will demonstrate their wisdom.

The final Q pericope (Q 16.16) is problematic not only because Matthew and Luke provide different versions and settings for it, but also because of its ambiguous nature.[13] A discussion of these problems is beyond our scope, but we can make two observations concerning Q's presentation of Jesus' view concerning John: his ministry is the eschatological turning point which inaugurates the kingdom of God, and the ministries of both John and Jesus are the focus of opposition.[14]

To summarize, in Q John is a great prophet and the eschatological messenger of Yahweh, and thus he is implicitly identified as Elijah-*redivivus*. He proclaims imminent judgment and calls the people to repentance, as well as announcing the imminent arrival of a figure who will judge and restore. John's ministry introduces an eschatological crisis which inaugurates the kingdom of God. Q presents Jesus as fulfilling John's expected figure and Jesus' ministry as resolving the eschatological crisis. Both their ministries are placed on a similar footing, yet John is carefully subordinated to Jesus. In Q nothing is made of John's baptizing ministry; it is only mentioned in passing (Q 3.7a, 16a), and John is never identified as 'the Baptist' in Q. Furthermore, we are provided with little indication of a positive response to John's ministry other than the mere mention that he had disciples (Q 3.19). Therefore, Q focuses only upon

---

11  The term 'Elijah-*redivivus*' is the scholarly designation for the Jewish expectation that a (literally) 'renewed' Elijah would come, that is, the return of Elijah or the coming of an Elijah-like figure. For further discussion of this expected figure see §7.7.

12  On whether or not this statement goes back to Jesus, and whether the comparative μικρότερος (lit. 'lesser') should be understood as a superlative ('least') see, for example, Wink, *John the Baptist*, 23-25; Fitzmyer, *Luke*, 1.675.

13  For a history of interpretation and extensive discussion of this problematic text, see Cameron, *Violence and the Kingdom*.

14  Wink, *John the Baptist*, 21-22; Kloppenborg, *Formation*, 114-15.

John's eschatological role as the prophet who introduces Jesus and the kingdom of God. Q has *described* John primarily in his own terms (esp. Q 3.7-9, 16-17); that is, John has not been Christianized. Yet, 'John is *evaluated* wholly in terms of his relationship to the Gospel and the kingdom of God' (esp. Q 7.18-35).[15]

### 3.3 *The Portrayal of John the Baptist in Mark*

The Gospel of Mark contains nine pericopae referring to John the Baptist.[16] They may be summarized as follows:

| Subject | Mark |
|---|---|
| 1. John preaches a baptism and baptizes the people | 1.2-6 |
| 2. John announces a coming figure | 1.7-8 |
| 3. John baptizes Jesus | 1.9-11 |
| 4. Jesus goes into Galilee after John's arrest | 1.14 |
| 5. Jesus comments on John's practice of fasting | 2.18-22 |
| 6. Public opinions concerning Jesus and Herod's opinion in light of having imprisoned and executed John | 6.14-29 |
| 7. Public opinions concerning Jesus and Peter's confession of him as Messiah | 8.27-30 |
| 8. Jesus explains that Elijah has already come | 9.9-13 |
| 9. Jesus disputes over the authority of John's baptism | 11.27-33 |

Mark introduces us to the figure of John as one whose ministry fulfils prophetic scripture by preparing the way for the coming of the Lord (1.2-3). As a wilderness figure in prophetic garb (1.4a, 6), John calls the people to 'a baptism of repentance for the forgiveness of sins' (1.4b). The response to John is overwhelming as people flock from all around to be baptized in the Jordan river (1.5). But not only is this baptismal ministry preparatory, John also prepares the people by announcing the coming of a mightier figure who will baptize them with the Holy Spirit (1.7-8). Jesus then arrives on the scene from Galilee and is also baptized by John. He receives the Spirit and hears a heavenly voice declaring: 'You are my beloved son, with you I am well pleased' (1.9-11). Events quickly climax in this introductory section to Mark's Gospel. Sometime after Jesus' temptation in the wilderness (1.12-13) John is arrested, and then Jesus returns to Galilee where he proclaims the gospel: 'The time has been fulfilled and the kingdom of God is at hand; repent and believe the gospel' (1.14-15).

15  Wink, *John the Baptist*, 26; my emphasis.
16  Other, more extensive discussions of John the Baptist in Mark's Gospel include Lohmeyer, *Johannes der Täufer*, 13-17; Marxsen, *Mark*, 30-53; Wink, *John the Baptist*, 1-17; Bammel, 'The Baptist', 96-99; Wolff, 'Bedeutung Johannes des Täufers', 857-65; Lupieri, *Giovanni Battista*, 21-52; Ernst, *Johannes der Täufer*, 4-38.

In this opening section of Mark's Gospel, John is the forerunner who prepares the way for the Lord, that is Jesus. His prophetic announcement of a coming figure is implicitly fulfilled in Jesus[17] who comes to bring God's salvation. The description of John's baptizing ministry prepares the reader for the baptism of Jesus, and thus it allows for the narration of the Spirit's descent and the heavenly announcement of Jesus' identity as the Son of God. But Mark quickly removes John from the scene once his preparatory ministry as forerunner is completed, so that Jesus can now announce the beginning of the eschatological era and the inbreaking of the kingdom of God. Mark uses John's ministry christologically to support his view that this is 'the beginning of the gospel of Jesus Christ, the Son of God' (1.1).

Other than the account of his death, the remaining pericopae in Mark's Gospel which mention John focus upon the views of others concerning John, especially as they relate to their understanding of Jesus.

In Mk 2.18-22 people ask Jesus why the disciples of both John and the Pharisees fast but Jesus' disciples do not.[18] This brief reference to John's lifestyle may be linked to the previous description of his diet in 1.6b, but it functions here to provide an opportunity for Jesus to describe his own ministry as a wedding feast, and thus it belongs to the eschatological age of salvation (2.19).[19] So his ministry, which is 'new', is incompatible with that which is 'old' (1.21-22), that is, the ministries of John and the Pharisees.

The first part of the next pericope (6.14-16) records various opinions concerning Jesus as his fame spreads because of his miracles: Jesus is either Elijah or a prophet (6.15). But others believe that 'John the baptizer has risen from the dead' (6.14), an opinion which is held by Herod Antipas (6.16). This first part functions to highlight the spread of Jesus' fame, but it also serves to provide the setting for the account of John's death (6.17-29).[20] John rebukes Herod for marrying Herodias, the former wife of his brother Philip, which angers Herodias. Herod has John

---

17 This identification is not made explicit, and neither is the identification of John with Elijah-*redivivus* in 9.9-13. Bammel ('The Baptist', 97) explains this phenomenon by describing Mark's Gospel as 'the gospel of indirect christology'.

18 It is grammatically possible to understand οἱ μαθηταὶ Ἰωάνου καὶ οἱ Φαρισαῖοι in Mk 2.18a to be the subjects of the verbs ἔρχονται καὶ λέγουσιν in 2.18b (i.e. the identity of those who come and question Jesus). However, the subject of those verbs is better understood to be indefinite (i.e. 'and people came and said. . .'), because in the question itself the disciples of John and of the Pharisees are referred to in the third person. Luke makes such a distinction clear (Lk. 5.33), whereas Matthew specifically identifies the questioners as the disciples of John (Mt. 9.14). Cranfield, *Mark*, 108; Lane, *Mark*, 109; Pesch, *Markusevangelium*, 1.171; Gnilka, *Markus*, 1.112; against Guelich, *Mark*, 1.109.

19 On this imagery see Guelich, *Mark*, 1.110-11.

20 For a brief discussion of the historical issues behind this account, cf. §10.7.

arrested, but does not want to execute John. At a banquet celebrating Herod's birthday the daughter of Herodias dances in a way which pleases Herod so much that he vows to give her anything she wishes. Upon prompting from Herodias, she requests the head of John. Not wishing to break his vow in front of his guests, Herod commands the execution to take place. Afterwards, John's disciples take his body and bury it. Mark's account portrays the unjust death of a righteous prophet at the hands of a wicked man through the instigation of a vindictive woman.

In 8.27-30 the disciples respond to Jesus' question, 'Who do people say that I am?' with the same opinions listed in 6.14-16; he is either John the Baptist, Elijah or one of the prophets. Jesus then asks the disciples for their own opinion, to which Peter responds: 'You are the Messiah'. This passage thus focuses upon Jesus' messianic identity, and John is only mentioned in passing, but it does serve to strengthen John's standing as a popular prophetic figure in Mark.

After the transfiguration of Jesus (9.1-8), in which Moses and Elijah appear and talk with him, Jesus commands them not to tell anyone what they have seen 'until the Son of Man had risen from the dead' (9.9). This prompts the disciples to question the meaning of this resurrection (9.10). They also ask Jesus, 'Why do the scribes say that Elijah must first come?' (9.11). Jesus' answer is somewhat problematic due to the interjection of a reference to the sufferings of the Son of Man.[21] With respect to Jesus' three statements concerning Elijah, the first confirms the belief in an Elijah-*redivivus* figure (9.12a), the second asserts that this figure has already come, and the third states that 'they did to him whatever they wished, as it is written concerning him' (9.13). While it is not made explicit by Mark, Jesus is implicitly identifying John the Baptist as Elijah-*redivivus*, and referring to John's suffering and death at the hands of Herod and Herodias.[22] The interjected reference to the suffering of the

---

21 Wink (*John the Baptist*, 13-17) proposes that originally the reference to the Son of Man in this saying was not to Jesus but to Elijah, the sense of the phrase being '*that* Son of Man', and referring back to Elijah as the antecedent in language reminiscent of Ezekiel's use of the term (e.g. Ezek. 2.1-3). While this is an interesting proposal, our concern here is with Mark's portrayal of the matter. For further discussion see the commentaries, e.g. Lane, *Mark*, 322-27, esp. nn. 28, 36.

22 There is no clear evidence of a pre-Christian Jewish belief that Elijah-*redivivus* would suffer. Jeremias ('Ἠλ(ε)ίας', 2.939-40) claims that the Apocalypse of Elijah provides support for the pre-Christian concept of a suffering Elijah-*redivivus*, but the text in question appears to be a Christian expansion based on Rev. 11.3-12; cf. Wink, *John the Baptist*, 14 n. 2 (cf. the translation of *Apoc. Elij.* 4.7-19 in *OTP* 1.747-48, and the text and another translation of *Apoc. Elij.* 15.8–17.3 [is different line numbering but is the same text as 4.7-19] in Pietersma, Comstock and Attridge, *Apocalypse of Elijah*, 49-53). Lane's explanation (*Mark*, 326 n. 35) that 'the phrase "even as it is written of him" has reference to the prophet Elijah in the framework of his historical ministry' is quite plausible and receives support from the Elijah-typology found elsewhere in Mark's Gospel.

Son of Man evidently signifies a parallel between John's suffering and death as Elijah-*redivivus* and Jesus' predicted suffering and death as the Son of Man (cf. 8.31). John's suffering and death as 'Elijah' paves the way for, and prefigures, the similar fate of Jesus as the Son of Man.[23]

With the identity of John as Elijah-*redivivus* and the use of John's suffering and death to prefigure Jesus, the significance of earlier references to John becomes clearer. For example, the inclusion of Mal. 3.1 in the introductory quotation in 1.2-3, a prophetic expectation which John fulfils, could be intimating a link with the expectation of Elijah-*redivivus* in Mal. 4.5-6. Secondly, the mention in 1.6 that 'John was clothed with camel's hair and a leather belt around his waist' probably is included by Mark to identify John as a prophet, and possibly to hint as well at John's identity as Elijah-*redivivus* (cf. 2 Kgs 1.8).[24] Thirdly, Mark's extended narration in 6.14-29 of John's imprisonment and death which highlights his sufferings because of a revengeful woman who schemes for his death, parallels Elijah's sufferings due to Jezebel's scheming (cf. 1 Kgs 19.1-3). This story was also included by Mark to support further his use of John's sufferings and death to pre-figure those of Jesus.[25]

The final mention of John the Baptist in Mark's Gospel concerns a conflict between the temple leadership and Jesus during his final week of ministry in Jerusalem (11.27-33). While in the temple they question Jesus concerning his action of clearing the moneychangers and merchants from the temple courts and teaching in the temple: 'By what authority are you doing these things, or who gave you this authority to do these things?' Instead of answering, Jesus responds with his own question, so that, if his opponents will answer his question, he will answer theirs. He asks them, 'Was the baptism of John from heaven or from men?' (11.29-30). Discussing among themselves they realize that, if they answer 'from heaven', Jesus will rebuke them for not believing him, and, if they answer 'from men', they would offend the people who believed John was a prophet (11.31-32). So the temple leaders say they do not know, and Jesus in turn refuses to answer their question. This pericope reveals little new concerning John. It confirms the impression gleaned

---

23　For further discussion of this parallel in terms of Mark's messianic secret and Elijah-incognito, see Wink, *John the Baptist*, 13-17; Ernst, *Johannes der Täufer*, 30-34.

24　John's dress is that of the nomad in the wilderness as well as that of the prophetic role in particular (Zech. 13.4; Heb. 11.37). While some see this description as an allusion to Elijah (cf. Wink, *John the Baptist*, 3), others see little basis for such a claim (cf. Guelich, *Mark*, 1.20-21).

25　Guelich, *Mark*, 1.328, 331; Wink, *John the Baptist*, 11. The pre-figuring of Jesus' sufferings and death by John's fate probably also explains the unusual use of the verb παραδίδωμι in Mk 1.14 to describe John's arrest: as John is 'handed over' to suffering and death, so is Jesus (cf. the same verb used for Jesus in Mk 3.19; 9.31; 10.33; 14.10, 11, 18, 21, 41, 42, 44); cf. Cranfield, *Mark*, 62; Lupieri, *Giovanni Battista*, 30-33.

elsewhere of the people's opinion of John's prophetic status, but shows that this was evidently a matter of debate. The context in which Jesus asks this question indicates that he viewed John as an ally,[26] and that his own authority could be considered in similar terms.

In summary, Mark portrays John in the dual role of prophet and baptizer. He calls the people to repentance and baptism, and he announces the imminent arrival of a figure who will inaugurate God's salvation by bestowing the Spirit (1.4-8). The response from the people is positive, and they hold him in high esteem (1.5; 6.14; 8.28; 8.30-32), but the Jewish leaders do not accept his message (11.30-33). John is also a wilderness figure with ascetic practices (1.6), and he has disciples who join him in this lifestyle (2.18). John is presented as the forerunner of Jesus; he prepares the way for the arrival of Jesus Messiah, Son of God, and in so doing, he himself fulfils scripture (1.2-4). But he is also Elijah-*redivivus* whose sufferings and death prefigure the similar fate of Jesus (9.9-13; cf. 6.17-29). John is closely identified with Jesus by functioning as his forerunner and ally (1.2-8; 11.27-33), and his ministry fulfils scripture (1.2-4), and thus he contributes to the arrival of the eschatological time of salvation (1.14-15) and participates in 'the beginning of the gospel' (1.1). Yet, since this 'new' time of salvation is centered in the ministry of Jesus, John's 'old' ministry is carefully distinguished from it in time (1.14-15) and focus (2.18-22).[27]

Mark's presentation differs from Q's in several respects. First of all, Mark focuses much more on John's baptizing ministry (1.4-5, 9-11; 11.30-32) and does not mention John's announcement of imminent judgment (1.7-8; cf. Q 3.7-9, 16-17). Secondly, while both Q and Mark understand John to be Elijah-*redivivus*, it is Mark who interprets this role to include suffering and death which prefigure Jesus' own passion. Thirdly, in contrast to Q, Mark appears more concerned to separate John's ministry from that of Jesus (1.14-15; 2.18-22), and yet, Mark does not appear as concerned (at least explicitly) to subordinate John to Jesus, as does Q (e.g. Q 7.28).

### 3.4 *The Portrayal of John the Baptist in Matthew*

In Matthew's Gospel there are 16 pericopae containing references to John the Baptist.[28] They are as follows:

---

26 Lane (*Mark*, 413) points out that the temple leaders' 'decision about John will determine their decision about him'.

27 Cf. Wink, *John the Baptist*, 5-7; Robinson, 'Problem of History', 69-74. Ernst, (*Johannes der Täufer*, 37) concludes that 'Johannes ist nach des Intentionen des Markus der Mann "zwischen den Zeiten" '.

28 More complete discussions of Matthew's portrayal of John the Baptist may be found

| Subject | Matthew | Source |
| --- | --- | --- |
| 1. John preaches repentance and baptizes the people | 3.1-6 | Mk 1.2-6 |
| 2. John preaches repentance and imminent judgment | 3.7-10 | Q 3.7-9 |
| 3. John announces a coming figure | 3.11-12 | Mk 1.7-8 & Q 3.16-17 |
| 4. John baptizes Jesus | 3.13-17 | Mk 1.9-11 |
| 5. Jesus goes into Galilee after John's arrest | 4.12 | Mk 1.14 |
| 6. Jesus comments on John's practice of fasting | 9.14-17 | Mk 2.18-22 |
| 7. John questions Jesus' identity | 11.2-6 | Q 7.18-23 |
| 8. Jesus testifies concerning John | 11.7-11 | Q 7.24-28 |
| 9. Jesus relates John to the Law and Prophets and to the kingdom | 11.12-13 | Q 16.16 |
| 10. Jesus identifies John as Elijah | 11.14-15 | |
| 11. Jesus describes responses to John and himself | 11.16-19 | Q 7.31-35 |
| 12. Herod's opinion of Jesus in light of having imprisoned and executed John | 14.1-12 | Mk 6.14-29 |
| 13. Public opinions concerning Jesus and Peter's confession of him as Messiah | 16.13-16 | Mk 8.27-30 |
| 14. Jesus explains that Elijah has already come | 17.9-13 | Mk 9.9-13 |
| 15. Jesus disputes over the authority of John's baptism | 21.23-27 | Mk 11.27-33 |
| 16. Jesus applies the parable of two sons to different responses to John | 21.28-32 | |

In these 16 pericopae Matthew has utilized all pericopae available to him from Mark and has added to them two units which are unique to his own Gospel.[29] Since these pericopae have already been summarized in the preceding discussion, it would be needlessly repetitive to do the same for Matthew (and Luke as well). Therefore, I refer the reader to the preceding discussion for those summaries, and focus here upon Matthean emphases.

In 3.1-6 Matthew introduces John as a wilderness preacher who proclaims: 'Repent, for the kingdom of heaven is at hand' (3.1-2). In describing John's message this way, Matthew has altered Mark's description of John 'preaching a baptism of repentance for the forgiveness of sins' (Mk 1.4) to a message which is identical to the message proclaimed by

in Trilling, 'Täufertradition', 271-89; Wink, *John the Baptist*, 27-41 (who follows Trilling closely); Bammel, 'The Baptist', 101-104; Meier, 'John the Baptist', 383-405; Krentz, 'John the Baptist', 333-38; Lupieri, *Giovanni Battista*, 13-43, 81-113; Ernst, *Johannes der Täufer*, 155-85; cf. Nepper-Christensen ('Taufe', 189-207) who focuses upon the relationship of traditions concerning John to Christian baptism.

29   Whether he utilized all the pericopae available from Q is impossible to determine for, by definition, Q is material found in both Matthew and Luke. In the discussion in §3.5 concerning Luke's presentation of John I do mention that Lk. 3.10-14 may be Q material which Matthew had not used, but this is speculative.

Q has six pericopae and Mark nine, but Matthew has only 16 rather than the 17 we might expect (if we added 6 [Q] + 9 [Mk] + 2 [Mt.] = 17). This is because Mt. 3.11-12 is one pericope combining two pericopae from his sources (Q 3.16-17; Mk 1.7-8).

Jesus (4.17). In so doing, Matthew aligns John even more closely with Jesus than Mark did, but he also carefully subordinates John to Jesus by attributing forgiveness of sins exclusively to the death of Jesus (26.28).[30] Matthew states that John's ministry fulfils Isa. 40.3 (3.3). In this way, he makes John's fulfilment of prophetic scripture explicit, whereas Mark only implied it. Matthew's quotation of this prophecy does not blend Mal. 3.1 and Exod. 23.20 with Isa. 40.3 as did Mark (Mk 1.2-3), thus removing an indirect reference to Elijah-*redivivus* at this point (though he does cite these texts in 11.10, making explicit the identification of John as Elijah-*redivivus*).

Though many came to be baptized by John (3.5-6), Matthew reports that Pharisees and Sadducees came to observe John's baptismal practice, evidently with a critical attitude (3.7).[31] Matthew follows Q 3.7-9 closely in reporting John's condemnation of them and his announcement of imminent wrath.

In 3.11-12, Matthew evidently has two sources at hand, but chooses to follow Q more closely than Mark. The only alteration to his sources which is significant at this point is his addition of the phrase 'for repentance' in John's statement concerning his baptism: 'I baptize you with water for repentance'. Matthew evidently does so to clarify that John's baptism is a baptism of repentance, because in 3.2 he removed such a reference from his source (Mk 1.4) to make John's preaching consistent with Jesus' preaching of the kingdom of heaven.[32]

John's ministry having been described, the reader is now introduced to the adult Jesus, whose ministry begins with his being baptized by John (3.13-17). This baptismal scene serves a similar function in Matthew as it did in Mark: Jesus is anointed by God's Spirit and is declared to be the Son of God. However, Matthew's alteration of Mark's 'you are my beloved Son' to '*this is* my beloved Son' (3.17) makes the event more public than does Mark's account. Since John and Jesus have engaged in conversation, it may be that Matthew is suggesting that John, and possibly the crowds, also heard the voice.[33] The conversation between John

---

30  Wink, *John the Baptist*, 35. Matthew has already aligned John with Jesus by introducing him with the clause 'in those days came John . . .' (3.1); 'those days' being the days of Jesus the Messiah, which were introduced as beginning with Jesus' birth in Matthew's infancy narrative.

31  This is the best sense of Matthew's use of ἐπί in the clause ἐρχομένους ἐπὶ τὸ βάπτισμα. Cf. Hill, *Matthew*, 92; Davies and Allison, *Matthew*, 1.303-304; Gundry, *Matthew*, 46. For further discussion of John's audience in this pericope, cf. §6.2.3.

32  Cf. Gundry, *Matthew*, 48.

33  Cf. Hill, *Matthew*, 97; Davies and Allison, *Matthew*, 1.330. Luz (*Matthew*, 1.180) suggests that 'in Matthew, Jesus was already from the beginning, from his birth, the Son of God and did not become such through baptism. So the heavenly voice is no longer directed to Jesus, who knows his own identity, but rather to John the Baptist and particularly to the crowds who have to be considered as present since 3.5. . .'

and Jesus is reported only in Matthew and suggests that Jesus' baptism
has become a matter of embarrassment to the early church by this time.
The cause of this embarrassment may be either that receiving John's
baptism—a baptism of repentance for the forgiveness of sins—brought
into question the belief in Jesus' sinlessness, or else that receiving John's
baptism suggested that Jesus was inferior to John.[34] In spite of these
potential problems, Matthew does utilize this tradition. In this conversation, John recognizes Jesus, and thus he becomes a witness to Jesus.
John's subordinate position relative to Jesus is emphasized by John's
words, but by contrast Jesus' response, 'it is fitting for *us* to fulfil all righteousness' (3.15), emphasizes that John and Jesus together carry out
God's salvific plan.[35]

After his account of Jesus' temptation (4.1-11), Matthew follows Mark
in reporting that Jesus returned to Galilee following John's arrest, but he
makes the causal relationship between the two events more explicit:
'Now when he heard that John had been arrested, he [i.e. Jesus] withdrew into Galilee' (4.12).

In 9.14-17, Matthew follows Mark closely in describing Jesus' response
to the question concerning why his disciples did not fast though John's
disciples and the Pharisees did so. In contrast to Mark, Matthew makes
clear that it is John's disciples who actually ask the question concerning
themselves and the Pharisess (9.14; in Mk 2.18 the questioners are left
unidentified).[36] Jesus responds with a question, which Mark expresses as
'Can the wedding guests fast . . . ?' (2.19), but which Matthew alters to
'Can the wedding guests *mourn* . . . ?' which suggests the issue is not fasting itself, but fasting as an expression of sorrow. Such fasting would be
incompatible with the presence of Jesus Messiah at the messianic banquet.[37] In spite of these changes, Matthew's thrust in the passage is
essentially the same as Mark's.

In 11.2-19, Matthew follows the Q tradition concerning John's question to Jesus from prison and Jesus' view of John. His introductory
clause emphasises that the issue is the messianic identity of Jesus: 'Now

---

34  Cf. the denial that Jesus was baptized by John in the *Gospel of the Nazareans*
    (§3.7.3). Luz (*Matthew*, 1.177, his emphasis) states that 'the idea of the *sinlessness of
    Jesus*, which has always played a decisive role for the church interpretation of our
    passage, is not at all expressed by Matthew or the Synoptics. . .' While Matthew does
    not *state* the idea of Jesus' sinlessness in this pericope, his handling of it does suggest
    that he is sensitive to the problems associated with Jesus' baptism by John. Cf. Bon-
    nard, *Matthieu*, 39-40; Hill, *Matthew*, 95-96; Davies and Allison, *Matthew*, 1.320-27.
35  Meier, 'John the Baptist', 391-92.
36  Gundry (*Matthew*, 169) points out that Matthew alters the questioners so that there is
    a progression from the scribes (9.1-8) to Pharisees (9.9-13) to John's disciples (9.14-
    17).
37  Hill, *Matthew*, 176.

when John heard in prison about the deeds of the Messiah . . .' (11.2). Matthew's major addition to this series of pericopae makes explicit the Elijianic identity of John which was left implicit in Q. Not found in Q, and so unique to Matthew, is 11.14-15: 'And if you are willing to accept it, he [i.e. John] is Elijah who is to come. The one who has ears to hear, let that one hear.'

Matthew's presentation in 14.1-12, concerning Herod's opinion of Jesus in light of having imprisoned and executed John, follows Mk 6.14-29 but edits it to make it shorter. For example, he does not mention the various opinions people held concerning Jesus (Mk 6.14-15). He removes Mark's suggestion that Herod liked and feared John, and that it was Herodias who held a grudge against him (Mk 6.19-20). Rather, in Matthew, it is Herod himself who wants to kill John, but he fears the people because of their high opinion of John. The only alteration Matthew makes concerning John himself is to make explicit that the people 'held him to be a prophet' (14.5). Matthew also adds to the end of the pericope that, after burying his body, John's disciples 'went and told Jesus' (14.12b). This Matthew offers as the reason for Jesus' withdrawal 'to a deserted place apart' (14.13a; by contrast, in Mark Jesus withdraws with his disciples after their mission two by two into the Galilean villages, Mk 6.30-31). By this causal relationship, Matthew is adding to the parallel between John's fate as a prophet and that expected for Jesus.[38]

While Matthew has altered the pericope concerning public opinions of Jesus and Peter's confession of Jesus as Messiah (16.13-16; cf. 16.17-20), it does not affect Matthew's presentation of John.

Matthew's account concerning the disciples asking Jesus about Elijah's coming (17.10-13) clarifies the somewhat problematic text in Mark (esp. 9.12). He removes the reference concerning the Son of Man's suffering from the middle of Mark's explanation concerning Elijah's return and places it at the end. Thus he makes clear and explicit what was rather tortuously suggested in Mark; that is, as Elijah has come and suffered because he was not recognized, 'so also the Son of Man will suffer at their hands' (17.12b). Matthew also makes explicit what Q had left implied: 'Then the disciples understood that he spoke to them about John the Baptist' (17.13).

Matthew's account of Jesus' using the question about the source of John's baptism in his dispute with the temple leadership over his authority (21.23-27) does not vary significantly from Mark's account. But Matthew does append to the account a parable unique to his Gospel (21.28-

---

38 Matthew places the story of John's death immediately after Jesus' saying concerning a prophet being without honour (13.57). Wink, *John the Baptist*, 27; Trilling, 'Täufertradition', 272-74; Bonnard, *Matthieu*, 217.

32), which Jesus addresses to these same temple leaders. Two sons are told to go work in the vineyard by their father. One refuses, but later repents and goes. The other agrees, but does not go. In response to Jesus' question, these leaders agree that it was the first son who did the will of the father. Jesus then likens them to the second son, but identifies tax collectors and prostitutes with the first son: 'Truly I say to you, the tax collectors and prostitutes enter into the kingdom of God before you' (21.31b). To support this statement, Jesus applies it to the temple leaders' rejection of John's baptism in their dispute with Jesus. They did not believe John, and even when the tax collectors and prostitutes believed, they still 'did not repent afterward and believe him' (21.32). This pericope continues the view of John which was intimated in the preceding one. John is viewed as Jesus' ally against the Jewish leaders who have rejected them both. It also identifies one of the segments of the population among which John had success, the marginalized persons within Jewish society.

Thus, Matthew's *presentation* of John himself and his ministry does not differ markedly from that of his sources. He portrays John as both baptizer and prophet, and adds one further element: John not only drew crowds, but this positive response to John included the marginalized members of society. But Matthew's *interpretation* of John is somewhat different: he makes more explicit John's identity as Elijah-*redivivus*, an identification already implicit in his sources. As well, Matthew so shapes his sources as to reinterpret John's role with respect to Jesus. While John is more clearly subordinated to Jesus (to protect the uniqueness of Jesus), John is also more completely identified and associated with Jesus not only as his ally, but as the one who prefigures Jesus' death.[39]

### 3.5 *The Portrayal of John the Baptist in Luke/Acts*

Material concerning John the Baptist may be found in 28 pericopae in Luke/Acts.[40] These may be summarized as follows:

| Subject | Luke/Acts Source |
| --- | --- |
| 1. John's birth is predicted to Zechariah, and Elizabeth conceives | 1.5-25 |
| 2. John's conception revealed to Mary | 1.36 |

---

39 It is Meier ('John the Baptist', 383-405) who argues most convincingly that Matthew presents John as both subordinate to, and parallel with, Jesus.

40 Discussions of Luke's presentation of John the Baptist include Lohmeyer, *Johannes der Täufer*, 21-26; Conzelmann, *Luke*, 18-27; Wink, *John the Baptist*, 42-86; Bammel, 'The Baptist', 105-109; Mattill, *Luke*, 13-25; Böcher, 'Lukas', 27-44; Bachmann, 'Johannes der Täufer', 123-55; Lupieri, *Giovanni Battista*, 53-80; Fitzmyer, *Luke the Theologian*, 86-116; Ernst, *Johannes der Täufer*, 81-154.

| | | |
|---|---|---|
| 3. Mary visits Elizabeth while pregnant with John | 1.39-45 | |
| 4. John is born, and Zechariah prophesies | 1.57-79 | |
| 5. John grows up in the wilderness | 1.80 | |
| 6. John preaches a baptism of repentance | 3.1-6 | Mk 1.2-6 |
| 7. John preaches repentance and imminent judgment | 3.7-9 | Q 3.7-9 |
| 8. John replies to questioners | 3.10-14 | |
| 9. John announces a coming figure | 3.15-18 | Mk 1.7-8 & Q 3.16-17 |
| 10. John is imprisoned by Herod | 3.19-20 | Mk 6.17-18 |
| 11. John baptizes Jesus | 3.21-22 | Mk 1.9-11 |
| 12. Jesus comments on John's practice of fasting | 5.33-39 | Mk 2.18-22 |
| 13. John questions Jesus' identity | 7.18-23 | Q 7.18-23 |
| 14. Jesus testifies concerning John | 7.24-28 | Q 7.24-28 |
| 15. The people have accepted John's baptism, but the Pharisees and Scribes did not | 7.29-30 | |
| 16. Jesus describes responses to John and himself | 7.31-35 | Q 7.31-35 |
| 17. Public opinions concerning Jesus and Herod's opinion in light of having imprisoned and executed John | 9.7-9 | Mk 6.14-16 |
| 18. Public opinions concerning Jesus and Peter's confession of him as Messiah | 9.18-21 | Mk 8.27-30 |
| 19. Jesus' disciples ask to be taught to pray as John taught his disciples | 11.1 | |
| 20. Jesus relates John to the Law and Prophets and to the kingdom | 16.16 | Q 16.16 |
| 21. Jesus disputes over the authority of John's baptism | 20.1-8 | Mk 11.27-33 |
| 22. Jesus explains that John's baptism was with water, but disciples will be baptized with the Holy Spirit | Acts 1.5 | |
| 23. The new apostle chosen was to have been with them from baptism of John | 1.21-22 | |
| 24. Peter explains that the gospel began after John's baptism | 10.37 | |
| 25. Peter remembers Jesus' statement concerning John's baptism and disciples being baptized with the Holy Spirit | 11.16 | |
| 26. Paul summarizes John's preaching a baptism of repentance and a coming figure | 13.24-25 | |
| 27. Apollos preaches Jesus, but knows only John's baptism | 18.25 | |
| 28. Paul meets disciples in Ephesus who have only received John's baptism | 19.1-7 | |

Luke's presentation of John the Baptist is similar to that of Matthew, for they both utilize the same two sources, Mark and Q. However, Luke's portrayal is more extensive because he has incorporated additional material concerning John into both his infancy narrative[41] and the book of Acts.

Following his prologue (1.1-4), Luke begins his Gospel in 1.5-25 with an angelic revelation to an elderly priest named Zechariah while he is serving in the temple, that his formerly barren wife, Elizabeth, will have a child (1.5-14). Zechariah is told that the child will be named John, and

---

41 An examination of the possibility of a Baptist source behind Lk. 1 is beyond the limits of this chapter, and it is not relevant to our concerns here. For further discussion and bibliography on the issue see Wink, *John the Baptist*, 60-72. More recent bibliography may be found in Brown, 'Gospel Infancy Narrative Research II', 660-70.

that he will be Spirit empowered and will fulfil the prophecy concerning the coming of Elijah in Mal. 4.5-6 (1.15-17). Zechariah, having been struck dumb as a sign that God would accomplish his word (1.18-22), returns home and his wife conceives a child (1.23-25).

In the annunciation to Mary, she is told that Elizabeth has conceived a son in her old age (1.36). Subsequently, upon being visited by Mary, Elizabeth's baby leaps in her womb (1.39-41). Inspired by the Spirit, Elizabeth prophesies concerning Mary's blessed privilege (1.42-45).

When Elizabeth gives birth to the child, Zechariah writes that he is not to be named after himself, but to be named John instead. Zechariah then receives the power of speech again (1.57-64). These events cause amazement throughout the region (1.65-66). Zechariah, filled with the Spirit, prophesies, describing the coming of a Davidic Messiah (1.67-75) and portraying the role of his son, John, as a prophet who prepares the way for the coming of the Lord (1.76-79).

Luke's portrayal of John in the infancy narrative concludes with the brief announcement that John 'was growing and becoming strong in the Spirit, and he lived in the wilderness places until the day of his public appearance to Israel' (1.80).

In this infancy narrative, John is portrayed in terms with which we are familiar; he is a prophet and forerunner, and is to be identified as Elijah-*redivivus*.[42] But, as distinct from his portrayal elsewhere and due to the very nature of the material, a new side of John is seen. His coming is the result of direct, angelic revelation in addition to OT prophecy (as in Mark and Matthew) and his conception is the result of divine intervention. He is of priestly descent, but he lives in the wilderness prior to beginning his ministry. Due to the relationship between Elizabeth and Mary, John is related to Jesus. His conception, birth and youth are also portrayed by Luke to parallel closely the conception, birth and youth of Jesus, but in each instance he is carefully subordinated to Jesus.[43]

In 3.1-6 Luke prefaces his use of Mk 1.2-6 with a six-fold synchronism to date the beginning of John's ministry (3.1-2a),[44] and then he introduces John's ministry in terms clearly reminiscent of the OT prophets: 'the word of God came to John the son of Zechariah in the wilderness' (3.2b; cf. Jer. 1.1 LXX). So John begins his ministry of 'preaching a bap-

42  John's Elijianic role is clearly stated in 1.16-17. Conzelmann (*Luke*, 22-27) is often cited to support the view that Luke does not identify John with Elijah (e.g. Wink, *John the Baptist*, 42-43). While it is true that Luke has not emphasized this role as much as Matthew did, we should not ignore this clear statement in the infancy narrative, as did Conzelmann (22 n. 2) who admits he ignores Lk. 1–2 entirely. Cf. Oliver, 'Lucan Birth Stories', 202-26; Brown, *Birth*, 275-79.
43  For a discussion of this parallelism see Brown, *Birth*, 248-53.
44  Cf. Finegan, *Biblical Chronology*, 259-80; Hoehner, *Chronological Aspects*, 29-44; Sherwin-White, *Roman Society*, 166-67.

tism of repentance for the forgiveness of sins' (3.3), which Luke attributes to the fulfilment of prophecy, as does his source, Mk 1.2-3. However, Luke excises from Mark's OT citation the use of Exod. 23.20 and Mal. 3.1 (as did Matthew), but he extends the quote of Isa. 40.3 to include vv. 4-5, which describe the results of this preparatory ministry: the way is made smooth and straight, and 'all flesh shall see the salvation of God' (3.4-6). Luke does not use Mark's description of John's baptizing ministry, the people's response to John (but cf. 3.7), and John's dress and diet. Thus, Luke has focused the pericope to portray John coming as a prophet announcing the word of God to a particular historical situation in fulfilment of OT prophecy. His extension of the Isaianic quotation to 40.5 links John's proclamation with the inauguration of God's salvation and highlights the extension of this salvation to include the Gentiles, a Lukan emphasis (cf. Acts 28.28).[45]

In 3.7-9, Luke portrays John addressing the multitudes coming to be baptized and proclaiming the necessity of repentance in the face of imminent judgment. The account of John's speech follows Q 3.7-9 closely (cf. §3.2).

In 3.10-14, three groups of people ask John what they should do, evidently in response to John's call to 'bear fruits that befit repentance' (3.8). These three groups are the multitudes, the tax collectors and the soldiers. John's reply in each case involves a practical response to the problems of economic deprivation. This pericope is unique Lukan material.[46]

Luke prefaces his use of Mk 1.7-8 and Q 3.16-17 with two observations concerning the people: they were in a state of expectation, and they wondered whether John was the Messiah (3.15). With this preface Luke shapes John's announcement of a coming figure to be an explicit denial of his own messianic status, but this in turn suggests an implicit interpretation of the expected figure as messianic (3.16-17). Luke concludes his account of John's preaching with the observation that John also proclaimed 'many other exhortations' to the people, and in so doing, 'he preached good news' (εὐηγγελίζετο). By employing this verb to summarize John's message, Luke links John's 'evangelizing' with Jesus' own preaching the good news of the kingdom (e.g. 4.43; cf. 4.18; though they are kept distinct, cf. 16.16).[47]

---

45 Fitzmyer, *Luke*, 1.460-61; Marshall, *Luke*, 136-37.
46 It is quite possible that 3.10-14 may have originally been found in Q. However, since Matthew omitted it, then direct evidence for its presence in Q is lacking; cf. Davies and Allison, *Matthew*, 1.311; Kloppenborg, *Q Parallels*, 10.
47 Wink (*John the Baptist*, 52) supports the significance of this observation to indicate that John 'is already participating in the period of fulfilment even while preparing for it. . .' However, while clearly linked with Jesus' own proclamation, Wink goes too far when he concludes that 'the Christian message of salvation is indicated. . .' On the

From its later position in Mark (6.17-18), Luke inserts at this point in his narrative the summary of John's rebuke of Herod and Herod's response by imprisoning John (3.19-20). Its position here is an example of John's 'other exhortations' mentioned in 3.18, and contrasts the people's response to John's ministry (3.10-14, 15) with Herod's response. It also suitably completes Luke's summary of John's ministry. The one addition Luke makes to his source is the comment that John not only rebuked Herod for marrying Herodias, but also 'for all the wicked things which Herod had done' (3.19b). Furthermore, by placing John's imprisonment at this point, Luke *thematically* separates John's ministry from that of Jesus (which began with his baptism). Within Luke's schema of salvation-history, the epoch of fulfilment—primarily consisting of Jesus' ministry—begins with John's preparatory ministry, but his ministry comes to an end before Jesus' ministry in this epoch begins.[48]

After completing the narrative concerning John's ministry, Luke presents a brief account of Jesus' baptism. He makes several minor changes, but none of these are significant to us here. We may simply observe that Luke is interested in what happens after Jesus has been baptized and while he is at prayer.[49] It has often been observed that the account does not state that Jesus was baptized 'by John', and that the pericope has been placed by Luke *after* John has been imprisoned by Antipas. Walter Wink draws a conclusion from this observation which others have made as well; he states that Luke 'completely separates John from Jesus in 3.1-20; by a literary *tour de force* John is imprisoned *before* he baptizes Jesus. . .'[50] He also states that 'βαπτισθέντος is intended as middle ("baptized himself") since no one else is there to baptize him'.[51] While it may be true that Luke places a clear division between the minis-

other hand, Fitzmyer (*Luke*, 1.475) understands the verb here to simply indicate 'to preach or exhort' without any special significance at all (cf. Conzelmann, *Luke*, 23 n. 1). For support of the special significance of the verb see Chamblin, 'Gospel and Judgment', 7; Marshall, *Luke*, 149; Lohmeyer, *Johannes der Täufer*, 46; Friedrich, 'εὐαγγελίζομαι', 2.717-21; Becker, 'Gospel: εὐαγγέλιον', 2.112-13; Schürmann, *Lukasevangelium*, 1.186.

48  Fitzmyer (*Luke the Theologian*, 105-106) states: 'in depicting John imprisoned by Herod even before the baptism of Jesus takes place, Luke has in effect finished off the story of John's ministry and removed him from the scene before the ministry of Jesus itself begins'.

49  Marshall, *Luke*, 150-52.

50  Wink, *John the Baptist*, 46.

51  Wink, *John the Baptist*, 83 n. 1. Cf. Mattill (*Luke*, 16) who states that placing Jesus' baptism after John's arrest avoids 'the embarrassment John's baptism of Jesus was causing Christians. . .' Jesus' baptism is mentioned only in the temporal use of the genitive-absolute clause καὶ Ἰησοῦ βαπτισθέντος, identifying that Jesus was baptized at the same time as the other people in the preceding clause. Cf. BDF, §404; Ellis, *Luke*, 92; Leaney, *Luke*, 109; Marshall, *Luke*, 150-52, etc.

try of John and Jesus, such a statement fails to appreciate the literary style by which an author may jump back and forth chronologically in order to link themes together. We observed above that Luke places John's imprisonment at the end of his summary of John's ministry for thematic reasons. Having concluded his presentation of John, Luke begins his presentation of Jesus' ministry, appropriately enough with Jesus' baptism, though he chooses to focus rather on Jesus' anointing by the Spirit and the heavenly voice. But Luke's introductory statement to this pericope clearly shows that he is jumping chronologically back to the time prior to John's imprisonment when other people were being baptized by John: 'Now it happened when all the people were baptized and when Jesus had also been baptized . . .' (3.21a). Thus, Luke is not attempting to suggest that Jesus was actually baptized after John had been imprisoned. Thematic placement should not be confused with chronological order.[52]

Luke's presentation of the question concerning the disciples of John and the Pharisees fasting (5.33-39) makes few alterations to his source (Mk 2.18-22; cf. §3.3). Three may be observed here. First of all, Luke adds to the description of the disciples: 'the disciples of John fast *often and offer prayers*' (5.33). Secondly, Mark's presentation of the 'old' and 'new' only portray them as different from one another and incompatible (Mk 2.21-22). Luke adds a third element, whereby clinging to the 'old' effectively cuts a person off from the 'new' (5.39).[53]

The account by Luke of John's question from prison concerning Jesus' identity (7.18-23) adds explanatory notes (esp. 7.20-21), but otherwise it differs little from its source in Q (cf. §3.2). The same may be said of Jesus' testimony to John (7.24-28). However, Luke does append at this point an observation concerning the response to Jesus' words: 'When all the people and the tax collectors heard, they acknowledged God's justice, having been baptized with John's baptism. But the Pharisees and scribes rejected God's purpose for themselves, not having been baptized by him' (7.29-30). In a way similar to Mt. 21.31-32, this pericope identifies the segment of the population among whom John has his appeal and success, and contrasts it with rejection by those in leadership. It should be noted, however, that Luke, in using Q 7.26-27, does continue the tradition which identifies John as more than a prophet and one who fulfils Mal. 3.1, which may imply that John was Elijah-*redivivus*.[54]

---

52  Wink (*John the Baptist*, 46), even though he makes this assertion concerning John being imprisoned before baptizing Jesus, does admit that John's 'presence is assumed in 3.21f'. See the more nuanced statement by Conzelmann, *Luke*, 21. See further the discussion above concerning the *thematic* reasons for placing the account of John's imprisonment where it is.

53  Fitzmyer, *Luke*, 1.597; Schürmann, *Lukasevangelium*, 1.300.

The pericope concerning Jesus' description of responses to both John and himself (7.31-35) has not been significantly altered by Luke. However, having been positioned to follow 7.29-30, the pericope could be understood to expand upon, and condemn, the rejection by those Pharisees and scribes mentioned in vv. 29-30.

Luke follows Mark's order and places the account of the people's opinions concerning Jesus (9.7-9; Mk 6.14-16) immediately after the sending out of the twelve (9.1-6; Mk 6.6b-13), even though he moved the pericope concerning John's rebuke of Herod, which was positioned here in Mark (6.14-16), to its location in 3.19-20 at the conclusion of John's ministry. Luke's account records similar opinions by the people concerning Jesus: he is John raised from the dead, or Elijah-*redivivus*, or else one of the prophets. However, while Mark states that Herod believes Jesus to be John raised, Luke leaves Herod in a state of perplexity (9.7), with the question, 'I myself had John beheaded; but who is this about whom I hear such things?' Luke also states that Herod 'was trying to see him', which prepares the reader for Jesus' interview with Herod during his trial, an account found only in Luke (23.6-12).

Luke's account in 9.18-21 of public opinions concerning Jesus differs little from his source in Mark (8.27-30; cf. §3.3). He places the original question concerning people's opinion of Jesus in a context in which Jesus is praying alone with his disciples (9.18). Referring to Jesus praying is a well-known Lukan emphasis (cf. 3.21). Peter's confession is also slightly different: Jesus is 'the Messiah *of God*' (9.20).

In 11.1, Jesus has been praying, and one of his disciples comes to him, requesting, 'Lord, teach us to pray, just as John also taught his disciples'. In response, Jesus teaches them what is popularly known as 'the Lord's prayer' (from Q 11.2-4). Just as Luke introduced the observation that John's disciples prayed as well as fasted in the question to Jesus concerning fasting (5.33), he also introduces John's disciples as praying in this pericope as well. In both places, this introduction probably forms part of Luke's emphasis upon prayer.

Lk. 16.16 forms part of a series of sayings which, in Luke, are in the context of Jesus responding to the Pharisees who are scoffing at him because of his teaching concerning money (16.1-13). Much of this material is unique to Luke, and in those instances where the material is also found in other Gospels, it is in different locations.[55] Thus, while Q

---

54 This pericope provides further support that Luke does perceive John to be Elijah-*redivivus*, though he does not emphasize it as much as Matthew does (cf. the comments above on Luke's infancy narrative, esp. 1.16-17).

55 The unique Lukan material includes 16.1-9, 10-12, 14-15, 19-31. The different locations for the Lukan material for which parallels exist are Lk. 16.13 = Mt. 6.24; Lk. 16.16 = Mt. 11.12-13; Lk. 16.17 = Mt. 5.18; Lk. 16.18 = Mt. 19.9 = Mk 10.11-12.

16.16 is found in Mt. 11.12-13, in a context in which Jesus is testifying to John's greatness before the people, Luke uses Q 16.16 in this quite different context. Moreover, Q 16.16 also has a significantly different form in Luke than it has in Matthew, which is complicated by the enigmatic nature of the statement concerning violence. The examination and resolution of these issues are beyond the confines of this chapter's purpose. Fortunately, the statement concerning John itself is somewhat less problematic: 'the law and the prophets were until John; since then the good news of the kingdom of God is proclaimed. . .' The saying clearly reveals the place of John within salvation-history. Hans Conzelmann, who argues that Luke conceives of the history of salvation in three epochs, places John in the first epoch on the basis of 16.16.[56] However, he offers no exegetical support for his interpretation of this verse.[57] It would appear rather that, in Luke, John is a

> transitional figure who inaugurates the second period and introduces Jesus. . . In this sense, John is a precursor of Jesus, not as a . . . kingdom-preacher himself, but the Jewish reform-preacher who prepares Israel for the preaching of the kingdom.[58]

The final pericope in Luke's Gospel which concerns John the Baptist is the dispute between Jesus and the temple leaders concerning Jesus' authority, in which Jesus asks them concerning the authority of John's baptism (20.1-8). Luke's version does not differ significantly from that of his source, Mk 11.27-33 (cf. §3.3).

There are a number of brief references to John the Baptist in Luke's second volume, the book of Acts. They add nothing to our understanding of John himself, but they do help to fill out the early church's interpretation of John, as presented by Luke.

In Acts 1.4-8 the resurrected Jesus addresses his disciples just prior to his ascension. Included in these final instructions is the command to remain in Jerusalem for the Holy Spirit (1.4). By way of explanation, in 1.5 Jesus says, 'for John baptized with water, but you will be baptized with the Holy Spirit not many days from now'. This is clearly a reference to the coming of the Spirit at Pentecost, but, by being contrasted with

---

56  Conzelmann, *Luke*, 20-27, esp. 23.
57  Minear ('Birth Stories', 122) comments: 'It must be said that rarely has a scholar placed so much weight on so dubious an interpretation of so difficult a logion'.
58  Fitzmyer, *Luke*, 2.1115. For further support of this interpretation of Lk. 16.16 see Wink, *John the Baptist*, 51-57; Marshall, *Luke*, 628-29. This interpretation of John's role in Luke's view of salvation-history finds corroboration elsewhere in Luke, for which see Wink, *John the Baptist*, 51-57. However, I realize that the interpretation of this saying and its parallel in Mt. 11.12-13 has numerous difficulties; for an extensive discussion of these and a history of interpretation, see Cameron, *Violence and the Kingdom*.

John's baptism with water, Pentecost is being interpreted as the fulfilment of John's proclamation of an expected figure who will baptize with
holy spirit and fire (Lk. 3.16-17).

After Jesus' ascension, and while waiting for the promised Holy Spirit,
Peter addresses the disciples and explains the need to have a new disciple chosen to replace Judas Iscariot. It is necessary that this person be
someone who was in the company of the disciples during the entire ministry of Jesus, with the starting point identified as 'beginning with the
baptism of John' (1.22a). With this time reference Luke understands the
ministry of John to be linked with Jesus' own ministry, and so it was
necessary that witness also be borne to John's ministry. This reference to
John provides further confirmation to the point made above in discussing
Lk. 16.16, that Luke understands John's ministry, not as part of the epoch
of the law and prophets, but rather as introducing Jesus' ministry.[59]

In 10.34-43, Peter addresses Cornelius and his household, presenting
the Christian kerygma. This summary of Jesus' life and ministry begins
with his ministry in Galilee; the explicit time reference is 'after the baptism which John proclaimed' (10.37b). But the starting point in the next
verse begins with Jesus' baptism by John, at which time he was anointed
with the Spirit. Thus integral to the beginning of the early Christian
kerygma's content was the ministry of John, especially his baptism of
Jesus.[60] This conforms to the emphasis observed in 1.22.

After the events in Caesarea with Cornelius, Peter reports to the Jerusalem church what had happened (11.1-18). He interprets the Holy
Spirit falling upon Cornelius' household: 'I remembered the word of the
Lord, how he used to say, "John baptized with water, but you will be baptized with the Holy Spirit" ' (11.16). As a reference to Jesus' saying in
1.5, 11.16-17 interprets the fulfilment of John's proclamation to be found
not only in the coming of the Spirit at Pentecost, but also in other 'com-
ings' of a similar nature, such as happened with Cornelius' household.

Paul, while addressing the synagogue in Pisidian Antioch on his first
missionary journey, makes reference to the expectation of a Davidic
Messiah and identifies this Messiah as Jesus (13.22-23). Paul then refers
in 13.24-25 to John's proclamation of a baptism of repentance, and to
John's denial that he was the Messiah but that one was coming after him
who was more worthy than he. This summary of John's ministry uses
specifically the imagery of John being unworthy to untie the expected figure's sandals. The reference to John's denial that he was the Messiah
echoes Lk. 3.15-16.

59   Wink (*John the Baptist*, 54-55) states concerning Acts 1.22: 'The *arche* of the Gospel
     is set at Luke 3.1ff.; the appearance of John upon the stage of world history sets the
     *terminus a quo* of the church's apostolate!'
60   Bruce, *Acts*, 46, 212-13.

In 18.25, Apollos, an evangelist who went to Ephesus, is described as one who 'was speaking and teaching accurately the things concerning Jesus' and yet he 'knew only the baptism of John'. It is not quite clear what this signifies. It is possible that Apollos had only been baptized with John's form of baptism—a baptism of repentance (whether by John himself or someone else is not stated). Or it could suggest that, in his ministry, Apollos proclaimed and practised John's form of baptism. In either case, Apollos is not aware of Christian baptism in the name of Jesus as proclaimed by Peter in 2.38. Yet, Luke evidently understands Apollos to be a Christian.

When Paul arrives in Ephesus (19.1-7), he meets a dozen 'disciples', of whom he inquires whether they had received the Holy Spirit when they believed. Their negative reply[61] prompts Paul to inquire concerning what baptism they had received. Finding out that they had received John's baptism, Paul explains that 'John baptized with a baptism of repentance, telling the people to believe in the one coming after him, that is, in Jesus'. Hearing this, these disciples were baptized in the name of Jesus. Whether these are disciples of John or of Jesus is not entirely clear. The fact that they had received John's baptism suggests that they had been at one time followers of John. But describing them as 'disciples' without qualification does suggest that Luke understood them to be disciples of Jesus; they were, in some sense, Christians. This understanding is strengthened by the wording of Paul's first question concerning whether they had received the Spirit, 'when you believed'.[62] Yet, these were 'deficient' Christians, because they had not received Christian baptism, nor had the Spirit come upon them.[63] The pericope suggests that John's ministry and baptism continued to have an influence in the early church, even as far away as Ephesus, and that the assimilation of John's disciples was a matter of concern in the early church.

To summarize, Luke's presentation of John the Baptist is the most extensive account of all the Gospels. He incorporates most of the material found in his sources, as well as presenting new traditions in his infancy narrative, in the rest of the Gospel itself and in the book of Acts. In contrast to Matthew, who presents John as a kingdom-preacher whose ministry parallels and foreshadows Jesus' ministry, Luke portrays John as a reform-preacher whose ministry prepares the way for Jesus' ministry.[64]

---

61 For discussion of the significance of their answer, cf. §8.2.1.
62 Bruce, *Acts*, 363; Haenchen, *Acts* 553.
63 For a variety of interpretations concerning the historical situation of this passage, see especially Dibelius, *Johannes dem Täufer*, 88-94; Käsemann 'Disciples of John', 136-48; Haenchen, *Acts*, 554-57; Barrett, 'Apollos and the Twelve Disciples', 1.29-39. These issues are not relevant to our concerns here.
64 Conzelmann (*Luke*, 22-26) argues that Luke rejects the forerunner role for John, but we have seen above that the evidence from Luke/Acts does not support Conzelmann

Thus, while he understands John to be part of the epoch of fulfilment, nevertheless, Luke carefully separates the ministry of John from Jesus in that epoch.[65] It is sometimes asserted that Luke rejects the interpretation of John as Elijah-*redivivus*. It is true that he does not develop this theme as much as Matthew does, nor does he utilize Mk 9.9-13 in which this identification is made implicitly (by contrast, in Mt. 17.9-13 Matthew used this tradition and made the identification explicit). However, in both the infancy narrative (1.16-17) and the latter portion of the Gospel (7.26-27), Luke does place John in the role of Elijah-*redivivus*.[66]

### 3.6  The Portrayal of John the Baptist in the Fourth Gospel

There are ten pericopae containing references to John the Baptist in the fourth Gospel.[67] These may be summarized as follows:

| Subject | John |
|---|---|
| 1. John is a witness to the light | 1.6-9 |
| 2. John is a witness to Jesus' superiority | 1.15 |
| 3. John answers questions about his identity | 1.19-23 |
| 4. John answers questions about his baptism and announces a coming figure | 1.24-28 |
| 5. John witnesses to Jesus' identity | 1.29-34 |
| 6. John witnesses to Jesus' identity to two disciples who follow Jesus | 1.35-42 |
| 7. Jesus is baptizing, and John responds to his disciples' question | 3.22-30 |

---

at this point. See also Wink, *John the Baptist*, 42-58; Bachmann, 'Johannes der Täufer', 123-55; Fitzmyer, *Luke the Theologian*, 106-109.

65  Wink, *John the Baptist*, 51-55. On the other hand, John may be understood as a transitional figure, spanning the periods of promise/Israel and fulfilment/Jesus (cf. Fitzmyer, *Luke the Theologian*, 107-10; Ernst, *Johannes der Täufer*, 110-12, 153-54). While this view explains the data somewhat differently, the result is actually quite similar. Mattill (*Luke*, 21-25) also places John within the period of fulfilment, but his periodic structure is somewhat different than that proposed by Conzelmann (*Luke*, 16-18; cf. the revisions by Wink, *John the Baptist*, 55-57; Fitzmyer, *Luke*, 1.181-87).

66  So Fitzmyer, *Luke the Theologian*, 103-109; Mattill, *Luke*, 17-18; against Wink, *John the Baptist*, 42-45.

67  I would normally use the name 'John' to identify the author of the fourth Gospel, though in doing so I would not be making any assertion concerning the actual identity of the author, as I have done with the authors of the three synoptic Gospels. However, due to the confusion between the two 'Johns' with which we are dealing (the Baptist and the Evangelist), I will use the term 'the Evangelist' to identify the author, and reserve the name 'John' for 'John the Baptist' (though it should be pointed out that the Evangelist never uses the title 'the Baptist' for John). I realize that there may have been more than one author (e.g. the author of the Prologue and the redactor who inserted the material concerning John the Baptist), but the examination here is concerned with the final form of the text.

Other, more comprehensive studies of John the Baptist in the fourth Gospel include Lohmeyer, *Johannes der Täufer*, 26-31; Brown, 'John the Baptist in the Gospel of John', 132-40; Wink, *John the Baptist*, 87-106; Bammel, 'The Baptist', 109-13; Ernst, *Johannes der Täufer*, 186-216.

8. Pharisees hear that Jesus was baptizing more people than John, so Jesus   4.1-3
   goes to Galilee
9. Jesus has other witnesses to himself than John   5.33-36
10. Jesus goes to where John baptized   10.40-42

It is commonly recognized that 1.6-9 and 1.15, both of which concern
John the Baptist, have been combined with an originally separate poem
to form the Prologue to the fourth Gospel.[68] Though added, they are
related to their context within the poem and have a valid function within
the final form of the fourth Gospel.[69] In the second strophe, 1.3-5, the
theme is the Word's relation to creation. In 1.5 the Word's gift of light
shines into the opposing darkness, but the darkness was not able to over-
power that light. In the third strophe, 1.10-12b, the Word enters the
world and is rejected by some but received by others. Between these two
strophes John the Baptist is presented as the one who prepares for the
coming of the light of the Word.[70] He was a man who had been sent
from God (1.6; cf. 1.33; 3.28) with the express role of being a witness to
that light in order that people might believe (1.7). The Evangelist adds
nothing substantively new in 1.8, except to deny that John was the light
and to reiterate John's role as witness.[71]

The fourth strophe (1.14, 16) of the Prologue is concerned with the
Christian community (cf. the use of the first person) experiencing 'the
Word become flesh'. As 1.6-8 was concerned with John the Baptist's role
as witness, the interpolation in v. 15 concerns one aspect of this witness.
John identifies the one who was 'the Word become flesh' as the same
one about whom he had previously said: 'The one coming after me ranks
ahead of me, because he existed before me'. This statement has been
taken from the narrative concerning John's witness to Jesus' identity
(1.29-34; esp. v. 30). It functions here to emphasize that, though he may
have begun his ministry after John and might even have appeared to be

---

68 On the problems and issues surrounding the Prologue to the fourth Gospel, see the
survey and literature cited by Brown, *John*, 1.3-37; Schnackenburg, *John*, 1.221-81.
For the sake of convenience, I have followed Brown's analysis (*John*, 1.3-37) of the
strophe and interpolations of the Prologue. It is quite possible that, as Robinson
('Relation of the Prologue', 65-76) argues, the 'insertions' were actually first and the
poem was subsequently woven around them. These issues are not relevant to our
purpose here.
69 Cf. the chiastic structure proposed by Boismard, *Prologue*, 73-81. Recent studies of
the structure of John's Prologue include those by Culpepper, 'Pivot', 1-31; Giblin,
'Literary Structures', 87-103; Staley, 'Structure', 241-64.
70 Brown, *John*, 1.27.
71 It is often stated on the basis of 1.8 that the Evangelist is polemicizing against later
disciples of John the Baptist who claimed that John was the Messiah (and possibly
described John as 'the light'); cf. Brown, *John*, 1.28; Schnackenburg, *John*, 1.252-53.
However, Wink (*John the Baptist*, 88) suggests that this verse could 'be understood as
simply a Christological safeguard to preserve the uniqueness of Jesus. . .'

John's disciple, 'the Word become flesh' is qualitatively superior to John because of his pre-existence.

After the Prologue, the Evangelist begins his Gospel narrative with four pericopae which encapsulate 'the witness of John' (1.19a). In the first two, 1.19-23 and 1.24-28, Jewish authorities[72] have sent priests and Levites as well as Pharisees to interrogate John. The questions from the priests and Levites concern John's identity with respect to expected eschatological figures (1.19b). John rejects for himself the roles of the Messiah, Elijah-*redivivus* and the eschatological Prophet (1.20-22), but rather perceives himself as the wilderness herald crying, 'Make straight the way of the Lord' (1.23; cf. Isa. 40.3). This pericope agrees with Lk. 3.15 by indicating that there was speculation concerning John's eschatological identity. However, it is different from the synoptic portrayal of John's role in two respects. First of all, all three of the synoptic Gospels portray John in the role of Elijah-*redivivus*, while in the fourth Gospel John rejects that role for himself.[73] Secondly, all three of the synoptic Evangelists quote Isa. 40.3 to explain John's wilderness ministry, but the fourth Evangelist attributes this quotation to John the Baptist himself.

The second group of emissaries were Pharisees, who questioned John's authority to baptize (evidently understood to be an eschatological act) if he did not claim to be fulfilling any eschatological role (1.24-25). Their concern over John's authority to baptize is echoed in Jesus' debate with the temple leadership over his own authority (Mt. 21.23-27 = Mk 11.27-33 = Lk. 20.1-8). John's answer limits the importance of his baptism by describing it as 'with water' and by announcing one who comes after him (1.26-27). John's response here is similar to the proclamation of an expected figure who will baptize attributed to John in the synoptic Gospels. In both, John contrasts himself and his baptism with a coming figure, and describes his own inferiority in terms of a servant unworthy to even untie the thong of his master's sandal. However, in the fourth Gospel, several features have been omitted, such as the expected figure baptizing with a Holy Spirit and fire (though partially referred to in v. 33b), and the comparative 'mightier than I'. One significant element is present here which is not found in the synoptic Gospels. John initially describes this coming figure by stating that 'among you stands one whom you do not know' (v. 26b). This may be interpreted as a reference to that strain of Jewish expectation which understood the presence of the Messiah to be hidden until he would be suddenly revealed,[74] or as a rebuke

---

72  Brown (*John*, 1.42-43) points out that 'the Jews' in the fourth Gospel is the term used for 'the religious authorities hostile to Jesus, particularly those in Jerusalem. . .'

73  Wink (*John the Baptist*, 89) suggests that the Evangelist does not present John the Baptist in the role of forerunner because 'the Logos is already πρῶτός [sic] (1.15, 30) and can have no forerunner'.

to these emissaries for their profound ignorance of the identity of the one in their midst and who are therefore estranged and unbelieving.[75] The first alternative fits better the context of John the Baptist's own ministry (for he admits his own prior ignorance in v. 33), but the second alternative is more appropriate to the function of the pericope in the fourth Gospel, for John is already aware of this figure's identity through divine revelation (as is made clear in 1.31-34), but his vagueness in answering the emissaries suggests their inability to receive and believe such divine revelation.[76] The Evangelist appends to the narrative the observation that this event took place in Bethany beyond the Jordan River, which is where John was baptizing.

In the next pericope, 1.29-34, John, perceiving Jesus approaching, proclaims, 'Behold the Lamb of God who takes away the sin of the world' (1.29),[77] and identifies Jesus as the expected figure he had been announcing and describing as pre-existent (1.30).[78] John states that he had not immediately perceived Jesus as this figure, but then explains how he came to this realization through his baptismal practice, the purpose of which was 'that he might be revealed to Israel' (1.31).[79] This rather enigmatic explanation is clarified in vv. 32-33. John's witness to Jesus includes his having seen the Spirit descend as a dove upon Jesus, an oblique reference to Jesus' baptism. John could witness to Jesus' identity because it had been revealed to him by God that the one upon whom he saw this taking place, 'this is the one who baptizes with the Holy Spirit' (1.33). This reference to baptizing with the Holy Spirit is an aspect of Jesus' ministry which could have been mentioned in the contrast in 1.26-

---

74 So Brown, *John*, 1.53; Dodd, *Historical Tradition*, 289-90; for further description see Mowinckel, *He that Cometh*, 304-308; Schürer, *History*, 2.524. This may be expressing in different words the similar idea in the synoptic Gospels which stresses the imminence of the expected figure's arrival and judgment (esp. Mt. 3.10, 11-12 = Lk. 3.9, 16-17).

75 So Schnackenburg, *John*, 1.294-95; Wink, *John the Baptist*, 90.

76 Wink (*John the Baptist*, 90) points out that 'this statement and the reference to "the Jews" suggest that the chief opponents of the church in the Evangelist's day were Pharisees and not Baptists'.

77 The significance of the term 'Lamb of God' in this context has been a matter of debate, often in conjunction with discussions of its historicity. For discussion see the commentaries as well as Barrett, 'Lamb of God', 210-18; Virgulin, 'Lamb of God', 74-80; Burrows, 'Lamb of God', 245-59; Carey, 'Lamb of God', 97-122. Cf. the relevant note in §8.2.1.

78 Jn 1.30 is essentially the same as the witness borne by John in 1.15, except that, while v. 15 identifies the figure with an articulated participle: ὁ . . . ἐρχόμενος ('the one who is coming'), v. 30 is more specific with its use of a noun and verb construction: ἔρχεται ἀνήρ (a man comes). For discussion see on 1.15 above.

79 Schnackenburg (*John*, 1.303) and Brown (*John*, 1.56) point out that, while 'the Jews' is a negative term in the fourth Gospel, 'Israel' has a positive sense, indicating the chosen people of God.

27 between John and the expected figure, as it was in the synoptic Gospels, but the fourth Evangelist sees fit to reserve it for mention here. John's explanation of how he came to recognize Jesus as the expected figure subordinates John's baptism to function merely as the means by which Jesus is revealed to John and, consequently, to Israel. John's witness in this pericope concludes with his statement that he has borne witness to Jesus' identity as the Son of God, an echo of the heavenly voice reported by the synoptic Evangelists.[80]

In 1.35-42, John fades from the scene. He again identifies Jesus as the Lamb of God, at which point two of John's disciples leave John and follow Jesus. The narrative continues with Jesus beginning to gather around him a group of his own disciples (1.40-51). The initial portion of this pericope indicates that the early followers of Jesus had been disciples of John.

Having introduced Jesus and his first disciples, the Evangelist focuses his narrative upon Jesus' ministry, including his miracle at the wedding feast in Cana (2.1-12), his cleansing of the temple (2.13-25), and his discussion with Nicodemus concerning the birth from above (3.1-21). The next pericope concerns Jesus' early ministry and the responses to that ministry by John's disciples and John himself. Jesus goes with his disciples into Judea where he engages in a baptizing ministry (3.22).[81] At the same time, John, for he is not yet imprisoned, also engages in a baptizing ministry nearby (3.23-24). A dispute arises between John's disciples and 'a Jew' concerning purification (3.25). While a difficult verse in itself, the fact that in the following narrative John's disciples return to John and report to him concerning Jesus' baptizing ministry suggests that this debate with a Jew about purification was prompted by Jesus' baptizing ministry.[82] John's disciples report to him that Jesus, to whom John had earlier borne witness, is now practising a baptizing ministry himself. In hyperbole derived from envy, they state 'all are coming to him' (3.26),

---

80  The third edition of the UBS text reads ὁ υἰὸς τοῦ θεοῦ, a reading which Metzger (*Textual Commentary*, 200) supports 'on the basis of age and diversity of witnesses . . .' (cf. also Haenchen, *John*, 1.154). However, several commentators prefer to read ὁ ἐκλεκτὸς τοῦ θεοῦ on the basis that it is the more difficult reading (e.g. Brown, *John*, 1.57; Schnackenburg, *John*, 1.305-306; Barrett, *John*, 178). This variant, while important, is not relevant to our purposes here.

81  The verbs διέτριβεν and ἐβάπτιζεν are singular and in the imperfect tense, thus indicating that Jesus himself was baptizing, and that he engaged in the practice over a period of time.

82  Schnackenburg, *John*, 1.413. The identity of the Jew in 3.25 cannot be ascertained. It could have been someone who simply saw or perhaps received Jesus' baptism, or one of Jesus' disciples (3.22), or even Jesus himself (e.g. Goguel, *Jesus*, 274-75), but proof is not forthcoming. However, it may be reasonably concluded that the debate concerning purification resulted from a difference between the teaching that John had given to his disciples and that which was now being propounded by Jesus to his own

suggesting that they perceived Jesus' baptizing ministry to be in competition with their own. John's response reminds them that one's ministry is God-given, and that this applies equally to himself as well as Jesus. John's own role is to be sent before the Messiah (3.27-28). Utilizing imagery which suggests Jesus is the bridegroom and he is only the bridegroom's friend, John expresses joy at Jesus' ministry, realizing that the focus of attention is upon Jesus as the 'bridegroom' (3.29). John therefore concludes, 'He must increase, but I must decrease' (3.30).[83]

In 4.1-3 Jesus discovers that the Pharisees have heard that he is baptizing more disciples than John, and so he leaves Judea and returns to Galilee. The Evangelist utilizes this brief reference to introduce and explain Jesus' trip through Samaria (4.4), and therefore it is difficult to understand precisely why Jesus leaves Judea. This passage once again, as in 3.22-26, portrays Jesus engaged in a baptizing ministry, which was perceived by some to be associated with John's ministry and perhaps in competition with it as well. Interrupting the narrative flow in an attempt to modify the statements in 3.22, 26 and 4.1 that Jesus baptized, an editorial remark is made to indicate that Jesus himself did not actually baptize, only his disciples did (4.2).

In 5.30-47 Jesus evaluates various witnesses to himself, one of whom is John the Baptist. He states that John's witness to himself was true, but he has a greater witness than John (5.33-34, 36). Jesus then describes John as a burning and shining lamp.

In 10.40-42, following a debate with the Jews in Jerusalem, Jesus withdraws beyond the Jordan, 'to the place where John was first baptizing' (10.40). In so doing, the Evangelist reminds the reader of the reference in 1.28 to the place where John not only baptized, but also bore witness to Jesus. Those who came to Jesus realize that 'everything John said concerning him was true' (10.41), and, as a consequence, 'many believed in him there' (10.42). In this final reference to him in the fourth Gospel, John once again functions as a witness to Jesus, and because his witness is true, he leads people to faith in Jesus.

To summarize the portrayal of John the Baptist in the fourth Gospel requires only one word: witness. This word itself has been used repeatedly to describe John's function, and in other texts which may not have this term, the idea is still there.[84] Even John's baptizing ministry

disciples.

83   In 3.31-36 no change of speaker is indicated, and so it is possible that John is still the speaker (so Barrett, *John*, 224). However, the language so closely resembles the speech attributed to Jesus in 3.1-21 that it would be too speculative to consider vv. 31-36 in relation to John the Baptist (cf. Brown, *John*, 1.159-60).

84   John is described as a witness using the μαρτυρ- word group in Jn 1.7 (2x), 8, 15, 32, 34; 3.26; 5.33, 34, 36, and possibly 3.32 (2x), 33 as well. The idea is also found in 1.35-37; 3.27-30; 10.41.

and his prophetic proclamation have been subordinated to his role as
witness to Jesus (1.19-34).[85]  By portraying John as one who witnesses in
order that others might come to faith in Jesus (1.7; 10.42), the Evangelist
has incorporated John's ministry into his over-arching purpose: 'that you
might believe that Jesus is the Christ, the Son of God' (20.31).  In so
doing, John has been 'made the normative image of the Christian
preacher, apostle and missionary, the perfect prototype of the true
evangelist, whose one goal is self-effacement before Christ. . . His whole
function is to 'witness', that others might believe through him. . .'[86]

It is sometimes asserted that the Evangelist's portrayal of John is a
polemic against a Baptist sect who have developed a rival 'christology'.[87]
However, Walter Wink has pointed out that

> it is methodologically illegitimate . . . to reconstruct the views of John's dis-
> ciples by reversing every denial and restriction placed on John in the Fourth
> Gospel. . . By [this] line of reasoning, John was worshipped as Elijah, pro-
> phet, messiah, the Light and the Life of men, a wonderworker, the pre-
> existent Logos through whom all things were made, indeed, even as the
> Word made flesh!
>     If such an advanced 'John-cult' had in fact antedated the fourth Gospel,
> John would never have been conferred such an exalted role by the
> Evangelist.[88]

The issue at stake in the Evangelist's portrayal of John, as in much of the
rest of his Gospel, is the christological uniqueness of Jesus.  This issue
appears in the synoptic Gospels' accounts of John as well, though somewhat muted in comparison to the fourth Gospel.  Just as 'the Synoptics
reflect, on the whole, not polemic, but rather the need to place Christo-

---

85  The corollary to this emphasis is the downplaying of John's role as forerunner.  Wink
    (*John the Baptist*, 89) states that 'the Evangelist . . . sharply contradicts the earlier
    tradition that John was Elijah.  For him the idea of a forerunner is anathema. . .'  It is
    true that John the Baptist rejects for himself the identity of Elijah-*redivivus* (1.21),
    but the more general concept of forerunner is not entirely absent from the fourth
    Gospel, for in 3.28 John says to his disciples: 'You yourselves bear witness to me that
    I said, "I am not the Messiah", but, "I have been sent before him" '.  This first state-
    ment refers back to John's witness to the first emissaries in 1.20.  It is probable that
    the second statement ('I have been sent before him'), which incorporates a forerun-
    ner role, refers back to John's identity of himself as the Isaianic voice in the wilder-
    ness in 1.23.  Thus, though his identity as Elijah-*redivivus* is rejected, John's role as
    forerunner is still present, but muted.
86  Wink, *John the Baptist*, 105; cf. 106.
87  For example, Bultmann (*John*, 17-18, cf. 48-52) comments that Jn 1.6-8, 15 are
    'polemical: to dispute the claim that the Baptist has the authority of Revealer.  This
    authority must therefore have been attributed by the Baptist sect to their master;
    they saw in him the ϕῶς, and thus also the pre-existent Logos become flesh.'  Wink
    (*John the Baptist*, 98 n. 2) traces this view back to Baldensperger, *Prolog* (1898), and
    Michaelis, *Einleitung*, (1788).
88  Wink, *John the Baptist*, 102.  For an example of the type of argumentation Wink con-
    siders 'methodologically illegitimate' see Bultmann, *John*, 17-18.

logical safeguards on John's exalted role', the fourth Evangelist does the same, except his safeguards are more pronounced due to the explicit and developed christology of his Gospel.[89]  Thus one alternative explanation is presented by Wink who argues that 'the Fourth Evangelist is still in dialogue with these Baptists, countering their hyper-elevation of John and wooing them to the Christian faith'.[90]  However, a more plausible alternative may be to perceive the issue of John the Baptist being but one of the many points of contention in the debate between the Johannine church and the Jewish synagogue.  Each group perhaps claiming John the Baptist in support of its own point of view: the synagogue arguing that John's ministry was prior to that of Jesus and that Jesus was John's disciple, to which the church countered by arguing that Jesus was prior because he was the Word and that John witnessed to Jesus' superiority.[91]  Whichever explanation is used, we may conclude that the Evangelist has effectively 'Christianized' John.[92]

### 3.7  *The Portrayal of John the Baptist in Extra-Canonical Gospels*

In addition to the accounts concerning John in the four canonical Gospels, references may be found in several extra-canonical Gospels as well as other extant Christian literature from the first centuries CE. Since the purpose of this chapter is to lay the groundwork for a socio-historical investigation of John the Baptist in his first-century Palestinian context, I will not examine all these references, but limit this brief survey to those Gospels which may be dated to the middle of the second century CE or before.  The Gospels surveyed here include: the *Gospel of Thomas*, the *Gospel of the Ebionites*, the *Gospel of the Nazareans* and the *Protevangelium of James*.[93]

---

89  Wink, *John the Baptist*, 104.
90  Wink, *John the Baptist*, 105.  Similarly, Dodd (*Historical Tradition*, 299-300) concludes that 'the Baptist therefore is not treated as a rival who must be subpoenaed to give evidence in favour of Christ.  He is claimed as one of Christ's own people.  The *Sitz im Leben* which we should infer is one in which it was desired that persons who had followed the Baptist should be regarded as the adoptive members of the Church.'
91  Cf. Kysar, *Maverick Gospel*, 34.  For further discussion defending the position that the fourth Gospel's portrayal of John the Baptist is not primarily polemic against John's followers, cf. Smalley, *John: Evangelist and Interpreter*, 125-28; Robinson, *Priority*, 170-72; Ernst, *Johannes der Täufer*, 215-16.
92  Wink, *John the Baptist*, 106.  Dibelius (*Johannes dem Täufer*, 143) concludes his work on John the Baptist with this comment on the portrayal of John in the fourth Gospel: 'Ja, die Christen gingen in der Christianisierung der Johanneserzählungen noch weiter: da die Vorläuferstellung des Täufers die Würde des Herrn gefährdete, wurde Johannes neben Jesus gestellt, der Täufer ward zum 'Freunde', der Vorläufer zum 'Zeugen', der Prophet zum Heiligen'.

### 3.7.1  *The Gospel of Thomas*

The *Gospel of Thomas* contains a collection of 114 wisdom and prophetic sayings of Jesus which portray him as a teacher of wisdom. The work claims to have been composed by Didymus Judas Thomas, a disciple of Jesus. It may reasonably be dated to the second half of the first century CE, or possibly even to the first half.[94] Its existence has been known for some time from a few Greek fragments, but now is available in its entirety in a Coptic translation discovered as part of the Nag Hammadi Library.[95] The Gospel contains little narrative due to its focus on Jesus'

---

93  I do not examine the references to John within the Gnostic literature found in the Nag Hammadi Library (except the *Gospel of Thomas*) or in *Pistis Sophia*. Though these references mention John's parents, his baptism of repentance, his preaching of a coming figure, the Elijah-*redivivus* theme, and his baptism of Jesus, no additional historical information is presented; rather, the exclusive interest is in a Gnostic interpretation of the Christian tradition. Keck ('John the Baptist', 192) states in his discussion of the Gnostic references to John: 'In short, the historical questions connected with John are ignored entirely and attention is focused on the one moment when the careers of Jesus and John intersect, and even here attention is concentrated on Jesus'. He concludes (194) that these 'treatments of John show an attempt to come to terms with the Christian tradition'. The references to John the Baptist in the Gnostic literature found in the Nag Hammadi Library (except the *Gospel of Thomas*) include: *Ap. Jas.* (NHC I,2) 6.28-34; *Exeg. Soul* (NHC II,6) 135.19-26; *Gos. Eg.* (NHC III,2) 65.23-26; *Treat. Seth* (NHC VII,2) 63.26-64.6; *Testim. Truth* (NHC IX,3) 30.18-31.5; 39.15-40.1; 45.6-22; *Val. Exp.* (NHC XI,2) 41.10-38. The references in *Pistis Sophia* include: *Pis. Soph.* 7, 60–62, 133, 135. For discussion see Keck, 'John the Baptist', 184-94; Ernst, *Johannes der Täufer*, 228-36. On the relationship between the Nag Hammadi texts and the synoptic Gospels, see Tuckett, *Nag Hammadi*. The translations of these texts may be found in Robinson, *Nag Hammadi Library*; Mead, *Pistis Sophia*; the text and translation of *Pistis Sophia* in Schmidt and MacDermot, *Pistis Sophia*.

Neither do I examine *Gos. Heb.* 2, which is an expansion of the heavenly words which are spoken after Jesus' baptism, because no mention is made of John the Baptist or of him baptizing Jesus. Furthermore, I do not examine the fragmentary Papyrus Cairensis 10 735.2, which is an expansion of the angelic messenger's announcement to Mary that Elizabeth is pregnant, and which describes John as a 'servant who go[es before his Lord's] coming. . .' On both the *Gospel of the Hebrews* and the Papyrus Cairensis 10 735 see Hennecke, Schneemelcher and Wilson, *New Testament Apocrypha*, 1.114-15, 158-65; Funk, *New Gospel Parallels*, 2.359, 372-77; Cameron, *Other Gospels*, 83-86; Koester, *Introduction*, 2.223-24.

For a description of John's portrayal among the later church fathers, see Lupieri, 'John the Baptist: The First Monk', 11-23.

94  For a discussion of the issues and problems of dating the *Gospel of Thomas*, see Robinson, 'From Q to the Gospel of Thomas', 142-64.

95  Guillaumont (*Gospel according to Thomas*) provides the Coptic text and an English translation. The English translation used here is that by Lambdin in Robinson, *Nag Hammadi Library*, 124-138; this translation is found in Funk, *New Gospel Parallels*, 2.93-187; Cameron, *Other Gospels*, 23-37 (though they quote the first edition of *Nag Hammadi Library*, not the second as is done here). Helpful introductions and studies include Wilson, *Gospel of Thomas*; Grant and Freedman, *Secret Sayings*; Gärtner, *Gospel of Thomas*; Wilson, 'Gospel of Thomas'; Koester, 'One Jesus'; Koester, *Introduction*, 2.150-54.

The sayings I examine here may be cited more exactly according to the codex, page sayings, and so there are no narrative references to John the Baptist. Neither does the Gospel contain any sayings of John. The only references to John are contained in logia of Jesus.

*Gospel of Thomas* 46 states:

> Jesus said, 'Among those born of women, from Adam until John the Baptist, there is no one so superior to John the Baptist that his eyes should not be lowered (before him). Yet I have said, whichever one of you comes to be a child will be acquainted with the kingdom and will become superior to John.'

Like Mt. 11.11 = Lk. 7.28, this passage reports Jesus expressing an exalted opinion of John the Baptist, but this is balanced by the statement that those within the kingdom are greater than John. In contrast to the synoptic form of this balancing statement ('the one who is lesser in the kingdom is greater than he'), the form in *Gos. Thom.* 46 is similar to another saying of Jesus in Mt. 18.3 = Mk 10.15 = Lk. 18.17, of which the Markan form states: 'Whoever does not receive the kingdom of God like a child shall not enter it'. In the synoptic context, however, this saying has nothing to do with John the Baptist. As in the Q and synoptic versions of this saying, John is held in high esteem, and yet he is carefully subordinated to Jesus.

The next saying in the *Gospel of Thomas*, that is, *Gos. Thom.* 47, is concerned with the impossibility of serving two masters, to which is appended sayings concerning drinking old wine rather than new, not putting new wine in old wineskins or sewing an old patch on a new garment. The synoptic accounts of these latter sayings have been placed in a context which associates them with Jesus' response to the question concerning John's disciples fasting while his disciples do not (Mt. 9.14-17 = Mk 2.18-22 = Lk. 5.33-39). Although *Gos. Thom.* 47 immediately follows a saying which refers to John the Baptist, there is no explicitly stated link with John the Baptist as is found in the synoptic Gospels, though the reference to old wine or a second master could be interpreted to imply a link. Similarly, *Gos. Thom.* 104 states: 'They said to Jesus, "Come, let us pray today and let us fast". Jesus said, "What is the sin that I have committed, or wherein have I been defeated? But when the bridegroom leaves the bridal chamber, then let them fast and pray." ' This saying approximates the synoptic context of the question concerning John's disciples fasting, but there is no reference to John or his disciples in this saying in the *Gospel of Thomas*.[96]

and line numbers (e.g. *Gos. Thom.* 46 = NHC II,2 41.6-12), but I will use the numbers of the sayings instead for the sake of simplicity.

96  Cf. a similar statement on fasting by Jesus in *Gos. Thom.* 27.

*Gospel of Thomas* 78 states:

> Jesus said, 'Why have you come out into the desert? To see a reed shaken
> by the wind? And to see a man clothed in fine garments [like your] kings
> and your great men? Upon them are the fine garments, and they are
> unable to discern the truth.'

A similar question and response are given by Jesus in the synoptic
account of Jesus praising John (Mt. 11.7-11 = Lk. 7.24-28), so that the
reference to a man in the desert whom the people went out to see refers
to John. However, in *Gos. Thom.* 78, if no knowledge of the synoptic
accounts is assumed, then the question appears to be asked by Jesus
about himself; there is no reference to John the Baptist.[97]
Thus, there are several sayings which are identified with John in some
way in the synoptic accounts, but similar sayings in the *Gospel of Thomas*
have no such explicit connection. On the other hand, *Gos. Thom.* 52,
which has no close canonical parallel, may be a reference to John:

> His disciples said to him, 'Twenty-four prophets spoke in Israel, and all of
> them spoke in you'.
> He said to them, 'You have omitted the one living in your presence and
> have spoken (only) of the dead'.

This saying could refer to John the Baptist in one of two ways. Since the
reference to prophets is to those who have spoken 'in Jesus', it is possible
that the reference to a living prophet is not to Jesus himself, but to one
contemporaneous with Jesus, and the most plausible candidate is John
the Baptist.[98] On the other hand, if Jesus is referring to himself as the
living prophet, the twenty-fourth prophet may be a reference to John.[99]
    The *Gospel of Thomas* reveals little real interest in John. It does not
describe him, nor does it quote any of his sayings. The focus is exclusively upon Jesus. John is only referred to because he is mentioned in
Jesus' sayings, and in these he only functions as a pointer to Jesus.[100]
Several sayings in the synoptic tradition which are connected with John
have parallels in the *Gospel of Thomas*, but here they lack an explicit
connection. Thus, from the *Gospel of Thomas* we may conclude little
concerning its portrayal of John other than the fact that he is apparently
a prophet who speaks of Jesus (*Gos. Thom.* 52). He was a great man, but
he is subordinate to anyone acquainted with the kingdom (*Gos. Thom.*

---

97  Similarly, *Gos. Thom.* 11a echoes Lk. 16.17 which is associated with a reference to
    John the Baptist in 16.16 (though not in the parallel in Mt. 5.18), but no such associa-
    tion with John is present in *Gos. Thom.* 11a. Also, *Gos. Thom.* 51 is reminiscent of
    Mt. 17.9-13 = Mk 9.9-13, but no reference to John is present in *Gos. Thom.* 51 (but
    cf. the possible reference to John in *Gos. Thom.* 52 discussed below).
98  Cf. Bammel, 'The Baptist', 115 n. 4; against Gärtner, *Gospel of Thomas*, 156.
99  Grant and Freedman, *Secret Sayings*, 153.
100 Ernst (*Johannes der Täufer*, 227) concludes that in the *Gospel of Thomas*, 'das Bild

46). On the other hand, the lack of any explanation in the references to John suggests that the author of the Gospel assumed the readers had some knowledge of him.

### 3.7.2 *The Gospel of the Ebionites*

The *Gospel of the Ebionites*, which may be dated to the first half of the second century, is extant only in quotations provided by Epiphanius in his work *Panarion*. The Ebionites were a heretical Jewish-Christian sect, probably located east of the Jordan. Their Gospel apparently drew upon Matthew and Luke, and possibly Mark as well. The extant fragments contain no independent traditions, though alterations to the synoptic accounts have been made for theological reasons. Since the fragments quoted by Epiphanius contain his own comments, I distinguish his statements from the quotes themselves by placing his comments in italics.[101]

*Gospel of the Ebionites* 2–3 is a description of John and his baptizing ministry. *Gos. Eb.* 2 states:

> *And*
> It came to pass that John was baptizing; and there went out to him Pharisees and were baptized, and all Jerusalem. And John had a garment of camel's hair and a leathern girdle about his loins, and his food, as it saith, was wild honey, the taste of which was that of manna, as a cake dipped in oil.
> *Thus they were resolved to pervert the word of truth into a lie and to put a cake in the place of locusts.*

### *Gospel of the Ebionites* 3 states:

> *And the beginning of their Gospel runs:*
> It came to pass in the days of Herod the king of Judaea, [when Caiaphas was high priest,] that there came [one], John [by name,] and baptized with the baptism of repentance in the river Jordan. It was said of him that he was of the lineage of Aaron the priest, a son of Zecharias and Elisabeth; and all went out to him.

*Gospel of the Ebionites* 4 is an account of Jesus' baptism by John. The account is somewhat extended due to the threefold repetition of the heavenly voice—a repetition which appears to be a result of amalgamat-

---

des Täufers ist verblaßt. . .'

101 The full title of Epiphanius' work is *Panarius seu adversus lxxx haereses*, and is commonly abbreviated *Haer.* An English translation and introduction to the extant fragments of the *Gospel of the Ebionites* in *Panarius* is available in Hennecke, Schneemelcher and Wilson, *New Testament Apocrypha*, 1.153-58 (which has been cited here), and is reproduced in Funk, *New Gospel Parallels*, 2.364-70; Cameron, *Other Gospels*, 103-106. See also the discussions by Koester, *Introduction*, 2.202-203; Cameron, 103-104. For a discussion of the description of the Ebionites in the patristic literature as well as the relevant texts and translations, see Klijn and Reinink, *Jewish-Christian Sects*, 19-43, 178-81. *Gos. Eb.* 2 is a quotation from Epiphanius, *Haer.* 30.13.4-5, *Gos. Eb.* 3 from *Haer.* 30.13.6, and *Gos. Eb.* 4 from *Haer.* 30.13.7-8.

ing the three synoptic accounts, including John's desire to be baptized by
Jesus as suggested by Mt. 3.14.

If Epiphanius is correct that *Gos. Eb.* 3 was the beginning of this
Gospel, then the author has not incorporated the infancy narratives of
both Matthew and Luke. However, the names of John's parents are
mentioned, as is his priestly lineage, which may be a summary derived
from Luke 1. The picture of John in this Gospel focuses upon his baptizing ministry, which is described in essentially the same terms as in the
synoptic Gospels. While this Gospel is based upon a reading of the
synoptic Gospels, the author has not reproduced exactly what the sources
indicated. The reference to John's food in *Gos. Eb.* 2 describes the
honey, but fails to mention the locusts, probably because the group
responsible for the Gospel was vegetarian.[102] They have made an addition to the description of the honey: 'and his food, as it says, was wild
honey, the taste of which was that of manna, as a cake dipped in oil' (καὶ
τὸ βρῶμα αὐτοῦ, φησί, μέλι ἄγριον, οὗ ἡ γεῦσις ἡ τοῦ μάννα, ὡς
ἐγκρὶς ἐν ἐλαίῳ). This addition is based upon two descriptions of the
manna provided for Israel in the wilderness; in Exod. 16.31 the manna's
'taste was like wafers with honey', and in Num. 11.8 it was 'like the taste
of cakes baked with oil'. This description of the honey was evidently produced by reading the reference to ἀκρίς ('locust') in Matthew or Mark as
ἐγκρίς ('cake'). In light of the OT descriptions of manna, this alteration
to the text of the synoptic Gospels suggests that the author was interpreting John's description to be part of a wilderness motif.[103] Epiphanius
comments on this addition, that 'they were resolved to pervert the word
of truth into a lie and to put a cake in the place of locusts'.[104]

In the *Gospel of the Ebionites*, then, John is portrayed as a priest with

---

102 Hennecke, Schneemelcher and Wilson, *New Testament Apocrypha*, 1.156. More
explicit support for the Ebionites being vegetarian is found in Epiphanius, *Haer.*
30.15.3-4.

103 Other examples of not exactly reproducing the synoptic Gospels include *Gos. Eb.* 3,
which states that John baptized 'in the days of Herod the king of Judaea' which may
have been derived from Lk. 1.5. But in Lk. 1.5 it is the date for the *birth* of John, and
not his *ministry* (cf. the date provided by Luke in 3.1-2). Also, *Gos. Eb.* 2 states that
'there went out to him Pharisees and were baptized' which is evidently derived from
Mt. 3.7, but there the Pharisees come to observe John's baptismal practice, evidently
with a critical attitude (cf. §3.4).

104 Epiphanius' criticism of the addition to *Gos. Eb.* 2 is not quite accurate. The reference to a cake in oil is not a *replacement* for locusts in John's diet; that is, *Gos. Eb.* 2
does not say that John ate wild honey *as well as* cakes in oil. It is rather a comparative explanation (the ὡς is functioning as a comparative particle) describing the
manna, and, thus, is part of a midrashic-style description of the honey and not a
replacement for locusts at all. This interpretation is contrary to what is commonly
stated concerning *Gos. Eb.* 2. For example, Enslin ('Ebionites', 2.6) states that in
this text they 'replace the locusts which John the Baptist was said to have eaten with
honey cakes. . .' See further, Luz, *Matthew*, 1.168 n. 15.

a wilderness lifestyle who baptizes with a baptism of repentance. Many come to be baptized by him, including Jesus. No mention is made of John preaching or being a prophet, though this might be due to the fragmentary nature of the extant text.[105]

### 3.7.3 *The Gospel of the Nazareans*

The *Gospel of the Nazareans* appears to have been an Aramaic, or possibly Syriac, translation and expansion of the Greek Gospel of Matthew. Most of the early, extant fragments are derived from the writings of Jerome. The *Gospel of the Nazareans* may be dated to the first half of the second century, CE.[106]

*Gospel of the Nazareans* 2 states:

> Behold, the mother of the Lord and his brethren said to him: John the Baptist baptizes unto the remission of sins, let us go and be baptized by him. But he said to them: Wherein have I sinned that I should go and be baptized by him? Unless what I have said is ignorance (a sin of ignorance).

It is quite evident that Jesus' baptism by John was a source of difficulty for some persons within the early church, not only because it suggested that Jesus was a disciple of John's and thus inferior, but also because a baptism of repentance for the forgiveness of sins placed in question the doctrine of Jesus' sinlessness. This pericope eliminates this problem rather drastically, by having Jesus deny his need to be baptized at all, precisely because of his own sinlessness. The passage does portray John as a baptizer, whose baptism was characterized by forgiveness of sins.[107]

### 3.7.4 *The Protevangelium of James*

The *Protevangelium of James* is a work which may be dated about the mid-point of the second century CE. It purports to have been written by James, the half brother of Jesus. It is concerned primarily with exalting Mary, and does so by narrating her birth and early life. Extensive use is

---

105 However, while Mk 1.4 and Lk. 3.3 describe John as 'preaching a baptism of repentance', the *Gos. Eb.* 3 only states that John baptized with such a baptism. Also, while *Gos. Eb.* 2 evidently picks up the reference to Pharisees from Mt. 3.7a, it does not mention what John said to them in 3.7b-10.

106 For an introduction to, and text of, the *Gospel of the Nazareans*, see Hennecke, Schneemelcher and Wilson, *New Testament Apocrypha*, 1.139-53 (which has been used here); Cameron, *Other Gospels*, 97-102. This translation is also found in Funk, *New Gospel Parallels*, 2.378-89. The fragment *Gos. Naz.* 2 cited below was originally derived from Jerome, *Adv. Pel.* 3.2. A description of the Nazareans in the patristic literature as well as the Latin text of this fragment and another translation may be found in Klijn and Reinink, *Jewish-Christian Sects*, 44-52, 226-29.

107 *Gos. Naz.* 8 records a variant to Mt. 11.12, the context of which in Matthew refers to John the Baptist. However, *Gos. Naz.* 8 is too brief to demonstrate such a reference: 'The Jewish Gospel has: [the kingdom of heaven] is plundered'.

made of infancy narratives similar to those found in Matthew and Luke as well as OT parallels.[108]

In *Prot. Jas.* 8.2-3 Zechariah, who later is identified as the father of John the Baptist, is the high priest (cf. Lk. 1.8-9). While functioning as high priest, Zechariah is struck dumb when the lot falls to Mary that she should weave the colours purple and scarlet into the new veil for the temple (*Prot. Jas.* 10.1-2; cf. Lk. 1.20-22). After receiving an angelic messenger who announces that she will have a child (*Prot. Jas.* 11.1-3), Mary visits her relative, Elizabeth, whose baby leaps in her womb when Mary arrives (*Prot. Jas.* 12.2; cf. Lk. 1.39-45). After Mary's child is born and the wise men have visited him, Herod commands all children two years and under to be killed. Elizabeth flees with her child, John, into the hill country, and, when she finds nowhere to hide, a mountain miraculously splits apart to hide her (*Prot. Jas.* 22.1-3). Herod seeks to kill John because he was less than two years old, so he sends officers to inquire concerning his location from Zechariah, who denies knowing his location. After being threatened, Zechariah still refuses and is killed inside the temple (*Prot. Jas.* 23.1-3; cf. Mt. 23.35).

The extensive differences between the *Protevangelium of James* and the canonical infancy narratives of Matthew and Luke suggest that the author of the *Protevangelium* may not have had access to these narratives directly, but rather to certain oral traditions similar to those found in Matthew and Luke. What is interesting to observe is the contrast between the *Protevangelium* and Luke in their emphases. In Luke's infancy narrative the emphasis is upon John, his miraculous birth and his role as forerunner, while in the *Protevangelium* the focus is upon Zechariah and Elizabeth. Neither John's conception nor his birth are mentioned. There are no expectations of him and he has no future role with respect to Jesus. He is not a baptizer, nor is he really anything else. He only leaps in his mother's womb when Mary enters the room, flees as a baby, is miraculously protected and is indirectly the cause of his father's death.

### 3.7.5 *Summary*

The extra-canonical Gospels do not contain the quantity of data concerning John the Baptist found in the canonical Gospels. Their concern appears to focus more exclusively upon the relationship between John and Jesus, whereas the canonical Gospels provide some description of John himself and his ministry. Thus, the *Gospel of Thomas* and the

---

108 For further introduction and text see Hennecke, Schneemelcher and Wilson, *New Testament Apocrypha*, 1.370-88; Cameron, *Other Gospels*, 107-21; for text and parallels see Funk, *New Gospel Parallels*, 2.263-86. On John in the *Protevangelium* see Ernst, *Johannes der Täufer*, 237-39.

*Gospel of the Nazareans* only contain sayings of Jesus about John, and they are concerned with christological issues. The *Gospel of the Ebionites* does describe John and his baptizing ministry, but it is evidently dependent upon the canonical Gospels for this material, and it has been shaped to be consistent with the Ebionite lifestyle. The *Protevangelium of James* on the other hand appears to be largely independent of the canonical Gospels, but John has no role explicitly attributed to him.

### 3.8 *The Use of These Traditions in a Historical Investigation*

Since the purpose of this work is to investigate the ministry of John the Baptist in its own social, cultural and historical context, we must briefly consider whether it is possible to utilize these sources for such a historical investigation. Before pursuing this question further, three comments are in order. First of all, the observations I make here are general in nature. When specific texts are discussed in detail at appropriate points throughout this work, specific comments concerning historicity are made then. Secondly, as I mentioned above (§1.2), this investigation focuses upon the ministry of John before Jesus' ministry began. Therefore, I am not concerned with the relationship between Jesus and John, nor with the opinions Jesus expresses concerning John, except as these might shed light on John's ministry itself. Thirdly, we must distinguish between questions which are primarily theological in nature and those which are primarily historical. For example, the question 'Was John the Baptist Elijah-*redivivus*?' is in essence a theological question because it requires an evaluation of John from a faith perspective (though such a question may have historical elements). Whereas the question 'Did Jesus consider John to be Elijah-*redivivus*?' is primarily a historical question since it requires the examination of historical data apart from a particular theological opinion concerning the question at hand (though such a question may have a theological component).[109]

In the ensuing discussion I first make some observations concerning the Gospels in general, but these apply particularly to Q and the synoptic Gospels. Then I address the more specific problems associated with the fourth Gospel and the extra-canonical Gospels.

As a source of information concerning John the Baptist, the Gospels

---

109 Cf. Runciman (*Social Theory*) for a helpful discussion of the different types of questions to be asked and answered in all the sciences of humankind (including sociology, anthropology and history). He argues that an appropriate methodological framework must distinguish between reportage, explanation, description and evaluation. Cf. Rogerson's application ('Use of Sociology', 245-56) of Runciman's work to OT studies, and Fowl's application ('Reconstructing', 319-33) to the quest for the historical Jesus.

are limited because the Evangelists' interest in John is more or less limited to christological concerns. This focus of their interest limits the information they provide in two ways. First of all, their christological concerns have limited the *amount* of information they provide. They selected the material which served their purposes, probably leaving much unreported which would assist us, but which did not contribute to their interests.

Secondly, their christological concerns led to a process of adaptation in order to interpret the ministry of John for their readers. Their adaptation has produced a Christian perspective on John. However, while christological concerns dominate the Evangelists' portrayal of John, this does not mean that every detail in their portrayal necessarily has christological significance. Some aspects may have been included simply for the colour they add to the picture, or they may have been in the source used by an Evangelist and simply not removed. Or, more likely, some details were included in order to explain John himself. For example, the explanation of John's baptism as 'a baptism of repentance for the forgiveness of sins' (Mk 1.4 = Lk. 3.3) serves no explicit christological purpose. In fact, it became a problem and a source of embarrassment; but it is still preserved within the Gospel tradition.

Yet, on the other hand, even if an element has been included due to a christological or theological concern, this does not necessarily mean that it has no historical basis in the ministry of John and must have been a creation of the early church or the Evangelist. The evidence in these cases must be individually and carefully weighed before pronouncing a historical judgment on their probability. For example, the description of John's clothing (Mt. 3.4 = Mk 1.6) may have been provided by the Evangelists to support their interpretation of John as Elijah-*redivivus*. But from such an observation it does not *necessarily* follow that John did not in fact dress in such a fashion! The Elijah-*redivivus* interpretation may explain why the Evangelists included it, but it is too vague a reference to Elijah to be interpreted as a Christian creation. If they were *creating* an allusion to Elijah, we would expect the Evangelists to select something more explicit, such as a mantle, which was Elijah's trademark (cf. 1 Kgs 19.13, 19; 2 Kgs 2.8, 13-14). And we would not expect a reference to John's diet of locusts and wild honey, which has nothing to do with Elijah at all. Therefore, in this particular instance, it is more probable that John did dress this way, but it has been included to support the Evangelists' purposes.

We must not be critical of this process of selection and adaptation, because all good historical narrative must involve this process.[110] But on

---

110 On history-writing and historiography in the Greco-Roman world see Fornara,

the other hand, this limitation necessarily leaves many questions unanswered concerning John, with the result that it is impossible to write in any sense a biography of him.

While the synoptic Gospels are limited as historical sources for John the Baptist because of this editing process of selection and adaptation, they should still be taken seriously as historical sources with respect to John. A number of factors make this a reasonable basis from which to work. First of all, while the survey made above has shown how the Evangelists portrayed John in order to present an *interpretation* of him, there is no obvious reason why most elements of historical data contained within those portrayals should be considered a *creation* of the traditioning process.[111] Any number of reasons could be suggested for wholesale creation of these Baptist traditions, but careful examination of those reasons usually reveals their implausibility.[112]

Secondly, the broad outline of John's portrayal in the Gospels relates quite believably to certain elements within late Second Temple Judaism.[113] The fact that such an interpretive context may be found for John indicates that the Gospels' portrayal has not transformed him, but only interpreted him.

Thirdly, independent corroboration of the Gospels' presentation of John is provided by Josephus' account. Though Josephus also selected and adapted his material concerning John, his account nevertheless is in accord with the Evangelists' accounts. Such corroboration indicates that the Evangelists were controlled in their process of selection and adaptation.

Fourthly, the accounts of both the Evangelists and Josephus indicate that John had gathered around him a group of disciples, and they, as well as the crowds at large, were interested in John's teachings. This interest, combined with the existence of disciples, suggest that John's teachings would be remembered and could later be passed on with a degree of accuracy appropriate to such a context. It is also not impossible that certain elements may even have been written down by disciples, but there is no compelling evidence for direct Baptist sources within the Gospels, apart from the probable use of Baptist traditions supplied by former dis-

---

*Nature of History*; Gabba, 'Literature', 1-79, and the bibliography there. For surveys of Jewish historiography see Attridge, 'Jewish Historiography', 311-43; Attridge, 'Historiography', 157-84, and the bibliographies he provides. With respect to the Gospels in particular, and their relationship to types of history-writing during this period see the survey article by Kee, 'Synoptic Studies', 253-59. For a survey of various approaches to understanding the Gospels as history, especially with respect to the historical Jesus see McArthur, *Historical Jesus*.

111 With respect to the Jesus tradition, cf. Meyer, *Aims*, 60-94, esp. 72-75.
112 Cf. the detailed analyses of relevant pericopae in §6.2, 8.2.
113 This is a major focus in Parts II and III of this work.

ciples of John. The continued existence of John's disciples after John's death, especially those who were absorbed into the Christian movement, indicates that reliable traditions would have been available as sources for the Evangelists.

Fifthly, the continued existence of John's disciples may have provided a control upon any editing process.[114] The general point of view of the early Christian movement towards John was a positive appreciation, but they carefully kept John in a subordinate position with respect to Jesus. If the portrayal of John in early Christian tradition or by the Evangelists had been seriously altered in order to substantiate the Christian perspective of John, then that portrayal would have neither won Baptist disciples to the Christian faith, nor encouraged Christians who were former Baptist disciples that the superiority of their Christian faith was indeed correct. Furthermore, the continued respect shown to John by both his disciples and the Jews in general (as evidenced in the accounts of both the Gospels and Josephus) suggest that serious alteration of John's image would have been immediately apparent and unacceptable, at least during the first century CE when John could be remembered first hand by those who lived during his ministry and may have even been eyewitnesses.[115]

These general observations substantiate as a working premise that the synoptic accounts are generally reliable sources for information concerning John the Baptist. They should therefore be taken seriously, though at the same time they need to be taken critically, in recognition of their limitations mentioned above.[116]

---

114 On the control of a community on oral tradition, see the comments by the classicist Schadewaldt, 'Reliability', 108-10; the editor of that work draws the reader's attention to Boman, *Jesus Überlieferung*. Cf. also Riesenfeld, 'Gospel Tradition', 1-29; Gerhardsson, *Gospel Tradition*; for creative interaction with Gerhardsson, see Davids, 'Gospels and Jewish Tradition', 1.75-99; Kelber, *Oral and Written Gospel*, 1-43. A helpful introduction to oral history and its relationship to the Gospels is provided by Lord, 'Gospels as Oral Traditional Literature', 33-91; cf. esp. 36-39 on historicity.

A helpful survey of recent folklore studies and the question of oral history with respect to the OT is provided by Kirkpatrick, *Folklore Study*, 97-112. It must be observed, however, that the oral history referred to in such studies is usually at least several generations removed from the events being narrated, whereas the synoptic Gospels are literary products produced while some of the first generation, including eyewitnesses, are still alive.

115 Cf. the portrayal of John in these Gospels with the traditions concerning John in later literature, such as that of the Mandaeans. John's disciples would hardly recognize him.

116 These conclusions concerning utilizing the Gospels for data concerning John the Baptist, while being more or less acceptable to many biblical scholars, would find sharp disagreement from Enslin ('Once Again: John the Baptist', 557-66) who argues that the portrait of John by Josephus is 'good, solid historical reporting', but that the picture in the Gospels is a Christian creation which 'attempts to bring this figure into a relationship with Jesus which in sober fact did not exist' (557). However, Enslin brings no evidence to bear in support of his case, except for his own conjectural

The portrayal of John the Baptist in the fourth Gospel is problematic from a historical point of view, particularly due to the differences between John's preaching as recorded in the fourth Gospel compared with that recorded within the synoptic Gospels. For example, the general outlook of the synoptic Gospels is that the expected figure proclaimed by John is Jesus, but this identification is made explicit *by the Evangelists* and not by John himself.[117] By contrast, in the fourth Gospel it is *John the Baptist himself* who explicitly identifies Jesus as his expected figure (1.31-33; 3.26-30), as well as witnessing that Jesus is the Lamb of God (1.29, 36), the Son of God (1.34) and the Messiah (3.28). It may be argued that such christological statements in John the Baptist's sayings could arise in John's own historical situation, though the Evangelist may have attributed a different significance to them than did John.[118] However, in light of the explicit christological orientation of the fourth Gospel,[119] it may be prudent to view this evidence as having less probability as a historical expression of John's ministry, and to consider it rather as the Evangelist's development of the theological implications of John's ministry.[120] This decision is not as crucial methodologically as it might first appear, since I am focusing on John's ministry prior to the beginning of Jesus' ministry, and the christological statements which John makes in the fourth Gospel are directed explicitly toward Jesus; they are not expansions of John's preaching concerning his expected fig-

hypotheses. Cf. his later article ('John and Jesus', 1-18) which is little better.

117 The only exception is Mt. 3.14-15, but this is generally considered to be a redactional addition by Matthew which attempts to alleviate the problem of Jesus' baptism by John; cf. Bonnard, *Matthieu*, 39-40; Davies and Allison, *Matthew*, 1.320, 323-27. John considers the possibility that Jesus may be identified as his expected figure, but he is portrayed as questioning or doubting (Mt. 11.3 = Lk. 7.19-20).

118 Brown's thesis ('John the Baptist in the Gospel of John', 134) is that 'the statements were actually made by [John the Baptist], but that he intended by them a meaning perfectly consonant with the Synoptic picture of his expectations of the one to come. With slight adaptation these statements were incorporated into the fourth Gospel because in the light of Christian faith they were seen to be even more applicable to Jesus than [John the Baptist] realized.' More specifically, it is sometimes argued that John the Baptist did actually identify Jesus as 'the Lamb of God', with the discussion focusing upon whether its significance is paschal, Isaianic or apocalyptic. For discussion see Dodd, *Interpretation*, 230-38; Dodd, *Historical Tradition*, 269-71; Barrett, 'Lamb of God', 210-18; Burrows, 'Lamb of God', 245-4; Brown, 136-38.

119 Jn 20.31: 'these things have been written in order that you might believe that Jesus is the Christ, the Son of God. . .' Note that in the fourth Gospel, John the Baptist is a witness to precisely these christological formulations (1.34; 3.28).

120 This statement may be considered a specific application of Dunn's more general statement ('Let John be John', 338): 'If we are to do justice to the Johannine distinctives, we have to see them as a development of the Jesus-tradition designed to express the truth of Jesus as understood within the Johannine circle'. Dodd (*Historical Tradition*, 298) concludes that the *explicit* identification of Jesus by John 'is put into the mouth of the Baptist and so becomes part of his testimony'.

ure prior to the baptism of Jesus. On the other hand, the fourth Gospel
is still of great value historically. If, as many believe, this Gospel is not
dependent upon the synoptic Gospels,[121] then it would be an independent witness to several elements of John's proclamation which are also
found in the synoptic Gospels. Examples include the proclamation of an
expected figure, whose sandals John is not worthy to untie, and who will
baptize with the Holy Spirit (Jn 1.26-27, 33; cf. Mt. 3.11-12 = Mk 1.7-8 =
Lk. 3.16-17).[122] This suggests that the fourth Evangelist did have access
to reliable traditions concerning John the Baptist, and therefore other
traditions in the fourth Gospel about John's ministry which have no
explicit christological significance may be taken more seriously as reliable historical data concerning John. Examples include the geographical
locations of John's ministry (1.28; 3.23), that the first disciples of Jesus
were former disciples of John (1.35-42), and Jesus' own baptizing ministry paralleling John's (3.22-24).[123]

The traditions in the extra-canonical Gospels are interesting and
worth careful examination, but there are problems with using them as
prime historical sources concerning John the Baptist. The *Gospel of
Thomas* shows no interest in John himself, focusing rather on sayings by
Jesus concerning John's role and place in the kingdom. The *Gospel of
the Ebionites* is dependent upon the synoptic Gospels for its traditions
concerning John. This demonstrates appreciation for the synoptic traditions concerning John, but the book's very dependence renders it of little
value as a separate historical source. On the other hand, the *Gospel of
the Nazareans* contains an independent tradition that Jesus was not baptized by John, a tradition which historically is implausible.[124] But it does
provide further support for the synoptic picture of John's baptism being
linked with the forgiveness of sins. The *Protevangelium of James* is to a
large part independent of the synoptic Gospels, but it presupposes the
infancy narratives of Matthew and Luke, and thus is of little value as an

121 For a review of the discussion concerning the relationship between the fourth Gospel
and the synoptic Gospels, see Kysar, *Fourth Evangelist*, 54-66; and more recently,
Smith, 'John and the Synoptics', 425-44. An interesting example of the fourth Gospel
being independent of the synoptic Gospels, yet dependent upon a common Aramaic
tradition is argued by Lindars, 'John and the Synoptics', 287-94.
122 For discussion, see Dodd, *Historical Tradition*, 251-61.
123 For further discussion, see Dodd, *Historical Tradition*, 248-312; Robinson, *Priority*,
172-89. Morris (*Studies*, 139-42; cf. 139-214) has argued that some of this material
concerning John the Baptist in the fourth Gospel is based on eyewitness testimony,
as is other portions of the Gospel as well. In the judgment of Robinson (159-60, esp.
n. 2) Morris builds a 'formidable case', but this is a 'notoriously difficult category to
establish to general satisfaction'.
   On the problems and possibilities of the fourth Gospel as a historical source, see
the articles reproduced in McArthur, *Historical Jesus*, 82-108.
124 Against Cadoux, *Jesus*, 44-47.

independent witness concerning John the Baptist, who plays little role in the work anyway. Therefore, in comparison with Josephus, Q and the canonical Gospels, the traditions of the extra-canonical Gospels are of little help in a historical investigation of John's ministry.

### 3.9 *Conclusion*

In this chapter we have surveyed the portrayal of John the Baptist in the earliest Gospels, both canonical and extra-canonical. The three synoptic Gospels and Q are quite similar in their portrayal of John himself, though they shape and nuance their portrayals to suit their own theological interests and viewpoints. The issue at hand for these Evangelists was not so much how John was to be portrayed historically, as how he was to be interpreted theologically, especially with respect to the ministry of Jesus and the kingdom of God. Thus, they were concerned with issues such as John's role as the forerunner of Jesus, whether he was Elijah-*redivivus*, and whether his ministry was to be associated with the new inbreaking of God's kingdom or the old epoch. When such theological interests are taken into account, the three synoptic Gospels and Q can provide data for a historical investigation of John.

The fourth Evangelist paints a similar picture of John himself, but a somewhat different picture of John's relationship to Jesus—a picture in which John is re-presented as an explicit witness to Jesus as the Messiah, the Son of God. The theological interests with respect to John are quite different in the fourth Gospel as compared with Q and the synoptic Gospels, and it is these interests which have led to the reshaping of the John's relationship with Jesus in this account. Yet, in many respects, the fourth Evangelist has included traditions which provide both independent corroboration for elements in the synoptic Gospels as well as additional material of historical value.

The extra-canonical Gospels, when they portray John at all, portray him in terms similar to Q and the synoptic Gospels. As sources for additional or corroborative historical evidence concerning John, these extra-canonical Gospels are, unfortunately, of little value.

Therefore, in the ensuing investigation, I rely for evidence primarily upon Josephus, Q and the synoptic Gospels, and utilize the fourth Gospel mostly as an independent, corroborative witness to these other sources.

# PART II

## JOHN AS BAPTIZER

## Chapter 4

## ABLUTIONS IN THE OLD TESTAMENT
## AND SECOND TEMPLE JEWISH LITERATURE

### 4.1 *Introduction*

It is common practice to nickname someone by reference to a distinctive or prominent element in his/her person or role. So John received his nickname 'the Baptizer' ('Ιωάννης ὁ βαπτίζων),[1] probably because this was a memorable, prominent and rather distinctive characteristic of his ministry. In Chapter 6 we examine in detail the evidence concerning his baptizing activity and seek to determine the functions of that baptism. In anticipation of that discussion, we may summarize in the most general terms (in order not to predispose our inquiry) the central elements of John's baptismal practice: his baptism was a bath or immersion in flowing water, usually the Jordan river, and was associated in some way with repentance and forgiveness of sins.

In this chapter we survey the Jewish literature of the OT and Second Temple period in order to ascertain the types of ablutions which were performed and their various functions. In the next chapter we examine the special case of the ablutory practices of the Qumran community. This community is a special case, not because its practices are necessarily different, but because the evidence concerning its understanding of the function of those ablutions is more extensive and so merits separate treatment.

While John's baptism was evidently an immersion, I broaden the scope of our inquiry at this point to include all forms of ablutions. This enables us to determine more precisely the function of immersions within the broader compass of other types of ablutions.[2]

---

1 Cf. the introductory remarks in §6.2.
2 Discussion of these matters is often confused by use of the terms 'baptism' or 'lustration', for these have become technical theological terms suggesting a particular function. Thus, I avoid them in the ensuing discussion of Jewish ablutions, though I continue to use the term with respect to John's immersion, because in all our sources, including Josephus, it is so labelled. As an alternative, I use 'ablutions' to refer generally to any use of water for the purpose of cleansing. The type of ablution may be made more specific by use of one of these terms: 'immersions' refer to bathing the entire body (and so is equivalent to the terms 'bath' and 'bathe'); 'washings' cleanse part of the body (e.g. hands) or an object (e.g. vessel), and 'sprinkling' refers to partial application of water by the means implied by the term.

The purpose of this chapter and the next is to determine as clearly as possible the Jewish milieu with respect to ablutions in John's day. This will enable us to appreciate the possible influences upon John in the development of his baptismal practice and its functions, as well as the ways in which his audience may have perceived its significance.

### 4.2 *Ablutions in the Old Testament*

#### 4.2.1 *Cleanness and Uncleanness*
To appreciate the significance of ablutions, the concepts of clean and unclean need to be understood. Jacob Neusner states that they

> are not hygienic categories and do not refer to observable cleanliness or dirtiness. The words refer to a status in respect to contact with a source of impurity and the completion of acts of purification from that impurity. If you touch a reptile, you may not be dirty, but you are unclean. If you undergo a ritual immersion, you may not be free of dirt, but you are clean.[3]

Thus, clean and unclean are considered to be opposite states in which cleanness is the norm (cf. Lev. 10.10). Most things and persons are intrinsically clean, though some things are permanently unclean (e.g. certain animals, Lev. 11).[4] Most uncleanness is a temporary, abnormal condition which is contracted by contact with uncleanness (e.g. a corpse, Num. 19; discharges, Lev. 15), by developing uncleanness (e.g. leprosy, Lev. 14; discharges or menstruation, Lev. 15), or by committing certain immoral acts (e.g. sexual immorality, Lev. 18).[5] To be restored from the state of uncleanness to cleanness requires some process of cleansing. This process may include a waiting period (until evening, or a set number of days), a cleansing agent (water, Lev. 15; prepared water, Num. 19; blood, Lev. 14.5-7; fire, Num. 31.23), and a sacrifice (e.g. Lev. 14.19; 15.14-15). Cleansing a *person* from uncleanness usually involves only a waiting period and the cleansing agent of water or prepared water. When a sacrifice is also required, the explanation given is that the sacrifice did not function only to cleanse (as was the function of the water); rather, the sacrifice functioned to make atonement before Yahweh because of the person's uncleanness (Lev. 14.19-20; 15.15, 30).[6]

---

3    Neusner, *Idea of Purity*, 1.
4    Permanently unclean animals cannot be cleansed (Lev. 11). Contact with them does not make a person unclean (as does contact with temporary uncleanness), rather they are simply not to be eaten. However, contact with a corpse of an unclean animal defiles (11.8, 11, 24-28, 31-35, 38), but this applies equally to contact with the corpse of a clean animal (11.39).
5    On sin as a cause of uncleanness, see Wright, *Disposal of Impurity*, 17-20.
6    The atonement provided on the Day of Atonement includes a similar element. In Lev. 16.16 (cf. v. 19) the sacrifice of the goat is said to 'make atonement for the holy place, because of the impurities of the sons of Israel, and because of their transgres-

From this brief summary of cleanness and uncleanness in the OT we can make two generalizations concerning *human* cleanness and uncleanness which are relevant to our concerns here. First of all, there are two agents by which a person is made unclean: physical contagion and moral contagion.[7] This does not, however, imply two types of uncleanness, only two types of contagion. Secondly, there are two primary agents which make a person clean: water (or prepared water) and blood. In some cases, sacrifice has the supplemental role of providing atonement.

It is not necessary for our purposes here to attempt a complete analysis of the OT regulations and practices concerning cleanness and uncleanness, nor their relationship with holiness and commonness.[8] For our purposes we only need to examine how *ablutions with water* function within this larger structure.

The evidence for the use of ablutions in the OT may be categorized according to the recipient of the ablution (object or person), the ablutory method (sprinkling, washing or immersion)[9] and whether an additional rite is added to the ablution (e.g. sacrifice or anointing with oil). There is a further category in which ablutory language is used metaphorically.

### 4.2.2 *Ablutions of Objects*
Objects may be either sprinkled or washed. An example of *sprinkling* is found in Num. 19.18, whereby the tent and furnishings which have had

sions, in regard to all their sins; and thus he shall do for the tent of meeting which abides with them in the midst of their impurities'. Wenham (*Leviticus*, 228, cf. 233) explains that this rite is designed to 'cleanse the sanctuary from the pollutions introduced into it by the unclean worshippers... The aim of these rituals is to make possible God's continued presence among his people.' Wright (*Disposal of Impurity*, 17-20) points out that the sanctuary required cleansing because certain sins are specifically identified as defiling the sanctuary (e.g. Lev. 15.31; 20.3; Num. 19.13, 20).
   Occasionally, the sacrifice of atonement is said to be involved in the cleansing itself; cf. the discussion concerning Deut. 21.1-9 in §4.2.4.
7   Cf. Neusner (*Idea of Purity*, 11; cf. 11-25) who states that 'the biblical corpus of ideas about purity may be divided into two distinct parts, the interpretation of purity as a metaphor of morality, on the one hand, and the specific laws about purity and impurity in connection with the Temple cult, on the other'.
8   Discussions which I find helpful, and which were used in preparing this summary include Wenham, *Leviticus*, 15-29; Toombs, 'Clean and Unclean', 1.641-48; de Vaux, *Ancient Israel*, 460-67. For more detailed discussion see the recent works by Neusner (*Idea of Purity*) and Wright (*Disposal of Impurity*). De Vaux (460) states that 'this impurity is not to be understood as a physical or moral defilement, and this kind of holiness is not to be understood as a moral virtue: they are rather "states" or "conditions" from which men must emerge in order to re-enter normal life'.
9   In this survey of the OT, the following verbs (and their related word groups) have been examined: רחץ ('to bathe'), כבס ('to wash'), שטף ('to wash off' or 'wash over'), דוח ('to rinse'), זרק ('to throw' or 'sprinkle'), and נזה ('to sprinkle'). Words such as 'purify' or 'cleanse', which describe the function of the ablutions, have also been examined, but only when the text specifies one of the ablutory methods listed here. On the verb טבל, 'to dip', see the relevant note in §4.2.5.

contact with a dead body must be sprinkled with the water of the red heifer rite in order to be made clean.[10]

The *washing* of objects is used in two situations. The first concerns an object which has been defiled by contact with something or someone unclean. For example, in Lev. 15.4-12, 20-27 persons with a discharge and women who are menstruating render clothing, vessels and other objects unclean. These objects must be washed to be made clean.[11] A second situation is the washing of the legs and entrails of the sacrificial animal for the burnt offering (e.g. Lev. 1.9, 13).[12] The reason why just these parts were washed when the entire animal was burnt in the sacrifice is not stated. But these parts of the animal are those most susceptible to being soiled by excrement prior to or during the act of slaying the animal, and therefore they would require washing to cleanse them before being burnt upon the altar.[13] In each of these situations the reason for sprinkling or washing the object was to cleanse it from uncleanness.[14]

### 4.2.3 *Sprinkling Water upon a Person*

Sprinkling water upon a person is used in only two situations. In the first, Yahweh instructs Moses to cleanse the Levites: 'sprinkle upon them waters of cleansing' (Num. 8.7). The second is Num. 19.18, in which the water of the red heifer rite is sprinkled upon a person who has contracted corpse uncleanness.

---

10  Num. 31.19-24 refers to the sprinkling of the booty gained in battle with the water to remove uncleanness (מֵי נִדָּה) of the red heifer rite because these objects had probably been in contact with corpses. Another example of sprinkling objects with water concerns a leprous house, but this sprinkling includes the blood of a slain bird as well as running water (Lev. 14.50-53). The act of sprinkling is more commonly used with blood or oil (e.g. Lev. 1.5, 11; 3.2, 8, 13; 4.6, 17; 5.9; 9.12, 18; 14.7, 16, 27).

11  Cf. also Exod. 19.10; Lev. 6.28; 11.25, 28, 32, 40; 13.6, 34, 58; Num. 31.20, 23. A special case concerns the washing of clothes in conjunction with the immersion of an unclean person. If the person is unclean, then their clothing is also unclean by contact (e.g. Lev. 15.16-17). For discussion of immersion of an unclean person, see §4.2.5. For immersion in conjunction with washing clothing see Lev. 14.8-9; 15.5-13, 17, 21-22, 27; 16.26, 28; 17.15-16; Num. 8.7, 21; 19.7-10, 19, 21; 31.24 (cf. v. 19).

12  For the washing of the legs and entrails of the animal for the burnt offering see Exod. 29.17; Lev. 1.9, 13; 8.21; 9.14; 2 Chron. 4.6; Ezek. 40.38.

13  Wenham, *Leviticus*, 54 n. 5.

14  The only possible exception to this is Exod. 19.10 in which, just prior to delivering the Law at Mount Sinai, Yahweh instructs Moses concerning the people to 'consecrate them today and tomorrow, and let them wash their garments'. However, washing clothing required only a short time, while consecration took two days. If the washing of their clothes is combined with Moses' instruction in v. 15 not to engage in sexual intercourse, then they both may be understood to ensure that the people are in a state of cleanness (cf. Lev. 15.16-18).
     In a few situations objects are washed, but the act is simply for cleanliness and lacks any cultic context. Cf. 2 Sam. 19.24; 1 Kgs 22.38; Song 4.2; 6.6.

In the first example the water for cleansing the Levites is designated as מֵי חַטָּאת, which is literally 'waters of sin' and signifies 'waters to purify from sin'. The water of the red heifer rite is designated מֵי נִדָּה, which is literally 'waters of uncleanness', and similarly signifies 'waters to remove uncleanness' (cf. Num. 31.19, 23). This water is also referred to as חַטָּאת (vv. 9, 17), that is, dealing with sin or purification from sin. In the case of the red heifer rite, however, the water is designed to remove corpse impurity, which is not a 'sin' or 'ethical trangression' in our modern, western sense of the term. The term חַטָּאת may be used in a non-ethical sense to identify that which is 'contrary to the norm', or, in this context, 'uncleanness'.15

The use of מֵי חַטָּאת in Num. 8.7 is probably used in a sense similar to Num. 19. This is suggested by observing that the purpose of the water is to cleanse the Levites (טָהֵר, 8.6, 7), and the sprinkling is combined

---

15 The Hebrew words derived from the root חטא are the most common terms in the OT for 'sin'. There is, however, a problem sometimes in translating this term due to the exclusive ethical and theological orientation of the term 'sin' in modern, western thought, probably due, no doubt, especially to the influence of the NT as well as the prophetic literature of the OT. It is often pointed out that the basic meaning of this root is 'to miss the mark or the way' as suggested by its usage in Judg. 20.16; Job 5.24; Prov. 8.35-36; 19.2; cf. BDB, 306; Livingstone, 'חטא', 1.277; Quell, 'ἀμαρτάνω', 1.271-72. Koch ('חטא', 4.311) suggests this may be simply a 'metaphorical' use rather than a 'basic meaning'. In any case, when we appreciate that this is in essence a 'term for what is contrary to the norm' (Quell, 1.278), then the use of חַטָּאת, or 'sin' language in Num. 19.9, 17 (cf. 8.7) to apply to the removal of corpse impurity becomes understandable. To touch a corpse is 'contrary to the norm' and makes one unclean—a state which is also 'contrary to the norm'. Therefore, the water removes this state of being 'contrary to the norm'; that is, it cleanses the person from the uncleanness.

This understanding may be associated with the concept of breaking a tabu. Newing ('Religions of Pre-Literary Societies', 41) explains that 'where *mana* [i.e. spiritual power] is concentrated in a particular person or thing it is considered dangerous—it becomes tabu. . . A whole range of people, things and places are thus prohibited [including among other things] . . . the dead and all that belongs to them; . . . all these and many others are hedged round with myriads of tabus for the protection of the communities and their members.' For further discussion, see Koch, 4.311; Beasley-Murray, *Baptism*, 3-7. Neusner (*Idea of Purity*, 8-13) compares a tabu understanding with a demonic understanding of the categories of clean and unclean. Wright (*Disposal of Impurity*, 72-74, 273-74) rejects the demonic viewpoint.

Interpreting חַטָּאת in this way only removes the ethical and theological orientation associated with the term 'sin'; it does not make the state 'contrary to the norm' any less serious, for in Num. 19.13 those who neglect to be cleansed from this state of uncleanness are to be 'cut off from Israel'. For further discussion of this element of the OT's understanding of sin, see de Vries, 'Sin', 4.361-63; Eichrodt, *Theology*, 2.380-82, 423-24.

Milgrom ('Sin-Offering or Purification-Offering?' 237-39) argues on contextual, morphological and etymological grounds that the red heifer rite (Num. 19.9, 17) should not be called a 'sin offering' but a 'purification offering'; cf. Budd, *Numbers*, 213-14, cf. 72.

with both shaving their entire bodies and washing their clothes. Following this cleansing, two bulls were to be sacrificed 'to make atonement for the Levites' (v. 12; cf. vv. 8-12). Thus, the prior sprinkling of מֵי חַטָּאת in vv. 6-7 is better understood as cleansing from uncleanness rather than cleansing from sin.[16]

### 4.2.4 *Washing Parts of a Person's Body*

Washing parts of persons' bodies is primarily a priestly regulation. For example, in Exod. 30.18-21 the priests were to wash their hands and feet in the bronze laver when entering the tabernacle (or temple) and approaching the altar.[17] While the purpose of this action is not stated, it is most probably undertaken to ensure the clean state of the priest during the exercise of his duties, as suggested by the clause 'when they approach . . . to minister' (v. 20).[18]

The only other context involving the washing of parts of the body is a regulation in Deut. 21.1-9 concerning atonement for a murder in which the murderer remained unknown. The elders of the nearest city were to take a heifer to a valley with running water, break the heifer's neck and wash their hands in the water over the heifer while declaring their innocence by stating 'our hands have not shed this blood, nor did our eyes see it', and requesting that Yahweh forgive his people, Israel. The function of the handwashing itself is not entirely clear, but the purpose of the whole rite is explained in 21.8b-9a: 'And the bloodguiltiness shall be forgiven them [i.e. his people, Israel]. So you shall remove the guilt of innocent blood from your midst. . .' However, the *hand*washing itself is probably to be linked with their statement 'our *hands* have not shed this blood', and, thus, is most probably a symbolic declaration of innocence.[19] The fact that the handwashing is performed 'over the heifer' further suggests that the 'bloodguiltiness' is transferred to the heifer.[20] While the washing of hands is linked with a process which provides atonement, we should not conclude that the ablution itself provided atonement, because the presence of the heifer with its neck broken should be understood as the means of atonement, this being a form of sacrifice which is the usual means of atonement.[21]

---

16  Budd, *Numbers*, 93, cf. 72.
17  For other examples of priests washing their hands and feet see Exod. 40.30-32; 2 Chron. 4.6. In Job 9.30 reference is made to cleansing hands with lye, but in this context, such a reference is unclear and probably not relevant to our concerns.
18  Cassuto, *Exodus*, 395-96.
19  Cf. Pss. 26.6; 73.13; *Ep. Arist.* 305-306; Philo, *Vit. Mos.* 2.138; Mt. 27.24. Driver, *Deuteronomy*, 243; Craigie, *Deuteronomy*, 279-80.
20  Driver, *Deuteronomy*, 243; Mayes (*Deuteronomy*, 297-99) points to a similar transferal of guilt in the scapegoat (Lev. 16.20-22), but in Deut. 21.1-9 those who wash

### 4.2.5 *Bathing a Person's Body*

The immersion or bathing of the entire body[22] is used quite extensively. Its occurrences may be divided into three categories depending upon whether the immersion is combined with some form of sacrificial rite, other forms of ablutions, or used only by itself.

An example of bathing combined with a sacrificial rite is the cleansing of a leper in Leviticus 14. The cleansing of the leper included bathing, but it also involved two birds of which one was sacrificed, the sprinkling of the person with the blood of one of the birds and the release of the other bird, as well as washing the clothes and shaving the hair of the person. Seven days later the person was again to shave, wash his/her clothes and bathe. After these baths the person was clean. On the eighth day sacrifices were to be offered and the person was to be anointed with oil as well as blood; these rites were to make atonement for the person (Lev. 14.10-32). Another example is in Leviticus 15 which relates to persons having a discharge or women who are menstruating. These persons were unclean and the uncleanness could be passed on to other objects which would then require washing (cf. §4.2.2). The unclean person with the discharge was not cleansed until the seventh day when

their hands are innocent, which is not the case with respect to Lev. 16.20-22.

21 This observation is strengthened by a survey of atonement in the OT (the various forms of the root כפר), which yields the general observation that in no OT text is an ablution with water the means of atonement. The most common means of atonement is with a sacrifice or the blood of a sacrifice, though less conventional means are occasionally mentioned (cf. Exod. 30.15-16; Num. 16.46-47 [17.11-12]; 31.50). A passage similar to Deut. 21.1-9 is Num. 8.5-13, which describes the consecration of the Levites; it also combines an ablution with a sacrifice. The Levites are sprinkled with the water of cleansing (cf. §4.2.3), and then they shave and wash their clothes—the stated purpose of this is to 'cleanse themselves' (v. 7). Then two bulls are offered as sacrifices which make atonement for them (v. 12). The later summary of these actions (vv. 20-22) also separates the ablutions from the sacrifice, though in v. 22 the atoning sacrifice is said to also cleanse them. It was recognized above (§4.2.4) that a sacrifice which atones may be involved in the cleansing process in addition to an ablution. The point of the careful delineation made here is that, while an atoning sacrifice may cleanse (or be involved with an ablution in cleansing), the reverse cannot be said concerning the ablution; that is, ablutions cleanse, but they do not atone.

All other examples of washing parts of the human body are derived from non-cultic or non-ritualistic situations; cf. Gen. 18.4; 19.2; 24.32; 43.24, 31; Judg. 19.21; 1 Sam. 25.41; 2 Sam. 11.8; 2 Kgs 3.11; Song 5.3.

22 I am using the terms 'immersion' and 'bathing' as synonyms here. In most cases the verb is רחץ, which may refer to the washing of a part of the body (e.g. Gen. 18.4; Ps. 26.6), but in most cases the reference is to performing the ablution upon him/herself or his/her flesh (e.g. Lev. 15.5, 6, 7, 8, 10, 11, 13, 16, 18, 21, 22, 27; 16.4, 24, 26, 28 etc.), which is understood to be an action involving the bathing of the entire body and so may be considered an immersion. Cf. the concern for the size of immersion pools expressed in *m. Miq.* 2.1-2, and the importance of the water touching every portion of the person's body in *m. Miq.* 8.5.

he/she was to bathe in water which was to be 'running [lit. living] water' (15.13). On the eighth day the person was to offer two birds as a sacrifice for atonement.

A somewhat different example concerns the ordination of priests which began with an immersion, but also included sacrifices, anointing with oil, and dressing them in their priestly robes (Exod. 29.4 [cf. vv. 1-37]; 40.12 [cf. vv. 12-15]; Lev. 8.6 [cf. vv. 1-36]). The stated purpose of the entire procedure is to ordain them (יָד אֶת מִלֵּא, piel of מלא, lit. 'to fill the hand'; Exod. 29.9, 29, 35; Lev. 8.22, 33), though it is also described as an act to consecrate them (קִדֵּשׁ, piel of קדשׁ; Exod. 29.1; 40.13; Lev. 8.12). However, if the constituent parts are examined, the function of the anointing with oil appears to be specifically linked with consecration (cf. Exod. 29.21; 40.13, 15; Lev. 8.11), and the function of the sacrifices is to provide atonement (cf. Exod. 29.33; Lev. 8.14, 34). Therefore, the specific function of the immersion was most probably to ensure the cleanness of the priests as the process of ordination began, though there is no explicit statement to this effect.[23]

In most examples, not only is the cleansing included in a larger process involving sacrifice, but washing one's clothes was involved as well. Washing clothes is an example of the second form, which combines an immersion with some other form of ablution. A person who had contact either with a person having a discharge or an object touched by such a person became unclean and so he/she was to bathe, wash his/her clothes, and remained unclean until evening (Lev. 15.7-12, 19-24, 27). Another case is the ruling in Lev. 17.15, in which any person who ate an animal which was injured or already dead had to bathe, wash his/her clothes, and wait until evening before becoming clean.[24]

In other cases, only the bathing is referred to explicitly, but by implication the washing of clothes would also be required. For example, contact with a seminal emission only required bathing, but washing the clothes was also required if they had been in contact with the emission (Lev. 15.16-18). Another example is Lev. 22.4-7 which requires that priests who were unclean had to bathe and wait until evening before they could eat of the holy gifts. However, the ways specified elsewhere by which the priest could be made unclean require both an immersion and the washing of clothes (e.g. Lev. 15).[25] Therefore, while washing clothes is not mentioned in these texts specifically, cleansing most probably entailed a combination of both bathing and washing the clothes.[26] In addition, a

---

23	Wenham, *Leviticus*, 139-45.
24	Other examples include Lev. 15.16-18; 16.26, 28; 19.7-10, 19-21; 31.19, 24; cf. 2 Sam. 11.8.
25	A similar argument could be made for the soldier who has had contact with a nocturnal emission (Deut. 23.9-11; cf. Lev. 15.16-17).

period of waiting was involved in these cases.

Since most bathing appears to have included washing the clothes, there are actually only two cases in which *only* an immersion was performed. The first case is the high priest on the Day of Atonement who immersed himself on two occasions (Lev. 16.4, 24). No washing of clothes was required because upon completion of each immersion he changed into other attire, the first of which was already holy (v. 4), and the second of which could be presumed clean and therefore did not require washing (v. 24).[27] But even in this example clean attire was a requirement. The high priest's second bath was performed after he had finished atoning for the holy place and had confessed the sins of the nation over the head of the scapegoat (vv. 20-22). He was clean prior to performing these actions, and it is quite clear that neither of these actions were defiling.[28] So the second bath, performed 'in a holy place' before coming out to the people in the court (a less holy place), was evidently performed to remove the effects of being in contact with the Divine.[29]

The only other example of an immersion by itself is the story of Naaman, and this is the only example in the OT in which an immersion is performed and the cleansing of clothing is not an issue at all. Naaman was told by Elisha to wash himself seven times in the Jordan river to be healed from leprosy (2 Kgs 5.9-14). The verb used in Elisha's instructions is רחץ ('to bathe'), which is the same verb as is used with respect to the instructions in the holiness code concerning the bathing by a leper (Lev. 14.8). But, when describing Nathan's action in the Jordan, the narrative uses the verb טבל, ('to dip') rather than רחץ. The verb טבל in this context is unusual, because it is normally used for dipping an object in a liquid and is not a synonym of 'washing' or 'bathing'. Its most common use is in cultic contexts, referring to the dipping of an object (finger or hyssop) into a liquid (blood, oil or water) with the intent of sprinkling that liquid upon an object (altar, person or house).[30] Its use here indi-

26 Cf. Wright, *Disposal of Impurity*, 185-86 nn. 38-39.
27 This is in contrast to the other persons involved with the scapegoat, who were required to bathe and wash their clothes (Lev. 16.26, 28). Cf. Wright, *Disposal of Impurity*, 218 n. 100.
28 Wright, *Disposal of Impurity*, 218, esp. n. 100.
29 Cf. Ezek. 44.16-19 in which the priests, upon leaving the sanctuary, must leave their linen garments inside the holy place and put on other garments 'so that they do not transmit holiness to the people with their garments' (v. 19). Cf. Beasley-Murray, *Baptism*, 5.
30 Other than here in 2 Kgs 5.14, the verb טבל ('to dip') is used 15 times in the OT. It is used in a cultic context eight times: Exod. 12.22; Lev. 4.6, 17; 9.9; 14.6, 16, 51; Num. 19.18. This cultic use of the action of dipping is subservient to that of sprinkling, which is the action used to actually apply the liquid. Non-cultic uses of the verb are similar, describing the dipping an object into a liquid: Gen. 37.31; Deut. 33.24; Josh.

cates that Naaman, in bathing himself, did so by immersing himself.

It is also interesting to observe that, in contrast to Naaman's pride and anger in v. 12, v. 14 states: 'so *he went down* and he dipped' (וַיֵּרֶד וַיִּטְבֹּל), which T.R. Hobbs suggests may have a double meaning: 'Naaman descended to the Jordan and also demonstrated his humility'.[31] The purpose of the immersions is twofold: 'your flesh shall be restored to you and you will be clean' (v. 10; cf. v. 14). This immersion is different from that performed by the leper in Lev. 14. In that case the immersion (in combination with other rites) cleansed a leper who had already been healed of his/her leprosy. But in Naaman's case, the immersions both healed and cleansed.[32] It is also interesting to observe that, after his immersion, Naaman confessed, 'now I know that there is no God in all the earth except in Israel' (2 Kgs 5.15), and made the commitment that he would 'never again make any burnt offering or sacrifice to other gods, only to Yahweh' (v. 17). This is probably an early example of conversion to Yahwism.[33]

### 4.2.6 *Metaphorical Use of Ablution Language*

Ablution language is sometimes used in the OT to refer to cleansing from sin,[34] but the ablution language is being used metaphorically—a literal or physical ablution was not performed.[35] This metaphorical use may be categorized according to whether the cleansing was a present experience for the person or nation, or whether it was a future or eschatological cleansing. Passages indicating a present cleansing may refer to an appeal to Yahweh for cleansing as in Ps. 51.2, 7, or refer to Yahweh's having cleansed Jerusalem (Ezek. 16.4, 9). But in most cases the 'washing' is self-performed.[36] By contrast, the future or eschatological ablu-

---

3.15; Ruth 2.14; 1 Sam. 14.27; 2 Kgs 8.15. Only in Job 9.31 is a person 'dipped'. In this context Job is concerned with moral cleanness (vv. 28-30), but in spite of his attempts to become clean, he complains that God is still able to 'plunge me into the pit', implying he would become unclean again.

31 Hobbs, *2 Kings*, 65. Cf. Jer. 13.18; Ezek. 30.6 for examples of the verb יָרַד indicating humility.

32 The verb טָבַל, 'to dip', is usually translated in the LXX by the verb βάπτω, 'to dip'. However, 2 Kgs 5.14 is the only place where טָבַל is translated by the intensive form βαπτίζω. The employment of this verb in the LXX form of this story may have suggested the use of the Jordan river as a site for immersions in later Judaism. It also might have influenced early Christian thought to use this form of the verb to refer to its own rite.

33 Other examples of immersion in the OT are derived from non-cultic or non-ritualistic situations; cf. Exod. 2.5; Ruth 3.3; 2 Sam. 12.20; Ezek. 23.40.

34 I am using the term 'sin' here in its conventional ethical and theological sense of moral failure. This is in contrast to the special, non-ethical sense of the term noted earlier with respect to the red heifer rite in Num. 19 (§ 4.2.3). On the 'interpretation of purity and impurity as a metaphor of morality', see Neusner, *Idea of Purity*, 11-16.

35 Against Büchler, *Sin and Atonement*, 245-61.

tion is always performed by Yahweh.[37]

With respect to those cases in which the ablution is self-administered, the metaphorical 'washing' is performed by the person ceasing to commit certain sins and acting righteously. For example, Isa. 1.16-17 states:

> Wash yourselves, make yourselves clean;
>> Remove the evil of your deeds from my sight.
> Cease to do evil,
>> Learn to do good;
> Seek justice,
>> Correct oppression;
> Defend the orphan,
>> Plead for the widow.

The one example in which God performs the metaphorical ablution in the person's present experience is in Ps. 51.1-2. This example implies that cleansing from sin's defilement includes forgiveness:

> Have mercy on me, O God, according to your unfailing love;
>> According to the greatness of your compassion wipe away my transgressions.
> Wash me thoroughly from my iniquity,
>> And from my sin cleanse me.

In those contexts in which the metaphorical ablution is an eschatological expectation, Yahweh performs the ablution. The cleansing may involve causing certain sins to cease, but the emphasis is the removal of the defilement caused by the sin. For example, with reference to an eschatological cleansing Ezek. 36.25-26 states:

> Then I will sprinkle clean water on you, and you will be clean; from all of your uncleannesses and from all your idols I will cleanse you. And I will give you a new heart and a new spirit I will put within you, and I will remove the heart of stone from your flesh and give you a heart of flesh.

Similarly, Isa. 4.2-4 describes the day when Yahweh's Branch will be with the remnant of Israel, a day in which 'Yahweh will wash away the filth of the daughters of Zion, and he will cleanse the blood of Jerusalem from her midst by a spirit of judgment and a spirit of burning' (v. 4).

---

36  Pss. 26.6; 73.13; Prov. 30.12; Isa. 1.16-17; Jer. 4.14.
37  Cf. Isa. 4.4; Ezek. 36.25; Mal. 3.2-3. See also the reference to an eschatological hope for a 'fountain . . . for sin and uncleanness' in Zech. 13.1 as well as a stream of 'living waters' flowing out of Jerusalem in Zech. 14.8; cf. also Ezek. 47.1-12; Joel 3.18. In Isa. 52.15 Yahweh's servant performed the ablution, which may have been understood eschatologically.

These are all the references in which ablution language is used explicitly (i.e. bath, wash, sprinkle) in the metaphorical sense of cleansing from sin and its defilement. However, this metaphorical use of ablution language is related to the more general use of the words 'purify' and 'cleanse' for the removal of sin and its defilement. Cf. for example, Ps. 18.20, 24; Jer. 33.8; Ezek. 24.13; 37.23.

### 4.2.7 *Summary*

We may summarize our survey of ablutions, especially with respect to persons. *Sprinkling* persons with water is used in only two contexts: cleansing the Levites prior to service (Num. 8.7) and cleansing corpse impurity in the red heifer rite (Num. 19.18). In both cases additional cleansing procedures were involved (8.7-8; 19.12, 19). In the latter case, specially prepared 'water for uncleanness' was used. *Washing* parts of persons' bodies is exclusively a priestly regulation related to the performance of their cultic duties (e.g. Exod. 30.18-21), except for the handwashing performed by elders declaring their innocence with respect to an unsolved murder (Deut. 21.6). In most other cases, cleansing from uncleanness required an *immersion*, but cleansing in these cases involves the additional requirements of washing of one's clothing and waiting for a period of time (e.g. contact with discharges, Lev. 15.1-12, 16-24). In certain cases, usually for a higher degree of uncleanness, this cleansing was part of a larger process in which a sacrifice was required to provide atonement (e.g. leprosy, Lev. 14.1-32). Only in the cases of the high priest on the Day of Atonement (Lev. 16.4, 24) and the example of Naaman (2 Kgs 5.10, 14) are immersions performed without other requirements. Ablutory language is also used *metaphorically* to signify cleansing from sin in contexts indicating present experience (Ps. 51.1-4) as well as eschatological expectation (e.g. Ezek. 36.25). In present experience the ablution is mostly self-performed, while in eschatological expectation it is Yahweh who will perform the ablution.

From this survey of the uses of ablutions in the OT we are able to make certain observations concerning their functions. First of all, the predominant function of ablutions in the OT is to cleanse an unclean person; that is, by cleansing a person from uncleanness, that person's status is changed from unclean to clean. While at times this cleansing function is a preliminary stage of a larger process (e.g. ordaining priests, Lev. 8.6), nevertheless, the ablution still maintains this basic cleansing function. In most cases, it appears that the process by which the cleansing takes place deals with the *state* of uncleanness (changing the status from unclean to clean), but it is not designed to deal with the *cause* of the uncleanness. For example, with respect to the leper, the person must have been healed prior to being cleansed (Lev. 14.3), or, with respect to the menstruating woman, the period of menstruation must have ceased prior to her being cleansed (Lev. 15.28). The one exception is the case of Naaman's cleansing (2 Kgs 5), in which the bathing did deal with the cause of uncleanness. While most ablutions cleanse in order to change a person's status from unclean to clean, in one case, the high priest on the Day of Atonement (Lev. 16.24), the bath appears to remove the vestiges of special holiness derived from contact with the Divine prior to having contact with the common people in the outer court.

Secondly, while the two types of contagion (physical and moral) may make a person unclean, this survey has shown that ablutions were used only to cleanse uncleanness which was caused by physical contagion.[38] In contrast, when the state of uncleanness was caused by moral contagion (e.g. sexual immorality, Lev. 18.20-30; sin, Ps. 51.1-4), the responses varied,[39] but actual ablutions were not prescribed in such cases,[40] though the metaphorical, ablutory language was sometimes still used. Dealing with sin itself usually required a sacrifice to provide atonement. Some cases of uncleanness caused by physical contagion also required an atoning sacrifice (e.g. leprosy, Lev. 14.1-32).[41]

Thirdly, while we have perceived the distinction whereby ablutions appear to be performed only when the uncleanness is caused by a physical contagion rather than a moral contagion, the metaphorical use of ablutory language indicates the perception that sin makes a person unclean and requires a metaphorical 'ablution'. This metaphorical ablution appears to have had two elements; a self-administered 'ablution' in which the person 'washed away' the sin by turning from it, and a divinely administered 'ablution' in which the person was forgiven and blessed by God.

Fourthly, as a specific type of ablution, bathing appears to have been the most general form of ablution for the common person; sprinkling and washing were used in more specialized situations. But in almost all cases

---

38  Cf. Neusner, *Idea of Purity*, 11-25, esp. 11; he has not observed the specific function of ablutions with respect to these types of contagion, but that is because his focus is upon purity itself rather than ablutions.

39  When the state of uncleanness was caused by moral contagion, the responses included being 'cut off' (e.g. Lev. 18.20-30) and confession to God and requesting forgiveness (e.g. Ps. 51.1-4).

40  Wright (*Disposal of Impurity*, 85; cf. 73) points out that 'the Priestly system . . . only perceives cultic impurity, not moral impurity (= sins) or disease, to be the object of purification in its purgation rituals'. The one exception Wright makes to this statement (85, 72-74) is the scapegoat rite, which removes the impurities caused by the sins of the people. However, this is irrelevant to our concern here, because the removal of impurities by the scapegoat does not involve water ablutions as the means of cleansing.

41  On the role of sacrifice with respect to cleansing, see Wenham, *Leviticus*, 25-29. Sacrifice in addition to an ablution appears to be required when the degree of impurity is greater. For example, *bathing and a sacrifice* is required when a person with a discharge (considered unnatural) is healed (Lev. 15.13-15), as well as when a woman who has been bleeding at a time other than her normal menstrual period (considered unnatural) is healed (Lev. 15.25-30). But, after a man has had a seminal emission or a woman has had her menstrual period (both considered natural), they are only required to bathe; *no sacrifice* is mentioned (Lev. 15.16-19). Wenham (221) suggests that sacrifice is required in these and other, similar circumstances because 'the uncleanness lasts more than a week'.

these immersions were linked with other cleansing elements. While immersions had a different form from the other ablutions, they do not seem to have had a particular function which would distinguish them from those other forms of ablution. The fact that an immersion by itself was not common in the OT highlights the distinctiveness of the two examples where this was the case.

Fifthly, a few cases specify the use of 'living' or running water, which indicates the employment of water from a stream or river.[42] These appear to be cases in which the uncleanness caused by the contagion was particularly severe.

Finally, the regulations concerning ablutions function as part of the ideology concerning clean and unclean. General statements, especially the Holiness Code, suggest that the focus of this ideology of clean and unclean was primarily priestly. For example, at the conclusion of Leviticus 15, which regulated natural and unnatural discharges, v. 31 states: 'So you shall keep the people of Israel separate from their uncleanness, lest they die in their uncleanness *by defiling my tabernacle that is in their midst*'. Jacob Neusner says that 'here in a single sentence is the complete priestly ideology of purity. All matters of purity attain importance because of the cult.'[43] While this reflects the priestly orientation of the Holiness Code, the implications of these purity regulations not only protect the temple from defilement, but also separate between clean and unclean among non-priestly people. Thus, Neusner also states that, for example,

> the menstrual taboos were observed by people who had no intention whatever of entering the Temple. We certainly cannot maintain, therefore, that purity was primarily a cultic concern, or important only when a non-priest intended to go to the Temple. The contrary was in fact the case.[44]

### 4.3 *Ablutions in Second Temple Jewish Literature*

#### 4.3.1 *Passing References to Washings and Immersions*
The evidence concerning ablutions in the Jewish literature of the Second Temple period is somewhat fragmentary, but this is understandable when we realize that most of the OT evidence is contained within the legislative material of the Torah. The other OT references to ablutions are often made in passing, and the same applies to similar references in the later literature of the Second Temple period, to which we now turn.

---

42  Lev. 14.5-6, 50-52; 15.13; Num. 19.17; Deut. 21.4.
43  Neusner, *Idea of Purity*, 20. Cf. Lev. 16.16; 20.3; Num. 19.13, 20. Cf. also Wright's discussion (*Disposal of Impurity*, 231-77) of a map of cultic topography which distinguishes holy, clean and unclean places.
44  Neusner, *Idea of Purity*, 30.

As in the OT, handwashing and footwashing were associated with priestly duties in the temple.[45] Footwashing is also mentioned as a demonstration of hospitality, and it was a sign of subservience when performed by another person.[46] Handwashing was practised in two other contexts which may have special significance. First of all, handwashing is mentioned as an ablution practised in conjunction with prayer. *Ep. Arist.* 305-306, in describing the men who translated the LXX, states:

> Following the custom of all the Jews, they washed (ἀπονιψάμενοι) their hands in the sea in the course of their prayers to God, and then proceeded to the reading and explication of each point. I asked this question: 'What is the purpose of washing (ἀπονιζόμενοι) their hands whenever they say their prayers?' They explained that it is evidence that they have done no evil, for all activity takes place by means of the hands.[47]

Secondly, there is evidence that some people practised handwashing before eating.[48] Apparently, handwashing developed in conjunction with the idea that minor uncleannesses could affect only one part of the body, and this was associated particularly with the hands because 'oral law held that the hands were impure as a rule because they thouched [sic] things automatically and so came under suspicion'. Thus, the Torah regulations concerning immersions were extended especially to the hands, so that 'washing the hands was really a token bath'.[49]

---

45  *Eupol.* 9.34.9 (v. 7 in *OTP*, 2.869); *Jub.* 21.16b; *T. Levi* 9.11b; 18.2B20-21, 26, 53-54 (an addition to 18.2 in *Test. XII Patr.* MS e; see the discussion of *T. Levi* 2.3B in §4.3.4); *Ant.* 8.87; Philo, *Vit. Mos.* 2.138; cf. *m. Tam.* 1.4; 2.1.

46  *T. Job* 25.6; *T. Abr.* A 3.7, 9; 6.6; *T. Abr.* B 3.6, 8-9; 6.13; *Jos. Asen.* 7.1; 13.15; 20.2-5; Lk. 7.44; Jn 13.1-17.

47  Josephus (*Ant.* 12.106) describes similar ablutory practices by the translators, but does not mention prayer: 'And early each day they would go to the court, pay their respects to Ptolemy and then go back to the same place and, after washing ἀπονιπτόμενοι) their hands and purifying (καθαίροντες) themselves, would betake themselves in this state to the translation of the laws'.
   Marcus (*Josephus*, 7.52-53 note c) cites Sukenik's observation (*Ancient Synagogues*, 49-50) that Hellenistic Jews often built their synagogues near water (cf. *Ant.* 14.258; Acts 16.13), which he suggests may have been motivated by their perception of Gentile lands as unclean. It is not clear how common was this practice of locating synagogues near natural bodies of water, but provision was made for ablutions in conjunction with synagogue worship; cf. Safrai ('Synagogue', 2.941, cf. 2.937-42) who observes that 'only the Amoraim held that the hands had to be washed before prayer. But there is much to indicate that this was an ancient custom, dating from the period of the Second Temple.' He also mentions that 'bathing pools are often found near ancient synagogues in Palestine' (2.942 n. 2), thus suggesting this was a Palestinian custom as well (cf. Schürer, *History*, 2.440-41, esp. n. 65). Other references to ablutions prior to prayer may be found in Jdt. 12.6-8; *Sib. Or.* 3.591-93; for rabbinic references see Safrai, 'Religion', 2.829-31.

48  Mk 7.2-5; Mt. 15.2; Lk. 11.38; cf. the addition of bathing and washing in Tob. S 7.9. For rabbinic references, see Safrai, 'Religion', 2.802 nn. 2-4.

49  Safrai, 'Religion', 2.829, 831. Sanders (*Jesus*, 185-86) suggests the adoption of the practice of handwashing among certain laypeople (especially the ḥabirim) developed

Bathing was also practised in several contexts. Priests bathed prior to beginning their daily ministry in the temple, as apparently did the people.[50] Bathing is also mentioned with respect to cleansing from leprosy and after sexual intercourse and nocturnal emissions, etc.[51] Furthermore, bathing is described as the means of cleansing from corpse uncleanness.[52] This is noteworthy in light of the fact that this is not the means prescribed in the OT.[53] In Numbers 19, corpse uncleanness required the sprinkling of the specially prepared 'water for uncleanness' (מֵי נִדָּה) upon the unclean person; there is no mention in Numbers 19 that the person needed to bathe. Most specific references to cleansing from corpse uncleanness specify bathing, though more general references still refer to sprinkling specially prepared water. This does not mean that 'the water for uncleanness' was never used, only that bathing became an acceptable alternative.[54]

out of their desire to live as priests did in the temple, whom they perceived ate the heave-offering with washed hands.

Several other references to washing contribute little to our understanding of their function during the Second Temple period; these include *Jos. Asen.* 18.8-10; 29.5. Cf. also Josephus' references to washing during the OT period in *Ant.* 3.114; 6.120; 7.106; 8.79-87, 417; 10.145. An interesting reference is found in *Jos. Asen.* 14.12-15, in which Aseneth receives a heavenly visitor who tells her that her time of confession and repentance is finished; she is now to take off the sackcloth and ashes and 'wash your face and your hands with living water' and dress in new clothes. While the context is significant, this washing appears to function only to remove the dust of the ashes.

50  On priests bathing, see *T. Levi* 9.11 (cf. 8.5); *Jub.* 21.16a; cf. *m. Yom.* 3.3; *m. Tam.* 1.1-2. Josephus mentions in *War* 5.227 that 'those priests undergoing cleansing [καθαρεύοντες]' were not allowed to enter the inner court of the temple; in *War* 6.426-27 defiled common people were prevented from entering the temple (cf. *Apion* 2.1-3). On the common people bathing prior to entering the temple, see Philo, *Spec. Leg.* 1.269; *Deus Imm.* 7-8; POxy840 2.104.

51  On cleansing from leprosy, see *Apion* 1.282. On bathing after sexual intercourse, see *Apion* 2.198, 203; *Ant.* 3.263; after a nocturnal emission, see Philo, *Spec. Leg.* 1.119; after child-birth, see *Apion* 2.198. Josephus mentions in *War* 5.227 that women while menstruating were not allowed into the temple, and men who were not clean (μὴ καθάσιαν) were barred from the inner court of the temple.

52  Sir. 34.25 (31.25); Tob. BA 2.5; Tob. S 2.9; *Apion* 2.198; cf. *Ass. Mos.* 9.4.13; *Ant.* 18.36-38. Josephus describes cleansing the temple of corpse impurity in *War* 1.148-53, but he does not specify the method used.

53  But, cf. the regulation in Lev. 22.4-6, whereby if a *priest* touches a corpse (or becomes unclean in another way), he is not allowed to eat of the holy foods unless he has first bathed.

54  For discussion of Num. 19 see §4.2.3. Three possible exceptions could be raised against this observation that there are no specific references to physical sprinkling of water for uncleanness. First of all, the phrase 'waters for uncleanness' (מֵי נִדָּה) is found in 1QS 3.4b, 9a, but I argue in §5.3.1.3 that this is a metaphorical use of the phrase, and is not referring to the physical application of the waters for uncleanness at all. Secondly, in *Ant.* 4.79-81, Josephus describes the red heifer rite, but he does so only in the course of summarizing the OT text; he is not describing its practice in the Second Temple period. It is interesting to observe that, contrary to Num. 19.17

As with handwashing, bathing was also practised prior to both praying and eating. The evidence is stronger for bathing in these contexts than is handwashing. For example, with respect to praying, Jdt. 12.6-8 states that Judith, after she requested permission from Holofernes to pray, went each evening and 'bathed (ἐβαπτίζετο) in the spring'; then she returned and prayed.[55] Another example is *Sib. Or.* 3.591-93, in which the Jews are eulogized as persons who 'lift up holy arms to heaven at dawn [having just arisen] out of bed, always cleansing the body with water [χρόα ἀγνίζοντες ὕδατι]'.[56]

Metaphorical use of ablution language is also found. For example, Philo states in *Deus Imm.* 7 that 'if we cultivate the spirit of rendering thanks and honour to Him, we shall be pure from wrongdoing and wash away the filthiness which defiles our lives in thought and word and deed'.[57]

in which running water is added to the ashes in a vessel, Josephus states that 'a little of the ashes are thrown into running water [εἰς πηγήν] and the hyssop dipped [βαπτίσαντες]' (*Ant.* 4.81). Philo similarly describes the red heifer rite in Philo, *Spec. Leg.* 1.267-68; *Somn.* 1.209-12. Thirdly, *m. Par.* 3.5 states that five (or seven) red heifers were burnt since the time of Ezra. But this reference is not part of the literature of the Second Temple period, and I am not claiming that the rite was never practised during this period, only that actual references to corpse uncleanness in the literature of this period refer to bathing as the means of cleansing rather than the specially prepared water for uncleanness. For a discussion of the early rabbinic references to the red heifer rite, see Bowman, 'Red Heifer', 74-81. Safrai ('Temple', 2.876-77) describes the use of this water for uncleanness in conjunction with temple worship, and mentions that this water was kept throughout Palestine, and after the destruction of Jerusalem is found elsewhere as well; he cites *t. Par.* 3.14; 10.2; 5.6; 7.4. In 11QTemple 49.16-20; 50.10-15 sprinkling with water for uncleanness is combined with bathing and washing one's clothes; cf. §5.2.1.

55 In Tob. S 7.9 both bathing and washing are mentioned prior to eating. Cf. the discussion of *T. Levi* 2.3B1-19 in §4.3.4; in this instance bathing precedes prayer, but it has an additional significance.

56 While it is not entirely clear, the use of the participle (ἀγνίζοντες) suggests that the cleansing is associated with the activity of the finite verb (ἀείρουσι, 'they lift up'); that is, the cleansing is associated with prayer. Cf. Josephus' description of the Essenes in *War* 2.128 discussed in §4.3.3.

References are also made to the presence of baths in Palestine. For example, *Ph. E. Poet* 9.37.1-3 refers to fountains, the ruler's baths, and the high priest's fountain in Jerusalem; cf. also healing baths in *War* 7.189; *Ant.* 18.249. On the presence of baths in Palestine, see the discussion by Wood, 'To Dip or Sprinkle?' 45-60; Avigad, *Discovering Jerusalem*, 139-43.

Other references to bathing contribute nothing to our understanding of their function during the Second Temple period; these include Sus. 15, 17; *T. Reub.* 3.11; *Ezek. Trag.* 9.28.2; *Apoc. Mos.* 37.3; *War* 1.340; 7.189; *Ant.* 14.462-63; 18.203, 249; 19.96, 98; Philo, *Cher.* 95; *Det. Pot. Ins.* 20; *Deus Imm.* 8. Cf. also Josephus' references to bathing during the OT period: *Ant.* 7.130; 8.356, 417; 11.163.

57 Cf. also Philo, *Spec. Leg.* 1.257-60, and Neusner's discussion of Philo in *Idea of Purity*, 45-50. Cf. references to the flood cleansing the earth of sin in *Jub.* 7.20-21; *1 En.* 10.18-22.

Several descriptions of immersions are more extensive and explicit, and they merit closer attention. To these we now turn.

### 4.3.2 *Immersions Performed by Bannus*

Prior to becoming a Pharisee, Josephus was for three years a follower of Bannus. He described his experience in *Life* 11-12:

> On learning of someone named Bannus, who dwelt in the wilderness, using for clothing what trees provided and for food what grew by itself, and in cold water day and night frequently bathing for the sake of purity [ψυχρῷ δὲ ὕδατι τὴν ἡμέραν καὶ τὴν νύκτα πολλάκις λουόμενον πρὸς ἁγνείαν], I became his zealous follower [ζηλωτής].

This tantalizingly brief description raises more questions than it answers, but we may make a few observations. The description of the clothing and food suggest an ascetic lifestyle, which may also be linked to Bannus' dwelling in the wilderness. The frequency of the ablutions and the fact that they were baths indicates a constant supply of water in a wilderness locality, which suggests that Bannus was probably located in the lower portion of the Jordan river valley.[58] The reference to ablutions 'day and night' suggest a regular cycle of bathing morning and evening at least. We are told Bannus bathed out of a concern for purity, but we do not know if Bannus thought he was being made unclean daily or whether the bathing merely ensured a state of purity whether he had actually been made unclean or not. If Bannus' concern was with continually being made unclean, we might ask what physical contagion would cause uncleanness on such a regular basis, particularly with an ascetic lifestyle in the wilderness? The ascetic lifestyle and frequency of the ablutions might imply that Bannus was primarily concerned with impurity caused by moral contagion; this might also explain why Josephus became a 'zealous follower' of Bannus. While it is plausible that Bannus' concern was with moral contagion, the evidence to substantiate this explanation further is lacking. On the other hand, Bannus' practice may be parallel to that of the Essenes who bathed morning and evening prior to their meals.[59] We might also observe that, while Bannus appears to be alone, the fact that Josephus was a 'zealous follower' (ζηλωτής) of Bannus for three years suggests that there was some form of group gathered around this figure, though we know nothing further about such a group.[60]

---

58  Josephus mentions that the water was cold. He describes the water used by the Essenes for their ablutions in the same way in *War* 2.129; cf. *Ant.* 3.263; 7.130. In *m. Par.* 8.8-9 warm water is considered invalid for use in the red heifer rite.

59  Cf. the discussion of *War* 2.129 in §4.3.3.

60  Thomas (*Mouvement baptiste*, 33-34) considers the possibility that Bannus may represent another class of Essene, but he is hesitant because Josephus does not identify him as such. If, however, we consider Essenism to be a generic term for a type of

### 4.3.3 *Immersions Performed by the Essenes*

The evidence concerning the ablutory practices of the Essenes, provided particularly by Josephus, also merits closer attention.[61] While he mentions them briefly in *Ant.* 18.18-22 (see below), Josephus' extended description of the Essenes in *War* 2.119-61 mentions several different ablutory practices. In the first instance, 'they consider oil defiling, and anyone who is accidentally anointed washes the body (σμήχεται τὸ σῶμα), for to be dry [of skin] is held to be good, as well as always wearing white' (2.123). This avoidance of oil appears to be the result of the belief that oil touched by an unclean person is rendered unclean, so that the oil would become a source of contagion.[62] Bathing the body removed the oil and presumably restored the person to a state of cleanness.

Secondly, they practise 'a special piety toward the divine being' in which they get up before sunrise and offer prayers (2.128).[63] After a period of work, they gather once again and 'having girded themselves with linen cloths, they bathe the body (ἀπολούονται τὸ σῶμα) in cold water' (2.129).[64] After this 'purification' (τὴν ἁγνείαν) which has rendered them 'clean' (καθαροί), they gather in a dining hall, pray, and eat the breakfast meal in which only the members of the group may participate. Their evening meal involves a similar practice (2.129-32). This description shows a concern for bathing to ensure purity for eating (and possibly for prayer as well), which was practised by other persons.[65]

movement of which there may have been several different examples rather than a term identifying a single, unified movement, then this hypothesis is plausible. However, we are once again limited by how little we know of Bannus.

Rajak (*Josephus*, 34-39) thinks that some form of group gathered around Bannus, and suggests they may have been 'a group of political activists' (38). If so, then Josephus rejected this point of view by leaving Bannus.

61  Cf. references in §5 to ablutions in the Qumran literature.

62  Cf. CD 12.15-17, and the concern for the purity of oil in *m. Toh.* 9-10; Baumgarten, 'Essene Avoidance of Oil', 183-93; Beall, *Josephus' Description*, 45-46.

63  Josephus states in *War* 2.128 that these prayers are offered to the sun, 'as though beseeching it to arise'. Cf. a similar description in *Sib. Or.* 3.591-93; cf. also Ezek. 8.16; *m. Suk.* 5.4. Schürer (*History*, 2.573) denies that there was any sun-worship among the Essenes, due to their essential Jewish character, and suggests that Josephus' statement 'cannot be meant in the sense of adoration but only of invocation. It seems more probable that Josephus is describing here an Essene custom in a form intelligible to Hellenistic readers, rather than defining the meaning it had for the Jewish sect itself.' For further discussion, and a survey of various positions on this matter, see Beall, *Josephus' Description*, 52-54.

64  I understand ψυχροῖς ὕδασιν to be a dative of place rather than a dative of means; that is, as signifying 'in cold water' rather than 'with cold water'. In light of contemporary Jewish practices with respect to bathing, the former is more probable, though the latter is possible. Cf. Beall, *Josephus' Description*, 55; Sutcliffe ('Baptism', 187) is hesitant, but his grounds are questionable.

65  Cf. §4.3.1. The comment is made in Schürer (*History*, 2.569 n. 44) concerning this text that 'the obligation to take a ritual bath, instead of merely washing the hands,

Josephus also states that a person desiring admission to the group is placed on probation for one year, after which he/she 'partakes in the cleaner water for purity' (καθαρωτέρων τῶν πρὸς ἀγνείαν ὑδάτων μεταλαμβάνει). The person is still not a fully accepted member, however, because he/she is not yet allowed to attend the group's meetings (*War* 2.138). The purpose of 'partaking in cleaner water for purity' is unclear. It might be assumed that it is the same as the bathing for purity before a meal mentioned earlier (2.129),[66] but Josephus states here that it is still two more years before they are allowed to touch the communal food (2.139), and the purpose of the daily bathing for purity in 2.129 was to allow participation in that communal meal. Therefore, in this context the purpose of this cleansing is not clear; we can only conclude that partaking of the immersion indicates that the first, probationary year, during which the person remained excluded from the community, is now over (2.137-38).

Josephus' fourth statement, in *War* 2.149, is that, after having a bowel movement, disposing of the excrement in a hole and covering it over, an Essene must 'bathe after it as defiled' (ἀπολούεσθαι μετ' αὐτὴν καθάπερ μεμιασμένοις). The instruction here for disposing of the excrement follows Deut. 23.12-13, but this OT text makes no mention of bathing afterwards. An explanation might be perceived in the regulations for levitical sacrifices which required that the entrails were washed (e.g. Lev. 1.9), evidently because of contact between the sacrificial animal and its own excrement.[67]

Fifthly, Josephus states that the Essenes are divided into four grades, in which the senior members are vastly superior to the lower grades, so that 'if [seniors] are touched by them [i.e. the juniors], they must bathe (ἀπολούεσθαι) just as if contacted by a foreigner' (*War* 2.150).[68] In this instance, a bath is required to remove the uncleanness derived from contact with a junior member who is evidently not considered to be fully cleansed yet. This suggests that after the probationary year the cleansing process may have included something in addition to the use of the

---

implies that the Essene meal was endowed with a sacred character'. Cf. *m. Hag.* 2.5.

66  Cf. Beall, *Josephus' Description*, 73-74.
67  Cf. *m. Yom.* 3.2 which requires the priest in the temple to bathe after excreting, and to wash his hands and feet after urinating.
68  Josephus states (*War* 2.150) that 'they have been divided according to the duration of [their] training into four grades'. Thus, these four grades correspond to the initial probationary period (first grade) followed by two additional years during which the person is tested (second and third grades) after which the person is finally a full member (fourth grade; 2.137-39). A survey of less probable alternatives for understanding these four grades is presented by Beall, *Josephus' Description*, 99.

'cleaner water for purity' (2.138). For the junior members were cleansed when they employed these waters, yet they were still not pure enough to have physical contact with the senior members without making them unclean.

Sixthly, Josephus has been describing up to this point the Essenes who do not marry (*War* 2.120; cf. 2.160).[69] According to Josephus (2.160-61), another group of Essenes exist who do marry, but only out of concern for propagation. With this group, which otherwise is the same as the non-marrying type of Essene (2.160), both the men and women bathe, but 'in the bath (λουτρά) the women are covered in a garment just as the men [are covered] in a loincloth' (2.161). This is probably related to the description Josephus gave in 2.129 describing their bathing practices prior to meals. By clarifying that the women 'are covered in a garment' and the men are clothed as well, Josephus is probably stressing the propriety of their bathing in this way.[70]

Finally, in the much briefer description of the Essenes in *Ant.* 18.18-22, Josephus mentions that the Essenes, though they sent sacrifices to the temple, were excluded from it due to 'a difference concerning the purifications which they practised' (διαφορότητι ἁγνειῶν, ἃς νομίζοιεν; 18.19).[71] Since it appears that, according to Josephus, they were excluded (εἰργόμενοι) from the temple over this issue rather than refusing to enter the temple themselves,[72] it suggests that some aspect of their

---

69  Pliny, in *Nat. Hist.* 5.15.73, also mentions this fact concerning the Qumran community: 'it has no women and has renounced all sexual desire. . .' He does not mention their ablutory practices.

70  Beall (*Josephus' Description*, 112; citing Moehring, 'Marriage Customs', 124 n. 22) comments that 'this Essene practice is in marked contrast to the customs of the Greeks, and perhaps that is why Josephus mentions it here'.

71  Feldman (*Josephus*, 9.15-17) translates 18.19 as follows: 'They send votive offerings to the temple, but perform their sacrifices employing a different ritual of purification. For this reason they are barred from those precincts of the temple that are frequented by all the people and perform their rites by themselves.' Unfortunately there is a major textual problem in the first sentence, in that both E and Lat. have a negative, so that it would be translated: 'they do not offer sacrifices'. Good cases can be made either way. Arguments for the inclusion of οὐκ have been made by Thomas (*Mouvement baptiste*, 12-19), Wallace ('Essenes and Temple Sacrifice', 335-37), and Nolland ('Misleading Statement', 558-61), while arguments for its exclusion have been made by Strugnell ('Josephus and the Essenes, 113-15) and Black (*Scrolls*, 39-42); for further references, see Beall, *Josephus' Description*, 115 n. 302. Due to this difficulty, I do not think a case should be made from this passage concerning the Essene view of sacrifice. This difficulty, however, does not affect the observation made here that, according to Josephus, it was the issue of purification which led to the Essenes being excluded from the temple. Nolland ('Misleading Statement', 555-62) presents an interesting case that Josephus' *tendenz* in presenting the Essenes in a positive light has led him to mislead his Roman readers; the actual Essene attitude was not as positive as Josephus suggests.

72  This is based on the assertion of Marcus ('Pharisees', 158) that εἰργόμενοι 'is always passive, never middle voice in Josephus', and so should be translated 'they were

view or practice of purification rendered them unclean in the eyes of the temple authorities. But it is unclear what the problem was to which Josephus is referring, especially in light of the evident concern for purity manifested by the Essenes' use of ablutions.[73]

Philo also provides a description of the Essenes in *Omn. Prob. Lib.* 75-91 as an example of 'nobleness and goodness' manifested in Palestine (75); to Philo, the Essenes are 'athletes of virtue' (ἀθλητὰς ἀρετῆς; 88). Philo describes the three standards by which they judge all things as 'love of God, love of virtue and love of persons' (83). In further defining these three, the first characteristic demonstrating love of God is their concern for 'continuous purity' (ἐπάλληλον ἁγνείαν; 84). While Philo does not expand this point, it is most probably a reference to the concern for purity demonstrated by their bathing.[74] Philo makes no other references to their ablutions, but he does mention that 'they have become especially devout in the service of God, not by sacrificing animals, but considering it worthy to make their thoughts holy' (75). Philo does not actually state that they have explicitly rejected animal sacrifice; rather, the focus of their divine service was holiness of mind rather than on animal sacrifice.[75]

### 4.3.4 *Immersions in the Addition to* T. Levi *2.3 in Manuscript E*

The 11th century CE manuscript of the *Testaments of the Twelve Patriarchs* from the Monastery of Koutloumous on Mount Athos in Greece has three extensive additions not found in other manuscripts of this document.[76] Of these three,[77] it is the first which merits our closer

excluded' rather than 'they removed themselves'. This assertion is cited frequently by others; e.g. Nolland, 'Misleading Statement', 557 n. 11; Beall, *Josephus' Description*, 115 n. 303. While this observation makes it probable that Josephus is using the verb in a passive sense here as well, it does not entirely exclude the possibility of a reflexive sense in this one instance (cf. a possible exception to Marcus' rule in *Ant.* 19.267).

73   The explanation provided by Feldman (*Josephus*, 9.17 note b) appears too speculative. Perhaps the most probable explanation is that the Essenes did in fact sacrifice in the temple, but simply avoided contact with other worshippers whom they might consider as a source of physical contagion. This may be supported by the fact that there was a specific gate to the temple area called the gate of the Essenes (*War* 5.145), and specific Essenes are mentioned as being present in the temple area (e.g. *War* 1.78; 2.562-67). Cf. Black, *Scrolls*, 39-41; Baumgarten, 'Essenes and the Temple', 62-67; Beall, *Josephus' Description*, 119. Wallace ('Essenes and Temple Sacrifice', 335-38) argues that the Essenes abandoned temple sacrifice altogether.

74   Colson (*Philo*, 9.58-59 note b) points out that if this was a general concern for purity of living, it would have been listed under 'love of virtue' rather than 'love of God'.

75   Beall (*Josephus' Description*, 118) concurs: 'this does not necessarily imply that the Essenes did not sacrifice, but rather that sacrifice was not the focal point of their worship. Hence, there is no inherent contradition between Josephus (and Philo) and the Qumran community on the matter of sacrifices.' Cf. also Marcus, 'Pharisees', 158.

attention, for in it Levi performs ablutions and prays.

The reader might immediately object that this evidence is very late and quite irrelevant to our concerns here. However, the Aramaic Qumran fragment 4QTLevi ar[a] closely parallels not only this addition to the Greek *T. Levi* 2.3 (identified as 2.3B),[78] but also the immediate context of the addition in the Greek *Testament of Levi* 2. J.T. Milik's examination of 4QTLevi ar[a] led him to conclude that it may be dated between the end of the second century BCE and the beginning of the first century BCE.[79] Unfortunately only partial lines remain in the two largest fragments of 4QTLevi ar[a]; nevertheless, the parallels between the extant portions of 4QTLevi ar[a] and *T. Levi* 2.3B are very close. For example, we can compare in both texts the end of Levi's preparation and the beginning of the prayer which he prays. In such a comparison we observe that all of the extant text of 4QTLevi ar[a] is represented in *T. Levi* 2.3B3-5a. I highlight this by italicizing these parallels in the translations:

4QTLevi ar[a] 1.8-10:

| | |
|---|---|
| ארי̇ן עיני ואנפי ]נטלת לשמיא | ] 8 |
| [ואצבעת כפי וידי | ] 9 |
| וצלית ו]אמרת מרי אנתה | ] 10 |

| | | |
|---|---|---|
| 8 | [ | Then my eyes and my countenance] *I lifted up to the heavens* |
| 9 | [ | ] *and the fingers of my palms and my hands* |
| 10 | [I stretched out . . . | I prayed and] *I said, 'My Lord, you* |

*T. Levi* 2.3B3-5a:

3B3 τότε τοὺς ὀφθαλμούς μου καὶ τὸ πρόσωπόν μου ἦρα πρὸς τὸν

---

76  De Jonge, *Testaments: Critical Edition*, xvii.  De Jonge identifies this manuscript by the siglum e.

77  The second addition occurs after *T. Levi* 18.2.  It is paralleled by the Aramaic fragments discovered in the Cairo Genizah, now held in the Bodleian Library.  This addition concerns priestly ordinances, including washings in the course of priestly duties; cf. references in §4.3.1.  The text of this addition is found in de Jonge, *Testaments: Critical Edition*, 46-48; Denis, *Concordance*, 837.  For a translation see Charles, *APOT*, 2.364-65; for discussion see Grelot, 'Notes', 391-406.  The third addition appears to be a Christian interpolation.

78  De Jonge (*Testaments: Critical Edition*, 25) provides the text of the addition in a footnote with versification from v. 1 to v. 19, but this makes references to these additional verses confusing.  I have followed the reference system of Denis (*Concordance*, 835), whereby the 19 verses of the addition are prefixed by 3B; so, for example, vv. 1-3 of the addition would be fully identified as *T. Levi* 2.3B1-3.  The text is provided by de Jonge and Denis, as well as by Charles, *Greek Versions*, 29.  A (rather poor) translation may be found in James, *Lost Apocrypha*, 19-20.

I am using the text and translation of 4QTLevi ar[a] provided by Fitzmyer and Harrington, *Aramaic Texts*, 88-91; cf. Milik, 'Testament de Lévi', 400.

79  Milik, 'Testament de Lévi', 399.

οὐρανόν, καὶ τὸ στόμα μου ἤνοιξα καὶ ἐλάλησα,
3B4 καὶ τοὺς δακτύλους τῶν χειρῶν μου καὶ τὰς χεῖράς μου ἀνεπέτασα
εἰς ἀλήθειαν κατέναντι τῶν ἁγίων. καὶ ηὐξάμην καὶ εἶπα·
3B5 Κύριε, γινώσκεις. . .

3B3 Then my eyes and my countenance *I lifted up to heaven*, and I opened
my mouth and spoke,
3B4 *and the fingers of my hands and my hands* I stretched out for truth in
the sight of the saints; and I prayed and *I said,*
3B5 'Lord, you know. . .

Parallels may also be observed in the content of the prayer itself. For
example, in 4QTLevi ar[a] 1.17-18 Levi prays: '[    do] not let any adversary have power over me [    to] me, my Lord and draw me near to be
for you', while the parallel in *T. Levi* 2.3B10-11 states: 'and *do not let any
adversary have power over me* to lead me astray from your way, and have
mercy on me *and draw me near to be your* servant. . .' Similar parallels
may also be seen in the surrounding narrative, including the mention of a
specific location: in *T. Levi* 2.3 it is identified as ʾΑβελμαούλ (Abel-
Maoul; cf. 2 Chron. 16.4) and 4QTLevi ar[a] 2.13 mentions אבל מין
(Abel-Main). Similarly, in both texts Levi has a vision of the heavens
and receives an angelic messenger (4QTLevi ar[a] 2.15-18 = *T. Levi* 2.6-
8).[80] In light of this evidence I would conclude that the additional text in
*T. Levi* 2.3B probably represents a pre-Christian tradition.

Unfortunately, the beginning of the first column of 4QTLevi ar[a] is
extremely fragmentary, and this is the point at which immersions are
mentioned in *T. Levi* 2.3B. 4QTLevi ar[a] 1.8 has been reconstructed with
the following reading: אתרח[עת וכל    ]. This may be translated
'[    I washed my]self, and all. . .' However, *T. Levi* 2.3B1-2 reproduces what little remains of the Aramaic fragment:

[1]τότε ἐγὼ ἔπλυνα τὰ ἱμάτιά μου, καὶ καθαρίσας αὐτὰ ἐν ὕδατι καθαρῷ
[2]καὶ ὅλος ἐλουσάμην ἐν ὕδατι ζῶντι· καὶ πάσας τὰς ὁδούς μου ἐποίησα
εὐθείας.

[1]Then I washed my clothes and cleansed them in pure water, [2]and in living
water I wholly bathed my*self, and all* my ways I made straight.

Certain elements within the prayer itself indicate that one thrust of the
prayer is confession and the desire for cleansing from sin along with a
commitment to God; for example, *T. Levi* 2.3B7-8, 11, 14 states:

[7]μάκρυνον ἀπ᾽ ἐμοῦ, κύριε, τὸ πνεῦμα τὸ ἄδικον καὶ διαλογισμὸν τὸν
πονηρὸν καὶ πορνείαν, καὶ ὕβριν ἀπόστρεψον ἀπ᾽ ἐμοῦ. [8]δειχθήτω μοι,
δέσποτα, τὸ πνεῦμα τὸ ἅγιον, καὶ βουλὴν καὶ σοφίαν καὶ γνῶσιν καὶ
ἰσχὺν δός μοι. . . [11]καὶ ἐλέησόν με καὶ προσάγαγέ με εἶναί σου δοῦλος

---

80  For further parallels, see Milik, 'Testament de Lévi', 398-406; cf. also de Jonge,
'Notes', 252-58.

καὶ λατρεῦσαί σοι καλῶς. . . [14]καθάρισον τὴν καρδίαν μου, δέσποτα, ἀπὸ πάσης ἀκαθαρσίας, καὶ προσάρωμαι πρός σε αὐτός·

[7][Remove] far away from me, Lord, the spirit of unrighteousness and evil thought and sexual immorality, and remove arrogance from me, [8]and make known to me, Lord, the spirit of holiness, and give to me resolution and wisdom and knowledge and strength. . . [11]And have mercy on me and bring me to be your servant and to worship you correctly. . . [14]Cleanse my heart, Lord, from all uncleanness, and I will be joined to you myself.[81]

Levi performs his immersion prior to praying, but in contrast to most descriptions of bathing before prayer (cf. §4.3.1), Levi's immersion is unusual in two respects: he also washes his clothes, and his immersion is in 'living' water; that is, water which is flowing and this usually signifies a river. The combination of washing one's clothing and bathing was a frequent combination in the OT (cf. §4.2.5). But the additional requirement of immersing in *running* water is made only in the case of a person with a discharge (Lev. 15.13; cf. Naaman in 2 Kgs 5.9-14). Yet in this case other elements are also required for cleansing, and, thus, does not directly apply to Levi's immersion. However, in Lev. 15.13 and other texts, flowing water is associated with more serious cases of defilement,[82] and it is probable that the mention of running water is meant to imply that here. Therefore, while Levi's immersion precedes his prayer, preparation for prayer probably does not fully provide its significance.

The content of Levi's prayer is more helpful in this regard. He seeks from God cleansing from sin and desires to commit himself to God (vv. 3B11, 14), and desires a transformation of his life described in terms of God removing a spirit of evil and giving a spirit of holiness as well as other graces (vv. 3B7-8). This transformation of life combined with a commitment to God could be described as a conversion. Since he appeals to God to cleanse his heart, the immersion is not understood to accomplish the cleansing in a magical or mechanical sense. Nevertheless, his ablutions may be understood to symbolize or signify Levi's desire for God's forgiveness and a conversion of his life. What appears to have happened in this text is the bringing together of two streams of evidence which we observed in the OT: the actual use of immersions for cleansing from physical contagion, and the use of metaphorical language of ablutions to describe cleansing from sin. Thus, in this addition to *T. Levi* 2.3, an actual immersion is performed in running water to symbolize cleansing from sin and conversion to God.[83]

---

[81] Parallels to these verses may be observed in 4QTLevi ar[a] 1.12-15.
[82] Cf. running water in other contexts: Lev. 14.5-6, 50-52; 15.13; Num. 19.17; Deut. 21.4; cf. also *m. Miq.* 1.8.
[83] Further associations may be found in the eschatological orientation to the prayer in *T. Levi* 2.3B and the eschatological expectation such as a stream of 'living waters will flow out of Jerusalem in that day' in Zech. 14.8; cf. Zech. 13.1; Joel 3.18; Ezek. 47.1-

This text is particularly significant, for it clearly antedates John's baptismal practice. There are other texts which are significant for understanding immersions, but the dating of these is somewhat problematic. To these we now turn.

### 4.3.5 *Immersions in* Sibylline Oracles *4*
In *Sib. Or.* 4.152-61 the sibyl describes the impiety and evil of humankind in the last times and the wrath of God against the entire world. There follows in 4.162-70 an exhortation:

> 162 Ah, wretched mortals, change [μετάθεσθε] these things [i.e. the
> wickedness and impiety in 4.152-61], and do not
> 163 lead the great Great God to all sorts of anger, but abandon
> 164 daggers and groanings, murders and outrages,
> 165 and wash [λούσασθε] your whole bodies in perennial rivers.
> 166 Stretch out your hands to heaven and ask forgiveness [συγγνώμην
> αἰτεῖσθε]
> 167 for your previous deeds and make propitiation [ἰλάσκεσθε]
> 168 for bitter impiety with words of praise; God will grant repentance
> [μετάνοιαν]
> 169 and will not destroy. He will stop his wrath again if you all
> 170 practice honorable piety in your hearts.

The immersion in a river is associated with changing one's behavior from impious deeds to piety and with receiving forgiveness from God. The urgency of this exhortation is heightened by the threat of judgment by fire: 'But if you do not obey me ... there will be fire throughout the whole world ...' (4.171-73).[84] The understanding expressed here of immersion, forgiveness and propitiation is probably linked to the other distinctive element in the ideology of *Sibylline Oracles* 4, which is the rejection of temple worship and animal sacrifice (4.8, 27-30). The immersion, together with seeking forgiveness and propitiation, may have been understood as a replacement for the temple cultus.

According to John Collins' analysis, *Sibylline Oracles* 4 is a composite work consisting of an early political oracle describing the four kingdoms of Assyria, Media, Persia and Macedonia (4.49-101) which has been

12; Isa. 4.4, etc.
   We should also observe that there is no connection between this immersion and problems with the temple and/or the sacrificial system. In *T. Levi* 2, following this prayer, Levi ascends to heaven in a vision, in which he is told by the angel that he shall be the Lord's priest (2.5-10). It is possible that Levi's cleansing and conversion are in preparation to being told that he will become the Lord's priest, but it is unlikely that his immersion is to be equated with priestly preparations for temple service.

84 It is interesting to observe in *Sib. Or.* 4 that, after the whole earth is destroyed by fire (4.171-78), God raises the dead, judging the wicked and the pious (4.178-83). The wicked are punished (4.184-86), but the pious live on the earth and God gives them '*spirit* and life and favor' (4.187-90).

expanded with a brief description of the rise of Rome (4.102-14) and an extensive description of the destruction of Jerusalem (4.115-29). That this later addition is distinctly Jewish is substantiated by the interpretation of the eruption of Mount Vesuvius and other calamities as divine judgment for Rome's destruction of Jerusalem (4.130-51). The polemic against idolatry and temple worship, and the praise of righteous living which begin *Sibylline Oracles* 4 (1-48), as well as the eschatological orientation linked with exhortations to piety which conclude *Sibylline Oracles* 4 (152-92), are probably also part of this later Jewish addition, or at least extensively redacted from a Jewish point of view.[85] The references to the destruction of Jerusalem in 70 CE (4.115-19, 125-28) and the eruption of Mount Vesuvius in 79 CE (4.130-35) indicate that the Jewish redaction, including the reference to immersions, may not be dated prior to 80 CE.[86] While the redaction must be dated post-70 CE, it is possible that it reflects a pre-70 Jewish practice.[87]

### 4.3.6 *Immersions in the* Life of Adam and Eve (Apocalypse of Moses)

In the *Life of Adam and Eve* (using here the Greek text known as the *Apocalypse of Moses*)[88] Adam and Eve were cast out of Paradise after being judged for their sin (*Apoc. Mos.* 24.1–29.6) and 'came to be on the earth' (29.6). They are now hungry, but they find no food (29.7-8). In

---

85  *OTP*, 1.381-83; Collins, 'Fourth Sibyl', 365-80. Collins (374) suggests that vv. 174-92 are the work of the Hellenistic oracle rather than the later, Jewish sibyl, though these may have been redacted by the Jewish sibyl.

86  Thomas (*Mouvement baptiste*, 48) points out 'd'autre part, il n'est rien dit de l'incendie de Rome en août 80 ni de la mort de Titus survenue au début de 81 ...' and, therefore, 'la rédaction du quatrième livre sibyllin doit donc se placer dans la première moitié de l'an 80'.

87  Collins (*OTP*, 1.382) states with respect to the geographical provenance that 'most scholars locate it in Syria or the Jordan Valley because of the importance attached to baptism, and, while the evidence is less than conclusive, this position carries the balance of probability'. Cf. also Thomas, *Mouvement baptiste*, 48-49.

88  The Greek text of the *Life of Adam and Eve* has been known as the *Apocalypse of Moses*, while the Latin text was named *Vita Adae et Evae*. Johnson's recent translations of these Greek and Latin texts (*OTP*, 2.249-95) are both labelled the *Life of Adam and Eve*, but sub-titled 'Apocalypse' and '*Vita*' respectively (I will use the more commonly used abbreviation *LAE*). This confusion between *Apoc. Mos.* and *LAE* is unfortunate, but this is not the proper context in which to attempt a correction. Since the Greek recension is shorter and simpler in nature, and the Latin recension was probably translated from a Greek version, I utilize the Greek text here, identified as *Apoc. Mos.* For a general introduction, see Schürer, *History*, 3.757-61; Johnson, *OTP*, 2.249-57. The Latin version, while different in minor ways in the passage relevant here (*LAE* 4-8), does not contain anything substantively different with respect to its understanding of immersions. Charles (*APOT*, 2.128-29) considers the *Apocalypse of Moses* to be older; cf. also Schürer, *History*, 3.758-59. The versification of the *Apocalypse of Moses* is not consistent. I have followed the versification used in Johnson's translation (*OTP*, 2.249-95), but this differs somewhat from that found in, for example, Denis, *Concordance*, 815-18.

despair, Eve asks Adam to kill her, but Adam refuses (29.9-10) and in 29.11-13a responds:

> $^{11}$'Rather, let us repent (μετανοήσωμεν) for forty days in order that God might have compassion on us and give to us food better than that of animals. I will do forty days but you [will do] thirty-four days, because you were not formed [until] the sixth day in which God completed his creation. $^{12}$But arise and go to the Tigris river, and take a stone and place [it] under your feet, and stand clothed in the water up to [your] neck [στῆθι ἐνδεδυμένη ἐν τῷ ὕδατι ἕως τοῦ τραχήλου], and do not let a word escape out of your mouth, for we are unworthy and our lips are not clean [οὐκ ἔστι καθαρά]'.[89] $^{13}$But Adam went to the Jordan river . . . and was praying in the water. . .[90]

This passage is interesting for it presents the view that an immersion in water may express repentance in combination with praying. This combination with bathing may be linked to the view that, as a consequence of the disobedience in the fall, they are 'not clean'. Also significant is the mention of the Jordan river as a suitable river in which to express such an act of repentance, though this is not the only river used. But care must be taken in utilizing this text, because, first of all, standing for thirty-four or forty days in a river is rather more than a simple immersion; it is almost like an endurance test as a form of penance. The *Life of Adam and Eve* expresses this quite clearly, for Adam states, 'let us repent with a great penitence', to which Eve responds, 'tell me, what is repentance and what kind of penitence should I do' (*LAE* 4.3–5.1). Yet, the idea of immersing in water to express repentance is still there. Secondly, dating the *Life of Adam and Eve* (and the *Apocalypse of Moses*) is very difficult, due to the lack of explicit historical references. It may be dated in the first century CE, but more probably to the second half. A later date is also possible.[91]

### 4.3.7 *The Immersion of a Jewish Proselyte*

For a Gentile to be fully accepted as a Jewish proselyte the rabbinic literature requires that the Gentile be circumcised, perform an immersion,

---

89  According to Johnson (*OTP*, 2.261) Eve prays as well, for manuscript F adds: 'But cry silently to God (saying), "O God, be gracious to me" '.

90  This translation is from the Greek text of *Apoc. Mos.* 29.10-11a supplied in Denis, *Concordance*, 816, which is equivalent to 29.11-13a in *OTP*, 2.259-61. Johnson's translation is somewhat different, due to the use of different Greek texts, but these differences do not alter the basic thrust in the passage concerning immersions.

91  In comparison with other ancient literature, Johnson (*OTP*, 2.252) dates it between 100 BCE and 200 CE and probably in the second half of the first century CE. Charles (*APOT*, 2.126-29) dates it between 60 and 300 CE, 'and probably in the earliest years of this period' (129). Cf. also Schürer, *History*, 3.758-59. Since it may have originated in the first century, we use it here, though with caution. To ignore it would be equally unwise.

and offer a sacrifice in the temple, though a woman was only required to perform the latter two.[92] A debate has raged among scholars concerning whether or not proselyte immersion was a requirement during the Second Temple period and antedates the baptisms of John the Baptist and the early Christian community.[93] Joachim Jeremias has advanced the most comprehensive case for an early date for proselyte immersion. His arguments are basically four: (1) proselyte immersion must antedate Christianity because the influence of Christian baptism on the development of a Jewish rite 'must be excluded as impossible';[94] (2) by the end of the first century BCE a Gentile was considered unclean, and therefore a proselyte would need to be cleansed; (3) certain texts demonstrate the early practice of proselyte immersion, especially *T. Levi* 14.6, and also *Sib. Or.* 4.162-70; Epictetus, *Diss.*, 2.9.19-21, and earlier rabbinic texts, including *m. Pes.* 8.8 = *m. 'Ed.* 5.2; and (4) Christian baptism has many contacts with proselyte baptism in its terminology, rites, catechetical instruction and theology.[95]

A careful examination of these arguments demonstrate that they are less than convincing. The first argument assumes that one rite directly influenced the other, and concludes a priori that the influence could only be one direction. The rites may have developed without direct dependence on each other, and, thus, both the assumption and conclusion cannot stand without actual evidence.[96]

With respect to his second argument, the issue of Gentile uncleanness is not as clear as Jeremias would make it. First of all, as late as the end of third century CE, rabbinic discussion was not decided on this matter. For example, *b. Pes.* 92a states concerning a proselyte that 'the previous year he was a heathen and not susceptible to uncleanness, whereas now

---

92  Cf. *b. Yeb.* 46a-47b; *b. Ger.* 60b (2.5); Schürer, *History*, 3.173-76; Moore, *Judaism*, 1.323-53.

93  Jeremias (*Infant Baptism*, 24-37) puts forth the best case for an early date for proselyte baptism, while Smith ('Proselyte Baptism', 13-32) provides the best argument for a late date. Other examples of those arguing for an early date: Abrahams, *Studies*, 1.36-46; Gavin, *Jewish Antecedents*, 26-58; Leipoldt, *Urchristliche Taufe*, 1-25; Jeremias, 'Johannestaufe', 312-20; Rowley, 'Proselyte Baptism', 313-34; Marsh, *Baptism*, 7-13; Flemington, *Baptism*, 3-12; Jeremias, 'Proselytentaufe', 418-28; Moore, *Judaism*, 1.331-38; Torrance, 'Proselyte Baptism', 150-54; Daube, *Rabbinic Judaism*, 106-13; Vermes, 'Baptism', 308-19; Levison, 'Proselyte', 45-56; Oepke, 'βάπτω', 1.535-36; Schürer, *History*, 3.173-74; Pusey, 'Proselyte Baptism', 141-45. Other examples of those arguing for a later date include: Brandt, *Jüdischen Baptismen*, 57-62; Zeitlin, 'Halaka', 357-63; Zeitlin, 'Baptism', 78-79; Thomas, *Mouvement baptiste*, 356-74; Taylor, 'Proselyte Baptism', 193-98; Beasley-Murray, *Baptism*, 18-31; Scobie, *John the Baptist*, 95-102.

94  Jeremias, *Infant Baptism*, 24.

95  Jeremias, *Infant Baptism*, 24-37; Cf. also Jeremias, 'Johannestaufe', 312-20; Jeremias, 'Proselytentaufe', 418-28.

96  Cf. Smith, 'Proselyte Baptism', 14.

he is an Israelite and susceptible to uncleanness'.[97]

Secondly, Jeremias' argument[98] is heavily dependent on the statement in *m. 'Ed.* 5.1 ( = *m. Nid.* 4.3) that 'the blood of a non-Jewess and the blood of the purification of a leprous [Jewish] woman—the School of Shammai pronounce clean, but the School of Hillel say, [The blood] is like to her spittle and like to her urine'.[99] Jeremias states that these texts 'ascribe to a Gentile woman the permanent impurity of a menstruous person'.[100] But this is highly questionable, because the texts are discussing the menstrual blood of a Gentile woman being unclean (cf. Lev. 15.19-24), and are making no statement about the Gentile being in a state of permanent, menstrual uncleanness at all. The Hillelite position that the Gentile woman's menstrual blood 'is like to her spittle and like to her urine' is only asserting that 'just as the saliva and urine are unclean only when they are moist and not when they are dry, even so the blood in these cases is unclean only when moist'.[101] Therefore, Jeremias' conclusion is invalid when he states that the Arab who spat upon the high priest Simeon and made him unclean (*t. Yom.* 4.20) was himself unclean 'because he is constantly made so by his wife, who is in a permanent condition of Nidda [i.e. a menstruous woman]'.[102] The texts he cites simply do not support his view.

It is true, however, that certain texts do suggest that uncleanness may have been attributed to Gentiles,[103] but this is certainly not a universal point of view, and, furthermore, the nature of that uncleanness is uncertain. David Daube concludes that 'pagans were not susceptible to *Levitical* uncleanness' and therefore, 'in principle there was simply no room for purification'.[104] Derwood Smith suggests that 'while the Gentile was

---

97 Jeremias (*Infant Baptism*, 25, my emphasis) notes this text and others, and comments that 'according to the older view, *demonstrably still dominant* as late as the third century AD, a Gentile who was not under the law could not be legally impure'. Yet, Jeremias takes no further notice of this in his discussion of Gentile uncleanness. Cf. also *m. Neg.* 7.1; *t. Ohol.* 1.4.

98 Jeremias, *Infant Baptism*, 25-26.

99 Danby (*Mishnah*, 431) mistranslates *m. 'Ed.* 5.1, which states, בֵּית שַׁמַּאי מְטַהֲרִין, 'the School of Shammai *declare it clean*'; whereas Danby translates the participle 'unclean'. The statement in *m. Nid.* 4.3 is identical except that it uses the Hebrew form of the participle (מְטַהֲרִים) rather than the Aramaic as in *m. 'Ed.* 5.1. My argument is supported by the text and translation of Blackman (*Mishnayoth*, 4.422; 6.613), which I have used here.

100 Jeremias, *Infant Baptism*, 25.

101 Blackman, *Mishnayoth*, 4.423 n. 10. Blackman states elsewhere (6.613) that the Hillelite position is still more lenient with respect to a Gentile woman than with a Jewish woman, because 'the menstrous blood of a Jewess conveys uncleanness whether wet or dry'.

102 Jeremias, *Infant Baptism*, 26.

103 E.g. *War* 2.150; *t. Yom.* 4.20; Jn 18.28; Acts 10.28.

104 Daube, *Rabbinic Judaism*, 107, my emphasis.

*legally* reckoned to be clean, he was at times treated by Jews as though he were unclean. Or it may be necessary to distinguish between the kinds of uncleanness attributed to a Jew and a Gentile.'[105]

Jeremias' third argument, that certain texts support an early date for proselyte baptism, also fails under the weight of scrutiny. He places a great deal of emphasis upon *T. Levi* 14.6. In the context Levi addresses his children (the priests), warning them that 'in the last days you will act impiously against the Lord' (14.1), and then he identifies the ways they will do this, including abuse of the law (v. 4) and the sacrifices (v. 5), as well as through sexual sins (v. 6) and pride (vv. 7-8). Among the sexual sins listed is the statement: 'You will take daughters of Gentiles for wives, cleansing them with an unlawful cleansing (καθαρίζοντες αὐτὰς καθαρισμῷ παρανόμῳ), and your sexual intercourse will become like Sodom and Gomorrah in impiety'. Jeremias' interpretation is that 'its author opposes the introduction of proselyte baptism because he fears that it encourages mixed marriages, and he appeals to the fact that it lacks scriptural support (παρανόμῳ)'.[106] But there is nothing in the text to actually identify the cleansing as a reference to proselyte immersions. The vague reference could be describing 'purification after the menses',[107] or 'lax observance of customary purifications'.[108] G.R. Beasley-Murray judiciously observes that 'a saying whose significance and origin are so dubious as this has no claim to confidence as a means of determining so complex an issue as that under review'.[109]

The two Mishnaic references commonly cited to support Jewish proselyte immersions also require careful examination. The statements in both *m. Pes.* 8.8 and *m. 'Ed.* 5.2 are essentially the same:

105 Smith, 'Proselyte Baptism', 17, my emphasis. Cf. also Beasley-Murray, *Baptism*, 21-22 n. 2; Büchler, *Sin and Atonement*, 212-18. Moore (*Judaism*, 1.331-35) also argues that the function of the proselyte's immersion was not purification from Gentile uncleanness but only initiation into Judaism.

106 Jeremias, *Infant Baptism*, 27.

107 Zeitlin, 'Baptism for Proselytes', 79.

108 Charles, *APOT*, 2.313. Cf. Finkelstein ('Baptism for Proselytes', 205) who emends the text to read 'betrothing them against the law'. Certain manuscripts do not contain this clause (cf. de Jonge, *Testaments: Critical Edition*, 42), which may be the reason that Kee did not include this clause in his translation in *OTP*, 1.793. Equally problematic is Jeremias' dating of *T. Levi* to first century BCE (*Infant Baptism*, 26-28). This date is also important for his argument, for if it is much earlier, then it would negate his argument concerning Gentile uncleanness developing at the same time, and if it is much later, then it would not antedate Christian baptism. For discussion, see Smith, 'Proselyte Baptism', 19; Beasley-Murray, *Baptism*, 23. On dating the *Testaments of the Twelve Patriarchs*, see note in §7.3.

109 Beasley-Murray, *Baptism*, 23. Neither do Jeremias' two other texts support proselyte immersion; on *Sib. Or.* 4.162-70, see §4.3.5. It is not clear that Epictetus, *Diss.*, 2.9.19-21 refers to proselyte immersion at all, and the text is post-70 CE; cf. Smith, 'Proselyte Baptism', 20.

> The School of Shammai say: If a man became a proselyte on the day before
> Passover he may immerse himself and consume his Passover-offering in the
> evening. And the School of Hillel say: He that separates himself from his
> uncircumcision is as one that separates himself from the grave.

In *m. 'Ed.* 5.2 the statement is the last in a list of 'six opinions in which
the School of Shammai follow the more lenient and the School of Hillel
the more stringent ruling'. These are six unconnected rulings, and, therefore, this context is of no help in understanding the statement. However,
the tractate *Pesahim* regulates the Feast of Passover, and this provides
the larger context for this statement. The first portion of *m. Pes.* 8.8
(which is often not cited in discussions of proselyte immersion) states:

> He that mourns his near kindred may, after he has immersed himself, eat
> the Passover-offering in the evening, but he may not eat of [other] Hal-
> lowed Things. If a man heard of the death of one of his near kindred or
> caused the bones of his dead to be gathered together, he may, after he has
> immersed himself, eat of Hallowed Things. The School of Shammai say: If
> a man became a proselyte on the day before Passover he may immerse
> himself and consume his Passover-offering in the evening. And the School
> of Hillel say: He that separates himself from his uncircumcision is as one
> that separates himself from the grave.

In this immediately preceding context, regulations are given whereby
*Jews as well as new proselytes* were required to immerse (in all three cases
identified identically as טוֹבֵל, 'one who bathes') before eating their Passover offering. Another passage, *m. Hag.* 3.3, explains why:

> Dry foodstuffs that are Heave-offering may be consumed with unwashed
> hands, but it is not so with Hallowed Things. He that mourns his near of
> kin [even though he has not contracted corpse uncleanness] and he whose
> atonement is yet incomplete, needs to immerse himself for Hallowed
> Things, but not for the Heave-offering.

The Passover-offering was a 'Hallowed Thing', and, according to *m. Hag.*
3.3, to eat the Passover, if either in mourning (cf. Deut. 26.14) or not
having completed an atonement, required an immersion prior to con-
sumption. There were four situations in which one might not yet have
completed an atonement, including the proselyte, who has been circumcised, but has not yet offered the required sacrifice (*m. Ker.* 2.1).

In light of these two other passages, the situation in *m. Pes.* 8.8 may
now be explained. In *m. Pes.* 8.8a, the Jews who are mourning are
required to immerse themselves before eating the Passover offering
because it is a Hallowed Thing (*m. Hag.* 3.3). Similarly, the new
proselyte who has just been circumcised the day before is required to
immerse himself (*m. Pes.* 8.8b), because he has not yet offered his
sacrifice (*m. Ker.* 2.1) and so his atonement is not yet complete (*m. Hag.*
3.3). The immersion performed by the Jew and the one performed by

the proselyte have exactly the same function and are performed for exactly the same reason. Therefore, these passages, which are often cited to support proselyte immersion, do not refer to it at all, thus leaving proselyte immersion without Mishnaic support.[110]

In light of the collapse of Jeremias' first three points, his final point, that there are many points of contact between Jewish proselyte immersion and Christian baptism, provides no evidence for an early date of proselyte immersion.[111]

In addition to these criticisms of the arguments of Jeremias (and others) may be brought one other 'small' piece of evidence. A search of Jewish literature prior to 70 CE reveals a total silence concerning proselyte immersions.[112] While an argument from silence by itself holds no weight, it does have significance if a text is silent on a subject when

---

110 Daube (*Rabbinic Judaism*, 109-11) interprets the stricter Hillelite viewpoint given at the end of *m. Pes.* 8.8, 'he that separates himself from his circumcision is as one that separates himself from a grave', as an expression that circumcision was understood as a passage from death to life, which he relates to the later interpretation of the proselyte coming up out of the water as a newborn child. Thus, he perceives a reference to proselyte immersion in *m. Pes.* 8.8. While it appears probable that the Hillelites were understanding circumcision in this way, it does not necessarily follow that the passage refers to proselyte immersion. Rather, the Hillelites were claiming that, since the proselyte is as one who has contracted corpse impurity on the preceding day when he was circumcised, then he needs to be sprinkled with water for uncleanness on the third and seventh day before he is pure, and so should not eat a Passover-offering; cf. Danby, *Mishnah*, 148 n. 4; Blackman, *Mishnayoth*, 2.208 n. 7.

This Hillelite position with respect to sprinkling the proselyte for corpse impurity might suggest the historical cause for the rise of proselyte immersion. We saw in §4.3.1 that an immersion was a frequent substitute for cleansing from corpse impurity. When in close proximity to the temple it would be natural still to utilize the levitical method of sprinkling with the water for uncleanness, as suggested by *m. Pes.* 8.8 (cf. the Mishnaic tractate *Parah* on the red heifer rite in general). But when the temple was destroyed in 70 CE, then the specially prepared water for sprinkling was no longer available, but since an immersion was already perceived as an acceptable substitute for sprinkling, it quickly became associated with cleansing the proselyte.

Cf. the rabbinic discussion of this passage in *b. Pes.* 92a; Taylor, 'Proselyte Baptism', 195; Smith, 'Proselyte Baptism', 21; Scobie, *John the Baptist*, 98-99. Beasley-Murray (*Baptism*, 24) states that 'in the Mishnah, a discussion is recorded . . . as to the relative importance of circumcision and baptism', but he is mistaken, for the discussion he cites is Talmudic, *b. Yeb.* 46a. Sometimes *y. Pes.* 8 and *t. Pes.* 7.13 are cited as evidence of pre-70 CE proselyte immersions (e.g. Abrahams, *Studies*, 1.37; Beasley-Murray, *Baptism*, 24-25). These passages refer to Roman soldiers guarding the gates of Jerusalem who were immersed prior to eating their Passover meal. But this context is *exactly* the same as that in *m. Pes.* 8.8, and therefore cannot be used to support a pre-70 CE date.

111 For critical interaction with this final point, see Smith, 'Proselyte Baptism', 22-27; Beasley-Murray, *Baptism*, 25-31.

112 Noted by Plummer ('Baptism', 1.239), and confirmed by others, including Taylor, 'Proselyte Baptism', 195; Beasley-Murray, *Baptism*, 19-20; Smith, 'Proselyte Baptism', 14.

that subject is directly relevant and necessary to the subject at hand. For example, Emil Schürer, who argues for a pre-Christian date, states 'the *argumentum e silentio* from Philo and Josephus would be valid only if it could be shown that reference to proselyte baptism is absent from passages where it should have appeared'.[113] While such relevance cannot be 'proven', its probability can be established and, thus, be significant. One example is the conversion of Izates, King of Adiabene, in *Ant.* 20.34-48 (during the reign of Claudius Caesar, 41–54 CE). This example is particularly significant because at issue is precisely what rite was necessary for Jewish proselytism. Josephus' discussion however, revolves exclusively around circumcision without any mention of a proselyte immersion. Furthermore, Izates' mother Helena is also converted to Judaism, but does not want Izates to be circumcised. No mention is made of her being immersed; the existence of this rite could have been used as an argument to prevent Izates' circumcision.[114] A similar example is the conversion of Azizus, King of Emesa, in *Ant.* 20.139-140 (c. 53 CE).[115]

Similarly, in the NT Paul often raises the issue of the relationship between circumcision and conversion in the context of Jewish or Jewish-Christian theology. Yet a proselyte immersion is never mentioned as an issue.[116] Joachim Jeremias argues that the use of the middle voice of βαπτίζω in 1 Cor. 10.2 and Acts 11.16 demonstrates a link with proselyte baptism.[117] While it is evident that Christian baptism was influenced by Judaism and OT levitical ablutions, the middle voice of βαπτίζω is used of Jewish ablutions generally.[118]

While this is only an argument from silence, in this instance, the silence is quite deafening. Thus, the evidence compels us to conclude that proselyte immersion, as described in rabbinic texts such as *b. Yeb.* 46a-47b and *b. Ger.* 60a-61b, was most probably not practised prior to 70 CE,[119] and that the destruction of the temple probably provided the most compelling reason for its emergence.[120]

---

113 Schürer, *History*, 3.174 n. 89.
114 Zeitlin ('Halaka', 359) concludes that this example comes close to meeting Schürer's condition. He states that 'had baptism at this time been required, Josephus would not be silent at this point'.
115 Cf. also Jdt. 14.10. In *Jos. Asen.* 8–15 the conversion of a Gentile woman is extensively described, but without mentioning a proselyte immersion.
116 Smith, 'Proselyte Baptism', 15.
117 Jeremias, *Infant Baptism*, 29.
118 Cf. in the LXX Jdt. 12.7; Sir. 34.25 (31.25); 2 Kgs 5.14.
119 Cf. Beasley-Murray (*Baptism*, 19) who points out that the two most extensive works on 'baptism among Jews and Jewish sects show a marked caution in this respect and incline to minimize the extent to which proselyte baptism was practised in the first half of the first century A.D.' He is referring to Brandt, *Jüdischen Baptismen*, 57-62; Thomas, *Mouvement baptiste*, 356-74.

While proselyte immersion is probably a post-70 CE practice, it may be instructive to mention briefly its significance, merely for comparative purposes, because the foundation upon which it developed would have already been laid in the Second Temple period. Two problems emerge which make establishing the significance of proselyte immersion difficult. The discursive nature of the rabbinic literature cites a wide variety of opinions, so that it is almost impossible to say that one statement is 'the rabbinic position' or 'the correct significance'. Also, it is difficult to establish what is the precise significance of the proselyte immersion as distinct from the other two elements in the proselyte process: circumcision and sacrifice.[121] In light of these two problems, I would *suggest* that proselyte immersion functioned, first of all, as an initiatory rite for, along with circumcision and a sacrifice, it was the means by which a Gentile entered the covenant community; *b. Ker.* 9a states: 'As your forefathers entered into the Covenant only by circumcision, immersion and the sprinkling of the blood, so shall they [i.e. proselytes] enter the Covenant only by circumcision, immersion and the sprinkling of the blood'.[122] Secondly, 'one who has become a proselyte is like a child newly born' (*b. Yeb.* 22a, 48b; cf. *b. Ger.* 61a [2.6]) evidently signifies their new status of having passed from death into life and having their previous sins forgiven.[123] Thirdly, proselyte immersion may have functioned as a purificatory immersion as well, though this is a matter of debate between scholars. It was an immersion bath like those practised by Jews regularly, but it also required the presence of three witnesses (*b. Yeb.* 46b). It was probably perceived as purificatory, at least by some, but what had

120 Cf. Taylor, 'Proselyte Baptism', 196-97; cf. Zeitlin ('Halaka', 361) and Gavin (*Jewish Antecedents*, 55) who attribute the rise of proselyte immersion to the attitude manifested in Jewish nationalism which viewed Gentiles as unclean; thus, they date the rise of proselyte immersion to 65 CE. This is, however, a dubious argument in light of the problems with establishing an extensive view that Gentiles were unclean. Cf. my suggestion in a preceding note in this section for the rise of proselyte immersion after 70 CE, when the water for impurity from the red heifer rite was no longer available.

    To my mind, the one problem with a post-70 CE date for the emergence of proselyte immersion is that of women, who, of course, could not be circumcised. How were they brought into the community of Israel? Yet our sources are silent! Perhaps the answer may be sought in the sacrifice associated with proselytism, or in the example of the repentance shown by Aseneth in *Jos. Asen.* 10–14. Beasley-Murray, *Baptism*, 25 n. 2; Daube, *Rabbinic Judaism*, 106.

121 Cf. Gavin, *Jewish Antecedents*, 53; Smith, 'Proselyte Baptism', 24-25.

122 Rowley, 'Proselyte Baptism', 327; Moore, *Judaism*, 1.331-35; Pusey, 'Proselyte Baptism', 143-45.

123 *M. 'Ed.* 5.2 = *m. Pes.* 8.8; (cf. discussion above); cf. *Jos. Asen.* 15.2-8; Abrahams, *Studies*, 1.39-42; Rowley, 'Proselyte Baptism', 328-29; Daube, *Rabbinic Judaism*, 109-13. The statement in *b. Yeb.* 47b, 'when he comes up after his ablution he is deemed to be an Israelite in all respects', Daube (111) considers significant, for 'coming up' was the decisive moment; it signified resurrection from the dead.

caused the uncleanness in the first place may be debated.[124]

### 4.4 *Conclusion*

Several observations may be drawn at this point concerning the ways in which the practice and function of ablutions developed from the OT through the Second Temple period.

First of all, in some respects the ablutory practices during this period were *consistent* with OT law. Handwashing and footwashing continued to be practised by the priests in connection with the temple cultus. Bathing is mentioned with respect to cleansing before beginning the priestly service in the temple, and after leprosy and sexual intercourse.

Secondly, with respect to corpse uncleanness, bathing became an *acceptable alternative*, at least in some circles, to the OT regulation requiring the sprinkling of the specially prepared water for uncleanness.

Thirdly, the use of ablutions was *expanded* in certain circumstances and among certain circles. This may be observed in handwashing, which in the OT was almost exclusively a priestly ablution, being extended in some circumstances to be an ablution performed prior to prayer and eating. This may have been understood as a token bath. This same expansion may be observed even more clearly with respect to bathing prior to prayer and eating.

Fourthly, we have observed that within the Judaism of the late Second Temple period at least two groups used bathing extensively as a means of cleansing: Bannus and the Essenes. Of course, other persons and groups may have done so as well.[125] The evidence from both these groups indi-

---

124 The cause of the uncleanness may have been *later* understood as general Gentile uncleanness, but we noted earlier that such a view was both late and not held universally. It is more probable that the uncleanness was associated with the turning from death associated with proselytism generally and circumcision particularly (cf. discussion above of *m. Pes.* 8.8; *m. 'Ed.* 5.2). Smith, 'Proselyte Baptism', 24-25; Blackman, *Mishnayoth*, 2.208 n. 7. Bamberger (*Proselytism*, 44) suggests that it cleansed the proselyte from the defilement of idolatry. In *Jos. Asen.* (e.g. 8.6; 11.9, 16; 12.5) Aseneth's mouth is unclean because she has eaten food sacrificed to idols, but there is no explicit evidence that she was unclean as a Gentile *per se*; neither is there any reference to proselyte immersion in the book.

For arguments against it having purificatory significance, see Moore, *Judaism*, 1.331-35; arguments for, see Bamberger, *Proselytism*, 44; Averbeck, 'Focus of Baptism', 274-77; Pusey, 'Proselyte Baptism', 143-45. Schürer (*History*, 3.173) assumes it is purificatory without discussion.

125 It is most probable that the Pharisees also practised bathing, but the evidence for such practice is drawn primarily from the rabbinic material—a realm which is beyond the confines of this study. Older works are often unhelpful in this respect, due to an uncritical use of the sources. For recent, more careful examination of the Pharisees and purity rules in the Second Temple period, see Neusner, *Idea of Purity*, 65-71; Neusner, *Evidence*, 63-69; Saldarini, *Pharisees*, 212-20. Neusner (*Evidence*, 49-50) considers the Mishnaic Division of Purities to represent the most developed

cates the prominence of daily immersions, including at morning and evening. The Essenes bathed at other times as well. Additionally, after the first probationary year, the initiate is allowed to 'partake in cleaner water for purity', which appears to mark the end of that first year. Bannus' immersions were probably performed in or around the Jordan river.

Fifthly, we have observed in a few texts that immersion was associated with the expression of repentance, seeking forgiveness and conversion. Additionally, immersions in rivers is specified, with the Jordan river being identified in one case (*Life of Adam and Eve*) and possibly others (e.g. Bannus).[126] However, while the evidence from one text does antedate John the Baptist, the evidence derived from the other texts is somewhat problematic with respect to dating the traditions and practices.

Sixthly, in at least two cases, the Essenes and *Sib. Or.* 4.162-70, the bathing is associated with a criticism of at least some aspect of the temple establishment and/or the sacrificial system.[127] Jacob Neusner points out that, since purity rules were closely associated with protecting the temple's holiness, this had two effects in the Second Temple period: first of all, 'a characteristic charge of a sect against its opponents is that of

---

aspect of pre-70 CE material in the Mishnah. An examination of these works suggest that the pre-70 evidence would not substantively alter the conclusions being drawn in this chapter.

Thomas in his massive work, *Mouvement baptiste*, argues for a widespread Jewish baptizing movement, and he is often cited for support. But, unfortunately, he is frequently cited in a superficial manner, for Thomas is *not only* examining movements in Palestine and those which pre-date the rise of Christianity, as is clearly revealed by the full title of his book: *Le mouvement baptiste en Palestine et Syrie (150 av. J.-C. – 300 ap. J.-C.)*. Thus, much of his discussion is quite irrelevant for the more limited focus we have here, such as an examination of the Elchasaites, Ebionites, Mandaeans, etc. (cf. 140-267). Furthermore, I have not examined the references to the Jewish sects which practised immersions and are polemically described by the church fathers, including the Hemerobaptists, Nazarenes, Masbuthaeans and Sabaeans (cf. the list of Hegesippus cited by Eusebius, *Hist. Eccl.* 4.22.7), and the brief references to groups such as the morning bathers (e.g. *t. Yad.* 2.20), because it is highly questionable that these movements are actually early enough to be relevant, and the evidence concerning them is both very limited and biased. Kraeling (*John the Baptist*, 112) states: 'How early such groups came into existence is not known. The evidence about them belongs to the middle of the second century A.D.' For further discussion of these movements, see Thomas, *Mouvement baptiste*, 34-45; Brandt, *Jüdischen Baptismen*, 90-122; Black, *Scrolls*, 48-74. On the possibility of similar groups practising immersions among the Samaritans, see Montgomery, *Samaritans*, 252-65; Black, 62-66.

126 The Mishnaic passage, *m. Par.* 8.10, is sometimes cited to state that the Jordan river was considered unclean for cleansing purposes (e.g. Ernst, *Johannes der Täufer*, 332 n. 207). But this text does not concern cleansing in general but rather the use of the Jordan's water for the red heifer rite. Cf. Abrahams, *Studies*, 1.33; Blackman, *Mishnayoth*, 6.443.

127 Cf. the conclusions of Thomas (*Mouvement baptiste*, 425-30) concerning the replacement of sacrifice with immersions.

polluting the Temple', and secondly

> sectarian laws about purity would serve to differentiate from those who accept the predominant cult both priests and laymen who rejected the regnant priesthood or its conduct of the cult or its view of purity, and who therefore coalesced to form a sect.[128]

Seventhly, in many cases, the primary function of the ablutions in the Second Temple period is the same as that in the OT: *restoration* from a state of uncleanness to a state of cleanness. However, their function appears to have expanded. The prescribed daily ablutions prior to prayer and meals appears to function more to *maintain* cleanness against the possibility of having been defiled, rather than the certainty of defilement.

Eighthly, the function of immersions in particular appears to be also expanding as an expression of repentance and conversion, and perhaps in symbolizing cleansing from sin. In this sense, the metaphorical use of ablution language in the OT to express cleansing from sin is being linked to the actual use of ablutions as cleansing from uncleanness.

---

128 Neusner, *Idea of Purity*, 27-28; cf. 108-12.

Chapter 5

# ABLUTIONS IN THE QUMRAN LITERATURE

## 5.1 *Introduction*

In the preceding chapter we examined the practices and functions of ablutions reflected in the Jewish literature of the OT and Second Temple period. However, this discussion of immersions was limited by two factors. References in the literature to immersions were often made in passing without an explanation of either their function or their relation to the ideology of those who practised them (which is very much our interest here). An explanation would not be needed for the writers or readers because ablutions were an accepted part of their culture and so in many cases required no explanation. Also, some references to, and explanations of, the immersion practices of specific groups were made by those outside the group (e.g. Josephus explaining Essene practice). The Qumran literature is at the same time similar to, and distinct from, this other literature. Often references are made in passing to ablutions without further explication. But on the other hand, a few texts within this literature do give us some insight into the function and ideology of those ablutions; these texts are especially helpful because the ablutions are explained by those within the group itself. Such an explanation may be of particular value when interpreting John's baptism.

The use of ablutions by the Qumran community has been the subject of much scholarly discussion, which has generally revolved around the question of the significance of these immersions, especially whether or not they have an initiatory function. The purpose of such discussion is usually to determine the extent to which these immersions contribute to understanding the origin and significance of the baptismal practices of John the Baptist and/or the Christian church.[1] Though studies which use the Qumran texts for comparative purposes may be helpful and illuminating, they are often too brief and fail to provide adequate exegetical support for the positions taken. Thus, some suffer from a lack of a careful, complete examination of the Qumran literature on its own. This chapter attempts to fill this gap with an extensive examination of the relevant passages in the Qumran literature in order to ascertain more precisely the practice and function of immersions within the community

---

1  Numerous studies have been devoted to this subject; cf. those cited in §6.5.

and their relation to the broader ideology of the community. This purpose is achieved by a discussion of purity and ablutions in the Qumran literature followed by a more extensive examination of those passages in 1QS which are central to the discussion of immersions at Qumran.[2]

## 5.2 *Purity and Ablutions in Various Qumran Scrolls*

### 5.2.1 *General References to Purity and Ablutions*

The Qumran community exhibited a concern for purity which may be observed in numerous references throughout its literature.[3] This concern is epitomized by the command to 'those who have entered the New Covenant' (CD 6.19) that they are required 'to distinguish between the unclean and the clean and to make known (the distinction) between sacred and profane' (CD 6.17-18; cf. 12.19-20). Many specific examples of the community's concern for purity can be observed. For example, the warriors and the camp itself must be pure, even when fighting in the eschatological battle, (1QM 7.3-7). Also, the state of those who were in fellowship within the community is repeatedly described in 1QS as 'the purity of the many'.[4] Furthermore, one of the responsibilities of meeting

2  The translation of those passages in columns 3 through 5 of 1QS dealing with immersions are my own. Otherwise, for translations of 1QS I cite Leaney, *Rule of Qumran*. Translations of 11QTemple are by Maier, *Temple Scroll*. All other translations are from Dupont-Sommer (*Essene Writings*) because of his inclusion of line numbers (which I also indicate, but only in longer quotes). Other translations consulted include Brownlee, *Manual of Discipline*; Wernberg-Møller, *Manual of Discipline*; Guilbert, 'Règle de la Communauté', 1.9-80; Lohse, *Texte aus Qumran*; Vermes, *Dead Sea Scrolls*; Gaster, *Dead Sea Scriptures*; Knibb, *Qumran Community*.

3  In this survey I use the Damascus Document (CD), which, while present among the Qumran scrolls, is not exclusively a Qumran document since another manuscript had been discovered earlier in the Cairo Geniza. But its presence at Qumran and the possibility that the Qumran community arose out of an earlier community reflected in the Damascus Document (cf. Davies, *Damascus Covenant*, 203-204) suggest a close enough link between it and Qumran, so that the simple observations I make here concerning purity and ablutions probably reflect an understanding of them which is compatible with the Qumran community. I also use 11QTemple and 1QM in this survey, both of which reflect the community's understanding of an idealized or future setting. Thus, these two documents probably do not provide evidence of how those at Qumran practised ablutions, but they do suggest ways in which they understood ablutions did, or ought to, function.

In the ensuing discussion I am examining the ideology of the literature discovered in the caves surrounding Khirbet Qumran. The literature is often viewed as a whole and understood to represent the unified ideology of a single community. Such a view has methodological and conceptual weaknesses, but it is beyond the limits of this work to examine this problem here. It is sufficient to observe that, while I refer to a number of different Qumran scrolls, this chapter focuses upon a single scroll, 1QS. Thus in discussing the ideology of the 'Qumran community', I am referring primarily to the ideology of the community reflected in this document.

4  1QS 6.16-17, 25; 7.3, 16, 19; cf. 5.13; 8.17; on this phrase, cf. §5.2.2.

in the council was to render decisions concerning issues of purity (1QS 6.22; cf. 6.24–7.25). In contrast, those outside the community were considered to be impure. For example, 1QS 3.2-3 states that the non-member 'ploughs with evil step and defilement clings to his drawing back'. In addition, the language of cleansing from defilement is frequently utilized metaphorically to describe cleansing from sin. For example, 1QH 4.37 states: 'For Thou pardonest iniquity and clean[sest m]an of sin by Thy righteousness'.[5]

In contrast to the centrality of purity in the ideology and practice of the community's members, their ablutory practices are somewhat less obvious in their literature. E.F. Sutcliffe observes:

> In view of [the] . . . widespread use of ablutions among the general population one would expect more numerous and more stringent regulations among the particularly law-observant inhabitants of Qumran. And it is surprising to find how few are the references to ablutions.[6]

Sutcliffe qualifies his observation by stating that 'not all the daily practices and customs of a Community find their way into writing; and, of course, we may not possess all that did'.[7] However, his observation fails to recognize adequately that within most Jewish circles ablutions are a necessary corollary to purity because ablutions were the usual means whereby purification was achieved. Thus, the centrality of a concern for purity by those at Qumran points to the corresponding (though dependent) importance of ablutions in their practice.

Ablutions are referred to in a number of contexts within the Qumran literature. Purity regulations are provided for washing clothes (CD 11.3-4; 1QM 14.2-3), and reference is made to washing vessels as well (CD 10.12).[8]

With respect to the practice of immersions, CD 10.10-13 regulates the proper cleanliness, sufficient quantity and correct use of water for immersions:

> Let no man [11]bathe in dirty water or in a quantity too little to cover a man completely.

5   Cf. 1QS 3.7; 4.5, 21; 11.14; 1QH 1.32; 3.21; 5.16; 6.8; 7.30; 11.10, 30; 16.12; 4Q504 fr.1-2 6.2-6.
     Buchanan ('Role of Purity', 397-406) discusses how the concern for purity also contributes to the structure of the Qumran community with respect to its communistic economy, monasticism and rejection of slavery. See also the emphasis on purity in 11QTemple, and the discussion by Milgrom in 'Temple Scroll', 501-23, esp. 512-18. On purity generally in the Qumran scrolls, see Neusner, *Idea of Purity*, 50-54.
6   Sutcliffe, 'Baptism', 181-82.
7   Sutcliffe, 'Baptism', 182.
8   The background to 1QM 14.2-3 is found in Num. 19.16; 31.19-20, and for CD 10.12 in texts such as Lev. 11.33-34; 15.12; Num. 19.15; cf. Mk 7.4. On CD 11.3-4 see Schiffman, *Halakhah*, 106-109.

> [12]Let no man purify a vessel with this water.
> And any pool in a rock in which there is not enough water [13]to cover <a man> completely, if an unclean person has touched it he defiles the water of the pool <as> he would defile the water in a vessel.

The necessity of sufficient water to ensure a complete immersion is similar to the Mishnaic requirement that an immersion pool must contain at least forty seahs of water (*m. Miq.* 1.7; 2.1-4; 7.6). The warning in CD 10.12-13 that insufficient water would be defiled if touched by an unclean person is also similar to rabbinic concerns (*m. Miq.* 1.1-4) though perhaps slightly stricter (cf. *m. Miq.* 1.4).[9]

Another text, CD 10.23–11.2, regulates Sabbath observance (cf. 10.14):

> And let no man drink if he is not in the camp. [11.1]<But if a man is> travelling and goes down to bathe, he may drink there where he is; but let no (water) be drawn up (to be poured) into [2]any vessel.

Drawing water was work and therefore forbidden on the Sabbath; it had to be done the day before.[10] According to this regulation, a person who was travelling (i.e. not at home and so experiencing difficulties in making preparations) could drink if he was immersing himself, but to use a vessel would be work and thus was still forbidden. In this text the practice of immersion is assumed and only forms the background for regulating the Sabbath.

CD 11.21-22 states: 'And whoever enters the House of Prostration, let him not enter in a state of uncleanness; let him wash himself'. The term 'the House of Prostration' is probably a reference to the temple because the previous regulation (CD 11.18-21) required that sacrifices being sent to the altar be delivered by a person who was not defiled.[11] If so, this regulation may have required an immersion prior to temple worship (cf. §4.3.1). However, this regulation uses the verb כבס which is usually used of washing clothes, and, therefore, the passage may refer to the need for the person to wash his/her clothes rather than immerse him/herself.[12]

---

9   Neusner (*Evidence*, 49-50) considers the Mishnaic Division of Purities (סדר טהרות) to represent the most developed aspect of pre-70 material in the Mishnah.

10  Cf. *Jub*.2.29; 50.8. With respect to related regulations concerning not preparing food on the Sabbath, see CD 10.22; *Jub*.2.29; 50.9; *War* 2.147; cf. Exod. 16.5, 22-30; 35.3. On this text see Schiffman, *Halakhah*, 102-104.

11  These regulations evidently related to a period in the history of the Qumran community prior to its break with the temple. Vermes (*Qumran in Perspective*, 105) explains such a reference by distinguishing between the Qumran community which separated itself from the temple and the town sectaries (as evidenced in CD) who participated in temple worship. On the relationship between the Qumran community and the temple see Baumgarten, 'Sacrifice and Worship', 39-56; Baumgarten, 'Essenes and the Temple', 57-74; Davies, 'Ideology of the Temple', 287-301.

12  Sutcliffe, 'Baptism', 185. However, we observed in §4.2.5 that in the OT bathing usually required washing one's clothes as well.

In either case, an ablution was required.[13]

In 11QTemple, certain regulations require both the washing of a person's clothes and bathing the body. For example, 11QTemple 45.7-10 states:

> And if o[ne] has an emission of a semen in the night, then he may not enter [8]the whole sanctuary until he has [com]pleted three days. He shall wash his clothes and bathe [9]on the first day, and on the third day he shall wash his clothes {and bathe}, and after the sun has set, [10]he may come to the sanctuary.

Such a regulation is similar to that in Lev. 15.16-17 and Deut. 23.10-11. 11QTemple requires that one be sprinkled with water for uncleanness as well as the washing of one's clothes and the bathing of one's body to cleanse from corpse-contamination.[14]

Against the background of the community's concern for purity, these references to washings and immersions in the Qumran literature suggest that such ablutions were an integral part of the community's lifestyle. The members were evidently concerned with the application of temple and priestly purity to everyday life, and so meticulously observed the laws concerning cleanness and uncleanness. They were certainly motivated by a commitment to the Torah, but other factors which may have contributed to this emphasis include the priestly orientation of their community coupled with their rejection of the contemporary temple and its priesthood which they believed to be defiled. However, the passages examined thus far reveal little about the function of immersions at Qumran. Those passages in 1QS which are more illuminating for this concern are examined in the next section, but before examining them we must deal with two problematic issues.

---

13 Cf. the discussion in §4.3.1 concerning handwashing prior to prayer. It is possible that 'the House of Prostration' could refer to a synagogue, and so this regulation would then refer to washing one's hands prior to prayer. This might be a more natural explanation of the verb נכס. However, the contextual references to sacrifice still make a reference to the temple more probable. Cf. Davies, 'Ideology of the Temple', 293.

14 11QTemple 49.16-20; 50.10-15; 51.3-5. Num. 19 required sprinkling but not bathing or washing clothes. In contrast, we observed in §4.3.1 that in the Second Temple period bathing was an acceptable alternative to sprinkling with water for uncleanness. Here both are combined. To include all references to ablutions in 11QTemple is beyond the limits of this chapter, and not strictly necessary because they are regulations for an idealized Jerusalem as a temple-city, and probably did not apply directly to members of the Qumran community. However, they are relevant here as examples of the community's concern for purity, and the role they believed ablutions had for cleansing. For a discussion of the differences between these regulations concerning immersions in 11QTemple and those in the OT see Milgrom, 'Temple Scroll', 512-18. For a survey of purity concerns in 11QTemple, see Yadin, *Temple Scroll*, 170-91.

### 5.2.2 *Issues Related to the Practice of Immersions at Qumran*

Two points need to be examined briefly because they are sometimes used to support the practice of immersions at Qumran, but their use in this respect is incorrect.

First of all, some scholars have suggested that in 1QS the phrase טהרת הרבים ('the purity of the many') and those similar to it refer to the process of cleansing or to the purificatory immersions of the community.[15] While in the OT the word טָהֳרָה may signify the act of cleansing (e.g. 1 Chron. 23.28), it does not necessarily have this significance all the time (e.g. Lev. 12.4-5). In rabbinic literature it was also used of the state of cleanness (*m. Hag.* 2.7), but it had particularly become a technical term for food which was pure along with the vessels and utensils in which it was held, as well as clothing. But טָהֳרָה was distinguished from מַשְׁקֶה, that is, liquids, because they are more susceptible to contracting uncleanness (*m. Hag.* 2.7; *m. Toh.* 8.6-7).[16] Several lines of evidence suggest that the phrase 'the purity of the many' should be understood in a manner similar to this rabbinic sense. First of all, in two passages in 1QS (6.16-17, 20-21; 7.19-20) the 'purity of the many' is distinguished from the 'the drink of the many' (משקה הרבים). A novice or a member under discipline was kept from both, but if upon examination he/she was found acceptable, he/she was allowed to touch the purity of the many after one year, and only after two years was allowed to touch the drink. Thus, to touch 'the drink of the many' required a higher degree of purity than to touch 'the purity of the many'. The 'purity of the many' included the 'drink' as a broader category incorporating within itself a more specialized category. Therefore, this phrase most probably refers to objects succeptible to impurity, particularly to the food served at the community's fellowship meal (cf. 1QSa 2.17-18).[17]

Secondly, 1QS 5.13 states that immersion was a condition for touching the purity of the many which implies that the two are different things: '[Such a man] shall not enter the waters to approach the purity of the men of holiness'.[18]

---

Cf. also the fragmentary text, 4Q512, which may be a purification ritual.

15   These passages include 1QS 5.13-14; 6.16-17, 24-25; 7.3, 16, 19-20; 8.17, 24. E.g. Dupont-Sommer, *Essene Writings*, 83 n. 1; Huppenbauer, 'טהר und טהרה', 350-51; Rowley, 'Baptism of John', 220; Kuhn, 'Lord's Supper', 67-68.

16   Vermes, *Qumran in Perspective*, 95.

17   It is possible that the term may be understood at two levels. First of all, it would be a reference to the physical objects or food which were clean and susceptible to contracting uncleanness. Secondly, it could also refer to a more abstract concept of the community's corporate cleanness which was symbolized by the concern for the cleanness of the physical objects or food.

18   The infinitive construct of the verb נגע with ל (לגעת, 'to touch') most naturally indicates the purpose or aim of the previous clause. Cf. the discussion of the passage in Knibb, *Qumran Community*, 108, 110-11.

Thirdly, in half of the references in 1QS to 'the purity of the many' and similar phrases, the verb used in conjunction with it is נגע ('to touch').[19] If the phrase refers to the process of cleansing, it is difficult to see how one could 'touch' a process. If it refers to the actual water itself, it is difficult to understand the concern, because water used for immersions was not susceptible to contracting uncleanness if there was sufficient water (cf. CD 10.12-13). In fact, the purpose of water used for immersions was to 'touch' those who were unclean and render them clean. Therefore, 'the purity of the many' should be understood not as a reference to the community's immersions or immersion pools, but to the objects within the community which were susceptible to defilement, particularly the food served at its fellowship meals.[20]

The other issue is the conjecture that some of the water cisterns at Qumran functioned as ceremonial immersion pools, and this has been used to support an interpretation of the immersions.[21] The archaeological remains at Khirbet Qumran do clearly indicate the presence of some pools with steps leading down to them, making it probable that they functioned as immersion pools, but it is also possible that they were used simply for water storage.[22] CD 10.12-13 refers to the use of pools in rocks for immersions, while 1QS 3.4-5 refers to immersing 'in seas or rivers'. The archaeological remains at Khirbet Qumran, as well as the presence nearby of the Wadi Qumran, demonstrate that immersions were possible at or near Qumran.[23] However, this evidence is not able to further our understanding of the ideology and function of immersions within the Qumran community.

All the texts discussed thus far demonstrate the community's concern for purity and the use of both washings and immersions for achieving or maintaining that purity. But these texts have not been very helpful in identifying the function of those immersions or any underlying ideology expressed by such practices. However, there are three other passages in 1QS which are more relevant to this concern. To these we now turn.

---

19   1QS 5.13-14; 6.16-17; 7.19-20; 8.17.
20   Cf. Newton, *Concept of Purity*, 10-26.
21   E.g. Black, *Scrolls*, 95-96.
22   De Vaux (*Archaeology*, 132) concludes that two small cisterns 'were certainly baths, but archaeology is powerless to determine whether the baths taken in them had a ritual significance'. But in a more recent study, Wood ('To Dip or Sprinkle?' 45-60) argues that the cisterns did indeed have a ritual purpose based upon two kinds of evidence: '(1) the design and evolution of the [water] system, and (2) the subsistence requirements of the community' (46).
23   The Jordan river, over 10 km away, would be too far to be used for regular immersions (against Scobie, *John the Baptist*, 106), though a trip of this length could be made for an immersion of special significance. On the other hand, 3 km to the south

### 5.3 *Immersions in 1QS*

The Qumran scroll known as The Community Rule (1QS) contains two passages which discuss the practice of immersions in an ideological context and a third passage which expresses the hope for an eschatological ablution; these are 1QS 2.25–3.9; 5.7-15, and 4.19-22.

#### 5.3.1 *1QS 2.25–3.9*
In 1QS 2.25–3.9 those who refuse to enter the new covenant are denounced. Incorporated into this denunciation is an explanation of the reasons why an immersion by such a person would be ineffective. The part of the passage relating to these immersions is 3.4-9:

> He will not be made guiltless by atonement and he will not be purified in waters for purification; he shall not sanctify himself in seas [5]or rivers nor will he be purified in all the waters of cleansing. Unclean, unclean shall he be all the days of his rejection of the precepts [6]of God with its refusal to discipline himself in the community of his counsel. For in a spirit of true counsel about the ways of man will all his iniquities find atonement, [7]that he may look upon the light of life; and in a holy spirit of being united with his truth he will be purified from all [8]his iniquities, and in a spirit of uprightness and humility his sin will be atoned. In subjection of his soul to all the ordinances of God his flesh will be purified [9]in being sprinkled with waters for purification and by sanctification in waters of purity.

5.3.1.1 *The identity of the persons referred to in 1QS 2.25–3.9.* To understand the passage correctly it is important to ascertain as precisely as possible the type of person to which the passage refers.[24] In 2.25-26 they are identified: 'Everyone who refuses to enter [26][the covenant of G]od in order to walk in the stubbornness of his heart shall not [. . . the com-]munity of his truth'. This statement itself could refer to three possible types of people: (1) people in general who are not members of the community; (2) members of the community who refuse to take part in the annual renewal of the covenant;[25] or (3) candidates who refuse to complete their initiation into the community by entering the covenant. The expression 'to enter [the covenant of G]od' could refer either to the can-

was Ain Feshka, an oasis with a spring.

24  In the ensuing discussion the level of membership in the Qumran community is distinguished by the following terms: 'candidate' refers to a person who is not yet a member because he/she has not fulfilled the conditions for membership but is either being taught or examined for acceptability. A 'novice' is a person who has fulfilled conditions for membership, is a member of the community, but is still going through stages of training before being recognized as a full member. To distinguish a novice from a person who has been fully trained and accepted I use the term 'full member', though the term 'member' can be used to refer to both a novice and a full member.

25  This alternative assumes that such a renewal ceremony was practised by the Qumran community, an assumption which may not be justified.

didate's initial entry into the covenant or to the renewal of the covenant by the members of the community. The preceding context enables us to decide which of these alternatives is more probable, because it contains the liturgy for entry into the covenant (1.16–2.18). The introduction to this liturgy specifically states: 'all who enter the order of the community shall enter into a covenant in the presence of God . . .' (1.16), which indicates that the liturgy is recorded at this point in 1QS to portray the entry into the covenant by candidates. The content of the liturgy itself indicates the same function by distinguishing the candidates from the priests and Levites who were involved with them in performing the liturgy (cf. 1.18-20). But most of the liturgy could be used either for entry by candidates or for covenant renewal by members. Nevertheless, its use in this context in 1QS is for entry by candidates.[26]

The liturgy (1.16–2.18) is followed by a description of the ceremony for the annual assembly by the members of the community (2.19-25).[27] In this passage the priests, Levites and the people all 'shall enter' in their correct order. This idea of entering could refer to entering the covenant at a covenant renewal ceremony. The verb in 2.19 is עבר, which is the same as that used at 1.16, 18 in the liturgy for entry into the covenant by the candidates. Also, the designation of this assembly as 'year by year' (2.19), implying a special annual gathering, suggests that this passage may be describing the annual ceremony of covenant renewal[28] or some other annual event. Against this interpretation is the fact that the emphasis of the passage is on the order of the persons in the assembly, and the purpose is that each person 'may know . . . the place of his standing' (2.22). For example, 2.19-22 explains that

> the priests shall enter [20]first, in order, according to their spiritual status one after the other. And the Levites shall enter after them. [21]And all the

26  The confession in 1.24-26 would be more appropriate for candidates, but it would still be possible for those who were already members to make the same confession, though in a more general sense only (cf. 2.25-26 which could hardly be said by those who were full members). The same holds true for 2.11-14, which could apply more specifically to novices rather than members. On the other hand, in 2.1-2, the priests bless the participants who are described as 'all the men of the lot of God who walk perfectly in all his ways'. This description would be more appropriate for members than for candidates, yet it could be said by the candidates in an anticipatory sense.

27  This section begins with ככה which could be referring to the succeeding instructions for assembling the members (i.e. '*as follows* shall they do year by year . . .'), or it could be referring to the preceding liturgy for candidates' entrance being performed at this annual assembly (i.e. '*in the way just stated* shall they do year by year . . .'). While the first alternative is a more common use of ככה, either alternative is possible in this case. Therefore, the reference of ככה cannot be used to determine the link with the preceding context, though other factors may assist in deciding which sense of ככה is being used here.

28  Cf. Leaney, *Rule of Qumran*, 95-107, 135.

people shall enter third in order, one after the other, by thousands and hun-
dreds [22]and fifties and tens, so that every man of Israel may know each the
place of his standing in the community of God. . .

This emphasis on order expresses the classification of the community
members according to their spiritual state (cf. 5.20-24). This classification was the basis for the order of entering, sitting, and speaking at community gatherings.[29] Therefore, the repeated expression 'shall enter' in
2.19-25 more probably refers to the act of entering the meeting place at
the important annual assembly than entry into the covenant.[30] The function of this passage is by no means clear, but its context suggests that it
identifies the assembly at which the immediately preceding liturgy for
candidates joining the covenant (1.16–2.18) would be performed.[31]

We may now return to the question concerning the type of person in
2.25-26 'who refuses to enter [the covenant of G]od'. Since the preceding context is primarily concerned with the candidate entering the community by entering the covenant, the natural contrast to a candidate
entering the covenant is a candidate who refused to do so. Therefore,
the contrast implied by the clause 'who refuses to enter' is best understood as referring to a candidate who refuses to enter rather than a member who refuses to *re*-enter. Such an understanding is confirmed by the
description of this person in the succeeding context. For example, 3.2
states that 'his knowledge and his power and his wealth shall not come
into the counsel of the community'. If the person was already a member,
the concern would be to excommunicate the person,[32] but that is not the
case here. If the person had been a full member, his wealth would
already have been added to the community's resources (6.19-23). The
whole tenor of the passage is concerned with preventing a person enter-

29   1QS 6.1-4, 8-11; cf. 1QSa 2.11-17, 21-22; CD 14.3-6.
30   While I consider this interpretation more probable, the alternative is possible. Either
     way, the identity of the person referred to in 2.25-26 is not wholly dependent on this
     point (cf. §5.3.1.2). Knibb (*Qumran Community*, 89) opts for the alternative inter-
     pretation 'based on the assumption that we have here a technical term for admission
     to the covenant', but considers the interpretation argued here to also be possible. Cf.
     also Dimant, 'Qumran Sectarian Literature', 500 n. 84; Dupont-Sommer, *Essene
     Writings*, 76. Wernberg-Møller (*Manual of Discipline*, 56 n. 52) cites *m. Sanh.* 2.1 to
     indicate 'that the custom of "passing by, one after another" was well known among
     the Jews and used on occasions other than the one here mentioned'.
31   However, 1QS 1.12-20 and 5.7-8 could be understood to imply that only the candi-
     dates were present with the priests and Levites at the ceremony for entering the cov-
     enant (cf. Leaney, *Rule of Qumran*, 171). However, Vermes (*Qumran in Perspective*,
     95) understands the entry to the covenant to take place before the whole community,
     because he interprets 6.14 (the candidate 'shall be examined by the man who is the
     officer at the head of the many') to refer to the examination taking place while he is
     at his place during a session of the council. Thus, for Vermes the process of entering
     the covenant in 6.14-15 ('if he passes the test he shall bring him into the covenant')
     would take place at the same session of the council.

ing the community rather than excommunicating someone from the community. Thus, the second alternative for the type of person 'who refuses to enter', (i.e. a person who was already a community member) is inadequate.

The first alternative for the type of people referred to in 2.25-26 (i.e. people in general who are not members of the community) may be eliminated by observing that the phrase describes the person, not as one 'who does not enter', but one 'who *refuses* to enter' (וכול המואס לבוא), which implies a conscious decision to reject the community and the covenant. That the person has at least some knowledge of the community with its beliefs and practices is implied by the immediately succeeding explanatory clause: 'for his soul has revolted at the disciplines involved in the knowledge of precepts of righteousness . . .' (2.26–3.1). Therefore, the type of person 'who refuses to enter [the covenant of G]od' is best understood to be the candidate who refuses to enter the covenant and thus has refused to become a member of the community.[33]

5.3.1.2 *An analysis of 1QS 2.25–3.6.* Having ascertained the type of person to which the passage refers, we may now observe that the passage outlines the reasons for the candidate's refusal (2.26–3.1) and the consequences of that refusal (3.1-6). Of the numerous consequences listed, two are pertinent here. First of all, 'with Israel he shall not be counted' (3.1), and later in a similar vein, 'in the well of the perfect he will not be counted' (3.3-4). Both these clauses point to the community's belief that only they were the true Israel and those outside the community were not.[34] As a corollary, the second interesting consequence is that 'he ploughs with evil step and defilement clings to his drawing back' (3.2-3),[35] which relates to the rebellious candidate being described as one who 'has not mastered his backslidings' (3.3). Thus, the rebellious candidate is also evil, defiled and backslidden. These consequences of the candidate's refusal do not suggest that by his/her refusal the candidate has changed status and become a non-Israelite, evil, defiled and backslidden. Rather, each of these terms describes the community's sectarian view of those outside the community. The refusal does not *change* the candidate's status; rather, it *confirms* the status he/she already had as a non-member.

32  As in 1QS 7.1-2, 16-17, 22-25; cf. CD 19.32–20.13.
33  This interpretation follows Leaney (*Rule of Qumran*, 137) rather than Flusser ('Baptism of John', 217, as cited by Leaney, 137), who interprets the person 'who refuses to enter' as a member of the sect.
34  Though outsiders were not considered members of the 'true Israel', there is no evidence that the community considered them to be Gentiles; cf. 4QpNah 3.4-5; 1QSa 1.1-6.
35  On the significance and translation of this difficult passage, see Draper, 'Targum of

Having confirmed his/her status as a non-Israelite, evil, defiled and backslidden, the following consequences follow for the candidate:

> He will not be made guiltless by atonement and he will not be purified in waters for purification [ולוא יטהר במי נדה]; he shall not sanctify himself in seas or rivers [ולוא יתקדש בימים ונהרות] nor will he be purified in all the waters of cleansing [ולוא יטהר בכול מי רחץ].
> Unclean, unclean shall he be all the days of his rejection of the precepts [6]of God with its refusal to discipline himself in the community of his counsel [3.4-6].

The candidate's refusal is not only viewed as sin, it effectively cuts the person off from the means of atonement. Furthermore, until the sin had been atoned, the immersion which would have rendered the person clean has no effect. It is important to observe carefully that in this passage sin does not render a clean person unclean; it only confirms the prior unclean state by making any cleansing immersion of no value.[36] So, with this passage, the community rejects the efficacy of purificatory rites outside the Qumran community. The impurity of the candidate is not a result of refusing to enter the covenant but of the unclean state of everyone who was not a member of the sect.

### 5.3.1.3 *The sense of 'waters for impurity' in 1QS 3.4, 9.* In both 1QS 3.4 and 3.9 ablutions are referred to by the phrase 'waters for impurity'. Lines 8-9 state that 'his flesh will be purified when sprinkled with waters for impurity and consecrated with waters for cleansing'. The clause 'when sprinkled with waters for impurity' could refer to the red heifer rite in Numbers 19 in which specially prepared water was sprinkled upon a person who had been defiled with corpse uncleanness (cf. §4.2.3, 4.3.1). This interpretation would be supported by the fact that the phrase מי נדה is used in the OT exclusively with reference to the red heifer rite. Furthermore, this phrase is used here in 1QS in conjunction with the verb נזה ('to sprinkle') which is the specified means of applying these waters for impurity. However, it is better to interpret the clause as a reference to cleansing immersions in general. The word נדה is also used in the OT to refer to the state of impurity incurred by women during menstruation or childbirth.[37] It is also used metaphorically of the defilement produced by Israel's sins, especially that of idolatry.[38] Furthermore, both Ezek. 36.25 and Zech. 13.1 express the hope of an eschatological cleansing by water from this defilement. In particular, Ezek. 36.25

---

Isaiah', 265-69.

36  This observation is not to deny that other texts do in fact suggest that the Qumran community held to the idea that sin rendered a person unclean. See for example, 1QS 3.4-6a, 7b-8a; 5.13b-14a; 8.16-19.

37  E.g. Lev. 12.2, 5; 15.19-20, 26.

38  E.g. 2 Chron. 29.5; Ezra 9.11; Ezek. 36.17; Zech. 13.1.

uses language reminiscent of the red heifer rite: 'I will sprinkle clean water upon you, (וְזָרַקְתִּי עֲלֵיכֶם מַיִם טְהוֹרִים) and you shall be clean from all your uncleannesses, and from all your idols I will cleanse you'. The term נדה is used in the Qumran literature in this latter sense of the defilement caused by sin.[39]

Since נדה is being used here in 1QS to refer to the defilement of sin, the red heifer rite is not applicable because it was specifically designed only for corpse uncleanness. There is no evidence elsewhere that the use of this 'water for uncleanness' was broadened to include forms of defilement other than corpse uncleanness. It is more appropriate to view the use of this clause here in 1QS as the application of red heifer *terminology* to the defilement of and cleansing from sin *without the application of the actual rite itself* in the cleansing procedure.

Further support for this interpretation may be observed in the use of red heifer terminology to apply to an eschatological cleansing from sin in both Ezek. 36.25 as well as 1QS 4.21-22: 'He will sprinkle upon him a spirit of truth like waters for purification from all abominations of falsehood and his contamination with the spirit of uncleanness'. However, since immersions were used at Qumran for cleansing, it would be appropriate for the members to apply the terminology of the red heifer rite to these immersions, particularly in light of the fact that the method of cleansing from נדה-type defilement was by immersion.[40] Furthermore, we observed earlier that immersions became an acceptable alternative for cleansing from corpse uncleanness, and, therefore, it would be natural to extend red heifer terminology to immersions.

A second line of evidence for interpreting the clause 'when sprinkled with waters for impurity' as a reference to the practice of immersions is found in the parallelism of the sentence in 3.8-9:

> his flesh will be purified
> [9]when sprinkled with waters for impurity and
> when consecrated with waters for purification.

This same parallelism is also found in 3.4-5 (though in the negative) where it expresses the fact that the rebellious candidate will not be cleansed:

> He will not be absolved by atonement, and
> he will not be cleansed by waters for impurity, and
> he will not be consecrated in seas [5]or rivers, and
> he will not be cleansed in any waters for washing.

In both cases 'waters for impurity' (מי נדה) stands in parallel with other

---

39 E.g. 1QS 4.5, 10, 21-22; 10.24; 11.14; 1QH 1.22; 11.11; 12.25; 17.19; CD 2.1; 3.17. Cf. Leaney, *Rule of Qumran*, 141.
40 E.g. Lev. 19.24; *m. Nid.* 10.7-8.

terms indicating immersions ('waters for purification', and 'waters for washing'). Therefore, the clause 'when sprinkled with waters for impurity' is to be understood as a reference to purificatory immersions as are the other terms used here for the same immersions.[41] The function of these passages is not to make fine distinctions between types and/or methods of purification, but to assert polemically that only their community's immersions are efficacious and only when entered with a proper spirit.[42]

5.3.1.4 *An analysis of 1QS 3.6-9.* Having denounced those who refuse to enter the community and explained that as a consequence atonement and purification are impossible, the passage continues by explaining why these are now impossible: atonement and purification require a person to exercise God-given spiritual virtues in order for the atonement and purification to be efficacious, and these essential spiritual virtues are only available upon, and demonstrated by, entering the community. Therefore, a rebellious candidate, by the very fact of refusing to enter the community, must remain unatoned for and unclean because he/she fails to meet these conditions. The implication is that the candidate could return and, by meeting these requirements, would receive atonement and purification.[43]

1QS 3.6-9 consists of four statements which explain how atonement and purification function. For the sake of clarity, I will label these state-

---

41 Furthermore, *m. Par.* 3.5 states that only five (or seven) red heifers had been burnt since the days of Ezra. This may imply that the rite was not in common use during the Second Temple period. It also suggests that the use of the red heifer rite had not expanded to fulfil other purposes. On the other hand, it is possible that others did not know that the Qumran community burnt the red heifer. However, such conjecture becomes highly speculative and flies in the face of a careful reading of 1QS. For further discussion and support for this interpretation see for example, Newton, *Concept of Purity*, 30-32; Ringgren, *Faith of Qumran*, 221. In contrast, Bowman ('Burn the Red Heifer?' 73-84) argues that the Qumran community did in fact burn the red heifer and these references in 1QS are used in support. However, while Bowman's article is an excellent discussion of the red heifer rite, his argument concerning 1QS is unconvincing.

42 The use of the verb קדשׁ in the hithpael in 1QS 3.4, 8, translated 'consecrate' probably does not signify a state of sanctification in distinction to the state of purification. Rather, the terms 'cleanse', 'purify', and 'consecrate' are more probably synonyms in this context. This use is supported by their use in both texts. Also, 3.9 states that the water is 'water for purification'. Furthermore, in 2 Sam. 11.4 the same verb is used in the hithpael to refer to the purification of a woman following menstruation, which is understood elsewhere as purifying rather than consecrating. But the most decisive point in support of this argument is that Qumran was a priestly community which was keeping the sanctity of the temple within its own community. For them to purify was to consecrate.

43 This implication follows from the polemic nature of the passage observed in §5.3.1.2: only the community's immersions are efficacious and only when entered with a proper spirit.

ments S1, S2, S3 and S4 in my translation and the following discussion. A parallel display clarifies the close relationship between the alternate statements (S1 with S3, and S2 with S4):

כיא

.S1 ברוח עצת אמת אל דרכי איש יכופרו כול 7עוונותיו
להביט באור החיים

.S2 וברוח קדושה ליחד באמתו יטהר מכול 8עוונותו

.S3 וברוח יושר וענוה תכופר חטתו

.S4 ובענוות נפשו לכול חוקי אל יטהר 9בשרו להזות במי
נדה ולהתקדש במי דוכו

For

S1. by a spirit of true counsel concerning[44] the ways of man all his iniquities will be atoned 7so that he may look on the light of life; and

S2. by a holy spirit of the community in his truth[45] he will be cleansed from all 8his iniquities; and

S3. by a spirit of uprightness and humility his sin will be atoned; and

S4. by humility of his soul towards all the precepts of God his flesh will be cleansed 9when sprinkled with waters for impurity[46] and consecrated with waters for cleansing.[47]

---

44 It is possible to read אל as אֵל (cf. Lohse, *Qumran Texte*, 10) and translate it 'the spirit of God's true counsel' (cf. Brownlee, *Manual of Discipline*, 12; Wernberg-Møller, *Manual of Discipline*, 24). However, this leaves דרכי איש without an explicit connection with the previous clause, which requires some interpolation or emendation of the text. Therefore, it is better to read אל as the preposition אֶל and translate it as has been done here.

45 The sense of this clause is difficult to determine with precision, because ליחד is problematic. The noun יחד normally is used in 1QS as a term identifying the 'community' (e.g. 1.1, 12, etc.). Combined with ל to form ליחד ('to the community'), it probably signifies that it is a holy spirit which is specifically identified with the community in its application of God's truth (possibly as a polemic against possible claims of a spirit of holiness operating outside the community; cf. the contrast between 3.6b and 3.6a). Thus, the clause וברוח קדושה ליחד באמתו could probably be translated 'and by a holy spirit of the community in his [or: its] truth . . .' (supported by Dupont-Sommer, *Essene Writings*, 77; Wernberg-Møller, *Manual of Discipline*, 61 n. 18; Lohse, *Qumran Texte*, 11). However, it is possible that ליחד is being used as a verb, or at least in a verbal sense, and not as a term for the community (for a discussion of the alternatives see Wernberg-Møller, 61-62 n. 21). If so, the clause could be translated 'and by a holy spirit uniting him to his truth . . .' (supported by Vermes, *Dead Sea Scrolls*, 64; Leaney, *Rule of Qumran*, 137; Knibb, *Qumran Community*, 90-91).

In light of these difficulties, Thiering ('Inner and Outer Cleansing', 266-77) is incorrect to base so much of her argument on translating the clause: 'in the Spirit of holiness (which is given) to the community in its truth, he will be purified . . .' (267), and interpreting it to refer to a spirit which cleanses within the community and is not given to the individual in contrast to the other spirits which are virtues operating within the individual (cf. 268-70). Her argument is also based on the variant reading קורשו in 4QS^a rather than קרושה in 1QS. No reason for preferring this reading is given.

46 The translation here of במי נדה literally as 'with waters for impurity' is to make clear that this particular phrase is used in this passage. Normally it is appropriate to translate it as 'waters of purification'.

An analysis of these four statements reveals certain parallels between them. Each statement begins with the instrumental use of the preposition בּ followed by a statement concerning a spirit which is the instrument accomplishing the action of the verb. The verbs in S1 and S3 are the same (pual imperfect of כפר, 'will be atoned'), and the verbs in S2 and S4 are also the same (niphal imperfect of טהר, 'will be cleansed'). The statements S1 and S4 conclude with the preposition ל with an infinitive construct (S4 actually concludes with two such constructions). In S1 the clause with this construction most probably signifies the consequence or result of the main part of the statement. In S4 they indicate the attendant circumstances of the main part of the statement.

With respect to S1 and S3, the distinction between these two statements is the description of the spirit as well as the object of atonement.[48] The object of the atonement is עוונותיו ('his iniquities') in S1, while

---

47   This word could be read as either רוכי or רוכו. Brownlee (*Manual of Discipline*, 13 n. 17) reads it as רוכי, understands it a term perhaps drawn from Ps. 93.3 ('waves') and parallel to the phrase 'seas or rivers' in 1QS 3.4-5. He thus translates it as 'rippling water'. He rejects the reading רוכו which he states is equivalent to the Aramaic רכו ('purification'). While Dupont-Sommer (*Essene Writings*, 77) agrees with Brownlee and translates this phrase as 'flowing water', most translators prefer the other option and translate it as 'waters of purity' or something similar (e.g. Wernberg-Møller, *Manual of Discipline*, 25; Vermes, *Dead Sea Scrolls*, 64; Leaney, *Rule of Qumran*, 137; Knibb, *Qumran Community*, 91). Whether the word is understood as a reference to the purpose of the water (i.e. cleansing) or to the type of water (i.e. rippling), it still is a reference to cleansing waters. Therefore, while it is difficult to choose between these two options, I have chosen the translation here because it probably best communicates the intention of the passage.

48   The understanding of atonement by the members of the Qumran community is not entirely clear due to their rejection of the temple. Evidently the Qumran community understood itself as the temple and their activities as a separated community would provide atonement for the land. Their verbal worship was itself a sacrifice (cf. 1QS 8.1-10a; 9.3-6). Cf. §5.4.1; Vermes, *Qumran in Perspective*, 180-82. On this subject see Garnet, *Salvation and Atonement*; Gärtner, *Temple and the Community*.
     It is unclear whether רוח קרושה in 3.7 should be understood as a reference to the spirit of God, or to a person's spirit or moral disposition. The use of קרש to describe רוח usually indicates God's spirit, though in this instance קרשה is syntactically indefinite, and is parallel to the two statements following in 3.8a-9a which clearly emphasize a person's moral disposition. It is more probable that the two concepts are actually closely linked. Leaney (*Rule of Qumran*, 34) explains that the 'conception of spirit is that which sees it as the source of all life and therefore as that by which (not until the NT can we say "by whom") God bestows on man all the powers which man possesses'. Therefore, in 3.6-8 it is God's spirit which bestows upon the members these spiritual qualities. In this instance it would probably do damage to the sense of the passage to attempt to separate the moral qualities from the source of those qualities, though each phrase may emphasize one aspect more than the other; cf. Sekki, *Meaning of RUAH*, 92, 106-108. See also 1QS 3.6-8; 8.16; 9.3; 1QH 7.6-7; 9.22; 12.11-12; 13.19; 14.13; 16.2, 3, 7, 11-12. Such a conception of spirit relates most specifically to OT passages such as Isa. 44.3; Ezek. 36.27; 37.6, 14; Joel 3.1-2. For a full discussion of the concept of spirit in the Qumran literature, see Sekki.

in S3 the object of atonement is חטאתו ('his sin'). The instrument of the atonement in S1 is 'a spirit of true counsel concerning the ways of man', while in S3 it is 'a spirit of uprightness and humility'. While differences between these two statements suggest nuanced distinctions in meaning, they fundamentally state the same thing: by means of spiritual virtues given by God, a person's sins are atoned.[49]

S2 and S4 demonstrate similar parallels with respect to the required spiritual virtues as well as the object of cleansing. In S2 it is 'a holy spirit of the community in his truth' which cleanses the candidate. This phrase suggests that only the virtue of holiness as practised by the community in its application of God's truth is able to cleanse.[50] Such a claim by the Qumran community may be a polemic against possible claims by non-members that the virtue of holiness could be practised outside the community. In S4 the instrument of cleansing is 'humility of his soul towards all the precepts of God'. This latter phrase does not use the term 'spirit', but it nevertheless refers to a spiritual virtue in parallel with the other statements.[51] The only distinction between this phrase and the three previous 'spirit' statements is the clear emphasis that the virtue is being demonstrated by the person rather than a virtue given by God. The virtue in S4, which is the instrument of cleansing, is the candidate's submission to the Torah as interpreted by the community. This virtue of submission by the candidate stands in contrast to the rebellious candidate who is described in 3.5-6 as 'unclean, unclean shall he be all the days of his rejection of the precepts of God'. Thus, while in S2 and S4 the terminology for the virtues which cleanse are different, their significance is quite similar. Essentially they both require a whole-hearted commitment to the community's regulations. S2 focuses on holiness as the orientation of those regulations, while S4 focuses on submission as the response to those regulations.

S2 and S4 also demonstrate parallels with respect to the object of cleansing. In S2 the object of cleansing is simply the person identified as 'he', and that from which the person is cleansed is 'all his iniquities'. The iniquities which required atonement in S1 have also defiled the person, and thus he/she requires cleansing from that defilement. In S4 the object cleansed is 'his flesh', but the statement does not identify from what the flesh is cleansed. It could be argued that the distinction between 'he' in S2 and 'his flesh' in S4 indicate two different objects of cleansing as well as two different means of cleansing; that is, an inward cleansing by spiritual virtues and a separate outward cleansing by an

---

49   A discussion of the possible nuanced distinctions between these two statements is not necessary for this examination of immersions and will not be entered into here.
50   Cf. Garnet, *Salvation and Atonement*, 58.
51   Cf. 'humility of his soul' here in S4 with a 'spirit of . . . humility' in S3.

immersion. For example, B.E. Thiering makes such a distinction which leads her to argue that, as they are separate and distinct, they take place at two different times in the process of the candidate becoming a member.[52] However, the distinction between S2 and S4 is better interpreted as emphasizing two aspects of one cleansing. On the one hand, S2 emphasizes that the cause of defilement is iniquities, and these defile the whole person including the flesh. So S2 correspondingly emphasizes that cleansing the candidate from this defilement requires spiritual virtues. On the other hand, S4 emphasizes the role of an immersion in the cleansing from this defilement, and so S4 correspondingly emphasizes that it is the flesh of the person which is cleansed. These are not two separate cleansings but two aspects of the same cleansing, because both aspects have the same cause of defilement: the person's iniquities. Also, both aspects require the person to exhibit spiritual virtues. Furthermore, to imagine a person who is inwardly clean from his/her iniquities, but remains for some time outwardly unclean because of those same iniquities, is incongruous. Therefore, S2 and S4 should be understood as complementary, presenting two aspects of one cleansing.

With respect to immersions in this passage, the issue is not their use or non-use. That an immersion was to be used is taken for granted. Rather, at issue is the question, what is required for an immersion to be effective in cleansing the candidate? The answer given is that, because the person has been defiled by his/her iniquities, efficacious cleansing requires the immersion to be accompanied by spiritual virtues. The appropriate spiritual virtues are those which indicate a commitment to obey the community's sectarian interpretation of the Torah. Thus, 1QS 3.6-9 explains that with these spiritual virtues the submissive candidate is cleansed by an immersion. On the other hand, for the candidate who refuses to enter the community, any purificatory immersion in which he/she engages will not be efficacious because it is not accompanied by

---

52   Thiering ('Inner and Outer Cleansing', 266-71) argues for such a difference by claiming that 'the passage deals with two different *objects* of cleansing and with two corresponding *instruments* of cleansing' (267, her emphasis). She thus separates 1QS 3.6b-8a, identified as (A) from 3.8b-9a, identified as (B). However, her distinctions seem to confuse the different roles played by atonement and purification in the passage, and they fail to take into account the parallels between S1 and S3 as well as S3 and S4. Furthermore, she places too much weight upon a peculiar translation and interpretation of 1QS 3.7b (cf. my discussion in the relevant note in §5.3.1.4). I do not wish to deny that elsewhere this distinction may be made. However, forcing such a distinction on this passage obscures its sense. It is interesting to observe that Thiering argues that her distinction is not found in 4.18-22, even though according to her translation objects of cleansing include 'the works of man', 'the frame of man', as well as 'flesh'. Her later article ('Qumran Initiation', 615-31) builds upon the distinctions made in the earlier article, and therefore its argument is flawed as well.

the correct spiritual virtues (3.1-6). S4 stresses the correct spiritual virtue to be 'humility of his soul towards all the precepts of God' because
this is precisely the failure of the rebellious candidate: he/she refuses to
humble him/herself to the commandments of the community which
express their sectarian nature (cf. 3.1, 5-6).

One further question needs to be explored briefly. What is the relationship between the atonement in S1 and S3 and the purificatory
immersion in S2 and S4? Though the members of the Qumran community did not sacrifice at the temple (cf. §5.4.1), they still employed atonement language, and in this context the atonement is closely associated
with the purificatory immersion which cleanses the candidate. The
atonement and purification are closely linked because they are both
dealing with the same sins and their effects upon the same person. Also,
the expression of very similar spiritual virtues effects the atonement as
well as rendering the immersion efficacious. It would be quite easy to
conclude at this point, with Paul Garnet, that 'atonement is mentioned
here alongside of cleansing as a synonym. . .'[53] This might be supported
by the references to cleansing from sin which parallel statements concerning forgiveness or atonement.[54] However, while here in 3.6-9 (cf.
3.4) atonement and purification are closely related, it is going beyond the
statements to identify them with each other as synonyms, for they are
kept distinct structurally.

The close link between atonement and purification might be
explained here by observing that sin in this context is fundamentally the
prior rebellion of the person against God and his Torah; thus, sin is primarily an action by a person against God, affecting his/her relationship
with God. Consequently, by demonstrating appropriate spiritual virtues,
a person effects atonement which is primarily directed toward God,
whereby God now recognizes the sins to be 'covered' and allows a relationship to be established between the person and himself. But the same
sins also render a person unclean, which primarily affects his/her relationship with other people. Thus, when the person performs an immersion accompanied by appropriate spiritual virtues which render the
immersion efficacious, it allows a relationship to be established with the
other people in the community. So atonement establishes a divine relationship while purification establishes human relationships.

But it is possible to take this matter one step further, for, as we
observed, the spiritual virtues which effect atonement and purification
are very similar. Atonement is 'by a spirit of true counsel' (S1) and 'by a
spirit of uprightness and humility' (S3), while purification is 'by a holy

53   Garnet, *Salvation and Atonement*, 59; cf. Ringgren, *Faith of Qumran*, 120-23; Kuhn,
'Communal Meal', 68; Scobie, *John the Baptist*, 107-108.

spirit of the community' (S2) and 'by humility of his soul toward all the precepts of God' (S4). If the person exhibits this piety while bathing to render the immersion efficacious, then probably it is this same piety which God recognizes as atoning for the person's sins. It would be incorrect to say that the immersion atoned; rather, the person's sins were recognized as atoned for by God on the basis of the same piety demonstrated at the time of the immersion.

To summarize, several points arise out of our discussion of this passage which are relevant to interpreting immersions practised by the members of the community at Qumran. First of all, the passage is particularly concerned with the candidate who refuses to enter the community. It explains the consequences of such refusal by describing the conditions of entry, particularly in terms of atonement and purification. Secondly, prior to entering the community, the candidate (as well as everyone outside the community) is a non-Israelite, evil, defiled and backslidden. Thirdly, the person's iniquities are understood to cause that person to be unclean. Fourthly, for a candidate to enter the community his/her iniquities must be atoned by means of the spiritual virtues given to the person by God's spirit—virtues the candidate is expected to manifest. Fifthly, to enter the community a candidate must also be cleansed of the defilement caused by his/her iniquities and status as a non-Israelite, evil and backslidden. Sixthly, efficacious cleansing requires that the purificatory immersion be accompanied by correct spiritual virtues. Seventhly, atonement is closely linked to purification, for the candidate's sins were recognized as atoned for by God on the basis of the same spiritual virtues which rendered efficacious the candidate's purificatory immersion. Finally, only purificatory immersions practised by the community are efficacious; any other immersion does not work because it lacks the necessary accompanying spiritual virtues given by God's spirit, and because it is not done in submission to the community's sectarian interpretation and application of the Torah.

### 5.3.2 *1QS 5.7-15*

A text similar to the one just analysed is 1QS 5.7-15. The preceding context (5.1-7) explains the general functioning of the community, stressing the principles of separation, obedience and piety. The matters raised briefly in this introductory paragraph are developed in columns 5 through 7. The statement in 5.7 provides the transition from these introductory principles to their development in the succeeding sections: 'This is the course of their ways, according to all these ordinances, when they join the community'. The specific development of these principles begins

---

54   E.g. 1QS 11.13-15; 1QH 4.35-37; cf. §4.2.6.

in 5.7-15 with the oath required by the candidate at his/her entry into the community. The oath stresses the principle of obedience (introduced in the preceding introductory passage):

> Everyone who approaches the council of the community [8]shall enter the covenant of God in the sight of all who offer themselves; and he shall take upon his soul with a binding oath to return to the Law of Moses, according to all that he commanded, with all [9]his heart and all his soul, and to all that has been revealed from it to the sons of Zadok, the priests who keep the covenant and who seek out his will . . . [5.7-9].

This oath was taken in the presence of the other candidates (5.8), and probably took place during the liturgy described in 1.16–2.18 at which were present the priests and Levites who performed the liturgy with the candidates.[55] The oath was to obey not only the Torah (5.8) but also other commandments given by the Zadokite priests which expressed the sectarian nature of the community (5.9). This oath encapsulated a 'return' to Torah obedience. The verb used is שוב, signifying 'to repent' or 'to be converted to'.[56]

The passage continues by describing a major implication of this oath of obedience to the sectarian principles of the community: the principle of separation (which was also mentioned in the preceding introductory section):

> By the covenant he shall take upon his soul to be separate from all the men of perversity who walk [11]in the way of wickedness, for they are not reckoned in his covenant because they have not enquired nor sought among his ordinances to discover the hidden things in which they have erred [12]to their guilt, while in the things revealed they have acted with a high hand; so that wrath arises for judgment to wreak vengeance by the curses of the covenant, to bring upon them great punishments [13]to annihilate them for ever without remnant [5.10-13].

The candidate's oath led him/her to be separate from all who were not members of the community because of the wickedness of these people due to their disobedience of the Torah (5.12) as well as their failure to seek the hidden principles of the Torah—the sectarian doctrines and practices of the Qumran community (5.11; cf. 5.9). Those who were not members of the community were considered to be non-Israel: they were outside the covenant (5.11); they would be judged for their disobedience (5.12); and their punishment would 'annihilate them for ever without remnant' (5.13).

The principle of separation is amplified by a number of regulations in the succeeding context, including not joining with non-members in work

---

55  See the discussion of 1QS 2.19-25 in §5.3.1.1, which indicates that the entire community was probably present at this oath-taking ceremony.

56  Cf. 1QS 5.14. For a discussion of repentance, see §6.4.1.

or possessions (5.14-15), rejecting the authority of non-members (5.15-16), refusing to eat or drink with them (5.16), and refusing to take anything from them except in payment for something (5.16-18). However, the first amplification of the principle of separation is in 5.13-14 and concerns immersions:

אל יבוא במים לגעת בטהרת אנשי הקורש כיא לוא יטהרו
14כי אם שבו מרעתם כיא טמא בכול עוברי דברו

He shall not enter the waters in order to touch the purity of the men of holiness, because they will not be cleansed [14]unless they turn from their wickedness, because [they are] unclean among all those who transgress his word.

This regulation (as well as those which follow) stresses the strictness of the principle of separation. However, the identification of the person described as 'he shall not enter' is not immediately evident. It clearly does not refer to the candidate taking the oath described in the preceding context (5.7-13), because the person is described as unrepentant (5.14). Michael A. Knibb suggests that these lines are a redactional layer which was

> originally concerned with the person whose conversion was insincere. . . [T]he members of the community were to keep away from such a man; it is this point, the demand for separation, which led to the inclusion of this passage here.[57]

While the redactional character of the passage is probably correct, it has a more immediate significance in this context than Knibb suggests. In light of the severity of the separation required in the context (including separation with respect to business, property and table fellowship), the person referred to as 'he shall not enter the waters' could be a non-member who wanted to bridge the separation between him/herself and a member(s) of the community in order to participate in a communal meal (cf. 'the purity of the many'). He/she might offer to undergo an immersion at Qumran.[58] This is the implication of the purpose clause which expresses the inadequate motive for undergoing the immersion: 'He shall not enter the waters in order to touch the purity of the men of holiness'.[59] If interpreted in this way, 5.13-14 makes the application of separation in this section even more absolute.

57  Knibb, *Qumran Community*, 111. Cf. Wernberg-Møller, *Manual of Discipline*, 95 n. 51.
58  This offer could be made if the person observed that the members immersed themselves before the communal meal (cf. *War* 2.159).
59  Cf. Baumgarten, 'Sacrifice and Worship', 48. In the preceding context (5.10-13) non-members were referred to in the plural because they were the group from which the candidate was taking the oath to separate. In 5.13 the non-member is referred to in the singular because the passage is not dealing with all non-members, but with a par-

A non-member could not undergo an immersion in order to have contact with the community members or objects and food susceptible to defilement.[60] The reason given is that the non-member, by virtue of being a non-member, has not yet repented of his/her wickedness and thus remains unclean as are all transgressors. The statement that '[they are] unclean among all those who transgress his word' implies that it is their transgression of God's law (as interpreted by the community) which defiles them, and thus an immersion (i.e. 'enter the waters') is not able to cleanse them without a corresponding repentance from their wickedness. Here once again (as 2.25–3.9) we find the belief that moral failure renders a person impure. Since it is moral failure which defiles, purification cannot take place simply by an immersion; it must be accompanied by the corresponding moral or spiritual dispositions of repentance and obedience.

The logical implication of this prohibition is that the only way a non-member could have the type of contact described here with a member was to repent, obey God's law (as interpreted by the community) and undergo a purificatory immersion. The repentance and obedience would make the purificatory immersion efficacious. In essence, what was required for a non-member to have fellowship with a member was that he/she become a member. While this passage is not specifically describing the process of membership, nevertheless it is implying at least one aspect of what would be required to join the community: a change from a state of impurity to purity, involving an immersion.[61]

A final implication lies behind the expressed belief that non-members were impure because of their disobedience of God's law. With this assertion the members of the Qumran community denied the efficacy of all purificatory immersions other than their own.

From our examination of this passage we may conclude that members of the Qumran community were committed to separation from all non-members because the latter were impure. Secondly, all non-members were in a state of impurity caused by their transgression of God's law (as interpreted by the community). Thirdly, purificatory immersions outside the community were not efficacious because they were not linked with repentance and obedience to the community's sectarian commandments.

ticular case or type of non-member: one who wished to have contact with the community. The text switches back to the plural to express the reason for not allowing this particular non-member to 'enter the waters' because it applies to this particular case a general principle which is relevant to all non-members.

60  Cf. the discussion of the phrase 'the purity of the many' in §5.2.2.
61  This is further strengthened by the similarity of the clause 'to touch the purity of the men of holiness' in 5.13 to the statement in 6.16-17 concerning a new member: 'At his approaching the council of the community he shall not touch the purity of the many. . .'

Finally, the community's immersions were efficacious because, when combined with repentance and obedience, they dealt with the true cause of the impurity: transgression of God's law.

### 5.3.3　*1QS 4.19-22*

The final passage in 1QS which mentions ablutions is contained in the section discussing the doctrine of the two spirits: the spirit of perversity and the spirit of truth (3.13–4.26).[62] In the closing portion of this section their final end is portrayed. God will destroy the spirit of perversity and give the spirit of truth to those whom he has purified. This granting of the spirit of truth is described in 4.19-21:

> Then shall come forth for ever truth upon the earth, for it has been contaminated with the ways of evil during the dominion of perversity until [20]the set time which has been decreed for judgment. Then God in his truth will make manifest all the deeds of man and will purify for himself some from mankind, destroying all spirit of perversity, removing all blemishes of [21]his flesh and purifying him with a spirit of holiness from all deeds of evil.

This does not refer to the granting of a new spirit because the spirit of truth is already present with some persons in either small or great measure (cf. 4.16). While the passage is not entirely clear, it would seem that those who possess the spirit of truth in sufficient measure (presumably the members of Qumran; cf. 3.6-9) are those who will be the 'some from mankind' purified completely at the end time from all vestiges of contamination by the spirit of perversity (4.20-21).[63] Thus, this passage expresses the community's hope in an eschatological purification, the corollary of which is that those who are not purified will be destroyed (4.23-26; cf. 5.13).

1QS 4.21-22 continues by describing this purification more explicitly:

> ויז עליו רוח אמת כמי נדה מכול תועבות שקר והתגולל
> [22]ברוח נדה להבין ישרים בדעת עליון וחכמת בני שמים
> להשכיל תמימי דרך

> And he will sprinkle upon him the spirit of truth like waters for impurity from all abominations of falsehood and being contaminated [22]by the spirit of impurity, so that the righteous will gain insight into the knowledge of the Most High, and the perfect of way will understand the wisdom of the sons of heaven.[64]

---

62　For discussion of the meaning of 'spirit' in this section, see Sekki, *Meaning of RUAH*, 193-219; Licht, 'Two Spirits', 88-100.

63　For discussion of the interpretive problems in this passage, see Leaney, *Rule of Qumran*, 154-61.

64　This last clause may be variously translated depending upon whether וחכמת בני שמים ('the wisdom of the sons of heaven') should be understood as continuing the object of the previous clause (e.g. Brownlee, *Manual of Discipline*, 16; Wernberg-Møller, *Manual of Discipline*, 27), or as the object of the final clause (e.g. Dupont-

In the preceding discussion of 3.8-9 we saw that the term 'waters for impurity', though reminiscent of the red heifer rite, is actually a reference to cleansing from the defilement of sin (§5.3.1.3). This use of red heifer terminology to refer to an eschatological cleansing is similar to and almost certainly derived from Ezek. 36.25-27, particularly in light of the connection with the granting of God's spirit in both passages. Thus, the Qumran community expressed its hope in an eschatological cleansing using terms which were the same as those used to describe its own immersions. It is interesting to observe that other parallels exist between this eschatological cleansing and the description of immersions in 3.6-9. In both, the spirit is described as holy, the spirit cleanses from sin, and the person receives God's truth in some way. On the grounds of this parallelism in both concepts and terminology, it is quite possible that the community's practice of immersions as described in 3.6-9 foreshadowed this eschatological expectation of a greater, spiritual cleansing.[65]

The examination of this passage demonstrates that, first of all, the Qumran community hoped for an eschatological cleansing which would purify its members from all defilement. Secondly, evidently only the community members would be purified; those outside would be destroyed. Finally, their hope in an eschatological cleansing was expressed with the same terminology and concepts as those used to describe their purificatory immersions, so that the latter probably foreshadowed their expected, eschatological purification.

## 5.4 *The Ideology and Function of Immersions*

In order to appreciate fully the function of immersions within the Qumran community, it would be helpful to summarize certain elements of the community's ideology relating to immersions which have arisen from the discussion of these passages in 1QS.

### 5.4.1 *Ideological Concepts Relating to Immersions at Qumran*
The community's ideology concerning immersions arose out of its understanding of the relationship between sin and defilement. The members

Sommer, *Essene Writings*, 22; Knibb, *Qumran Community*, 101), or as the subject of the final clause (e.g. Leaney, *Rule of Qumran*, 22; Vermes, *Dead Sea Scrolls*, 66). The choice is complicated by whether or not to understand להשכיל to signify 'understand' (e.g. Brownlee, 16; Wernberg-Møller, 27; Dupont-Sommer, 82; Knibb, 101) or 'give understanding', i.e. teach (e.g. Leaney, 154; Vermes, 66).

65  Betz ('Proselytentaufe', 220-21) understands the Qumran community's immersions to be linked with the eschatological cleansing, but only in terms of the eschatological cleansing being much greater. Vermes (*Qumran in Perspective*, 182) draws a similar inference concerning the similarities between the community's fellowship meal and the eschatological Messianic meal (1QS 6.4-5 with 1QSa 2.17-21).

held to a common Jewish view derived from the OT that clean objects and persons could be defiled by contact with uncleanness and thus become unclean. We observed in examining the OT that it usually distinguishes between the two forms of contagion leading to the state of uncleanness: physical contagion and moral contagion. Uncleanness caused by physical contagion required cleansing, usually using an immersion with other elements (e.g. Lev. 15). But uncleanness caused by moral contagion did not require ablutions for cleansing, and the sin itself required atonement, usually involving repentance and sacrifice (e.g. Lev. 16). The distinction between these two categories is not absolute because the language of uncleanness is occasionally used to describe the consequence of sin (e.g. Lev. 18.24-30), but more often in a metaphorical sense (e.g. Isa. 1.16; 6.5-7). In these situations ablutions were not used as a means of cleansing. If the uncleanness was caused by sin, then cleansing required other means (e.g. Ps. 51; cf. §4.2.6, 4.2.7).

But the situation reflected in 1QS is somewhat different. Its community believed that sin resulted in a state of being both sinful and unclean. This is itself not essentially different from the OT, though perhaps they placed greater stress upon it. However, the community was distinctive in its belief that the uncleanness caused by sin required an immersion, and that immersion had to be coupled with repentance (or similar spiritual dispositions) in order for the immersion to be efficacious.[66]

The second aspect of the community's ideology relevant to a full appreciation of the function of immersions is its self-understanding, which may be summarized as having a number of elements. First of all, we saw that the community viewed itself as the true Israel in contrast with all those outside the community who were not true Israel. As the true Israel, they had a relationship with God based upon a new covenant which incorporated both a return to Torah-obedience and an intensification of the Torah as interpreted by the community's leadership. Secondly, those who were non-Israel and outside the community were in a

---

66   This requirement of repentance was most probably necessary only in those cases where the uncleanness had been caused by sin. For those cases in which the uncleanness had been caused by a physical contagion, then repentance was probably irrelevant.

The explanation provided here of the Qumran community's distinctiveness in this matter differs slightly from that provided by Leaney (139; following Flusser, 'Baptism of John', 209-38). He explains that 'ritual acts cleanse from ritual defilement, repentance from moral defects. The sect is the first group within Judaism of whom we know who believed that moral failure . . . incurred ritual defilement. They taught that to be cleansed from sin required *both* repentance *and* ritual purification.' This view depends upon distinguishing ritual defilement from moral defilement. However, it is probably better to understand uncleanness to be one condition, but with two possible causes: physical contagion and moral contagion. Cf. also Neusner (*Idea of Purity*, 54) who expands on this point.

continual state of impurity because they were wicked and rebellious, while the members were righteous and obedient to God's Torah. Thirdly, as the true Israel, the members of the Qumran community believed they were pure and had the means to maintain that purity, that is, by their immersions. In contrast, those outside the community (i.e. non-Israel) were impure and had no means by which to be cleansed. The members of the community claimed that their immersions worked and everyone else's did not. Finally, the way in which one changed one's status from being non-Israel, outside God's covenant, impure, wicked and rebellious to being true Israel, in God's covenant, pure, righteous and obedient was by becoming a member of the community.

Another aspect of the community's ideology which we must briefly note is their attitude to the temple.[67] They rejected the validity of the current Jerusalem temple, because they considered it to be defiled (1QpHab 12.7-10; cf. CD 6.11-20[68]). Evidently they looked forward to the day when they would be able to return to the temple, cleanse it, and reinstitute correct worship under their own direction as the sons of Zadok (cf. 1QM; 11QTemple). In the meantime, they considered their own community to be a spiritual temple of God, 'a house of holiness for Israel, a company of holy of holies for Aaron' (1QS 8.5-6; cf. 8.8-9; 1QpHab 12.3-4[69]), and their worship and prayers were 'like a sweet-savoured offering of righteousness' (1QS 9.5; cf. 8.8-9). Their own community was to be a sacrifice which atoned for the sins of the land (1QS 8.4-5), and this atonement was evidently accomplished by the perfection and holiness with which they conducted themselves in their community as governed by meticulous observance of their interpretation of the Torah (1QS 8.9-19; cf. 8.1-5; 9.3-6).

### 5.4.2 *The Function of Immersions at Qumran*
These three aspects of the community's ideology enable us to clarify the function of immersions. The community's view of the temple may be linked to its understanding of immersions in two ways. First of all, in 1QS 3.6-9, we concluded, atonement is closely linked to purification, for the candidate's sins were recognized by God as having been atoned for on the basis of the same spiritual virtues which rendered efficacious the candidate's purificatory immersion. Though the members of the commu-

---

67  See Baumgarten, 'Sacrifice and Worship', 39-56; Gärtner, *Temple and the Community*, 1-46; Vermes, *Qumran in Perspective*, 180-82.

68  The evidence of the Damascus Document indicates that though defiled, the temple was still utilized (cf. CD 11.19-20). Cf. observations on CD 11 in §5.2.1; Davies, 'Ideology of the Temple', 287-301.

69  Cf. discussion in Vermes, *Dead Sea Scrolls*, 50-51; Vermes, *Qumran in Perspective*, 181; Schüssler Fiorenza, 'Cultic Language', 164-68.

nity rejected the current temple, they were still concerned about atonement, and in this text, that atonement was based upon spiritual virtues demonstrated at the time of the candidate's immersion. The rejection of the Jerusalem temple and the view of the community as a spiritual temple probably led them to take this view of the atonement of the candidate. Secondly, the community's desire to atone for the land by its concern for holiness and meticulous observance of the Torah, as well as its view of the community as a spiritual temple, no doubt contributed to the concern for purity within the community and, thus, the importance of purificatory immersions.

In light of the community's self-understanding, the process of membership (that is, initiation) was a change of one's status from a candidate to a member. Such a change of status involved a change from being a non-Israelite and impure to being a true Israelite and pure. This initiation involved two elements, both linked with this change of status. First of all, the candidate entered the covenant. In 1QS 5.7-10 the process by which the person 'shall enter the covenant of God' (5.8) involved an oath expressing the person's repentance or conversion: to 'return' to obedience of the Torah as well as the doctrines and practices of the community. The second element of the initiation was to cleanse the candidate from the impurity caused by sins committed as a non-Israelite.[70] This cleansing was accomplished by an immersion accompanied by appropriate spiritual virtues. Both passages relevant to the ideology of immersions (1QS 3.6-9; 5.13-14) are contained within contexts discussing the initiation of a candidate and relate to that fundamental change of status from an impure non-Israelite to a pure Israelite. Therefore, because of the fundamental change of status involved in the first purificatory immersion by the candidate, that first immersion also functioned as an initiatory immersion.[71]

---

70  Vermes (*Qumran in Perspective*, 96) distinguishes between entering the covenant (1QS 5.10-11) and entering the community (5.20), arguing that they take place at two different times. However, 5.20 ('when a man enters the covenant to act according to all these statutes, to be united with the community of holiness . . .') suggests rather that they are two aspects of the same thing. The candidate, having taken the oath and undergone immersion, is both a member of the covenant and consequently of the community as well (cf. 1.16). Perhaps it could be understood that establishing the relationship with God (i.e. entering the covenant) produces a relationship with the community (i.e. entering it). There is no evidence for certain persons being members of one without the other. However, the novice (i.e. the candidate who has completed entering and is a member) still has further training to undergo before being allowed to sit at the council of the community and participate fully at the meals (i.e. become a full member; cf. 1QS 5.7-10; 6.13-23).

It is unclear precisely when this initiatory immersion for purification took place. However, since the oath and the immersions were closely linked ideologically, then it is reasonable to presume that they took place in the same ceremony.

71  For support, cf. e.g. Cullmann, 'Beginnings of Christianity', 21; Black, *Scrolls*, 92-97;

Once the candidate's status had been changed in this manner, he/she would remain a member of the true Israel. His/her status would not change, and therefore, the special nature of the cleansing which took place at that initiatory immersion would not be repeated. However, purification would still be required by the community's members if they contracted uncleanness. If the uncleanness was caused by a moral failure, then presumably the principles in 3.6-9 would equally apply. A purificatory immersion would be required accompanied by those spiritual virtues. That purificatory immersion would change the member's *state* from unclean to clean, but it would not involve the more fundamental change of *status* undergone by the candidate. Therefore, community members would continue to practise immersions, whose function was purificatory (but no longer had the unique, initiatory function of the first immersion).[72]

The relationship between these immersions and the community's belief in an eschatological cleansing by God is not entirely clear, but we did observe that both the immersions and the eschatological cleansing are described in similar terms and have a number of other parallels between them. We may reasonably infer that the immersions of the Qumran community were understood as prefiguring the eschatological cleansing.

## 5.5 Conclusion

This analysis of immersions in 1QS has demonstrated their close relationship to two aspects of the community's ideology. First of all, the Qumran community believed that moral failure caused defilement and that cleansing from such impurity required an immersion made efficacious when accompanied by appropriate spiritual virtues. Secondly, they believed that only their community was the true Israel and pure, in contrast to all those outside the community who were non-Israel and impure. Also, only their own immersions were able to cleanse; all others were useless.

In light of the community's ideology, we are able to conclude that the function of its immersions was purificatory. The candidate's first immersion was purificatory, but due to the special nature of the change of

Beasley-Murray, *Baptism*, 15-17; Scobie, *John the Baptist*, 104-108; against e.g. Rowley, 'Baptism of John', 218-29.

72  These purificatory immersions could be understood to be of two types, depending upon whether the defiling agent was a physical or moral contagion. The emphasis in 1QS is upon cleansing from moral contagion, though the Qumran community evidently practised immersions which cleansed from physical contagion as well; cf. the survey in §5.2.1.

status involved, this immersion was also an initiatory immersion. This initiatory immersion cannot be entirely separated from the regular purificatory immersions. However, they were two distinct, though related, types of immersions. The first immersion changed the candidate's status from an impure non-Israelite to a pure Israelite, while the other immersions only changed a member's state from an impure member to a pure one. This difference between these two changes is significant, thus justifying our conclusion that they were two different, though related, types of immersions.

Chapter 6

THE ADMINISTRATION AND FUNCTIONS OF JOHN'S BAPTISM

## 6.1 *Introduction*

In the preceding two chapters we have laid the groundwork for under-standing John's baptism within his social, cultural and historical context by examining ablutions in the Jewish literature which formed John's socio-religious heritage as well as his contemporary milieu. Now we turn to John's baptism itself and consider it in the light of this context. To accomplish this will take four stages. First of all, we examine the sources concerning John's baptism in order to determine what evidence may be taken as historically reliable. Secondly, we consider this evidence to ascertain how John's baptism was administered. Thirdly, we examine the evidence to determine the functions of John's baptism. Finally, we com-pare these functions with the use of immersions within John's heritage and contemporary milieu.

## 6.2 *The Evidence for John's Baptism*

One of the most secure pieces of historical data we possess concerning John is that he performed a water rite identified as a 'baptism'. This claim may be substantiated in three ways. First of all, four independent sources explicitly refer to his baptism. Josephus describes it, and refer-ences to it are found in all layers of NT tradition, including Q, Mark and the fourth Gospel.[1]

Secondly, this baptismal rite was so integrally linked with John that it led to his nickname 'the baptizer' and then to the title 'the Baptist', which is also evidenced by both Josephus and the NT.[2] As a corollary,

---

1  Cf. §2.3, 2.4 and 3.8 for discussion of the authenticity of these traditions and their use for historical data.
2  Cf. the introductory remarks in §4.1. While each of the synoptic Gospels use the title Ἰωάννης ὁ βαπτιστής, Matthew and Luke use it exclusively (Mt. 3.1; 11.11, 12; 14.2; 14.8 = Mk 6.25; Mt. 16.14 = Mk 8.28 = Lk. 9.19; Mt. 17.13; Lk. 7.20, 23). Mark uses Ἰωάννης [ὁ] βαπτίζων as well (Mk 1.4; 6.14, 24). It is interesting to observe that in a number of passages Matthew and/or Mark use the titles but Luke does not (Mt. 3.1 = Mk 1.4 = Lk. 3.2; Mt. 11.11 = Lk. 7.28; Mt. 11.12 = Lk. 16.16; Mt. 14.2 = Mk 6.14 = Lk. 9.7). However, this may not have much significance because the reverse is also true (e.g. Mt. 11.18 = Lk. 7.33), and both Matthew and Mark also refer to John without any title (e.g. Mt. 3.4 = Mk 1.6). It is of greater significance that the Gospel of John uses neither title at all. Such elimination of the title may be serving the

his baptismal practice is given the descriptive nomenclature 'the baptism of John'. Both this title and description are used in the Gospel narratives in connection with diverse groups of people, including John's disciples, Jesus' disciples, the common people, the temple leadership, tax-collectors and Herod Antipas.[3]

Thirdly, the Gospels record that Jesus was baptized by John (Mt. 3.13-17 = Mk 1.9-11 = Lk. 3.21-22). It is highly unlikely that the early Christians would have created such a story because it could be construed to imply that Jesus was subordinate to, or a disciple of, John. We observed earlier that Matthew's addition of the conversation between John and Jesus at Jesus' baptism (Mt. 3.14-15) is probably an attempt to counter this embarrassment. By the second century, the *Gospel of the Nazareans* (in *Gos. Naz.* 2) denied that Jesus was baptized at all because of this embarrassment (cf. §3.4, 3.7.3).

But not only is John's baptismal ministry a relatively secure datum, it is also an important one; that is, John's baptism is a central element in his ministry. This may be observed from John's nickname as well as from the fact that his baptism became a subject of controversy in both the life of Jesus and the early church.[4] Furthermore, elements of his baptismal practice and aspects of its function appear distinctive in comparison with immersions as practised commonly within Palestinian Judaism of his day—distinctive, though not so unique that it is incomprehensible in a Jewish context. This, of course, we explore further in this chapter, but it is the importance and distinctiveness of John's baptism which make it worthy of careful examination.

Where we must tread more carefully is with respect to the descriptions of John's baptism provided by our sources, particularly descriptions of its significance. The reason is that we have no source coming *directly* from John himself or one of his followers. Both Josephus and the NT provide explanations of John's baptism, supposedly explaining its significance from John's point of view. But neither Josephus nor the NT pro-

Evangelist's purpose of stressing the subservient role of John as the one who bears witness to Jesus. Cf. Wink, *John the Baptist*, 89-90.

Hollenbach ('Social Aspects', 851 n. 1) suggests that the participial form of the nickname 'the baptizer' (ὁ βαπτίζων; cf. Mk 1.4; 6.14, 24) stresses John's activity and so is a functional description. Thus, it is probably earlier than the more formal, substantival form 'the Baptist' (ὁ βαπτιστής; e.g. Mt. 16.14 = Mk 8.28 = Lk. 9.19). This is a reasonable conjecture, but there is nothing to prevent an early development of the substantival form, and its use as early as the ministry of John himself.

3   Cf. with John's disciples: Lk. 7.19-20; Acts 18.24; 19.3; with Jesus' disciples: Mt. 16.14 = Mk 8.28 = Lk. 9.19; Mt. 17.13; Acts 1.22; 10.37; 19.4; the common people: Mt. 11.7, 11-12; (cf. = Lk. 7.24, 28); the temple leaders: Mt. 21.25 = Mk 11.30 = Lk. 20.4; tax-collectors: Lk. 7.29; Herod Antipas: Mt. 14.1-2 = Mk 6.14 (cf. = Lk. 9.7). Josephus uses the same title in *Ant.* 18.116.

4   Cf. Mt. 21.23-27 = Mk 11.27-33 = Lk. 20.1-8; Acts 18.24-26; 19.1-7.

vide a biographical account of John for his own sake; rather, they are utilizing a selective description of John for their own purposes. So, when examining our sources, we must take into account their agendas which may have shaped the accounts of John's baptism and its significance. This becomes particularly important when we observe that our sources describe the significance of John's baptism in different ways. This difference is most clearly observed when Josephus' statement that John's baptism was '*not* for seeking pardon of certain sins' (*Ant.* 18.117) is compared with Mark's statement that the baptism *was* 'for the forgiveness of sins' (Mk 1.4 = Lk. 3.3). Therefore we must examine more closely the statements in our sources concerning John's baptism.

### 6.2.1 Ant. *18.117*

Josephus describes John's baptismal ministry in *Ant.* 18.117 as follows:

> κτείνει γὰρ δὴ τοῦτον Ἡρώδης ἀγαθὸν ἄνδρα καὶ τοῖς Ἰουδαίοις κελεύοντα ἀρετὴν ἐπασκοῦσιν καὶ τὰ πρὸς ἀλλήλους δικαιοσύνῃ καὶ πρὸς τὸν θεὸν εὐσεβείᾳ χρωμένοις βαπτισμῷ συνιέναι· οὕτω γὰρ δὴ καὶ τὴν βάπτισιν ἀποδεκτὴν αὐτῷ φανεῖσθαι μὴ ἐπί τινων ἁμαρτάδων παραιτήσει χρωμένων, ἀλλ' ἐφ' ἁγνείᾳ τοῦ σώματος, ἅτε δὴ καὶ τῆς ψυχῆς δικαιοσύνῃ προεκκεκαθαρμένης.

> For Herod indeed put him to death, who was a good man and one who commanded the Jews to practise virtue and act with justice toward one another and with piety toward God, and [so] to gather together by baptism. For [John's view was that] in this way baptism certainly would appear acceptable to him [i.e. God] if [they] used [it] not for seeking pardon of certain sins but for purification of the body, because the soul had already been cleansed before by righteousness.

Josephus briefly describes John's ethical proclamation and its relationship to baptism. Baptism was part of the message John proclaimed and was closely related to his ethical demand.[5] Having introduced baptism, Josephus then expands upon its significance. He states that the baptism must be used correctly; that is, 'not for seeking pardon of certain sins but for purification of the body'. The reason for making this distinction is *not* because pardon for sin was unimportant or unrelated to John's ministry; rather, he explains that pardon was accomplished another way: 'by righteousness'. The righteousness which accomplishes this pardon is defined in the context by John's ethical proclamation. In other words, responding to John's call to a righteous lifestyle results in pardon for sins, while the baptism itself functions to purify the body. A correct understanding of the baptism is important, because only if it is used correctly will the baptism 'appear acceptable to him [i.e. God]'.[6]

---

5    Cf. §6.4.1, 6.4.2, 6.4.3 for further discussion of this text.

6    It is syntactically possible that αὐτῷ could refer to John rather than God. However, τὸν θεόν is the closer antecedent. As well, the concern here is for pardon for sins as

The question which arises at this point is whether this explanation of the significance of John's baptism should be accepted as an explanation from John's point of view (as Josephus indicates[7]) or actually as an explanation from Josephus' point of view. Final judgment on this matter cannot be made until we compare this account with the evidence of the NT, but several preliminary observations may be made concerning Josephus' text itself.

We observed above that Josephus' description of John's ethical proclamation had been Hellenized in order for it to be understood by his Gentile, Roman audience (cf. §2.2). It is possible that a similar transformation has taken place with respect to his description of John's baptism. For example, the reference to the baptism being 'acceptable to him [i.e. God]' (ἀποδεκτὴν αὐτῷ) appears at first glance to be unusual terminology. However, this is precisely the terminology used in the OT for the correct observance of procedure in the temple and the sacrificial system, and of a sacrificial animal being 'accepted by the Lord'.[8] Furthermore, this is the only place Josephus uses this compound adjective, and he never uses the simple form, which suggests that this term and concept is actually consistent with Judaism and is not part of Josephus' Hellenized description of Jews and Judaism evidenced elsewhere in his literature. The noun παραίτησις, meaning 'supplication, entreaty, intercession' or with ἁμαρτ- words 'pardon'[9] or better 'seeking pardon' is unusual in this context of seeking pardon from God.[10] Though the term may be unusual, the desire for, and granting of, forgiveness is certainly a Jewish concept. Similarly, the terms and concepts of sin, purification, cleansing and righteousness are certainly Jewish as well. Furthermore, Josephus' use of the verb βαπτίζω to identify John's baptism is highly unusual, for this term and its cognates were often associated in a Hellenistic context with death and destruction, usually being employed to describe the sinking of a ship or a flood, but they were not used to describe an immersion ritual.[11] Yet the term is Jewish, and was used in the LXX to signify just such an immersion (e.g. 2 Kgs 5.14; Jdt. 12.7). It might almost be argued

---

well as purifying the body, which suggests that acceptance to God has more relevance and significance in this context that acceptance to John.

7    The infinitive construction with φανεῖσθαι continues the idea of indirect discourse from κελεύοντα.

8    Josephus uses the compound adjective ἀποδεκτός, meaning 'acceptable', while the LXX uses the simple form of the adjective, δεκτός. There is no significant difference in their meanings, and the use of δεκτός in the LXX is the same as Josephus' use of ἀποδεκτός here; cf. Exod. 28.34; Lev. 1.3, 4; 19.5, etc.

9    LSJ, 1311.

10   The noun παραίτησις is not used in the LXX, but the related verb, παραιτέομαι, is used a few times, though primarily of entreating a king; e.g. 1 Sam. 20.6; Est. 4.8; 7.7.

11   LSJ, 305-306; Ysebaert, *Greek Baptismal Terminology*, 12-19.

that this is evidence of Christian interpolation or at least of a Christian source. However, Josephus' use of the derived nouns βάπτισις and βαπτισμός are not particularly Christian. The noun βάπτισις is not used in the NT or other early Christian literature, and βαπτισμός is not the normal term used in the NT for either John's baptism or Christian baptism (cf. §2.3). And this unusual sense of the verb βαπτίζω to indicate an immersion is a Jewish usage, evidenced prior to the Christian utilization of the term. These observations are certainly not evidence of Josephus Hellenizing Jewish concepts for a Gentile audience. Perhaps the only evidence of Hellenizing is the separation of the soul and body, for in Josephus' explanation baptism purifies *the body*, but righteousness cleanses *the soul*. While in Jewish thought the body and soul were distinguished, it is unlikely that in Palestinian Jewish thought (John's context) they would be separated in the way Josephus has done.[12] In our examination of OT and Second Temple Jewish literature, ablutions cleansed *the person*. The separation between body and soul which Josephus makes suggests that in this instance he is adapting his explanation to a Hellenistic, Gentile audience.[13]

This examination of the concepts and terminology indicates that in most respects Josephus has not Hellenized his discussion of John's baptism, except for making a body–soul dichotomy in explaining forgiveness and purification—a dichotomy quite understandable in his Hellenistic world. In fact, his use of βαπτίζ- terminology indicates that he is retaining distinctive Jewish thought forms. Thus far, we may conclude that Josephus' account of the significance of John's baptism is thoroughly Jewish (apart from the body–soul dichotomy) and therefore probably reliable.

The next question which naturally arises concerns the source for

---

12  With respect to OT thought concerning cultic acts, Eichrodt (*Theology*, 1.100; cf. 2.147-50) states: 'Because the physical and spiritual sides of human life have not as yet been violently dissociated, but man is still taken seriously in his totality as a psychosomatic being, his sensory life also plays its part in this relationship with God. In the outward actions of the cult the power of divine blessing is communicated to the actual mode of man's existence.' Similarly, Beasley-Murray (*Baptism*, 7, his emphasis) states that 'the Jew maintained a sense of the unity of being which is not native to us. . . The remarkable feature of this is not that the Jew or later Judaism *could* not distinguish between outer and inner but that he *would* not separate them when he did understand the distinction.'

13  Cf. §6.4.3. Josephus probably introduced this dichotomy between body and soul which separated the forgiveness of sins from John's baptism in order to distinguish John's 'Jewish' baptism (which he presents in a positive light) from other immersion practices which may have been known to his Gentile audience. He may be attempting to distinguish John's baptism from Christian claims concerning their baptism (cf. Scobie, *John the Baptist*, 111), or from the claims made concerning the immersion practices of the mystery religions (cf. Kraeling, *John the Baptist*, 121).

Josephus' description. We have argued that the text is not a Christian interpolation, and the same arguments indicate that Josephus' source is not a Christian one either. We do know that Josephus had direct knowledge of the immersion practices of both Bannus and the Essenes.[14] In both cases, his description of their significance identified only their purificatory nature, and in neither case did he mention forgiveness of sins anywhere in the context as he does here with John's baptism.[15] In contrast, Josephus' knowledge of John's baptism could only come second hand, for he was born in 37 or 38 CE (*Life* 5), several years after John had died, and it was not until he was 16 years old that his interest in the Jewish sects manifested itself (53–54 CE; *Life* 9), some 20 years after John's death. Yet, according to his own statement (*Ant.* 18.116) John the Baptist was a well-known figure, whose memory lingered in Jewish circles. So, while Josephus would not have had first-hand knowledge, he evidently had access to popular Jewish traditions concerning him. If John was as popular as both Josephus and the NT indicate, it is quite plausible that Josephus would have met people who heard John and had even been baptized by him.

In light of this discussion, Josephus' description of John's baptism should be accepted as a reliable historical source, apart from those elements which bear evidence of being Hellenized.

### 6.2.2  *Mt. 3.1-6 = Mk 1.2-6 = Lk. 3.2b-6*

References to John's baptism are scattered throughout the Gospels and Acts, but the NT evidence concerning the significance of that baptism is encapsulated in three pericopae.[16] The first and most extensive description may be set forth as follows:

| Matthew 3 | Mark 1 | Luke 3 |
|---|---|---|
| (cf. v. 3) | 2-3(Quotation Mal. 3.1; Isa. 40.3) | (cf. vv. 4-6) |
| 1Ἐν δὲ ταῖς ἡμέραις ἐκείναις παραγίνεται Ἰωάννης ὁ βαπτιστὴς κηρύσσων ἐν τῇ ἐρήμῳ τῆς Ἰουδαίας 2[καὶ] λέγων, Μετανοεῖτε, ἤγγικεν γὰρ ἡ βασιλεία τῶν οὐρανῶν. | 4aἐγένετο Ἰωάννης [ὁ] βαπτίζων ἐν τῇ ἐρήμῳ 4bκαὶ κηρύσσων βάπτισμα μετανοίας εἰς ἄφεσιν ἁμαρτιῶν. | 2bἐγένετο ῥῆμα θεοῦ ἐπὶ Ἰωάννην τὸν Ζαχαρίου υἱὸν ἐν τῇ ἐρήμῳ. 3aκαὶ ἦλθεν εἰς πᾶσαν [τὴν] περίχωρον τοῦ Ἰορδάνου 3bκηρύσσων βάπτισμα μετανοίας εἰς ἄφεσιν ἁμαρτιῶν, |

14  *Life* 9-12; cf. §4.3.2, 4.3.3.
15  This is in distinction to the interpretation given to immersions in 1QS 3–5 by the Qumran community; cf. §5.3.
16  These three pericopae are Mt. 3.1-6 = Mk 1.2-6 = Lk. 3.2b-6; Mt. 3.7-10 = Lk. 3.7-9, and Mt. 3.11-12 = Mk 1.7-8 = Lk. 3.15-18. The significance of John's baptism is also described in the fourth Gospel (e.g. Jn 1.25-27, 33), but it adds little to what may be gleaned from the synoptic Gospels; cf. §3.6, 3.8.

| | | |
|---|---|---|
| ³(Quote Isa. 40.3) | (cf. vv. 2-3) | ⁴⁻⁶(Quote Isa. 40.3-5) |
| ⁴(John's dress, food) | (cf. v. 6) | |
| ⁵τότε ἐξεπορεύετο πρὸς | ⁵ᵃκαὶ ἐξεπορεύετο πρὸς | |
| αὐτὸν Ἱεροσόλυμα καὶ | αὐτὸν πᾶσα ἡ Ἰουδαία | |
| πᾶσα ἡ Ἰουδαία καὶ πᾶσα ἡ | χώρα καὶ οἱ Ἱεροσολυμῖται | |
| περίχωρος τοῦ Ἰορδάνου, | πάντες, | |
| ⁶καὶ ἐβαπτίζοντο ἐν τῷ | ⁵ᵇκαὶ ἐβαπτίζοντο ὑπ' | |
| Ἰορδάνῃ ποταμῷ ὑπ' | αὐτοῦ ἐν τῷ Ἰορδάνῃ | |
| αὐτοῦ ἐξομολογούμενοι | ποταμῷ ἐξομολογούμενοι | |
| τὰς ἁμαρτίας αὐτῶν. | τὰς ἁμαρτίας αὐτῶν. | |
| (cf. v. 4) | ⁶(John's dress, food) | |
| | | |
| (cf. v. 3) | ²⁻³(Quotation of Mal. 3.1; | (cf. vv. 4-6) |
| | Isa. 40.3) | |
| ¹Now in those days John the | ⁴ᵃJohn the baptizer | ²ᵇthe word of God came to |
| baptist came preaching in | appeared in the wilderness, | John the son of Zechariah |
| the wilderness of Judea | | in the wilderness; ³ᵃand he |
| | | went into all the region |
| | | around the Jordan, |
| ²saying, 'Repent, for the | ⁴ᵇpreaching a baptism of | ³ᵇpreaching a baptism of |
| kingdom of heaven is at | repentance for the for- | repentance for the for- |
| hand'. | giveness of sins. | giveness of sins. |
| ³(Quote Isa. 40.3) | (cf. vv. 2-3) | ⁴⁻⁶(Quote Isa. 40.3-5) |
| ⁴(John's dress, food) | (cf. v. 6) | |
| ⁵Then Jerusalem and all | ⁵ᵃAnd all the country of | |
| Judea and all the region | Judea and all the people of | |
| around the Jordan went out | Jerusalem went out to him, | |
| to him, | | |
| ⁶and they were being bap- | ⁵ᵇand they were being bap- | |
| tized in the Jordan river by | tized by him in the Jordan | |
| him, confessing their sins. | river, confessing their sins. | |
| (cf. v. 4) | ⁶(John's dress, food) | |

Utilizing the hypothesis of Markan priority (cf. §3.1), a comparison of these three accounts indicates that in reality we have one source, Mark, which has been utilized in Matthew and Luke.[17] Lk. 3.3b reproduces verbatim Mk 1.4b, that John was 'preaching a baptism of repentance for the forgiveness of sins' (κηρύσσων βάπτισμα μετανοίας εἰς ἄφεσιν ἁμαρτιῶν). Lk. 3.2b is the product of Lukan redaction and introduces John as a prophet in the style of OT prophecy. On the other hand, Mt. 3.2 does not reproduce Mk 1.4b, replacing it with a statement of John's preaching without mentioning baptism: 'Repent, for the kingdom of heaven is at hand' (Μετανοεῖτε, ἤγγικεν γὰρ ἡ βασιλεία τῶν οὐραν-

---

17  In this pericope there are two agreements between Matthew and Luke against Mark. Both Matthew and Luke excise the citation of Mal. 3.1 in Mk 1.2-3 and place the remaining quote of Isa. 40.3 after the description of John's preaching. They both use the phrase 'all the region around the Jordan', but in different contexts (Mt. 3.5b; Lk. 3.3a). This suggests that a similar pericope might have existed in Q. For arguments pro and con see Kloppenborg, *Q Parallels*, 6. But such a possibility does not assist us here.

ὧν). While it is theoretically possible that Matthew has another source for this statement concerning John's preaching, the use of the Mattheanism 'kingdom of heaven' and the parallel between this account of John's preaching and that of Jesus (Mt. 4.17) indicate that this is probably Matthean redaction.[18]  Mt. 3.5 expands Mk 1.5a to include an additional geographical region, but the sense is not significantly different. Mt. 3.6 reproduces Mk 1.5b exactly apart from a minor alteration of word order.  Therefore Mk 1.4-5 is the source for the synoptic Gospels' account of John's baptism, and it is primarily this source that we subject to further analysis (cf. §3.3, 3.4, 3.5).

In Mk 1.4-5 there are three elements which contribute to the NT's presentation of the significance of John's baptism: (1) John was preaching and baptizing in the wilderness along the Jordan; (2) John's baptism was a baptism of repentance for the forgiveness of sins; and (3) the people were baptized by John in the Jordan river confessing their sins. Each of these must be examined in turn.

The first aspect, that John preached and baptized in the wilderness along the Jordan, is somewhat problematic because each Evangelist explains John's wilderness/Jordan ministry slightly differently (this issue was not mentioned above when arguing that Mk 1.4-5 was the primary source), which led Willi Marxsen to question the authenticity of the wilderness tradition.[19]  However, as we will conclude below (§10.5), his arguments prove inadequate; that John's baptismal ministry was located in the wilderness along the Jordan river may be accepted as historically reliable data.

The second element in the NT's presentation of John's baptism explains its significance.  Mk 1.4b (= Lk. 3.3) states that John was 'preaching a baptism of repentance for the forgiveness of sins' (κηρύσσων βάπτισμα μετανοίας εἰς ἄφεσιν ἁμαρτιῶν).  Is this a Christian formulation, or may it reasonably be accepted as representing John's explanation of his baptism?  Such a question is difficult to answer simply, because repentance and forgiveness are ideas current in both Judaism

---

18  Matthew's rejection of this description of John's baptism has a corresponding Matthean emphasis elsewhere that it is through Jesus that sins are forgiven; cf. 1.21; 26.28.  Cf. Davies and Allison, *Matthew*, 1.389-92.  Cf. §3.4 on the parallelism between John and Jesus in Matthew's Gospel.

 Two qualifications must be placed upon this conclusion. First of all, I am not saying John *could not* have spoken of 'the kingdom of God/heaven' with his disciples. He could very well have done so, but the evidence of this is too weak because Mt. 3.2 bears strongly the evidence of Matthew's theology and emphases. Secondly, from the point of view of the early Christian movement, John's ministry could legitimately be *interpreted* in light of Jesus' preaching of the kingdom, and thus as a Christian interpretation, Matthew's formulation is illuminating.  Cf. Marsh, *Baptism*, 82-94 who argues John did preach the kingdom of God.

19  Marxsen, *Mark the Evangelist*, 34-38.

and early Christianity. The precise phrase εἰς ἄφεσιν ἁμαρτιῶν ('for the forgiveness of sins') is rather abstract in nature, and in Mark it is only used to explain John's baptism, whereas in Matthew it is only found in the words Jesus used to institute the Lord's supper (Mt. 26.28). Other, more concrete, statements are made about Jesus who is able 'to forgive sins' (ἀφιέναι ἁμαρτίας; Mt. 9.6 = Mk 2.10 = Lk. 5.24). In contrast, the precise phrase εἰς ἄφεσιν ἁμαρτιῶν is a Lukan emphasis, and is also linked several times with repentance.[20] Furthermore, in his speech in Acts 2.38, Peter exhorts the people: 'Repent, and let each of you be baptized in the name of Jesus Christ for the forgiveness of your sins, and you shall receive the gift of the Holy Spirit'. In this explicitly Christian context, repentance and forgiveness of sins are linked with Christian baptism. In light of this Lukan emphasis and special terminology it would be possible to conclude that the formula 'a baptism of repentance for the forgiveness of sins' is an early Christian formulation attributed to John the Baptist or a Christian explanation of John's baptism.

However, other evidence mitigates this skeptical conclusion. First of all, if we were dependent upon Luke alone for this formulation of the significance of John's baptism, then, in light of his theological interest, we would be led to draw that conclusion. But this clause is also attested to in Luke's source for Lk. 3.3, that is, Mk 1.4, and Mark betrays no special interest in the phrase or its terminology.

Secondly, the phrase εἰς ἄφεσιν ἁμαρτιῶν in the other Lukan contexts is consistently given a specifically Christian orientation by being joined to christological phrases such as 'in the name of Jesus Christ' (Lk. 24.27; Acts 2.38; 10.43), or 'believes in him' (Acts 10.43), or 'through him' (Acts 13.38).[21] This Christian orientation is a fundamental shift from the significance of John's baptism. For John it was 'a *baptism* of repentance for the forgiveness of sins', whereas the Christian emphasis is *faith in Jesus Christ* with repentance which leads to forgiveness. In Acts 2.38, the phrase εἰς ἄφεσιν ἁμαρτιῶν is used in the context of baptism, but even here the Christian orientation is evident in the clause 'be baptized in the name of Jesus Christ'. Thus, Luke is careful to distinguish not only between John's use of the phrase 'repentance for the forgiveness of sins' and Christian usage, but also between the conditions and significance of John's baptism and Christian baptism.[22] Since in his account of

---

20  The phrase is not only used parallel to Mk 1.4 = Lk. 3.3, but also in special Lukan material within the Gospel (Lk. 1.77; 24.47) as well as in Acts (2.38; 5.31; 10.43; 13.38; 26.18). As in Mk 1.4 = Lk. 3.3, it is also linked with repentance in Lk. 24.27; Acts 2.38; 5.31. It is only found once elsewhere in the NT (Col. 1.14; cf. Eph. 1.7).

21  Cf. also Acts 5.31; 26.18.

22  Other texts in which Luke distinguishes John's baptism from the Christian interpretation of baptism include Acts 1.5; 11.16; 18.25-26; 19.3-5.

early Christianity Luke is so careful to make these distinctions, it is unlikely that theological concepts which were so important in the early church would have been anachronistically used to describe John's baptism.

Finally, it is highly unlikely that the early Christians would willingly attribute forgiveness to any means other than faith in Jesus Christ. To do so would have gone against the exclusive claims for their Lord.[23]  In fact, it is somewhat surprising that the synoptic Gospels retained such a (from their point of view, almost heretical) description of John's baptism. Hartwig Thyen concludes with respect to this phrase in Mk 1.4:

> Because of the tendency, shared by Mark with the entire Christian tradition, to make John the forerunner of Jesus and because of the story of the healing of the paralytic which reaches its high point in the question τίς δύναται ἀφιέναι ἁμαρτίας εἰ μὴ εἷς ὁ θεός; . . . we must assume that the expression βάπτισμα μετανοίας εἰς ἄφεσιν ἁμαρτιῶν was so fixed a designation for John's baptism that it could hardly be suppressed.[24]

Therefore, we may conclude that the NT description of John's baptism as 'a baptism of repentance for the forgiveness of sins' probably reflects the significance of John's baptism as John proclaimed it, rather than reflecting a Christian interpretation.

The final element in Mk 1.4-5 concerns the popular response of the people of Judea and Jerusalem, and a statement concerning John's baptismal practice.  There is no reason to doubt that John became known throughout Judea, and that many came to participate in his baptism or at least observe out of curiosity.  But the hyperbolic *'all . . . went out to him'* (Mk 1.5a = Mt. 3.5) is intended to stress John's popularity with the people.[25]  Mk 1.5b (= Mt. 3.6) describes John's baptismal practice: 'they were being baptized by him in the Jordan river, confessing their sins' (καὶ ἐβαπτίζοντο ὑπ' αὐτοῦ ἐν τῷ Ἰορδάνῃ ποταμῷ ἐξομολογούμενοι τὰς ἁμαρτίας αὐτῶν).  In light of the preceding conclusion that John's baptism as 'a baptism of repentance for the forgiveness of sins' is a historically reliable tradition, this description is consistent and plausible. It is unlikely that the confession of sins while being baptized is a Christian creation.  It adds nothing to the Christian interpretation of John and contributes to the theological problems associated with Jesus having received this baptism.

Mk 1.4-5 is included in the introduction to Mark's Gospel because it

23  Cf. Mt. 9.1-8 = Mk 2.1-12 = Lk. 5.17-26; Acts 4.12.
24  Thyen, 'ΒΑΠΤΙΣΜΑ', 132 n. 4; cf. 138.
25  This hyperbole concerning Jesus' forerunner prepares the reader for the initial popularity of Jesus. Brower ('Elijah', 87-88, his emphasis) suggests that *'all* came to be baptized because the Baptist is to fulfil Elijah's role as the restorer of *all* things'; cf. Mk 9.8-9. Davies and Allison, *Matthew*, 1.297-98; Guelich, *Mark*, 1.20.

explains the baptismal ministry of Jesus' forerunner and provides the context for Jesus being baptized. Its inclusion by Mark and its framework (esp. vv. 1-3, 9-11) demonstrate that this narrative has been selected by Mark to suit his theological purposes (cf. §3.3), but the data concerning John and his baptism may be accepted as historically reliable tradition.

### 6.2.3 *Mt. 3.7-10 = Lk. 3.7-9*

The second NT pericope which is relevant for appreciating John's baptism is this summary of John's preaching of repentance:

| Matthew 3 | Luke 3 |
|---|---|
| 7a Ἰδὼν δὲ πολλοὺς τῶν Φαρισαίων καὶ Σαδδουκαίων ἐρχομένους ἐπὶ τὸ βάπτισμα αὐτοῦ εἶπεν αὐτοῖς, | 7a Ἔλεγεν οὖν τοῖς ἐκπορευομένοις ὄχλοις βαπτισθῆναι ὑπ' αὐτοῦ, |
| 7b Γεννήματα ἐχιδνῶν, τίς ὑπέδειξεν ὑμῖν φυγεῖν ἀπὸ τῆς μελλούσης ὀργῆς; 8 ποιήσατε οὖν καρπὸν ἄξιον τῆς μετανοίας· | 7b Γεννήματα ἐχιδνῶν, τίς ὑπέδειξεν ὑμῖν φυγεῖν ἀπὸ τῆς μελλούσης ὀργῆς; 8a ποιήσατε οὖν καρποὺς ἀξίους τῆς μετανοίας· |
| 9 καὶ μὴ δόξητε λέγειν ἐν ἑαυτοῖς, Πατέρα ἔχομεν τὸν Ἀβραάμ, λέγω γὰρ ὑμῖν ὅτι δύναται ὁ θεὸς ἐκ τῶν λίθων τούτων ἐγεῖραι τέκνα τῷ Ἀβραάμ. | 8b καὶ μὴ ἄρξησθε λέγειν ἐν ἑαυτοῖς, Πατέρα ἔχομεν τὸν Ἀβραάμ, λέγω γὰρ ὑμῖν ὅτι δύναται ὁ θεὸς ἐκ τῶν λίθων τούτων ἐγεῖραι τέκνα τῷ Ἀβραάμ. |
| 10 ἤδη δὲ ἡ ἀξίνη πρὸς τὴν ῥίζαν τῶν δένδρων κεῖται· πᾶν οὖν δένδρον μὴ ποιοῦν καρπὸν καλὸν ἐκκόπτεται καὶ εἰς πῦρ βάλλεται. | 9 ἤδη δὲ καὶ ἡ ἀξίνη πρὸς τὴν ῥίζαν τῶν δένδρων κεῖται· πᾶν οὖν δένδρον μὴ ποιοῦν καρπὸν καλὸν ἐκκόπτεται καὶ εἰς πῦρ βάλλεται. |
| 7a But seeing many of the Pharisees and Sadducees coming to his baptism he said to them, | 7a He said therefore to the crowds going out to be baptized by him, |
| 7b 'You brood of vipers! Who warned you to flee from the wrath to come? | 7b 'You brood of vipers! Who warned you to flee from the wrath to come? |
| 8 Therefore, bear fruit in keeping with repentance, | 8a Therefore, bear fruits in keeping with repentance, |
| 9 and do not presume to say to yourselves, "We have Abraham as our father"; for I say to you that God is able from these stones to raise up children to Abraham. | 8b and do not begin to say to yourselves, "We have Abraham as our father"; for I say to you that God is able from these stones to raise up children to Abraham. |
| 10 And the axe is already laid at the root of the trees; every tree therefore that does not bear good fruit is cut down and thrown into the fire.' | 9 And also, the axe is already laid at the root of the trees; every tree therefore that does not bear good fruit is cut down and thrown into the fire.' |

Of the 63 (Matthew) or 64 (Luke) words in this citation of John's preaching 60 words are identical.[26] Thus, for the preaching itself Matthew and

---

26  Matthew has the singular καρπὸν ἄξιον ('fruit in keeping with'), while Luke's version is the plural καρποὺς ἀξίους ('fruits in keeping with'). In Matthew John tells his audience μὴ δόξητε λέγειν ('do not *presume* to say'), while in Luke it is μὴ ἄρξησθε λέγειν ('do not *begin* to say'). Finally, in Luke's account the conjunctions beginning

Luke clearly have a common source in Q for this material. The minor distinctions do not significantly alter the sense of the statements, but in terms of style, the original form of Q is generally considered to be represented more closely by Matthew, which I therefore follow.[27]

Rudolf Bultmann understands these sayings to be a Christian compilation because of a 'desire to have some record of his preaching of repentance', and so he concludes that 'we must reckon it as quite accidental that Jesus is not said to have uttered these warnings'.[28] However, Bultmann provides no evidence to substantiate these claims, and neither of them appears historically plausible. Why should the early church create a call to repentance and place it in John's mouth when their concern was Jesus' call to repentance, and salvation by faith in him?[29] There is nothing distinctively Christian in this pericope. The imagery and ideology expressed here fit well within certain strands of Second Temple Jewish thought as well as with what is known elsewhere of John's preaching of judgment and repentance. The content of John's call to repentance in this pericope may be regarded as authentic tradition concerning John—a verdict supported by most scholars.[30]

It is been observed that Q 3.8b, with its use of Abraham and stone imagery, interrupts the flow of thought from Q 3.7b-8a to Q 3.9 with its emphasis upon judgment and fruit-bearing, and, thus, two or more sayings of John have probably been combined.[31] John would most probably have used this imagery repeatedly in statements such as these, and thus this is probably a summary of a couple of his more memorable sayings. However, whether this is a single saying or a combination of sayings does not alter materially the sense of the pericope because it does not present one sustained logical argument, but a series of discrete state-

---

v. 9 are δὲ καί ('and also'), while Matthew (v. 10) has only δέ ('and').

27   E.g. Fitzmyer, *Luke*, 1.465, 468; cf. literature and discussion by Marshall, *Luke*, 140.

28   Bultmann, *Synoptic Tradition*, 117; cf. Thyen, 'ΒΑΠΤΙΣΜΑ', 137 n. 26.

29   Wink (*John the Baptist*, 19 n. 1) disagrees with Bultmann's judgment by observing that 'the church is not likely to have suggested . . . that simple repentance would suffice for salvation apart from faith in Jesus as the Christ'.

30   E.g. Davies and Allison, *Matthew*, 1.301; Marshall, *Luke*, 137-38; Nolland, *Luke*, 1.147; Beare, *Matthew*, 93; Hill, *Matthew*, 92-93; Becker, *Johannes der Täufer*, 16 n. 21; Goppelt, *Theology*, 1.33. Schulz (*Q*, 371-72) argues this text is a Hellenistic Jewish Christian contribution to Q, and Schürmann (*Lukasevangelium*, 1.181-83) finds elements of a pre-Christian baptismal instruction in the pericope. However, Marshall (*Luke*, 138) points out that we must distinguish between the source of the tradition and how it might later have been used in communities which preserved those traditions. Black (*Aramaic Approach*, 144-45) observes Semiticisms in the pericope, which, while not proving authenticity, suggests a Palestinian milieu.

31   Davies and Allison, *Matthew*, 1.307; Beare, *Matthew*, 93; Marshall, *Luke*, 137-40. The combination of sayings may be indicated by the seemingly extraneous conjunctions introducing Mt. 3.10 = Lk. 3.9: δέ in Matthew and δὲ καί in Luke.

ments complete in themselves, though of course they do shed light on each other.

The major difference between Matthew and Luke in this pericope is their respective introductory statements. Matthew identifies the audience which John addresses as 'the Pharisees and Sadducees' and states that they were 'coming to his baptism' (ἐρχομένους ἐπὶ τὸ βάπτισμα αὐτοῦ) to observe it critically.[32] On the other hand, Luke identifies the audience as 'the crowds' who were actually 'going out to be baptized by him' (τοῖς ἐκπορευομένοις ὄχλοις βαπτισθῆναι ὑπ' αὐτοῦ).

Matthew's 'Pharisees and Sadducees' may be due to Matthean redaction, because in a number of passages he shows a heightened interest in the Pharisees.[33] Also, Matthew adds Sadducees in 16.1-12 where his source (Mk 8.11-21) only mentions Pharisees. The addition makes John's opponents here in Mt. 3.7-10 parallel the opposition faced later by Jesus.[34] This evidence may be taken to suggest that Matthew's intro-

---

32  It is possible that Matthew's phrase may be interpreted as indicating essentially the same thing (e.g. the *RSV* and *NRSV* translates Matthew 'coming for baptism' and Luke 'came out to be baptized'). But this is unlikely. Matthew should be translated 'coming to his baptism', indicating they came to where John was baptizing or were coming to observe John performing his baptism, but not necessarily to be baptized themselves. The first clue is the pronoun αὐτοῦ, which, while missing in some texts, is most probably authentic. Metzger (*Textual Commentary*, 9) observes that αὐτοῦ would be easily dropped from the text as inappropriate or unnecessary. This would be true especially if harmonization with Luke was taking place, so that Matthew's phrase would mean 'for baptism'. As a possessive pronoun, αὐτοῦ indicates the baptism is identified with John, and may more subtly suggest that the Pharisees and Sadducees did not wish to be identified with the baptism. The preposition ἐπί with the accusative more commonly indicates movement 'to' somewhere rather than purpose or reason (i.e. 'for'; even 'against' is possible here); cf. BAGD, 288-89; Davies and Allison, *Matthew*, 1.304. This use makes perfect sense here. Furthermore, Matthew's view of the Pharisees would hardly allow him to portray 'many' of them showing repentance by submitting to John's baptism. Therefore, Matthew is probably portraying the Pharisees and Sadducees as coming to observe critically John's baptism. Cf. Hill, *Matthew*, 92; Gundry, *Matthew*, 46; Davies and Allison, 1.303-304.
33  In Matthew, the Pharisees are present in pericopae where other identifications are given to the persons in the parallel passages, or the emphasis on Pharisees is heightened: Mt. 9.34 = Mt. 12.24 = Mk 3.22 = Lk. 11.15; Mt. 21.45 = Lk. 20.19; Mt. 23.13 = Lk. 11.52; Mt. 23.14 = Mk 12.38, 40 = Lk. 20.46, 47; Mt. 23.26 = Lk. 20.40; Mt. 23.27 = Lk. 20.44; Mt. 23.29 = Lk. 20.47. Also, the Pharisees are present in material unique to Matthew, both in redactional comments as well as traditional material: Mt. 5.20; 15.12; 22.41; 23.2, 15; 27.62.
34  Matthew has added Sadducees in 16.1 as well as vv. 6, 11, 12, but these form part of the same pericope. Therefore, in reality, Matthew had added Sadducees to a reference to Pharisees in his source only once. On the parallel between John and Jesus in Matthew, see §3.4.
    In Mt. 22.34 Sadducees are mentioned with Pharisees, but they are not linked together, and Matthew is only summarizing the preceding narrative, which mentioned both Sadducees and Pharisees (in Matthew as well as his source, Mk 12.13-27). The only other place in the NT in which they are mentioned together is Acts 23.6-8, but in this context they are in conflict with each other.

ductory phrase is the product of his redactional emphasis, and Luke's identification of a general audience is more authentic.[35]

But other evidence indicates that this conclusion is somewhat premature. Luke, who identifies the audience generally as τοῖς . . . ὄχλοις, employs the term ὄχλος frequently in contexts in which it is absent in the parallel accounts in the other Gospels,[36] as well as in pericopae found only in Luke.[37] In many of these contexts it is evident in the source that a large group of some form is actually present. Luke highlights this feature by introducing the term itself, which he may have done in this context as well to emphasize the popular response to John.[38] Therefore, both Matthew and Luke's identification of the audience manifests their own particular redactional tendencies.

Turning to the sayings in Q 3.7b-9 themselves may assist in this dilemma. The address 'you brood of vipers!' fits Matthew's audience better than Luke's. First of all, Jesus uses the same term of Pharisees once and of scribes and Pharisees in another context, and in both passages he is describing them in opposition to his ministry (but only in Matthew: 12.34; 23.33). Secondly, the address itself more adequately describes those in opposition rather than those who gather for baptism.[39] If the audience was the crowds coming for baptism, but they were misunderstanding John's message and baptism (if Q3.7b-9 is read as referring to them), then this address appears unduly harsh.[40]

---

35   This is the opinion of most scholars; cf. Davies and Allison, *Matthew*, 1.303-304; Luz, *Matthew*, 1.170; Hill, *Matthew*, 92; Gundry, *Matthew*, 46; Marshall, *Luke*, 139; Nolland, *Luke*, 1.146-48; Schulz, *Q*, 366-67. Fuchs ('Intention', 62-75) argues that it is implausible that Sadducees and Pharisees united in opposition to John. But Matthew only states both were present, not that they were working in concert. Kazmierski ('Stones of Abraham', 27-29) follows Fuchs (63-65) in rejecting the audiences identified by both Matthew and Luke.

36   Lk. 3.7 = Mt. 3.7; Lk. 4.42 = Mk 1.36; Lk. 5.3 = Mt. 13.2 = Mk 4.1; Lk. 5.3 = Mt. 13.3 = Mk 4.2; Lk. 5.15 = Mk 1.45; Lk. 5.29 = Mt. 9.10 = Mk 2.15; Lk. 6.19 = Mk 3.10; Lk. 7.9 = Mt. 8.10; Lk. 9.18 = Mt. 16.13 = Mk 8.27; Lk. 12.54 = Mt. 16.2.

37   Lk. 3.10; 5.1; 7.11, 12; 11.27, 29; 12.1, 13; 13.14, 17; 14.25; 19.3, 39; 22.6; 23.4, 48.

38   Lk. 3.6, 10-14, 18, 21. Fitzmyer (*Luke*, 1.467) suggests that Luke is stressing 'the popular, universal reaction to the ministry of both John and Jesus'. Cf. Fuchs, 'Intention', 63-64.

39   Cf. the term 'offspring of asps' (ἔκγονα ἀσπίδων) in the LXX of Isa. 14.29; 30.6 (cf. 59.5) to describe those who oppose Israel. Beare, *Matthew*, 93; Fitzmyer, *Luke*, 1.467.

40   So Fitzmyer, *Luke*, 1.467; Beare, *Matthew*, 93; Hollenbach, 'Social Aspects', 860-61; against, Marshall, *Luke*, 139; Gundry, *Matthew*, 47. I contend that this address is unduly harsh, not simply because it 'feels' too harsh, but because in Lk. 3.10-14, which is the one other pericope in which John addresses questioners who did not fully understand repentance or the implications of John's preaching, no such attitude is expressed. Rather, John addresses their questions with care and sensitivity. This contention in no way alleviates the severity of John's preaching of repentance and coming judgment.

The rhetorical question John asks, 'Who warned you to flee from the wrath to come?' implies that it was certainly not John. If the question was addressed to the Pharisees and Sadducees, then the question is both sarcastic and ironic, for John evidently had not warned them and their critical attitude to John's baptism indicates that they were certainly not fleeing the wrath to come at all. If the question is addressed to crowds who have come to be baptized, then the implication that it was not John who warned them makes the question appear somewhat incongruous, for John certainly did warn people about coming judgment. Commentators who argue that Luke's 'crowds' is authentic resort to reading ideas into the question to remove this incongruity. For example, I. Howard Marshall paraphrases the question: 'Who has shown you how to flee from the wrath to come (merely by being baptised or by feigning conversion)?'[41] But there is no evidence in John's speech or in Luke's identification of the audience that they were feigning conversion or misusing baptism. Similarly, John Nolland suggests that John's ministry was

> initially restricted to wilderness-dwellers, like those in the Qumran community, who were already alert to the need for renewal in the wilderness. John would be surprised and skeptical, at least at first, about this wider impact of his preaching and inclined to treat the response as of dubious sincerity.

But this is only speculative, which Nolland admits by introducing this idea by stating that 'it is tempting to think . . .' this.[42] It is the assumed audience which requires these suggestions, but, as observed above, if addressed to Matthew's audience, John's question both makes sense and requires nothing to be added (or speculated).

The command to 'bear fruit in keeping with repentance' (Q 3.8a) and the description of imminent judgment in Q 3.9 fit either audience equally well and so do not help us here. Q 3.8b, in which John tells his audience 'do not presume to say to yourselves "We have Abraham as our father"; for I say to you that God is able from these stones to raise up children to Abraham', might apply to either audience. But it is a more relevant rebuke to those who are presuming that their Abrahamic descent makes baptism irrelevant for them than to those who are coming and seeking baptism.[43]

Therefore, the statements in Q 3.7b and 3.8b are more appropriate for Matthew's audience than Luke's, whereas Q 3.8a and 3.9 are general in nature and could apply to either audience. It was observed above that v. 8b interrupted the flow of v. 8a and v. 9. If, as we have suggested, vv. 7b,

---

41 Marshall, *Luke*, 139.
42 Nolland, *Luke*, 1.147-48.
43 We could also observe that Jewish leaders might be more likely to make this type of theological argument than the common people.

8b are understood to be directed toward Matthew's audience, then our examination has strengthened that observation. It suggests that vv. 7b, 8b were addressed originally to an audience like that suggested by Mt. 3.7a, and another saying of John's was inserted later which, since it is more general in nature, was probably the type of repentance preaching he normally delivered to his audiences.

Therefore, I would conclude, preliminarily, that Matthew's audience is more authentic than Luke's, at least for Q 3.7b, 8b. However, we must still deal with the major criticism of this position noted earlier: Matthew highlights Pharisees by frequently adding them to his text. This redactional characteristic is probably at work in this case as well, but that does not necessarily mean that he added Sadducees also. It is quite plausible that in Q the original audience for this saying was only Sadducees. Since Matthew shows no particular interest in Sadducees themselves, he probably added Pharisees (which is his particular redactional interest) to this text in order to make John face a united front of opposition from these two groups. Later, in Mt. 16.1-12 (the only other text where these two groups are brought together) Matthew added Sadducees, not because he was interested in them particularly, but because he wished to present Jesus facing the same united front of opposition that John had faced, thus contributing further to his theme of paralleling John and Jesus (cf. §3.4). Luke, on the other hand, generalizes this specific audience to 'crowds' to suit 'his general stress on the popular, universal reaction to the ministry of both John and Jesus'.[44] The sayings in Q 3.7b, 8b would be particularly appropriate (from John's point of view) for the Sadducees. Addressing someone as 'viper' is 'to castigate him as evil in his innermost being'.[45] As those who were the religio-political Jewish leaders in Judea with their power centered in the temple, the Sadducees would be the most appropriate recipients of such a label. John's condemnation of claiming ethnic privilege would fit the Sadducees as well. Since John's proclamation and ministry was a threat to the power of the temple establishment, it would be very appropriate for them to come out to where John was preaching in order to observe critically John's ministry (cf. §6.4.6, 10.6.2). Therefore, we may conclude that the most probable original audience for Q 3.7-9, and 3.7b, 8b in particular, was the Sadducees.[46]

---

44   Fitzmyer, *Luke*, 1.467.
45   Kraeling, *John the Baptist*, 48; cf. Hollenbach, 'Social Aspects', 860.
46   Fitzmyer (*Luke*, 1.467) as well as Ellis (*Luke*, 89) view the Matthean audience as authentic, but they do not make the distinction between Matthew's Pharisees and Q's Sadducees which I have argued for here. Cf. also the delegation of priests and Levites sent to John in Jn 1.19; as priests and Levites sent from Jerusalem, they were

### 6.2.4 *Mt. 3.11-12 = Mk 1.7-8 = Lk. 3.15-18*

The third NT pericope which is relevant for appreciating John's baptism is the explanation of his own baptism 'with water' in contrast with an expected figure who 'will baptize you with a holy spirit and fire'. Since the focus of this sentence is upon John's proclamation of an expected figure, I examine it in detail in Chapter 8 (§8.2.1). In anticipation of those results, to which I refer the reader, I am able to state here that this contrast drawn by John is found in two sources, Mk 1.7-8 and Q 3.16-17, and may be taken to reflect an authentic Baptist tradition.

### 6.2.5 *Summary*

Our examination of the descriptions of John's baptism in Josephus' *Antiquities* and the synoptic Gospels leads us to conclude that these sources reveal their own interests and biases which must be taken into account. But, in general, these sources reflect authentic traditions concerning John the Baptist and may be utilized as data in a historical examination of the practice and significance of John's baptism. Specifically these sources are *Ant.* 18.117, Mk 1.4-8 and Q 3.7-9, 16-17, and these form the basis for the ensuing discussion of the administration and function of John's baptism.

At this point the reader might raise the objection that two of these sources are in conflict with each other, for Josephus stated that 'baptism certainly would appear acceptable to him [i.e. God] if [they] used [it] not for seeking pardon of certain sins but for purification of the body' (*Ant.* 18.117), whereas the NT source stated that John's baptism was 'a baptism of repentance for the forgiveness of sins' (Mk 1.4). At this point I can only respond that each source, *taken by itself*, appears to reflect reliable historical tradition. Consequently, I suspend judgment on this issue until we can discuss the significance of John's baptism with respect to this particular aspect.

### 6.3 *The Administration of John's Baptism*

In this section we examine several aspects of the actual administration of John's baptism. Some of these are interesting in and of themselves, while others contribute to an appreciation of the baptism's significance.

First of all, several lines of evidence suggest that the mode of John's baptism was by immersion. Both Josephus and the NT use the verb βαπτίζω to describe John's baptism, and this term is not commonly used

---

probably Sadducees.

For support of a Sadducean audience, see Kraeling, *John the Baptist*, 45-50, and more recently, Hollenbach, 'Social Aspects', 860-61; Horsley, *Bandits*, 178-79; Evans, 'Evidence of Corruption', 538.

to refer to a ritual ablution.[47]  When describing an action, this verb signifies 'to dip', 'to immerse', 'to plunge into' or 'to submerge'.[48]  Therefore, John's baptism was probably by immersion since this particular verb
and its associated word group is used to describe it.  Other phrases in the
NT support this conclusion.  The people were baptized 'in the river' (ἐν
τῷ . . . ποταμῷ; Mk 1.5), and after his baptism Jesus is described as
'coming up out of the water' (ἀναβαίνων ἐκ τοῦ ὕδατος; Mk 1.10).  This
was not an unusual feature of John's baptism, because the evidence concerning ritual ablutions for the whole body in Second Temple Judaism
indicates that immersion was the normal mode of performing a ritual
bath (cf. §4.3).  Since John's baptism was in a river, immersion would be
a natural mode of performing this ablution.[49]  Effusion may have been
involved as well, but specific evidence is lacking.[50]

Secondly, John's baptism is consistently described as being administered 'by John' (ὑπ᾽ αὐτοῦ; Mk 1.5; cf. v. 9), and John himself states: 'I
baptize' (Q 3.16; Mk 1.8).[51]  This feature is quite unusual, and in fact
could very well be John's innovation, because in Jewish circles there is no
evidence of the immersion being administered by another person.[52]  This
feature of John's baptism no doubt contributed to him receiving the nickname 'the baptizer' (Mk 1.4).[53]  There are parallels: in Num. 19.19 it was
neccessary that a clean person sprinkle the water for uncleanness upon
the person who had contracted corpse uncleanness, and it is possible that
the initiatory/purificatory immersion by the candidate into the Qumran
community was witnessed by the other members of the community.[54]

---

47  Beasley-Murray ('Baptism, Wash: βαπτίζω', 1.143) points out that the verb λούω is
    the most common verb for complete washing, while νίπτω is used for partial wash-
    ings.
48  BAGD, 131; LSJ, 305-306; Oepke, 'βάπτω', 1.529-38; Beasley-Murray, 'Baptism,
    Wash: βαπτίζω', 1.143-50.
49  Cf. Scobie, *John the Baptist*, 92-93; Kraeling, *John the Baptist*, 97; Marsh, *Baptism*,
    74-75, Ernst, *Johannes der Täufer*, 331, etc.
50  For literature supporting effusion, see Nolland, *Luke*, 1.142.
51  Cf. the comparison with the expected figure who performs the baptism with a holy
    spirit and fire (Q 3.16; Mk 1.8).
52  The only other examples are the references to Jesus and/or his disciples baptizing
    (Jn 3.26; 4.1-2) and the baptismal practice of the early church (e.g. Acts 8.38).  But
    both these cases have been quite evidently influenced by John's method of adminis-
    tering baptism. Ysebaert (*Greek Baptismal Terminology*, 16) notes that the practice
    of immersions among Gentiles was that 'usually the person concerned bathed him-
    self, but in a few cases the intervention of a priest is mentioned: θύει ιαρρεὺς καὶ
    ἀπορραίνεται θαλάσσα SIG 1026.23f., cf. Athenaeus Dipn. 9.410a'. But this is rather
    distant from John's Jewish practice.
53  Scobie, *John the Baptist*, 102; Stauffer, *Theology*, 22. Dibelius (*Johannes dem Täufer*,
    135) states that John's baptism was a self-baptism performed in John's presence, and
    points to the reading in D: βαπτισθῆναι ἐνώπιον αὐτοῦ. Marsh (*Baptism*, 77-82)
    also considers this possible. But this is unlikely as Thyen ('ΒΑΠΤΙΣΜΑ', 132 n. 3)
    indicates.

But these parallels are rather distant. Jewish practice was a self-administered immersion, evidently with the understanding that by one's own act of immersing one was capable of cleansing oneself by performing the act. That John administered his baptism suggests in contrast that the immersion signified something that the person being baptized could not do for him/herself. Therefore, the act of being baptized by another probably points to some aspect of the symbolic nature of John's baptism in particular.

There is no evidence in our sources to suggest how John performed the baptism. He might have dipped the person into the water, or pushed him/her under; he could have led the person into the water by the hand and held it while he/she was immersed; John may have held out his hands and pronounced a benediction. It is also possible that he himself did not always perform the baptism, but had his disciples assist him. These suggestions simply indicate that we do not know precisely how John performed the baptism, and we would do well not to read later Christian practices back into the evidence.

Thirdly, John's baptism was performed in a river (Mk 1.5; cf. vv. 9-10) which is flowing or 'living' water. While the evidence does not state he baptized *only* in a river, it is consistent in describing John's baptism as a river baptism. In the OT, 'living' water was required in cases of the most severe uncleanness.[55] Our survey of Second Temple literature did not find many explicit references to running water, especially rivers, but there were three, and in all three cases they were associated with repentance and confession as well as a desire for forgiveness. *T. Levi* 2.3B2 states 'in *living water* I wholly bathed myself, and all my ways I made straight', and the prayer of Levi pleads for God to remove the spirit of unrighteousness, the granting of the spirit of holiness and inward cleansing (2.3B7-8, 14; cf. §4.3.4). *Sib. Or.* 4.165-67 exhorts the readers to 'wash your whole bodies in *perennial rivers* ... ask forgiveness [and] ... God will grant repentance' (cf. §4.3.5). In *Apoc. Mos.* 29.11-13 Adam and Eve realize they are unclean and repent of their rebellion by immersing in rivers (cf. §4.3.6). This evidence suggests that John baptized in a river because in Jewish thought of his day an immersion in running water or rivers was associated with severity of uncleanness as well as with repentance, confession and the desire for forgiveness and inward cleansing. We pursue this matter further in discussing the significance of John's baptism.[56]

---

54 Cf. discussion of 1QS 5.7-15 in §5.3.2. A similar parallel may be drawn from the requirement of three witnesses at a proselyte's immersion; cf. *b. Yeb.* 46b.

55 Lev. 14.5-6, 50-52; 15.13; Num. 19.17; Deut. 21.4.

56 It is sometimes observed that *m. Par.* 8.10 states: 'The waters of the Jordan ... are invalid because they are mixed waters'. But the context is not discussing whether the

Fourthly, Mk 1.5 states that the people were 'confessing their sins' while being baptized.[57] This description strengthens the parallels just made between John's baptism and *T. Levi* 2.3B, *Sib. Or.* 4.162-70 and *Apoc. Mos.* 29.11-13. We do not know, however, whether the confession was made audibly or silently, whether to God, to John or both. But the fact that confession of sins is contemporary with John's baptism contributes to an appreciation of its significance.[58]

Fifthly, not only was John's baptism performed in a river, but that river is always identified as the Jordan river (Mk 1.5; cf. v. 9). It is possible that no significance should be attached to this datum; John is in the wilderness, and the Jordan was the most convenient body of water around. We did observe above that the Jordan river is specified in the case of Naaman's immersions,[59] as well as in *Apoc. Mos.* 29.13, and it is probably the location used by Bannus, and possibly the Qumran community on special occasions (cf. §4.3.2, 4.3.6, 5.2.2). I discuss below the importance of the wilderness and the Jordan river in the ideology of prophetic movements as symbols of the Exodus/Conquest, and this may contribute to understanding John's baptism in the Jordan (cf. §10.5).

While it is evident that John baptized in the Jordan river, it is quite possible that much of his time was spent on the east bank of the river. First of all, John was critical of Herod Antipas (Mk 6.18) who ruled Perea, the border of which was the Jordan river. It would be most natural for John to publicly criticize the ruler of the territory in which he was located. Secondly, John was arrested by Antipas (*Ant.* 18.118-19; Mk 6.17), which would have required John to be within his territory. That this was Perea rather than Galilee is indicated by the fact that John was incarcerated and executed in Machaerus, Antipas' fortress in southern Perea, east of the Dead Sea (*Ant.* 18.119). Furthermore, the geographi-

---

Jordan river could be used for cleansing generally, but only whether or not it could be classified as 'living water' which could be used to mix with the ashes of the red heifer (cf. *m. Par.* 8.8-9; Blackman, *Mishnayoth*, 6.443). So, for example, *m. Par.* 8.8 states that 'all seas are valid as a ritual bath ... but they are invalid ... for [using their] water to mingle with the ashes of the [red heifer] sin offering'. This could suggest that the Jordan river was excluded only for mixing with the ashes of the red heifer, or that the Jordan river was not considered to be valid 'living water'. While the latter is more probably the case, it is unlikely that John or those receiving the baptism would have been concerned with such Pharisaic/rabbinic distinctions, and it is not even known that such an opinion was current in his day. Cf. *m. Miq.* 1.6-8 for a graduated scale of types of water valid for cleansing, with 'living water' the best.

57   The present tense of the participle ἐξομολογούμενοι indicates that the activity of confession was contemporaneous with the baptism.

58   Kraeling (*John the Baptist*, 97) suggests other liturgical elements were involved, but of them we know nothing.

59   The LXX describes his immersion using the same unusual verb βαπτίζω in 2 Kgs 5.14; cf. §4.2.5.

cal indications in the fourth Gospel place John on the eastern side of the Jordan; for example, Jn 1.28 states: 'These things happened in Bethany beyond the Jordan, where John was baptizing' (cf. Jn 3.26; 10.40).[60] When John was baptizing on the eastern side of the Jordan, those who came to be baptized from Jerusalem and Judea (Mk 1.5) would be required to go through the wilderness and cross the Jordan to be baptized, and then re-cross the Jordan to enter Judea.[61] The links with Exodus/Conquest motifs are very suggestive; they are explored below (§10.5).

Sixthly, we should examine the question of whether John's baptism was an act to be repeated or was a single, unrepeatable rite. The data are not clear on this matter. The only specific clue is that the Gospel narrative implies that Jesus was only baptized by John once (Mk 1.9-11), but this is hardly conclusive. More generally, while some disciples may have stayed with John, most of those who were baptized appear to have returned to their homes.[62] Our examination of the function of John's baptism may shed more light on this question (cf. §6.6).

Finally, his baptism was not only something which John administered, it was also something which he preached. In *Ant.* 18.117 Josephus explains that John 'commanded the Jews to practise virtue . . . and [so] to gather together by baptism'. Similarly, Mk 1.4 declares that John was 'preaching a baptism . . .' These texts indicate that not only was baptism important in John's thought, but it was something which he believed was necessary for his audience to receive. Evidently his audience was not aware of the necessity of receiving John's baptism prior to his preaching, which suggests that John attached some significance to his immersion which was different from the common understanding. Thus, John would preach, calling the people to be baptized, and that would involve explaining to them the signficance of the baptism as well as its necessity.[63]

## 6.4 *The Functions of John's Baptism*

In this section we examine the evidence concerning John's baptism in order to ascertain the functions of that baptism. This evidence suggests that the baptism functioned in six interrelated ways. Each of these may

---

60 On the reliability of these geographical indications see the discussion of John's Gospel in §3.8. The location of 'Aenon near Salim' mentioned in Jn 3.23 is not known for certain; arguments may be made for it being on either side of the Jordan; cf. Brown, *John*, 1.151. For arguments locating it in Samaria, see Albright, 'Observations', 193-94; Albright, 'Discoveries', 159; Scobie, *John the Baptist*, 163-64.

61 Marsh (*Baptism*, 38 n. 1) cites Badcock ('Baptism of Christ', 155-60) in this regard.

62 Scobie, *John the Baptist*, 91-92.

63 Ernst, *Johannes der Täufer*, 333-34.

be compared with the functions of immersions within the larger Jewish context (cf. §6.5).

### 6.4.1 *An Expression of Conversionary Repentance*

I concluded above that the NT summary of John's ministry as 'proclaiming a baptism of repentance for the forgiveness of sins' (Mk 1.4) is a historically reliable description (cf. §6.2.2). This conclusion is substantiated by Josephus' description that John 'commanded the Jews to practise virtue and act with justice toward one another and with piety toward God, and [so] to gather together by baptism' (*Ant.* 18.117), though we did observe that Josephus had Hellenized John's ethical proclamation for his Gentile audience. But the sense of this ethical imperative leading to baptism closely parallels the NT's 'proclaiming a baptism of repentance'. Since the NT's description is Jewish in orientation in contrast to Josephus' Hellenistic description, our analysis begins with the NT phrase.

The analysis by J. Behm and E. Würthwein of the concept of repentance within Judaism identifies two broad strands of thought derived from the OT. The first strand viewed repentance as contrition or penitence; that is, feelings of remorse because of one's sins. This type of repentance was often identified with rituals such as fasting, sackcloth and ashes. Thus, they describe it as 'cultic' or 'ritual' repentance, but perhaps the term 'penitential repentance' is more explicit. The second strand is represented particularly by OT prophets who called the people to repent, using especially the verb שוב, signifying 'to return' or 'to go back'. They criticized the penitential form of repentance as inadequately superficial. For them, repentance was not contrition, but a 'turning'—a reorientation of all spheres of a person's life to a new relationship with Yahweh, or in a single word, a 'conversion'.[64] This conversion has two aspects; frequently it is spoken of as having a negative element of 'turning' from sin, but the positive side in the OT is almost exclusively a 'turning' to God.[65] In contrast to penitential repentance, this concept of repentance might be identified by the term 'conversionary repentance'. William L. Holladay's analysis has demonstrated that this form of repentance had a covenantal orientation: it was a radical return to Yahweh restoring covenant loyalty.[66] The people are called to turn from evil and turn to God in obedience and trust.[67] Looming judgment is often a threat against those

---

64  E.g. Isa. 30.15. Behm and Würthwein, 'νοέω', 4.980-99; cf. Laubach and Goetzmann, 'Conversion: μετάνοια', 1.353-59.

65  Behm and Würthwein ('νοέω', 4.984) point out that when repentance is referred to absolutely or an object is specified to which one returns, the implied or specified object is always Yahweh, with only one exception: in Neh. 9.29 the object to which they 'return' is the Torah.

66  Holladay, *Root subh*, 120, cf. 116-57.

67  Cf. Isa. 10.20-21; Jer. 3.22-23; 18.8; 26.3-5; 34.15; Zech. 1.3-4; Mal. 3.7.

who refuse to repent.[68] By contrast, to those who do repent God grants forgiveness, remission of judgment and life.[69] Sometimes the restoration of a remnant from exile is associated with repentance.[70] God uses those in prophetic ministry to call people to repent.[71] They address the message to all Israel, but call for individual response. Sometimes it is Yahweh who is viewed as the one who gives the impulse to such radical returning.[72] Repentance is not only a human 'turning'; God must accept those who return and complete the transformation of the person by giving them a new heart.[73] There is within the prophets a recognition that repentance is at times not possible and judgment is certain.[74] Yet they expected in the last days there would be a final time of repentance.[75]

John's call to repentance (Q 3.8a; Mk 1.4) is clearly to be understood as conversionary repentance. He is a prophet who addresses his message of repentance to all Jews (*Ant.* 18.117a; Mk 1.5). The repentance must not be superficial or temporary, but instead it must 'bear fruit' (Q 3.8a; cf. *Ant.* 18.117a). The call to repent is in light of imminent judgment (Q 3.9, 17). No one is exempt; even the pious who might claim Abrahamic descent are called to repent (Q 3.8b).

The imagery of repentance, that is 'turning', implies a turning from one object to another object. We observed above that in the OT one usually turned from some form of sin. This accords well with John's preaching which was concerned with forgiveness of sins, and to which people responded by confessing their sins (Mk 1.4-5). We also observed that when 'turning' was used absolutely it implied the turning was to Yahweh, and when the object of turning is identified it is always Yahweh (with only one exception: the Torah, in Neh. 9.29). Both statements con-

---

68   E.g. Amos 4.6-8; Hos. 11.5-6; Ezek. 33.9-11.
69   E.g. Isa. 55.7; Jon. 3.9-10; Ezek. 33.13-16.
70   E.g. Jer. 12.15-16; Isa. 10.20-22.
71   E.g. Zech. 1.3-6.
72   E.g. Jer. 31.18-19; Lam. 5.21.
73   E.g. Jer. 24.7; 31.33-34; Ezek. 36.22-29.
74   E.g. Hos. 5.4; Isa. 6.10.
75   E.g. Deut. 4.30; Isa. 59.20; Hos. 3.4-5; Mal. 4.5-6; *Jub.* 1.15, 23. Cf. Behm and Würthwein, 'νοέω', 4.980-99; Laubach and Goetzmann, 'Conversion: μετάνοια', 1.353-59.

In extra-canonical Greek the verb μετανοέω means 'to change one's mind' or 'to regret', representing more the OT idea of penitential repentance. The LXX does not translate the verb שׁוּב by μετανοέω (except Isa. 46.8) but by ἐπιστρέφω or ἀποστρέφω, 'to turn back' or 'to turn away'. Instead, it uses μετανοέω in the classical Greek sense of 'to change one's mind' in order to translate the verb נחם, meaning 'to regret' or 'to be sorry'. But the Jewish literature of the Second Temple period provides ample evidence of a shift to μετανοέω to represent שׁוּב with the OT sense of repentance (e.g. Pr. Man. 7; Sir. 48.15). While the classical Greek sense is found in the NT (e.g. Lk. 17.3-4), it usually uses μετανοέω to express the idea of conversionary repentance. Cf. Behm and Würthwein, 'νοέω', 4.989-95.

cerning John's conversionary repentance in the NT (Mk 1.4b; Q 3.8a) use the term absolutely. In light of this absolute use in the OT, John's similar use indicates that he was calling the people to turn from sin and turn to God with a total reorientation of their relationship with God characterized by obedience and trust. But this repentance had an ethical component. Though repentance itself was a turning to God, true repentance would have its consequences in changed ethical relationships with other people.[76] John is concerned that people 'bear fruit in keeping with repentance' (Q 3.8a); that is, show with visible deeds the reality of conversion. Josephus' description of John's preaching emphasizes this ethical element: '[He] commanded the Jews to practise virtue and act with justice toward one another and with piety toward God . . .' (*Ant.* 18.117a).

But what is the relationship between this repentance and John's baptism, as expressed in the phrase 'a baptism of repentance for the forgiveness of sins' (βάπτισμα μετανοίας εἰς ἄφεσιν ἁμαρτιῶν; Mk 1.4)? Ernst Lohmeyer argues on the basis of εἰς μετάνοιαν in the expression ὑμᾶς βαπτίζω ἐν ὕδατι εἰς μετάνοιαν ('I baptize you in water unto repentance') in Mt. 3.11 that this conversionary repentance is the act which God performs when a person is baptized: 'Nicht der Mensch entschließt sich zur Umkehr, sondern Gott kehrt durch die Taufe des Menschen Sinn und Wesen um'.[77] While this might be the sense of the phrase in Mt. 3.11, the addition of εἰς μετάνοιαν in this clause is probably due to Matthean redaction (cf. Mk 1.8 = Lk. 3.16), introducing repentance in connection with baptism because he had deleted it from his source in 3.2 (cf. Mk 1.4). Lohmeyer's position is, however, a less probable explanation of the expression βάπτισμα μετανοίας in Mk 1.4, which I have argued is the more reliable historical tradition.[78]

The phrase βάπτισμα μετανοίας more probably signifies a baptism which expresses repentance.[79] Such a view may be supported on several grounds. First of all, in the above discussion of the meaning of repent-

---

76 Goppelt, *Theology*, 1.34.

77 Lohmeyer, *Johannes der Täufer*, 68; cf. Lohmeyer, *Markus*, 14.

78 For criticism of Lohmeyer's position see Ernst, *Johannes der Täufer*, 344. Beasley-Murray (*Baptism*, 34-35) criticizes Lohmeyer in this regard, and understands repentance to have the human element of turning to God, but points out that God's activity is also presumed, for he 'accepts the baptized man turning to Him'. Beasley-Murray (33-34) criticizes Brandt (*Jüdischen Baptismen*, 78, 84) for holding a position similar to Lohmeyer.

79 E.g. Ernst, *Johannes der Täufer*, 334; Kraeling, *John the Baptist*, 120-22; Scobie, *John the Baptist*, 80-81, 112; Beasley-Murray, *Baptism*, 34-35; Marsh, *Baptism*, 40-43; Guelich, *Mark*, 1.19. Merklein's suggestion ('Umkehrpredigt', 36-37) that the 'fruit' of repentance in Q 3.8a is baptism itself is interesting but lacks specific evidence for such a concrete identification; cf. Sato, *Q*, 212.

ance we observed that at times God was understood to give the impulse for repentance, and this would support Lohmeyer's position. However, the prophetic orientation usually emphasized calling people to return, and condemning them for not doing so. Without clear evidence to the contrary, we would expect John to remain part of this Jewish prophetic orientation. Secondly, the specific evidence concerning John supports this contention: so, John's command to 'bear fruit in keeping with repentance' (Q 3.8a) suggests that this is an activity he expects of his audience, not one performed by God on their behalf. Thirdly, the associated activity of confessing their sins while being baptized (Mk 1.5) suggests that an inward conversion is taking place which leads to this action, rather than a conversion accomplished by God upon performance of the baptism.[80] Yet, we must not eliminate the ministry of God from conversionary repentance altogether, because ultimately it is God who must accept the conversion, and the ministry of God is required to complete the transformation which the conversion involves (cf. §6.4.4, 8.4).

We observed above that Josephus' *terminology* had been Hellenized (§2.2), but we should still examine briefly whether Josephus' *description* in *Ant.* 18.117 is consistent with our analysis of the NT evidence. Josephus states that John was one who

> τοῖς Ἰουδαίοις κελεύοντα ἀρετὴν ἐπασκοῦσιν καὶ τὰ πρὸς ἀλλήλους δικαιοσύνῃ καὶ πρὸς τὸν θεὸν εὐσεβείᾳ χρωμένοις βαπτισμῷ συνιέναι.

> commanded the Jews to practise virtue and act with justice toward one another and with piety toward God, and [so] to gather together by baptism.

This description has been understood in two ways. A few scholars interpret the participles ἐπασκοῦσιν ('practising') and χρωμένοις ('acting with') to be attributive (or 'adjectival') participles modifying τοῖς Ἰουδαίοις ('the Jews'). Thus F.J. Foakes-Jackson and K. Lake translate Josephus and then argue:

> '[John was] one who commanded the Jews, training themselves (epaskousi) in virtue and practising righteousness to one another and piety towards God, to come together for baptism. . .'
> . . . It would rather seem that Josephus means that John preached originally to those who were already making especial practice of virtue—'ascetics' in the original sense of the word. . .[81]

---

80 The most probable alternatives for the genitive μετανοίας are either a genitive of description or purpose. Maloney (*Semitic Interference*, 165-69) argues that this genitive is an example of a Semiticism in Mark, but is still a genitive of purpose. Guelich (*Mark*, 1.16, 18-19) understands it to be a genitive of description, translating the phrase 'repentance-baptism'. Turner (*Grammar*, 3.211) on the other hand understands it as a subjective genitive; that is, baptism 'does not lead to, but springs from, repentance'. These syntactical alternatives in this case do not alter substantively the sense of the expression.

In this view, the participles are describing Jews who were already living a righteous lifestyle. Thus the righteous lifestyle describes the audience and is not part of John's message.

The second view interprets the participles ἐπασκοῦσιν and χρωμένοις to be adverbial (or 'circumstantial') participles modifying the infinitival construction βαπτισμῷ συνιέναι ('to gather together by baptism'), which is the direct object of indirect discourse of the substantival participle κελεύοντα ('one who commanded'). In this view, rather than describing the recipients of the message, the participles are part of the message itself. This view is presented in Louis H. Feldman's translation of the passage:

> [John] had exhorted the Jews to lead righteous lives, to practice justice towards their fellows and piety towards God, and so doing to join in baptism.[82]

In this view, John's exhortation to the Jews is that practising virtue and acting with justice toward one another and with piety toward God must accompany the baptism. Thus the righteous lifestyle is part of the message.

The second of these two views is to be preferred. Syntactically, the participles are adverbial rather than attributive because they are in the predicative position rather than the attributive.[83] Thus they should be understood to modify the infinitival construction βαπτισμῷ συνιέναι.[84]

---

81   Foakes-Jackson and Lake, *Beginnings*, 1.102. Farmer ('John the Baptist', 2.959) translates similarly: 'he was bidding the Jews who practiced virtue and exercised righteousness toward each other and piety toward God, to come together for baptism'.

82   Feldman, *Josephus*, 9.81-83. Similarly, Whiston's translation (*Josephus*, 3.72) is: '[John] commanded the Jews to exercise virtue, both as to righteousness towards one another, and piety towards God, and so to come to baptism'.

83   Attributive participles are in the attributive position, whereas adverbial participles are in the predicative position; cf. Smyth, *Grammar*, §2049, 1166, 2054. They are in the predicative position because τοῖς Ἰουδαίοις is articulated and the participles follow later in the sentence and are anarthrous. Attributive position may take one of four forms (where t = article, a = attributive adjective or participle, n = noun): t-a-n, t-n-t-a, n-t-a, n-a. Cf. Funk, *Grammar*, §774.1.

84   The verb κελεύω may either be followed by the accusative and usually the infinitive, or by the dative either alone or with the infinitive; cf. Smyth, *Grammar*, §1465; BDF, §187.5. The use of κελεύω with the accusative is the more classical of the two forms. In *Antiquities* Josephus uses both forms (e.g. with the accusative, *Ant*. 18.83; 18.186: 18.304; with the dative, *Ant*. 18.96: 18.166; 18.180; 18.334). In *Ant*. 18.117 Niese (*Iosephi*, 4.161) lists the Epitome (E) text as correcting all three participles to accusatives and Eusebius as correcting only χρωμένοις to χρωμένους. This textual reading most probably reflects a scribal correction to the classical usage.

   Word order could also support this conclusion. The separation of the participial clauses from τοῖς Ἰουδαίοις by the insertion of the substantival participle κελεύοντα between them, and the inclusion of the participial clauses between κελεύοντα and βαπτισμῷ συνιέναι suggests that the participles explain κελεύοντα ... βαπ-

The syntactical relationship between the participles describing the ethical imperative and the infinitival construction referring to John's baptism indicate that they are related in a manner similar to that found in the NT. Thus, according to Josephus, an integral part of John's call to baptism was an ethical imperative 'to practise virtue and act with justice toward one another and with piety toward God'. Since the precise terminology used by Josephus to describe the content of John's ethical imperative reflects categories which would be more understandable to Josephus' Roman audience than those which may have been actually used by John, John's proclamation could best be summarized as a call to a righteous lifestyle.[85] This summary is suggested by Josephus' own summary of John's ethical imperative when he states later in 18.117 that 'the soul had already been cleansed before *by righteousness*'. If this is what John called the people to do, then it suggests he believed they were not living righteously, and that he was calling them to 'turn' to a different lifestyle. While Josephus' description contains both 'piety toward God' and 'justice toward one another', it lacks the radical orientation of conversionary repentance indicated by the NT evidence, but this lack is probably due to Josephus' Hellenizing of John's message. However, John's concern that people 'bear fruit in keeping with repentance' (Q 3.8a) indicates that John's view of conversionary repentance had a strong ethical element in it (cf. Lk. 3.10-14). Therefore, while Josephus' description of John's proclamation is not oriented precisely towards conversionary repentance, it is, nevertheless, similar enough to be considered supportive of the interpretation of John's baptism as functioning as an expression of conversionary repentance.

We may conclude that individuals within John's audience heard John proclaim imminent judgment and summon them to a baptism of repentance, to which they responded by being turned around, or converted, and they expressed that conversion by submitting to John's baptism. The confession of sins which accompanied the baptismal act formed part of this expression of repentance. For John baptism was not an option: the expression of repentance required baptism, and the efficacy of the baptism required repentance. These two are inextricably linked, which perhaps may be expressed by identifying John's baptism as a 'repentance-baptism',[86] or, alternatively, a 'baptismally-expressed repentance'. The repentance focused on turning from sin and turning to a new relationship with God in obedience and trust which was to have ethical consequences.

τισμῷ συνιέναι rather than τοῖς Ἰουδαίοις.
85  It is possible that 'virtue' is Josephus' general term, and the expressions 'justice toward one another' and 'piety toward God' define the two aspects of that virtue.
86  Cf. Guelich, *Mark*, 1.18-19.

### 6.4.2 *A Mediation of Divine Forgiveness*

Mk 1.4 states that John's baptism which expressed conversionary repentance was 'for the forgiveness of sins' (εἰς ἄφεσιν ἁμαρτιῶν). Forgiveness is the divine response to those who responded to John's message. While this is quite clear, two questions do arise at this point. First of all, is the forgiveness of sins to be understood as the goal of the repentance or of the baptism?[87] Let us examine our sources in turn.

In his explanation of John's baptism, Josephus states that it was 'not for seeking pardon of certain sins but for purification of the body' (*Ant.* 18.117). But this does not mean that in Josephus' account 'seeking pardon of certain sins' was unimportant. His account of John's message was that John called the people to a righteous lifestyle because he believed they were not living righteously; if so, then seeking pardon for their former unrighteous lifestyle would presumably be quite important. Josephus' explanation suggests that pardon of sins was in fact part of John's message. But if, according to Josephus, John's baptism was not used to seek this pardon, then what did effect the pardon? Josephus provides the answer with the causal clause which immediately follows: the baptism was 'not for seeking pardon of certain sins but for purification of the body, *because* the soul had already been cleansed before by righteousness'. In this clause Josephus is evidently equating 'pardon of sins' with 'cleansing the soul', though the expressions use different imagery. The 'pardon of sins/cleansing the soul' is accomplished by righteousness; that is, by the person's response to John's ethical imperative, and this 'pardon of sins/cleansing the soul' precedes the baptism which purifies the body.

Two interesting points arise from Josephus' explanation. First of all, though pardon is separated from the baptism, the pardon for sins is still described employing ablutory language: 'the soul has been *cleansed* before (προεκκεκαθαρμένης). . .' Secondly, it is interesting that the correct use of baptism is necessary to ensure that it is acceptable to God. Therefore, Josephus' answer to our question is that pardon for sins is effected by the person's turning to a righteous lifestyle, or, in the language of the NT, forgiveness of sins is the goal of the repentance rather than the baptism.

---

87   It is clear that εἰς is expressing the goal; that is, 'with a view to' forgiveness. More precisely, the εἰς expresses the purpose of the repentance-baptism from the human perspective; they responded to John's message in order to receive the forgiveness of sins. But the εἰς expresses the result of the repentance-baptism when viewed from the divine perspective; that is, the repentance-baptism resulted in God forgiving their sins. Since we are examining the function of John's baptism from the human perspective, εἰς ἄφεσιν ἁμαρτιῶν expresses purpose.

Ernst (*Johannes der Täufer*, 345 n. 17) correctly rejects the interpretation of εἰς ἄφεσιν ἁμαρτιῶν as a person 'putting away' his/her sins.

The phrase in Mk 1.4, 'a baptism of repentance for the forgiveness of sins' is ambiguous with respect to this question. However, since John's concern is calling the people to a conversionary repentance in the face of judgment, he probably associated the divine response of forgiveness with the expression of repentance in a manner consistent with the prophetic orientation of conversionary repentance. For example, Isa. 55.7 associates forgiveness with repentance:

> Let the wicked forsake his way,
>     and the evil man his thoughts;
> And let him return [יָשֹׁב; LXX: ἐπιστραφήτω] to Yahweh,
>     and he will have mercy on him;
> And to our God,
>     for he will abundantly pardon/forgive their sins [לִסְלוֹחַ; LXX: ἀφήσει τὰς ἁμαρτίας ὑμῶν].[88]

Therefore, both Josephus and the NT support the view that forgiveness of sins is the goal of repentance. But this does not answer the question completely. While the forgiveness of sins is more closely associated with the repentance than with baptism, nevertheless, there is probably a relationship between the baptism itself and the forgiveness. Two earlier observations point in this direction. First of all, repentance and baptism are inextricably linked to each other (it is a 'repentance-baptism', a 'baptismally-expressed repentance'), and so it is probable that in some way the forgiveness of sins is associated with the baptism itself, and this may explain why in fact the baptism was essential in the first place. The explanation may be derived from a second earlier observation: John's baptism was distinctive due to the fact that it was not a self-baptism, but rather performed by John upon the person being baptized. Since this feature was distinctive of John's baptism, it was no doubt significant, but we are not told explicitly what that significance was. That the person could not baptize him/herself but had to receive the baptism from another suggests the baptism symbolized that which the person received as a consequence of the repentance-baptism, namely, the forgiveness of sins. In other words, being baptized by John symbolized being forgiven by God, and the act of baptism provided the person with the assurance that he/she had indeed been forgiven. But since the baptism was essential to express repentance, the baptism did more than *symbolize* the forgiveness, in some way it *mediated* the forgiveness; that is, as a requirement for forgiveness, the repentance-baptism was the *necessary channel* for that forgiveness. Also, since the one baptized received the baptism from John, John could then be considered a *mediator* of the forgiveness.[89]

---

88  Cf. Hos. 14.1-2.
89  Goppelt, *Theology*, 1.36; Becker, *Johannes der Täufer*, 38, 40; cf. Beasley-Murray's

But this view that John's baptism mediated forgiveness is contrary to Josephus' statement that the baptism was 'not for seeking pardon of certain sins but for purification of the body, because the soul had already been cleansed before by righteousness' (*Ant.* 18.117). However, a couple of observations suggest that Josephus' dissociation of forgiveness from the baptism probably does not reflect accurately John's point of view on this matter. First of all, in separating forgiveness from baptism Josephus is by implication also separating the idea of repentance from baptism. But we have seen (§6.4.1) that for John repentance and baptism were inextricably linked: the expression of repentance required baptism, and the efficacy of the baptism required repentance; it was a baptismally-expressed repentance.[90] Secondly, our examination of the reliability of Josephus' description concluded that it was reliable except at one point: Josephus' separation of the body from the soul (§6.2.1). It is precisely this separation which dissociates the forgiveness from the baptism. Therefore Josephus, by separating forgiveness from John's baptism, is not expressing John's view of the matter but his own. However, in our examination of the passage here, we observed that Josephus still used ablutory language to describe the forgiveness ('the soul had been *cleansed*'), and that the correct use of the baptism was to ensure that it was acceptable *to God*. Both these observations are consistent with the view of John's baptism proposed here.

An interesting parallel arises at this point between this idea of mediation in John's baptism with the mediation of forgiveness in the OT sacrificial system. For example, in Leviticus 5 a guilty person confesses his/her sin (v. 5), brings a sacrifice to the priest who, in a mediatorial

discussion (*Baptism*, 43) of prophetic symbolism with respect to John's baptism. Concerning the mediatory role of such symbolism Beasley-Murray (43 n. 2) cites Robinson ('Symbolism', 132): 'The prophet might equally well have said "Thus doth Yahweh", of his own prophetic act, as he does say, of his own spoken word, "Thus saith Yahweh" '. On prophetic symbolism with respect to John's baptism see also Flemington, *Baptism*, 18-21; Scobie, *John the Baptist*, 113; Ernst, *Johannes der Täufer*, 332-34.

A topic of discussion concerning John's baptism which frequently arises at this point is whether or not John's baptism is 'sacramental'. I find this discussion unhelpful, because it appears to me to be the attribution of what is primarily a Christian theological concept to a pre-Christian phenomenon, and what clouds the issue further is one's own conception of sacramentalism in Christian theology. While it was popular at one time to refer to John's baptism as an 'eschatological sacrament' (e.g. Bultmann, *Jesus*, 23; Thyen, 'ΒΑΠΤΙΣΜΑ', 132), this terminology has more recently been rejected (e.g. Becker, 39; Ernst, 335).

90   This was supported in §6.4.1 not only from the NT, but from the syntactical relationship in Josephus' statement between the participles describing the ethical imperative and John's call to baptism.

role, offers that sacrifice to God as an atonement for the sin (vv. 6-9), and the person's sin is forgiven (v. 10). This parallel is particularly interesting in light of the NT tradition that John was a member of a rural priestly family (Lk. 1.5, 23).[91] But John did not go to the temple to perform his priestly duties of offering sacrifices and pronouncing the sinner forgiven; rather, he called people to a repentance-baptism for the forgiveness of sins. These parallels and John's priestly background suggest that John's baptism was probably understood to function in a manner similar to the OT sacrifices. We could speculate that in his role as baptizer, John, the mediator of forgiveness, might have pronounced the person forgiven, just as a priest pronounced a person forgiven after offering a sacrifice in the temple. Such speculation is supported by observing that 'confessing their sins' (Mk 1.5b) was actually part of the 'liturgy' associated with the baptismal rite.

The second question is, when was the forgiveness of sins understood to have taken place? In other words, were the person's sins forgiven when being baptized, or, even though forgiveness was the goal of the repentance-baptism, were the person's sins actually forgiven at a future time? For example, Josef Ernst argues that the forgiveness of sins is not actually received at the baptism; rather it refers to a promise of forgiveness at the coming judgment, when the expected figure will baptize with a holy spirit.[92] However, there is no actual evidence for this in the data concerning John's baptism. What appears to lead to this position is the incorrect equation of forgiveness of sins with salvation in general, particularly with escaping judgment through the expected figure (Q 3.16-17) and the blessings of eschatological restoration (cf. §8.4). The confession of sins which accompanied John's baptism suggests that those sins were forgiven at that time. In the prophetic orientation of conversionary repentance, forgiveness of sins was usually received upon repentance. Other eschatological blessings were still reserved for the future. With respect to John's baptism, rather than *forgiveness* being reserved until the eschatological judgment by the expected figure, it is more probable that the completion of conversionary repentance and its fruits are not actually seen in all their fulness until those baptized received the eschatological blessing of a holy spirit from the expected figure.[93]

Therefore, John's baptism had two closely related functions: it was a

---

91  While some scholars reject the historical reliability of the Lukan infancy narratives (e.g. Hollenbach, 'Social Aspects', 852-53), nevertheless, many accept that John came from a family of rural priests (e.g. Hollenbach, 852-53); cf. Fitzmyer, *Luke*, 1.317; Marshall, *Luke*, 52; Kraeling, *John the Baptist*, 21-25; Scobie, *John the Baptist*, 55-57; Ernst, *Johannes der Täufer*, 269-72, Horsley, *Liberation*, 91-92.

92  Ernst, *Johannes der Täufer*, 335; cf. Guelich, *Mark*, 1.19-20.

93  On the eschatological gift of the spirit see §8.4.1. Cf. §6.4.1 on conversionary repentance being completed by God; Beasley-Murray, *Baptism*, 35, 39 n. 2.

repentance-baptism which mediated forgiveness; that is, it was an immersion which expressed conversionary repentance, and as such was the channel through which God forgave the person his/her sins.[94]

### 6.4.3 *A Purification from Uncleanness*

The preceding survey of ablutions in the OT and Second Temple Jewish literature demonstrates the predominant conception that ablutory rites purified a person from uncleanness. In fact, if John's baptism—an immersion performed in the context of Jewish culture—did not have a cleansing function, this would probably be the most surprising and distinctive feature. However, the evidence indicates John's baptism did have a purificatory function.

It is Josephus who provides the most explicit statement on this subject in *Ant.* 18.117b:

> οὕτω γὰρ δὴ καὶ τὴν βάπτισιν ἀποδεκτὴν αὐτῷ φανεῖσθαι μὴ ἐπί τινων ἁμαρτάδων παραιτήσει χρωμένων, ἀλλ᾽ ἐφ᾽ ἀγνείᾳ τοῦ σώματος, ἅτε δὴ καὶ τῆς ψυχῆς δικαιοσύνῃ προεκκεκαθαρμένης.

> For [John's view was that] in this way baptism certainly would appear acceptable to him [i.e. God] if [they] used [it] not for seeking pardon of certain sins but for purification of the body, because the soul had already been cleansed before by righteousness.

This text is frequently interpreted in a way which suggests that Josephus attributes forgiveness to the person's response to John's ethical call (or, in NT terms, 'repentance') and relegates John's baptism to a purificatory role which cleanses from physical contagion like many other forms of Jewish immersions.[95] However, such a view is too simplistic, for it fails to take into consideration the question, what causes the uncleanness from which John's baptism purifies? Josephus' description of John emphasizes his calling the people to a righteous lifestyle (18.117a). The associated terms Josephus used to explain John's baptism suggest the focus of John's concern (and the concern of those who were baptized) was for forgiveness of sins and cleansing which may be accomplished by righteousness. Since it is righteousness which cleanses the soul, that which has made it unclean is probably unrighteousness, that is, moral contagion, or in other words, the sin which is pardoned. So Josephus' description of John's ministry and baptism emphasizes its ethical orientation. Therefore, when Josephus describes John's view of baptism as one which is 'for purification of the body', the context implies that the con-

---

94  So Thyen, 'ΒΑΠΤΙΣΜΑ', 132-33 n. 6; Kraeling, *John the Baptist*, 121-22. For further discussion of John's baptism in terms of atonement (in comparison with 1QS 3.6-9), see §6.5.

95  E.g. Scobie, *John the Baptist*, 95; Ernst, *Johannes der Täufer*, 336.

cern is also for cleansing from moral contagion rather than physical contagion, but it is now the body being cleansed rather than the soul.[96] In separating the cleansing of the body from the cleansing of the soul (both were made unclean by the moral contagion), and placing the 'pardon of sins/cleansing the soul' temporally prior to cleansing the body by baptism, Josephus is probably trying to clarify for his Gentile Roman readers that the Jewish rite of John's baptism was not a magical rite which Jews simplistically believed could pardon sins.

Therefore, according to Josephus' explanation, the baptism of John cleansed the *body* from *moral* contagion. But we observed above (§6.2.1) that Josephus' explanation is probably inaccurate in separating the body from the soul. It was a device necessary for his explanation to a Gentile audience, but it is unlikely that John made such a separation. Thus, in order to understand John's baptism within his Jewish context, we could remove this element. Then the evidence in Josephus indicates that *the person* is forgiven his/her sins through the response to John's ethical demand, and *the person* is cleansed of the uncleanness caused by his/her sins through baptism.

In the NT, a similar significance may be observed (though here the baptism is more closely associated with repentance and forgiveness). John's concern is ethical, he preaches repentance, and those baptized confess their sins. No explicit reference is made to cleansing, but in Jewish culture immersions had primarily a purificatory function, and sin was understood to cause uncleanness (cf. §4.2.6, 4.2.7, 4.4). John's concern with repentance and forgiveness, associated with a purificatory immersion, suggests that the baptism functioned to cleanse a person from uncleanness caused by moral contagion; that is, the life from which he/she is 'turning' and the sins which he/she is confessing. This implication is confirmed by the parallel between John baptizing 'with water' and the expected figure's baptizing 'with a holy spirit and fire' (Q 3.16). I argue below that the agricultural imagery of the threshing floor in Q 3.17 expresses similar ideas to those expressed by the expected figure's baptizing ministry (§8.4; cf. §8.2.1). The expected figure's ministry is also to cleanse: 'His winnowing shovel is in his hand and he will clean (διακα-θαριεῖ) his threshing floor'.[97]

The seriousness of the uncleanness (i.e. from moral contagion) may partially explain why John's baptismal ministry is associated with the Jordan river. The Jordan was 'living' or flowing water which was required in serious cases of uncleanness in the OT and was associated with cleansing from uncleanness caused by moral contagion and with repentance in the

---

96  On physical and moral contagion, see §4.2.1.
97  Others who perceive John's baptism to function as a cleansing include Beasley-

literature of the Second Temple period (cf. §6.5).

While John's baptism functioned to cleanse a person from uncleanness caused by the moral contagion of his/her sins, I am not suggesting that John had no concern for cleansing from uncleanness caused by physical contagion. In all likelihood he practised ablutory rites which were common in the Judaism of his day.[98] But this does not appear to have been associated with his baptismal ministry.

### 6.4.4 *A Foreshadowing of the Expected Figure's Ministry*
Another focus of John's ministry was the announcement of an expected figure (Q 3.16-17; Mk 1.7-8), which we examine in Chapters 8 and 9.[99] We need merely to observe at this point that John portrays the expected figure's ministry in terms of a baptizing ministry which is explicitly compared with his own ministry: 'I baptize you with water, but the one who is coming after me is mightier than I, whose sandals I am not worthy to carry, he will baptize you with a holy spirit and fire' (Q 3.16). Not only is the expected figure mightier and more worthy than John, but this figure's baptizing with a holy spirit and fire is contrasted with John's baptism which is 'only' with water. This explicit comparison of their ministries and the identification of them both as baptizing ministries indicates that John's baptism is a foreshadowing of the expected figure's greater baptism. John's baptism is the final preparation for the imminent, eschatological culmination of judgment and restoration by the expected figure.[100]

This aspect of John's baptism places it in an eschatological context, along with the proclamation of imminent wrath as the motivation for the repentance-baptism. The conversionary repentance expressed by the baptism indicated a radical turning from sin to a transformed relationship with God. But the expected figure's greater baptism with a holy spirit was probably to complete the transformation. Thus, while John's baptism expressed the human 'turning' to God, in foreshadowing the coming baptism John's repentance-baptism was foreshadowing the completion of the process begun with that conversion.[101] John's baptism also

Murray, *Baptism*, 39; Scobie, *John the Baptist*, 112-14, etc.

98  This might find support from his ascetic lifestyle (Mk 1.4a; 2.18), as well as the reference to 'a debate between some of John's disciples and a Jew concerning purification' in Jn 3.25. Cf. Scobie, *John the Baptist*, 95.

99  For the historical reliability of this material, see §8.2.1; cf. §6.2.4.

100  So Goppelt, *Theology*, 1.37-38; Beasley-Murray, *Baptism*, 32; Ernst, *Johannes der Täufer*, 333. Cf. the OT prophets who performed acts of prophetic symbolism to prefigure coming events; Napier, 'Prophet', 3.912-13.

101  Cf. the prophetic orientation of conversionary repentance discussed above in §6.4.1, which included the need for a human 'turning' to God as well as the realization that God had to complete the process by giving his people a new heart.

Other aspects of John's foreshadowing the expected figure's baptism include the

cleansed the person, but the expected figure would render the person completely cleansed.

### 6.4.5 *An Initiation into the 'True Israel'*

John proclaimed the necessity for everyone to undergo conversionary repentance and express that repentance by receiving his baptism which symbolically mediated the forgiveness given to the person by God and cleansed the person from the uncleanness caused by his/her sins. By so doing, the person would be prepared for the imminent, eschatological judgment and restoration carried out by the expected figure John announced.[102] John's baptizing ministry, therefore, created a fundamental distinction between two groups of people: those who received the repentance-baptism and those who were unrepentant; those who were forgiven and those who were unforgiven; those who were purified and those who were unclean; those prepared to receive the expected figure's ministry of restoration and those who would be judged and face that figure's wrath. While John addressed his message to all Israel, the effect of that message was to divide them into these two sets of people.

The effect of this division could be interpreted either individualistically or corporately. In other words, did a person who received John's repentance-baptism perceive him/herself only as an individual who had been forgiven and so would escape the coming wrath, or did that person perceive him/herself as becoming part of a prepared, and so distinct, group? This question is examined from the perspective of John's prophetic ministry in Part III (§8.4, 8.5, 10.2, 10.3); here we wish to examine it only in terms of the function of his baptism. If the effect of John's baptizing ministry is interpreted from a corporate point of view, then the baptism could have the additional function of an initiation rite into the group (I use the term 'initiation rite' to refer to an external action which serves to change the status of a person from a non-member to that of a member[103]). But if interpreted individualistically then his baptism would not have this function.

The individualistic interpretation may be supported by observing that the message requires an individual response and grants forgiveness to individuals, so preparing individuals for the coming wrath. With such an

---

elements of cleansing and separation, but discussion of these must be reserved for an examination of the expected figure; cf. §8.4.

102 In the analysis of that ministry of judgment and restoration (§8.4) I conclude that the imagery of 'baptizing with a holy spirit' refers to the eschatological blessing of those prepared by John's ministry, while the 'baptizing with fire' refers to the eschatological judgment of those who rejected John's ministry; that is, the unrepentant.

103 On types of initiation, see Bleeker, 'Initiation', 18-19; on the subject generally, see the entire volume, Bleeker, *Initiation*.

emphasis, several scholars reject the interpretation of John's baptism as an initiation rite. For example, Jürgen Becker states:

> Die Taufe is ferner ebensowenig Initiationsritus. Die damit gesetzte ekklesiologische Dimension der Taufe verfehlt gerade das johanneische Denken. Johannes hat keine geschlossene Gemeinde gegründet, sondern alle einzelnen Israeliten, die seinem Ruf Folge leisteten, vor dem Zorn bewahren wollen. Angesichts der Nähe des Gerichts wäre eine Gemeindegründung ein Anachronismus. . .
> Die Taufe führt zu keiner Pauschalamnestie des Volkes, sondern erzwingt die Individualisieruung des einzelnen Israeliten. . . Diese Einzelnen werden von Johannes nirgends durch eine soziologisch überindividuelle Kategorie in eine neue Gemeinschaft integriert.[104]

This interpretation suffers from a number of weaknesses. For example, it assumes that an initiation rite only initiates a person into a 'closed community', as perhaps exemplified by the Qumran community, and, since John did not create a segregated and organized community, his orientation was solely individualistic. However, the sectarian nature of Second Temple Judaism reveals quite clearly that groups were formed who maintained some form of identity and yet remained integrated into Jewish society, such as the Pharisees, the town-dwelling Essenes, and the early Christian movement. Even entrance into Judaism itself by a Gentile has a similar perspective. Secondly, this interpretation focuses upon John as a preacher of judgment, and that his message was only 'escape the coming wrath!'[105] But John also proclaimed a message of imminent restoration, and it was those who received John's repentance-baptism who were restored.[106] In view of the self-understanding of Jews as the elect, covenant people of God, with the abiding hope for national restoration, John's proclamation of imminent judgment *and restoration* would be understood by first-century Jews as a restoration of a corporate body, and thus, his baptism would function to form the group which would escape the judgment and experience the restoration. Not only does the concept of restoration point to a corporate view of John's ministry, but John's preaching of judgment does as well. For, from John's point of view, *all Israel* was facing imminent wrath, not just certain

---

104 Becker, *Johannes der Täufer*, 39-40. Other scholars also recognize that John's baptism creates a separation, but, strangely, do not accept the corporate implication; e.g. Ernst, *Johannes der Täufer*, 340; Goppelt, *Theology*, 1.35.

105 For example, Becker (*Johannes der Täufer*, 38-39) states: 'Der Täufer formuliert keine positive Aussage über die Zukunft!' Such a truncated view of John's message leads to an inadequate perception of the function of his baptism. Cf. §8.4, 8.5, 10.3 on the positive aspects of John's expectation.

106 If the unrepentant are judged (and presumably removed) by the expected figure, what happens to the repentant if they are viewed only from an individualistic point of view? Only 'individual' forgiveness of sins? Such a view lacks a sense of concreteness.

impious individuals. While he called for an individual response, it was Israel *as a corporate body* which was under judgment. If John viewed the problem fundamentally from a corporate point of view, then it would be consistent and plausible for his solution to have a corporate aspect (cf. §8.4, 8.5, 10.2, 10.3).

Thus far we may conclude that, first of all, in the environment of Second Temple Judaism sectarian movements flourished which distinguished themselves in some way from ethnic Israel as a whole, and yet the individuals remained as functioning members of society. Thus, the social environment of John's ministry allowed for this type of group formation. Secondly, the framework of John's proclamation contributed to the separation of a group who would not be judged but who would receive eschatological blessings from the expected figure. Since repentance-baptism is the required rite for membership in this group, that baptism is functioning as an initiatory rite. Explicit evidence for this interpretation of baptism is provided by Josephus' statement in *Ant.* 18.117 that John was one who

> τοῖς Ἰουδαίοις κελεύοντα ἀρετὴν ἐπασκοῦσιν καὶ τὰ πρὸς ἀλλήλους δικαιοσύνῃ καὶ πρὸς τὸν θεὸν εὐσεβείᾳ χρωμένοις βαπτισμῷ συνιέναι.

> commanded the Jews to practise virtue and act with justice toward one another and with piety toward God, and [so] to gather together by baptism.

In the structure of this sentence, βαπτισμῷ συνιέναι ('and [so] to gather together by baptism') is the object of the substantival participle κελεύοντα (i.e. John was 'one who commanded'). The expression βαπτισμῷ συνιέναι is most unusual if all Josephus meant was that John commanded them to be baptized. The verb σύνειμι means 'to come together' or 'to gather together'.[107] It implies a common purpose and the coming together is to accomplish this purpose.[108] The dative, βαπτισμῷ, is usually translated 'in baptism', 'for baptism', or 'to baptism'.[109] While each of these is possible, they do not explain adequately the unusual construction with συνιέναι.[110] It is possible that it refers to group baptism, but as Louis H. Feldman comments: 'The translation "to be united by baptism" seems unlikely, since there is no indication that John championed group baptism'.[111] While this observation with respect

107 BAGD, 787; LSJ, 1705.
108 Cf. the only NT use of this verb in Lk. 8.4 in which a large crowd 'gathers together' to hear Jesus.
109 Respectively, Feldman, *Josephus*, 9.83; Farmer, 'John the Baptist', 2.959; Whiston, *Josephus*, 3.72.
110 The conjectural emendation of ἐπί before βαπτισμῷ (by both Richards and Shutt, in Feldman, *Josephus*, 9.80 n. 4) is an attempt to explain this unusual construction. However, such emendations should only be employed in a last resort, when no reasonable explanation can be made otherwise; but this is not the case here.

to group baptism is correct, Feldman has too hastily rejected the translation 'by baptism'. It is equally possible that the dative, βαπτισμῷ, is
being used in the sense of instrumental of means: 'by means of baptism'.
This alternative is more probable because it is used with the verb σύνειμι which, as a compound verb with σύν, frequently takes the instrumental.[112] As the object of κελεύοντα, the verb συνιέναι implies that
the 'gathering together' is important. John was calling for his audience
to 'gather together' into some form of group and that baptism is the
means whereby the group was gathered, or from the individual's point of
view, baptism was the means whereby a person entered this 'gathered'
group. Therefore, both semantically and syntactically, this clause is best
understood to signify that John commanded the Jews 'to gather together
*by means of* baptism'.

Confirmation of this significance may be found in Josephus' use elsewhere of this same verb, σύνειμι, to refer to joining a group or party, or
to the meeting together by such a group. For example, *War* 4.132 portrays the rivalry dominating certain Judean cities because their inhabitants joined (συνιὼν) different parties in order to oppose one another.
It is interesting to note that Josephus in this context identifies στάσις
('strife') as the result of people joining these parties (*War* 4.133, 137) just
as with John the Baptist in *Ant.* 18.117-18. Similarly, *Ant.* 18:315 describes two brothers, Asinaeus and Anilaeus, who became armed bandits,
and 'young men of the poorest class gathered together [συνῇεσαν]
around them' and formed a peasant army. Also, in *War* 2.129, Josephus
describes the Essene practice of gathering together (συνίασιν) after the
morning's work to bathe in cold water in order to purify themselves for
their communal meal. In these first two examples, the verb σύνειμι signifies the joining of an individual to a group, while in the third example,
the verb indicates the meeting together with a group. It is more probable that the first two examples are closer parallels, since Josephus attributes the gathering together to be the consequence of a renewed righteous lifestyle rather than an act which allows them to do something
together. Also, the fact that Josephus attributes strife to be the consequence of John's ministry closely parallels the first two examples. It is
more probable that forming a group with socio-political sensitivities
would lead to στάσις than individuals simply meeting together. In fact,
Josephus' statement may suggest that he considered the gathering
together into a group to be of greater significance than the baptism itself,
at least from his point of view. This may be due to his concern to describe the causes and effects of στάσις in Palestine.[113] Formation of

111 Feldman, *Josephus*, 9.82 n. a.
112 Smyth (*Grammar*, §1548) states that verbs which are 'compounds of σύν take the

groups with expectations of change creates στάσις, but an ablutory rite by itself does not. Nevertheless, we may conclude that Josephus provides evidence to confirm that John's baptism did indeed function as an initiatory rite.[114]

A second line of evidence for understanding John's baptism as an initiatory rite is provided indirectly by the prophetic concept of conversionary repentance—it was sometimes associated with a return to covenant faithfulness and the formation of a faithful remnant (cf. §6.4.1). Since John proclaimed a baptism which expressed conversionary repentance, his call to repentance could suggest the formation of just such a group. This implication is suggested by the statement in Q 3.8:

> Therefore, bear fruit in keeping with repentance, and do not presume to say to yourselves, 'We have Abraham as our father'; for I say to you that God is able from these stones to raise up children to Abraham.

This saying is sometimes interpreted to indicate that John rejected ethnic Israel, viewed them as equivalent to Gentiles, and, therefore, that he was universal in his appeal.[115] However, this is unlikely. John is not repudiating God's promises to Israel, for he says that 'God is able . . . to raise up children to Abraham'.[116] Rather, John is actually reaffirming the covenant promises, but is condemning those who claim that simply being a Jew—a member of ethnic Israel—is sufficient.[117] For John, only the

---

instrumental'.

113 Cf. the context of *Ant.* 18.116-19 described in §2.2.1.

114 Marsh (*Baptism*, 64) supports this interpretation of the clause βαπτισμῷ συνιέναι and cites older authorities in support; cf. also Goguel, *Jean-Baptiste*, 16 n. 1; cf. 19; Lohmeyer, *Johannes der Täufer*, 31-32. On the other hand, Scobie (*John the Baptist*, 131-32) states that 'the argument is a weak one, however, and most likely the phrase means simply "that the people were invited to come as a people must, in numbers rather than each one separately" '. However, the only support Scobie offers for either his contention or this interpretation is his statement that 'having received baptism, they [i.e. the people] returned to their daily tasks'. But this argument (used frequently by scholars) misrepresents the sectarian character of first-century Judaism: members of most sects went about 'their daily tasks'! Cf. Kraeling, *John the Baptist*, 119; Ernst, *Johannes der Täufer*, 255. This argument also assumes, incorrectly, a monastic model for group formation, which has been unfortunately perpetuated by describing the members of the Qumran community as 'monks'.

115 E.g. Eisler, *Messiah Jesus*, 268-69; Leipoldt, *Urchristliche Taufe*, 26-27. This view is usually associated with the interpretation of John's baptism as a proselyte baptism, but I have demonstrated above (§4.3.7) that there is no evidence that proselyte baptism antedated John's baptism.

116 Kraeling, *John the Baptist*, 72-73; Scobie, *John the Baptist*, 83; cf. Davies and Allison, *Matthew*, 1.307-309; Hill, *Matthew*, 93; Fitzmyer, *Luke*, 1.468; Nolland, *Luke*, 1.148.

117 For example, *m. Sanh.* 10.1, even though it mentions exceptions to this principle, does state that 'all Israel have a portion in the world to come. . .' and cites Isa. 60.21 in support: 'your people shall *all* be righteous. . .'. Cf. Isa. 51.2-3 in which the promises to Abraham are the grounds for the restoration of Zion; cf. also *T. Levi* 15.4; *Pss. Sol.* 18.1-4; Jn 8.33, 39; Rom. 9.6-9. On the doctrine of the merits of the fathers, see Davies, *Paul*, 268-73; Moore, *Judaism*, 1.536-45; cf. also Str-B, 1.116-21.

repentant, those who had returned to Yahweh in covenant faithfulness, are the true 'children of Abraham'. So only this repentant remnant constitutes the true Israel which will be preserved and restored, receiving the eschatological, covenant promises. The Jewish people strongly identified themselves with their corporate identity as an elect people, a group chosen and set apart by God. If John is rejecting the notion of ethnic Israel receiving the covenant promises but still asserting that those promises will be fulfilled for the true, repentant 'children of Abraham', then John is clearly constituting those who do repent as a corporate entity. To deny the corporate nature of those who received repentance-baptism would require explicit evidence of John individualizing both the judgment and restoration as well as the covenant promises, ideas which would be quite distinctive in John's Palestinian Jewish context. However, no such evidence exists. The individual element in John's ministry is the call for individuals to respond to his proclamation of judgment and restoration, but this is quite understandable within a Jewish environment. John does not name this group or expand upon it; therefore, it is difficult to know what to call it. Since John thought in terms of traditional identifying terms, such as 'children of Abraham' (Q 3.8), it is probably appropriate to use the terms 'remnant', 'true Israel' or eschatological community to identify it.[118] But in so doing, we must recognize that we are the one's applyi⸗ ⸗ these terms, not John.

This evidence only provides indirect support for interpreting John's repentance-baptism to function as an initiatory rite; the direct evidence is found in Josephus' account. This NT evidence confirms that John's ministry was forming a group. Since baptismally-expressed repentance was required by John, the rite of baptism may be considered to initiate a person into the true, remnant Israel.

To conclude then, an initiatory rite is an external action which serves to change the status of a person from a non-member to that of a member. With John's baptism in particular, it changed the status from that of a non-member who is unrepentant, unforgiven, impure and facing imminent wrath to the status of a member who is repentant, forgiven, pure and assured of being preserved from the coming wrath and receiving the expected figure's eschatological blessing reserved for the true Israel.[119]

---

118 Cf. Lk. 1.17 which describes the purpose of John's ministry as one which is 'to make ready for the Lord a prepared people'. Black (*Scrolls*, 97) views the self-understanding of both the Qumran community and John to be the formation of 'a new Covenanted Israel' or 'the new Israel'. Reicke ('John's Baptism', 214) states that 'the Baptist's intention was to create a new community within Israel, a congregation of individuals purified and justified'. Cf. Beasley-Murray, *Baptism*, 32-33.

119 Examples of those who interpret John's baptism as an initiatory rite include Scobie, *John the Baptist*, 114-16; Cullmann, 'Significance', 215; Benoit, 'Qumran', 7-9;

### 6.4.6 *A Protest against the Temple Establishment*

We have observed that John's baptism functioned as a rite which mediated divine forgiveness and John, in the role of baptizer, appears to function as a mediator of that forgiveness. As such, John's baptism is significantly parallel to the atoning sacrifices of the temple cult which also mediated God's forgiveness to the person offering the sacrifice. Thus, John's baptism provided an alternative to the temple's sacrificial system as a means of forgiveness. But what reason would John have for offering such an alternative? Was his baptism simply an alternative; that is, from John's point of view was his baptism one way to receive forgiveness and a temple sacrifice was another, equally valid way? Or, was the alternative of John's baptism actually implying some type of criticism of the temple? If so, was John's problem with the sacrificial system itself, possibly considering it obsolete in face of the imminent arrival of the expected figure? Or did he conceive of the current high priesthood as illegitimate, so their officiating over the temple service was wrong? Unfortunately, the extant, fragmentary evidence concerning John contains no explicit reference to the temple itself, but indirect evidence does suggest that the broad outlines of an answer may be made.

In the Judaism of John's day the temple was not only the religious center of Judaism, it was also the social and cultural focus for Palestinian Jews as well as the center for the political authority of the ruling priestly aristocracy. In light of the socio-political realities of the first century CE, the temple was perceived in two quite different ways. It expressed the greatness of the Jewish faith as well as symbolizing the political hopes and aspirations of a people under foreign occupation. On the other hand, the temple was also a visual reminder of the way in which the temple authorities, who were the Jewish political leaders, accomodated and capitulated to the foreign occupying power.[120] Furthermore, the priestly aristocracy was frequently perceived as wealthy and corrupt, and sometimes as greedy and violent. Criticism of the temple was not focused on the building itself (though its opulence was sometimes criticized) or the concept of a sacrificial system, for both of these were central and integral to the Jewish faith. Rather, the focus of criticism was upon the temple establishment—the priestly aristocracy for whom the temple was the

---

Brownlee, 'John the Baptist', 36-39; Heron, 'Baptism', 40-41; Robinson, 'Baptism', 16-19; Oepke, 'βάπτω', 1.537; Goguel, *Jean-Baptiste*, 291; Marsh, *Baptism*, 44, 64; Reicke, 'John's Baptism', 214-19. Examples of those who oppose such an interpretation include Kraeling, *John the Baptist*, 119-20; Thyen, 'ΒΑΠΤΙΣΜΑ', 132-33 n. 6; Becker, *Johannes der Täufer*, 39; Sutcliffe, 'Baptism', 180; Pyrke, 'John the Baptist', 492; Ernst, *Johannes der Täufer*, 340.

120 Cf. the offering of two daily sacrifices for Caesar and Rome, which would have been offensive to many Jews; *War* 2.197; *Apion* 2.77.

center of their religious and political authority.[121]

We concluded above that Q 3.7-9, and 3.7b, 8b in particular, was probably addressed originally to the Sadducees (§6.2.3). Little is known of this group, but Josephus does state that they were the aristocrats and the wealthy (*Ant.* 18.17). This suggests that they either belonged to or were associated with the high-priestly families, for the temple and the high-priestly families were a locus of both Jewish power and wealth in Palestine. The close connection between the Sadducees and the temple establishment is confirmed by both Josephus and the NT (*Ant.* 20.199; Acts 5.17). Therefore, while the Sadducees were probably a broader group than just the priestly aristocracy, the temple establishment formed the core and power base of the Sadducees. Thus, the popular perception of the Sadducees appears to have equated them with the focus of power and wealth—the temple establishment.[122]

John's baptism, functioning to mediate forgiveness, offered an alternative to a primary function of the temple, and so was a threat to the temple establishment. As John grew in popularity, he would probably have been perceived as a real threat to those whose authority was grounded in the temple. Thus, it is very understandable for members of the Sadducean party to be 'coming to [observe critically] his baptism' (Q 3.8a; cf. Mt. 3.7a; cf. §3.4). John's words in Q 3.7b-8b take on greater specificity and significance when read as addressed to those associated with the temple establishment:

> You brood of vipers! Who warned you to flee from the wrath to come? . . .
> Do not presume to say to yourselves, 'We have Abraham as our father'; for
> I say to you that God is able from these stones to raise up children to
> Abraham.

When associated with other elements of John's proclamation, including the universal call to a conversionary repentance and the announcement of imminent judgment and restoration, this saying implies that John is denying to them their claim to power and respectability, pronouncing them under the judgment of God, and suggesting their removal from their position of authority was imminent.

---

121 E.g. 1QpHab 8.8-13; 9.4-7; 10.1; 11.4-8, 12-14; 12.2-10; 4QpNah 1.11; *T. Mos.* 5.1-6; 7.1-10. For other evidence and recent discussion see Evans, 'Evidence of Corruption', 522-39. Cf. also Horsley, 'High Priests', 23-55; Horsley, *Spiral of Violence*, 7-15; Smallwood, 'High Priests', 14-34. Jesus' action in the temple is a central feature of Sanders' interpretation (*Jesus*, 61-76) of Jesus' ministry. He argues (61-69) that there was little wrong with the temple establishment which would require a 'cleansing' by Jesus. But see the extensive criticism of Sanders' view by Evans, 'Cleansing', 237-70, esp. 256-64.

122 On the Sadducees see Schürer, *History*, 2.404-14; Stern, 'Aspects of Jewish Society', 2.561-630, esp. 609-12; Jeremias, *Jerusalem*, 228-32. For a more sceptical point of view, see Saldarini, *Pharisees*, 298-308.

Why John condemned them specifically is not clear. However, this condemnation does indicate that John's baptism is not offered as an alternative to an equally valid temple rite, but it is probably a replacement for the temple rite, at least temporarily.[123] It does not appear that John was against the temple or its rites *per se*. Since his condemnation is of the priestly aristocracy and he has replaced a prime function of the temple itself, it is probable that John conceived the priestly aristocracy's presence or actions as in some way defiling the temple or invalidating the temple rites. In light of the coming wrath, John offered a replacement which prepared people to be preserved through that wrath.

If this reconstruction is correct, those Jews who received John's baptism were no doubt aware that, in receiving forgiveness of sins through a repentance-baptism, they were bypassing or eliminating the temple rite, one which had previously been a focus of their Jewish heritage. If so, John would have had to explain why this was so to his audiences. Therefore, a person receiving John's baptism would probably be in agreement with John's criticism of the temple establishment. So, receiving John's baptism probably functioned as a form of protest against the temple establishment, at least a protest by John as well as by some who were baptized and were aware of this significance.[124]

---

123 Thomas (*Mouvement baptiste*, esp. 280-81) concludes that ablutions sometimes took the place of sacrifices among certain groups. But much of his evidence is later than John the Baptist. Cf. the discussion of Thomas' work in §4.4.

124 This particular function of John's baptism has generally been neglected by scholars. For example, Thyen ('ΒΑΠΤΙΣΜΑ', 151) describes John's baptism as 'a polemic substitute for temple-sacrifice', but he does not explore this further.

What led to John's opposition to the temple establishment is unknown. Kraeling (*John the Baptist*, 15-27) traces John's wilderness existence to 'some bitter experience' (16) which alienated him as a rural priest from the temple establishment, though what this experience was is unknown (cf. the agreement by Hollenbach, 'Social Aspects', 853-55). To understand John as alienated from the urban, priestly aristocracy is a most plausible reconstruction and quite helpful, though tracing that alienation to one particular experience might be unwarranted; cf. §10.6.2.

Lohmeyer's entire discussion (*Johannes der Täufer*) of John the Baptist is guided by the question, 'why did John abandon the priesthood?' Unfortunately, his question has coloured his exegesis, so that everything is read in terms of the temple. For example, the tree which the axe is about to chop down is the Herodian temple (62-67). Lohmeyer perceives John prophecying the destruction of Judaism and creating a new religion (146-47). For a summary and critique of Lohmeyer, see Wink, 'John the Baptist and the Gospel', 35-41.

For an analysis from a sociological perspective which views the critique of the temple in terms of perceiving oneself cut off from the means of redemption, see Isenberg, 'Millenarism', 30-38; Isenberg, 'Power', 2.24-52.

## 6.5  *The Jewish Context of John's Baptism*

I have argued that John's baptism had six interrelated functions. A comparison of these functions with Jewish immersions is illuminating, both in terms of their similarities and differences.[125]

### 6.5.1  *The Context of the Old Testament*

Just as John was concerned with repentance, forgiveness and cleansing, etc., the OT is also concerned with similar issues. But John's conceptual framework is somewhat different from the OT. For example, the OT is concerned with both repentance and forgiveness as was John, but in the OT forgiveness was understood to be mediated through the sacrificial system, and the prophetic orientation concerning repentance did not require the performance of any particular religious rite. Yet links with OT thought may be traced in the function of John's baptism. One possible parallel is the immersion of Naaman (2 Kgs 5.10, 14), but his 'conversion' (5.15-19) was a consequence of being miraculously healed through his immersions and not an expression of that conversion, and his immersions did not mediate forgiveness. Nevertheless, the story of Naaman draws together the ideas of conversion, immersion and the Jordan river in Jewish tradition.[126]

We also observed that immersions in the OT were performed to cleanse from uncleanness caused by physical contagion, but that, while the OT used ablutory language metaphorically to portray cleansing from uncleanness caused by moral contagion, it did not use actual ablutions to accomplish such cleansing (§4.2.6). John drew these two strands of Jewish thinking together, performing an actual immersion to cleanse a person from uncleanness caused by moral contagion. In linking these two strands, and in light of John's emphasis on ethical transformation as the fruit of repentance (Q 3.8; cf. *Ant.* 18.117a; Lk. 3.10-14), texts such as Isa. 1.16-17 may have formed a background for John and/or his audience:

> Wash yourselves, make yourselves clean;
> > Remove the evil of your deeds from my sight.
> Cease to do evil,
> > Learn to do good;

125 It is not my purpose to examine the 'origins' of John's baptism. I find such discussion is frequently inadequate methodologically and reductionist. John's baptism has to be understood for itself. The purpose of comparing his baptism with its larger context is to highlight its similarities and differences within John's Jewish milieu. These similarities and differences demonstrate the Jewish orientation of John's baptism and the plausibility of the interpretation provided in this chapter of its functions, and yet leave room for John to stand out as a distinct individual within his Jewish milieu.

126 Cf. the discussion in §4.2.5. of Naaman 'going down' to the Jordan river as a suggestion of humility.

> Seek justice,
>> Correct oppression;
> Defend the orphan,
>> Plead for the widow.

To link actual cleansing from physical contagion and metaphorical cleansing from moral contagion is not unique to John, for we have observed similar ideas in the Second Temple Jewish literature.[127]

John's baptism also foreshadowed the greater baptizing ministry of the expected figure. The OT also conveys a hope in a greater eschatological ablution, such as that expressed in Ezek. 36.25-26:

> Then I will sprinkle clean water on you, and you will be clean; from all of your uncleannesses and from all your idols I will cleanse you. And I will give you a new heart and a new spirit I will put within you, and I will remove the heart of stone from your flesh and give you a heart of flesh.[128]

Leonhard Goppelt states that 'John offered the first part of Ezekiel's prophecy, namely, the cleansing water bath; the renewing bestowal of the Spirit would be brought by the One to come'.[129]  While it perhaps goes beyond the evidence to tie John's baptism to Ezekiel's prophecy in particular, nevertheless John did conceive of his own baptism as foreshadowing the OT expectation of an eschatological ablution.

### 6.5.2 *The Context of the Second Temple Jewish Literature*
But John's baptism must be compared particularly with the immersions described in the literature of the Second Temple period, for this is his more immediate context. Levi explains concerning his immersion in *T. Levi* 2.3B2 that 'in living water I wholly bathed myself, and all my ways I made straight'.  The idea of 'making one's ways straight' suggests an extensive change in ethical behavior, but the prayer following indicates that a reorientation towards God was being sought (cf. 2.3B7-8, 11, 14), thus suggesting that this is a reference to a concept similar to conversionary repentance.  However, the prayer emphasizes the need for God to remove 'the spirit of unrighteousness' and replace it with 'the spirit of holiness'.  This recognizes that, while a person may 'make his/her ways straight', it requires God to make such a repentance complete by transforming the person's spirit.  This conception is similar to John's idea that the expected figure's baptism will complete the transforming process by

---

127 E.g. 1QS 3.6-9; *T. Levi* 2.3B; *Sib. Or.* 4.162-70. Collins ('Fourth Sibyl', 378 n. 72) suggests that Isa. 1.16 may have provided the biblical basis for both the sibyl and John to link an immersion with repentance.

128 Cf. similar expectations in Isa. 4.4; Joel 3.18; Zech. 13.1; 14.8; Mal. 3.2-3, and the discussion in §4.2.6.

129 Goppelt, *Theology*, 1.38.  Goppelt's observation could be applied to the understanding of the Qumran community as reflected in 1QS 3.6-9 and 4.19-22; cf. §5.3.1, 5.3.3, 5.4.2.

baptizing the people of the true Israel with a holy spirit. In both cases the agent of final transformation is 'a spirit of holiness' (*T. Levi* 2.3B8; Q 3.16b; Mk 1.8b). But in *T. Levi* 2.3B there is no explicit indication of the immersion *mediating* forgiveness; it appears rather to symbolize the desire for God to cleanse from sin (which is essentially similar to forgiveness). In both *T. Levi* 2.3B and John's baptism the immersion is performed in 'living' or running water, suggesting a link between the need for such water and the themes of repentance and cleansing from moral contagion.

In *Sib. Or.* 4.162-64 the sibyl's exhortation to 'change' (μετάθεσθε) from the wickedness and impiety described in 4.152-61 and to 'abandon' moral outrages is a call to a form of repentance, but the emphasis is upon ethical transformation rather than a radical 'turning' to God. Following this ethical transformation is a command to 'wash [λούσασθε] your whole bodies in perennial rivers . . . and ask forgiveness [συγγνώμην αἰτεῖσθε]' (4.166-67). The immersion probably cleanses from uncleanness caused by the moral contagion of their wickedness, and symbolizes the desire for forgiveness which is further expressed in the petitions offered to God. The immersion, while symbolizing the desire for forgiveness, probably did not mediate the forgiveness itself because 'propitiation [ἱλάσκεσθε] for bitter impiety' is accomplished 'with words of praise' (4.167-78) rather than the immersion. This verbalization of 'words of praise' probably links the atonement and forgiveness to the plea for forgiveness which expressed the repentance. While the reader is exhorted to 'change . . . abandon . . . wash . . . ask forgiveness . . . and make propitiation . . .', the actual conversion is something God must provide: 'God will grant repentance [μετάνοιαν] and will not destroy' (4.168-69). Thus, in a way similar to John, the audience is called to transform, but God is understood to complete this process of transformation. Here the completion of that process is described as 'repentance', while in John's baptism, the term 'repentance' describes the human act of turning. The terminology is the same, and the process is similar, but the terms are applied to different elements of that process. We also observed in *Sib. Or.* 4.8, 27-30 a rejection of the temple and animal sacrifice, and suggested that the use of immersions in conjunction with seeking forgiveness and making propitiation may have been a substitute for the temple cultus. A similar relationship was observed with respect to John's baptism, though he was evidently opposed to the temple establishment rather than the building itself and its sacrifices. As with *T. Levi* 2.3B, this immersion was to be performed in flowing water of a river.

In the *Life of Adam and Eve* (*Apoc. Mos.* 29.11-13a) the immersion is an expression of repentance ('let us repent', μετανοήσωμεν; 29.11), but the idea of repentance here is not conversionary repentance but rather penitential repentance, which is probably why the immersion is for 40 days.[130] That which leads Adam and Eve to this repentance is not a radical 'turning' to God but a need for food. Nevertheless, the immersion may be for cleansing from moral contagion because Adam states that 'our lips are not clean' (29.12). Again, the immersion took place in a river and is linked with the themes of repentance and cleansing from moral contagion, though the concept of repentance here is quite different from John's conversionary repentance.

Though I argued above that proselyte immersion within Judaism is a post-70 CE phenomenon, nevertheless it may be profitably compared with John's baptism. Our examination above suggested that proselyte immersion functioned as a rite initiating Gentiles into the covenant community of Israel, as well as symbolizing forgiveness of sins and cleansing the person, though the precise nature of this cleansing is unclear (§4.3.7). John's baptism also initiated people into the true Israel, but there is no evidence that he considered all Jews to be Gentiles. Thus, while John's rite was an initiatory baptism it was not a 'proselyte' baptism. That such a concept could arise after John in mainstream Judaism indicates that the constituent elements were probably already existing in Judaism (and did not have to be 'borrowed' from Christianity). It is also interesting to observe that proselyte baptism probably did not arise until after the destruction of the temple, thus suggesting that within Jewish thinking generally there were the seeds already existing whereby an immersion could be an alternative to a temple rite. Of course, I have suggested that John's use of baptism was as a critical protest against the temple establishment, and the use of proselyte baptism arose in quite different circumstances. Nevertheless, the parallel relationship between an immersion and a temple rite remains.

### 6.5.3 *The Context of the Qumran Literature*
While these texts are similar in some respects to John's baptism, the closest parallel is the initiatory immersion practised by the Qumran community. In 1QS 3.6-9 the expression of spiritual virtues by the person has two results: the immersion is efficacious to purify the person, and the person's sins are atoned. Unfortunately this Qumran text relates various spiritual virtues to *atonement* and an immersion, while John's baptism relates repentance to *forgiveness* and an immersion. Can these really be compared? I think they can be compared, but with care. We saw above

---

130 Cf. references to penitence in *LAE* 4.3-5.1; on the difference between conversionary and penitential repentance, see §6.4.1.

that the spiritual virtues were given to the person by God's spirit, but they were virtues that the candidate was expected to manifest.[131] Elsewhere, the members of the Qumran community considered themselves to be 'the repentant' or 'the converted' (שבי).[132] The focus of their 'returning' was to 'turn' from evil and to 'turn' to the Law.[133] In 1QS a candidate was one who was expected 'to turn [לשוב] from all evil and cling to all His commands' (1QS 5.1) and the oath the candidate took upon entering the covenant community is an oath 'to return [לשוב] to the Law of Moses' (5.8), and the candidates are not cleansed 'unless they turn [שבו] from their wickedness' (5.14). Thus, the spiritual virtues described in 1QS 3.6-9 may be understood as expansions detailing just what the conversionary repentance by the candidate entailed.

The other difference is that in 1QS 3.6-9 the sin is *atoned* by the spiritual virtues (or, the repentance), while in John's proclamation the sin is *forgiven* by God as a response to the repentance-baptism. While related, atonement and forgiveness are different. The sin had to be 'covered' (כפר, 'to atone') in order for the person to be 'released' or 'pardoned' (סלח, 'to forgive') from the consequences of that sin.[134] 1QS 2.8 states that God will 'forgive by atoning your iniquities' (יסלח לכפר עווניך),[135] and in 1QH 14.24 God is described as the one 'who forgives those who repent of transgression' (הסולח לשבי פשע). Therefore, while 1QS 3.6-9 only states that God views the candidate's sins as atoned for by the repentance expressed, it is reasonable to assume that the person is also being forgiven by God at the same time.

Thus, within the Qumran community the conceptual framework appears to have been that a person turns from sin to Torah-obedience which is demonstrated by appropriate spiritual virtues (i.e. repentance) and a commitment to enter the covenant/community. This repentance atones for the person's sins and the person is forgiven by God thus establishing a relationship between the person and God. This same repentance makes efficacious the immersion which cleanses the person thus establishing a relationship with the other purified members of the com-

---

131 Cf. the discussion of the specific spiritual virtues in §5.3.1.4.

132 4QpPs37 3.1; cf. CD 4.2; 6.4-5; 8.16; but cf. the discussion by Davies (*Damascus Covenant*, 92-94) concerning the alternative interpretations of the term שבי ישראל in CD.

133 Turn from evil: 1QS 5.14; 10.20; 1QH 2.9; 6.6, 14; 14.24; CD 2.5; 20.17; turn to the Law: 1QS 5.8; CD 15.12; 16.1-2, 4; both turning from evil and turning to the Law together: 1QS 5.1; 6.15; 4QpPs37 2.2-4; CD 15.7-9. References to 'returning' to God are rare (1QH 16.17; 4Q504 fr.1-2 5.11-14), but even in these cases the return includes returning to obeying the Law. This stands in contrast to the OT, in which the return is almost always a return to Yahweh; cf. §6.4.1.

134 Cf. Lev. 4.26, 31; 5.10.

135 In 1QS 2.8 the statement is in the negative, describing what God will not do to the ungodly.

munity. The conceptual framework for John, on the other hand, is slightly different. With John, a person turns from sin to God which is expressed by an immersion. To this repentance-baptism God responds by forgiving the person's sins; at the same time, this repentance-baptism cleanses the person. Therefore, the understanding of repentance differs somewhat, but more importantly, the function of the immersion with respect to forgiveness is different. This difference may be diagrammed:

QUMRAN COMMUNITY:

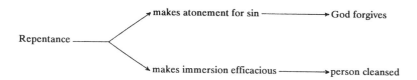

Repentance
- makes atonement for sin ⟶ God forgives
- makes immersion efficacious ⟶ person cleansed

JOHN THE BAPTIST:

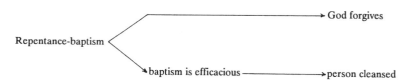

Repentance-baptism
- ⟶ God forgives
- baptism is efficacious ⟶ person cleansed

In this discussion and these diagrams I have altered the Qumran community's vocabulary in order to compare it with John's concepts, but a comparison of these two diagrams causes us to consider reversing the alteration temporarily to consider whether John's repentance-baptism 'makes atonement for sin' as repentance did for those at Qumran. While our evidence concerning John does not use this term, it is possible that John's baptism may be understood in this way. We observed above that the mediation of forgiveness in the OT sacrificial system was paralleled by John's baptism mediating forgiveness and John's participation in the act of baptizing as the role of mediator (cf. §6.4.2). The primary difference between the two is that in the first a mediating priest performs a sacrifice which atones for the sin resulting in God forgiving the person, while in the other John as a mediator (priest) performs a repentance-baptism resulting in God forgiving the person. Therefore, while atonement is not explicitly mentioned with respect to John's baptism, John's baptism could have been conceived of as a rite of atonement in parallel with both the OT sacrificial system as well as the understanding of atonement and immersions in the Qumran literature.

John's baptism also parallels the Qumran community's immersion in that both are understood to cleanse the person from uncleanness caused by moral contagion. In this they appear identical, but the thought is not unique to them, for we have observed similar ideas in other Jewish literature.

Both John's baptism and the Qumran community's initial immersion of the candidate function as an initiatory rite. At Qumran the initial purificatory immersion fundamentally changed the candidate's status from an impure non-Israelite to a pure member of the true Israel—a member of the Qumran community (1QS 3.6-9; 5.7-15). Similarly, we concluded that John's baptism changed the status of a person from a non-member who is unrepentant, unforgiven, impure and facing wrath to one who was a repentant, forgiven, pure member of the true Israel who was assured of being preserved from the coming wrath and would receive the expected figure's eschatological blessing. Neither the Qumran community nor John perceived outsiders as equivalent to Gentiles, but they both interpreted Israel's eschatological expectations to be reserved for their group alone. Thus, while John's baptism and the Qumran community's immersions differ in other ways, in this respect they are quite similar.

1QS 4.21-22 expressed the expectation of an eschatological cleansing which was described with ablutory language derived from Ezek. 36.25-27—the same language utilized to portray the initiatory immersion of a candidate in 1QS 3.6-9. We concluded above on the grounds of both similar concepts and terminology that it is possible that the community's purificatory immersion was understood to foreshadow this eschatological cleansing (cf. §5.3.3, 5.4.2). It was evidently the members of the Qumran community who were expected to receive this eschatological cleansing, even though the community considered themselves already pure; thus, this passage expresses the hope for a complete purification from all vestiges of contamination. This eschatological purification completed the purificatory process already begun by their own purificatory immersions. While this foreshadowing of the eschatological purification by their purificatory immersions may be implied from 1QS, the foreshadowing of the baptizing ministry of John's expected figure by John's own baptizing ministry is explicit in Q 3.16-17 and Mk 1.7-8. Interestingly, the agent in both cases is 'a spirit of holiness'.[136] The Qumran community was primarily concerned with purity, and so the focus of its own immersions as well as the eschatological ablution was upon purification. John's focus was more upon conversionary repentance and its fruits, though he

136 1QS 4.21; Q 3.16b; Mk 1.8b; cf. *T. Levi* 2.3B8; 1QS 3.7; cf. §8.2.1, 8.4.1.

was evidently concerned with purity as well, but not in quite the same sense as those at Qumran. Therefore, while John's baptism foreshadowed the expected figure's baptizing ministry in a way similar to that which may have existed among the members of the Qumran community, the precise elements being foreshadowed are not the same.

We also observed that at Qumran was a community which was critical of the temple establishment. Their understanding of repentance provided an alternative to the use of a temple sacrifice as a means of atonement and forgiveness. While their use of immersions did not function directly as a means of forgiveness as did John's baptism, nevertheless, their understanding of immersions was closely related to their alternative means of achieving forgiveness and thus was part of the conceptual framework which included their criticism of the temple establishment.[137]

This comparison of the functions of John's baptism with the functions of immersions practised by other individuals and groups within Second Temple Judaism demonstrates that in certain respects John's baptism was different from these other practices. Yet, for each of the functions which we have observed, similarities with John's baptism may be found within his Jewish heritage and contemporary environment. John was a creative innovator and yet he remained very much within the social and cultural milieu of first-century Judaism.

## 6.6 *Conclusion*

In this chapter I have argued that both Josephus' *Antiquities* and the NT may be utilized as reliable historical sources for data concerning John's

---

137 The literature comparing John with the Qumran community is extensive. Significant studies include: Brownlee, 'Comparison of the Covenanters', 50-72; Lieberman, 'Discipline', 199-206; Brownlee, 'John the Baptist', 33-53; Cullmann, 'Significance of the Qumran Texts', 18-32; Rabin, *Qumran Studies*, 1-21; Robinson, 'Baptism of John', 11-27; Betz, 'Proselytentaufe', 213-34; Rowley, 'Baptism of John', 218-29; Sutcliffe, 'Baptism', 179-88; Black, *Scrolls*, 91-101; Flusser, 'Baptism of John', 209-38; Gnilka, 'Essenischen Tauchbäder', 185-207; Braun, 'Täufertaufe', 1-4; Delcor, 'Vocabulaire juridique', 109-34; Pyrke, 'John the Baptist', 483-96; Dupont-Sommer, 'Culpabilité', 61-70; Braun, *Qumran*, 2.1-29; Harrison, 'Rites and Customs', 26-36; Scobie, *John the Baptist*, 102-16; Scobie, 'John the Baptist', 58-69; Reicke, 'Jüdischen Baptisten', 76-88; Thiering, 'Inner and Outer Cleansing', 266-77; Badia, *Qumran Baptism*; Thiering, 'Qumran Initiation', 615-31. Cf. the bibliographic survey by É. Cothenet, 'Qumran et le Nouveau Testament: A. Jean-Baptiste', 9.980-96.

Since the discovery of the Qumran scrolls several scholars have suggested that John may have at one time been a member of the Qumran community; e.g. Brownlee, 'John the Baptist', 33-53; Robinson, 'Baptism of John', 11-27; Geyser, 'Youth of John', 70-75. However, concrete evidence is lacking, and even if John had been a member at one time, the certain elements of his public ministry are sufficiently different from the ideology of the Qumran community to indicate that he must have broken with them. Therefore, while an interesting hypothesis, this idea must remain merely speculative. Cf. the extensive critique by Wink, 'John the Baptist', 75-103.

baptism, provided that we take into consideration the aims and emphases of these sources. On the one hand, Josephus, in writing for his Roman audience has Hellenized John's message and certain aspects of John's baptism. In so doing, Josephus has at the same time heightened the ethical orientation of John's ministry and removed the eschatological orientation of John's ministry, both of which are evident in the Gospels. On the other hand, the Evangelists, in writing for their audiences, have Christianized elements of John's message and baptism. At the same time they have downplayed the socio-political implications and consequences of John's ministry which are portrayed by Josephus. None of our sources claim to be presenting an 'objective' biography of John; rather, all sources have, not unreasonably, portrayed John for their own purposes and from their own points of view. When these purposes and points of view are taken into account, and our sources carefully gleaned for what data they may provide us, we arrive at a more extensive and rounded portrayal of John (though still incomplete and fragmentary) than any one of our sources provides.

On the basis of these sources I have argued that several elements contribute to appreciating how John's baptism was administered. John's baptism was an immersion performed in 'living' or flowing water, which was probably associated with expressing repentance and being cleansed. This flowing water is usually identified as the Jordan river, with John sometimes being found on the eastern bank; but we have not yet discussed the significance of this (cf. §10.5). In conjunction with being baptized, the people confessed their sins, which relates to the baptism expressing repentance and mediating forgiveness. This feature also suggests some form of liturgy might have been used. The most distinctive feature of John's baptism is that he administered it to the person being baptized rather than the immersion being self-administered. The method by which he administered the baptism is unknown, but the fact that he did so appears to be a symbolic portrayal of the baptism mediating divine forgiveness and so, in baptizing the people, John is functioning in a mediatorial role himself. Finally, John not only administered a baptism, he proclaimed it, suggesting that it was not only an essential requirement, but that the significance of its functions required explanation.

I have argued that John's baptism functioned in six interrelated ways.[138] First of all, it expressed the person's conversionary repentance,

---

138  I could be accused of committing the semantic error of attributing all possible meanings of a word to its use in a particular case, or what is known as 'illegitimate totality transfer' (cf. Carson, *Fallacies*, 62; Silva, *Biblical Words*, 25-27). However, this is not actually the case. First of all, with John's baptism we are dealing with the action of baptizing and its attendant elements, not the word 'baptism'. Secondly, I have not

in which a person, realizing the imminence of the coming judgment, turned from his/her past life perceived now as sinful, and turned to a new relationship with God which was to produce a new, righteous lifestyle. The expression of repentance required the baptism, and the efficacy of baptism required the repentance; thus, it was a repentance-baptism. Secondly, God responded to the repentance-baptism by forgiving the person's sins. The baptism itself and its administration by John assured the person of divine forgiveness. Since repentance-baptism was the required channel for forgiveness, it mediated the forgiveness, and John functioned in a mediatorial role. Thirdly, the past, sinful life of a person was understood to be moral contagion which rendered the person unclean. Therefore, John's baptism cleansed the person from that uncleanness.

Fourthly, John's baptism foreshadowed the expected figure's greater baptism; it was the final preparation to be made before the imminent arrival of this figure. What John's baptism did in part, the expected figure's baptism would complete. John's baptism expressed a person's turning to God, but the expected figure will complete the conversion by baptizing the person with a holy spirit. John's baptism cleansed the person but, through the expected figure's ministry, the cleansing will be full and final. Fifthly, the responses to John's ministry separated the repentant from the unrepentant, and it was the repentant who were prepared to receive the expected figure's ministry of restoration. As a corporate body, these prepared ones constituted the eschatological community of the true, remnant Israel, and it was the baptism which prepared them, and so initiated them into this community. Finally, John's repentance-

gathered all possible significances for an immersion and read them into John's baptism. Rather, I have demonstrated how these various functions arise out of the evidence at hand. Thirdly, I have also shown how similar functions may be seen in other ablutory practices, with these other immersions also having several functions at the same time. Finally, these functions may be understood to be perceiving John's baptism from the point of view of different relationships, including the person's relationship with God, other persons, one's past heritage, one's future expectations and the temple establishment.

There are functions of John's baptism which have been suggested by other scholars but supporting evidence is, I think, lacking; they have not been included in the preceding discussion. For example, it has been suggested that John's baptism symbolized a death and resurrection (but cf. Beasley-Murray, *Baptism*, 41 n. 1). As well, Kraeling (*John the Baptist*, 117-18) argued that for John the Jordan river represented the fiery river of apocalypticism, and that a voluntary immersion in the Jordan now saved a person from a later involuntary immersion in the fiery river. So John's baptism was 'a rite symbolic of the acceptance of the judgment which he proclaimed' (118; but cf. Thyen, 'ΒΑΠΤΙΣΜΑ', 132-33 n. 6; Becker, *Johannes der Täufer*, 39). I have also avoided discussions of the 'origin' of John's baptism, for these are generally unhelpful and often reductionist.

baptism, as a rite which mediated forgiveness indicated that the usual means of forgiveness, the temple cultus, had been made invalid, probably by the actions and policies of the temple establishment. Thus, John's baptism functioned as a protest against the perceived abuses by the temple establishment.[139]

A comparison of the administration and functions of John's baptism with the evidence provided by the OT and Second Temple Jewish literature indicate that each element of John's baptism is quite understandable within his Jewish milieu. Yet, John's baptism manifests distinctive features which indicate that he was a creative and innovative person who was able to formulate from within his heritage and milieu a coherent response to the problems he perceived among his people.

---

139 Some of these functions suggest that John's baptism was administered only once to a
person, especially the functions of expressing conversionary repentance and initiating
into the true Israel. Therefore, while the evidence is not conclusive, it would seem
that John's baptism was probably only administered once (cf. Scobie, *John the Baptist*, 115). This does not preclude the probability that John practised other immersion
and ablutory rites, but these would have been distinct from 'John's baptism'.

# PART  III

# JOHN AS PROPHET

Chapter 7

## JUDGMENT/RESTORATION FIGURES
## IN THE OLD TESTAMENT
## AND SECOND TEMPLE JEWISH LITERATURE

### 7.1 *Introduction*

In Part II we considered John in one of his major, and in some senses, his most distinctive role: 'the baptizer'. In our analysis of his baptismal ministry we came to appreciate that baptism was integrally related to John's eschatological orientation, and it was something which he proclaimed. But John proclaimed more than just his baptism. In fact, the NT quite unequivocally reports that John was understood by large segments of the population to be a prophet.[1] John's role as prophet forms the heart of our investigation here in Part III. In Chapters 7 and 8 we first turn our attention to the content of his prophetic proclamation and concentrate upon his announcement of an expected figure[2] within the wider contours of his eschatological expectation. Then in Chapters 9 and 10 we broaden our horizons and consider John's prophetic ministry in the light of other prophetic figures in existence during the latter portion of the Second Temple period.

In this chapter we survey the types and characteristics of Jewish eschatological figures portrayed in the OT and Second Temple Jewish literature. However, a broad survey of these figures without any guidelines directing our investigation would be beyond the confines of this work. Therefore, we must allow the description of John's figure in the two primary NT sources (Mk 1.7-8; Q 3.16-17) to provide preliminary guidelines for this survey. In the next chapter we subject to careful analysis these NT sources which describe John's announcement of an expected figure in order to ascertain as far as possible their original form and whether or not they may be utilized as historically reliable sources (§8.2). This survey of Jewish expected figures will contribute to making informed historical judgments concerning the NT data.

---

1   Cf. §9.1; e.g. Lk. 7.26 = Mt. 11.9; Mk 11.32 = Mt. 21.26 = Lk. 20.6.
2   In §8.2.1 I analyse the descriptions 'Coming One' and 'Mighty One' and conclude that neither within Judaism nor with John are these actual titles. In order not to perpetuate this misconception and possibly prejudge the material, I refrain from making a title out of either of them. I will use the term 'expected figure' instead. I employ the term 'figure' in its broadest possible sense to indicate an individual—but an indi-

John proclaimed the coming of a figure whose activities would involve what may be broadly described as judgment and restoration. While the term 'judgment' may refer to rendering a legal verdict (i.e. guilty or not guilty of certain sins or crimes), or pronouncing a sentence upon the guilty party, it may also refer to the execution of punishment. As a term to describe the activity of John's expected figure, judgment may refer to any of these elements, but the emphasis in John's description seems to be upon the latter sense of executing punishment (Q 3.16d-17; cf. Q 3.9). John is sometimes considered to be exclusively a prophet of judgment or doom.[3] But this is not an accurate portrayal, because the figure he proclaimed also had a ministry of restoration. This is indicated by the reference to 'he will gather the wheat into his granary' (Q 3.17c), and might also be implied by the baptism with a holy spirit (if such a baptism is understood to have a gracious sense, but this has yet to be explored; cf. §8.4.1). I have chosen to use 'restoration' as an inclusive term, indicating a return to a state of blessing. It may include the ideas associated with more specific terms such as salvation, purification and vindication, and may have political, social and spiritual connotations as well. How John's description of his expected figure is to be specifically interpreted within these broad parameters of a figure of judgment and restoration is explored in the next chapter.

It is possible that John proclaimed a figure of judgment and restoration who was totally distinct from any form of expectation current in Jewish thought of his day. However, this is highly unlikely, and must be set aside as an alternative unless all other possible alternatives have been rejected. As a Jew speaking primarily to Jews, John would use imagery and themes which arose out of his Jewish heritage. Since his portrayal does not go to great lengths to describe the figure itself, but uses traditional Jewish imagery to call the people to repentance, he is most probably referring to expectations already current among the people of his day. This does not preclude of course the likelihood that John developed his own ideas and emphases even though he employed this traditional material. It is to this Jewish thought that we now turn in order to ascertain to which figure(s) his audience would have understood him to be referring.

The NT interprets John's expected figure to be the Messiah (e.g. Lk. 3.15), and, while this is one possibility, the evidence concerning Jewish thought in the OT and the literature of the Second Temple period betrays an almost bewildering variety of figures who were expected to

vidual who may be human (e.g. a human messianic figure), supernatural (e.g. an angelic figure) or even divine (e.g. Yahweh himself).

3    E.g. Becker, *Johannes der Täufer*, 38-39.

exercise a role of judgment and restoration. In addition to Yahweh himself, there are supernatural agents including angels generally, as well as specific angels such as Michael. Other supernatural figures include the Son of Man and Melchizedek. Human agents who exercise these functions include both Davidic and Aaronic messianic figures, as well as prophetic figures such as the eschatological prophet or Elijah-*redivivus*. Judgment and restoration could also be carried out by the people themselves, or the nation, or even a remnant within the nation.

A description and analysis of each of these types is beyond the scope of this work, but this list does demonstrate the difficulty of the task at hand, and this is compounded by the fact that John apparently does not explicitly identify to which of these figures he is referring. The only way to proceed is to narrow the field of possibilities by identifying those figures whose descriptions correspond at least to some extent with the elements used in John's description of his expected figure. A preliminary reading of the NT sources (Josephus does not mention this element of John's ministry) indicates that John's description included the following five elements: (1) he is coming; (2) he is mightier than John; (3) John was unworthy to be even his servant; (4) he will baptize with a holy spirit and fire; (5) his ministry includes both judgment and restoration and is portrayed in terms of a farmer cleaning his threshing-floor, gathering the wheat into the granary, and burning the chaff. But the third element is essentially a characteristic of John rather than of his expected figure, and thus it plays no direct role in our search for antecedents (though it may be relevant for choosing between those antecedents). For the purposes of our search, the second element (the figure is mightier than John) must be altered to a figure described as mighty in order to remove the reference of comparison with John. With respect to the fourth element, we must consider the possibility that the term πνεῦμα could have originally signified either 'wind' or 'spirit', and that the adjective 'holy' was not original.[4] Thus, if the expected figure John proclaimed is to be identified in the minds of his audience with a figure already current in contemporary eschatological expectation, as evidenced in the OT and the Second Temple Jewish literature, then the data at hand concerning this figure are that: (1) his activities include judgment and restoration; (2) he is coming;[5] (3) he is mighty; (4) he will baptize with a (holy) spirit/wind and fire; and (5) his judgment and restoration is portrayed employing threshing-floor imagery.

---

4    Cf. §8.2 for an examination of the historicity of these various elements.
5    The notion of a figure 'coming' is somewhat vague and may actually be used in at least two ways which differ in their nuance: (1) the figure, once absent, could

## 7.2 Yahweh

In both the OT and Second Temple Jewish literature[6] the most prominent figure who was expected to act in judgment and restoration was
Yahweh.[7] He had done so in the past,[8] and he was expected to do so in
the future. He would judge not only his people,[9] but also the Gentile
nations[10] and even the whole earth.[11] He was also expected to purge
Israel, separating the wicked from the righteous; the wicked would be
punished or destroyed, and the righteous would be restored and blessed.
For example, *Pss. Sol.* 2.33-35 states:

> Praise God, you who fear the Lord with understanding,
>     for the Lord's mercy is upon those who fear him with judgment.
> To separate between the righteous and the sinner

approach someone/somewhere and arrive (emphasizing physical presence with
others), or (2) the figure, once unrecognized, could appear (emphasizing manifesta-
tion to others). Both of these senses are used with respect to the figures we will be
examining, but it is not necessary to distinguish between them.

6    Jewish expectation concerning Yahweh's coming judgment and restoration involves
     many diverse themes and is evidenced in a multitude of references. It is not possible
     to elucidate the details of these themes nor provide all relevant references within the
     scope of this work; neither is this necessary, because the function of this section is
     merely to establish that Yahweh was indeed such a figure and then explore the more
     specific elements for which we are searching.

7    The expected coming of Yahweh in judgment and restoration forms part of a larger
     motif of theophany in the OT. A survey of the OT evidence may be found in
     Schnutenhaus, 'Kommen', 1-22. He concludes (21) that theophany is 'Gottes
     Selbsterweis mitten im geschichtlichen, weltlichen Geschehen'. Jenni ('Kommen',
     254-54) observes that, when the verb 'to come' is used with God as subject, three
     contexts may be distinguished in which God comes: (1) revelation meetings; (2) the
     coming of God in cultic events; and (3) God's coming for judgment and salvation. It
     is this last group that is the center of attention here. For discussion and other litera-
     ture, see Beasley-Murray's discussion (*Kingdom*, 3-10) of 'Theophany in the Old
     Testament'. Cf. also the definitive treatment of Jeremias (*Theophanie*) which he
     summarizes in 'Theophany', 896-98.
         Integrally related to Yahweh's role as one who judges and restores is the kingship
     of Yahweh over his people as well as the whole earth; e.g. Isa. 6.5; Zech. 14.9, 16-17;
     Wis. 6.3-5; *1 En.* 12.3; 81.3; *T. Mos.* 10.1; *Pss. Sol.* 2.30-32; *Sib. Or.* 1.7, 65, 73; CD
     12.7; 19.1. For further references and discussion, see Becker, *Expectation*, 52-53;
     Beasley-Murray, *Kingdom*, 17-20; Buber, *Kingship*. On the Psalms portraying the
     enthronement of Yahweh, see Westermann, *Praise and Lament*, 242-45; Eaton, *King-
     ship*. The theme of Yahweh's kingship is often related to other motifs including the
     exaltation of Zion, the defeat of the nations and their pilgrimage to Jerusalem.
     These are often linked in what is known as the Zion tradition, on which see Roberts,
     'Zion in the Theology', 93-108; Roberts, 'Davidic Origin', 329-44.

8    Cf. the themes of exile and restoration of Israel which permeate Jewish literature;
     e.g. Deut. 29–31; Isa. 29; 54; Jer. 30–31; Neh. 9; Dan. 9; Bar. 2, 4–5; *Jub.* 1; *Pss. Sol.*
     3; *Sib. Or.* 3.265-94; CD 1.3-8.

9    E.g. Joel 2.1-11; Mal. 4.1; *1 En.* 90.26-27; *Pss. Sol.* 8.26.

10   E.g. Isa. 13.1-16; Ezek. 21.1-23; *Sib. Or.* 3.295-572.

11   E.g. Isa. 24.1-23; 63.1-6; Joel 3.2-21; Sir. 36.1-10; *1 En.* 1.3-10; *Pss. Sol.* 2.30-35;
     1QpHab 13.1-4.

> to repay sinners forever according to their actions
> And to have mercy on the righteous (keeping him) from the humiliation of
>   the sinner,
> and to repay the sinner for what he has done to the righteous.[12]

Yahweh's restoration of his people has a physical dimension whereby he delivers them from their enemies and blesses them.[13] From a spiritual perspective, he was expected to purify his people, forgiving their sins and cleansing them.[14] The universal horizon is emphasized by the reversal of Israel's relationship with the nations.[15] Each of these perspectives has eschatological elements, but the eschatological perspective in some texts is oriented beyond the earthly dimensions (which concentrated on restoration to the land, etc.) by highlighting paradisal descriptions of nature, references to a new heaven and earth, as well as descriptions of eternal life and/or resurrection.[16]

Thus, clearly Yahweh fulfils the first element: he is a figure of judgment and restoration. Similarly, with respect to the second through fifth specific elements of John's proclamation concerning the expected figure, each of them appears with reference to Yahweh's judgment and restoration of his people. Thus, with respect to the second element, Yahweh is identified as one who is coming. For example, in a context describing restoration Isa. 40.10 proclaims:

> Behold, the Lord Yahweh will come with might,
>   with his arm ruling for him.
> Behold, his reward is with him,
>   and his recompense is before him.

Similarly, the opening chapter of *1 Enoch* describes God coming, though the context describes world-wide judgment prior to restoration:

---

12  E.g. Ezek. 20.33-38; Mal. 3.5; 4.1-3; *1 En.* 1.7-10; 5.4-10; CD 1.6-9; 1QMyst 1.5-7.

13  E.g. Ezek. 34.11-31; Joel 2.18-27; Bar. 4.21–5.9; *Jub.* 1.15-18; *Pss. Sol.* 11.2-8; *Sib. Or.* 3.282-94; 1QM 1.4-14.

14  Jer. 31.34; Ezek. 11.17-20; 36.25, 29; *Jub.* 1.23; 1QS 4.10-21; 1QH 6.6-10. Yahweh renews his covenant or establishes a new covenant with them; e.g. Jer. 31.31-34; Ezek. 16.59-63; Bar. 2.35; *1 En.* 60.6; *T. Mos.* 12.13; 1QS 4.22-23; CD 3.12-20. Sometimes Yahweh's restoration (whether physical or spiritual) is conditional upon repentance; e.g. Jer. 3.11-14, 21-23; Joel 2.12-17; Tob. 13.5-6; Bar. 1.10–3.8; *Jub.* 1.15, 23; *Sib. Or.* 3.624-34; 4.162-70; 1QS 2.24–3.12.

15  The nations are expected to come to Israel, sometimes bringing their wealth; e.g. Isa. 2.2-4; 60.5-11; Zech. 8.20-22. In other texts, the nations are converted to worshipping Yahweh; e.g. Isa. 56.1-8; Zech. 14.16-19; *1 En.* 10.21. Israel will rule the nations, or foreigners will serve them; e.g. Isa. 14.1-2; 61.5-7; Wis. 3.8; *1 En.* 90.30. Yahweh was also expected to rule the nations, resulting in world-wide peace; e.g. Isa. 2.2-4; Dan. 2.44-45.

16  E.g. Isa. 65.17-25; 66.18-23; *1 En.* 10.17-22; 45.4-5; 102.4–104.6; *Pss. Sol.* 3.12; *Jub.* 23.27-29; *Ps.-Philo* 3.10; *Sib. Or.* 2.313-38; 1QS 11.6-9; CD 7.5-6. This eschatological dimension is also evidenced in the radical separation of the righteous from the wicked mentioned above.

> The God of the universe, the Holy Great One, will come forth from his dwelling. And from there he will march upon Mount Sinai and appear in his camp emerging from heaven with a mighty power... And there shall be a great judgment upon all, (including) the righteous. And to all the righteous he will grant peace... Behold, he will arrive with ten million of the holy ones in order to execute judgment upon all ... [*1 En.* 1.3-4, 7-9].[17]

Thirdly, Yahweh is frequently described as mighty when he judges and restores his people. This feature may be observed in both of the preceding quotations.[18]

Fourthly, while God's spirit was granted to individuals in special circumstances in the OT, one element of eschatological expectation was that Yahweh would bestow his spirit as a blessing upon *all* his people. For example, in Ezek. 36.26-27 Yahweh promises:

> And I will give to you a new heart, and a new spirit I will put within you; and I will remove the heart of stone from your flesh and give you a heart of flesh. I will put my spirit within you and cause you to walk in my statutes, and you will be careful to observe my ordinances.

A similar promise by Yahweh is expressed in *Jub.* 1.23:

> But after this they will return to me in all uprighteousness and with all of (their) heart and soul. And I shall cut off the foreskin of their heart and the foreskin of the heart of their descendants. And I shall create for them a holy spirit, and I shall purify them so that they will not turn away from following me from that day and forever.[19]

This latter quotation links Yahweh's spirit to the ministry of cleansing his people from their wickedness. In Isa. 4.4 this cleansing spirit is a 'spirit of burning'.[20]

The specific language of 'baptizing with' is not associated with Yah-

---

17  Cf. e.g. Isa. 26.11; 35.4; 62.11; 63.1; 66.15; Mic. 1.3; Zech. 14.3-4; Wis. 6.5; Sir. 35.17; *1 En.* 25.3-5; 90.15, 18; 91.7; *T. Mos.* 10.3, 7; 12.13; *Liv. Proph.* 2.12; 1QS 3.18; 4.19; CD 7.9; 8.2-3. In these references the language of 'coming' may vary to include 'go forth', 'visit', etc.

18  E.g. Isa. 10.21; 33.13; 49.26; 62.8; 63.1, 15; Jer. 16.21; Ezek. 20.33-34; Sir. 36.3, 8; *1 En.* 84.2; *Pss. Sol.* 2.29; *Liv. Proph.* 2.12; 1QS 10.16-17; CD 2.5; 1QM 3.5-6; 12.9-10; 13.13-16; 18.11-14; 1QH 6.30; 4Q181 fr.1 2. The expression 'Mighty One' comes close to being used as an actual title in 1QM 12.10: 'Rise up, O Hero/Mighty One! [קומה גבור] Lead away your captives, O glorious Man!' But the usage in the preceding line of this same word גבור ('hero, valiant, mighty') makes it unlikely that it is here an actual title. Cf. the discussion in §8.2.1.

19  In *Jub.* 1.23 the statement 'create for them a holy spirit' is not specifically referring to Yahweh *bestowing* his spirit. The text suggests, however, that it is this created holy spirit which purifies the people, and so this statement may be taken to infer that Yahweh bestows this spirit upon his people. E.g. Isa. 32.15; 44.3; Ezek. 11.19; 37.14; 39.29; Joel 2.28-29; Zech. 12.10; *Sib. Or.* 4.46, 189; 1QS 4.20-21.

20  Furthermore, the spirit is also a special endowment Yahweh bestows upon human agents to enable the restoration of his people; e.g. Isa. 11.2; 42.1; 61.1; *Pss. Sol.* 17.37; 1QSb 5.25-26; 4QpIsa^a fr.8-10 11-12; 11QMelch 2.18.

weh's bestowal of the spirit, but water/ablution imagery is employed to portray this bestowal with expressions like 'poured out', 'sprinkled' and 'cleansing'. For example, Joel 2.28-29 twice declares: 'I will pour out my spirit. . .' 1QS 4.21 portrays Yahweh cleansing his people when 'he will sprinkle upon him a spirit of truth like waters for purification. . .'[21] In the OT, Yahweh's spirit is described as 'holy' in a few texts, but these are not within the context of eschatological expectation.[22] However, in Second Temple Jewish literature, a '*holy* spirit' (or spirit of *holiness*) is the object of eschatological expectation. This may be observed in the above quote of *Jub.* 1.23. Similarly, 1QS 4.20-21 states:

> Then God in his truth will make manifest all the deeds of man and purify for himself some from mankind, destroying all spirit of perversity, removing all blemishes of his flesh and purifying him with a spirit of holiness from all deeds of evil.[23]

The imagery of the wind is also used to portray Yahweh's judgment. For example, Isa. 27.8b states: 'he removed them with his fierce blast in the day of the east wind'. In a similar vein Sir. 39.28 states that

> there are winds that have been created for vengeance, and in their anger they scourge heavily; in the time of consummation they will pour out their strength and calm the anger of their Maker.[24]

As far as I am able to determine, however, wind imagery is not used to portray restoration, only judgment, nor is it linked with water/ablution imagery,[25] though it is occasionally linked with the terminology of burning.[26] By itself, fire (without wind imagery) is commonly used to portray

---

21  For the immediately preceding context of this quotation see the extended quote of 1QS 4.20-21 below. Cf. e.g. Isa. 32.15; 44.3; Ezek. 36.25-26; Zech. 12.10. The Qumran literature speaks frequently of Yahweh's spirit, but generally does so in the context of the community's present situation rather than some eschatological future. However, the community's eschatology reflects a belief that they were living in a time of eschatological fulfilment, and therefore their use of spirit-language in their current context is relevant for our purposes; e.g. 1QS 3.7-9; 1QH 16.12; 17.26.

22  Ps. 51.11; Isa. 63.10, 11.

23  Cf. *Pss. Sol.* 17.37. Cf. the prominent use of the term in the Qumran literature, though in contexts reflecting the community's current situation (as noted in a preceding footnote): CD 2.12; 5.11; 7.4; 1QH 7.6-7; 9.32; 12.11-13; 14.13; 16.7, 12; 17.26; 4Q504 fr.1-2 5.15-16; fr.4 5; 1Q34^bis 2.7.

24  Cf. e.g. Isa. 27.8; 29.6; 30.27-28; 40.24; 57.13; Jer. 18.17; 49.32, 36; Ezek. 13.11, 13; Hos. 13.15; Nah. 1.3; Zech. 7.14; Sir. 39.28; 43.16-17; *4 Ezra* 13.20, 27. Winds are also portrayed as serving God generally; e.g. *1 En.* 18.1-4; 60.11-22; 76.1-14.

25  The only possible exception I found was Ezek. 37.5-10, in which 'breath' coming from the four 'winds' is the agent by which the dry bones live in Ezekiel's vision (both are the same Hebrew term, רוּחַ, and are translated in the LXX by πνεῦμα). However, the breath and wind here are the visionary symbols for what is going to be accomplished in actuality by Yahweh's spirit, as Yahweh explains to Ezekiel the meaning of the vision: 'I will put my spirit within you, and you shall live, and I will place you in your own land' (37.14a).

judgment, and in some contexts this includes water imagery (though without ablution language) by describing the fire as a 'river of fire'. For example, *Sib. Or.* 2.196-282 vividly describes such judgment:

> And then a great river of blazing fire
> will flow from heaven, and will consume every place. . .
> All the souls of men will gnash their teeth,
> burning in a river, and brimstone and a rush of fire
> in a fiery plain, and ashes will cover all. . .
> And then all will pass through the blazing river
> and the unquenchable flame. And the righteous
> will be saved, but the impious will then be destroyed . . . [2.196-97, 203-205, 252-54].[27]

Finally, imagery from the threshing floor is used to portray Yahweh's judgment upon his people. For example, Jer. 15.7 states:

> I will winnow them with a winnowing fork
>     in the gates of the land;
> I will bereave them, I will destroy my people;
>     they did not turn from their ways.[28]

More commonly, however, threshing-floor imagery is combined with either wind or fire to portray judgment. For example, Mal. 4.1 combines threshing floor imagery with the imagery of fire:

> For behold, the day comes, burning like an oven, when all the arrogant and all evildoers will be stubble; the day that comes shall burn them up, says Yahweh of hosts, so that it will leave them neither root nor branch.[29]

An example of the combination of wind with threshing-floor imagery is Jer. 13.24 in which Yahweh judges his people for turning from him: 'I will scatter you like chaff driven by the wind from the desert'. Similarly, in Wis. 5.23 Yahweh's coming in wrath against his enemies is described thus: 'a mighty wind will rise against them, and like a tempest it will winnow them away. . .'[30]

This type of imagery is usually reserved for portraying judgment, but in one text, Isa. 27.12-13, the imagery of gathering the wheat after it has been threshed and winnowed is employed to portray restoration:

---

26  E.g. Isa. 29.6; 66.15; Ezek. 5.2; Amos 1.14.
27  Cf. e.g. Isa. 66.24; Jer. 4.4; Ezek. 31.31-32; Jdt. 16.17; Wis. 16.16-27; Sir. 36.9; Bar. 4.35; *1 En.* 1.6; 10.14; 90.26-27; 91.9; *Sib. Or.* 2.315, 332; 3.618; 4.173-78; 1QS 2.8, 15; 4.13; CD 2.5; 17.13; 1QH 17.13. Cf. 1QH 3.28-31 for similar imagery.
28  Cf. Jer. 51.2, 33; Nah. 1.10.
29  Cf. Isa. 5.24; 33.11; 47.14; Joel 2.5.
30  Cf. Isa. 17.13; 29.5; 40.24; Jer. 4.11-13; 13.24; Dan. 2.35; Hos. 13.15; Zeph. 2.2; Wis. 5.14, 23. The only Qumran text I have found with this imagery is 1QH 7.22-23, in which the author describes the victory over his enemies: 'and the lords of my dispute are like chaff before the wind' (כמוץ לפני רוח). But this example is clearly not eschatological, but personal, and it is not even clear whether it is the Lord who

> In that day from the river Euphrates to the Brook of Egypt Yahweh will thresh out the grain, and you will be gathered one by one, O people of Israel... [A]nd those who were driven out to the land of Egypt will come and worship Yahweh on the holy mountain at Jerusalem.[31]

A somewhat surprising observation has to be made at this point concerning the use of threshing-floor imagery: it is used quite frequently in the OT to portray Yahweh's judgment and (rarely) restoration, but this metaphorical usage is largely absent from Jewish literature of the Second Temple period, though, as has been seen in the preceding discussion, Yahweh's judgment and restoration continue to be prominent themes in this literature.[32]

accomplishes the victory or the Psalmist through the strength given to him.

31  Cf. Joel 2.24. Israel's exile and restoration is sometimes described using the language of 'scattering' and 'gathering'. Occasionally the associated terminology makes clear that the scattering/gathering is utilizing threshing-floor imagery, as in Isa. 27.12-13 quoted here. However, the scattering/gathering language is also associated with the scattering and gathering of a flock of sheep (e.g. Jer. 10.21; 23.2; 31.10; Nah. 3.18). Therefore, we cannot attach any significance to those cases where scattering and/or gathering language is used without reference to specific metaphorical imagery (either of the threshing-floor or flock; e.g. Ezek. 11.17; 20.34, 41; 28.25; Joel 3.2; Sir. 36.11; Bar. 2.29; 3.8; 2 Macc. 1.27; *Jub.* 1.13, 15). In these cases any possible metaphorical reference is probably a dead metaphor, or else the references are simply to a physical scattering and/or regathering without a metaphorical reference at all. For example, on the trumpets used for breaking camp during the eschatological warfare in 1QM 3.5 is inscribed: 'The mighty deeds of God to scatter the enemy'. This verb, פוץ, may be used of scattering chaff (e.g. Isa. 41.16) but it is commonly used for scattering sheep (e.g. Ezek. 34.6). The only other use of this verb in the Qumran literature (that I know of) is in CD 19.8 which quotes Zech. 13.7, and here it employs the scattering-sheep imagery: 'Strike the shepherd that the sheep may be scattered...' Cf. the same problem with the verb אסף ('to gather') in 1QM 3.10.

32  The only clear exception I have been able to find is Wis. 5.23 quoted above, though *Liv. Proph.* 3.5 refers to the 'scythe which desolates to the end of the earth...' Wis. 3.7 and *1 En.* 48.9 refer to the people rather than God being the agents of judgment using this language; Wis. 3.7 says that they 'will run like sparks through the stubble'. According to the translations in Charles (*APOT*) and Charlesworth (*OTP*), the land of Israel in *1 En.* 56.6 is compared to a threshing floor when the Parthians and Medes trample it (the translations by Black [*Enoch*] and Milik [*Enoch*] use 'trampling-place' and 'tramping-ground' respectively). Cf. also the discussion of 1QH 7.22-23 and 1QM 3.5, 10 in the preceding two notes.
   The imagery of harvest and the threshing floor is used elsewhere in the literature, but it is usually in wisdom sayings of an ethical nature; e.g. Wis. 5.14; Sir. 5.9; 7.3; *T. Levi* 13.6; Philo, *Conf. Ling.* 152; *Mut. Nom.* 269; 1QS 10.8, 22; 1QH 1.28. The language is of course used literally, as in *War* 3.223, 513; *Ant.* 4.281; 20.181, 206; etc.; 1QS 10.7; 1QDM 2.10-11; 3.3. It is found in post-70 CE apocalyptic literature (e.g. *4 Ezra* 4.28-32; 9.17; 15.61; 16.6; *2 Bar.* 70.2; *Apoc. Elij.* 5.23) as well as in the NT (e.g. Mk 4.29; Mt. 13.24-30; Rev. 14.15-16; in these last two examples the angels are the agents of judgment), but the date of this literature and its context render it of little explicit help for the purposes of understanding John the Baptist.

### 7.3 *The Expected Davidic King/Davidic Messiah*

Before examining the next expected figure of judgment and restoration, the Davidic Messiah, it is necessary to discuss briefly the concept of the Messiah in the OT, because the subsequent examination of this figure will combine evidence from both the OT and Second Temple Jewish literature. Such a presentation of the evidence would fail to bring to light the historical development of Jewish thought concerning this figure.

'Messiah', the anglicized form of the Hebrew word מָשִׁיחַ, means 'anointed'. In physical terms it indicates that oil has been poured over or rubbed on a person or object. As a symbolic action performed on a person it signifies divine appointment to a particular role or office. For example, the related verb, מָשַׁח, is used of anointing Aaron and his sons, consecrating them to the priesthood,[33] as well as of Saul, David, Solomon, and kings of both Judah and Israel, appointing them to kingship.[34] Although it is a prophet who is anointing a person to be king, in several cases the prophet asserts that it is Yahweh who is actually anointing. For example, in 2 Sam. 12.7 Nathan announces in an oracle to David: 'Thus says Yahweh the God of Israel, "I [i.e. Yahweh] anointed you king over Israel . . ."'[35] This evidence indicates that in the OT anointing does not identify a person as having a particular role or office, but rather signifies divine appointment to a role or office.

The significance of the 39 instances of the word מָשִׁיחַ in the OT lies in its being simply an extension of the verb. The word identifies a person as one who has been anointed, indicating an appointment to a role or office. In four cases it refers to a priest,[36] and twice it is used with reference to the patriarchs who are called, somewhat anachronistically, prophets.[37] Most of the remaining passages refer to a king. Many of these apply either to Saul or David in their role as king, that is, as 'Yahweh's anointed'.[38] In Isa. 45.1 Yahweh refers to Cyrus, the Gentile king of Per-

33  Exod. 28.41; 29.7, 21, 29; 30.30; 40.13, 15; Lev. 8.12, 30; 16.32; 21.10.
34  1 Sam. 9.16; 10.1; 15.1, 7; 16.3, 12, 13; 2 Sam. 2.4, 7; 5.3, 17; 19.10; 1 Kgs 1.34, 45; 5.1; 19.15-16; 2 Kgs 9.3, 6, 12; 11.12; 23.30; 1 Chron. 11.3; 14.8; 29.22; 2 Chron. 23.11 cf. also Judg. 9.8, 15. The verb is also used to denote the anointing of objects which consecrates them (e.g. Gen. 31.13; Exod. 40.9-15; Lev. 2.4). Oil was also used for anointing oneself in the course of physical hygiene; in these cases it lacks the symbolic significance discussed here (e.g. Ruth 3.3; 2 Sam. 12.20).
35  Cf. 1 Sam. 10.1; 15.17; 1 Chron. 22.7. In other cases it is Yahweh who sends the prophet to anoint on his behalf (1 Sam. 9.16; 15.1; 16.3-13). It is interesting to note that in 1 Chron. 22.7 Jehu is referred to as having been anointed by Yahweh as king, but this is followed by a statement indicating the anointing had a specific purpose: 'to destroy the house of Ahab'.
36  Lev. 4.3, 5, 16; 6.22.
37  1 Chron. 16.22 = Ps. 105.15.
38  Saul: 1 Sam. 12.3, 5; 24.6 (2x), 10; 26.9, 11, 16, 23; 2 Sam. 1.14, 16; Saul's shield: 2 Sam. 1.21; David: 1 Sam. 16.6; 2 Sam. 19.21; 22.51; 23.1; Ps. 18.50, and possibly

sia, as 'his anointed'. Other texts do not relate to a specific king, but rather refer to the current Israelite ruler in a liturgical context, and so have a theological significance.[39] The final two uses are in Dan. 9.25-26. In v. 25 a cryptic reference is made to an anointed one, who is described as a prince (נָגִיד; lit. 'leader'), and v. 26 mentions an anointed one who 'will be cut off'. It is not clear whether these two references refer to the same person, nor whether a royal or priestly role is being implied, though the latter is more probable. A definite identification of the figures is not possible though suggestions may be made.[40] It is possible, though, that this is an early appearance of the more developed use of the term מָשִׁיחַ. In most of these references the anointed one is a person who has literally been anointed with oil in order to indicate symbolically a divine appointment to a role or office. The few passages which do not refer to a literal anointing still retain, nevertheless, the symbolic significance attached to the use of the term. For example, in Isa. 45.1, Yahweh's purpose will be fulfilled by Cyrus, his anointed one—the one whom God has appointed to allow the remnant to return and Jerusalem to be rebuilt.

This survey clearly indicates that nowhere in the OT is the term 'Messiah' used in the technical sense it was to develop in later literature of the Second Temple period and in the NT. However, the roots of this later messianic expectation are found in the OT, especially in the royal ideology associated with David. In 2 Sam. 7.8-17 the prophet Nathan announced the establishment of a covenant in which Yahweh promised to maintain the Davidic dynasty forever.[41] To this hope was attached the glorious successes associated with the reigns of David and Solomon. The king was Yahweh's anointed one as well as his adopted son. As such, he was expected to rule righteously on behalf of Yahweh. The ideology of kingship was gloriously positive, but the historical realities were another matter.[42] Two major problems arose. First of all, the actual kings failed

Solomon in 2 Chron. 6.42 (but cf. = Ps. 132.10).

39  1 Sam. 2.10, 35; Pss. 2.2; 20.6; 28.8; 84.9; 89.38, 51; 132.10 (but cf. = 2 Chron. 6.42); 132.17 (or possibly a reference to David); Lam. 4.20; Hab. 3.13. Gowan (*Eschatology*, 33) states that Ps. 28.8 and Hab. 3.13 refer to the people of God as anointed, but this applies the poetic parallelism of these references too strictly. These two passages speak of Yahweh acting to save not only his people, but his anointed king as well; cf. Craigie, *Psalms 1–50*, 240; Smith, *Micah-Malachi*, 116.

40  For discussion see Lacocque, *Daniel*, 194; Klausner, *Messianic Idea*, 232-35; Montgomery, *Daniel*, 376-83. Hartman and Di Lella (*Daniel*, 250-52) argue that the first anointed figure (v. 25) is probably Joshua, the first high priest of the restored temple (cf. Zech. 4.14) while the latter figure (v. 26) should be identified as the high priest Onias III who was murdered in 171 BCE; cf. Goldingay, *Daniel*, 260-62. Cf. the possible messianic interpretation of Dan. 9.25 in 11QMelch 2.18; cf. Fitzmyer, 'Further Light', 40.

41  Cf. 1 Chron. 17.1-15; Pss. 89; 132.11-18.

42  It should be observed that this royal ideology was not universal. Judg. 8.22-23 and 1 Sam. 8.1-22; 10.17-27; 12.1-25 indicate an ideology which could be considered anti-

to achieve the righteous ideals expected of them.[43]  Secondly, the destruction of Jerusalem in 587 BCE saw the removal of the final Davidic king and the elimination of the last vestiges of the Davidic kingdom.  These realities of history, contrasting with the ideology of kingship, led to the expectation of a future righteous king reigning over a restored kingdom.[44]  Out of this expectation of a future Davidic king arose the later hope for a Messiah.  But a description of the OT evidence itself reveals the expectation of a future Davidic king, and not the expectation of the Messiah.[45]

However, our concern here is not only with the OT expectation of a future Davidic king, but with this OT evidence *and* its development into the messianic expectation of the Second Temple period viewed especially from the point of view of Jews living at the turn of the era.  Since this is the perspective required for our discussion here I use the term 'Messiah' to identify this expected figure, though it is, strictly speaking, anachronistic to speak of a Messiah in the OT.[46]

We now turn to the Messiah as an expected figure and the specific features listed above.

The expectation of a future king or Messiah is usually associated explicitly with the restoration of a Davidic king.[47]  He is given titles other

monarchic or at least very critical of royal ideology. For discussion see Becker, *Expectation*, 14-17.

43  E.g. Jer. 22; Ezek. 34.1-10; Mic. 3.1-4; Sir. 47.12-25, and the evaluations of the kings in 1–2 Kgs and 1–2 Chron.

44  Another, more immediate, contributory cause may have been anti-priestly reactions after the decline of the Hasmonean dynasty; cf. Schürer, *History*, 2.503.

45  For discussions of these issues see Gowan, *Eschatology*, 32-34; Green, 'Messiah', 1-2. Cf. the literature cited by Charlesworth, 'Concept', 189-90, n. 4.

46  Evidence that OT texts describing the expected Davidic king were interpreted as referring to the Davidic Messiah may be found in 4QFlor, 4QTest, 4QPBless, as well as the NT, especially the Gospels.

47  Examples of explicit references to a Davidic king or a reaffirmation of the Davidic covenant include Isa. 9.1-7; Jer. 23.3-8; Ezek. 34.23-24; Hos. 3.5; Mic. 5.1-4; Hag. 2.20-23; Zech. 12.7–13.1; Sir. 47.11, 22; *Pss. Sol.* 17.4; 4Q504 fr.1-2 4.6-8; 4QPBless 1-4. Texts which fail to identify the king specifically as Davidic do not make a different explicit identification and are consistent with the Davidic references; e.g. Isa. 4.2-4; Jer. 3.15-18; Zech. 3.6-10. Therefore, we are justified in speaking of the expectation of a king to be a Davidic king.

A few texts imply that the expected king is David himself (Jer. 30.9; Ezek. 34.23-24; 37.24-25; Hos. 3.5), and it has been argued that these texts reflect an expectation of a David-*redivivus* (e.g. Moore, *Judaism*, 2.326), but it is more probable that this is simply a vivid expression for a king in the Davidic line (cf. Mowinckel, *He That Cometh*, 163-64).

Certain texts are not considered here because in their original setting they do not refer to a future Davidic king, though they may have been understood much later to have application to an expected figure. Their primary reference is to the current period or current king, though spoken of in an idealistic manner; for example Pss. 2; 45; 72; 110; Isa. 7.10-17. For discussion see Mowinckel, *He That Cometh*, 11-12, 110-

than king, such as prince and messiah, as well as metaphorical titles, such as branch, shoot, shepherd and servant.[48]

In the OT several texts indicate that Yahweh comes to judge and restore his people and then establishes his king upon the Davidic throne to rule, thus suggesting that the Davidic king was a figure of restoration but not of judgment.[49] However, other OT texts do explicitly indicate that the king is involved in judging as well. For example, in Isa. 11.4 the king reverses the fortunes of the poor and downtrodden, and judges the wicked oppressors:

> but with righteousness he shall judge the poor,
>     and decide with equity for the meek of the earth;
> and he shall smite the earth with the rod of his mouth,
>     and with the breath of his lips he shall slay the wicked.[50]

In later literature this role of the Messiah was expanded.[51] He will not only judge and/or destroy the enemies of his people, he will also judge Israel and purge the sinners from within it. Both these judgmental roles are described in the *Psalms of Solomon* 17. In vv. 22-25 the Psalmist prays that God would

> undergird him with the strength to destroy the unrighteous rulers,
>     to purge Jerusalem from gentiles
> who trample her to destruction;
>     in wisdom and in righteousness to drive out
> the sinners from the inheritance;

19; Gowan, *Eschatology*, 33-35.
    The literature of the Second Temple period reveals a related expectation of an Aaronic and Davidic Messiah (or, 'Messiah of Aaron and Israel'). This expectation is discussed in §7.4, but the evidence is included here since it relates to the expectation of the Davidic Messiah.
48  E.g. king: Isa. 32.1; Jer. 23.5; Zech. 9.9; *Pss. Sol.* 17.21, 32; prince: Ezek. 37.25-48; *Jub.* 31.18; 1QSb 5.20; CD 7.20; 1QM 5.1; messiah: *Pss. Sol.* 17.32; 18.5, 7; *1 En.* 48.10; 52.4; 1QS 9.11; 1QSa 2.12, 14, 20; CD 12.23; 14.19; 19.10-11; 20.1; 4QPBless 3; (cf. later refs., e.g. *2 Bar.* 29.3; 30.1; 39.7; 40.1; 70.9; 72.2; *4 Ezra* 7.28-29; 12.32); branch: Isa. 4.2; 11.1b; Jer. 23.5; Zech. 3.8; 4QPBless 3; 4QFlor 1.11; 4QpIsaª fr.8-10 11; shoot: Isa. 11.1b (on the use of 'shoot' in 1QH 6.15; 7.19; 8.6, 8, 10, see the relevant footnote at the end of this section); shepherd: Jer. 3.15; 23.4; Ezek. 43.23; *Pss. Sol.* 17.40-41; 4Q504 fr.1-2 4.6-7; 1Q34ᵇⁱˢ 2.8; servant: Ezek. 34.23-24; 37.24-25; Zech. 3.8. Often these titles are combined, as in Ezek. 37.24-25: 'My servant David shall be king over them; and they shall all have one shepherd. . . ; and David my servant shall be their prince for ever'.
49  E.g. Isa. 16.4-5; Jer. 23.3-4; 30.1-9; Ezek. 34.22-23; 37.21-22.
50  Cf. Isa. 9.7; Jer. 23.5-6; 33.15-16; Zech. 9.9-10. In the OT, while the king was expected to defeat Israel's enemies and restore Israel, there is no explicit reference to the king judging or purging Israel itself.
51  While the Messiah's role was expanded, and the word itself developed into a technical term, the expression 'Messiah' is found in relatively few places in the literature of the Second Temple period, and its use in these contexts is not consistent. Cf. §7.3, 7.4, and especially de Jonge, 'Word "Anointed" ', 132-48.

> to smash the arrogance of sinners
>   like a potter's jar;
> To shatter all their substance with an iron rod;
> to destroy the unlawful nations with the word of his mouth;
> At his warning the nations will flee from his presence;
>   and he will condemn sinners by the thoughts of their hearts.[52]

Similarly, in vv. 26-27a he judges Israel:

> He will gather a holy people
>   whom he will lead in righteousness;
> and he will judge the tribes of the people
>   that have been made holy by the Lord their God.
> He will not tolerate unrighteousness (even) to pause among them,
>   and any person who knows wickedness shall not live with them.[53]

Related to the judgmental role for the Messiah is that of restoring Israel. Elements of this restorative ministry include the gathering of the people to the land, saving Israel from their enemies, restoring the kingdom, the temple and the covenant. Several of these restorative elements are drawn together in 1QSb 5.21-23 in which the Messiah, called here the Prince of the Congregation, is blessed in order

> that he may restore the kingdom of His people for ev[er]
> [and judge the poor with justice,]
> [22][and] that he may rule with e[quity the hum]ble of the land
> and walk before Him perfectly in all the ways [of truth. . .]
> [23]and that he may restore [His holy] Coven[ant at the time] of the distress
>   of those who seek [Him].[54]

The most prominent characteristic of this king is the fact that his rule will be, in contrast with the historical reality of Israel's kings, a reign of justice and righteousness. Jer. 23.5 states that he 'will reign as king and act wisely, and he will execute justice and righteousness in the land'. Similarly, *Pss. Sol.* 17.37 describes him as 'wise in the counsel of understanding, with strength and righteousness'.[55] Under his reign Israel expe-

---

52  Cf. e.g. *Pss. Sol.* 17.29; *Jub.* 31.20; 1QSb 5.24, 27; 4QpIsa[a] fr.8-10 17-21.

53  Cf. *Pss. Sol.* 17.36; 18.7; CD 7.20–8.2; 14.19; 19.10-13. On *Pss. Sol.* 17–18 see Nickelsburg, *Literature*, 207-209; Davenport, 'Anointed', 67-92; de Jonge, 'Word "Anointed" ', 136; Klausner, *Messianic Idea*, 323-24.

54  Cf. Isa. 9.7; Jer. 23.5-6; 33.15-16; *Pss. Sol.* 17.26, 28; *Jub.* 31.19; 4QFlor 1.13. In Zech. 6.12-13, the Branch was expected to rebuild the temple which is also part of the restorative process. It is possible that Zech. 6.12-13 originally might have referred to Zerubbabel (cf. the relevant footnote at the end of this section), but the canonical form of the passage most probably points to a more distant time. Smith, *Micah-Malachi*, 218-19.

55  Isa. 9.7; 11.3-5; 16.5; 32.1-2; Jer. 23.5; 33.15; *Pss. Sol.* 17.23, 26, 29, 37, 40; 18.7; 1QSb 5.25-26. In *Pss. Sol.* 17.36 he is 'free from sin'. While many of the motifs in the expectation of a future king may be drawn from Israel's experience of kingship, other motifs were included which may be traced to earlier periods of Israel's history, especially the period of the Exodus and judges. For further discussion see Harrelson, 'Nonroyal Motifs', 147-65.

riences peace and security as well as fruitfulness and prosperity.[56] The eschatological horizon, looking forward to the new age, becomes more explicit in those texts which describe this king's rule as having universal dominion, enduring forever, and as sometimes producing idyllic conditions in creation.[57] Clearly then, the first of the criteria for which we are searching has been met. The Davidic Messiah is an expected figure of both judgment and restoration.

Secondly, this figure is also described as one who is coming. For example, Zech. 9.9 exclaims:

> Rejoice greatly, O daughter of Zion!
>     Shout aloud, O daughter of Jerusalem!
> Lo, your king comes to you;
>     triumphant and victorious is he. . .

Similarly, 1QS 9.11 speaks of the community being governed by the first precepts 'until the coming of the prophet and the Messiahs of Aaron and Israel'.[58]

Thirdly, the descriptive language of might and power is used in portraying this figure. For example, the ruler who comes from Bethlehem Ephrathah in Mic. 5.2 is described thus in v. 4: 'And he shall arise and feed his flock in the strength of Yahweh. . .' *Pss. Sol.* 17.40 describes him as 'mighty in his actions and strong in the fear of God'.[59]

Fourthly, the Davidic Messiah is himself endowed with Yahweh's spirit, so that, as stated in Isa. 11.2, he rules with wisdom and understanding.[60] However, nowhere is it *explicitly* stated that he is the one who bestows the spirit upon the people. Possible references may be found in the *Testament of Levi*, the *Testament of Judah* and 1QIsaᵃ, but these are problematic.[61] That the bestowal of the spirit upon the people

---

56  E.g. Isa. 11.6-9; 33.17-20; Jer. 23.4-6; 33.16; Ezek. 34.22-23; 37.26; Amos 9.11-15; Mic. 5.4; Zech. 9.10; *Jub.* 31.20; *Pss. Sol.* 17.32, 40-44; 18.6-9; 1QSb 5.20-23; cf. the tranquil scene portrayed in 1QSa 2.11-21. Cf. de Jonge, 'Word "Anointed" ', 135-37; Klausner, *Messianic Idea*, 323-24.

57  E.g. Isa. 9.7; 11.6-10; Jer. 3.17; Ezek. 37.25; Amos 9.12; Mic. 5.4; Hag. 2.22-23; Zech. 9.10; *Pss. Sol.* 17:29-31, 34; *Jub.* 31.18, 20; 1QSb 5.27-28; 4QpIsaᵃ fr.8-10 20-21.

58  The verb in both of these examples is בוא, 'to come', which is the same verb used in 1QSa 2.12 and CD 19.10-11. In Isa. 11.1; Jer. 30.21; and Mic. 5.2 (MT v. 1) the verb is יצא, 'to come out, come forth', while in Mic. 5.4 (MT v. 3); CD 12.23–13.1; 20.1; 4QpIsaᵃ fr.8–10 17, and 4QFlor 1.11 the verb is עמד, 'to arise, stand'. The synoptic Gospels use the verb ἔρχομαι to describe the coming of John's expected figure, which the LXX often uses to translate both the verbs בוא and יצא, though not the verb עמד. However, in the particular examples cited here, the LXX translates the verb בוא in Zech. 9.9 with ἔρχομαι, but in Isa. 11.1; Jer. 30.21; and Mic. 5.2 (MT v. 1) the intensive form of the verb, ἐξέρχομαι, 'to come forth', is used.

59  Cf. e.g. Isa. 9.6; 11.2; *Pss. Sol.* 17.22, 37-40; 18.7; *Jub.* 31.18; 1QSb 5.24-25; poss. 1QH 3.10.

60  Cf. Isa. 32.1-8; Jer. 3.15; 23.5; *Pss. Sol.* 18.7; 1QSb 5.25.

61  Two possible, though problematic, exceptions exist, but the evidence is admittedly

by Yahweh's anointed agent was a current possibility is indicated by CD 2.12: 'And he [i.e. God] made known to them his holy spirit by the hand of his anointed ones'. In this context the anointed figures are the OT prophets rather than an expected, eschatological figure, but the idea of an anointed figure in some sense bestowing the spirit is still present. Yet, the spirit with which the Messiah is endowed is explicitly identified as a 'holy' spirit in *Pss. Sol.* 17.37: 'for God made him powerful in the holy spirit. . .' I have not found the imagery of wind or fire used to explicate the ministry of the Davidic Messiah.[62]

slight. First of all, in *T. Levi* 18.11 the result of the ministry of the Aaronic Messiah is that 'the spirit of holiness shall be upon them [the saints]' (v. 11). In *T. Jud.* 24 a mosaic of OT eschatological promises are gathered concerning the Davidic Messiah. He is both a recipient of God's spirit, and 'he will pour out the spirit of grace on you' (v. 3). However, *Test. XII Patr.* do manifest later Christian interpolations (including an explicit interpolation in *T. Levi* 18.7b, which stands in close proximity to 18.11 cited here). Yet, there is no explicit evidence for these specific references being Christian, except for the assumption that such an idea is specifically Christian in the first place. The early date of *Test. XII Patr.* is suggested by fragments of scrolls similar to *Test. XII Patr.* which were found both in the Cairo Geniza and among the Qumran scrolls (cf. the discussion concerning 4QTLevi in §4.3.4). Cf. Collins, 'Testaments', 332-33; Dupont-Sommer, *Essene Writings*, 301-305; de Jonge, 'Testaments', 370-84. De Jonge (*Testaments: A Study*) has argued for the Christian origin of *Test. XII Patr.*, but this thesis is problematic. For further discussion of the date, composition, and provenance of *Test. XII Patr.* as well as a survey of recent research see Collins, 'Testaments', 325-44; Collins, 'Testamentary Literature', 268-76; Schürer, *History*, 3.767-81; Kee, 'Testaments', 2.775-81. For a recent summary of de Jonge's position see 'Testaments', 359-420.

Secondly, Brownlee ('Servant', 10-11; cf. 'John the Baptist', 43-44) has argued that in 1QIsa[a] 52.14-15 an anointed figure (here the Servant of Yahweh) 'because of his own anointing (= sprinkling) with the Spirit, will be qualified to sprinkle others with the spirit' ('Servant', 10). While this suggestion is intriguing, it remains problematic, and thus it cannot be used as direct or strong evidence here. For further discussion see Dunn, 'Baptism', 89-91.

62  The one possible exception is in 1QH 6.14-19. Dupont-Sommer (*Essene Writings*, 219 n. 2) argues that the reference to the shoot (נצר) in 6.15 (cf. 7.19; 8.6, 8, 10) is a messianic reference on the basis of the same word used as a messianic title in Isa. 11.1. If so, then the shoot grows into a large tree, whose shadow covers the whole earth and whose roots reach down into the Abyss. This tree produces a fountain of everlasting light as well as a fire which consumes all sinners. However, the preceding lines (6.7-14) refer to Yahweh's blessing the righteous and the response by the righteous. The beginning of line 14 is fragmentary and the end is missing; the legible text reads: [          ל]גור בריכה שריכה ויהיו כבודכה בפי ישיכו והם, which may be translated: 'and they will return/reply at [or: according to] your glorious word/mouth and they will become your princes in the lo[t of     ]'. Line 15 begins: פרח כצ[י]ץ ע[ר עולם לגדל נצר לעופי מטעח עולם. The first word after the lacuna at the end of line 14 is פרח which may be understood as the noun פֶּרַח, a bud or flower, or as some form of the verb פָּרַח (to sprout, bud, bloom). Either way, the 'flower' or 'blooming' probably refers back to the righteous of line 14. On this basis, the נצר in line 15 continues the same imagery and represents the community of the righteous. The background for such usage would, then, not be traced to Isa. 11.1 (against Dupont-Sommer), but to Isa. 60.21 in which the righteous people possess the land as the 'shoot' planted by Yahweh. Other verbal links exist between

With respect to the fifth element for which we are searching, I have not been able to find any use of threshing-floor imagery in association with the Davidic Messiah.

From this survey we are able to conclude that, with respect to the Davidic Messiah, evidence exists for three of the elements for which we are searching: he is an expected figure of judgment and restoration, he is coming, and he is mighty.[63] However, the more specific elements are largely lacking. He does not bestow the spirit, nor is threshing-floor imagery used to describe his ministry. He is, though, a recipient of the (holy) spirit.

### 7.4 *The Aaronic Messiah (with the Davidic Messiah)*

In a few instances along with the expectation of a Davidic king in the OT there is a closely related expectation of a high priest. However, this expectation is not developed enough in the OT for the priest to be identified as a separate expected figure of judgment and restoration. The texts pose problems of interpretation which are not relevant here; it is sufficient to observe the beginnings of this idea in the OT in light of its more developed forms in later literature. In Zech. 6.12-14 there is the expectation of a Davidic king with whom is associated an Aaronic priest in what might appear to be a dyarchy.[64] In a similar vein, Zech. 4.14

this passage in 1QH 6 and Isa. 60.19-22. This interpretation of 'shoot' is consistent with 1QH 8.6; 1QS 8.5; 11.8; CD 1.7; *1 En.* 10.16; 84.6; 93.2; *Pss. Sol.* 14.3-4; *Jub.* 1.16; 7.34; 21.24. Cf. Mansoor, *Hymns*, 143-44; Carmignac and Guilbert, *Textes*, 1.222-23, esp. n. 62.

63 These elements describe the *expected* Davidic Messiah, but in at least one instance there appears to have been the belief that the Messiah was actually in the *process of arriving*. The prophet Haggai, and possibly Zechariah as well, may have believed that they could be living in the period when these expectations of the future Davidic king would be fulfilled and the new age would begin. This hope was focused on Zerubbabel who had returned to Palestine as governor under the Persians. He was grandson of the exiled king Jehoiachin (1 Chron. 3.17-19) and thus was of Davidic lineage. Hag. 2.21-23 is an oracle from Yahweh to Zerubbabel expressing the hope being placed in him. In v. 23 Yahweh states: 'I will take you, O Zerubbabel, my servant, the son of Shealtiel, says Yahweh, and make you like a signet ring; for I have chosen you. . .' The reference to 'signet ring' is an allusion to the authority of kingship drawn from Jer. 22.24. It is somewhat problematic to determine to what extent this oracle should receive a political interpretation and thus to what extent it was fulfilled in Zerubbabel himself, because Zerubbabel never became Davidic king, and he passes silently from the pages of history. Ackroyd (*Exile*, 163-66, esp. 166) suggests that Haggai's point is to stress Yahweh's sovereignty over the world and that the negative judgment of Jer. 20.24-27 is now reversed and a new age has arrived. Similar expectation may be implied by Zech. 3.8; 4.5-10, 14; 6.12-13, but the final form of these texts make this less clear. Cf. Smith, *Micah-Malachi*, 162-63, 200-201, 205-206, 217-19; Mowinckel, *He That Cometh*, 119-22; Becker, *Expectation*, 64-67.

64 Cf. the relevant footnote at the end of §7.3.

identifies two figures who are anointed (not מָשִׁיחַ, but בְּנֵי־הַיִּצְהָר, lit.
'sons of oil'), who probably represent Zerubbabel and Joshua in the two
leadership roles, political and religious, of that day.[65] This close association of a high priest with the expected Davidic king or Messiah may possibly be traced back to the earlier practice of identifying the high priest
as 'anointed'. Thus they would share a common 'title'.[66] Also, in Jer.
33.14-26, the reaffirmation of the Davidic covenant to be fulfilled by the
coming of the righteous Branch is associated with a reaffirmation of the
continued role of the Aaronic priesthood.[67]

The Qumran literature provides clear evidence for the expectation of
two Messiahs, one functioning as priest and the other as king. They are
commonly identified in academic circles as the Aaronic (or Priestly)
Messiah and the Davidic Messiah, though in the Qumran scrolls the
terms are 'the Messiah(s) of Aaron and Israel'. For example, 1QS 9.11
refers to 'the coming of the prophet and the Messiahs of Aaron and
Israel' (בוא נביא ומשיחי אהרון וישראל). In this instance, the
term 'Messiah' is in the plural. However, in similar references in CD the
term is in the singular, such as in CD 20.1: 'there shall arise the Messiah
from Aaron and from Israel' (עמור משיח מאהרון ומישראל). It is
possible that CD reflects a different messianic expectation, whereby both
messianic roles are brought together in one person, i.e., one Messiah
functioning as both priest and king (or one Messiah for both priests and
laypersons). However, it is more probable that, though the term is
singular in CD, the Qumran community did expect two Messiahs.[68]

In the Qumran literature the Aaronic Messiah takes precedence over
the Davidic Messiah. In the description of the messianic banquet in
1QSa 2.11-21 the Priest (Messiah) enters first, leading his priests, and
only then does the Messiah of Israel enter followed by his commanders
and the laypersons.[69] In this meal it is the Priest (Messiah) who extends

65 For discussion see Smith, *Micah-Malachi*, 205-206; Becker, *Expectation*, 50. For the
link between the later expectation of a Aaronic Messiah with this earlier evidence
and the historical situation in the Maccabean period see Talmon, 'Waiting', 123-26.
66 Lev. 4.3, 5, 16; 6.22.
67 This text has a problematic textual history due to its absence in the LXX, but its
presence in the final form of the text is what is of interest here. Cf. Gowan, *Eschatology*, 35-36.
68 Kuhn ('Messiahs', 58-60) comes to this conclusion and suggests the singular form of
the term in CD is a result of a medieval copyist's emendation of the text. It is also
possible that the singular term is subsuming two persons in the two roles under one
'anointing'. For further support of the community's dual messianism see Talmon,
'Waiting', 122-31; Burrows, 'Messiahs', 203-204; Wcela, 'Messiah(s)', 340-49; Brown,
'Teacher', 41-44; Schürer, *History*, 2.550-52; for arguments against see Laurin,
'Problem', 39-52; Higgins, 'Messiah', 215-19. It is quite possible that theological
development on this issue may have taken place within the Qumran community; cf.
Wcela, 347-49; Starcky, 'Quatre étapes', 481-505.
69 For the importance of the order of entry into meetings see 1QS 2.19-23; cf. §5.3.1.1.

his hands over the bread and wine and blesses it, and only afterward does the Davidic Messiah do so. The Aaronic priest takes precedence not only in matters of form or liturgy, but also in matters of function. In 4QFlor 1.11-12 the Aaronic Messiah is called 'the Interpreter of the Law' (דורש התורה) who arises along with the Davidic Messiah. This title suggests that the Aaronic Messiah 'was to be the supreme authority in all matters of interpretation of the Torah, as also the guide and instructor in Torah of his lay partner', the Davidic Messiah.[70]

Since the quantity of data for the Aaronic Messiah is so limited, analysing it for the elements we seek produces rather fragmentary results. Furthermore, this issue is complicated by the fact that most references to the Aaronic Messiah combine this figure with the Davidic Messiah without distinguishing clearly between them. Such an analysis produces the following results.

First of all, there is little evidence that the Aaronic Messiah was an agent of judgment. It might be speculated that the references to the chief priest in 1QM refer to the Aaronic Messiah,[71] and so his role in the eschatological battle could be considered judgmental since he presides over the liturgical blessings of those going out to battle (15.4), those returning (16.13) and at the end of the day (18.5).[72] More certain is the

---

70  Schürer, *History*, 2.551. This role for the Aaronic Messiah is strengthened by 4QpIsaᵃ fr.8-10. Lines 11-24 are a messianic *pesher* on Isa. 11.1-5, in which lines 11-21 interpret the Isaianic passage with respect to the Davidic Messiah. Then, lines 21-24 quote Isa. 11.3b (though in fragmentary form) and interpret it to refer to the Davidic Messiah receiving instruction from the priests. Allegro (*DJD* 5.14) translates it: 'And as it says, "Not [. . .] or decide by what his ears shall hear": its interpretation is that [. . .] and according to what they teach him so shall he judge, and according to their command [. . .] with him, one of the priests of repute shall go out with garments of [. . .] in his hand [. . .' Similarly, in CD 6.10-11 the faithful follow the Law 'until the coming of the one who shall teach righteousness at the end of days'.

It is not our purpose here to discuss all elements of this dual messianic expectation or Qumran's messianism. For further discussion see the literature cited in the relevant footnote above. The *Test. XII Patr.* provides evidence of the expectation of both an Aaronic as well as a Davidic Messiah (e.g. *T. Jud.* 21.2-5). However, as discussed above, problems exist with using this evidence to elucidate pre-Christian Jewish expectation. Furthermore, it has little of specific value to contribute to the elements for which we are searching.

71  Cf. Vermes, *Scrolls*, 185; Brown, 'Teacher', 44; cf. parallel in *T. Dan* 5.10.

72  The element of judgment in the work of the Aaronic Messiah may be implied by 4QTest. This document is usually understood to be a collection of proof-texts for Qumran's expectation of various eschatological figures: the eschatological Prophet, the Davidic Messiah, and the Aaronic Messiah (cf. Knibb, *Qumran*, 263-64; Vermes, *Scrolls*, 80-81; against Brown, 'Teacher', 41 n. 11). After scriptural passages on each of the figures are cited, the text ends by quoting a curse by Joshua (Josh. 6.26). The relationship between this latter quotation and the earlier scriptural citations is unclear. However, Knibb, (*Qumran*, 263; cf. Dupont-Sommer, *Writings*, 317-18) points out that 'each of the messianic prophecies ends with a threat of judgement, that is, the three messianic figures are figures of judgement. It may be that part of

Aaronic Messiah's role as an agent of restoration, whereby he (with the Davidic Messiah) was expected to 'atone for the iniquity' of those who had lived according to the community's laws (CD 14.19). This restorative role is augmented by his other tasks within the new age: he teaches the law (4QFlor 1.11), he blesses the food and wine (1QSa 2.17-20), and he presides over the temple sacrifices (1QSb 3.1-2).[73]

Secondly, the Aaronic Messiah is also identified as one who is coming (along with the Davidic Messiah). For example, we observed above that 1QS 9.11 speaks of the community being governed by the first precepts 'until the coming of the prophet and the Messiahs of Aaron and Israel'.[74]

Thirdly, with respect to this figure being identified as mighty, the quotation of Deut. 33.8-11 in 4QTest 14-20, which is probably cited as a reference to the Aaronic Messiah, concludes with a prayer: 'Bless, O Lord, his power' (ברך . . . חילו).

With respect to the other elements for which we are searching, the Qumran literature does not provide any evidence. The only exception is the possibility that the Aaronic Messiah has the holy spirit bestowed upon him.[75] If the blessing in 1QSb 3.1-22 is the blessing of the Aaronic Messiah, and if that blessing began somewhere in the fragmentary column two, then the fragmentary text of 2.24 indicates just such a bestowal: 'may he graciously provide you with the spirit of holiness and kindness' ([    ר]יחונכה ברוח קודש וחסן).[76]

From this survey we may conclude that the Aaronic Messiah functioned in such a way that he may be described as judging and restoring. He is, however, closely related in most cases with the Davidic Messiah, and so he probably should not be considered a figure of judgment and restoration who functioned without the Davidic Messiah. The Aaronic

the purpose of 4QTestimonia was to announce judgement to those who epitomised evil and were regarded as arch-enemies of the community.' Thus, the section concerning the Aaronic Messiah is a citation of Deut. 33.8-11, which ends with a prayer for him: 'smite the loins of his adversaries, and let those who hate him rise no more' (4QTest 19-20; Knibb's translation, *Qumran*, 265).

73  This latter role is based on the reasonable assumption that the blessing pronounced in 1QSb 3.1-21 is the blessing of the high priest, the Aaronic Messiah. This reconstruction is based upon the order of the blessings which culminate in the blessing of the Davidic Messiah. The precise line numbers are difficult to reconstruct due to the fragmentary nature of the scroll. The blessings are: the faithful (1.1-?), the Aaronic Messiah (2.?-3.21), the priests (3.22-?), the Davidic Messiah (here, 'the Prince of the Congregation', 5.20-29). Cf. Dupont-Sommer, *Writings*, 110 n. 2; Vermes, *Dead Sea Scrolls*, 235.

74  The verb is בוא, 'to come', which is the same verb used in 1QSa 2.12 and CD 19.10-11. In CD 12.23–13.1; 20.1, and 4QFlor 1.11 the verb is עמד, 'to arise, stand'.

75  Cf. §7.3 concerning the possibility of the Davidic Messiah bestowing the spirit in certain texts.

76  Cf. Dupont-Sommer, *Writings*, 110 n. 2.

Messiah was described as coming. He possibly was described as mighty, and might have been understood to have been the recipient of the spirit. But evidence is lacking for the other specific elements for which we are searching.

## 7.5 *The Angelic Prince Michael/Melchizedek*

Angels are referred to quite frequently with respect to the judgment of the wicked and the restoration of God's people. However, these angels are not figures of judgment and restoration in the same sense as the other figures we are considering here, because they are portrayed primarily as agents carrying out God's instructions, and thus the judgment and/or restoration is considered to be God's judgment and/or restoration.[77]

Yet, certain texts provide evidence for the belief in a special, individual, angelic prince as a figure of judgment and restoration, usually named Michael. In Dan. 10.13, 21 Michael is 'one of the chief princes' who battles against evil angelic princes who were thought to be angelic rulers over the nations.[78] Thus, a celestial battle between opposing angelic forces was thought to correspond to the terrestrial conflict experienced by God's people. In Dan. 12.1-3 a brief and enigmatic description of the end time is given to Daniel, a description entailing judgment and restoration. The preceding context has outlined both the warfare which takes place 'at the end time' (11.35, 40) between the king of the North and the king of the South (i.e. between Ptolemy VI Philometor and Antiochus IV Epiphanes), as well as the suffering experienced by the Jewish people.[79] Dan. 11.45 ends with Jerusalem being threatened, but the assurance is given that 'he shall come to his end, with none to help him'. Then the next verse, 12.1, introduces Michael:

> At that time shall arise Michael, the great prince who has charge of your people. And there shall be a time of trouble, such as never has been since there was a nation till that time; but at that time your people shall be delivered, every one whose name shall be found written in the book.

The next verses describe the resurrection and final judgment with a division between those who receive everlasting life and those who receive everlasting contempt. It is not actually stated who is the agent of the deliverance, but the description of Michael in 12.1 as the 'prince who has

---

77   E.g. *1 En.* 10–11; 54–56; 62.9-11; 91.15-16; 100.4; *T. Mos.* 10.2; *Sib. Or.* 2.214-20; 1QS 4.11-14; CD 2.5-7; 1QM 7.6; 12.1-6; 11QMelch 2.14.

78   Cf. the 70 shepherds in *1 En.* 89.59-65. Cf. Hartman and Di Lella, *Daniel*, 282-84; Goldingay, *Daniel*, 290-92.

79   Hartman and Di Lella, *Daniel*, 300-302; Porteous, *Daniel*, 166; Goldingay, *Daniel*, 295-96, 300-305.

charge of your people' combined with the statement that 'Michael shall arise' clearly implies that it is Michael who delivers God's people and defeats their enemies as well as being involved in judging and purging.[80]

In 1QM 9.15-16 the warriors fighting in the eschatological battle are apparently assisted by Michael and three other angels whose names are inscribed on the warriors' shields. However, the role of Michael is enhanced later in the same text. The high priest[81] encourages the soldiers in 16.13–17.10 to be fearless. His reason is given in 17.5-8:

> This day is His (i.e. God's) hour to bend and bring low the Prince of the empire of ungodliness. He will send final succour by the power of the Great Angel to the lot whom He has [re]deemed, and to the servant of Michael by the everlasting light, to enlighten the Co[venant of I]srael with joy. Gladness and joy shall belong to the lot of God to raise up the servant of Michael in the midst of the gods, and the dominion of Israel shall be over all flesh.

As in Daniel, Michael is evidently battling with an evil angelic counterpart, here described as 'the Prince of the empire of ungodliness'. However, Michael is also the one whom God uses to strengthen the terrestrial warriors, enabling them to be victorious and achieve dominion.[82]

Another Qumran manuscript provides an interesting addition to our knowledge of this angelic figure, though the scroll is in a quite fragmentary state. 11QMelch portrays Melchizedek as a figure of judgment and restoration. Though not stated in the extant fragments, it is probable that Melchizedek is to be identified with Michael.[83] Paul J. Kobelski

---

80  Cf. also *T. Mos.* 10.1-2. For further discussion see Davies, *Daniel*, 112-18; Collins, *Imagination*, 87-91; Hartman and Di Lella, *Daniel*, 306; Lacocque, *Daniel*, 242; Goldingay, *Daniel*, 305-306. Collins (*Vision*, 136) suggests that the context of Dan. 12.1 denotes a military as well as a judicial connotation to Michael's intervention; cf. Nickelsburg, *Resurrection*, 11-14. For later references to Michael, see Jude 9; Rev. 12.7-10; *T. Levi* 5.6; *T. Dan* 6.2; *2 En.* 22.

   In other passages Michael is an exalted angel, but he does not have the unique status attributed to him here in Dan. 12.1. He is often linked with other angels who serve God in special roles, frequently meting out the judgment of God. For example, *Sib. Or.* 2.214-20 states:

>   Then the imperishable angels of the immortal God,
>   Michael, Gabriel, Raphael, and Uriel,
>   who know what evils anyone did previously,
>   lead all the souls of men from the murky dark
>   to judgment, to the tribunal of the great
>   immortal God. For one alone is imperishable,
>   the universal ruler, himself, who will be judge of mortals.

   Cf. *1 En.* 9.1; 10.11; 20.5; 24.6; 40.8; 54.6; 60; 68–71; 1QM 9.15-16.
81  This high priest is probably the Aaronic Messiah; cf. §7.4.
82  Michael is probably to be identified in 1QM 13.10 with the 'Prince of Light' whom God appointed 'to bring help' to his people. Cf. also 1QS 3.20, 24; CD 5.18. Cf. Dupont-Sommer, *Writings*, 194 n. 1; Kobelski, *Melchizedek*, 57-58, esp. n. 29.
83  Van der Woude, 'Melchisedek', 369-73; de Jonge and van der Woude, '11QMelch', 305-306; Kobelski, *Melchizedek*, 71-74. For a contrary opinion see Bampfylde,

provides an excellent summary of the manuscript:

> 11QMelch brings together and interprets in the light of the community's eschatological outlook several OT passages dealing with the jubilee year, the day of expiation, and judgment. Quotations from and allusions to Leviticus 25 are particularly important to the structure and contents of 11QMelch. The interpretation of the biblical passages features the eschatological figure Melchizedek, who is presented as a heavenly redeemer who secures liberty for those held captive by the power of Belial and who exacts the judgments of God against Belial and the evil spirits allied with him. Standing at the head of the good angels, the heavenly leader Melchizedek leads the forces of good against the forces of evil at the end of days.[84]

In this text, Melchizedek is the heavenly agent of both judgment and restoration.[85] The text presents the picture of God's people under the dominion of the evil angelic forces of Belial, separated from association with 'the sons of heav[e]n, and from the inheritance of Melchizedek' (2.4-5), and thus they were considered captives. But it is 'Melchiz]edek who will restore them, and proclaim liberty to them . . .' (2.5-6; cf. Lev. 25.10; Isa. 61.1). This restoration includes receiving forgiveness, for Melchizedek's restoration involves 'relieving them [of the burden] of their iniquities' (2.6; cf. 2.7-8). The restoration also liberates God's people by defeating and judging Belial and his forces: 'Melchizedek will exact the ven[geance] of E[l's] judgments [and he will protect all the sons of light from the power] of Belial and from the power of all [the spirits of] his [lot]' (2.13). Thus, Melchizedek is a figure of judgment and restoration, though the focus of that judgment is neither upon Israel nor their human enemies, but upon their angelic enemies.[86] Therefore, the heavenly being, Michael/Melchizedek, is considered to be a figure of judgment and restoration, thus meeting our first criterion.

---

'Prince', 129-34. Other major studies of 11QMelch include Fitzmyer, 'Further Light', 25-41; Delcor, 'Melchizedek', 115-35; Carmignac, 'Melkisédeq', 343-78; Milik, 'Milkî-ṣedeq', 95-144; Horton, *Melchizedek*, 60-82; Puech, 'XIQMelkîsédeq', 483-513. The text and translation used here is that by Kobelski, *Melchizedek*, 5-10.

84  Kobelski, *Melchizedek*, 3-4. Cf. also the importance of Isa. 61.1-2 for the text suggested by Miller, 'Function', 467-69. For the figure of Melchizedek himself, both Gen. 14.18-20 and Ps. 110 form the OT background; cf. Kobelski, 51-55. Melchizedek is also mentioned in the Qumran manuscript, 1QapGen, but it is a quite literal Aramaic translation of Gen. 14.18-20, and adds nothing to our discussion here; cf. Horton, *Melchizedek*, 61-64.

85  While not relevant for our discussion here, Melchizedek's role as a heavenly being in 11QMelch may be perceived in a variety of ways, including priest, king, and *elohim*. For further discussion of these issues, see Kobelski, (*Melchizedek*, 56-71) and the literature he cites.

86  However, it is the evil celestial forces of Belial who dominate and control the terrestrial sons of darkness, and it is these evil human forces who are responsible for the community's experiences of oppression and 'captivity'. Therefore, their belief in restoration must have included liberty from their terrestrial as well as celestial enemies. Yet, if the citation of Ps. 7.8 in 11QMelch 2.10 is applied to Melchizedek, then he is 'El' who 'judges the nations'.

Secondly, language associated with 'coming' is used to describe this figure. In Dan. 12.1 the expression 'Michael shall arise' (רַעֲמֹד מִיכָאֵל), uses the same verb also associated with the coming of Messianic figures discussed above.[87] Thirdly, the figure of Michael/Melchizedek is described as mighty. For example, 1QM 17.6 speaks of 'the might of the great angel'.[88]

With respect to our fourth and fifth criteria, little evidence exists. One of the fragments of 11QMelch states that 'Belial will be consumed with fire' (3.7). Since it is Melchizedek who judges Belial in the previous column (2.12-13), it is reasonable to assume that this later statement attributes the use of fire to the judgment by Melchizedek, especially when fire is traditionally associated with judgment by angels.[89] Other than this use of fire as an instrument of judgment, none of the other motifs for which we are searching exist with respect to the angelic prince, Michael/Melchizedek.[90]

### 7.6 *The Human-like Figure/the Son of Man*

The figure identified in Dan. 7.14 as כְּבַר אֱנָשׁ ('one like a son of man')

---

87  §7.3, 7.4. Cf. 11QMelch 2.10. The use of the verb עמד in the expression רַעֲמֹד מִיכָאֵל ('Michael shall arise', Dan. 12.1) probably indicates more than just arising, coming to prominence, or standing, since the same verb is used later in this same verse in the expression הָעֹמֵד עַל ('the one who stands over'). This latter expression indicates Michael's military and judicial role in the restoration of God's people; cf. Nickelsburg, *Resurrection*, 11-14.
88  Cf. 11QMelch 2.9.
89  E.g. *1 En.* 10.11-14; 54.6; *Sib. Or.* 2.286-90; CD 2.5-6.
90  11QMelch 2.15-16 quotes Isa. 52.7 which concerns the herald proclaiming peace and announcing 'your God is king', and 2.17-25 provides an interpretation of the text. It is quite clear in the preceding context (2.9-11) that Melchizedek is interpreted to be אלוהים. The statement in 2.15 that 'this is the day [of salvation about w]hich [God] spoke . . .', is referring to the preceding liberty brought by Melchizedek. Thus, the quotation of Isa. 52.7, which ends with the proclamation of salvation that 'your God is king', is probably being used with the understanding that in this quotation אלוהים is referring to Melchizedek. This interpretation may be reconstructed in the fragmentary text of 2.24-25: 'But "Your G[o]d" is [Melchizedek who will res]c[ue them from] the hand of Belial'. If this is the case, then the herald referred to in the quote of Isa. 52.7 is probably *not* Melchizedek, but another figure, since it is unlikely that the herald would be making such an announcement about himself in the third person. The herald is interpreted in 2.18: 'And the herald i[s the one an]ointed of the spir[it about] whom Dan[iel] said: ['Until an anointed . . .]'. Therefore, while 11QMelch does speak of an anointing with the spirit, it is probably not an anointing of Melchizedek. Thus, this text cannot be used for evidence of this feature. For further discussion, see van der Woude, 'Melchisedek', 367; de Jonge and van der Woude, '11Q Melchizedek', 304-307; Kobelski, *Melchizedek*, 21; Horton, *Melchizedek*, 78-79.

has received a great deal of scholarly attention, and the interpretive alternatives are legion. Concerning the identity of this human-like figure in Daniel 7 three main schools of interpretation currently exist (with many variations and other, minority alternatives): (1) a collective identification as Israel; (2) an angelic identification, usually Michael; (3) an individual identification, usually with some messianic connections.[91] While these issues of debate are essential for a full and correct interpretation of this figure, it is not necessary for our purposes here to discuss the alternatives and choose between them, because the evidence from the *Parables of Enoch* (*1 En.* 37–71) indicates that in the first century Daniel's human-like figure was understood, in one strand of interpretation at least, to be an individual heavenly figure of judgment and restoration—an interpretation which may not necessarily agree with any of the above modern schools of interpretation. It is, therefore, sufficient at this point to examine the function of this figure within Daniel 7.[92]

It is necessary first to consider the identity of 'the holy ones of the Most High' because they are the ones restored in Daniel 7 (vv. 18, 21-22, 27a), and judgment on their behalf is mentioned as well (v. 22). The most common view is that the holy ones are Israel, the earthly people of God, or something similar.[93] However, some scholars have argued that in this vision they are angels.[94] As a plural adjective functioning substantively in the phrase קַדִּישֵׁי עֶלְיוֹנִין, 'holy ones' indicates a group of beings who may be characterized as holy and who are identified as belonging to the Most High. As a substantive standing alone, the Aramaic adjective קַדִּישׁ and the Hebrew equivalent קָדוֹשׁ are clearly used to refer to angelic beings in Daniel. Yet, functioning adjectivally, these same words modify 'gods' and 'people' in Daniel. This linguistic

---

91  An example of a recent representative of the first alternative is Casey (*Son of Man*, 7-50); of the second alternative is Collins ('Son of Man', 50-66; *Vision*, 123-52), and of the third alternative is Caragounis (*Son of Man*, 35-82). For surveys of recent research see Colpe, 'ὁ υἱὸς τοῦ ἀνθρώπου', 8.400-30; Caragounis, *Son of Man*, 9-34; Davies, *Daniel*, 100-108; Ferch, *Son of Man*, 4-39; Hartman and Di Lella, *Daniel*, 85-102; Goldingay, *Daniel*, 167-72.

92  This figure in Dan. 7 is not *the* Son of Man, but is rather described as being 'like a son of man' (כְּבַר אֱנָשׁ), which indicates that in the vision this figure had the appearance of a human in contrast to the beasts of the vision who appeared to be 'like' different animals. Strictly speaking, therefore, it is anachronistic to speak of the Danielic figure as 'the Son of Man'. Therefore, in the ensuing discussion of Daniel I refer to 'the human-like figure'. But, when discussing the figure portrayed in the *Parables of Enoch*, I use the term 'Son of Man'. In summarizing the evidence concerning the five criteria for which we are searching, since the discussion combines the data from the various sources from a first-century point of view, I employ the later title, 'Son of Man'.

93  For example, Brekelmans, 'Saints', 305-29; Poythress, 'Holy Ones', 208-13; Hasel, 'Identity', 176-85.

94  For example, Noth, 'Holy Ones', 215-28; Dequeker, 'Saints', 108-87; Collins, 'Son of

information is not decisive, and the evidence from the rest of the OT cannot decide the issue either.[95]   Their identity must therefore be decided on the basis of how the holy ones function in Daniel 7 itself.[96] Most decisive are the statements in v. 21 that the little horn 'made war' with the holy ones, and in v. 25 that he 'shall wear out' the holy ones. As symbolic descriptions of the actions of Antiochus IV Epiphanes, these statements more probably refer to humans (his persecution of the Jewish people) than to angels. Furthermore, while it may be possible for angels to 'receive the kingdom' (vv. 18, 22, 27), the fact that the vision featured earthly, human kingdoms makes it more probable that it is God's people who are receiving the kingdom rather than angels.[97]  Therefore, in Daniel 7, 'holy ones' is better understood as referring to the people of God than to angels. Whether they may be more specifically identified (e.g. national Israel, faithful remnant, etc.) is not relevant to our discussion here. It is sufficient to identify them as Israel, or God's people.

Judgment and restoration are two themes running through the vision and interpretation of Daniel 7. In vv. 9-10 the Ancient of Days is portrayed in a court-room scene in which 'the court sat in judgment, and the books were opened' (cf. vv. 22a, 26a). While the judgment of the court is not stated, the execution of its verdict is described: the fourth beast is killed and its body burned, and the other beasts have their dominion taken away (vv. 11-12; cf. vv. 21-22a, 26). That their verdict also vindicates God's people is suggested in v. 22: 'and judgment was given for the holy ones of the Most High' (i.e. a favourable judgment on their behalf).[98]  Restoration is indicated by the repeated statement that 'the holy ones received the kingdom' (vv. 18, 22b, 27a).

Man', 50-66; Collins, *Vision*, 123-52.

95 Used substantively with reference to angels, the Aramaic קַדִּישׁ is used in 4.13, 17, 18, 23 (MT vv. 10, 14, 15, 20), and the Hebrew קָדוֹשׁ in 8.13 (2x). These words function adjectivally in 4.5, 6, 15 (MT vv. 8, 9, 18); 5.11; 8.24. Similarly, the Hebrew noun קֹדֶשׁ is used in Daniel to identify the temple (8.13, 14; 9.26) and to describe the hill of Jerusalem (9.16, 20; 11.45), the city of Jerusalem (9.24), the covenant (11.28, 30 [2x]), and the people of God (12.7). Elsewhere in the OT the adjective קָדוֹשׁ is used substantively to refer to both angels (Job 5.1; 15.15; Ps. 89.5, 7 [MT vv. 6, 8]; Zech. 14.5) and people (Deut. 33.3; Pss. 16.3; 34.9 [MT v. 10]; 106.16). Debatable references are Prov. 9.10; 30.3; Hos. 11.12 (MT 12.1); cf. also the nominal form in Exod. 15.11; Deut. 33.2. For apocryphal and pseudepigraphal references, see Brekelmans, 'Saints', 309-26.

96 The argument of Collins (*Vision*, 141-44), which requires the unity of Dan. 7–12, and from which he argues that the identity of 'a holy one' in 8.13 is the same as the 'holy ones of the Most High' in Dan. 7, is methodologically problematic. Cf. Davies, *Daniel*, 57-65, 101-104.

97 The phrase 'the people of the holy ones of the Most High' in v. 27 is ambiguous, and can be used to support either position. It also has problems textually; cf. Caragounis, *Son of Man*, 61-67.
   Goldingay (*Daniel*, 176-78) considers both alternatives as well as the possibility that the referent could include celestial beings and earthly beings at the same time. But

From this examination of judgment and restoration we should note that it is not the human-like figure, but rather the Ancient of Days (with the court sitting in judgment) who is the Judge and Restorer of God's people.[99] The human-like figure is presented to the Ancient of Days in what appears to be a royal investiture. He is given the royal prerogatives of 'dominion and glory and kingship' (v. 14a), presumably by the Ancient of Days. As a consequence of this investiture, the human-like figure is served by all nations, exercises an eternal dominion and a triumphant kingship (v. 14b). Thus, the human-like figure functions in Daniel 7 as part of the restoration brought about by God, rather than as a figure exercising the judgment and restoration.

Thus, strictly speaking, the human-like figure of Daniel 7 is not a figure of judgment and restoration at all, and so would not normally be considered here. However, since the Son of Man tradition in *1 Enoch* developed to a large extent out of this passage and its portrayal of the human-like figure, this background material is relevant and may be used in later discussion.[100]

In the *Parables of Enoch* (*1 En.* 37–71),[101] two central figures are pre-

---

he concludes that 'Dan. 7 is too allusive to enable us to decide with certainty. . .'

98  It is possible to read this clause to indicate that it is the authority to judge which is given to the holy ones. However, this is an unlikely interpretation. Cf. Montgomery, *Daniel*, 309-10; Lacocque, *Daniel*, 153.

99  It has been observed that in v. 9 'thrones' is plural, and yet only the Ancient of Days is seated on a throne. Thus another throne could be reserved for the human-like figure (cf. Mowinckel, *He That Cometh*, 352, 393; Rabbi Akiba understood this to be two thrones, one for God and one for David [*b. Sanh.* 38b]). While such a suggestion is possible, it must remain conjectural for there is no evidence in the text to warrant it. On the contrary, there is at least some evidence that the other thrones were for other members of the court, because v. 10 states that 'the court *sat*'. In any case, these thrones and anyone who might occupy them are not emphasized in the passage. Hartman and Di Lella, *Daniel*, 217; Porteous, *Daniel*, 108-109; Ferch, *Son of Man*, 147-50.

100 On the relationship between Dan. 7 and the *Parables of Enoch*, see Caragounis, *Son of Man*, 101-11.

101 The date of the *Parables of Enoch* (*1 En.* 37–71) has been a major topic of debate recently among scholars. Milik (*Enoch*, 89-96) has argued for a late date (c. 270 CE) for the *Parables* partially because no fragments of this section of *1 En.* have been found at Qumran, and historical allusions in the book must be traced to events in c. 249–259 CE. In similar fashion, Hindley ('Date', 551-65) has argued that the historical allusions in the *Parables* require a date after c. 120 CE. However, this late date has more recently been questioned by numerous scholars (cf. the review of opinions by Charlesworth, 'SNTS Pseudepigrapha Seminars', 320-22). Concerning the absence of evidence from Qumran, we should note that this is an argument from silence, which is especially questionable in light of the fact that these fragments reproduce only about 5% of the book—rendering this a rather dubious argument at best (cf. Black, 'Aramaic Barnāshā', 201; Black, *Enoch*, 1 [against his earlier position given in 'Parables', 6]; Greenfield and Stone, 'Enochic Pentateuch', 55-56). With respect to the historical allusions, Bampfylde ('Similitudes', 9-31) has argued that a more plausible analysis dates the latest allusions to c. 50 BCE. While a late date for

sented. God himself is primarily identified by the titles 'Lord of spirits' and 'Chief of Days'. Four titles are used for the other figure: 'Righteous One' and 'Anointed One' (i.e. Messiah) are each used twice, while 'Elect One' and 'Son of Man' are each used 16 times.[102] That these four titles refer to one and the same figure is quite evident in the text and is generally accepted by scholars.[103]

the *Parables* was a popular position, especially in light of the Qumran evidence (or lack of it!), a significant number of scholars have recently adopted an earlier date. Thus, the position of Black (*Enoch*, 188) is quite reasonable: 'a Hebrew *Urschrift* for the Book of the Parables... I would date to the early Roman period, probably pre-70 A.D.' If the *Parables* contain traditions reasonably considered to be pre-70 CE, they must be considered here as reflecting one possible type of expectation current during the first century CE. For recent support (after Milik, *Enoch*, published in 1976) of a pre-70 CE date see Schürer, *History*, 3.257-59; Nickelsburg, *Literature*, 221-23; Greenfield and Stone, 'Enochic Pentateuch', 51-60; Suter, *Tradition*, 23-32; Collins, *Imagination*, 142-43; Stone, 'Apocalyptic Literature', 397-400; Mearns, 'Parables', 118-19; Mearns, 'Similitudes', 360-69; Wilson, 'Son of Man', 39-40; Caragounis, *Son of Man*, 84-94; as well as Black; Charlesworth; Bampfylde. Knibb ('Date', 345-59) prefers a date c. 100 CE.

102 Righteous One: *1 En.* 38.2; 53.6 (poss. 38.3; cf. 39.6; 46.3); Anointed One: 48.10; 52.4; Elect One 39.6; 40.5; 45.3, 4; 49.2, 4; 51.3, 5; 52.6, 9; 53.6; 55.4; 61.5, 8, 11; 62.1; Son of Man: 46.2, 3, 4; 48.2; 62.5, 7, 9, 14; 63.11; 69.26, 27, 29 (2x); 70.1; 71.14, 17. A 17th example may be an expression similar to Son of Man in 46.1, where this title is first introduced in a scene reminiscent of Dan. 7 and with language similar to Daniel's 'human-like figure'; 46.1 states: 'with him was another whose countenance had the appearance of a man...'

103 The less common titles are used in contexts linking them with the more common titles, so that the Righteous One is identified with the Elect One (53.6; cf. 39.6) and the Son of Man (46.3), while the Anointed One is identified with the Elect One (52.4-6) and the Son of Man (48.2-10). Furthermore, the two common titles, Elect One and Son of Man are identified with each other, as in 62.1-7. In v. 1 the Lord of spirits commands the rulers of the earth: 'Open your eyes and lift up your horns, if you can, to acknowledge the Elect One'. Verses 2-5 describe the judgment and suffering of those rulers, after which they obey the command of v. 1 and 'glorify and bless and extol him who reigns over all, the One who hides himself'. The next verse (v. 7) explains: 'For from the beginning the Son of Man was hidden...' Thus, the Elect One whom they acknowledge is the Son of Man. That these four titles identify one figure is further substantiated by the fact that the main characteristics, privileges and actions of both the Elect One and the Son of Man closely match one another. Cf. the detailed analysis by Caragounis, *Son of Man*, 107-109; cf. also Collins, 'Son of Man', 112-13; Hooker, *Son of Man*, 36-41.

This figure is called Son of Man in our discussion because it is the introduction of this title to the figure which is probably the key feature of the *Parables*. Son of Man was evidently not a current or widespread messianic title in the author's day, but the titles Anointed One, Righteous One, and Elect One were evidently all identified with the expected Davidic king, who was the Messiah, the Righteous Branch, and possibly the Servant of Yahweh. Thus, the author transforms messianic expectation from the human Davidic king to the heavenly Son of Man. This is accomplished by identifying the figure with titles linked with the Davidic King, but describing the figure in terms of the Danielic human-like figure, and then introducing the title Son of Man for this figure. For further discussion see Caragounis, *Son of Man*, 109-11; Hartman, *Prophecy Interpreted*, 118-20; Black, *Enoch*, 189.

The Son of Man is supremely a figure of judgment and restoration. The Lord of spirits appoints him as judge and places him on a throne of glory.[104] He judges sinners and separates them from the righteous and elect ones, consigning the wicked to punishment and destruction. For example, *1 En.* 69.27-28 states:

> And he [the Son of Man] sat on the throne of his glory,
> And the sum of judgement was given to the Son of Man,
> And he will cause the sinners to pass away and be destroyed from off the
>     face of the earth,
> And those who have led the world astray, with chains shall they be bound,
> And in their assembling-place of destruction shall they be imprisoned,
> And all their works shall vanish from the face of the earth.[105]

Those who have power, such as rulers and the wealthy, are specially mentioned as the objects of the Son of Man's judgment.[106] He is also responsible for the judgment of the fallen angels, including Azazel and his company.[107]

The Son of Man is also a figure of restoration. He is the Righteous One, and as such, his reign is a reign of righteousness, victory, peace and blessedness, which stands in marked contrast to the suffering and oppression experienced by God's people prior to his coming to judge the wicked and restore the righteous. For example, *1 En.* 48.4 states that the Son of Man 'shall be a staff to the righteous whereon to stay [i.e. to rest, or lean] themselves and not fall', and 49.2 states that 'he is mighty in all the secrets of righteousness, and unrighteousness shall disappear as a shadow and have no continuance'. He will be victorious 'because the Lord of spirits has chosen him, and whose cause before the Lord of spirits triumphs by uprightness for ever'.[108] The righteous who have died prior to the Son of Man's reign are resurrected in order that they also may enjoy the blessings of his reign, and they receive eternal life.[109] He also functions as the one who reveals both wisdom and hidden treasures to the righteous.[110]

Clearly then, the Son of Man, as he received more developed expression in the *Parables of Enoch*, is a figure of judgment and restoration, and fulfils the first criterion for which we are searching.

Secondly, the Son of Man is described as coming. In Dan. 7.13 the

---

104 *1 En.* 41.9; 51.3; 61.8; cf. 45.3; 55.4; 62.5; 69.27, 29; poss. 62.2 when compared with vv. 1, 5.
105 *1 En.* 38.3; 45.2-3; 49.4; 50.2.
106 *1 En.* 38.4-6; 46.4-8; 48.8; 62.3-6; cf. 55.4.
107 *1 En.* 55.4; 61.8.
108 *1 En.* 46.3; cf. also 39.6-8; 45.4-5; 46.3-4; 48.7; 50.1-2; 51.3-5; 52.6-9; 61.14-15; 71.17.
109 *1 En.* 51.1-2; 61.5.
110 *1 En.* 46.3; 48.7; 51.3.

human-like figure is described as 'coming with the clouds of heaven'.[111] In *1 Enoch* the Son of Man is portrayed as both 'arising' and 'appearing'. For example, *1 En.* 69.29 states:

> And from henceforth there shall be nothing corruptible,
> For that Son of Man has appeared,
> And has seated himself on the throne of his glory,
> And all evil shall pass away and depart from before his face. . .[112]

Thirdly, the Son of Man is described as mighty. For example, in *1 Enoch* 52 Enoch has a vision of mountains of various metals melting and becoming useless—metals which had been used by those who were wealthy and powerful to support their wealth and power. The interpreting angel explains to Enoch that 'all these things which you have seen shall serve the dominion of his [i.e. the Lord of spirits'] Anointed One, that he may be powerful and mighty on the earth' (52.4). In 49.2-3 'he is mighty in all the secrets of righteousness . . . and his might [is] to generations of generations. And in him dwells . . . the spirit of understanding and of might. . .'[113]

Fourthly, there are no precise correlations of the imagery of 'baptizing with (holy) spirit/wind and fire' with the description of the Son of Man's ministry of judgment and restoration. However, there are a few more general observations that may be made. While the specific language of baptism is not used with respect to the Son of Man, the language of water and ablutions is used. For example, the blessings brought by the Son of Man are described as fountains of righteousness and wisdom at which the thirsty may drink. Also, because of the Son of Man, wisdom is poured out like water.[114] As far as I am able to determine, the imagery of fire is not used to describe the Son of Man's judgment, though in *1 Enoch* 53–54 a judgment scene is described in which angels carry out the punishment of the wicked (who have evidently been judged by the Son of Man) by casting them into fire (54.6).[115] While the Son of Man is not described as one who bestows the spirit upon the righteous, he is the recipient of the spirit himself. *1 En.* 62.2 uses ablution imagery to portray the bestowal of the spirit:

> And the Elect One sat on the throne of his glory,
> And the spirit of righteousness was poured out upon him,
> And the word of his mouth slays all the sinners,
> And all the unrighteous are destroyed from before his face.[116]

---

111 The Aramaic verb used in Dan. 7.13 is אָתָה, a derivative of the Hebrew verb אָתָה, which is one of the verbs used elsewhere in the OT for the coming of judgment/restoration figures.

112 Cf. *1 En.* 38.2; 51.5; 52.9.

113 Cf. also *1 En.* 69.29.

114 *1 En.* 48.1; 49.1; 53.7.

Fifthly, I know of no place where threshing-floor imagery is used with respect to the Son of Man's ministry. In *1 En.* 48.9, the punishment of the rulers and powerful is described with this imagery: 'I will give them over into the hands of my elect ones: as stubble in the fire so shall they burn. . .' Thus, threshing-floor imagery is used, but it is specifically associated with the participation of the righteous in the judgment, rather than the Son of Man himself.[117]

This discussion may now be summarized. While the human-like figure of Daniel 7 is not a judgment/restoration figure, this Danielic figure contributed to the development of the Son of Man as a figure of judgment and restoration, which is reflected in the *Parables of Enoch*.[118] The portrayal of the judgment and restoration ministry of this Son of Man uses the language of 'coming' and 'mighty'. He is the recipient of the spirit, and this receiving of the spirit involves ablution language, but he does not bestow the spirit. In portraying his ministry the imagery of water is used generally, but not specifically the imagery of fire. Finally, the imagery of the threshing floor is associated with his ministry only indirectly.[119]

---

115 In Dan. 7.11, the fourth beast is destroyed in fire.

116 Cf. *1 En.* 49.3 cited above. The text of *1 En.* 62.2 is somewhat problematic. The text suggests that it is in fact the Lord of spirits who sits on the throne, but this reading would make God the recipient of an anointing by the spirit, a concept which, upon reflection, is quite strange, and for which I know of no parallel. For this reason, the text has often been read that the Lord of spirits seats the Elect One (of 62.1) on the throne, and, thus, it is the Elect One who receives the spirit. For this reason, Black (*Enoch*, 59; cf. 235) translates 62.2 as has been cited here; cf. Charles, *APOT*, 2.227. On the other hand, Isaac (*OTP*, 1.43) and Knibb (*Enoch*, 2.150) support the first translation.

117 Also, it is unclear who is the 'I' in the quote; it could be either the Lord of spirits or the Son of Man. One other very vague reference is to the restoration and blessing of the righteous by the Son of Man being described in terms of being 'sown' or 'planted' in *1 En.* 62.8.

118 Contrary to recent scholarly opinion, which has rejected the view that the phrase 'the Son of Man' was a messianic title (e.g. Vermes, 'נשא בר/בר נשא', 327-28; *Jesus*, 162-77), Horbury ('Messianic Associations', 34-55) has attempted to reopen the question.

119 In *1 En.* 71.14 Enoch is told by the angelic messenger: 'You are the Son of Man who is born for righteousness'. This identification is problematic, and it is unclear how much it should guide the interpretation of the preceding *Parables* in *1 En.* 37–71. On the one hand, Black (*Enoch*, 188; cf. Black, 'Eschatology of the Similitudes', 1-10) argues that this identification represents 'an older and pre-Christian stratum of the Enoch tradition', in which the preceding Parables function as a theophany preceding the commission of a prophet, a form found elsewhere. On the other hand, Isaac (*OTP* 1.50 n. 71s) states that this expression 'son of man' is to be distinguished from the titular use of 'Son of Man' elsewhere in the *Parables*. Alternatively, *1 En.* 71 (and 70) may be considered later, redactional additions to the *Parables* (so Colpe, 'ὁ υἱὸς τοῦ ἀνθρώπου', 8.426-27; cf. Black's reversal of the opinion cited above, in 'Aramaic

## 7.7 *Elijah*-redivivus

The fourth disputation of Malachi (2.17–3.5) concerns God's justice which the audience has questioned by asking 'Where is the God of justice?' (2.17-18).[120] The response to this question is provided in 3.1-5, but the answer is not what the audience expects, for they themselves will be the recipients of judgment and purification.

Four figures are specified in v. 1 as participating in this judgment and purification: (1) the one identified by Yahweh as 'my messenger' (מַלְאָכִי) who 'will prepare the way before me'; (2) Yahweh ('me') who comes after his messenger to judge (v. 5); (3) the Lord (הָאָדוֹן) who 'will come to his temple'; and finally (4) the messenger of the covenant (מַלְאַךְ הַבְּרִית). It is very probable that 'the Lord' referred to in the third person in v. 1d is the same as the reference by Yahweh to himself in v. 1b, because הָאָדוֹן may refer to Yahweh (cf. Zech. 4.14; 6.5), and 'his temple' most naturally refers to Yahweh's temple (cf. the judgment of the temple activities in vv. 2-4). Furthermore, the reference to the audience in the description of the Lord as the one 'whom you seek' most naturally refers back to their question concerning 'the God of justice' in 2.17.

The identity of 'the messenger of the covenant' is more problematic. This could be a figure distinct from either Yahweh or Yahweh's messenger. However, good arguments may be brought forward for identifying this messenger with either of these two figures and, thus, this option may be disregarded.[121] Scholars have commonly identified the messenger of the covenant with Yahweh. This contention may be supported on the basis of the chiastic parallelism of the description of these two figures[122] as well as the probable dependence of Mal. 3.1a-b on Exod. 23.20.[123] However, these arguments are unconvincing. First of all, such chiastic parallelism does not *require* the identification of the two figures with each other; it can only support such an identification if it has first been based on other grounds. Secondly, Beth Glazier-McDonald's use of Exod. 23.20 actually parallels Mal. 3.1a-b which describes the מַלְאַךְ

---

Barnāshā, 201). Collins (*Imagination*, 151-53) considers this latter alternative to be the most plausible explanation. In any case, we are able to discuss the function of the Son of Man in the *Parables* without having to come to a firm conclusion concerning this Enochic identification.
120 Cf. Smith's discussion (*Micah-Malachi*, 299-300) on the structure of Malachi.
121 On the other hand, France (*Jesus*, 91-92 n. 31) suggests that all figures could be equated with one another, but this also appears unlikely.
122 Verhoff, *Haggai and Malachi*, 288-89.
123 Glazier-McDonald (*Malachi*, 131) argues on the basis of this similarity that in both passages 'the roles of Yahweh and his messenger seem to merge (22.21f)... [T]he messenger (מַלְאָךְ) is Yahweh's mode of self revelation.' The assertion which equates Yahweh with the 'angel of Yahweh' requires a more nuanced discussion due to the Israelite aversion to actually seeing God. Cf. Eichrodt, *Theology*, 2.23-29.

who precedes Yahweh, and does not parallel the description of the מַלְאָךְ הַבְּרִית in 3.1e-f. Yet she wishes to equate the מַלְאָךְ of Exod. 23.20 with the מַלְאָךְ הַבְּרִית of Mal. 3.1e-f and preserve the separate prophetic-forerunner identity of the מַלְאָךְ in 3.1a-b.[124] Thus, the parallelism of Exod. 23.20 with Mal. 3.1 cannot support the identification of the מַלְאָךְ with the אָדוֹן.[125]

On the other hand, the use of 'messenger' terminology in the phrase מַלְאָךְ הַבְּרִית is most naturally identified with the identical term 'my messenger' (מַלְאָכִי) found earlier in this same verse.[126] This interpretation may be further supported by observing that Yahweh refers to the מַלְאָךְ הַבְּרִית in the third person and states that 'he is coming', which strongly suggests that Yahweh is speaking of the מַלְאָךְ הַבְּרִית as a figure other than himself.[127] The structure of this passage is better understood with v. 1a-d presenting the summary of a double scenario which is then expanded in vv. 1e-5. The summary consists of the מַלְאָךְ clearing the way (v. 1a-b) for Yahweh (= אָדוֹן) to come to his temple (v. 1c-d). This scenario is then expanded in the same order. In v. 1e-f the מַלְאָךְ is further identified as the מַלְאָךְ הַבְּרִית, and in vv. 2-4 his pre-paratory ministry is described. Finally, the reference in v. 1c-d to Yah-weh's coming to his temple is expanded by v. 5 in which Yahweh declares his intention to judge the oppressors. This structure is further supported by the observation commonly made concerning the reference in v. 1a-b that the מַלְאָךְ is 'to prepare the way'. The imagery concerns the mes-senger of the king who prepares the highway down which the king will soon proceed to come to his palace or temple.[128] Thus, if the king in v. 1c-d is coming to the temple, then it implies that part of the messenger's preparatory work would be to prepare the temple for the king's arrival.

---

124 Glazier-McDonald, *Malachi*, 132-35.

125 Also, in Exod. 23.20-22 the messenger (whether understood as a human messenger or as the 'angel of Yahweh', מַלְאַךְ יְהוָה) is actually kept carefully distinct from Yahweh and functions as an agent of revelation. As an agent of revelation, such a messenger would naturally be closely associated with Yahweh and is used by Yahweh to reveal himself. From a theological perspective, such a messenger may be Yahweh in a representative form; cf. Smith, *Micah-Malachi*, 327-28. But to simply merge the two figures into one misses the intent of having such a messenger-type figure in the first place.

126 Petersen, *Prophecy*, 42-43; Blenkinsopp, *History*, 241. Malchow ('Messenger', 253) points out that the term 'messenger' is not applied elsewhere to God.

127 Rudolph (*Haggai-Sacharja-Maleachi*, 278) contends that Yahweh's use of the third person to refer to himself 'erhöht nicht nur die Feierlichkeit, sondern unterstreicht das Majestätische seiner Erscheinung. . .' But this contention does not alleviate the forced nature of the interpretation.

128 Glazier-McDonald, *Malachi*, 136-38; Verhoff, *Haggai and Malachi*, 287. The lan-guage used to describe the messenger's preparatory ministry is reminiscent of Isa. 40.3 and may have in fact been influenced by it; cf. Isa. 57.14; 62.10; Kaiser, 'Prom-ise', 225-26.

This is precisely the type of ministry which is ascribed to the מַלְאַךְ הַבְּרִית: 'he will purify the sons of Levi and refine them like gold and silver, till they present right offerings to Yahweh' (v. 3b; cf. v. 4).[129]

Thus, Mal. 3.1-5 introduces a messenger-figure who precedes Yahweh, and has a purificatory and preparatory ministry concentrated primarily upon the temple and its cultus. However, a more specific identification of this 'messenger of the covenant' is not possible because this title is not used elsewhere. Various possibilities have been suggested (other than those considered above), including Malachi himself,[130] a priestly messiah[131] and a future prophetic figure.[132] The last suggestion is the most probable, especially in light of the appendix to Malachi in 4.5-6. While this is most probably a later addition,[133] it does clearly identify the prophet Elijah with the מַלְאַךְ in 3.1.[134] Though a later addition, it represents the final form of the text which would have had impact upon Jewish thinking around the turn of the era.[135]

In Malachi the ministry of Elijah-*redivivus* is not strictly one of judgment, but is rather a preparatory ministry for the coming of Yahweh, who would act as judge. (3.1, 5; 4.5-6). However, while purification may be considered restorative, it does have a judgmental aspect to it, as reflected in the smelting imagery of Mal. 3.2-3. *Liv. Proph.* 21.3 states concerning Elijah: 'his dwelling will be light and his word judgment, and he will judge Israel'. Most manuscripts add that this judgment is 'with sword and fire'.[136]

In Malachi, the preparatory ministry of Elijah-*redivivus* is a ministry of restoration which has two foci. First of all, the restoration involves purification, especially of the temple, its priesthood and its cultus. The

---

129 This structure denies Rudolph's statement (*Haggai-Sacharja-Maleachi*, 278) that it is 'unmöglich' to identify the מַלְאַךְ of v. 1a-b with the מַלְאַךְ הַבְּרִית 'denn nachdem Jahwe selbst schon da ist, hat der Vorbote ausgedient'.
130 Mason, *Haggai, Zechariah and Malachi*, 152.
131 Malchow, 'Messenger', 253-55.
132 Mowinckel, *He That Cometh*, 298-99; Petersen, *Prophecy*, 43-45; Blenkinsopp, *History*, 241.
133 Following Smith, *Micah-Malachi*, 340-41; Smith, *Malachi*, 82-83; against Glazier-McDonald, *Malachi*, 244-45.
134 Support for this identification may be found in Smith, *Micah-Malachi*, 341-42; Glazier-McDonald, *Malachi*, 261-70; Mason, *Haggai, Zechariah and Malachi*, 160; Childs, *Introduction*, 495-96.
135 The messenger of Mal. 3.1-5 is equated with the Elijah of 4.5-6 in Mt. 11.10-14.
136 It is not entirely clear whether this is a reference to Elijah of the past or to Elijah-*redivivus*. This reference is an oracle received by Elijah's father which was meant to explain the unusual events surrounding Elijah's birth. So it could be a reference to Elijah's past. However, the reference that 'his dwelling will be light' suggests his translation to heaven without dying, and, thus, the description of his judgment, which follows his translation, would refer to his ministry as Elijah-*redivivus*. Hare (*OTP*, 2.396 n. 21f) understands this text to refer to Elijah-*redivivus*.

description of this purification (3.2-3) suggests that judgment may be included, but the emphasis is upon purification. Secondly, this ministry involved the restoration of unity among the people of Israel, portrayed here in familial terms.[137] It may have included the return of the people to their covenant obedience to Yahweh, as suggested by the use of the verb שׁוב in 4.6 (MT 3.24; cf. 3.7). Sir. 48.10 refers to this expectation of Elijah-*redivivus*:

> You [i.e. Elijah] who are ready at the appointed time, it is written,
>> to calm the wrath of God before it breaks out in fury,
> to turn the heart of the father to the son,
> and to restore the tribes of Jacob.

This last clause is an addition to the Mal. 4.5-6 text, and suggests that Elijah's ministry of restoration would include his involvement in the political re-establishment of Israel.[138] Thus, it may be concluded that Elijah-*redivivus* was perceived as a figure of judgment and restoration.

With respect to the second criterion, Elijah-*redivivus* is described specifically as one who 'comes' in Mal. 3.2 (cf. 4.5).[139] However, I find no evidence of Elijah-*redivivus* being identified as mighty, the third criterion.

For the fourth criterion, baptism with (holy) spirit/wind and fire, little evidence exists. Some stories concerning Elijah in the OT feature fire, such as the calling of fire from heaven upon a sacrifice (1 Kgs 18.38), or the chariot of fire which appeared when he was translated to heaven (2 Kgs 2.11).[140] Similarly, fire is associated with Elijah-*redivivus*. The

---

137 In the MT of Mal. 3.24 (ET 4.6), this restoration is portrayed purely in familial terms: 'He will turn the hearts of the fathers to the children, and the hearts of the children to their fathers. . .' But the LXX (= v. 23) translates the first half in similar, familial terms, but alters the second half to have larger social implications: 'and the heart of a man to his neighbour' (καὶ καρδίαν ἀνθρώπου πρὸς τὸν πλησίον).

138 The verb here is καθίστημι which indicates appointing, ordaining, or putting someone in charge. Cf. BAGD, 390; Skehan and Di Lella (*Wisdom*, 530, 534) translate it as 're-establish'. It is probably derived from the description of the Servant's ministry in Isa. 49.6.

139 Elijah-*redivivus* is also described as coming in *Sib. Or.* 2.187-89 and 2.245-47, but the immediate context of both these references probably contain Christian interpolations. Thus, these references should not be used to reflect Jewish expectation at the turn of the era.

In 1963 Starcky ('Quatre étapes', 497-98) announced an Aramaic Qumran fragment, 4QarP, which contained the line [ מ]קרד לאליה אשלח לכנ ('I will send you Elijah befo[re. . .]'). On the basis of the preceding line which read תמינ יא [ ]א והא לבחיר ('the eighth as an elect one; and behold [. . .]'), Starcky argued that the 'eighth' was a reference to David, Jesse's eighth son, and the succeeding line may be stating that Elijah was coming as the precursor of the Davidic Messiah. Unfortunately, as far as I am aware, this fragment has never been published in its entirety, and Starcky's interpretation is somewhat speculative based on the evidence provided. Nevertheless, the fragment does refer to the coming of Elijah-*redivivus*. Cf. the comments by Fitzmyer, 'Aramaic "Elect of God" ', 134, 137, 159 n. 31.

140 Cf. the prominence of fire in the summary of Elijah's ministry in Sir. 48.1-9.

description of purification in Mal. 3.2-3 uses the imagery of fire, and as noted above some manuscripts of *Liv. Proph.* 21.3 state that 'he will judge Israel with sword and fire'.

There is no specific use of threshing-floor imagery in relation to the figure of Elijah-*redivivus*. The burning of chaff is referred to in Mal. 4.1, but this is associated with the Day of Yahweh, while Elijah's ministry precedes that Day (cf. 4.5). The fire imagery associated with Elijah in Malachi is the fire which refines metals rather than that which burns chaff.

Thus, while Elijah-*redivivus* is a figure of judgment and restoration, there is little evidence for most of the criteria for which we are searching. The only ones found are that he is coming and that fire is associated with his ministry.[141]

### 7.8 *The Relationship between Yahweh and the Other Figures*

With respect to the relationship between Yahweh and the other figures, this survey of judgment and restoration figures considered each figure in isolation from the others, and so Yahweh was placed on a par with the other figures. However, we must now consider the relationship between Yahweh and the other expected figures, because within Jewish thought Yahweh and the other figures were not isolated from each other. An analysis of the data shows in fact that a relationship was thought to exist between Yahweh and the other figures.[142]

---

141 Most other references to Elijah in the literature of the Second Temple period are to the figure from the past, such as Jdt. 8.1; Sir. 48.1-9; 1 Macc. 2.58; 1 Esd. 9.27; *Apoc. Zeph.* 9.4; *Liv. Proph.* 9.2-4; 10.4-5; 21; *Asc. Isa.* 2.14-15. Other, veiled references are of no relevance to our concern here, such as *1 En.* 89.52; 90.31; 93.8. Other references may be to Elijah-*redivivus*, but the date of the literature is problematic, and therefore they are not used as evidence in the question being examined here; they include Lk. 1.17; Mt. 17.10-13 = Mk 9.11-13; Rev. 11.3-12; *4 Ezra* 6.26; *Apoc. Elij.* 4.7; 5.32; *m. 'Ed.* 8.7; *m. B. Mes.* 3.4-5; *m. Sot.* 9.15; on rabbinic literature see Str-B, 4.779-98; Klausner, *Messianic Idea*, 451-57. Unfortunately, older discussions concerning Elijah-*redivivus* fail to take into account the date of the texts and traditions concerned; cf. Klausner, *Messianic Idea*, 451-57; Jeremias, ''Hλ(ε)ίας', 2.928-34; Moore, *Judaism*, 2.357-62.

   The recent debate concerning the specific role of Elijah-*redivivus* as the precursor of a messianic figure is not relevant in this discussion, but it does show the problems with the eisegesis of texts as well as dating them. Cf. Faierstein, 'Scribes', 75-86; Allison, 'Elijah', 256-58; Fitzmyer, 'Elijah', 295-96.

   A related expectation featured the return of a prophet like Moses, which is based upon Deut. 18.15. However, there is little specific evidence for it in Second Temple Jewish literature (e.g. 1QS 9.11; 4QTest 5-8), and, thus, there is not enough relevant information for analysis. For further discussion and examination of other, later texts, see Teeple, *Prophet*, esp. 29-73.

142 The secondary literature usually discusses this issue with respect to the expectation of a future Davidic king in the OT, but this discussion may equally be applied to the

The preceding presentation of the data concerning figures of judgment and restoration gives the impression that these figures are, at least to a certain extent, either in conflict or in competition with each other. Thus, one text might highlight one expected figure, while another text presents another. For example, the *Psalms of Solomon* stress the Davidic Messiah, while the *Parables* of *1 Enoch* present the Son of Man. The Enochic Son of Man is a messianic figure and so presumably excluded the expectation of a Davidic Messiah. One might conclude from the preceding survey of expected figures that, just as the Davidic Messiah and the Son of Man are two different expectations which do not really complement each other, so also the expectation of Yahweh conflicts with the expectation of any one of the other figures. While this may be the case with the other figures, the evidence does not support such a conclusion with respect to Yahweh. Rather, the evidence demonstrates that, in the case of each of the other expected figures, *Yahweh was also expected* as a complementary figure. This contention may be supported on at least three grounds.

First of all, in the case of the other figures of judgment and restoration, Yahweh is also presented as judging and restoring along with the other figure. For example, in Ezek. 34.22-23 concerning the expected Davidic king/Davidic Messiah, Yahweh proclaims:

> I will save my flock, and they shall no longer be a prey; and I will judge between sheep and sheep. And I will set up over them one shepherd, my

other figures. The relationship between Yahweh and the expected Davidic king (and the other figures) may be basically explained in two different ways. On the one hand, Becker (*Expectation*, 48-53, 68-82) interprets two strands in the OT as evidence for a theocratic movement which was in conflict with restorative monarchism. He argues that restorative monarchism included the idea of a theocracy, but pure theocracy rejected the monarchy and expected the immediate kingship of Yahweh. Sometimes this involved foreign rulers also having earthly power. Similarly, Mowinckel (*He That Cometh*, 125-86, esp. 159-60) argues that messianic hope in the OT was essentially this-worldly and political, and that the Messiah was Yahweh's representative and channel of blessing to the people. But when the hope takes on a religious cast and is other-worldly, then the kingly rule of Yahweh is highlighted and the Messiah is superfluous. He argues that this was to change when the concept of the Messiah was transformed in later Judaism to an other-worldly savior and mediator (160, 261-79). On the other hand, Gowan (*Eschatology*, 37, cf. 34-37) perceives the two strands to be in greater harmony, though the role of the king is limited: 'he is not the agent by which God saves his people but is one of God's gifts of salvation, and he is a purely human figure, responsible for good government'. Similarly, Beasley-Murray (*Kingdom*, 22) states that 'the submission of the nations to God, and the establishment of the new order of the saving sovereignty are the effect of the working of Yahweh, and that the task of rule in the kingdom of God is given to the Messiah'. He supports this more harmonious view by observing that 'the principle of representation is deeply embedded in the faith and institutions of Israel, applying alike to priests and prophets and kings' (22). Cf. also Wolff's discussion ('Herrschaft', 191-202) of 'Messias als Erscheinungsform Jahwes des Herrn'.

> servant David, and he shall feed them: he shall feed them and be their
> shepherd.[143]

In this example, Yahweh judges and restores, but also establishes a
Davidic king on the throne. Similarly, in Isa. 9.2-7 the victory overthrow-
ing the oppressor in vv. 4-5 is best understood to have been accomplished by the coming of the king who is announced in vv. 6-7; he comes
to his kingdom 'to establish it, and to uphold it. . .' Yet, the oracle ends
with the statement that 'the zeal of Yahweh of hosts will do this' (v. 7).[144]
Yahweh is the figure who restores his people, but he does so through
another figure of restoration, the Davidic king. This point is closely
related to the idea that the king will rule with Yahweh's help or on Yahweh's behalf, because Yahweh is king.[145] Similarly, in the *Psalms of
Solomon* 17 Yahweh is the king and saviour who will judge and restore
his people (vv. 1-3). Yet this judgment and restoration is actually to be
accomplished by Yahweh raising up the Davidic Messiah who carries out
this judgment and restoration (vv. 21-46) with the strength and spirit of
God (vv. 22, 37-42). Another example is CD 19.10-11 which refers to the
time 'when the Messiah of Aaron and Israel comes'. The explanation
continues by stating that this 'will be the day when God will visit' (19.15;
cf. 7.20–8.3). Thus, the expectation was not that Yahweh was expected
to come in judgment and restoration as well as a messianic figure, but
that the coming of the messianic figures for judgment and restoration is
an expression and outworking of God coming in judgment and restoration.

Such a conclusion could be demonstrated for each of the other figures
of judgment and restoration examined above, but this would be needlessly repetitive. One other example is sufficient. With respect to the
figure of Michael/Melchizedek, 11QMelch 2.13 explains Melchizedek's
role as judge, that 'Melchizedek will exact the ven[geance] of E[l's] judgments. . .' Similarly, *T. Mos.* 10.2 makes reference to a messenger who is
usually identified as Michael.[146] *T. Mos.* 10.2-3 states:

> Then will be filled the hands of the messenger,
>      who is in the highest place appointed.
> Yea, he will at once avenge them of their enemies.
> For the Heavenly One will arise from his kingly throne.

---

143 Cf. Isa. 16.4-5; Jer. 23.3-4; 30.1-9; Ezek. 37.21-22.
144 Kaiser, *Isaiah 1–12*, 209-10; Mowinckel, *He That Cometh*, 107. Cf. Isa. 11.10-16.
145 Isa. 33.17, 22; Jer. 3.15, 17; 23.5-6; 30.9; 33.15-16; Ezek. 34.24; 37.24-28; Mic. 5.4.
    Yahweh, in establishing his universal kingdom, is the one who establishes his regent
    upon the throne, and this king's righteous rule is a blessing from Yahweh for the
    people. Cf. Isa. 9.7; 11.12 (cf. v. 10); Jer. 3.15; 23.4, 5; 30.9, 21; 33.15; Ezek. 34.23;
    Amos 9.11; Hag. 2.23; Zech. 3.8.
146 Cf. *OTP*, 1.932 n. 10a.

> Yea, he will go forth from his holy habitation
>> with indignation and wrath on behalf of his sons.

In v. 2 Michael as the messenger is an agent of judgment. Yet, Michael's role is explained in v. 3 as God coming in judgment on behalf of his people (cf. v. 10).

A second line of argument, by way of explanation of the above phenomenon, may be developed from the point of view of OT salvation history. Yahweh was understood to have been active in his people's past history with acts of both judgment and restoration. But these events were usually historical events within the natural flow of human history which were then interpreted theologically by Israel to have been caused by Yahweh. For example, the exile in historical terms was the military subjugation of Judah by a foreign power, Babylon, but in theological terms (i.e. salvation history) it was Yahweh's act of judgment which cast his people into exile for their idolatry and disobedience. Another example is David, whose rise to power led to the expansion of Israel's territorial dominion and its prosperity during his reign. These were consequences of his military strength and diplomatic leadership skills, but they were also understood to be evidence of Yahweh blessing his people. Thus, if the prophets interpreted the disaster and blessing (i.e. judgment and restoration) of both the past and present as signs of Yahweh working through the human agents and natural events of their history, so it would be natural for them to express the hopes and expectations for their future in terms of actions by Yahweh. This they certainly did; but such a hope, expressing in vivid terms Yahweh's future or eschatological judgment and restoration, was not a denial or rejection of the realization that such judgment and restoration would take place through Yahweh's agents and historical events. As Yahweh had participated in the life of his people in the past, so he would participate in the future.[147]

Thirdly, related to this conception of OT salvation history is this question: in the light of Israelite aversion to seeing God[148] or presenting him in visual form in any way (Exod. 20.4), what is actually being expressed when God is described as coming to judge and restore? The OT probably concentrates the expression of its hope in terms of Yahweh's actions because the high expectations (e.g. world dominion, world peace, altered creation) demanded his (miraculous) participation. But the references to other figures of judgment and restoration express similar hopes which acknowledge that Yahweh's actions would involve agents and historical

---

147 Cf. the use of the Exodus tradition in Deutero-Isaiah to express the expectation of a new Exodus accomplished by Yahweh through his anointed one, Cyrus (e.g. Isa. 44.24–45.7).
148 Cf. Eichrodt, *Theology*, 2.16-39.

events.

These three points indicate that, while different figures of judgment and restoration were expected, *Yahweh is the prime figure behind all of them*. It would seem that expression of an expectation depended upon whether an author wished to emphasize the divine/celestial involvement as prime cause, or the historical/terrestrial outworkings by secondary agents. As we saw above, an author could refer to both at the same time, demonstrating how the historical/terrestrial outworking was the result of divine/celestial involvement. George R. Beasley-Murray's comment concerning the Davidic Messiah is equally applicable to all the expected figures of judgment and restoration; each of them is 'the representative of Yahweh in his kingdom, in whom Yahweh is present and through whom he acts'.[149] Thus, in the OT and literature of the Second Temple period there exists an interplay in expectation: Yahweh as God will judge and restore his people, and his agents will carry out that ministry of judgment and restoration.[150]

---

149 Beasley-Murray, *Kingdom*, 22. Similarly, Roberts ('Divine King', 133) concludes that the expected king is 'the regent of the divine sovereign, participating in what is ultimately the divine rule. His authority comes from God and rests in the conformity of his human rule to the divine rule, a view of kingship adumbrated in the ancient Davidic covenant.' Cf. Childs, *Theology*, 119-20.

150 Though Yahweh was expected to be closely involved with his agents, there is little explicit textual evidence for Yahweh acting *directly* in judgment and restoration *to the explicit exclusion* of his agents. For example, Zech. 14.1-8 describes Yahweh coming to the Mount of Olives with the angelic forces and fighting against the nations who have surrounded Jerusalem. The language is vividly descriptive and one might cite this as evidence against my argument. However, elsewhere in Zechariah there is evidence of the expectation of human agents of restoration producing peace with the surrounding nations, including a king (9.9-10) and an army arising out of Judah and Ephraim (9.11-13), which Yahweh supports with miracles so that they are victorious (9.14-17). The one possible exception is when the restoration includes expectations such as the creation of a new heaven and new earth (e.g. Isa. 65.17-25). But even with such an expectation human agents are involved in the blessing. For example, in *1 En.* 45.3-5 the Lord of spirits describes how he will place the Elect One (i.e. the Son of Man) on the throne to judge sinners and to dwell among the elect ones as a blessing, at which time the Lord of spirits will transform heaven and earth.

Another possible case which might be cited against my argument here is Mal. 3.1-5, in which Yahweh comes to his temple (v. 1) and draws near for judgment (v. 5). This could be understood in light of the Shekinah glory in the temple (or tabernacle) visibly manifesting the presence of Yahweh (Exod. 40.34-38; 2 Chron. 7.1-3; Ezek. 9.3; 10.4, 18-19; 11.23; 43.2-5). Even though Yahweh was 'in his temple', he still functioned through human agents, especially Moses, Aaron, and later the other high priests. Thus, in Mal. 3.1-5, the coming of Yahweh does not preclude the use of secondary agents in the judgment and restoration. This is clearly not the case here, for Yahweh's messenger is very much involved in such activities, though he does so prior to Yahweh's arrival.

## 7.9 *Conclusion*

We have considered six figures who were expected to judge and restore Israel. We have examined them generally with respect to that ministry of judgment and restoration, and more particularly observed whether or not certain features found in John's portrayal of his expected figure were present in how they were portrayed. Perhaps the best way to summarize the results of this discussion is in chart form. In the following chart YH is Yahweh, DM is the Davidic Messiah, AM is the Aaronic Messiah, MM is Michael/Melchizedek, SM is the Son of Man, and EL is Elijah-*redivivus*. A 'Y' means 'Yes, this feature is found', a '?' indicates that this feature is possible, or the evidence is problematic, and a blank space indicates this feature is missing.

| | | YH | DM | AM | MM | SM | EL |
|---|---|---|---|---|---|---|---|
| 1. | Judge Israel | Y | Y | ? | Y | Y | Y |
| | Purify/Purge Israel | Y | Y | Y | Y | Y | Y |
| | Restore Israel | Y | Y | Y | Y | Y | Y |
| 2. | Coming | Y | Y | Y | Y | Y | Y |
| 3. | Mighty | Y | Y | Y | Y | Y | |
| 4. | *Bestow* spirit | Y | ? | | | | |
| | water/ablution imagery | Y | ? | | | | |
| | 'holy' spirit | Y | ? | ? | | | |
| | *Receive* spirit | | Y | ? | | Y | |
| | water/ablution imagery | | | | | Y | |
| | 'holy' spirit | | Y | ? | | | |
| | Other water/ablution imagery | Y | | | | Y | ? |
| | Wind | Y | | | | | |
| | with water/ablution imagery | ? | | | | | |
| | Fire | Y | | | Y | ? | Y |
| | with water/ablution imagery | Y | | | | | |
| 5. | Threshing-floor imagery (general) | Y | | | | | |
| | winnow grain | Y | | | | | |
| | burn chaff | Y | | | | ? | ? |
| | gather wheat | Y | | | | | |

Finally, we concluded that Yahweh, as Israel's God was not on a par with the other expected figures of judgment and restoration, because Yahweh was the prime figure behind all of them. An author could make reference to both Yahweh and an expected agent of Yahweh, sometimes both at the same time. By concentrating upon Yahweh, the author was stressing the theological necessity for divine involvement as the prime cause behind the eschatological judgment and restoration being hoped for. At the same time, by emphasizing other expected figures, the author was expressing the realization that Yahweh worked through these figures as his agents to bring about the historical and terrestrial expectations described.

Chapter 8

# JOHN'S PROCLAMATION OF AN EXPECTED FIGURE

## 8.1 *Introduction*

According to the NT, a central feature of John's eschatological proclamation was the announcement of the imminent arrival of an expected
figure. The Evangelists' accounts of John's ministry reflect the early
Christian belief that this anticipated figure was realized in Jesus. The
concern of this chapter is somewhat different. I am not interested here
in the fulfilment of John's proclamation. Rather, I wish to explore how
John's proclamation of an expected figure would probably have been
understood by his first-century Jewish audience. To ascertain this significance of John's proclamation we have surveyed in the preceding chapter
the varieties of expected judgment/restoration figures in Second Temple
Jewish literature. We now turn to John's proclamation. It is necessary
first of all to examine the NT evidence concerning this figure to determine as far as possible what John actually proclaimed. Secondly, we
compare the results of this examination with the different figures of judgment and vindication considered earlier in order to determine the
identity of John's figure. Thirdly, we examine John's description of the
activities of this expected figure. Finally, we consider the broader contours of the judgment and restoration John expected.

## 8.2 *The Evidence for John's Proclamation of an Expected Figure*

The NT Evangelists interpreted John's expected figure to be fulfilled in
Jesus. It would be reasonable to presume that they have selected and
shaped their presentation of John's proclamation to fit, at least to a certain extent, their belief in how that proclamation was fulfilled. We must,
therefore, examine carefully to what extent these NT accounts of John's
proclamation may be used as historical data for ascertaining the proclamation of John himself. I am not concerned here, however, to discover
the *ipsissima verba* of John the Baptist. To attempt such a task would
produce highly speculative results which would actually 'prove' or accomplish little. John presumably preached many times with messages much
longer than the summarizing snippets contained in the NT (each of
which may be spoken in less than 30 seconds), and he most probably
preached in Aramaic rather than Greek. Thus, our evidence for John's

preaching is but a translation of a brief summary which has been redacted to serve the interests of the Christian Evangelists. Therefore, our concern must be whether what the NT attributes to John may be taken with a reasonable degree of probability to reflect the sense of John's preaching.

### 8.2.1  *Mt. 3.11-12 = Mk 1.7-8 = Lk. 3.15-18*
In the NT John's announcement of an expected figure is found in all four Gospels and in Acts as well, but it is not mentioned by Josephus. It is, however, the pericopae within the synoptic Gospels which present the most complete account.[1] These pericopae may be set forth as follows:

| Matthew 3 | Mark 1 | Luke 3 |
|---|---|---|
| | | ¹⁵Προσδοκῶντος δὲ τοῦ λαοῦ καὶ διαλογιζομένων πάντων ἐν ταῖς καρδίαις αὐτῶν περὶ τοῦ Ἰωάννου, μήποτε αὐτὸς εἴη ὁ Χριστός, |
| ¹¹ᵃἐγὼ μὲν ὑμᾶς βαπτίζω ἐν ὕδατι εἰς μετάνοιαν· | (cf. v. 8a) | ¹⁶ᵃἀπεκρίνατο λέγων πᾶσιν ὁ Ἰωάννης, Ἐγὼ μὲν ὕδατι βαπτίζω ὑμᾶς· |
| ¹¹ᵇὁ δὲ ὀπίσω μου ἐρχόμενος ἰσχυρότερός μού ἐστιν, | ⁷ᵃκαὶ ἐκήρυσσεν λέγων, Ἔρχεται ὁ ἰσχυρότερός μου ὀπίσω μου, | ¹⁶ᵇἔρχεται δὲ ὁ ἰσχυρότερός μου, |
| ¹¹ᶜοὗ οὐκ εἰμὶ ἱκανὸς τὰ ὑποδήματα βαστάσαι· | ⁷ᵇοὗ οὐκ εἰμὶ ἱκανὸς κύψας λῦσαι τὸν ἱμάντα τῶν ὑποδημάτων αὐτοῦ· | ¹⁶ᶜοὗ οὐκ εἰμὶ ἱκανὸς λῦσαι τὸν ἱμάντα τῶν ὑποδημάτων αὐτοῦ· |
| (cf. v. 11a) | ⁸ᵃἐγὼ ἐβάπτισα ὑμᾶς ὕδατι, | (cf. v. 16a) |
| ¹¹ᵈαὐτὸς ὑμᾶς βαπτίσει ἐν πνεύματι ἁγίῳ καὶ πυρί· | ⁸ᵇαὐτὸς δὲ βαπτίσει ὑμᾶς ἐν πνεύματι ἁγίῳ. | ¹⁶ᵈαὐτὸς ὑμᾶς βαπτίσει ἐν πνεύματι ἁγίῳ καὶ πυρί· |
| ¹²ᵃοὗ τὸ πτύον ἐν τῇ χειρὶ αὐτοῦ, | | ¹⁷ᵃοὗ τὸ πτύον ἐν τῇ χειρὶ αὐτοῦ |
| ¹²ᵇκαὶ διακαθαριεῖ τὴν ἅλωνα αὐτοῦ, | | ¹⁷ᵇδιακαθᾶραι τὴν ἅλωνα αὐτοῦ |
| ¹²ᶜκαὶ συνάξει τὸν σῖτον αὐτοῦ εἰς τὴν ἀποθήκην [αὐτοῦ], | | ¹⁷ᶜκαὶ συναγαγεῖν τὸν σῖτον εἰς τὴν ἀποθήκην αὐτοῦ, |
| ¹²ᵈτὸ δὲ ἄχυρον κατακαύσει πυρὶ ἀσβέστῳ. | | ¹⁷ᵈτὸ δὲ ἄχυρον κατακαύσει πυρὶ ἀσβέστῳ. |
| | | ¹⁸Πολλὰ μὲν οὖν καὶ ἕτερα παρακαλῶν εὐηγγελίζετο τὸν λαόν· |
| | | ¹⁵Now while the people were in a state of expectation, and all were debating in their hearts concerning John, whether perhaps he might not be the Messiah, |

---

1   Mt. 3.11-12 = Mk 1.7-8 = Lk. 3.16-17; Jn 1.15, 26-27, 30; Acts 13.25; 19.4, with

¹¹ᵃ'I baptize you with water for repentance,
¹¹ᵇbut the one coming after me is mightier than I,
¹¹ᶜwhose sandals I am not worthy to carry;
(cf. v. 11a)
¹¹ᵈhe will baptize you with a holy spirit and fire.
¹²ᵃHis winnowing shovel is in his hand,
¹²ᵇand he will clean his threshing floor
¹²ᶜand gather his wheat into the granary,
¹²ᵈbut the chaff he will burn with unquenchable fire.'

(cf. v. 8a)
⁷ᵃAnd he preached, 'After me is coming the one mightier than I,
⁷ᵇthe thong of whose sandals I am not worthy to stoop down and loose.
⁸ᵃI have baptized you with water,
⁸ᵇbut he will baptize you with a holy spirit.'

¹⁶ᵃJohn answered them all, 'I baptize you with water,
¹⁶ᵇbut the one mightier than I is coming,
¹⁶ᶜthe thong of whose sandals I am not worthy to loose;
(cf. v. 16a)
¹⁶ᵈhe will baptize you with a holy spirit and fire.
¹⁷ᵃHis winnowing shovel is in his hand,
¹⁷ᵇto clean his threshing floor,
¹⁷ᶜand to gather the wheat into his granary,
¹⁷ᵈbut the chaff he will burn with unquenchable fire.'
¹⁸So, with many other exhortations, he proclaimed to the people.

According to Matthew, John explains the ministry of 'one who is coming after me' by drawing a series of related contrasts between himself and this expected figure:[2] (1) the expected figure is to come 'after' John; (2) the expected figure is mightier than John; (3) the expected figure is more worthy than John; and (4) John's baptism is 'with water', while the expected figure's baptism is 'with a holy spirit and fire'. This latter ministry is further described with the imagery of the expected figure cleaning the threshing floor, gathering the wheat into the granary, and burning the chaff. Matthew's description in vv. 11-12 follows immediately his account of John's denunciation of the religious leaders and his preaching of repentance in vv. 7-10. These two pericopae were probably not addressed to the same group of people as is suggested by the difference in tenor and stress between them. It is possible that they could have been said at the same time but to different segments within John's general audience. In fact, it is hard to conceive of a situation in which John could have been alone with those who had rejected his ministry. It is equally possible that these two pericopae were spoken at quite different times. If the elements within these two pericopae were central to John's proclamation, then it is quite possible he repeated them, especially the announcement of an expected figure.

echoes in Mt. 11.3 = Lk. 7.20; Lk. 7.19; Jn 1.24-28, 31-33; Acts 1.5; 11.16.
2    These contrasts are highlighted by the use of the μὲν . . . δέ construction and the emphatic pronouns ἐγώ and αὐτός.

Luke's account is quite similar to Matthew's, though he prefaces this pericope with the explanation in v. 15 that John's description of the expected figure was intended to refuse a messianic identification for himself.[3] Luke also supplements it with a summarizing statement in v. 18 that John's preaching included other elements; this statement also serves to introduce John's rebuke of Herod Antipas and subsequent arrest in vv. 19-20. The terminology Luke uses for two of his contrasts differs from Matthew's, but is closer to Mark's terminology. Luke's account also does not contain the first contrast.

Mark's account contains the same series of contrasts between John and the expected figure as found in Matthew, but his briefer description differs significantly in three respects. His terminology for two of the contrasts is different. Secondly, the expected figure's baptism is only with a holy spirit, lacking a reference to fire. Finally, Mark's account makes no reference to the picture of a farmer working at the threshing floor to describe the expected figure's ministry.

A comparison of Mt. 3.11-12 = Lk. 3.16-17 with Mk 1.7-8 reveals several agreements between Matthew and Luke against Mark. The cumulative force of these agreements indicates that the form of the saying in Matthew and Luke reflects their dependence on a Q tradition.[4] On the other hand, the same comparison reveals two extensive agreements between Mark and Luke against Matthew, while Mark and Matthew agree against Luke in only one point.[5] Where Matthew and Luke

3    This may have been a Q tradition which Matthew eliminated because he also did not use the tradition concerning John's ethical teaching (Lk. 3.10-14) which may also have been part of Q. Thus, by having no intervening material, Mt. 3.11-12 gives the impression that it is addressed to the same audience as in vv. 7-10; but, as I have argued, this impression is inaccurate. Luke's account, on the other hand, conveys a change of audience. See Schürmann, *Lukasevangelium*, 1.171; Marshall, *Luke*, 144-45.

4    These agreements include: (1) Matthew and Luke use the particle μέν to introduce John's baptism, but this is absent in Mark; (2) Matthew and Luke use the present tense of βαπτίζω for John's baptism, while Mark uses the aorist; (3) Matthew and Luke's word order emphasizes ὑμᾶς in the clause αὐτὸς ὑμᾶς βαπτίσει, while Mark places this pronoun after the verb; (4) the word order in Matthew and Luke's pericopae contrasts John's baptism in water with the coming one who is mightier and more worthy as well as with this expected figure's baptism, while Mark introduces the coming one who is mightier and more worthy, and then contrasts his own baptism with that of this expected figure; (5) Matthew and Luke's description of the expected figure's baptism include the phrase καὶ πυρί, which is missing in Mark; and (6) Matthew and Luke's description of the expected figure adds the imagery of the farmer cleaning the threshing floor, gathering it into the barn, and burning the chaff, which is also missing in Mark. Hoffmann, *Studien*, 18-19; Laufen, *Doppelüberlieferungen*, 93-94; Fleddermann, 'Coming One', 377. Fleddermann (377) adds the agreement of the preposition ἐν, but this is incorrect.

5    Mark and Luke agree against Matthew in the following: (1) the one who is coming (ἔρχεται) is identified as ὁ ἰσχυρότερός μου (the word order of the clauses is the same), while Matthew's figure is identified as ὁ ὀπίσω μου ἐρχόμενος and then

agree, we may reasonably assume this to be the basic form of the Q tradition. Minor variations of grammatical form or word order are probably due to either different versions of the Q tradition used by the Evangelists or else to stylistic alterations by either Matthew or Luke.[6]

The more substantive variations indicate the redactional tendencies of the Evangelists. The phrase εἰς μετάνοιαν, which is found in Mt. 3.11a but missing in Lk. 3.16a, has probably been added by Matthew rather than omitted by Luke.[7] The similarities of Lk. 3.16b-c to Mk 1.7 (the second and third contrasts) are generally recognized to be evidence of Luke following Mark at this point rather than Q, and thus Matthew's text should be understood to represent Q.[8] The phrase ὀπίσω μου (Mt. 3.11b = Mk 1.7a; the first contrast) was probably found in Q as well as Mark, and Luke omitted it because it might be understood to refer to Jesus as a disciple of John.[9] It is sometimes argued that πνεύματι ἁγίῳ καί in the phrase describing the expected figure's baptism (ἐν πνεύματι ἁγίῳ καὶ πυρί) is not original to Q. However, if this exact phrase is found in Mt. 3.11d = Lk. 3.16d in contrast to the one found in Mk 1.8b, then the weight of evidence must lie on the side of πνεύματι ἁγίῳ καί being present in Q.[10] Whether this phrase was actually used by John or was an early Christian interpretation is another matter.

---

described as ἰσχυρότερός μου; and (2) all three pericopae contain the statement of John's unworthiness (οὗ οὐκ εἰμὶ ἱκανός), but the expansion in Mark and Luke is λῦσαι τὸν ἱμάντα τῶν ὑποδημάτων αὐτοῦ (Mark adds the participle κύψας), while Matthew's is τὰ ὑποδήματα βαστάσαι. Matthew and Mark agree against Luke by including the phrase ὀπίσω μου in the clause describing the expected figure.

6    These minor variations include: (1) the word order of Mt. 3.11a = Lk. 3.16a; (2) the use of ἐν in Mt. 3.11a = Lk. 3.16a; (3) Matthew's use of finite verbs in 3.12b-c, when Luke uses infinitives in 3.17b-c; and (4) the different noun which αὐτοῦ modifies in Mt. 3.12c = Lk. 3.17c. These variations are of no interest to us here.

7    Schulz, *Spruchquelle*, 368; Hoffmann, *Studien*, 22; Gundry, *Matthew*, 48; Fleddermann, 'Coming One', 378.

8    Schulz, *Spruchquelle*, 368; Hoffmann, *Studien*, 22-23; Laufen, *Doppelüberlieferungen*, 95-97; Marshall, *Luke*, 146. The one exception concerns the infinitive clause describing John's unworthiness (Q 3.16c). Fleddermann ('Coming One', 379) follows Schürmann (*Lukasevangelium*, 1.173 n. 79) in concluding that Luke preserves Q because Luke's expression (λῦσαι τὸν ἱμάντα τῶν ὑποδημάτων αὐτοῦ) is more Semitic, and Matthew's expression (τὰ ὑποδήματα βαστάσαι) simplifies the image. However, these arguments are better taken to support the Lukan version as more closely representing John's words, than to support a version of Q.

9    Laufen, *Doppelüberlieferungen*, 96; Fitzmyer, *Luke*, 1.472; against Schulz, *Spruchquelle*, 368. Fleddermann ('Coming One', 378-79) points out that in Acts 13.25 and 19.4 'Luke twice substitutes the preposition μετά for ὀπίσω to make it clear that he means a temporal succession rather than a spatial following that might suggest discipleship'. Nolland (*Luke*, 1.151) suggests this omission is natural after the infancy narratives which stressed the presence of the saviour.

10   Fleddermann, 'Coming One', 379; Fitzmyer, *Luke*, 1.473; against Schulz, *Spruchquelle*, 368. Hoffmann (*Studien*, 29-30) accepts the phrase, but argues that ἁγίῳ is secondary. However, his reasoning applies more to whether or not it is authentic to

Thus a reconstruction of what the Q tradition (Q 3.16-17) probably looked like may be placed beside the other early source, Mk 1.7-8. In the following synopsis I have altered the order of the Markan text to parallel Q's order:[11]

| Q 3.16-17 | Mark 1.7-8 |
|---|---|
| [16a]ἐγὼ μὲν ὑμᾶς βαπτίζω ἐν ὕδατι, | [8a]ἐγὼ ἐβάπτισα ὑμᾶς ὕδατι, |
| [16b]ὁ δὲ ὀπίσω μου ἐρχόμενος ἰσχυρότερός μού ἐστιν, | [7a]ἔρχεται ὁ ἰσχυρότερός μου ὀπίσω μου, |
| [16c]οὗ οὐκ εἰμὶ ἱκανὸς τὰ ὑποδήματα βαστάσαι· | [7b]οὗ οὐκ εἰμὶ ἱκανὸς κύψας λῦσαι τὸν ἱμάντα τῶν ὑποδημάτων αὐτοῦ· |
| [16d]αὐτὸς ὑμᾶς βαπτίσει ἐν πνεύματι ἁγίῳ καὶ πυρί· | [8b]αὐτὸς δὲ βαπτίσει ὑμᾶς ἐν πνεύματι ἁγίῳ. |
| [17a]οὗ τὸ πτύον ἐν τῇ χειρὶ αὐτοῦ, | |
| [17b]καὶ διακαθαριεῖ τὴν ἅλωνα αὐτοῦ, | |
| [17c]καὶ συνάξει τὸν σῖτον εἰς τὴν ἀποθήκην αὐτοῦ, | |
| [17d]τὸ δὲ ἄχυρον κατακαύσει πυρὶ ἀσβέστῳ. | |

| | |
|---|---|
| [16a]I baptize you with water, | [8a]I baptized you with water; |
| [16b]but the one who is coming after me is mightier than I, | [7a]the one who is mightier than I is coming after me, |
| [16c]whose sandals I am not worthy to carry, | [7b]the thong of whose sandals I am not worthy to stoop down and untie, |
| [16d]he will baptize you with a holy spirit and fire. | [8b]but he will baptize you with a holy spirit. |
| [17a]His winnowing shovel is in his hand, | |
| [17b]and he will clean his threshing floor | |
| [17c]and gather the wheat into his granary, | |
| [17d]but the chaff he will burn with unquenchable fire. | |

The early Christian belief that this anticipated figure was realized in Jesus is indicated by the Evangelists in a number of ways, such as by the order of their accounts (Jesus 'comes after' John, e.g. Mk 1.14-15), by the fulfilment of prophecy (e.g. Mk 1.2-3 = Mt. 3.3 = Lk. 3.4-6), and by the baptism of Jesus (e.g. Mt. 3.14). In his proclamation John describes this figure, but it is the Evangelists' accounts which make explicit the identification of Jesus as the fulfilment of that figure. However, in the account of the proclamation of this expected figure in the fourth Gospel, the identification of Jesus as the fulfilment is uttered by John himself (1.29-34). The wording of John's description of his expected figure is somewhat different (1.26-27, 30, 33b), but also has significant similarities. The

John than to whether it was present in Q.

11  This reconstructed text is the same as Fleddermann's ('Coming One', 380) except for Q 3.16c which was discussed above. For discussion of the minor variations behind this reconstructed text see Fleddermann, 'Coming One', 378-80; Laufen, *Doppelüberlieferungen*, 93-97; Schulz, *Spruchquelle*, 368-69; Hoffmann, *Studien*, 18-25.

differences in the description are due to the fourth Gospel's probable independence from the synoptic Gospels and to the more explicit interpretation that the identity of John's expected figure is fulfilled in Jesus. The references to John's expected figure in Acts also reflect the same interpretive orientation (1.5; 11.16; 13.23-26; 19.4). While these accounts are important for discussing how the fulfilment of John's expected figure was conceived, especially among the early Christians, they contribute nothing further to our knowledge of John's description of his expected figure.[12] Therefore, the focus of our attention will be upon the information gathered from the synoptic Evangelists.

As observed above, the synoptic accounts of John's proclamation of the expected figure have been included by the Evangelists because the early Christians believed Jesus was the person to whom John was referring. It could be argued that these accounts of John's preaching were wholesale creations by early Christians. The identity of Jesus would be further enhanced if he fulfilled the prophetic message of a known, current prophet. Thus each of the elements in the Evangelists' accounts could be understood to be later creations. For example, the Evangelists knew that Jesus' ministry continued after John's at least to some extent, and so they could create a reference to 'one coming after' John. They believed Jesus to be mightier and greater than John, thus could create the references to 'mightier than I' and 'I am not worthy'. The early Christians also believed that the resurrected Jesus baptized them with the Holy Spirit, beginning with 'tongues like fire' at Pentecost, and thus could have placed on John's lips the proclamation that 'he will baptize you with the Holy Spirit and fire'. Finally, Jesus was to return as a future Judge of the unrighteous, and so expressed this as 'his winnowing shovel is in his hand. . .'

While each element of John's proclamation could be linked in this

---

12  In the narrative of the fourth Gospel John not only explicitly identified Jesus as the expected figure, he also described Jesus as 'the lamb of God who takes away the sin of the world' (Jn 1.29; cf. 1.36). The authenticity of this description is problematic due to its absence from all other sources concerning John the Baptist and to its christological perspective. Nevertheless, it is possible that John may have made such an announcement. For alternatives of interpretation, most of which view this description to be authentic in some sense, see Dodd, *Interpretation*, 230-38; Brown, 'John the Baptist', 136-38; Barrett, 'Lamb', 210-18; Burrows, 'Lamb', 245-49; Brown, *John*, 1.58-63; against Schnackenburg, *John*, 1.297-301; Lindars, *John*, 108-10. I mentioned above (§1.2) that our primary concern in this work is to analyse John the Baptist in relation to his context prior to his baptism of Jesus; that is, I do not wish to be sidetracked into the issues and problems surrounding John's relationship to Jesus. Since this terminology is used in the fourth Gospel only to portray John's description of Jesus, and it is not part of John's prior proclamation of his expected figure, I will not consider it further in elucidating John's proclamation. On the presentation of John the Baptist in the fourth Gospel generally, see §3.6; cf. §3.8.

way with some element of early Christian belief, a number of points make such an argument historically implausible. First of all, most of the elements of John's description of the expected figure are quite vague and could have many possible references. Many people 'came after' John, and of those who had political or religious leadership it could be said that they were 'mightier' and 'more worthy' than John. The more specific description concerning baptizing with a holy spirit and fire does not find Christian fulfilment in the earthly life of Jesus but in Christian belief concerning the post-resurrection ministry of Jesus. If this is the case, then we must ask, for whom were these traditions 'created'? As prophecies fulfilled by Jesus, they would convince few non-Christians because they were vague or were pointing to elements of Christian belief which non-Christians would either question or reject. Furthermore, if these statements were created by Christians to be prophecies which had been uttered by a well-known, current prophet (i.e. John), the strategy becomes questionable because the intended audience had in fact never heard John say these things. If prophecies were to be created by the early Christians to convince non-Christians, then they probably would have needed to refer to specific aspects of Jesus' earthly life to be effective to that end. If these prophecies would not convince non-Christians generally, they would certainly not convince disciples of John who would naturally deny that John said these things; they would know better than anyone else what John had said or expressly taught. And these prophecies would not have been needed to convince Christians because they already believed these things anyway. Furthermore, their acceptance of Jesus' post-resurrection identity, ministry and future role as Judge was based primarily on their interpretation of the OT and the teaching of Jesus himself.

Therefore, it seems highly implausible that the basic content of John's preaching concerning the expected figure was created by the early Christians. However, if John did preach these things concerning an expected figure, then it becomes quite understandable why they were remembered and used by the early church. They would be much more effective in convincing non-Christians if those non-Christians, and especially disciples of John, already knew that John's preaching did in fact include these elements. They would naturally be remembered by Christians because the similarities between John's preaching and their own belief concerning Jesus led them to perceive that Jesus was the expected figure John proclaimed.

A second reason for accepting the basic historicity of these accounts concerning John's proclamation of an expected figure is that not one of the elements of the proclamation is specifically Christian. Each one may be understood within the context of Second Temple Judaism (cf. §7, 8.4, 8.5).

It could be argued that the Evangelists' accounts of this matter are not historical because the description of John given by Josephus in *Ant.* 18.116-19 lacks any reference to John's message about an expected figure. However, Josephus has demonstrated elsewhere an antipathy to messianism, especially because of the role he perceived it had in inciting στάσις among the people.[13] His positive evaluation of John makes it impossible for him to attribute messianism or some other form of eschatological fervour to John. Yet Josephus' account indicates that the people around John were excited to a fever pitch and ready to do anything and that this led Herod to fear στάσις. Such a response by the people strongly suggests that John was preaching more than the rather general ethical message Josephus attributes to him. Thus, while Josephus does not mention John's preaching of an expected figure, his account of the social dynamics surrounding John's ministry indicates that some such message may have been involved. Therefore, Josephus' lack of reference to an expected figure cannot be used to argue for the non-historicity of the Evangelists' accounts. In fact, Josephus' account of the social and political dynamics associated with John is consistent with the NT accounts of the excitement generated by heightened eschatological expectation triggered by John's proclamation. Thus Josephus' account actually provides indirect, corroborative evidence for the type of eschatological expectation contained in the NT's accounts of John's proclamation of an expected figure.

It may finally be observed briefly that other features of John's ministry are consistent with this aspect of his message; for example, his presence in the wilderness and prophetic identity.[14]

While the fact that John proclaimed an expected figure may be accepted as authentic, certain specific elements reported by our sources require further examination concerning their reliability as historical data for John's proclamation. However, I must reiterate that I am not attempting to discover or reconstruct John's *ipsissima verba*.

It is quite evident that John announced a coming, mightier figure. But it is difficult to determine whether John's emphasis is reflected by the Q

---

13 Cf. Horsley, 'Messianic Movements', 471-95; Horsley and Hanson, *Bandits*, 88-134.

14 The essential authenticity of John's proclamation concerning the expected figure is accepted by most scholars. For example, Davies and Allison, *Matthew*, 1.311-20; Hill, *Matthew*, 88-89, 93-95; Bonnard, *Matthieu*, 36-38; Cranfield, *Mark*, 47-51; Nineham, *Mark*, 57-61; Schürmann, *Lukasevangelium*, 1.169-79; Fitzmyer, *Luke*, 1.466, 471-75; Marshall, *Luke*, 144-48; Scobie, *John the Baptist*, 60-73; Ernst, *Johannes der Täufer*, 305-308. On John's presence in the wilderness and prophetic identity, see §9.1, 10.2, 10.5.

version or the Markan version. The core of the Q tradition states ὁ ...
ἐρχόμενος ἰσχυρότερός ἐστιν, 'the coming one is mightier', but the
core of the Markan version states ἔρχεται ὁ ἰσχυρότερος, 'the mightier
one is coming'. While both statements express similar ideas, the first
emphasizes the characteristic of strength, while the latter emphasizes the
action of coming. Scholarly discussion of the alternatives usually concentrates on whether the title of John's figure was 'the Coming One' or
'the Mightier One' (or 'the Mighty One'). For example, Charles H.H.
Scobie argues that the Q version is probably authentic because it is
unlikely that John used 'Mightier One' as a messianic title, whereas
'Coming One' 'was current as a Messianic title'.[15] But the evidence he
cites is from the NT, and he does not provide substantiation that the
phrase was actually used as a title.[16] W.D. Davies and Dale C. Allison
turn Scobie's argument on its head by arguing that Matthew's version ( =
Q) 'comes closer to turning "the coming one" into a title',[17] thereby
implying that the Markan version is more authentic. While this may be
true, the reverse could equally well be argued: the Markan version
comes close to turning 'the mightier one' into a title. Thus their argument actually has little weight.

Arguments similar to these can be made on both sides of the issue,
but they miss the point because they seem to be concerned with identifying the *title* of John's figure.[18] However, there is little actual evidence
that either 'Mightier One' or 'Coming One' was a title in use in Jewish
circles in the Second Temple period to identify an expected figure.[19] If

---

15   Scobie, *John the Baptist*, 65.
16   For example, Scobie (*John the Baptist*, 65) cites Mk 11.9 ( = Mt. 21.9 = Lk. 19.38 =
     Jn 12.13), in which the crowds shout 'Blessed is he who comes [ὁ ἐρχόμενος] in the
     name of the Lord!' Each of the Gospels use other expressions to identify this figure
     as messianic: Matthew uses 'Son of David'; Mark uses 'kingdom of our father David';
     Luke uses 'the king', and John uses 'the king of Israel'. These are the titles which
     identify the figure. The simple expression 'he who comes' identifies the figure, but is
     hardly a title as such. Cf. Laufen, *Doppelüberlieferungen*, 95, 407-409 n. 12.
17   Davies and Allison, *Matthew*, 1.314.
18   For other arguments see Kraeling, *John the Baptist*, 54; Dibelius, *Johannes dem
     Täufer*, 55; Fleddermann, 'Coming One', 382-84.
19   In both the OT and the Jewish literature of the Second Temple period various fig-
     ures are described as 'coming' and 'mighty', but this evidence does not support the
     titular use of these words. This evidence was examined in the preceding chapter.
     For recognition that these expressions did not function as titles see Marshall, *Luke*,
     146; against Schneider ('ἔρχομαι,' 2.670) who only cites rabbinic evidence from
     Strack and Billerbeck (Str-B, 4.872ff). Cf. Laufen (*Doppelüberlieferungen*, 95, 407-
     409 n. 12) who attempts to muster an argument for the titular use of ὁ ἐρχόμενος,
     based solely on NT evidence, but who must nevertheless admit (407 n. 12) that ' "Der
     Kommende" ist nicht in derselben Weise Messiastitel wie ὁ υἱὸς τοῦ ἀνθρώπου, ὁ
     χριστός, oder ὁ κύριος.'
        The closest 'mighty' comes to being used as a title that I know of is in 1QM 12.10,
     in which God is addressed as גבור ('hero, valiant, mighty'): 'Rise up, O

this is the case, then it becomes less likely that John used either of these expressions as a form of titular shorthand corresponding to his audience's expectations. Furthermore, in both forms of the expression, the word which forms the supposed title is further qualified: ὁ ἰσχυρότερος is followed by μου, while ὁ ἐρχόμενος is modified by the phrase ὀπίσω μου.[20] If either of these were functioning as a title, then these explanatory additions would have been unnecessary. Therefore it is unlikely that either of these expressions was functioning as a formal title. If so, then the differences between the Q and Markan versions of the statement are not as great as they first appeared. They are not distinguished in their sense, only in their emphasis. Since we are not seeking the precise wording of John's saying here, it is sufficient for us to conclude that John proclaimed a figure who was both coming and mightier. And since evidence does not exist that either of these terms was an actual title within Judaism or for John, I will refrain from making a title out of them either. Therefore, I refer to an 'expected figure' rather than 'the Coming One' or 'the Mightier One'.

The statement in John's proclamation concerning his unworthiness is found in all layers of the tradition, but the Q version (3.16c) differs from the others by stating οὗ οὐκ εἰμὶ ἱκανὸς τὰ ὑποδήματα βαστάσαι ('whose sandals I am not worthy to carry'), while the Markan version (1.7b) states: οὗ οὐκ εἰμὶ ἱκανὸς κύψας λῦσαι τὸν ἱμάντα τῶν ὑποδημάτων αὐτοῦ ('the thong of whose sandals I am not worthy to stoop down and untie'). The participle κύψας is unique to Mark and is probably his redactional addition to emphasize John's inferiority. But the fact that the Markan version is found in Jn 1.27 and is syntactically difficult supports the originality of Mark's version, which Q (or Matthew?) has simplified.[21] In any case, whichever version John may have said, their

Hero/Mighty One! [קומה גבור] Lead away your captives, O glorious Man!' However, I am not convinced that this is an actual title, for it is picking up on the OT usage of גבור to describe Yahweh as a mighty warrior who battles for his people (Isa. 42.13; Zeph. 3.17; cf. other uses of this term to describe Yahweh as mighty: e.g. Isa. 10.21; Jer. 32.18), a usage found in the preceding line, 1QM 12.9: 'and the Hero/Mighty One of War [[וגבור הלח[מה]] is with our congregation'. Cf. 1QH 6.30.

20  Ernst (*Johannes der Täufer*, 49-51) argues that both μου and ὀπίσω μου are secondary, and that the comparative ὁ ἰσχυρότερος represents the superlative, 'the Mightiest One', which is a designation for God; cf. also Laufen, *Doppelüberlieferungen*, 112-14. However, both μου and ὀπίσω μου are firmly embedded within the traditions concerning John's preaching, and they hardly represent Christian ideas interpolated into John's message. Ernst's argument begins with the assumption that John's proclamation referred to God. He states (50): 'Ich möchte von einer verhüllenden Gottesaussage im Sinne der alttestamentlichen Redeweise von dem starken Gott ausgehen'. But this assumption is never proven.

21  Fleddermann, 'Coming One', 379; BDF, §297; Schürmann, *Lukasevangelium*, 1.173; Cranfield, *Mark*, 48. The sense of both λύω and βαστάζω might be equated here and

basic sense is the same, though the imagery may be slightly different.[22]

The most problematic variation in this saying of John is the description of the expected figure's baptism. That John did proclaim a future baptism by this figure is not questioned, but the precise content of that description has been the subject of much debate. The Q version (3.16d) states that αὐτὸς ὑμᾶς βαπτίσει ἐν πνεύματι ἁγίῳ καὶ πυρί ('he will baptize you with a holy spirit and fire') while Mk 1.8b is shorter: αὐτὸς δὲ βαπτίσει ὑμᾶς ἐν πνεύματι ἁγίῳ ('but he will baptize you with a holy spirit'). Setting aside for the moment the alternatives concerning the significance of 'fire' and 'holy spirit' (which are discussed later in this section), there are three alternatives for the original description of the expected figure's baptism: (1) with fire only; (2) with a holy spirit only; and (3) with both a holy spirit and fire. In these last two alternatives the presence of the adjective 'holy' is also debated.

The first alternative is a common position. It is argued that John's message was a message of judgment, and the figure John proclaimed was expected to judge with a baptism of fire. But 'the experience of the early Church led them to interpret "baptism with fire" as baptism with the Holy Spirit'.[23] Q conflated the traditions into the dual form, while Mark derived his version by deleting the original reference to fire, leaving only a baptism with a holy spirit. However, there are two fundamental problems with this reconstruction. First of all, James D.G. Dunn points out that 'the fact remains that we have no text which speaks of baptism in fire; it is a purely hypothetical construction'.[24] Secondly, Luke's account of Pentecost fails to support such a reconstruction. Luke does state in Acts 1.5 that Jesus applied John's message to Pentecost: 'John baptized with water, but you will be baptized with the Holy Spirit not many days from now'. But, if Luke understood Pentecost to be a 'baptism with fire', it is surprising that he fails to include a reference to 'fire' in Acts 1.5. Also, in the account of Pentecost (Acts 2.1-4) Luke's description fails to make any explicit link: it is *'tongues'* which are *'like* fire' (γλῶσσαι ὡσεὶ πυρός, v. 3), and the consequence of speaking in tongues is ascribed to being *'filled* with the Holy Spirit' (ἐπλήσθησαν πνεύματος ἁγίου, v. 4)

thus there is no difference in the statements (cf. Marshall, *Luke*, 146; BAGD, 137, §3a), but βαστάζω does more commonly mean 'to carry'. Or the variation may be explained as differing translations of a single Aramaic term (Hill, *Matthew*, 94, following McNeile, *Matthew*, 29).

22   For discussion of the servant's task of removing or carrying the sandals of his/her master see §8.3.

23   Manson, *Sayings*, 41; Cf. Bultmann, *History*, 111 n. 1, 246; Taylor, *Mark*, 157, and the literature cited by Dunn, 'Baptism', 82.

24   Dunn, 'Baptism', 84.

rather than a *'baptism* with the Holy Spirit'.[25] Therefore, while this reconstruction is possible, it must remain speculative because there is no direct evidence to marshall in support of it.

With respect to the second alternative, E. Earle Ellis states: ' "Fire" is absent in Mark and probably is a Christian *pesher*-ing to the Pentecostal fulfilment'.[26] But the use of 'fire' to describe the expected figure's baptism does not provide a clear interpretive link with Pentecost, because the use of fire imagery in both the preceding and succeeding contexts in John's preaching indicate a fire of judgment (Q 3.9, 17).

The third alternative understands John's description of the expected figure's baptism to have originally included references to both a holy spirit and fire. A number of objections are raised against this view, which include: (1) there were disciples of John who had not heard of the Spirit (Acts 19.1-7);[27] (2) the bestowal of the spirit was not traditionally associated with the Messiah;[28] and (3) a reference to a baptism with a holy spirit is a reference to the reception of the spirit in Christian baptism.[29] These objections are not as convincing as they appear at first. First of all, in Acts 19.2 the response of the Ephesian disciples to Paul's query about them receiving the Holy Spirit is quite emphatic. Not only had they not received the Spirit (the sense of ἀλλ' οὐδέ),[30] they had also not heard whether the Holy Spirit 'is' (ἀλλ' οὐδ' εἰ πνεῦμα ἅγιον ἔστιν ἠκούσαμεν). The sense given to ἔστιν to support this objection is 'exist', with the conclusion that the disciples in effect say 'we have not heard that there *exists* a Holy Spirit'. While this sense is semantically possible, it is culturally impossible. If these disciples were Jews, even a rudimentary knowledge of the OT would make them aware of a holy spirit. If they were Gentiles, but disciples of John, presumably they would have had some contact with the synagogue and OT teaching.[31] Therefore, in this context, the 'exist' sense of the verb εἰμί is not appropriate. This verb can also signify the occurrence of a phenomenon or event, as well as the presence, availability or provision of something.[32] In this context either of these makes much more sense, so that the disciples' statement

25 For further discussion of these and other problems with this position see Dunn, 'Baptism', 84-85.
26 Ellis, *Luke*, 90.
27 Dibelius, *Johannes dem Täufer*, 56; Manson, *Sayings*, 41; Best, 'Spirit-Baptism', 237.
28 Taylor, *Mark*, 157; Best, 'Spirit-Baptism', 236.
29 Bultmann, *History*, 246; Taylor, *Mark*, 157.
30 BDF, §448.6.
31 Cf. the discussion by Kleinknecht, 'πνεῦμα,' 6.332-59. Käsemann, ('Disciples', 138) makes a similar observation and concludes that 'these Ephesian disciples seem to be living in a vacuum'. Those who interpret Acts 19.2 in this sense do not argue the point, but rather assume the 'exist' sense of ἔστιν; e.g. Haenchen, *Acts*, 553.
32 BAGD, 223 §I.4, I.6; LSJ, 448 §A.I.2.

could be paraphrased as 'we have not heard that the Holy Spirit is come', or 'we have not heard that receiving the Holy Spirit is occurring'.[33] If this is the correct interpretation of Acts 19.2,[34] then this verse would actually support John's proclamation of a coming baptism with a holy spirit, because these disciples were aware of such an expectation, but they did not know about the Christian belief concerning its fulfilment in their reception of the Spirit.

The second objection, that evidence is lacking for identifying the bestowal of the spirit with the Messiah, suffers from a number of weaknesses. First of all, the objection assumes that the expected figure that John proclaimed must be identified with the traditional Davidic Messiah. But this is not necessarily the case. Discussion of this figure's identity must be reserved until later (§8.3). Secondly, even if such an explicit identification had not yet been made in Jewish thinking, all of the elements were present in the OT and evidenced in Second Temple Jewish literature.[35] The distance between the two ideas, the outpouring of the spirit in the last times and a spirit-anointed messianic figure, was not great and they were bound to be bridged sooner or later: The spirit-anointed figure would be the one to bestow the expected spirit.[36] With his emphasis on the rite of water-baptism and the proclamation of an expected figure, it is quite probable that John would link the two ideas and have the expected figure performing a baptism of a holy spirit. Thus, not only is it possible for John to have spoken of an expected figure baptizing with a holy spirit, but the particular matrix of John's proclamation and practice actually makes a union of these two ideas quite probable.

The third argument, that baptism with a holy spirit is a reference to the reception of the spirit in Christian baptism, fails to take careful note of the NT evidence. For example, Rudolf Bultmann based his argument

---

33   Cf. this same sense of εἰμί with the Spirit in Jn 7.39. Here the Evangelist is explaining Jesus' saying in vv. 37-38. Verse 39 states: 'But this he said concerning the Spirit, whom those who believed in him were to receive; for the Spirit was not yet (οὔπω γὰρ ἦν πνεῦμα), because Jesus was not yet glorified'. The Evangelist is not stating that believers had not received the spirit 'because the Spirit did not yet exist'. The context concerns *receiving* the Spirit, and the Evangelist is explaining that the believers had not yet received the Spirit because Jesus had not yet been glorified. In this context, οὔπω γὰρ ἦν πνεῦμα is best translated 'for the Spirit was not yet given'. Cf. RSV; NASB; Brown, *John*, 1.324; Barrett, *John*, 329.

34   Cf. Bruce, *Acts*, 385-86; Scobie, *John the Baptist*, 73 n. 1; Ernst, *Johannes der Täufer*, 306-307.

35   For example, the coming of the spirit was expected in the last days and was associated with 'water' language in Isa. 44.3; Ezek. 36.25-27; Joel 2.28-29; 1QS 4.21. In the OT is also the expectation of a variety of figures as agents of blessing, including an expected Davidic king (e.g. Isa. 11.6-9) who is the recipient of Yahweh's spirit (Isa. 11.2).

36   For possible references in the *T. Jud.*, *T. Levi*, 1QIsaᵃ, and CD see the discussion in §7.3. Cf. also Dunn, 'Baptism', 91.

on the assumption that 'the prophecy of baptism with the Spirit refers to Christian baptism which bestows the spirit'.[37] However, James D.G. Dunn demonstrates the inadequacy of Bultmann's position:

> It is particularly noticeable that the only two receptions of the Spirit specifically designated baptisms in Spirit (Pentecost and Caesarea) are the ones most clearly separated from and independent of Christian water-baptism (or any rite).[38]

Luke does interpret John's proclamation of the expected figure's baptism with a holy spirit as being fulfilled in a Christian's reception of the Spirit (Acts 1.5; 11.16). However, such a Christian interpretation is hardly support for John's reference to a baptism with a holy spirit being a Christian interpolation. The Christian interpretation is quite natural and understandable if John did in fact make such a proclamation, but if John did not make such a proclamation then for what reason would the early Christians make such an interpolation? They hardly needed support from John's preaching for the eschatological bestowal of the Spirit; they had the OT as a far more authoritative base upon which to support their belief. That they used the OT in this way is evidenced by the use of Joel 2.28-32 in the account of Peter's sermon in Acts 2.16-21. If John did not proclaim such a coming baptism, a Christian insertion of it into John's message would hardly convince disciples of John who would know what John taught better than other Jews. Therefore, early Christian belief concerning baptism with the Holy Spirit does not support the contention that the use of similar language by John is evidence of Christian interpolation.

Therefore, of the three options for John's description of the expected figure's baptism, the most plausible one is that it did in fact contain both elements. This is supported by most recent scholarly work on John's proclamation which comes to similar conclusions.[39]

We can now return to the problems of the significance of πνεῦμα ('wind' or 'spirit') and the authenticity of the adjective 'holy' to describe πνεῦμα. With respect to the first problem, it is sometimes argued that John's message originally contained only the word πνεῦμα and signified 'wind' (the adjective 'holy' would then be understood as a Christian interpolation). In this case John's message would be that the expected figure 'will baptize you with wind and fire'.[40] This position is usually supported

---

37 Bultmann, *History*, 246.
38 Dunn, 'Baptism', 85. On the relationship between John's baptism and Christian baptism see Dunn, *Baptism*, 18-22, 99-102.
39 E.g. Dunn, 'Baptism', 86-92 and the literature cited there; also Ernst, *Johannes der Täufer*, 306-308; Davies and Allison, *Matthew*, 1.316-18; Schürmann, *Lukasevangelium*, 1.175-77; Fitzmyer, *Luke*, 1.473-74; Marshall, *Luke*, 146-48; Goppelt, *Theology*, 1.38-39; Nolland, *Luke*, 152-53.

by claiming that the imagery of wind is implied in the next verse (Q 3.17): the farmer is winnowing the grain in the wind. While 'wind' is certainly a semantic possibility in the range of meanings for πνεῦμα, two arguments lead us to conclude that in this context it signifies 'spirit' instead. First of all, the preceding survey of expected figures demonstrated that in both the OT and Second Temple Jewish literature God's spirit was a common element in eschatological expectation. But wind was a less frequent element, and it does not appear to have had any special significance attached to it as did the eschatological spirit. Secondly, the principal reason for interpreting πνεῦμα in John's proclamation as a reference to wind is the contextual argument that the imagery of wind is implied in the next verse (Q 3.17) in the reference to winnowing. But, if wind was important in the link between v. 16 and v. 17, it is interesting that πνεῦμα is not mentioned in v. 17. While it is quite obvious that wind would have been used in the winnowing process, it is not obvious that *winnowing* is the process being referred to here at all. I argue below that Q 3.17 does not, in fact, refer to the process of winnowing, and so *wind is not even implied* in this context. In light of this, the use of the contextual argument is not valid in this case.[41]

With respect to the second problem, we cannot be quite as certain concerning the authenticity of the adjective 'holy' as a description of the eschatological spirit because the early Christian communities believed that they were the recipients of God's eschatological 'Holy' Spirit,[42] and at the same time, they were the ones who transmitted this tradition concerning John. But the term 'holy' may be understood without a specific Christian sense by interpreting it to describe the function of a spirit rather than the spirit itself in the form of a title (as it developed in Christian circles): it is 'a spirit of holiness' rather than 'the Holy Spirit'. This sense is essentially the same as that found in the OT and Second Temple Jewish literature. As a spirit of holiness, this spirit bestows holiness upon those who are its recipients. If understood in this way, the balance of probability is in favour of its authenticity. We may observe several points in support of this probability. First of all, both sources of this tradition (Q 3.16; Mk 1.8) as well as every level of the tradition in the NT reporting this element of John's proclamation does include the word 'holy'.[43] Secondly, we saw above that the concept of 'a holy spirit' was

---

40  For recent proponents of the view, see Best 'Spirit-Baptism', 236-43; Barrett, *Holy Spirit*, 125-26.

41  Cf. §8.4.2. For further bibliography and criticism see Dunn, 'Baptism', 82 n. 5, 85-86.

42  E.g. Acts 2.14; 1 Cor. 11.3; Eph. 1.13.

43  Mt. 3.11 = Mk 1.8 = Lk. 3.16; Jn 1.33; Acts 1.5; 11.16. Barrett (*Holy Spirit*, 126) observes that two manuscripts (mss 63, 64) and three church fathers (Tertullian, Augustine, and Clement of Alexandria) omit ἁγίῳ. While this might support the view that ἁγίῳ is a Christian interpretation if πνεῦμα is understood as a reference to

part of OT terminology, and that the literature of the Second Temple period expressed the eschatological expectation of the bestowal of a *holy* spirit.[44] Thirdly, since the activity of the expected figure is described as 'baptizing', the use of the term 'holy' to describe the effect of this baptism upon its recipients is quite appropriate in light of the ideology of purification associated with ablutions in the Judaism of the day; in some cases the precise term 'a holy spirit' was associated with the practice of immersions.[45] In light of this precise terminology and these precise associations existing in John's environment, the weight of evidence supports the term 'holy' being part of John's description of the expected figure's baptism.[46]

The description of John's expected figure in Q 3.17 as the farmer at the threshing floor is almost universally regarded as authentic to John.[47] It employs Palestinian farming techniques for its imagery and applies them in a manner consistent with similar usage in the OT. The minor variations between Matthew's and Luke's versions do not materially affect the sense and need not be examined here.

To summarize then, the data from our NT sources which are historically reliable and so may be used in our investigations include John's expectation and proclamation of a figure whose description involved the following elements: (1) he is coming; (2) he is mightier than John; (3)

wind, but without corroborative evidence, this manuscript tradition bears no weight in this discussion.

44  Ps. 51.11; Isa. 63.10, 11; *Jub.* 1.23; *Pss. Sol.* 17.37; 1QS 4.20-21; 1QSb 2.24; CD 2.12; 5.11; 7.4; 1QS 3.7; 1QH 7.6-7; 9.32; 12.11-13; 14.13, 25-26; 16.7, 12; 17.26; 4Q504 fr.1-2 5.15-16; fr.4 5; 1Q34[bis] 2.7; *T. Levi* 18.11; cf. §7.2, 7.3, 7.4.

45  E.g. *T. Levi* 2.3B8; 1QS 3.7. See the discussion of immersions in Part II.

46  Examples of other scholars who support its authenticity include Dunn, 'Spirit-and-Fire Baptism', 86-92; Ernst, *Johannes der Täufer*, 307; Scobie, *John the Baptist*, 70-71; Nolland, *Luke*, 1.147, 153; Fitzmyer, *Luke*, 1.473-74. It is possible that John's proclamation of an imminent baptism with a holy spirit and the early Christians' belief in their reception of the eschatological Holy Spirit may have been one of the contributory causes of them associating the ministry of John with their own Christian movement. From their point of view it was quite legitimate, therefore, to interpret John's proclamation to be fulfilled in their reception of the Holy Spirit (e.g. Acts 1.5; 11.16).

47  While the description of the expected figure's baptism is supported by both our primary sources, Q and Mark (and John as well), the pericope concerning the farmer at the threshing floor is dependent upon Q alone. I am aware of no one who rejects the authenticity of this saying.

It is sometimes asserted that John's ministry was exclusively negative: he only announced judgment. Such an assertion denies the authenticity of a baptism with a holy spirit (understood as a restorative act). But such an assertion fails to observe the positive nature of the threshing-floor imagery: the gathering of the grain is the prime function of a threshing floor. To those in John's audience from a rural, agricultural background, this would have a positive element to it. Cf. Beasley-Murray, *Baptism*, 32-33.

John was unworthy to be even his servant; (4) he will baptize with a holy spirit and fire; (5) his ministry includes both judgment and restoration which is portrayed in terms of a farmer working at the threshing-floor, gathering the wheat into the granary and burning the chaff.[48]

### 8.2.2 *Mt. 11.2-6 = Lk. 7.18-23*

This pericope, Mt. 11.2-6 = Lk. 7.18-23, forms the first of three pericopae concerning Jesus' relationship with John. The latter two pericopae (Mt. 11.7-15 = Lk. 7.24-30; Mt. 11.16-19 = Lk. 11.31-35) concern Jesus' opinion of John and so are not relevant for our investigation. But this first pericope is relevant, because it reports that John sent a delegation of his disciples to Jesus with the question 'are you the one who is to come, or shall we look for another?', to which Jesus provides a response. Since the initial question comes from John, it is necessary to consider whether the pericope yields historically reliable data. Since our primary concern is with John's question, our treatment of Jesus' reply will be brief. This pericope may be set forth as follows:

| Matthew 11.2-6 | Luke 7.18-23 |
|---|---|
| 2a Ὁ δὲ Ἰωάννης ἀκούσας ἐν τῷ δεσμωτηρίῳ τὰ ἔργα τοῦ Χριστοῦ 2b-3aπέμψας διὰ τῶν μαθητῶν αὐτοῦ 3aεἶπεν αὐτῷ, | 18aΚαὶ ἀπήγγειλαν Ἰωάννῃ οἱ μαθηταὶ αὐτοῦ περὶ πάντων τούτων. 18b-19aκαὶ προσκαλεσάμενος δύο τινὰς τῶν μαθητῶν αὐτοῦ ὁ Ἰωάννης 19aἔπεμψεν πρὸς τὸν κύριον λέγων, |
| 3bΣὺ εἶ ὁ ἐρχόμενος ἢ ἕτερον προσδοκῶμεν; | 19bΣὺ εἶ ὁ ἐρχόμενος ἢ ἄλλον προσδοκῶμεν; 20παραγενόμενοι δὲ πρὸς αὐτὸν οἱ ἄνδρες εἶπαν, Ἰωάννης ὁ βαπτιστὴς ἀπέστειλεν ἡμᾶς πρὸς σὲ λέγων, Σὺ εἶ ὁ ἐρχόμενος ἢ ἄλλον προσδοκῶμεν; 21ἐν ἐκείνῃ τῇ ὥρᾳ ἐθεράπευσεν πολλοὺς ἀπὸ νόσων καὶ μαστίγων καὶ πνευμάτων πονηρῶν, καὶ τυφλοῖς πολλοῖς ἐχαρίσατο βλέπειν. |
| 4καὶ ἀποκριθεὶς ὁ Ἰησοῦς εἶπεν αὐτοῖς, Πορευθέντες ἀπαγγείλατε Ἰωάννῃ ἃ ἀκούετε καὶ βλέπετε· 5τυφλοὶ ἀναβλέπουσιν καὶ χωλοὶ περιπατοῦσιν, λεπροὶ καθαρίζονται καὶ κωφοὶ ἀκούουσιν, καὶ νεκροὶ ἐγείρονται καὶ πτωχοὶ εὐαγγελίζονται· | 22aκαὶ ἀποκριθεὶς εἶπεν αὐτοῖς, Πορευθέντες ἀπαγγείλατε Ἰωάννῃ ἃ εἴδετε καὶ ἠκούσατε· 22bτυφλοὶ ἀναβλέπουσιν, χωλοὶ περιπατοῦσιν, λεπροὶ καθαρίζονται καὶ κωφοὶ ἀκούουσιν, νεκροὶ ἐγείρονται, πτωχοὶ εὐαγγελίζονται· |

48  We observed above that the fourth Gospel's description of John's proclamation contained both significant similarities and differences when compared with the accounts of the synoptic Evangelists. As an independent witness to John's ministry, the fourth Gospel may be used to support the basic authenticity of John's proclamation of an expected figure and certain of its specific features (cf. §3.6, 3.8). Brown, *John*, 1.51-54; Schnackenburg, *John*, 1.282-85, 293-95, and esp. Dodd, *Tradition*, 251-56. Cf. Barrett (*John*, 170-75) who supports this point, but suggests the fourth Gospel is probably using Mark at this point.

⁶καὶ μακάριός ἐστιν ὃς ἐὰν μὴ
σκανδαλισθῇ ἐν ἐμοί.

²ᵃNow when John heard in prison about the works of the Christ,
²ᵇ⁻³ᵃhe sent (word) by his disciples ³ᵃand said to him,
³ᵇ'Are you the one who is coming, or shall we look for another?'

⁴And answering Jesus said to them, 'Go and report to John what you hear and see:

⁵the blind receive sight and the lame walk, lepers are cleansed and the deaf hear, and the dead are raised up, and the poor have the good news preached to them.
⁶And blessed is the one who does not take offense at me.'

²³καὶ μακάριός ἐστιν ὃς ἐὰν μὴ
σκανδαλισθῇ ἐν ἐμοί.

¹⁸ᵃAnd his disciples reported to John concerning all these things,⁴⁹
¹⁸ᵇ⁻¹⁹ᵃAnd summoning two of his disciples, John ¹⁹ᵃsent them to the Lord, saying,
¹⁹ᵇ'Are you the one who is coming, or shall we look for another?'
²⁰And when the men had come to him, they said, 'John the Baptist sent us to you, saying, "Are you the one who is coming, or shall we look for another?"'
²¹In that hour he healed many of diseases and afflictions and evil spirits, and to many who were blind he granted sight.
²²ᵃAnd answering he said to them, 'Go and report to John what you have seen and heard:
²²ᵇthe blind receive sight, the lame walk, lepers are cleansed and the deaf hear, the dead are raised up, the poor have the good news preached to them.
²³And blessed is the one who does not take offense at me.'

In the Matthean version John, in prison, hears of 'the works of the Christ', and sends a delegation of his disciples to Jesus with a question, 'Are you the one who is coming, or shall we look for another?' With this question John is inquiring whether or not Jesus is the one who will fulfil John's proclamation of an expected figure. Jesus responds by telling them to report what they 'hear and see', and provides a summary list of his miracles, some of which allude to OT texts. This answer is somewhat enigmatic, for it neither clearly affirms or denies that he is John's expected figure. He then pronounces a beatitude on the person (in the singular, implying a reference to John) who does not take offense at his (i.e. Jesus') identity and ministry. In the Lukan version, John hears about Jesus' ministry (but no mention is made of Jesus performing 'the works of the Christ') via his disciples, and sends two of them to Jesus with the same question. Luke's account is longer than Matthew's because he narrates the disciples arriving and asking the question (v. 20), and reports that in the presence of John's disciples Jesus performed many miracles before providing essentially the same answer to John's question as recorded in Matthew and uttering the identical beatitude.

49 Unfortunately, the versification of English translations does not follow the Greek text at this point. Verse 18a in Greek is v. 18 in English, with the Greek v. 18b forming the first part of v. 19 in English; cf. RSV; NASB. To be consistent, I have followed the Greek versification in my translation, which is used by the NRSV.

A comparison of the Matthean and Lukan texts reveals that Mt.
11.3b-6 is virtually identical to Lk. 7.19b, 22-23. This indicates that both
Evangelists are using the common source Q at this point. Mt. 11.2-3a =
Lk. 7.18-19a are similar in content, though differing extensively in their
wording. The emphasis in Luke upon the disciples actually witnessing
the miracles of Jesus probably led Luke to compose the summary of
Jesus' miracles in v. 21 and to introduce the reference to 'two disciples'
probably to emphasize their role as witnesses (cf. Deut. 19.15).[50] Thus, it
is important for Luke's purposes to narrate the arrival of John's disciples
in v. 20; so this is probably Luke's redactional material as well.[51]  Most
scholars consider Mt. 11.2-3a = Lk. 7.18-19a to be from Q,[52] but the differences between them render it difficult to ascertain the original text of
Q.  We have seen that Luke's references to two disciples is probably his
insertion (v. 18b) and so also is his emphasis upon the role of the disciples (v. 18a, cf. vv. 20-21). But in the Matthean parallel of 11.2 the
expression 'the works of the Christ' is probably Matthew's construction.[53]
In light of Luke's more obvious additions and alterations, the Matthean
form probably reproduces Q more accurately, except for those cases we
have noted.  A reconstruction of Q for this pericope would look like the
following:[54]

| Q 7.18-19, 22-23 | Q 7.18-19, 22-23 |
|---|---|
| [18a]Ὁ δὲ Ἰωάννης ἀκούσας ἐν τῷ δεσμωτηρίῳ περὶ πάντων τούτων [18b-19a]πέμψας διὰ τῶν μαθητῶν αὐτοῦ [19a]εἶπεν αὐτῷ, [19b]Σὺ εἶ ὁ ἐρχόμενος ἢ ἕτερον προσδοκῶμεν; [22]καὶ ἀποκριθεὶς ὁ Ἰησοῦς εἶπεν αὐτοῖς, Πορευθέντες ἀπαγγείλατε Ἰωάνῃ ἃ ἀκούετε καὶ βλέπετε· τυφλοὶ ἀναβλέπουσιν καὶ χωλοὶ περιπατοῦσιν, λεπροὶ καθαρίζονται καὶ κωφοὶ ἀκούουσιν, καὶ νεκροὶ ἐγείρονται καὶ πτωχοὶ εὐαγγελίζονται· | [18a]Now when John heard in prison concerning all these things [18b-19a]he sent (word) by his disciples [19a]and said to him, [19b]'Are you the one who is coming, or shall we look for another?' [22]And answering Jesus said to them, 'Go and report to John what you hear and see: the blind receive sight and the lame walk, lepers are cleansed and the deaf hear, and the dead are raised up, and the poor have the good news preached to them. |

50  Fitzmyer, *Luke*, 1.663-67; Nolland, *Luke*, 1.328.
51  While most scholars consider Lk. 7.21 to be Lukan material, a minority do take v. 20
    to be Q material, though the rest consider it to be Lukan as well.  While it is possible
    that v. 20 was in Q, it is sufficiently questionable for us to not place it there.  For
    example, Marshall (*Luke*, 290) considers v. 20 in Q (but not v. 21), while Fitzmyer
    (*Luke*, 1.663, 667) and Nolland (*Luke*, 1.329) consider both to be Lukan. For other
    references on this issue, see Kloppenborg, *Q Parallels*, 52.
52  Cf. Kloppenborg, *Q Parallels*, 52; against Bultmann, *History*, 23.
53  Cf. the use of the term 'works' in 11.19 to refer to Jesus in a context unique to Mat-
    thew, and the same term referring to other persons: 5.16; 23.3, 5.  Cf. Hill, *Matthew*,
    197; Gundry, *Matthew*, 204.
54  Cf. the reconstructions by Schulz, *Q*, 190-92; Havener, *Q*, 128; Hoffmann, *Studien*,
    191-93.

<sup></sup>

| | |
|---|---|
| <sup>23</sup>καὶ μακάριός ἐστιν ὃς ἐὰν μὴ σκανδαλισθῇ ἐν ἐμοί. | <sup>23</sup>And blessed is the one who does not take offense at me.' |

The primary reason for questioning the authenticity of this pericope is the perception that, according to John Kloppenborg, this pericope in Q 'is a post-Easter creation, arising in the effort to attract Baptist disciples into the Christian fold'.[55] Kloppenborg argues that 'the story deliberately invokes Baptist expectations in its use of the title "the Coming One", but infuses the title with specifically Christian content'.[56] However, the reconstruction of Q I have proposed has removed the Matthean reference to 'the works of the Christ' (11.2a) and the Lukan statement that John sent the disciples 'to the Lord' (7.19a). Without these, the pericope lacks the 'specifically Christian content' Kloppenborg attributes to it.[57] It is quite clear that the early church believed Jesus fulfilled John's proclamation, and the synoptic Evangelists constructed the pericopae concerning John in such a way as to communicate this belief (cf. §8.2.1). It is possible to perceive how this pericope could be used to 'attract Baptist disciples': the summary of Jesus ministry in Isaianic terms implies that eschatological, kingdom events are occurring. But it is difficult to perceive the post-Easter Christian community creating this question from John which expresses doubt or even unbelief concerning Jesus' identity as John's expected figure, especially in light of their belief that John was Jesus' forerunner. Similarly, Rudolf Bultmann states that 'in all probability the Baptist's question is a community product and belongs to those passages in which the Baptist is called as a witness to the Messiahship of Jesus'.[58] But, as noted above, John is hardly a 'witness' here; he is rather a questioning seeker (or possibly even a disillusioned skeptic!) whose expectations were in conflict with events. Furthermore, it is quite unlikely that the use of the vague term, 'one who is coming', would be a creation of the early church as a witness to Jesus' messianic status, when the early church had access to other, more explicit, titles. In contrast to Kloppenborg and Bultmann, Werner Kümmel states:

---

55  Kloppenborg, *Formation*, 107. Kloppenborg (108 n. 25) also cites Stuhlmacher (*Paulinische Evangelium*, 1.218-25) in support.

56  Kloppenborg, *Formation*, 107. Strauss (*Jesus*, 230) questioned the historicity of the pericope, because if John was in prison, 'he could hardly, so situated, transmit and receive messages'. However, this is pure supposition.

57  Unless of course, he is considering the summary of Jesus' miracles in Q 7.22 to be christological. The precise formulation of 7.22 might have Christian influence, especially in employing Isaianic allusions. However, Jesus' activity as a miracle-worker, especially as a healer, is well attested and widely recognized as historical (e.g. Sanders, *Jesus*, 11, 157). If so, then Jesus could equally summarize his healing ministry in this way, and so this is hardly 'specific Christian content'.

58  Bultmann, *History*, 23.

> The Baptist appears here in no way as a witness to Christ, but as an un-
> certain questioner, which contradicts the tendency of the early Church to
> make him such a witness; moreover the story even lacks an ending giving
> the reaction of the Baptist to Jesus' message. Above all, Jesus' answer is
> unusual owing to its veiled style... So it is the most probable assumption
> that the story in its essentials represents an old reliable tradition.[59]

Therefore we can conclude that this pericope probably represents a historically reliable tradition: John did send a delegation to Jesus questioning whether or not Jesus was the expected figure, and Jesus did reply
by enigmatically referring to his healing miracles.[60]

To recapitulate, we have examined in this section the NT evidence for
John's proclamation of an expected figure of judgment and restoration
and concluded that certain features in this description of the figure may
be reasonably accepted as reliably representing John's proclamation.
We have also reached similar conclusions concerning one source in
which John questioned whether or not Jesus was the expected figure he
had previously proclaimed.

### 8.3 *The Identity of John's Expected Figure*

Having ascertained those traditions which may be accepted as historically reliable, we can now apply the analysis of expected figures of
judgment and restoration from the preceding chapter to this data. For
convenience, I reproduce here the summarizing chart from Chapter 7:

|     |                          | YH | DM | AM | MM | SM | EL |
|-----|--------------------------|----|----|----|----|----|----|
| 1.  | Judge Israel             | Y  | Y  | ?  | Y  | Y  | Y  |
|     | Purify/Purge Israel      | Y  | Y  | Y  | Y  | Y  | Y  |
|     | Restore Israel           | Y  | Y  | Y  | Y  | Y  | Y  |
| 2.  | Coming                   | Y  | Y  | Y  | Y  | Y  | Y  |
| 3.  | Mighty                   | Y  | Y  | Y  | Y  | Y  |    |
| 4.  | *Bestow* spirit          | Y  | ?  |    |    |    |    |
|     | water/ablution imagery   | Y  | ?  |    |    |    |    |
|     | 'holy' spirit            | Y  | ?  | ?  |    |    |    |
|     | *Receive* spirit         |    | Y  | ?  |    | Y  |    |
|     | water/ablution imagery   |    |    |    |    | Y  |    |
|     | 'holy' spirit            |    | Y  | ?  |    |    |    |

---

59  Kümmel, *Promise*, 110-11.
60  Numerous scholars accept the essential historicity of the pericope. For example,
Dibelius, *Johannes dem Täufer*, 33-39; Marsh, *Baptism*, 95-99; Manson, *Jesus*, 38-39;
Scobie, *John the Baptist*, 143-44; and more recently, Dunn, *Jesus*, 55-60; Fitzmyer,
*Luke*, 1.662-64; Marshall, *Luke*, 287-89; Nolland, *Luke*, 1.326-27; against Goguel,
*Jean Baptiste*, 60-63; Kraeling, *John the Baptist*, 130-31.

| | | | | |
|---|---|---|---|---|
| Other water/ablution imagery | Y | | Y | ? |
| Wind | Y | | | |
|    with water/ablution imagery | ? | | | |
| Fire | Y | Y | ? | Y |
|    with water/ablution imagery | Y | | | |
| 5. Threshing-floor imagery (general) | Y | | | |
|    winnow grain | Y | | | |
|    burn chaff | Y | | ? | ? |
|    gather wheat | Y | | | |

Different scholars have argued for John's expected figure to be identified with each of these figures, except perhaps for the Heavenly Prince Michael/Melchizedek. Two alternatives which are also discussed in the secondary literature have not been included in the preceding discussion. Some scholars have argued that John's expected figure is a disciple of John. However, to include such a figure here would confuse expected figures with John's understanding of how the expectation of the figure would actually be fulfilled.[61] Others have argued that John's figure cannot be identified with any one figure. However, this alternative cannot be considered until we have examined each of the specific alternatives.

This chart summarizing the results of the preceding survey shows quite conclusively that the figure which best meets all elements of John's description is Yahweh—in fact, the only figure who does so. Of the other alternatives, the Son of Man and the Davidic Messiah each has a greater number of the elements than do the rest, but these two figures still come a distant second to Yahweh. Therefore the preliminary conclusion derived from a survey of the descriptive elements used to portray different expected figures of judgment and restoration is that the figure which most closely matches John the Baptist's expected figure is Yahweh. Two of the most distinctive aspects of John's description support this conclusion: using ablution imagery to portray the bestowal of a spirit described as 'holy', and using the imagery of a farmer at the threshing floor to portray judgment and restoration. While there is some evidence identifying these two aspects with other figures, this evidence is problematic due to it either being unclear or of a late date. Yet these two most distinctive aspects are clearly identified with Yahweh's ministry of judgment and restoration.[62]

---

61  Grobel ('He that Cometh', 397-401) argued that the rabbinic expression 'walk behind' also signified 'to be a pupil of', and thus John could have been indicating one of his disciples would accomplish this ministry; cf. also Cullmann, "Ο ὀπίσω μου', 177-82; Dodd, *Tradition*, 272-74. This explanation is ingenious, but rather far-fetched, and has not found general acceptance; cf. Scobie, *John the Baptist*, 63-64; Davies and Allison, *Matthew*, 1.313.

62  Examples of scholars who support the interpretation of John's expected figure to be

While John is evidently describing the expected figure in terms most clearly identified with Yahweh, we must consider other data which have a bearing on John's portrayal of this figure in order to appreciate fully this figure's identity. Several elements of John's description suggest that John is describing a figure other than Yahweh.

First of all, John states that he is not worthy to untie (or carry) the sandals of this figure (Q 3.16c: οὗ οὐκ εἰμὶ ἱκανὸς τὰ ὑποδήματα βαστάσαι; the variant forms are irrelevant here). It has often been observed that this figure could not be God because he would not be described as wearing sandals.[63]  John H. Hughes, who argues that John's figure is Yahweh himself, answers this objection by citing Pss. 60.8 and 108.9: 'Moab is my washbasin; upon Edom I cast my shoe', and states that 'John's reference to the Coming One wearing sandals must not be pressed beyond the realm of metaphor where it belongs'.[64]  Hughes is correct to argue that one must not take literally an anthropomorphic expression. However, John's statement is *not* simply a descriptive statement concerning what the figure is wearing (as Hughes seems to imply), nor is it a description of what the figure does with his own sandals (as in the OT references cited by Hughes). Rather, John's words form an evaluative statement of his own unworthiness to perform an action with respect to this figure's sandals—an action which was the responsibility of a servant to perform for his/her master.[65]  The evaluation of John's unworthiness to perform such an action loses some of its significance if it is an action which it is impossible for him to actually do. I am not stating that it would be impossible to express unworthiness before God in these

---

Yahweh include: Bretscher, 'Whose Sandals?' 81-87; Hughes, 'John the Baptist', 191-219; Thyen, 'ΒΑΠΤΙΣΜΑ', 136; Ernst, *Johannes der Täufer*, 50, 305. However, in the succeeding discussion I take a different approach in my interpretation of this figure than these scholars do.

63  E.g. Scobie, *John the Baptist*, 66-67; Nolland, *Luke*, 1.151.

64  Hughes, 'John the Baptist', 196.

65  This task appears to have been quite specifically associated with the servant-master relationship in rabbinic discussion; there is no evidence that it was a general expression of humility; cf. *b. Sanh.* 62b; *b. Qid.* 22b; *b. Pes.* 4a; *b. B. Mes.* 41a; *b. 'Erub.* 27b; cf. Str-B, 1.121. In *Mek.* on Exod. 21.2 these tasks are specifically associated with the role of the Gentile slave: 'the sages said: A Hebrew slave must not wash the feet of his master, nor put his shoes on him, nor carry his things before him when going to the bathhouse. . .' One rabbinic discussion concerned distinguishing the roles of a servant and a disciple, so that *b. Ket.* 96a states: 'R. Joshua b. Levi ruled: All manner of service that a slave must render to his master a student must render to his teacher, except that of taking off his shoe'. On the basis of this reference Daube (*Rabbinic Judaism*, 266-67) suggested that Matthew altered the statement in Q 3.16 and Mk 1.7 ('the thong of whose sandals I am not worthy to *untie*') to 'whose sandals I am not worthy to *carry*', in order to represent John adhering to the principle that he was willing to do that which was appropriate for a disciple but not for a slave. Davies and Allison (*Matthew*, 1.315) correctly consider this suggestion to be 'too ingenious'.

terms; rather, I am suggesting only that the evaluative significance of the statement points in the direction of the referent being other than God. Such a direction is supported by the following observation.

Secondly, closely related to the preceding argument is the fact that John states that this figure is 'mightier than I' (Q 3.16b: ἰσχυρότερός μου). We saw above that all the figures of judgment and restoration are described as mighty (apart from Elijah-*redivivus*), including Yahweh, of course. But John's actual description is not one who is 'mighty', nor even a reference to the 'Almighty', but rather a comparison between himself and the expected figure. It is commonly observed that 'the comparison shows that the person in question is not God, for to compare oneself with God, even in the most abject humility, would have been presumptuous for any Jew in John's day'.[66] This observation is entirely valid, but John H. Hughes counters it with two arguments. First of all, he states that John could make this comparison 'between himself and God in order to reinforce the substantial difference between his own water baptism and God's baptism with holy spirit and with fire'.[67] However, the contrast is already quite clear from the descriptions of the two baptisms, as well as the use of the emphatic pronouns ἐγὼ . . . αὐτός as well as the contrasting conjunctions μὲν . . . δέ (Q 3.16; Mk 1.7-8). Also, however the statement is mitigated, it is in fact a comparison between the *persons* of John and the expected figure, not just their baptisms, though the difference between their baptisms explains why the expected figure is mightier than John. Furthermore, the comparative implies that John is actually a mighty figure, and that the expected figure is still mightier. The statement is a comparative one, and it should not be interpreted as if it were contrastive.[68]

Hughes suggests, secondly, that John may have been responding to speculation concerning his own identity (cf. Lk. 3.15; Jn 1.20-21), and so, he 'may have felt the need to make a direct comparison or contrast between himself and God in an attempt to stress to everyone that he himself was important only insomuch as he heralded the imminent coming of Yahweh'.[69] This explanation is quite plausible, if the figure John pro-

---

66  Kraeling, *John the Baptist*, 54; cf. Brownlee, 'John the Baptist', 41.
67  Hughes, 'John the Baptist', 197.
68  While Ernst (*Johannes der Täufer*, 50) interprets John's figure to be Yahweh, he appears to assume this rather than prove it: 'Ich möchte von einer verhüllenden Gottesaussage im Sinne der alttestamentlichen Redeweise von dem starken Gott ausgehen'. He states that originally the comparative form ἰσχυρότερος ('mightier') with μου ('than I') lacked this relative pronoun, and that the comparative form of ἰσχυρότερος represents the superlative, and so he translates John's proclamation: 'Es kommt der Stärkste'. But both of these contentions to support his translation lack any foundation. There is no textual evidence that μου is not authentic, and that the comparative form in this case is really signifying the superlative lacks support.
69  Hughes, 'John the Baptist', 197.

claimed was other than God, but Hughes' argument fails because it still does not stand up to the preceding observations. It also fails to explain why John would use such a generalized comparison if he wished to make such a specific contrast. Again, the weight of probability suggests that John is not referring to God, but to an agent of God.

Therefore, though John's proclamation concerning the expected figure employs descriptions and imagery which indicate that he is referring to Yahweh, other elements within that proclamation point to John's expectation that the fulfilment of Yahweh's coming to judge and restore would be achieved through an expected agent of Yahweh rather than Yahweh himself. This conclusion finds support in the later NT passage concerning John's question to Jesus from prison: 'Are you the one who is coming, or shall we look for another?' (Q 7.19b). The use of the expression 'the one who is coming' (ὁ ἐρχόμενος) is a clear reference back to John's proclamation concerning 'the one who is coming after me' (ὁ ὀπίσω μου ἐρχόμενος). That John could even consider the possibility that his proclamation might find fulfilment in Jesus indicates that John expected a figure who was an agent of God.

Therefore we may conclude that John's expected figure is described in terms of the coming of Yahweh himself to judge and restore his people. But John did not actually expect Yahweh himself, but rather, he expected an agent of Yahweh who, acting with God's authority and power, would come to judge and restore.

This conclusion is in complete accord with the results of the preceding chapter (esp. §7.8). We observed in the OT and Second Temple Jewish literature that, while different figures of judgment and restoration were expected, Yahweh is the prime figure behind all of them. The expression of an expectation depended upon whether a speaker or author wished to emphasize the divine/celestial involvement as prime cause (a theological orientation), or the historical/terrestrial outworking through secondary agents (a historical orientation). A person could refer to both at the same time, demonstrating how the historical/terrestrial outworking was the result of divine/celestial involvement. Thus there existed an interplay in Jewish expectation: God will judge and restore his people, and one of his agents will carry out that ministry of judgment and restoration. John the Baptist appears to have couched his description of his expected figure primarily in terms of a theological orientation: God was imminently going to judge and restore his people. But he betrays a historical/terrestrial orientation which indicates he expected an agent. The evidence pointing to an agent provides almost no clue as to which of the other expected figures John expected. The fact that he considered the possibility of Jesus fulfilling this figure indicates that this agent probably was not the figure of the heavenly prince Michael/Melchizedek. But, beyond this, there is little explicit evidence on which to choose between the other figures.[70]

A question arises naturally at this point: Why is it not possible to make a precise identification of John's expected figure? Three different answers may be suggested. First of all, our data may be too fragmentary; John may have had one particular figure in mind, but a clear statement by John was not included by the Evangelists in their accounts. Secondly, John may have been vague because he did not know which agent he himself expected. Thirdly, though he knew what agent he expected, he may have chosen to be deliberately vague for some reason.

The first alternative is always a possibility in cases such as this, but it is not as probable as it first appears. We do possess historically reliable material which portrays John's figure with quite specific imagery and details. In light of Christian belief that Jesus was both Messiah and Son of Man, it is extremely unlikely that they would have excised such specific identifications from John's message when these would have greatly strengthened the case they were making for Jesus fulfilling John's announcement. If John had explicitly identified the figure as Elijah-*redivivus*, then it is understandable that the Evangelists would not mention this because they interpreted John to be this figure. However, even this is not certain, because some scholars have argued that evidence exists in the NT of an interpretation of Jesus as Elijah-*redivivus*.[71] So, while this alternative must always remain possible, another of the alternatives may be more likely.[72]

The second alternative is even less probable than the first. With

70 Examples of scholars who have argued for different identifications of John's expected figure include the following, Davidic Messiah: Davies and Allison, *Matthew*, 1.313-14; Manson, *Sayings*, 41; Dunn, 'Spirit-and-Fire Baptism', 89-92; Scobie, *John the Baptist*, 62-73; Aaronic Messiah: Stauffer, *Theology*, 24; Davies and Allison (1.313) consider this as one alternative of the Messianic identity of the expected figure; Son of Man: Becker, *Johannes der Täufer*, 34-37; Lohmeyer, *Johannes der Täufer*, 157-60; Kraeling, *John the Baptist*, 51-64; Elijah-*redivivus*: Schweitzer, *Quest*, 372-73; Robinson, 'Elijah', 28-33; Brown, 'John the Baptist', 181-84.

71 Cf. Martyn, 'Elijah', 181-219; Robinson, 'Elijah', 46-48; Cullmann, *Christology*, 36-38; against Fuller, *Christology*, 126-27.

72 It is possible that John could have announced the coming of Yahweh at one time and at another time discussed this coming in terms of Yahweh's agent. Christian tradition or the Evangelists could have conflated the two, especially in light of the belief that Jesus is Lord. However, two factors stand against this possibility. First of all, in such conflation it is unlikely that the specifics with respect to the expected figure described as Yahweh would have remained specific and those elements specifically identifying Yahweh's agent would have been rendered so ambiguous. Secondly, the description of the expected figure is portrayed in different sources and it is unlikely that conflation would have taken place in essentially similar ways in all sources.

John's strong eschatological orientation and emphatic proclamation, it appears inconsistent to suggest that John did not have an opinion of the type of agent he was announcing. That he sent the delegation of disciples to Jesus (Q 7.18-19) indicates he was concerned about the way his proclamation would be fulfilled. In light of this concern, John probably had an opinion concerning the identity of Yahweh's agent, but this was not of prime importance for him.

The third alternative could be the most probable of the three. John did not wish to identify himself with any one particular form of Jewish expectation, but wished to emphasize the divine nature of the imminent judgment and restoration. To have engaged in eschatological speculation as to the type of agent may have sidetracked his audience from the prime issue at hand: repentance in the face of imminent judgment. To have been specific in his public proclamation concerning the agent's identity might have had the effect of alienating those who held to a different form of expectation—a concern which would be quite relevant in light of the wide variety of expected agents. Thus, the specificity with which he described judgment and restoration in terms of divine intervention when placed beside the lack of specificity in identifying Yahweh's agent is probably an aspect of the strategy John used in his approach. This strategy enabled him to address his message to all Israel and call all to conversionary repentance.[73]

Whatever the reason John had for announcing his expected figure the way he did, lack of hard data prevents us from making a firm choice between these three alternatives (though the third is the most probable), and we cannot press too far here without engaging in 'psychologizing'. It is sufficient to offer the firm conclusion that John announced an expected figure primarily with a theological orientation: Yahweh was coming to judge and restore his people. However, John also perceived that this judgment and restoration had a historical orientation and so conceived of Yahweh's judgment and restoration being carried out by an agent of Yahweh. While there is specific evidence that John expected such an agent, the data make it difficult to choose between the alternatives current in the Judaism of John's day. For our purposes it is not really necessary to choose between them anyway; it is sufficient to appreciate that, while John emphasized the celestial/divine orientation as the ultimate source of judgment and restoration, he was concerned about the terrestrial/historical outworking of that judgment and restoration.

---

73 Cf. Goppelt (*Theology*, 1.38) who states that John 'awaited the One who, in whatever form, should come to usher in God's conclusive encounter with his people and his creation'. Similarly, McNeile (*Matthew*, 35) concludes that 'John looked forward to

## 8.4 *The Activities of John's Expected Figure*

Having discussed the identity of John's expected figure, we now turn to examine the significance of the activities attributed to this figure. We consider here the final two elements, namely baptizing with a holy spirit and fire, as well as the imagery associated with the farmer cleaning the threshing floor. The first three elements (judging and restoring, coming, and mighty), because they are more general, are more appropriately considered when the general contours of John's perception of the judgment and restoration are examined (§8.5).

### 8.4.1 *Baptizing with a Holy Spirit and Fire*

In his proclamation John stated that the expected figure 'will baptize'. This term immediately associates this activity of the expected figure with the imagery of water ablutions. The activities of both John and the expected figure are thus portrayed in the same way, but there is one crucial difference: John's baptism was a literal ablution with water, while the use of βαπτίζω to describe the expected figure's activity is metaphorical. Evidently John described the expected figure's activity with the same terminology in order to provide continuity with his own ministry. Also, this metaphorical use is quite appropriate with respect to both the elements of a holy spirit and fire because the language of ablutions is associated in Jewish eschatological expectation with the bestowal of the spirit (e.g. Joel 2.28-29), and water imagery is sometimes used to describe the fire of judgment (e.g. 'river of fire'). However, the imagery associated with the expression 'will baptize' must not be pressed too far, especially in determining the sense of that with which the expected figure will baptize. James D.G. Dunn may be guilty of this when he states that

> the Coming One's baptism *is envisaged as a single baptism* ἐν πνεύματι καὶ πυρί. . . [W]hat John held out before his hearers was a baptism which was neither solely destructive nor solely gracious, but which *contained both elements in itself.* Its effect would then presumably depend upon the condition of its recipients: the repentant would experience a purgative, refining, but ultimately merciful judgment; the impenitent, the stiff-necked and hard of heart, would be broken and destroyed.[74]

Dunn had earlier rejected the possibility that these were two different baptisms because 'the πνεύματι ἀγίω and the πυρί are united into a single baptism both by the ὑμᾶς and by the solitary ἐν'.[75] The issue of the referent of the pronoun ὑμᾶς to two different sets of people (i.e. the

---

an undefined, but divinely sent, Personality'.

74  Dunn, 'Spirit-and-Fire Baptism', 86; my emphasis.
75  Dunn, 'Spirit-and-Fire Baptism', 84-85. Dunn is followed on this point by some commentators, e.g. Marshall, *Luke*, 147; Nolland, *Luke*, 1.152.

repentant and the unrepentant) is later admitted by Dunn, and so this does not really argue against πνεύματι ἁγίῳ and πυρί referring to two different baptisms.[76] But neither does the fact that a solitary ἐν governs both πνεύματι ἁγίῳ and πυρί require these two to be understood as referring to the same baptism. Greek grammarians often comment that when two or more nouns used with the same preposition are joined by a conjunction the preposition may but does not need to be repeated. In the NT repetition of the preposition in this situation is more frequent and this may be attributed to Semitic influence, *but it is not required.*[77] Therefore, the solitary ἐν should not be used to support a single baptism unless the context also requires this sense. If the sense of the context suggests that this clause indicates two baptisms, then the syntax of the solitary ἐν allows for this possibility. In the subsequent discussion we will see that the sense of the context does indeed point to two baptisms.

The discussion of this matter is often confused by a seemingly minor linguistic mistake. We should observe that John's statement does not describe a *baptism*, but rather one who *'will baptize'*. The statement uses the verb 'baptize' rather than the verbal noun 'baptism'. When the verb is made the equivalent of the noun, and the metaphorical nature of the baptizing is neglected, then one ends up with a single action encompassing both elements. Linguistically, the number of a verb is determined by the number of its subject rather than the number of its object. But with respect to a noun being further described by other nouns, the number of the first noun is determined by the number of the other nouns. For example, the verb 'baptize' could be replaced with one more neutral, such as 'give', so that the statement becomes 'he will give an A and a B'. In this statement it is not necessary to understand that A and B are involved in the same act of giving. But if the verb 'giving' is altered to

76  Dunn, 'Spirit-and-Fire Baptism', 86; cf. my discussion of the reference of ὑμᾶς immediately below.
77  Cf. Turner, *Grammar*, 3.275; Robertson, *Grammar*, 566; Smyth, *Grammar*, §1668; Harris, 'Prepositions', 3.1175; Black, *Aramaic Approach*, 114-15 (cf. the debate between Argyle, 'Alleged Semiticism [1]', 177; Turner, 'Alleged Semiticism', 252-54; Argyle, 'Alleged Semiticism [2]', 247. For examples of contexts in which the preposition is not repeated for the second noun, even when that noun is referring to a separate a distinct entity, with ἐν see Mt. 4.16; 11.21; Lk. 1.79; 10.13; Jn 1.45; 4.23; Acts 1.8; 7.22; 16.2; 1 Cor. 1.5; with other prepositions, see Lk. 21.26; Acts 24.16; 26.18; Rom. 15.19; in contrast to similar situations in which the preposition is repeated, see Mt. 23.20-21; Mk 5.5, etc. The preposition ἐν is often a translation of the Hebrew preposition בְּ; even in Hebrew the preposition need not be repeated, especially in cases of poetic parallelism (cf. Gesenius and Kautzsch, *Grammar*, §119hh; Waltke and O'Connor, *Syntax*, §11.4.2a; Davidson, *Syntax*, 138); e.g. with בְּ, Isa. 48.14; with לְ, Isa. 28.6; with מִן, Isa. 30.1. If a Semitic background can be detected in Q 3.16-17 and a poetic structure observed (cf. Black, 144), then the solitary use of ἐν in Q 3.16 might reflect the instrumental function of בְּ and the solitary use of the preposition in Hebrew poetic parallelism might have influenced this solitary use of ἐν.

the singular noun, 'gift', (as Dunn and others do by altering 'will baptize' to 'baptism'), so that the statement in our example becomes 'a gift of an A and a B', then linguistically, A and B have become two elements in one gift. But if in the preceding verbal statement ('he will give an A and a B') A and B are separate, then the noun form must be 'gifts (plural) of an A and a B'. John states that 'he will baptize with a holy spirit and fire' in which case the two elements of spirit and fire do not need to be understood as united in one 'baptism'.[78] Understood metaphorically, 'he will baptize with' most probably indicates the means by which the expected figure would accomplish the program of judgment and restoration. It takes the metaphorical imagery too literally when one expects the elements of spirit and fire to encompass two aspects of one action. Therefore, John's statement that 'he will baptize you with a holy spirit and fire' does not need to signify two aspects of one activity, and the arguments which support a single baptism are rather weak. But to understand the activity of John's expected figure we must examine the identity of the recipients as well as the significance of spirit and fire.

The perception of the expected figure's activity is affected by how one identifies the recipients of this figure's baptism. John states 'I baptize *you* . . . but he will baptize *you* . . .' (Q 3.16 = Mk 1.8). The close connection drawn between John's baptism and the expected figure's baptism implies that the 'you' in both statements refers to the same group of people. From this it could be argued that, if the first 'you' refers to those persons who have been baptized with John's baptism, then these same people (the second 'you') are the recipients of the expected figure's baptism. Thus, the expected figure's baptism would have to be interpreted as essentially restorative, though perhaps including a purgative element. However, the premise of this argument is faulty. While the first 'you' obviously includes those who have received John's baptism, it is better to understand this 'you' as referring to John's audience generally, including not only those who had been baptized, but also those who were interested but had not responded, as well as those who had already rejected John's message.[79] In the synoptic Gospels, the context of this pericope is John's public preaching to the crowds (in Lk. 3: ὄχλοις [v. 7] . . . τοῦ λαοῦ [v. 15] . . . ὑμᾶς [v. 16]), which included both the repentant and the unrepentant. There is nothing in this context or this pericope itself to indicate that the situation has changed to John's specific instruction to his followers only. This explanation of the contrast, and yet continuity,

---

78  I will refer to the expected figure's activity as a 'baptism' for the sake of convenience, but in so doing, I am not indicating that both elements express a single act.
79  So Dunn, 'Spirit-and-Fire Baptism', 86 n. 2; Beasley-Murray, *Baptism*, 38; Nolland, *Luke*, 1.153; Davies and Allison, *Matthew*, 1.312.

between John's ministry and that of the expected figure, especially in light of the continued explanation of the expected figure's role as the one who cleans the threshing floor (Q 3.17), best fits an original setting of a public explanation to the crowds of John's role within his understanding of God's eschatological plan. Luke's introduction to this pericope ('now while the people were in a state of expectation, and all were debating in their hearts concerning John . . .', 3.15), while it might be his own interpretation, nevertheless is the most plausible context in which such a statement would be made by John. Therefore, if the 'you' refers both to those who responded to John's message and to those who did not respond or else rejected it, then John's metaphorical reference to the expected figure's 'baptizing' activity should be interpreted as being administered to both groups of people. This conclusion finds further support by the distinction made in the next verse between the wheat and the chaff (cf. §8.4.2).

To this point then, I have argued that the expected figure's activity of baptizing need not refer to one activity of one baptism, and that the recipients of this figure's activity include both those who respond to, and those who reject, John's message and baptism. Therefore, the two elements with which the expected figure baptizes are probably best understood as referring to two different activities, one of which is expressed towards the one group and the other activity is toward the second group. This probability is strengthened by examining the sense of both elements, spirit and fire.

The expected figure baptizing 'with a holy spirit' is a metaphorical description of the gracious bestowal of a holy spirit upon the repentant, that is, upon those who had responded to John's message and been baptized with his water baptism. In the preceding survey of expected figures, the spirit was an expected eschatological blessing which God would bestow upon his people as well as upon his agents of judgment and restoration. As an object of eschatological expectation, the bestowal of a spirit may be perceived in various ways, such as an evidence of blessing generally or of the new prophetic role to be experienced by all people.[80] However, this baptism with a spirit in John's proclamation probably has a more specific significance if, as was suggested above, John described the expected figure's baptism to be 'with a spirit of *holiness*' (§8.2.1). Often references to the eschatological bestowal of the spirit upon the people of God emphasize that spirit's enabling them to live righteously before God.[81] In the later literature of the Second Temple period, when the eschatological spirit is referred to as a spirit *of holiness*, then the empha-

---

80   Isa. 32.15; 44.3; Ezek. 37.14; Joel 2.28-29.
81   E.g. Ezek. 11.19-20; 36.26-27; Zech. 12.10.

sis is upon *purifying* the people so that they may live righteously before God. For example, in *Jub*. 1.23 God promises:

> But after this they will return to me in all uprightness and with all of (their) heart and soul. And I shall cut off the foreskin of their heart and the foreskin of the heart of their descendants. And I shall create for them a holy spirit, and I shall purify them so that they will not turn away from following me from that day and forever.

In this passage, a spirit of holiness purifies all the people as part of a restoration of Israel. There does not appear to be any separation of some to punishment. But the end result is the creation of a pure humanity where wickedness is abolished. A similar use of the expression 'a spirit of holiness' occurs in 1QS 4.20-21, which states:

> Then God in his truth will make manifest all the deeds of man and purify for himself some from mankind, destroying all the spirit of perversity, removing all blemishes of his flesh and purifying him with a spirit of holiness from all deeds of evil.[82]

In our examination of this passage above (§5.3.3) we observed that those identified as 'some from mankind' were probably the members of the community. In contrast to these who have removed the last vestiges of the spirit of perversity and are purified with a spirit of holiness, those who have a spirit of perversity in greater measure will be destroyed (1QS 4.2-14, 23-26). In contrast with *Jub*. 1.23 quoted above, in this passage in 1QS a separation does take place, whereby the wicked are destroyed, and only those prepared receive this final cleansing. But the end result is the same in both examples: a pure humanity where there is no wickedness. In both cases, the spirit of holiness has the same purificatory function. But John's use of the expression is more closely paralleled by the passage in 1QS 4 rather than *Jubilees* 1, because in John's case the spirit is applied to a select group who have been previously prepared while the rest are destroyed. In light of these parallels to the purificatory function of 'a spirit of holiness' in John's milieu, it is probable that John's use of the term had a similar orientation, and thus one function of the spirit of holiness was the final purification of the people.

In discussing the function of John's baptism as the expression of a radical, conversionary repentance, we saw that this repentance was both the responsibility of the person to 'turn to God' and something which required the ministry of God in order to complete the transformation of conversion (§6.4.1, 6.4.4). Thus a second function of this spirit of holiness is probably to accomplish this completion of repentance, enabling them to live in righteousness and obedience before God. The purification by this spirit of holiness might also have a corporate element. In

---

82   Cf. 1QH 16.12; 17.26; *T. Levi* 2.3B7-8; *Sib. Or.* 4.188-89.

conjunction with the removal of the wicked from their midst, this spirit of holiness could be understood to create a holy people: they were prepared by John's baptism and constituted the true, remnant Israel. This purifying and restorative work by a spirit of holiness completes their transformation into the holy people of God. Beyond this personal and corporate understanding, the evidence is too scanty to ascertain what further significance John's expectation of a baptism with a spirit of holiness might have. The suggestions made here, however, do have links with our discussion in the rest of this chapter.

The description of the expected figure baptizing 'with fire' refers to this figure's destruction of the unrepentant. The imagery of fire itself could indicate the purifying of the righteous or the making of all people righteous, utilizing the imagery of refining gold and silver.[83] But the significance of a baptism 'with fire' must be determined first of all by John's use of the language of fire elsewhere in his preaching. In Q 3.9 the trees are thrown into the fire and burned, and in Q 3.17 the expected figure burns the chaff. In both cases the imagery anticipates the destruction of the wicked, not a purifying at all, and thus a baptism with fire must be understood to envision the destruction of the wicked. In the preceding survey of expected figures numerous references were made to the use of fire imagery to portray the punishment and/or destruction of the wicked. In the other cases in which John employs this imagery the fire destroys the object being burned. Therefore John's reference to the unrepentant being baptized with fire by the expected figure implies the removal and destruction of the unrepentant by the expected figure rather than their experiencing sustained punishment. The emphasis then is not so much on the fact that the wicked will get what they deserve (as would be suggested by an emphasis upon punishment), but that they will be done away with, and so are no longer present among the righteous. Since the baptisms with a holy spirit and fire are closely associated with one another, we might observe that the baptism with fire upon the wicked results in the creation of an environment for the righteous where the wicked are no longer present. Therefore it is possible to understand that part of the expected figure's ministry in which holiness is restored involves not only the creation of a holy people (i.e. baptizing with a spirit of holiness), but the creation of a holy environment, or in terms more in sympathy with Jewish thinking, the creation of a 'holy land'.

We should note that it is the people's response to John's preaching and baptism that has already distinguished between the two groups: the repentant and the unrepentant. The expected figure's baptism does *not* identify or produce these two groups; John's preaching and baptism had

---

83  E.g. Isa. 48.10; Zech. 13.9; Mal. 3.3.

already done that. Rather, the expected figure's baptism brings the process to its completion, resulting in each group realizing their end, whether restoration or judgment.[84]

This relationship between the expected figure's baptism and John's ministry implies that it is John's ministry which brings into existence the group which receive the expected figure's gracious ministry. Therefore, since John addressed himself to all Israel, a consequence of John's ministry is the creation of a group which was separate and distinct from the rest of Jewish society; they were the ones who would remain and receive the expected figure's gracious ministry while the rest would be removed and destroyed. This suggests that John's ministry was creating a sectarian movement.[85]

### 8.4.2 *Cleaning the Threshing Floor*

The picture painted in Q 3.17 is quite specific in its employment of agricultural imagery. The specificity with which John portrays the expected figure's ministry with this imagery requires clarification to be fully appreciated. In the process of harvesting, the grain is cut and gathered, threshed, winnowed and finally stored. Such a harvesting process is practised universally, but the specifics of the Palestinian procedure need to be highlighted.[86]

---

84  I have primarily used the terms 'repentant' and 'unrepentant' to describe these two groups because they are the most specific terms for each group using terminology derived from what we know of John's own proclamation. But since the repentant are forgiven and are promised restoration, while the unrepentant are unforgiven and will experience judgment, the more common Jewish terminology of 'the righteous' and 'the wicked' could be used as equivalents. I am not suggesting that such categories are absolute or objective. Rather, due to the nature of John's proclamation and the group formation which resulted, such categories are the result of insider-outsider distinctions. Viewing the unrepentant as 'the unrighteous' might be John's point of view and that of the repentant, but it would be quite implausible that the Sadducees addressed in Q 3.7-9 would have viewed themselves as the unrighteous!

85  Cf. §6.4.5, 10.2, 10.3, 10.4. It may be helpful to clarify some of the terms I am using: a 'group' is a collection of people who may or may not have some basis of commonality between them. A 'movement' is a group of people who are unified by a common ideology and programme. The analysis here and in §8.5, 10.3, 10.4, and 10.5 indicates that the term 'movement' may legitimately be applied to the group gathered around John (cf. the common use of the term 'Jesus movement'). By the term 'sectarian' I am indicating that John's movement conceived of itself as set apart and distinct from other people and movements in Palestine.

86  Bible dictionaries and works on biblical archaeology are sometimes helpful in this regard; cf. Richardson, 'Threshing', 4.636; Richardson, 'Winnowing', 4.854; Mihelic, 'Shovel', 4.340; Richardson, 'Chaff', 1.549; Wright, *Archaeology*, 183-87. But, due to the brevity of their description, their portrayal is inaccurate at times. The work of Dalman is much more helpful with respect to the specifics of Palestinian practice; the entire third volume of his series, *Arbeit und Sitte*, is dedicated to a description of the harvesting process in Palestine (*Arbeit*, 3.1-308; its subtitle is *Von der Ernte zum Mehl*); cf. also Mackie, *Manners*, 40-45.

First of all, it is interesting to observe in John's description that it is the owner of the grain who is performing the action. This is indicated by the possessive pronoun αὐτοῦ indicating ownership of the wheat (so Mt. 3.12) or the granary (so Lk. 3.17). Whether the pronoun modifies the wheat or the granary is irrelevant at this point (the owner of the farm would probably own both the grain and the granary); it is the owner of the farm who is performing the work. The common practice of using hired help is unmentioned in John's portrayal.[87]

The major point of confusion concerning the interpretation of Q 3.17 lies in ascertaining what precisely are the actions being performed by John's expected figure. The expression οὗ τὸ πτύον ἐν τῇ χειρὶ αὐτοῦ, καὶ διακαθαριεῖ τὴν ἅλωνα αὐτοῦ has commonly been interpreted to portray the process of winnowing; that is, the tossing of the harvested grain into the air, allowing the wind to separate the wheat from the chaff.[88] This interpretation is based on the assumption that πτύον refers to the instrument used for tossing the grain into the air and that the verb διακαθαίρω refers to action of tossing itself. However, a careful examination of the evidence does not support this interpretation. First of all, the significance of the verb διακαθαίρω[89] is 'to cleanse thoroughly', 'to clean out', or 'to prune', but there is no evidence that it signified 'to winnow'.[90] I suppose the sense in which this verb is understood by those proposing this interpretation involves the 'cleansing' of the wheat from the chaff.[91] But it is interesting to observe that it is *not the grain* which is the object of cleansing in John's description, but rather *the threshing-floor* (ἅλων).[92] By contrast, John's portrayal does not use the verbs commonly used to specify the action of winnowing, which include especially λικμάω, but also διασπείρω and its equivalent διασκορπίζω; each has the basic significance of 'to scatter' and is used with reference to winnowing.[93]

87  Dalman, *Arbeit*, 3.73.
88  E.g. Davies and Allison, *Matthew*, 1.318-19; Hill, *Matthew*, 95; Fitzmyer, *Luke*, 1.474; Marshall, *Luke*, 148.
89  Matthew's equivalent form, διακαθαρίζω, is not attested elsewhere; BAGD, 183; LSJ, 396.
90  BAGD, 183; LSJ, 396.
91  E.g. Davies and Allison, *Matthew*, 1.318-19.
92  The word ἅλων specifies the threshing-floor, but it may be used to refer by inference to the contents of the threshing-floor, that is, the grain, such as in Ruth 3.2 LXX: αὐτὸς λικμᾷ τὸν ἅλωνα, 'he winnows the threshing-floor'. But this inferential meaning cannot be used here (against Davies and Allison, *Matthew*, 1.318-19) because there is no specific evidence to cause that inference and suggest that ἅλων means anything other than threshing-floor, as there is in the example of Ruth 3.2 cited above.
93  For examples of λικμάω signifying 'to winnow' see in the LXX, Ruth 3.2; Isa. 17.13; 30.24; 41.16; Amos 9.9; Sir. 5.9; cf. BAGD, 474-75; LSJ, 1050. For the same sense with διασπείρω see in the LXX, Isa. 41.16; Jer. 15.7; cf. LSJ, 412, and for the equivalent διασκορπίζω, see Ezek. 5.2, 10; cf. BAGD, 188; LSJ, 412.

Thus, neither the action of cleansing nor the object cleansed actually indicate that winnowing is the activity being described.

But does not the πτύον (winnowing shovel) in the hand of John's expected figure indicate that the process is winnowing? Such an interpretation would be supported by the description of πτύον provided by BAGD: 'a fork-like shovel, with which the threshed grain was thrown into the wind. . .' However, the extensive work by Gustaf Dalman on Palestinian agricultural practices does not support this description. Two tools were evidently used on the threshing-floor, a winnowing fork (מִזְרֶה, θρῖναξ) and a winnowing shovel (רַחַת, πτύον).[94] The actual winnowing of the grain, that is, separating the wheat from the straw and chaff by throwing it up into the wind, was accomplished by means of the winnowing fork and not the shovel.[95] The shovel was used to heap up the grain before winnowing as well as to gather the wheat and straw into piles after the winnowing was completed. It was also used for the final clearing of the threshing floor and for moving the wheat in the granary.[96] Therefore, the fact that the word πτύον (winnowing shovel) is used in Mt. 3.12 = Lk. 3.17 rather than θρῖναξ (winnowing fork) provides further evidence that the activity being described here is not winnowing.

A close parallel combining both πτύον and διακαθαίρω is found in the Letters of Alciphron:

> Ἄρτι μοι τὴν ἅλω διακαθήραντι καὶ τὸ πτύον ἀποτιθεμένῳ ὁ δεσπότης ἐπέστη καὶ ἰδὼν ἐπήνει τὴν φιλεργίαν.
>
> I had just finished cleaning the threshing floor and was putting away my winnowing shovel when my master came suddenly upon me, saw what I had done, and proceeded to commend my industry [*Alciphr.* 2.23.1].

94  In Symmachus' translation of Isa. 30.24, the word πτύον translates רַחַת, or winnowing shovel, while θρῖναξ translates מִזְרֶה, winnowing fork. This is the only place in the OT where רַחַת is used; the LXX does not translate the word, only Symmachus does. This is also the only place the word πτύον appears in a Greek translation of the OT. Cf. the Palestinian Arabic term rāḥa for the winnowing shovel. The term מִזְרֶה is only used here and in Jer. 15.7, but is translated as θρῖναξ only by Symmachus in Isa. 30.24. In neither place does the LXX translate the word. Cf. the Arabic term miḍrā. Dalman, *Arbeit*, 3.116-25.

95  Dalman, (*Arbeit*, 3.116) states: 'Das eigentliche Gerät des Worfelns . . . d. h. des Hochwerfens des gedroschenen Getreides, is nicht eine Schaufel, sondern eine in das Getreide leichter eingreifende Gabel. . .' Cf. the pictures Dalman supplies of winnowing, nos. 28, 29 and especially 30. Cf. also the brief description in Mackie, *Manners*, 42.

96  Dalman, *Arbeit*, 3.116-24, 201, 253-54. Dalman (122) does mention that the shovel was used to winnow leguminous plants (such as beans or lentils) as well as to winnow the straw to produce fodder (after the wheat had been winnowed out with the fork). This explains the use of a winnowing shovel as a tool for winnowing along with a winnowing fork in Isa. 30.24, where the reference is to the production of fodder. Cf. Homer, *Il.* 13.588-90, where reference is made to a πτυόφιν (poetic form of πτύον) being used to winnow 'dark-skinned beans or pulse'.

In this example, just as in John's portrayal, the object being cleaned is the threshing floor, presumably after the winnowing had been completed, and the instrument used for this cleaning is the winnowing shovel.

This analysis of Q 3.17 indicates that John portrayed a scene quite different from that of winnowing. Rather, the winnowing has already taken place and the wheat and chaff already lie separated on the threshing floor. The owner now has in his hand the πτύον or winnowing shovel, the tool appropriate for the next stage of the process. He is poised with shovel in hand to clean out the threshing floor.[97] Now there are only two substances on the threshing floor from which it needs to be cleaned: the wheat and the chaff. Therefore, the statement διακαθαριεῖ τὴν ἅλωνα αὐτοῦ ('he will clean his threshing-floor') describes the action as it is performed with respect to the threshing-floor. Similarly the next two statements, συνάξει τὸν σῖτον αὐτοῦ εἰς τὴν ἀποθήκην ('he will gather his wheat into the granary') and τὸ δὲ ἄχυρον κατακαύσει πυρὶ ἀσβέστῳ ('but the chaff he will burn with unquenchable fire') refer essentially to the same action, but now it is described with respect to the wheat and chaff specifically. Thus, the statements concerning the wheat and chaff amplify the statement concerning the threshing-floor and explain why the winnowing shovel is in the owner's hand in the first place.

The significance of this portrayal of the expected figure's ministry is remarkably parallel to the significance already perceived with respect to the relationship between the baptizing ministry of John and that of the expected figure in Q 3.16. In John's portrayal of the threshing floor the wheat and the chaff have already been separated. The expected figure's ministry is to take these two groups to their end, whether to the granary or to the fire. If the wheat and chaff have already been separated prior to the arrival of the expected figure at the threshing floor, this suggests that it is John's own ministry which has effectively separated the wheat from the chaff, the righteous from the unrighteous. It is the people's response to his proclamation which distinguishes them. If they repent and are baptized, then they are the wheat, but if they refuse, then they are the chaff. Thus, as already perceived in the preceding section, it is John's ministry which creates this division between these two groups (§8.4.1). It is the response to John's ministry which has 'piled up the grain on the threshing floor'. This imagery also points to the fact that one effect of John's ministry is the creation of a sectarian movement (cf. §8.4.1).

---

97 Nolland (*Luke*, 1.153) states that 'the winnowing which makes it possible to gather up separately the grain and the chaff has already been done... The interest here is not, however, in a whole harvest process, with the point being made that its terminal phase is about to occur.' Cf. Schürmann, *Lukasevangelium*, 1.177-78.

In this interpretation, the imageries of baptizing and cleaning the threshing floor actually present the same picture of the role of John's expected figure as well as the role of John's own ministry. Utilizing the imagery of baptism, John's ministry prepares a group of the repentant who are distinguished from the unrepentant by proclaiming and administering a repentance-baptism, and the expected figure baptizes the repentant group with a spirit of holiness and the unrepentant with fire, thus taking each group to their end, either restoration or judgment. Employing the imagery of the threshing floor, John separates the wheat from the chaff so that the expected figure who stands poised at the threshing floor can now take each pile to its appropriate end.

In light of this parallel between the imageries of baptism and threshing floor which present basically a unified picture of the judgment and restoration, it is intriguing to ask what might be symbolized by the threshing floor itself, especially in light of the fact that the other elements in the picture have quite evident symbolism. Two possibilities could be suggested. First of all, the threshing floor might symbolize the temple. We have already seen how John's baptism functioned as a protest against the temple establishment which was often the focus of protest by individuals and groups in the Second Temple period (§6.4.6, cf. §10.6.2). Those who perceived problems with the current temple establishment often envisioned an eschatological purification of the temple and/or the priesthood.[98] The imagery of the threshing floor might have been suggested by the OT tradition that the temple site had originally been a threshing floor (2 Chron. 3.1). Yet, John's ministry was not addressed to the temple establishment specifically but to all Israel.

So on the other hand, the threshing floor might symbolize the land of Palestine as the place where the righteous and the wicked were together. This latter possibility is more probable in light of the use of threshing floor imagery in the OT to portray the experiences and expectations of the people of Israel, particularly in relationship with their land. For example, the fruits of the threshing floor was one of the images describing the bounty and fruitfulness of Israel in the land.[99] The removal of Israel and Judah from the land and the sufferings of their exilic experience are described as being threshed on the threshing floor.[100] With respect to eschatological expectations, the destruction of the world powers prior to the establishment of God's kingdom is described in Dan. 2.35 using threshing-floor imagery. Having been crushed, 'they became

---

98   E.g. Mal. 3.3-4; 1QM; cf. the description of the purification of the temple by the Maccabeans in 1 Macc. 4.36-61; *Ant.* 12.316-22.
99   Lev. 26.3-6; Num. 15.18-20; 18.26-30; Deut. 15.14.
100  Isa. 21.10; 28.28-29; Hos. 9.2-3.

like chaff on the summer threshing floors, and the wind swept them away
so that no trace of them was found . . .' (cf. vv. 44-45). In Isa. 27.12-13
God's people are portrayed as being threshed out of the foreign lands to
which they have been scattered and being regathered into their own
land. Future blessing of the people in the land is described as a bounti-
ful threshing floor in Joel 2.23-24. Furthermore, the imagery of threshing is used to portray the vengeance which Israel will exercise when they
gain the ascendancy over those who dominated them, took them out of
their own land and into captivity.[101] In light of this OT usage, John's use
of this imagery was probably associated with expectations of the eschatological future to be experienced by the restored people of God.[102] The
gathering of the grain into the granary symbolizes the positive act taken
by the expected figure to preserve the prepared repentant from the
imminent judgment which will fall upon the wicked. John has used this
imagery in a general way rather than associating it with a particular OT
passage which makes it difficult to be more specific concerning the precise symbolism. But perhaps greater specificity was not needed, for the
connections could be made by those being addressed without John being
too specific. The imagery was associated with their hopes for a better
future in the land and that was specific enough.[103]

I indicated above that the baptisms with a spirit of holiness and fire
created a purified, true Israel with the suggestion of creating a purified
environment, or holy land (§8.4.1). This suggestion becomes more probable in light of the possibility that the threshing floor symbolized the
land.

## 8.5 *John's Perception of the Judgment and Restoration*

The focus of John's eschatological proclamation was upon the ministry of
the expected figure and so that has been the center of our attention as
well. However, from certain elements in this figure's description as well

---

101 Isa. 41.15-16; Mic. 4.10-13.
102 Against Schürmann (*Lukasevangelium*, 1.177 n. 107) who states, without providing
  any reason, that 'das beliebte atl. Gerichtsbild vom Dreschen . . . wird hier nicht
  gemalt'.
103 McNeile (*Matthew*, 29) observed that 'to the Baptist the [threshing] floor must have
  meant Palestine, the scene of the final judgment'. But this suggestion does not seem
  to have been picked up by more recent commentators. Cf. another older com-
  mentator, Plummer, *Luke*, 95.
      Cf. the concerns for the purity of the land expressed in the Maccabean revolt; *Ant.*
  12.286: 'Judas with the ready assistance of his brothers and others drove the enemy
  out of the country, and made an end of those of his countrymen who had violated
  their fathers' laws, and purified the land of all pollution'. On the purity of the land,
  cf. Joel 3.17; Neh. 13.3; *Pss. Sol.* 17.28; *Jub.* 23.30; 50.5; 1QS 8.1-10a; 9.3-6; Schürer,
  *History*, 2.83-84; Hengel, *Zealots*, 186-228, esp. 198.

as from other elements of John's ministry we may glean clues concerning how John perceived the judgment and restoration itself.

First of all, the judgment and restoration are expected imminently. Several pieces of evidence support this conclusion. The use of the present tense of the verb ἔρχομαι to describe the coming of the expected figure, rather than the future tense, suggests that the figure may already be 'travelling' and that his arrival is imminent. Also, John's further portrayal of the expected figure as already standing at the threshing floor with the winnowing shovel poised in his hand vividly portrays the fact that everything was ready for the judgment and restoration to begin. However, the most explicit piece of evidence is John's statement in Q 3.9, that 'already the axe lies at the root of the trees. . .' In this word picture the farmer has observed that certain trees in the orchard are no longer bearing fruit. He has, therefore, brought an axe with which to chop down those unfruitful trees. The use of the verb κεῖμαι[104] might indicate that the farmer has 'laid down' the axe at the base of the tree, but it is more probable that the sense is that the axe blade has been placed against the root and the farmer is about to draw the axe back for the first swing. The emphatic position of the adverb ἤδη ('already') at the beginning of the sentence serves to highlight this sense of imminence.

Secondly, we have already seen that in the judgment and restoration John's expected figure brings about the removal and destruction of the unrepentant and the restoration and blessing of the repentant. These two groups might also be labelled the righteous and the wicked, which is common Jewish terminology entirely consistent with John's point of view, though there is no evidence he used these precise terms (cf. §8.4.1). Labels like these depend very much upon the point of view of the one using them, so that those who are the righteous or the wicked from John's point of view would not necessarily correspond with the perspective of others or even those so labelled. From John's perspective, those who accepted his message and underwent John's repentance-baptism were the righteous. However, from the point of view of those who believed they attained certain standards of righteousness in other ways (e.g. the Pharisees or the temple aristocracy) it might seem that those who were so baptized were merely seeking 'cheap grace' by only having to perform a baptism to be forgiven and prepared for the coming wrath. On the other hand, from John's point of view, those who were not yet baptized were the wicked, though these might be divided into two subsets, depending upon whether or not they believed that John's call to repentance applied to them. Thus, the first subset recognized their need

---

104 The verb κεῖμαι serves here as the perfect passive of τίθημι, for which see BAGD, 426.

to be baptized, but had not yet completed their response, for whatever reason. The other camp within those labelled 'wicked' would be those who believed that John's message did not apply to them, or disagreed with John's perception of the whole situation, or else were not even aware of John's message and ministry. On the assumption that those within this first group would eventually become part of John's righteous group, the latter group, then, consisted of those who either rejected or were ignorant of John's message. Thus, for example, John vilified those Sadducees—respected persons associated with the temple—who rejected his call to repentance by denouncing them as 'you brood of vipers!' (Q 3.7).

John's perception of the new situation involved the removal and destruction of these who were unrepentant and the purifying and blessing of John's righteous ones. This purifying and blessing of those who were righteous by the expected figure, otherwise summarized by the term 'restoration', involved a radically altered situation for these people. But of what did this new situation consist? From the preceding discussion we can make several summarizing observations. In the new situation there would be a new absence and a new presence. The new absence was the removal of the wicked. The new presence was the experience of purifying and blessing derived from a spirit of holiness, and the active presence of God's agent, the expected figure. We saw above that this was expected to have both individual and corporate consequences, and it also probably envisioned a situation in which the land of Palestine was made once again the place in which the true Israel, the people of God, could live as they should (§8.4.1). With John's emphasis upon conversionary repentance, the new life in the land was probably one in which the people had a right relationship with Yahweh, one of obedience and trust. But repentance was also to lead to changed ethical relationships with other people, a concern John demonstrated with his call to 'bear fruit in keeping with repentance' (Q 3.8a; cf. Lk. 3.10-14; *Ant.* 18.117). In light of the social injustices experienced by many Jews in Palestine, this concern manifested a hope for a new situation in which social justice would be experienced by the true Israel.

The new absence mentioned above involved generally the removal of the wicked, but who were the wicked? They were the unrepentant of course, but with John's concern for social justice and the hope for a new situation, the wicked would include particularly those who were responsible for the social injustices and the current situation, as perceived by those who considered themselves to be deprived and experiencing injustice. Three groups immediately suggest themselves: the temple establishment who controlled the wealth gathered there and sought to maintain the *status quo* with the Romans; the Herodian family (and supporters) who were the lackeys of Rome by serving as client rulers, and the Roman imperialists who occupied the Jews' land, offended their sensibilities and taxed them.[105]

We might ask, by what means was this judgment and restoration to be brought about? The obvious answer is by the expected figure, of course. But this really answers the question 'by whom' rather than 'by what means'. Our evidence does not answer this question. The only clue which might even give a hint is John's description of the expected figure as 'mightier' (Q 3.16; Mk 1.7). John is indicating that this figure is greater than he in terms of power, which indicates that the figure will have the power and authority necessary to carry out the judgment and restore the repentant to their new situation. It is possible that the NT's use of the term ἰσχυρός ('mighty') in the portrayal of John's preaching reflects the use of the גבר word group (though other word groups, such as חזק, are equally possible).[106] One of the assocations of the גבר word group is military might, especially since the term גבור was used to describe a warrior who is a hero in battle.[107] It is used to describe Yahweh as mighty when he fights on behalf of his people (i.e. acting as a figure of judgment and restoration).[108] In the preceding chapter, those texts in which the various expected figures of judgment and restoration were described as mighty, the גבר word group is represented frequently, and in contexts which have military overtones.[109] While it is clear that the term 'mighty' implied that the expected figure was eminently capable of carrying out the judgment and restoration, it is possible that John might have conceived of the expected figure being involved in some form of military endeavour in which he fought against and defeated the enemies of the righteous. It is also plausible, for if John conceived of the removal of the Roman occupying forces, then warfare could have been involved. But, the lack of evidence forbids us making this suggestion more than a speculative possibility.[110]

The description of the new situation presented here is somewhat

---

105 This is pursued further when we discuss the socio-political orientation to John's ministry in Chapter 10, esp. §10.3, 10.6.

106 In the LXX the Greek terms ἰσχύω, ἰσχυρός and ἰσχύς translate a wide variety of Hebrew words, of which several belong to the גבר word group, and the ἰσχυ- terms translate these frequently.

107 Cf. BDB, 150; e.g. Judg. 6.12; 1 Sam. 17.51; 2 Sam. 20.7; Isa. 21.17.

108 BDB, 150; e.g. Ps. 24.8; Jer. 32.18 (cf. vv. 18-21); Zeph. 3.17 (cf. vv. 15-20).

109 Examples of the גבר word group with Yahweh see the preceding note as well as Isa. 49.26; 1QM 12.9-10; with the Davidic Messiah: Isa. 9.6; with Michael/Melchizedek: 1QM 17.6. Military imagery is sometimes associated with these figures in other ways as well.

110 Cf. the discussion of the tactics of John's movement in §10.4.

vague, which is probably due to the fragmentary nature of our data as well as the fact that the two emphases in the data we do have is upon what people were to do now (repentance-baptism) and the heavenly/theological description of the eschatological expectation rather than a more concrete terrestrial/historical orientation. But we can clarify the expected situation in one other way by observing what this restoration is *not*. It is not the 'end of the world' or universal, cosmic judgment or the destruction of the earth by fire.[111] In both Q 3.9 and 3.17 the fire burns up the unfruitful trees and the chaff, but there is no hint that it consumes the orchard, the wheat or the threshing floor. The imagery of the fire in both instances is careful to portray only the destruction of the wicked. In both images the fruitful trees remain and the wheat remains. Thus, the righteous experience a reversal within their present environment, but this restoration involves in some sense a continuation of their present, human existence, and is not some type of translation into a new dimension of existence such as ascension to heaven or resurrection.

### 8.6 *Conclusion*

The application of the survey in the preceding chapter of expected figures of judgment and restoration to the evidence concerning John's expected figure reveals that John's conception of that figure is best understood at two levels, similar to the way expected figures were understood to function in other expressions of Jewish expectation. The most explicit elements of John's description indicate that he concentrated on the celestial/theological level by announcing that Yahweh was coming to judge and restore. Yet other, less explicit elements of John's proclamation indicate that at a terrestrial/historical level he understood that Yahweh's judgment and restoration would be carried out by Yahweh's agent. The evidence which supports this conclusion does not, however, indicate which of the other expected figures John had in mind. The only hint we may have is that John conceived of a human figure rather than a supernatural being. John's reason for being vague on this point was possibly because he wished to stress the call to repentance and to emphasize the divine nature of the judgment and restoration without identifying himself with one particular form of Jewish expectation.

John announced that his figure 'will baptize with a holy spirit and fire', which I argued was describing two separate, metaphorical baptisms. The

---

111 Against, for example, Kraeling (*John the Baptist*, 42, cf. 50, 63) who states that with John 'judgment has become a cosmic event of such scope and magnitude that it beggars analogy in terms of human experience'.

first portrayed the expected figure's gracious bestowal of a spirit of holiness upon the righteous, repentant people who constituted the true, remnant Israel. This spirit of holiness purified the people, completing the transformation begun by their conversionary repentance, enabling them to live in righteousness and obedience before God. While having an individual orientation, this purifying and transforming activity probably also had a corporate aspect as well: it created a holy people. On the other hand, the baptism with fire describes the expected figure's destruction of the unrighteous, unrepentant people. The emphasis appears to be upon their removal and destruction rather than upon their punishment. This removal of the unrighteous has a positive effect for the righteous who remain: their environment has been cleansed by this removal, thus suggesting that the figure's ministry of restoration might also be understood to create a holy environment, or a 'holy land'. It is the response to John's ministry which creates the fundamental distinction between the righteous repentant and the unrighteous unrepentant, thus providing further support for the conclusion that one effect of John's ministry is the creation of a sectarian movement.

The imagery of the farmer at the threshing floor does not portray the process of winnowing but the stage after winnowing, in which the farmer uses the winnowing shovel to clean the threshing floor by shovelling the wheat into the granary and the chaff into a pile to be burned. As with the imagery of baptism, this picture also portrays the expected figure's ministry of judgment and restoration. The wheat and chaff represent the repentant and unrepentant respectively. They have already been separated by their response to John's ministry. The expected figure takes each group to their appropriate end. It is possible that the threshing floor represents the land of Palestine which is cleansed by the expected figure through removing the unrighteous from it and destroying them. This might further support the idea that John conceived of a situation in which the expected figure not only purifies the true, remnant Israel, but also prepares for them a holy land in which to dwell. Again we observe that it is the response to John's ministry which separates the wheat from the chaff.

Miscellaneous observations on the judgment and restoration included the fact that John stressed its imminence. Also, while the unrighteous were expected to be destroyed and the righteous blessed, those who fit these categories did so according to John's schema. This was not necessarily the perception of those who rejected John's ministry; they probably had their own labels for both themselves and John's followers and these could very well have been the reverse of John's. I suggested that the restoration to be experienced by the repentant involved the creation of a new situation which incorporated the absence of the unrighteous, the presence of God's agent and a situation of holiness in which they would experience social justice. The removal and judgment of the wicked was possibly conceived of as the judgment of those who were viewed as wicked because they maintained the *status quo* in a situation of injustice: the temple establishment, the Herodian family and the imperialist power of the Romans. It is unclear by what means John conceived that the expected figure would achieve this judgment and restoration; it might have involved a military struggle, but this is speculative. Finally, we concluded that the restoration was probably a reversal of their situation which was experienced within their present, human existence.

Chapter 9

PROPHETIC FIGURES IN LATE SECOND TEMPLE JUDAISM

## 9.1 *Introduction*

In the preceding two chapters we examined the central elements of John's prophetic proclamation: his announcement of an expected figure of judgment and restoration as well as the description of the judgment and restoration itself. In this second half of Part III we turn to investigate the public role John fulfilled as he made this type of proclamation—the role of prophet.

Josephus describes John's public speaking in several ways: he was 'one who *commanded* (κελεύοντα) the Jews' (18.117); the audience who gathered around him were excited 'by listening to [his] *teachings*' (τῶν λόγων); they were evidently prepared to 'do everything which he *counselled* (συμβουλῇ)', and Herod was afraid that John's 'great *persuasiveness* (τὸ ἐπὶ τοσόνδε πιθανόν) with the people' would lead to strife (18.118). According to Josephus, public speaking and teaching was integral to John's ministry—it was the means by which he had an impact upon the people, and it evoked their excited response which contributed to John's arrest and execution. It is possible for anyone to speak in public at one time or another without functioning in a particular role, but when public speaking is a major feature of one's life, then that person is often perceived as fulfilling a particular role or type of public speaker. However, Josephus does not explicitly identify which *type* of public speaker John was. Within Palestine during the late Second Temple period, those who spoke or taught in public could fulfil one of several roles, such as scribe, charismatic holy man or prophet.[1] While each of these types engaged in teaching, they may be distinguished from one another in several ways, one of which may be according to the source of the authority for their teaching. The scribe's teaching emphasized the correct interpretation of the Law and Prophets;[2] the charismatic holy man's teaching (what little is known about it) appears to have been

---

1 On the scribe, see Moore, *Judaism*, 1.37-47; Jeremias, *Jerusalem*, 233-45; Urbach, *Sages*, 1.1-18; Schürer, *History*, 2.322-36; Saldarini, *Pharisees*, 241-76; Orton, *Understanding Scribe*, 39-133; on the charismatic holy man, see Büchler, *Palestinian Piety*; Vermes, *Jesus*, 58-82; Green, 'Palestinian Holy Men', 619-47; Freyne, 'Charismatic', 223-58; on prophets see the discussion below.

2 Schürer, *History*, 2.322-36; Orton, *Understanding Scribe*, 161-62.

closely related to his immediate contact with God which found expression in being a 'person-of-deed' or miracle-worker.[3] The prophet, on the
other hand, spoke with the immediate authority of God—as God's
spokesperson—providing insight or instruction derived from divine
inspiration. Within Josephus' account there is no evidence that John's
teaching was concerned with the interpretation of the OT, though
Josephus' description of John teaching the people 'to practise virtue and
act with justice toward one another and with piety toward God' suggests
(in Hellenized terms) a call to traditional OT moral values. There is no
evidence that he was a miracle-worker. The excitement generated
among the people by his teaching might suggest that he was claiming to
speak as God's spokesperson, but this is not clear. If in his public speaking John was functioning in a prophetic role, Josephus' negative view of
most post-canonical prophets may explain the ambiguity with which he
has described John.[4]

Upon turning to the NT evidence, the picture is not ambiguous at all.
The Gospels specifically identify John as a prophet. Jesus says to the
crowds after receiving the delegation from John, 'What did you go out to
see? A prophet? Yes, I tell you, and more than a prophet' (Lk. 7.26 =
Mt. 11.9). Similarly, the Gospels record that, when responding to Jesus'
question concerning the authority for John's baptism, the temple leaders
did not wish to admit that John's baptism was 'from men' because they
feared the people 'for they all considered John to be truly a prophet'

---

3    Vermes, *Jesus*, 69-78.
4    Josephus' primarily negative view of prophets during the Second Temple period (cf.
     §9.2.1; especially those I identify as 'popular prophets', cf. §9.5) may have been
     caused by his view that such minority, extremist groups were a major contributing
     cause to the first Jewish Revolt (cf. Rajak, *Josephus*, 65-103). However, in 11 CE
     Augustus Caesar issued an edict in which 'the seers were forbidden to prophesy to
     any person alone or to prophesy regarding death even if others should be present'
     (Cassius, *History* 56.25.5; quotation from Judge, 'Decrees of Caesar', 3). Judge (3)
     explains that this edict applied especially, but not exclusively, to prophets in Rome
     who speculated concerning the death of Caesar. In light of the increasing belief that
     one's life could be seen written in the stars, it was believed that suppressing such
     speculation would help to prevent those who might wish to usurp the throne. Paulus
     (early 3rd century CE, *Sententiae* 5.21.1; quotation from Judge, 5) explains that 'it has
     been decreed to expel from the city prophets who pretend to be inspired by a god,
     lest public morale by human credulity be seduced into hoping for some particular
     thing, or that the minds of the people, for certain, might be excited thereby. And
     thus first offenders are flogged with rods and expelled from the city, but persevering
     ones are thrown into public gaol, or deported, or at least banished.' Since Josephus
     is writing to a Roman audience who officially took such a negative view of prophets,
     he could describe negatively persons he identified as prophets (during his own era;
     those from past centuries would not be a matter of concern) since this was quite con-
     sistent with the viewpoint taken by his Roman audience. However, if he wished to
     present someone in a positive light, such as John the Baptist, then he could not
     identify that person explicitly in a prophetic role, for to do so would create the oppo-
     site effect upon his readers to that he wished his description to have.

(Mk 11.32 = Mt. 21.26 = Lk. 20.6). The Gospels also portray John as a prophet in the style of his teaching. Luke introduces John in a manner reminiscent of the classic OT prophets: 'the word of God came to John' (Lk. 3.2b). The sayings attributed to John in the Gospels suggest the declaration of a message from God, such as would be proclaimed by a prophet.

By itself, the identification of John as a prophet in the NT is neither a christological formulation, nor is it a particularly Christian perspective, because during this period of Jewish history the interpretation of certain figures as prophets was a frequent occurrence, as is demonstrated below (§9.3, 9.4, 9.5). The identification of John as a prophet found in the NT is better understood to be a popular Jewish opinion, though it was not a unanimous opinion, for John's role was a matter of debate.[5] The specific christological interpretation by the Evangelists is that, as a prophet (which, by their presentation, they assume is based upon popular Jewish opinion), John is interpreted eschatologically as the forerunner of the Messiah and as Elijah-*redivivus*. We saw above that it was these interpretive categories which are the heart of the NT's interpretation of John (§3, cf. §3.8); they shed much light on how John was interpreted, and consequently, NT scholars have often concentrated upon these same categories for discussing John.

However, such categories are less helpful for understanding John's ministry within its own socio-historical context. The focus of this chapter is, therefore, somewhat different. We investigate John's prophetic role, not in terms of eschatological expectations, but in comparison with other examples of actual historical prophets during the late Second Temple period.[6] In a similar study, though with respect to Jesus rather than John the Baptist, David Hill expresses agreement with such an approach when he states that

> what is distinctive, as well as what is characteristic, in Jesus' ministry must be argued within this context [i.e. historical 'messianic prophets'], rather than (or, at least as much as) in comparison with the expectations of messianic figures in Jewish apocalyptic literature.[7]

To accomplish such a comparison requires us, first of all, to examine briefly the sources at our disposal and to determine the categories by which the evidence is to be analysed. Secondly, we shall analyse the evidence according to those categories. The comparison of the results of this analysis with John's ministry is reserved for the next chapter.

5   Cf. Mt. 21.24-27 = Mk 11.29-33 = Lk. 20.3-8.
6   For a corresponding discussion of expected, eschatological prophetic figures see Aune, *Prophecy*, 124-26; Horsley, 'Popular Prophets', 437-43.
7   Hill, 'Messianic Prophets', 149.

## 9.2 *The Sources and Categories for Analysis*

### 9.2.1 *The Character of the Sources*

We must note certain limitations which are pressed upon us by our sources. First of all, we are limited primarily to the writings of Josephus and the NT. Furthermore, while the NT provides us with data concerning John the Baptist and, of course, Jesus, its references to other prophets during this period are brief, and add little to what is known from Josephus. They do, however, confirm their existence and the identity of three of them.[8] Therefore, we are left with Josephus as the primary source for our examination.

Another limitation of our sources is their biased perspective. Such a biased perspective is not necessarily wrong, neither is it impossible to eliminate, but it must be recognized and taken into account in our analysis. The christological interpretation of John which I mentioned above is an example of this bias in the NT (§3.8).

Concerning the prophets we will examine, it is obvious that Josephus is very biased in his portrayal. For example, he considers a certain Egyptian who was a prophet in Judea to be a 'false prophet' (ψευδοπροφή-της), brands him a 'charlatan' (γόης), and labels his followers as 'the deceived' (τῶν ἠπατημένων). Such bias may be understandable when we consider that Josephus was interpreting the unrest in Judea prior to the Jewish Revolt and the Revolt itself to be caused by agitation on the part of a few minorities, and these prophets fit his interpretation nicely.[9] Such bias could make us rather skeptical of Josephus' accounts, even though Josephus is generally a credible historian by the historiographic standards of his day (cf. §2.4). However, two factors suggest that, even though he is biased, Josephus may be used critically as a historical source concerning these prophets. First of all, in *Apion* 1.37-41 Josephus takes a 'canonical' perspective concerning prophets; that is, with the completion of the Jewish scriptures, prophetic ministry ceased as it was known in the OT period.[10] In his writings, Josephus uses the προφητ- word group

---

8    Cf. Theudas and Judas the Galilean in Acts 5.36-37; the Egyptian in Acts 21.38.
9    Cf. Rajak, *Josephus*, 78-103.
10   Having summarized the historical period covered by his canon of 22 books, which he states ended with the reign of Artaxerxes, Josephus explains in *Apion* 1.41: 'From Artaxerxes to our own time the complete history has been written, but has not been deemed worthy of equal credit with the earlier records, because of the failure of the exact succession of the prophets'. This viewpoint may reflect a position he held in common with other Pharisees, as it is reflected in later rabbinic literature (*t. Sot.* 13.3). It is often suggested that this was the common interpretation during the first century, but the evidence suggests otherwise. The rabbinic text usually cited is *t. Sot.* 13.3: 'When the latter prophets died, that is, Haggai, Zechariah, and Malachi, then the Holy Spirit came to an end in Israel'. But the text does not end here (though quotations of it in secondary literature often do). It continues: 'But even so, they

overwhelmingly with respect to the OT prophets. Yet, in spite of his canonical perspective with respect to prophecy, he uses this word group nine times to identify prophets relevant to our investigation.[11] That he uses the specific προφητ- word group to identify persons against whom he was deeply antagonistic strongly suggests that he is doing so because either his sources recognize these persons as prophets, or they were widely acclaimed to be such. Thus, Josephus' accounts of these prophets contain elements with which he disagrees, which suggests that, when their bias is taken into consideration, they may be taken as historically reliable.

A second reason for taking Josephus' accounts of these prophets as essentially reliable is suggested by his use of derogatory terms to describe them. These include γόης ('charlatan'), πλάνος ('deceiver'), ἀπατεών ('cheat') as well as the verb ἀπατάω ('to cheat' or 'deceive') indicating both the deceiver as well as the deceived.[12] Josephus uses these same three word groups with respect to Moses' contest with Pharaoh's magicians (and the Exodus in general). In *Ant.* 2.284 Pharaoh, having seen Moses' miraculous signs given him by God, accuses him of being 'a criminal, who had once escaped from servitude in Egypt and had now effected his return by fraud [ἐξ ἀπάτης]'. After Pharaoh's magicians turn their staffs into serpents, Moses responds (in *Ant.* 2.286) by stating that 'it is from no witchcraft [γοητείαν, 'magic' or 'deceit'] or deception [πλάνην] of true judgement, but from God's providence and power that my miracles proceed'. By contrast, in order to demonstrate that Pharaoh's magicians had operated from witchcraft and deception, Moses' serpent devours all the magicians' serpents.[13] Thus, Pharaoh's magicians

made them hear [heavenly messages] through an echo'. The text in *t. Sot.* 13.3-6 continues with examples of this 'echo' (i.e. קול בת; lit. 'daughter of a voice', a reference to the divine voice; cf. Jastrow, *Dictionary*, 1371) heard by various Rabbis, but balances this with the absence of the Spirit. Thus, while the passage still suggests the point of view that prophecy as known in the OT had ceased, nevertheless, God's word was still heard, though through a different medium. Furthermore, the existence of numerous prophets during the first century who were followed by large groups of people clearly indicates that Josephus' viewpoint is in the minority. Other texts usually cited in this discussion are 1 Macc. 4.45-46; 9.27; 14.41. For further discussion see Aune, *Prophecy*, 103-106; Greenspahn, 'Prophecy', 37-49.

11  Josephus uses the προφητ- word group 404 times (προφητεία 38x, προφητεύω 58x, προφήτης 289x, προφῆτις 3x, ψευδοπροφήτης 16x). The nine uses of the προφητ- word group which concern us are: *War* 1.68, 69; 2.161, 261; 6.285, 286; *Ant.* 13.299; 20.97, 169. Five references do not refer to OT prophecy, yet five are not relevant to our investigation. *War* 4.387 seems to refer to the OT, but no biblical source is found. *War* 2.159 is unclear whether OT prophets are referred to or not. *Ant.* 1.240; *Apion* 1.249, 312 refer to extra-canonical prophets which are irrelevant.

12  For γόης see *War* 2.261; *Ant.* 20.97; 20.167; 20.188 (cf. also *War* 2.264; *Ant.* 20.160); for πλάνος see *War* 2.259; for ἀπατεών see *War* 2.259; 6.288; *Ant.* 20.167; and for ἀπατάω see *War* 2.261; *Ant.* 20.98 (cf. also *Ant.* 20.160).

13  Josephus also defends Moses from the charge of γοητεία ('magic' or 'deceit') with

are charlatans, deceivers and cheats, but Moses is none of these; he is God's true prophet who leads the people of Israel in the Exodus. Later, when describing the prophets with which we are concerned, Josephus employs these same three derogatory terms. Yet the interesting point to observe is that the actions which are attributed to these 'deceiving, cheating' prophets are not actions parallel to Pharaoh's magicians, but rather actions reminiscent of Moses and the events of the Exodus/Conquest, such as leading people into the desert or crossing the Jordan. I examine this Exodus/Conquest motif below (§9.5.1, 9.5.3, 10.5). The point I wish to make here is that, while Josephus denounces these prophets with the negative terms which he attributes to Pharaoh's magicians, the fact that his accounts portray the prophets' actions in positive terms of Exodus/Conquest motifs is strong evidence that the descriptions of these actions may be taken as historically reliable.[14]

Finally, a third limitation of our sources lies in the amount of data they contain. For example, in the *Jewish War* Josephus is not attempting to write a history of prophetic movements, but a history of the period up to and including the first Jewish Revolt. He mentions these prophets primarily to illustrate the unrest among the Jewish people during this period. He also uses in the same way examples of other types of movements, including bandits, Messiahs, the fourth philosophy, the Zealots and the Sicarii (cf. *War* 2.253-63). Thus, the information Josephus provides concerning these prophets is scanty, due to the limited purpose they serve within his narrative. There is much more we would desperately like to know, but many questions simply have to be left unanswered. But Josephus' descriptions do provide sufficient data to answer certain questions.

### 9.2.2 *The Categories for Analysis*

Various categories have been suggested for a typology of prophecy and prophets during the Second Temple period. Most of these are broader than our concerns here since they include elements outside of Palestine (e.g. Philo), as well as phenomena other than historical persons (e.g. apocalyptic literature, or eschatologically-expected figures). A brief survey of several of these typologies reveals both their strengths and weaknesses and provides a basis upon which to construct the typology which will be used here.

---

respect to the Exodus from Egypt (*Ant.* 2.320), as well as from being a γόης ('charlatan') and a ἀπατεών ('cheat') in general (*Apion* 2.146, 161).

14  The basis for this argument was suggested by Horsley, 'Popular Prophets', 455; Horsley, 'Popular Prophetic Movements', 4-5; cf. Barnett, 'Jewish Sign Prophets', 683.

Rudolf Meyer's discussion of 'Prophecy and Prophets in the Judaism of the Hellenistic-Roman Period'[15] has made an important and influential contribution. After examining the issue of the existence of prophecy during this period, Meyer divides his discussion into two parts: historical manifestations and apocalyptic literature. Since the second part is beyond the confines of our discussion, we will concentrate only on the first. He categorizes the historical manifestations of prophecy into five areas. His first area is entitled 'prophetic experience according to Palestinian sources' which includes a discussion of Daniel, the Teacher of Righteousness, Essene seers, and Joshua ben Hananiah. This, however, is not really a separate type because he is discussing prophecy in a more general way, so that most of his examples are also included in his other sections. Meyer's next category is 'prophecy in the light of Alexandrian theology' which is an examination of the sapiential orientation of prophecy in Philo. This category is beyond the geographic confines of our discussion. His third category is 'seers and prophets' under which he discusses Essene seers, Pharisaic seers, rabbinic seers, Zealot prophets, and Joshua ben Hananiah. By his title he seems to imply that seers and prophets are distinct, but he does not distinguish between them for he uses the terms interchangeably. While these examples are relevant to our discussion, Meyer is combining types which would be better kept distinct. This will become clearer when I suggest an alternative typology below. His fourth category is 'the ruler with the threefold office' by which he is referring to John Hyrcanus. Again, this is an example which will also concern us, but it is unclear why this one example merits a separate category. We will see below that this example fits better as part of another category. Meyer's final category is 'messianic prophets' in which he includes the Samaritan, Theudas, the Egyptian, Jonathan of Cyrene, Simon bar Kochba, as well as other, later examples. This category is most appropriate, but the term he has used is unfortunate. While no doubt the role of prophet and Messiah may be seen in a single person (e.g. Jesus), it is better to keep these roles separate for the purposes of analysis; they are distinct social phenomena. In actual fact, Meyer's definition of a messianic prophet involves neither a messianic figure nor a ruler.[16] Furthermore, until Simon bar Kochba none of Meyer's examples have a specific messianic character to them.

Jürgen Becker has contributed a more extensive typology.[17] He pro-

---

15   Meyer, 'προφήτης', 6.812-28.
16   Meyer ('προφήτης', 6.826) explains that 'the orientation of the Messianic prophet is to the immediate future. He and his followers expect a miracle of accreditation whereby the legitimacy of the prophet will be demonstrated and the age of salvation will open.'
17   Becker, *Johannes der Täufer*, 41-54.

poses four basic types of prophets with a number of subcategories. (1) The prophet who, in continuity with the OT prophetic function, knows God's will for cases not provided for in the law by virtue of being endowed with the Spirit (1 Macc. 4.46; 14.41). (2) The prophet who may be characterized as political-nationalistic but without an eschatological self-understanding; this type has two subcategories: (a) those without a party program (e.g. the Essenes, Menahem and Simon, Josephus), and (b) those with a party program (e.g. Zealot prophets). (3) The eschatological prophet, of which there are five subcategories: (a) those who claim to perform wonders which make typological assimilations from Israel's time in the wilderness (e.g. Theudas, the Egyptian); (b) Elijah-*redivivus*; (c) messianic prophets (e.g. the Samaritan); (d) a prophet like Moses; and (e) Moses-*redivivus*. (4) Charismatic prophets who suppose that Israel has gambled away its claim to salvation and see a new way to escape judgment through a call to repentance (e.g. the Teacher of Righteousness, John the Baptist). Becker's typology suffers from a number of weaknesses. First of all, it confuses historical prophets with theoretical types as well as eschatologically expected prophets. For example, while Theudas is a historical prophet, the references in 1 Maccabees are only to a theoretical prophet, and the category of Elijah-*redivivus* expresses an eschatological hope. Such diverse references can hardly be considered aspects of one major category. A second criticism is that certain of his categories are questionable. For example, it is unclear what distinguishes his fourth category from the third, that is the charismatic prophets and the eschatological prophets. Also questionable is his category of Zealot prophets, for recent discussions of the identity and role of the Zealots render such a category obsolete.[18] Furthermore, as I suggested earlier, the idea of messianic prophets tends to confuse the two phenomena of prophets and Messiahs, and are better kept distinct from one another.[19]

David Aune's discussion is more sensitive to some of the issues which were weaknesses in the earlier discussions by Meyer and Becker.[20] He proposes four major types of prophecy. The first is apocalyptic litera-

18  Cf. Borg, 'Term "Zealot" ', 504-12; Smith, 'Zealots and Sicarii', 1-19; Horsley, 'Zealots', 159-92; against Hengel, *Zealots*.
19  For further discussion, see Aune, *Prophecy*, 107; Horsley, 'Popular Prophets', 445-46.
20  Aune, *Prophecy*. Chronologically prior to Aune's work is that by David Hill (*New Testament Prophecy*), but he provides no typological analysis of prophecy. Instead, he discusses prophecy in Second Temple Judaism primarily according to its various literary sources (e.g. intertestamental literature, Josephus, Philo, etc.). This different approach is probably due to his more narrow focus upon the phenomenon of prophecy in the NT. His discussion of the issues is still helpful even though it does not contribute a typology.

ture, in which he discusses apocalypticism's major literary and social features. The second category is eschatological prophecy, in which he distinguishes two forms: some eschatological prophecy exists outside of a millenarian movement (e.g. Joshua ben Hananiah), or as a focal feature of such a movement (e.g. Theudas, the Egyptian, the Samaritan, Judas the Galilean, etc.). However, his discussion of eschatological prophecy also includes the expectation of eschatological deliverers, whether messianic or prophetic. This is perhaps the weakest area in Aune's discussion. He has not distinguished messianic expectation from prophetic expectation, and he has placed eschatological expectation as a category parallel to historical phenomena. His third category is clerical prophecy, referring to those prophets who have priestly functions (e.g., Caiaphas, Josephus, Jadda). His fourth and final category is sapiential prophecy. In this category Aune distinguishes between Palestinian examples (e.g. Yohanan ben Zakkai, R. Eliezer ben Hyrcanus, various Essenes) and those in the Diaspora (e.g. Philo).

The most recent work in this area has been done by Richard A. Horsley, though his analysis is more limited, because he concentrates only on phenomena during the latter part of the Second Temple period within Palestine. He clearly distinguishes the ideal and eschatological types from concrete historical phenomena; the failure to make such a distinction was a weakness we noted with earlier suggestions. His analysis of prophets within Palestine classifies them into two broad groups which he labels seers and prophets.[21] He divides the prophets into two groups according to whether they were oracular prophets, that is individuals who pronounced oracles, and action prophets, that is individuals who led movements in '*actions* of deliverance as agents of God'.[22] His analysis is most helpful, and we will use his insights below. However, while I agree essentially with his analysis of the categories, his choice of terms is unfortunate. To identify oracular prophets by the term 'oracle' and action prophets by the term 'action' implies that action prophets did not pronounce oracles. Yet the very actions in which they were calling the people to become involved strongly suggest that the means of calling would have included some form of oracular message. Furthermore, the term 'action' and 'oracle' classify two different elements of the individual's prophetic ministry. 'Action' describes what the prophet did along with his audience, while 'oracle' describes what the prophet himself did. Another weakness of Horsley's proposed typology is its failure to recognize that he has included two forms in his category of seer which are probably better kept separate, as suggested by Aune's typology; that is,

---

21   Horsley, 'Popular Prophets', 435-63; Horsley and Hanson, *Bandits*, 135-89.
22   Horsley, 'Popular Prophets', 454, his emphasis.

the clerical and the sapiential types of prophet.

In light of the criticisms I have made, I would suggest that the best typology is one in which *parallel categories characterize the same element*. This approach prevents us from comparing apples with elephants, and it assists us in observing the same phenomena in each case. A typology could be constructed according to the content, form or nature of the prophecy; it could be according to the social role of the prophet, or even the type of response required by the prophecy. Therefore, from my point of view, there is no single best typology. Rather, one should construct a typology to suit one's perspective and purpose.[23] One appropriate typology is one in which the broadest categories are based upon the nature of prophecy, which I would understand to be three: (1) prophecy as literature (e.g. apocalyptic literature); (2) prophecy as concepts (e.g. OT forms as models, ideal forms, eschatological expectation); and (3) prophecy as persons. Since it is this last category that is heart of our concern, it must be developed further. These actual, historical prophets could be categorized in various ways, as I have suggested above. However, the most helpful for our purposes are terms identifying the social sphere or identity of the prophet. For this the categories offered by Aune are appropriate: (1) clerical prophets, and (2) sapiential prophets. The sapiential prophets could be sub-divided according to their sectarian affiliation, that is, Pharisaic or Essene. However, Aune's third category of eschatological prophets does not identify the social identity of these prophets. Therefore, I would suggest that a better characterization would be popular prophets, whose prophetic ministry involved them primarily with the common people. By 'popular' I do not mean that everyone liked them, but rather that their social sphere was primarily with the common populace—the peasants.[24] Both Aune and Horsley further divide these popular prophets according to their social role, but I argued above that their terminology was inappropriate. I would suggest instead the terms 'solitary' prophet and 'leadership' prophet. In both cases, the prophet announced oracles to the people, but these terms which I propose distinguish their social role with respect to those people. The solitary prophet

---

23  The typologies I have described, and the one I propose, are based upon etic categories; that is, categories of analysis which are foreign to the persons or culture being studied. It is possible to study the phenomenon of prophecy from the perspective of emic concerns (descriptions from the point of view of the native), but such an approach would not suit our concerns here. The sub-title of Barton's *Oracles of God* suggests such an emic approach: *Perceptions of Ancient Prophecy in Israel after the Exile*. For further description of emics and etics, and their application to biblical studies, see Brett, 'Four or Five Things', 357-77.

24  A common dictionary definition (e.g. *Collins English Dictionary*, 1193) for the word 'popular' is not only 'widely favoured or admired'; the term may also signify 'connected with, representing, or prevailing among the general public'. Cf. Horsley's use ('Popular Prophets', 437) of the term 'popular prophet'.

proclaimed a message to the people, but remained a lone individual, a solitary figure. The leadership prophet, on the other hand, also proclaimed a message to the people, but the role extended to include leading a large group of those people in a movement.[25]

John Elliott has recently proposed a matrix model for analysing various interest groups in first-century Palestine.[26] For the discussion to follow, I wish to use this as a guide for analysing the prophets with which we are concerned. Unfortunately, for many of the categories we simply have no data, while for others we are only able to make inferences. However, Josephus does provide us with enough data to make comparisons in a number of categories. These categories may be divided into two areas of social factors as well as ideology and strategy. We will consider the following social factors: (1) prophet's class and/or status; (2) group class and/or status; (3) group size; (4) geographic location; (5) support and alliances; and (6) opposition. We also examine the following elements of their strategy and ideology: (1) interests and goals; (2) tactics; (3) symbols; (4) beliefs; (5) nature of prophecy; (6) subjects of prophecy; and (7) methods of prophecy.[27]

The following analysis is based upon the typology and categories suggested above. We examine in turn clerical prophets, sapiential prophets and popular prophets.

### 9.3 *Clerical Prophets*

Of the nine times Josephus uses the προφητ- word group for extracanonical figures, three are with respect to John Hyrcanus I (135–104 BCE). He was not simply a prophet, but rather a prince and high priest with prophetic powers. He is particularly significant due to the fact that, not only does Josephus use the προφητ- word group to describe him, these are the only times Josephus uses this word group with a positive evaluation of the person.[28] He states in *War* 1.68-69 that John was

---

25  It should be noted that any typology designed for social analysis creates ideals. Historical reality does not necessarily conform to these ideal categories in every respect. For example, I discuss in §9.5.2 whether the unnamed prophet who proclaimed during the seige of Jerusalem in the first Jewish War (*War* 6.285) should be classified as a leadership or a solitary prophet.

26  Elliott, 'Social-Scientific Criticism', 18-21.

27  I have deleted a number of categories from Elliott's list because Josephus does not provide us with the necessary data for those categories, especially for the popular prophets. With respect to a discussion of Essenes and Pharisees, data would have been available for more of the categories, but a complete analysis of these sects are not necessary for the purposes of this work. Since this is specifically an analysis of prophets I have added three categories which examine the element of prophecy in particular; that is, the nature, subjects and methods of prophecy.

28  This positive evaluation is due no doubt to the fact that Josephus considered himself

> truly a blessed individual and one who left no ground for complaint against
> fortune as regards himself. He was the only man to unite in his person
> three of the highest privileges: the supreme command of the nation, the
> high priesthood, and the gift of prophecy [προφητείαν]. For so closely was
> he in touch with the Deity, that he was never ignorant of the future; thus he
> foresaw [προεῖδεν] and predicted [προεφήτευσεν] that his two elder sons
> would not remain at the head of affairs.

In the parallel passage in *Ant.* 13.299-300, Josephus explains that John

> was accounted by God worthy of three of the greatest privileges, the rule of
> the nation, the office of high-priest, and the gift of prophecy [προφητείας];
> for the Deity was with him and enabled him to foresee [πρόγνωσιν] and
> foretell [προλέγειν] the future; so, for example, he foretold [προεῖπεν] of
> his two elder sons that they would not remain masters of the state.

A little later, in *Ant.* 13.322, Josephus clarifies further how John's prophetic gift functioned in this instance:

> Of all his sons Hyrcanus loved best the two elder ones, Antigonus and
> Aristobulus; and once when God appeared to him in his sleep, he asked
> Him which of his sons was destined to be his successor. And when God
> showed him the features of Alexander, he was grieved that this one should
> be heir of all his possessions . . .

Under the leadership of John's father, Simon Maccabeus, the Hasmonean dynasty had been formed, combining the hereditary roles of high
priest and prince (1 Macc. 14.41; cf. *War* 1.53). Thus, Josephus' reference to John is in light of this dynasty as well as a positive recognition of
his prophetic gift. In Josephus' account it is quite evident that John's
roles of high priest and leader are associated with his prophetic gift.
That this is to be classified as clerical prophecy is made clear by the one
other example that Josephus provides of John's prophetic gift, for he
experiences a prophetic vision while engaged in his priestly duties:

> Now about the high priest Hyrcanus an extra-ordinary story is told how the
> Deity communicated with him, for they say that on the very day on which
> his sons fought with Cyzicenus, Hyrcanus, who was alone in the temple,
> burning incense as high priest, heard a voice saying that his sons had just
> defeated Antiochus. And on coming out of the temple he revealed this to
> the entire multitude, and so it actually happened [*Ant.* 13.282-83].

The other relevant example of clerical prophecy is Josephus himself.
Though he never uses the προφητ- word group of himself, it is evident
that Josephus considers himself to be a prophet. This requires clarification because, as we discussed above, Josephus took a canonical view of
prophecy; that is, prophecy had ended with the canonical prophets

> a clerical prophet, as well as a priest of the royal, Hasmonean line. Thus, John
> Hyrcanus I was very similar to Josephus' perception of his own identity.

(§9.2.1; cf. *Apion* 1.41). Yet Josephus believed that God still used 'certain individuals as instruments for revealing the course of the future and guiding the destinies of his people'.[29] The most well-known example of Josephus' exercise of this gift is his prophecy concerning Vespasian becoming Caesar. In a private audience with Vespasian Josephus quotes himself as saying:

> You imagine, Vespasian, that in the person of Josephus you have taken a mere captive; but I come to you as a messenger [ἄγγελος] of greater destinies. Had I not been sent on this errand by God, I knew the law of the Jews and how it becomes a general to die. To Nero do you send me? Why then? Think you that [Nero and] those who before your accession succeed him will continue? You will be Caesar, Vespasian, you will be emperor, you and your son here. Bind me then yet more securely in chains and keep me for yourself; for you, Caesar, are master not of me only, but of land and sea and the whole human race. For myself, I ask to be punished by stricter custody, if I have dared to trifle with the words of God [*War* 3.400-402].

The precise nature of this prophecy is not so much simple prediction, but predicting that an already known prediction would be fulfilled in a specific person.[30] The prior prediction was concerning the rise of a world ruler from the region of Judea.[31] Later, Vespasian released Josephus because his prophecy was fulfilled (*War* 4.622-29; cf. 3.407-408). Josephus also claims that 'he had foretold [προειπεῖν] to the people of Jotapata that their city would be captured after forty-seven days and that he himself would be taken alive by the Romans' (*War* 3.406-407).

In another passage, Josephus explains how he made his predictions. He is in a cave, surrounded by Roman soldiers, and is being urged to surrender. He states concerning himself that

> suddenly there came back into his mind those nightly dreams, in which God had foretold [προεσήμανεν] to him the impending fate of the Jews and the destinies of the Roman sovereigns. He was an interpreter of dreams and skilled in divining the meaning of ambiguous utterances of the Deity; a priest himself and of priestly descent, he was not ignorant of the prophecies

---

29  Blenkinsopp, 'Prophecy and Priesthood', 256.

30  Aune (*Prophecy*, 140-41) rightly considers the account to be essentially historical because it is confirmed by Suetonius (*Vesp.* 5.6) and Dio Cassius (65.1.4). A similar prophecy is supposed to have been made by R. Yohanan ben Zakkai (*A.R.N.* 4.5; *b. Git.* 56a-b). Aune points out that the form of the prophecy is that of a recognition oracle, similar to others in the OT.

31  In *War* 6.312-13 Josephus explains: 'But what more than all else incited them to the war was an ambiguous oracle, likewise found in their sacred scriptures, to the effect that at that time one from their country would become ruler of the world. This they understood to mean someone of their own race, and many of their wise men went astray in their interpretation of it. The oracle, however, in reality signified the sovereignty of Vespasian, who was proclaimed Emperor on Jewish soil.' A similar report is provided by Tacitus (*Hist.* 5.13) and Suetonius (*Vesp.* 4.5). On the relationship of Josephus' account to that of these two historians, see Thackeray, *Josephus*, 37-38.

in the sacred books. At that hour he was inspired [ἔνθους γενόμενος] to read their meaning, and, recalling the dreadful images of his recent dreams, he offered up a silent prayer to God. 'Since it pleases thee', so it ran, 'who didst create the Jewish nation, to break thy work, since fortune has wholly passed to the Romans, and since thou has made choice of my spirit to announce the things that are to come [τὰ μέλλοντα εἰπεῖν], I willingly surrender to the Romans and consent to live; but I take thee to witness that I go, not as a traitor, but as thy minister [διάκονος]' [*War* 3.351-54].

From this explanation, it becomes clear that Josephus claims to have understood himself to be God's servant (διάκονος), and that his gift was an inspired (ἔνθεος) interpretation of either dreams which he had received or of prophecies in scripture. Josephus believed that he possessed this gift because he was 'a priest himself and of priestly descent'.[32] While he does not identify this gift using the προφητ- word group, the nature of the gift is essentially the same as that in his description of John Hyrcanus I, and thus we may legitimately consider it to be 'prophecy'.[33]

Further support for considering Josephus under the rubric of clerical prophecy is provided by Joseph Blenkinsopp.[34] He demonstrates that Josephus portrayed the biblical prophets as historians, and that his own task as a historian was to complete Jewish history from the point where the canonical prophets left off. 'Josephus could find grounds in the biblical material and its interpretation in contemporary Judaism for the prophetic character of his life's work as historian.'[35] Blenkinsopp traces Josephus' prophetic self-understanding to his claim of priestly status through the Hasmoneans (*Life* 1-6). Thus Josephus not only perceived himself from a priestly point of view, but actually claimed to be in the royal lineage of the high priest.[36]

To summarize thus far, we may observe that clerical prophets in late Second Temple Palestine were priests, who exercised some form of prophetic gift which was associated with their priestly status. Those of whom we are aware were aristocratic priests, associated with the upper or ruling class.[37] Whether the prophecy was also associated with their upper class status is not clear, but no evidence of prophecy exists among the rural or common priests. These clerical prophets also had alliances

32  In *Life* 208-11 Josephus narrates his experience of another visionary dream.
33  Cf. the similar description of the sapiential prophets in §9.4.
34  Blenkinsopp, 'Prophecy and Priesthood', 239-62.
35  Blenkinsopp, 'Prophecy and Priesthood', 242.
36  Aune (*Prophecy*, 143) comments: 'His "prophetic" gifts were integrally related to his status as a priest, like Jeremiah and Ezekiel. In his religious party affiliation, therefore, Josephus is more closely associated with the Sadducees than with the Pharisees. . . [I]t appears that "with his priestly charismatic exegesis Josephus is separated from the exegesis of the Pharisees".' (In the latter portion of this quote Aune is citing Lindner, *Geschichtsauffassung des Flavius Josephus*, 146.) Cf. Attridge, *Biblical History*, ch. 3.
37  Cf. the example of Caiaphas in Jn 11.49-52; cf. Aune, *Prophecy*, 138-39.

with sectarian parties. The nature of the prophetic gift they exercised involved prediction, but also included related abilities such as knowing distant events as well as recognizing the fulfilment of earlier prophetic oracles. Their methods of prophecy included receiving and interpreting dreams, hearing heavenly voices as well as interpreting scripture. Their prophecies emphasized political and military subjects, especially the identity of political leaders and military victory or defeat. This may be presented in chart form according to the categories of social description I proposed above (§9.2.2).

Table 1: *Social Description of Clerical Prophets*

| | John Hyrcanus | Josephus |
|---|---|---|
| *Social Factors* | | |
| Prophet's Class, Status | ruling class, high priest | upper class, priest |
| Group Class, Status | | |
| Group Size | | |
| Geographic Location | Jerusalem | various |
| Support, Alliances | Pharisees, Sadducees | Pharisees |
| Opposition | | |
| *Strategy and Ideology* | | |
| Interests, Goals | | |
| Tactics | | |
| Symbols | | |
| Beliefs | | |
| Nature of Prophecy | prediction, know distant events | prediction, recognize fulfilment |
| Subjects of Prophecy | identify political leaders, military victory | identify political leader, military defeat |
| Methods of Prophecy | dream, voice from heaven | dream, interpret scripture |

From this examination of the clerical type of prophet, it is quite evident that at least one form that prophecy may take in our investigation is prediction, for Josephus has explicitly identified the predictions made by John Hyrcanus I to be a demonstration of the prophetic gift. For Josephus, then, prophecy may involve prediction. This perspective concerning prophecy within Josephus is strengthened by observing that Josephus presents the OT canonical prophets from a similar perspective. It is of course true that the canonical prophets did predict future events, but Josephus' 'haggadic embellishments added to the narrative' of the biblical story reveal quite clearly that, for him, 'prophecy consists principally in prediction. . .'[38] For example, in *Ant.* 4.303, Josephus explains that Moses has written a book 'containing a prediction [πρόρρησιν] of future events, in accordance with which all has come and is coming to pass, the seer having in no whit strayed from the truth'.[39] This view of prophecy was common in Jewish thinking of the Second Temple period, being found in other sources as diverse as Philo and the Qumran literature.[40]  We therefore include in this survey of prophets in this period examples of whom Josephus may not have used the προφητ- word group, but who nevertheless exercised this form of prophetic gift.

## 9.4  Sapiential Prophets

Sapiential prophets are so labelled because the social role they fulfil is that of a wise person.[41]  The evidence for such prophets in late Second Temple Palestine identifies them as members of sectarian groups, so I use this feature to distinguish between them.

### 9.4.1  *Essene Sapiential Prophets*
In his explanation of the four 'philosophies' or sects within Judaism, Josephus provides a brief description of the sapiential prophets among the Essenes.  He states in *War* 2.159 that

> there are some among them [i.e. the Essenes] who profess to foretell the future [τὰ μέλλοντα προγινώσκειν], being versed from their early years in holy books, various forms of purification and apophthegms of prophets; and seldom, if ever, do they err in their predictions [προαγορεύσεσιν].

From this description we may observe that Josephus identifies the nature of their prophetic gift to be prediction.  Josephus' explanatory phrase

38  Blenkinsopp, 'Prophecy and Priesthood', 242.
39  Cf. Blenkinsopp ('Prophecy and Priesthood', 241-46) for further discussion and other examples.
40  E.g. Philo, *Vit. Mos.* 2.2-3, 6, 187-287, esp. 253. For examples from the Qumran literature, see the discussion concerning prophecy among the Essenes and the Qumran community in §9.4.1. Cf. also the view of prediction evidenced in apocalyptic literature of the period.
41  In an account which is too brief to use otherwise in this analysis, Josephus describes the physical suffering Herod the Great experienced at the end of his life and mentions that certain persons believed this suffering was God punishing Herod for his impiety. In *Ant.* 17.170, Josephus states that this opinion was expressed 'by the men of God and by those whose special wisdom led them to proclaim their opinions. . .' The verb translated here as 'to proclaim' is προσαποφθέγγομαι, which Marcus and Wikgren (*Josephus*, 8.450 n. d) identify as a *hapax legomenon* in Josephus, and, therefore, one cannot be certain of its precise significance.  Marcus and Wikgren offer the alternative translation 'to predict', which is a reasonable deduction based on the compound of προ- ('before') plus ἀποφθέγγομαι ('to speak, declare'; LSJ [1469] translate προσαποφθέγγομαι as 'to declare before').  Yet, the context does not appear to be a 'predictive' situation.  Nevertheless, we may observe that those who predicted or proclaimed are identified by Josephus as θειαζόντων, which Marcus and Wikgren translated 'men of God', but this verb, θειάζω, signifies 'to be inspired, divinely inspired', or 'to prophesy' (LSJ, 787), which strengthens the notion of a predictive sense for προσαποφθέγγομαι in this context.  The interesting point to all of this is that these men who predicted or proclaimed did so 'by special wisdom' (σοφίᾳ); they were functioning explicitly in a sapiential mode.

'being versed from their early years in holy books . . .' indicates that their gift was exercised through the interpretation of scripture—a skill in which they have been specially trained.[42]

In the course of his writings, Josephus has occasion to describe three individual Essenes with this prophetic gift. The first is the prophecy of Judas the Essene concerning the murder of Antigonus by his brother Aristobulus I (who ruled Judea in 104–103 BCE, following the death of his father, John Hyrcanus I). After narrating how Antigonus died, Josephus explains that

> another feature of this case which may well excite astonishment was the conduct of Judas. He was of Essene extraction, and his predictions [ἐν τοῖς προσαπαγγέλμασιν] had never once proved erroneous or false. On this occasion, seeing Antigonus passing through the court of the temple, he exclaimed to his acquaintances—a considerable number of his disciples were seated beside him—'Ah me! now were I better dead, since truth has died before me and one of my prophecies [τι τῶν ὑπ᾿ ἐμοῦ προρρηθέν-των] has been falsified. For yonder is Antigonus alive, who ought to have been slain today. The place predestined for his murder was Strato's Tower, and that is 600 furlongs from here; and it is already the fourth hour of the day. So time frustrates the prophecy [τὸ μάντευμα].' Having said this, the old man remained plunged in gloomy meditation. A little later came the news that Antigonus had been slain in the underground quarter, also called, like the maritime Caesarea, Strato's Tower. It was this identity of names which had disconcerted the seer [τὸν μάντιν] [*War* 1.78-80].

The parallel account in *Ant.* 13.311-13 is essentially the same except for an addition by Josephus in which he explains more clearly the group which was gathered around Judas:

> But when he saw Antigonus passing by the temple, [he] cried out to his companions and disciples, who were together with him for the purpose of receiving instruction in foretelling the future [προλέγειν τὰ μέλλοντα] . . . [*Ant.* 13.311].

A couple of points are worth noticing from this example. First of all, Judas is clearly a wise man, who has gathered around him his disciples for the purpose of instructing them. While these disciples probably received instruction in other subjects related to being a wise person, the subject specifically mentioned is prediction. This complements well Josephus' description of Essene prophets as those who are 'versed from their early years in holy books' (*War* 2.159). We are not given any indica-

---

42 Thackeray, in the LCL edition cited here, reads the text as διαφόροις ἀγνείαις and translates it 'various forms of purification'. This however does not make good sense in the context. Blenkinsopp, ('Prophecy and Priesthood', 247) prefers the reading διαφόροις ἁγίαις and so translates this phrase as 'holy writings'. He thus sees these three phrases as a reference to the three parts of the OT canon—the law, the writings and the prophets. This makes better sense of the passage and provides further support for the view of prophecy being understood here.

tion of the method by which Judas made this particular prediction. Secondly, the subject of the prediction concerns the future of a political figure (in this case, the lack of a future!), one of the two elder sons of John Hyrcanus I.

The second example of an Essene prophet provided by Josephus is a man named Menahem, who predicted the rise of Herod (the Great) to kingship while Herod was still a boy (thus prior to 37 BCE, the beginning of Herod's reign). Josephus states that he wishes to explain why Herod held the Essenes in high respect, and then proceeds with the following story:

> There was a certain Essene named Manaemus [in Hebrew: Menahem] whose virtue was attested in his whole conduct of life and especially in his having from God a foreknowledge of the future [πρόγνωσιν ἐκ θεοῦ τῶν μελλόντων]. This man had (once) observed Herod, then still a boy, going to his teacher, and greeted him as 'king of the Jews'. Thereupon Herod, who thought that the man either did not know who he was, or was teasing him, reminded him that he was only a private citizen. Manaemus, however, gently smiled and slapped him on the backside, saying, 'Nevertheless, you will be king and you will rule the realm happily, for you have been found worthy of this by God. And you shall remember the blows given by Manaemus, so that they, too, may be for you a symbol of how one's fortune can change. For the best attitude for you to take would be to love justice and piety toward God and mildness toward your citizens. But I know that you will not be such a person, since I understand the whole situation. Now you will be singled out for such good fortune as no other man has had, and you will enjoy eternal glory, but you will forget piety and justice. This, however, cannot escape the notice of God, and at the close of your life His wrath will show that He is mindful of these things.' At the moment Herod paid little attention to his words, for he was quite lacking in such hopes, but after gradually being advanced to kingship and good fortune, when he was at the height of his power, he sent for Manaemus and questioned him about the length of time he would reign. Manaemus said nothing at all. In the face of his silence Herod asked further whether he had ten years more to reign, and the other replied that he had twenty or even thirty, but he did not set a limit to the appointed time. Herod, however, was satisfied even with this answer and dismissed Manaemus with a friendly gesture. And from that time on he continued to hold all Essenes in honour... [M]any of these men have indeed been [graciously granted] a knowledge of divine things [τῆς τῶν θείων ἐμπειρίας] because of their virtue [*Ant*. 15.373-79].

In this example, Menahem's gift is specifically associated with his being an Essene. Furthermore, Josephus associates the prophetic gift with Menahem's virtuous life, identifying Menahem as a wise man (or, in this case perhaps more accurately, a holy man). Josephus makes these links between being an Essene, a virtuous person and the prophetic gift even more explicit in his concluding summary concerning Essene prophets in general: 'many of these men have indeed been [graciously granted] a knowledge of divine things because of their virtue' (*Ant*. 15.379).

Unfortunately, we are not told the methods by which Menahem was able to make his prophetic announcement. But the type of prophecy is prediction and the subject once again concerns a political subject—the identity of a future political leader.

The third example of an Essene prophet concerns the final days of Archelaus' rule (4 BCE–6 CE). Certain leading Jews and Samaritans had brought charges before Caesar concerning Archelaus' brutal and tyrannical rule. Caesar sent a messenger to summon Archelaus to answer these charges. Josephus explains that

> before he was summoned to go up to Rome, Archelaus related to his friends the following dream that he had had. It seemed to him that he saw ten thick ears of wheat that had reached their full growth and were being eaten by oxen. And when he awoke, believing that the vision was of great import to him, he sent for those who were skilled in interpreting dreams. But they were in disagreement with one another, and their interpretations did not come to the same result. Thereupon a certain Simon, who belonged to the Essene sect, asked for a guarantee of safety and said that the vision portended a change in the situation of Archelaus and one that was not for the better. For the oxen signified suffering, since this animal is subject to painful labour, and they also signified a change in his situation, since the earth, when ploughed by their labour, cannot remain in the same state as before. The ears (of grain), of which there were ten, denoted the same number of years, since there is a harvest in the course of each year, and this meant that the term of Archelaus' rule had come to an end. This was how Simon interpreted the dream [ἐξηγήσατο τὸ ὄνειρον] [*Ant.* 17.345-47].

As in the previous examples, Simon is specifically identified as an Essene. Once again the type of prophecy is predictive, but the method of prophecy is through the interpretation of another person's dream. The subject of prophecy is, as in the examples above, of a political nature; this time, it is a political leader's fall from power.

Josephus' summary concerning Essene prophets as well as his three specific examples show a number of similarities with one another. But we should also notice that, with respect to the nature, subjects and method of prophecy, Essene sapiential prophecy is very similar to the examples of clerical prophecy provided by Josephus, especially his own view and experience of such prophecy. Furthermore, Josephus evidently had a positive view toward Essene prophets. This similarity could suggest that Josephus portrayed these prophets in his own image, or at least according to his own understanding of prophecy, and thus his accounts should be rejected. However, corroboration of this perspective on contemporary prophecy among the Essenes is provided by the Qumran literature.[43] They avoided using נביא ('prophet') or נבא ('to prophesy') for

43 This is based on the assumption that the Qumran community were Essenes. Such a simplistic equation may not be entirely correct, but it is reasonable to conclude that the Qumran community represents one form of a multifaceted Essenism. For dis-

their own experience of prophecy, yet believed they had access to revelation through the 'inspired interpretation of biblical texts with reference to present and future fulfilment'.[44] They believed that the biblical prophets did not understand how their prophecies would be fulfilled (cf. the confusion of Judas the Essene), and so they required later interpretation under divine inspiration. For example, 1QpHab 7.1-5 states:

> And God told Habakkuk to write down the things which will come to pass in the last generation, but the consummation of time He made not known to him. And as for that which He said, *That he may read it easily that reads it*, [citing Hab. 2.2] the explanation of this concerns the Teacher of Righteousness to whom God made known all the Mysteries of the words of His servants the Prophets.[45]

Therefore, while Josephus' portrayal of Essene sapiential prophecy is similar to that of his own experience of clerical prophecy, his descriptions of Essene sapiential prophecy may be accepted as reflecting the Essenes' own expression of the prophetic gift. That Essene sapiential prophecy was similar to his own experience probably explains why Josephus presents them in a positive light.

### 9.4.2 *Pharisaic Sapiential Prophets*

It is probable that a similar form of sapiential prophecy also existed among the Pharisees. In *Ant.* 17.41-45 Josephus explains that

> there was also a group of Jews priding itself on its adherence to ancestral custom and claiming to observe the laws of which the Deity approves, and by these men, called Pharisees, the women (of the court) were ruled. These men were able to help the king greatly because of their foresight [κἀκ τοῦ προὔπτου], and yet they were obviously intent upon combating and injuring him. At least when the whole Jewish people affirmed by an oath that it would be loyal to Caesar and to the king's government, these men, over six thousand in number, refused to take the oath, and when the king punished them with a fine, Pheroras' wife paid the fine for them.[46] In return for her friendliness they foretold [προὔλεγον]—for they were believed to have foreknowledge [πρόγνωσιν] of things through God's appearances to them—that by God's decree Herod's throne would be taken from him, both from himself and his descendents, and the royal power would fall to her and Pheroras and to any children that they might have... And the king put to death those of the Pharisees who were most to blame and the eunuch Bagoas and a certain Karos... He also killed all those of his household who approved of what the Pharisee said. Now Bagoas had been carried away by their assurance that he would be called the father and benefactor of him [or better: called father and benefactor by him][47] who

cussion of the relationship between the Essenes and the Qumran community see Schürer, *History*, 2.555-90, esp. 2.583-85; Beall, *Josephus' Description*.
44  Blenkinsopp, 'Prophecy and Priesthood', 247.
45  Cf. 1QpHab 2.1-10; 1QS 11.3-4.
46  Pheroras, the brother of Herod the Great, was made tetrarch of Perea by Herod in 20 BCE and died 5 BCE.
47  Schürer (*History*, 2.505 n. 20) disagrees with this translation arguing that it renders

would some day be set over the people with the title of king, for all the power would belong to him and he would give Bagoas the ability to marry and to beget children of his own.

These Pharisees were influential in the court of Herod in an advisory capacity. Thus it is appropriate for us to perceive them fulfilling the role of wise persons, and, consequently, to consider their prediction as an example of sapiential prophecy. In this example, no specific Pharisaic prophet is mentioned, because a group of them were evidently responsible for promoting this prophecy. It is worth noting, however, that Josephus does imply that one particular Pharisee may have been responsible for the origin of the prediction, because he states that Herod 'killed all those of his household who approved of what the Pharisee said [singular: ὁ Φαρισαῖος ἔλεγεν]' (*Ant.* 17.44).

The nature of the prophecy is prediction, and its method is evidently by means of visions. This is the most probable implication of Josephus' statement that 'they were believed to have foreknowledge of things through God's appearances to them' (17.43). The subject of the prophecy is a dynastic change in the political leadership of the country, from Herod's family to that of Pheroras. That this prophecy may also have had an eschatological orientation is suggested by the incident concerning the eunuch Bagoas. He had been led to believe through the Pharisees' prophecy (or at least Herod thought that he had) that this king would call him a father and would grant him the ability to marry and father children, because this coming king would have all power and thus the ability to perform such a miracle. This eschatological significance may have been derived from an interpretation based on Isa. 56.3c: 'Neither let the eunuch say, "Behold, I am a dry tree" ' (cf. Isa. 56.1-5).[48]

The other example of a Pharisaic sapiential prophet in Josephus' writings is a Pharisee named Samaias. Actually, Josephus refers to the incident twice, and the accounts conflict as to whether the prophecy was uttered by a Pharisee named Pollion (*Ant.* 15.3-4) or his disciple Samaias (*Ant.* 14.172-76). This conflict does not hinder our understanding of the text, and therefore, I will simply use the name Samaias.[49] Josephus is

προρρήσει incorrectly, 'advancing the nonsense that Bagoas is to be called the father of the king who restores to him his ability to beget children!' He prefers (2.505) to interpret the passage to mean that Bagoas 'would be named father and benefactor in a pronouncement made by the future king who, since all would lie in his hands, would grant him the ability to marry and to father children of his own'. Horsley and Hanson (*Bandits*, 108) concur with Schürer's translation.

48  For discussion of the messianic interpretation of this passage in *Ant.* 17.44-45 see Schürer, *History*, 2.505.

49  In *Ant.* 15.3-4, Pollion is named along with his disciple Samaias, but it is Pollion who utters the prophecy. This relationship between the men is strengthened by 15.370 which names these two men in the order Pollion then Samaias, but the passage suggests they each have their own disciples. Nevertheless, the tenor of the passage is

describing Herod's trial before the Sanhedrin. While Hyrcanus II was still ruling (63–40 BCE), Herod had been made governor of Galilee as a young man. With this authority he had captured and executed a bandit named Ezekias and his band. The Jerusalem aristocracy called Herod to account before the Sanhedrin, but when Herod arrived with his soldiers, he overawed them, casting them into confusion. In *Ant.* 14.172-76, Josephus explains that

> while they were in this state, someone named Samaias, an upright man and for that reason superior to fear, arose and said, 'Fellow councillors and King, I do not myself know of, nor do I suppose that you can name, anyone who when summoned before you for trial has ever presented such an appearance. For no matter who it was that came before this Synhedrion for trial, he has shown himself humble and has assumed the manner of one who is fearful and seeks mercy from you by letting his hair grow long and wearing a black garment. But this fine fellow Herod, who is accused of murder and has been summoned on no less grave a charge than this, stands here clothed in purple, with the hair of his head carefully arranged and with his soldiers round him, in order to kill us if we condemn him as the law prescribes, and to save himself by outraging justice. But it is not Herod whom I should blame for this or for putting his own interests above the law, but you and the king, for giving him such great licence. Be assured, however, that God is great, and this man, whom you now wish to release for Hyrcanus' sake, will one day punish you and the king as well.' And he was not mistaken in either part of his prediction [εἰρημένον; possibly better translated 'announcement']. For when Herod assumed royal power, he killed Hyrcanus and all the other members of the Synhedrion with the exception of Samaias. Him he held in the greatest honour, both because of his uprightness and because when the city was later besieged by Herod and Sossius, he advised the people to admit Herod, and said that on account of their sins they would not be able to escape him.

The parallel account in *Ant.* 15.3-4 is important for it identifies Samaias and Pollion as Pharisees. Except for the confusion of names it presents the same picture as in 14.172-76, although it lacks the speech attributed to Samaias. In this account Josephus is beginning his narration of how Sossius and Herod took Jerusalem. Because of the role played by Samaias (or Pollion?), Josephus explains that

> especially honoured by [Herod] were Pollion the Pharisee and his disciple Samaias, for during the siege of Jerusalem these men had advised the citizens to admit Herod, and for this they now received their reward. This same Pollion [or Samaias?] had once, when Herod was on trial for his life, reproachfully foretold [προεῖπεν] to Hyrcanus and the judges that if Herod's life were spared, he would (one day) persecute them all. And in time this turned out to be so, for God fulfilled his words.

such that it suggests that Pollion was the more senior of the two men. The text in 15.3 has textual variants which name Samaias as the one who pronounces the prophecy. This would make the text harmonize with the parallel account in 14.172-76.

Samaias was a Pharisee who, as a member of the Sanhedrin, was part of the ruling class. He was evidently quite influential because he was able to sway the people of Jerusalem to allow Herod to enter. Thus, as a Pharisee who was also a member of the Sanhedrin, Samaias may be considered to be functioning in some sense in a sapiential role. Samaias' prophecy consists of predicting the actions of a political leader, but we are not told the method by which he is able to make this prophecy. It is possible that it is an 'educated guess' by a wise man, which, when it proved accurate, was in retrospect considered to be a prophecy.

Richard A. Horsley's discussion of these two examples of Pharisaic sapiential prophecy tends to minimize their prophetic character. He argues concerning *Ant.* 17.41-45 that, since no particular Pharisaic prophet is mentioned, their prophecy 'appear[s] to have been a kind of political "lobbying" through application of their own or current "messianic" hopes'. For him, this incident is really only evidence of apocalyptic visions among the Pharisees and their 'manipulation of messianic expectations . . . in the thick Herodian-court intrigue'.[50] Horsley's criticisms are inadequate in at least three ways. First of all, he bases part of his argument on his observation that 'no particular Pharisaic seer is mentioned'. However, we observed above that, while no Pharisee is *named*, nevertheless, Josephus implies that the prophecy originated with one particular Pharisee.[51] Secondly, if, as Horsley admits, the incident is evidence of apocalyptic visions and messianic expectations among the Pharisees, then the incident involves a current understanding of prophecy: the interpretation of such visions and expectations to apply to particular incidents and persons with whom the Pharisees were in contact. It is similar to Josephus' declaration that Vespasian would become Caesar.[52] He was applying a current expectation to a well-known figure. Thirdly, Horsley's description of the Pharisaic prophecy as 'political "lobbying" ' and 'manipulation of messianic expectations' is a decision on his part concerning the motivation of these Pharisees and implies a value-judgment that such interpretation and application of visions and expectations is not appropriate and thus not 'real' prophecy. Yet, if some members of Herod's court believed these Pharisees, and evidently Herod took the Pharisees seriously enough to kill their supporters, then, whether we

---

50   Horsley, 'Popular Prophets', 449.

51   In their later work, Horsley and Hanson (*Bandits*, 108) mistranslate *Ant.* 17.44 as '[Herod] also killed every one of his household who approved what the Pharisees said'. In the Greek text, 'Pharisee' is singular, ὁ Φαρισαῖος.

52   In fact, this view of the interpretation of visions and expectations to apply to current persons or incidents is very similar to the Essene interpretation of scripture in a predictive way to apply to the current situation.

like it or not, they perceived these Pharisees to be functioning in some
form of prophetic capacity.

Horsley also finds little evidence for Pharisaic prophecy in the incident concerning Samaias' address to the Sanhedrin. He states that

> Josephus finds here another one of the predictions-come-true that form
> such a typical and frequent theme in his historical narrative. For this very
> reason it may be difficult to claim anything about the Pharisees' prophetic
> activity on the basis of this speech and narrative composed by Josephus (or
> his source).[53]

Again, Horsley's evaluation of the incident has its weaknesses. It is correct that 'predictions-come-true' is a common form in Josephus' re-
writing of the OT, but it is not as common as Horsley implies in his
account of the post-OT, Second Temple period. It is a mistake to
generalize on the basis of Josephus' portrayal of biblical history in order
to down-play a less common element in his portrayal of post-OT history.
Yet Horsley is certainly correct to minimize the historical accuracy of
Samaias' speech in light of Greco-Roman historiographic practice. But,
on the other hand, this point cannot be used to eliminate the incident as
irrelevant. We must remember that ancient historians, when re-creating
speeches, were generally concerned with faithfulness to the context of
the person into whose mouth the speech was being placed.[54] Even
though the speech was probably created by Josephus (or his source), the
incident itself was remembered. It was probably remembered because a
declaration was made concerning the future which later proved to be
correct.[55] Thus, at least with hindsight, some people would perceive
Samaias' declaration as prophetic. It must be admitted that Samaias'
'prophecy' does not seem to require much divine inspiration. It could be
perceived as simply an intelligent person's common sense, applicable just
as much today as then: 'If you let this man go free who has taken justice
into his own hands and killed many people, then he will do it again, and
it could be you!' Thus, to those present (and to Samaias himself?)
Samaias' declaration was probably perceived as a wise and influential
man's rhetorical attempt to be persuasive. Later, remembering the incident, some realized the prediction was accurate, perceived it anew as
prophecy, and passed it on as such. We must remember that a view of
prophecy in this period included the idea that a prophet did not necessarily understand to what he was referring. Samaias' declaration could
fit into this understanding of prophecy.

53  Horsley, 'Popular Prophets', 449.
54  Cf. the discussion of Josephus as a historian in light of Greco-Roman historiographic
    methods in §2.4. On the matter of speeches, see the recent article by Porter
    ('Speeches', 121-42) and the literature cited there.
55  If the confusion of the names (Samaias vs. Pollion) is derived from Josephus'

What can we conclude concerning sapiential prophecy among the Pharisees? From the two examples we have seen, these Pharisees may be perceived as functioning in a sapiential role.[56] Both incidents allow for some form of sapiential prophecy to be operative among them. Yet neither incident is as clear cut in its prophetic orientation as are the examples derived from the Essenes. Furthermore, such sapiential prophecy seems to be a characteristic mark of Essenism, but not of Pharisaism. We could perhaps say that the interests and emphases of the Pharisees were different from those of the Essenes, with the result that it was possible for prophecy to be found among the Pharisees, but it was not a characteristic mark of Pharisaism as it seems to have been among the Essenes.

To summarize our discussion concerning sapiential prophets in late Second Temple Palestine, we have observed that they were associated with certain of its sectarian groups.[57] Primarily, sapiential prophets were Essenes, among whom such prophecy was evidently a prominent feature. But sapiential prophecy could also be expressed among the Pharisees, though evidently it was neither as common nor as important among them as with the Essenes. As literate members of sectarian groups who functioned in a sapiential role, these prophets formed part of the small, intellectual elite of Palestine.[58] They sometimes had associations with the upper or ruling class in an advisory capacity, and in certain cases may be considered part of that ruling class. As prophets, they functioned alone, but some had small groups of disciples to whom they taught this skill. Their prophetic gift involved prediction and possibly the interpretation of earlier prophetic beliefs to be fulfilled in current events as well. The subject of their prophecies focused on the identity of, or future happenings to, political leaders. Most of this prophecy could be considered simply political, but one example had eschatological and messianic overtones. The method of prophecy was primarily the interpretation of scripture, but also included the reception of visions and the interpretation of dreams—skills which could evidently be taught.[59] This may be presented in chart form using the same categories of social description.

---

sources, then this suggests that it is the incident itself which was remembered rather than the specific person.

56   There is also the example of the Pharisee, Josephus. But we have seen that his form of prophecy is closely associated with his priestly identity rather than his possible sectarian membership. He is, thus, better understood as an example of clerical rather than sapiential prophecy.

57   Later, but during the same period, a similar form of predictive prophecy also was associated with another, similar group—Christians; cf. Agabus in Acts 21.9-14.

58   Cf. Horsley ('Popular Prophets', 444) who states that 'although there was really nothing like the modern 'middle class', there was in Palestinian Jewish society at least a tiny but distinctive middle *stratum* of literate groups, called 'philosophies' or

Table 2: *Social Description of Sapiential Prophets*

| | Essenes in General | Judas | Menahem |
|---|---|---|---|
| *Social Factors* | | | |
| Prophet's Class, Status | Essene | Essene, intellectual, wise man | Essene, intellectual, wise man |
| Group Class, Status | Essene sect | Essene sect | Essene sect |
| Group Size | | small (disciples) | |
| Geographic Location | | Jerusalem | |
| Support, Alliances | | | Herod? |
| Opposition | | | |
| *Strategy and Ideology* | | | |
| Interests, Goals | | | |
| Tactics | | | |
| Symbols | | | |
| Beliefs | | | |
| Nature of Prophecy | prediction | prediction | prediction |
| Subjects of Prophecy | | political leader's death | political leader's identity, leadership style |
| Methods of Prophecy | interpret scripture | taught to disciples? | knowledge given by God |

| | Simon | Group of Pharisees | Samaias (Pollion?) |
|---|---|---|---|
| *Social Factors* | | | |
| Prophet's Class, Status | Essene, wise man | Pharisees, wise men | Pharisee, wise man, ruling class |
| Group Class, Status | Essene sect | Pharisaic sect | Pharisaic sect |
| Group Size | | small (group) | small (disciples) |
| Geographic Location | | | |
| Support, Alliances | | court women, Pheroras' wife | Herod? |
| Opposition | Archelaus? | Herod | |
| *Strategy and Ideology* | | | |
| Interests, Goals | | | |
| Tactics | | | |
| Symbols | | | |
| Beliefs | | messianic? | |
| Nature of Prophecy | prediction | prediction, recognize fulfilment | prediction |
| Subjects of Prophecy | political leader's downfall | political leader's dynasty | political leader's actions |
| Methods of Prophecy | interpret dreams | visions | |

## 9.5 *Popular Prophets*

The third type of prophet operating in late Second Temple Palestine was the popular prophet. This term, as mentioned above (§9.2.2), identifies the social milieu of the prophet as being among the common people or populace. In an attempt to define the social role of these prophets more precisely, we further delineate them by observing that some of these prophets functioned socially as leaders of prophetic movements while others functioned alone. Thus I identify them by the nomenclature 'leadership popular prophets' and 'solitary popular prophets'. We examine these prophets in chronological order.

### 9.5.1 *Leadership Popular Prophets*
In Josephus' description of the unrest in Palestine prior to and during the first Jewish Revolt, he has occasion to mention a number of prophets who led large movements. His evaluation of them is consistently negative, and, therefore, we must sometimes read between the lines to discern some of the features of these prophets and their movements.[60]

The first such prophet is commonly identified as 'the Samaritan' who arose towards the end of the period during which Pilate was procurator of Judea (26–36 CE). In fact, it was Pilate's handling of the affair which, according to Josephus, led to Pilate being removed from power. Josephus has been telling of a number of incidents which led to Jewish unrest; he then proceeds as follows:

> The Samaritan nation too was not exempt from disturbance. For a man who had [no qualms about deceit][61] and in all his designs catered to the mob, rallied them, bidding them [κελεύων] go in a body with him to Mount Gerizim, which in their belief is the most sacred of mountains. He assured them that on their arrival he would show them the sacred vessels which were buried there, where Moses had deposited them. His hearers, viewing this tale as plausible, appeared in arms. They posted themselves in a certain village named Tirathana, and, as they planned to climb the mountain in a great multitude, they welcomed to their ranks the new arrivals who kept coming. But before they could ascend, Pilate blocked their projected route up the mountain with a detachment of cavalry and heavy-armed infantry, who in an encounter with the firstcomers in the village slew some in a pitched battle and put the others to flight. Many prisoners were taken, of whom Pilate put to death the principal leaders and those who were most influential among the fugitives [*Ant.* 18.85-87].

While this movement did not occur among the Jews proper, but rather among the Samaritans, it nevertheless is instructive concerning popular

'parties' by Josephus (and often 'sects' by modern scholars). . .'
59   The book of Daniel is an excellent example of this understanding of prophecy, and it is possible that Daniel came to be regarded as a prototype.
60   Cf. the discussion of Josephus' approach in §9.2.1.
61   I follow the translation by Horsley and Hanson (*Bandits*, 163) at this point because

prophetic movements in Palestine, because, while there was much animosity between the Jews and Samaritans, they both traced their heritage back to ancient Israelite history and tradition.[62]

The precise evaluation of this incident is made difficult by the lack of information concerning first-century Samaritan theology. This passage is sometimes interpreted in light of Samaritan eschatological expectation of the *Taheb* or Restorer.[63] However, Marilyn Collins has recently argued that the specific belief in the *Taheb* is probably later than the first century, but had developed by the fourth. In the first century, however, Samaritan eschatology included an expectation of a prophetic figure like Moses who would restore the hidden vessels of the temple, thus restoring true worship in an eschatological age.[64] It should be pointed out that it is a mistake to interpret either this eschatological prophet or the later *Taheb* as a messianic figure, because there is nothing in the Samaritan belief concerning an anointed king. Therefore, the incident of the Samaritan is not to be understood as a messianic movement but a prophetic one.

In Josephus' narrative, the Samaritan instigated a large peasant movement by calling the people to action and promising them events which appealed to their belief in an eschatological prophet who would restore them to an age of divine blessing. He appealed to their interest by using symbols important to their tradition—Mt Gerizim and sacred vessels hidden by Moses. That some of the people who gathered brought arms and fought against the Roman infantry suggests that their view of restoration included freedom from Roman rule.

Another prophet described by Josephus was named Theudas, who arose during the procuratorship of Fadus (44–46 CE).[65] In *Ant.* 20.97-98 Josephus states that

---

Feldman's translation ('who made light of mendacity') is, to say the least, rather obscure English.

62   Horsley and Hanson, *Bandits*, 162-63.

63   Cf. Gaster, *Samaritans*, 90-91.

64   Collins, 'Hidden Vessels', 97-116. For discussion of Samaritan eschatology and especially its belief in the *Taheb* and the coming eschatological age of blessing, see Collins, 97-116; Gaster, *Samaritan Eschatology*, 1.221-77; MacDonald, *Samaritans*, 359-71; Bowman, *Samaritan Documents*, 263-83.

65   A person named Theudas is also mentioned in Acts 5.36 as a person who gathered a group of about 400 persons around him, but he was killed and his followers scattered. This reference is problematic, for the reference in Acts is found within a speech attributed to Gamaliel reputed to have taken place around 37 CE, but the actions by the Theudas described in Josephus' account did not take place until the procuratorship of Fadus, in 44–46 CE. It has often been argued that Theudas is an uncommon name, and it is unlikely that two different persons are being referred to. It is, therefore, concluded that Luke has anachronistically placed this later event back into the mouth of Gamaliel; cf. Haenchen, *Acts*, 252 n. 7, 257-58; Feldman, *Josephus*, 10.53 n.

> during the period when Fadus was procurator of Judaea, a certain impostor named Theudas persuaded [πείθει] the majority of the masses [τὸν πλεῖστον ὄχλον] to take up their possessions and to follow him to the Jordan River. He stated that he was a prophet [προφήτης] and that at his command the river would be parted and would provide them an easy passage. With this talk [ταῦτα λέγων] he deceived many. Fadus, however, did not permit them to reap the fruit of their folly, but sent against them a squadron of cavalry. These fell upon them unexpectedly, slew many of them and took many prisoners. Theudas himself was captured, whereupon they cut off his head and brought it to Jerusalem.

In Josephus' narrative, Theudas claimed to be a prophet, which is one of the few times Josephus uses the προφητ- word group for an extra-canonical prophet, though of course he considers him to be an impostor (γόης). What we know of his prophecy consisted of a call for the people to follow him and a promise that certain events would follow: the Jordan River would part and they would cross it with ease. The intention of this activity appears to have been a symbolic action, but one which was to have practical consequences; this is implied by his instruction that the people were to bring their possessions. We do not have enough information to determine how the action of parting and crossing the Jordan was understood, except that it was clearly building on imagery from the Exodus/Conquest. Horsley suggests two possibilities: it could have been a reverse conquest, by which they withdrew into the wilderness in order to prepare for a new conquest, or secondly, a new Exodus and/or Conquest like the one in which Moses liberated them from Egypt or Joshua led them into the land. Horsley does point out that 'Exodus from Egypt and entry into the land had long been juxtaposed in Israelite-Jewish traditions. . .'[66] It is not necessary, therefore, to identify the precise historical analogy being made in order to conclude that Theudas and his movement were anticipating a new deliverance by God. The use of the Exodus/Conquest motif suggests that delivering the land of Palestine and the Jewish people from oppressive Roman rule was the type of deliverance in mind. The swift and cruel Roman response strengthens this conclusion. Whether Theudas and the people understood this deliverance to be eschatological or not is unclear, but it would be entirely possible. It is clear that they at least anticipated some form of divine inter-

d. However, since in Gamaliel's speech Theudas is placed before Judas the Galilean (6 CE), it is possible that this is a different Theudas whose movement may have been one of the many rebellious actions which took place following the death of Herod the Great (4 BCE); cf. *Ant.* 17.206-323; *War* 2.1-100; Schürer, *History*, 1.330-35 for descriptions of these disturbances. Cf. Bruce, *Acts*, 116 n. 57; Hemer, *Acts*, 162-63 for arguments that two different men named Theudas are indicated by these references. On Theudas being a more frequently used name that is generally recognized, see Horsley's selective (not exhaustive) list (*New Documents*, 4.183-85) of 34 different examples of this name in the papyri; other examples are provided in MM, 290; BAGD, 359-60.

vention, because parting the Jordan River involved the miraculous.

Josephus provides a summary description of several unnamed popular prophets who arose during the procuratorship of Felix (52–60 CE):

> Deceivers and impostors, under the pretence of divine inspiration [θειασ-μοῦ] fostering revolutionary changes [νεωτερισμοὺς καὶ μεταβολάς], they persuaded [ἔπειθον] the multitude to act like madmen, and led them [προῆγον] out into the desert under the belief that God would give them tokens [σημεῖα, 'signs'] of deliverance [ἐλευθερίας]. Against them Felix, regarding this as but the preliminary to insurrection, sent a body of cavalry and heavy-armed infantry, and put a large number to the sword [*War* 2.258-60].

The parallel passage in *Ant.* 20.167-68 provides further, complementary data:

> Impostors and deceivers called upon [ἔπειθον] the mob to follow them into the desert. For they said that they would show them unmistakable marvels and signs [τέρατα καὶ σημεῖα] that would be wrought in harmony with God's design [τὴν τοῦ θεοῦ πρόνοιαν]. Many were, in fact, persuaded and paid the penalty of their folly; for they were brought before Felix and he punished them.

While Josephus and probably others of the aristocracy considered these prophets to be deceivers and impostors (πλάνοι ἄνθρωποι καὶ ἀπατεῶν-ες; οἱ γόητες καὶ ἀπατεῶνες ἄνθρωποι), the large following they developed among the peasants (πλῆθος; τὸν ὄχλον) indicates that they did in fact believe these prophets were divinely inspired, though from Josephus' point of view, it was only 'the pretense of divine inspiration'. They evidently believed that in the wilderness God would act to begin their deliverance, which Josephus and the aristocracy perceived as 'revolutionary changes' and the Romans as 'the preliminary to insurrection'. The reference to 'signs and wonders' and 'signs of deliverance' combined with the symbol of wilderness again alludes to the events of the Exodus and Conquest. Horsley points out that

> Josephus' most striking phrase is 'wrought in harmony with God's design (providence)'. Read against the background of Jewish apocalyptic concepts, this would appear to be an allusion to the 'mystery (rāz/mystērion) of God', which figures so prominently in literature such as Daniel and the Qumran texts... [T]herefore, it is evident that the action-oriented prophets and their movements should be understood as apocalyptically inspired movements convinced that eschatological fulfilment was at hand.[67]

While Horsley perhaps goes beyond the evidence to conclude that these were specifically apocalyptic movements, he is no doubt correct to see them as at least eschatologically oriented.

Josephus' account of these several unnamed prophets is followed

---

66  Horsley, 'Popular Prophets', 457.
67  Horsley, 'Popular Prophets', 456.

immediately by the more specific example of an unnamed prophet from Egypt (thus commonly identified as 'the Egyptian'), whose prophetic ministry took place while Felix was still procurator (52–60 CE). He explains in *War* 2.261-63 that

> a still worse blow was dealt at the Jews by the Egyptian false prophet [ψευδοπροφήτης]. A charlatan, who had gained for himself the reputation of a prophet [προφήτου], this man appeared in the country, collected a following of about thirty thousand dupes, and led them by a circuitous route from the desert to the mount called the mount of Olives. From there he proposed to force an entrance into Jerusalem and, after overpowering the Roman garrison, to set himself up as tyrant of the people, employing those who poured in with him as his bodyguard. His attack was anticipated by Felix, who went to meet him with the Roman heavy infantry, the whole population joining him in the defence. The outcome of the ensuing engagement was that the Egyptian escaped with a few of his followers; most of his force were killed or taken prisoners; the remainder dispersed and stealthily escaped to their several homes.

The parallel account in *Ant.* 20.169-72 states that

> there came to Jerusalem from Egypt a man who declared that he was a prophet [προφήτης] and advised the masses of the common people [τῷ δημοτικῷ πλήθει] to go out with him to the mountain called the Mount of Olives, which lies opposite the city at a distance of five furlongs. For he asserted that he wished to demonstrate from there that at his command Jerusalem's walls would fall down, through which he promised to provide them an entrance into the city. When Felix heard of this he ordered his soldiers to take up their arms. Setting out from Jerusalem with a large force of cavalry and infantry, he fell upon the Egyptian and his followers, slaying four hundred of them and taking two hundred prisoners. The Egyptian himself escaped from the battle and disappeared.

As a specific example of the several unnamed prophets which Josephus had just finished describing, the Egyptian has a number of features in common with them. The reference to the walls falling down is another use of Exodus/Conquest symbolism. It is clearly reminiscent of the defeat of Jericho by Joshua's army in the Conquest. Whether the 'circuitous route from the desert' indicates a prior preparatory time in the wilderness or a symbolic march around the city is unclear. Whichever it is, this again incorporates the wilderness into their symbolism. The reference to the Mount of Olives as the location from which they would enter the city of Jerusalem probably indicates a belief in the fulfilment of Zech. 14.1-4 in which Yahweh is pictured standing on the Mount of Olives battling against the enemy nations who have occupied Jerusalem. While the description by Josephus involves 'forcing an entrance into Jerusalem and . . . overpowering the Roman garrison', this should not be interpreted simply as military revolt by the movement. Because of the imagery involved, and the statement that 'at his command Jerusalem's walls would fall down', it is quite clear that the Egyptian and his followers believed that God would miraculously intervene on their behalf in a struggle to free Jerusalem from foreign domination, just as he did at the defeat of Jericho and was prophesied doing in Zechariah 14.[68]

This was evidently a large movement, though Josephus' estimate of 30,000 may be an exaggeration.[69] That its members were drawn from among the peasants is indicated by Josephus' description of his audience as 'the masses of the common people'.[70] It is interesting that, in contrast to the peasants who joined with the Egyptian, Josephus states that 'the whole population joined [Felix] in the defence' of Jerusalem. By this he is most probably indicating that the aristocratic, pro-Roman elements among the Jews of Jerusalem were afraid of such a peasant movement and wholly supported Felix's actions.

The final example of a popular leadership prophet arose while Festus was procurator (60–62 CE). After describing how Festus was troubled by the Sicarii, Josephus explains that

> Festus also sent a force of cavalry and infantry against the dupes of a certain impostor who had promised them salvation and rest from troubles [σωτηρίαν αὐτοῖς ἐπαγγελλομένου καὶ παῦλαν κακῶν], if they chose to follow him into the wilderness. The force which Festus dispatched destroyed both the deceiver himself and those who had followed him [*Ant.* 20.188].

The brevity of this account makes it difficult to interpret it precisely, but the reference to the wilderness combined with promises of 'salvation and rest from troubles' suggests that this movement should be understood in a similar fashion to those which preceded it. It is evidently based upon Exodus/Conquest typology as were most of the other movements. The people's response to this promise of 'salvation and rest from troubles'

---

68  Horsley, 'Popular Prophets', 458-59. Horsley (458) also suggests that the name 'the Egyptian' may indicate more than the fact that he was from Egypt. It could be 'symbolic, in the typological sense of a leader like Moses and Joshua: having come out of Egypt, he was now leading the people'. While this is an interesting suggestion, it should not be used to support a particular interpretation of the significance of the Egyptian due to its speculative nature. Nevertheless, this suggestion is consistent with the clear presence in this movement of Exodus/Conquest symbolism.

69  The reference to the Egyptian in Acts 21.38 might be a more realistic estimate at 4,000.

70  Luke's brief reference in Acts 21.38 is usually understood to the same incident. He quotes the Roman commander who has rescued Paul from the mob in the temple as asking: 'Then are you the Egyptian who some time ago stirred up a revolt and lead four thousand men of the Sicarii out into the wilderness?' If this statement by the commander indicates a Roman perspective on the incident, then identifying the movement as composed of Sicarii could be a misunderstanding of the movement's composition by the Romans because of their preoccupation with the Sicarii—a movement which had only arisen a few years before. On the Sicarii see Horsley, 'Sicarii', 435-59; Horsley and Hanson, *Bandits*, 200-16.

indicates the feelings of oppression with which they were burdened. This suggests that the movement was composed of the peasant class. Furthermore, this phrase suggests that they expected some form of divine intervention which would bring this 'salvation and rest from troubles'.

### 9.5.2 *Solitary Popular Prophets*
In contrast to the leadership popular prophets, other prophets also had a ministry among the peasantry, but they remained alone, rather than leading a peasant movement. The first example of this form of prophecy takes place during the seige of Jerusalem by Herod (37 BCE). Josephus explains that

> throughout the city the agitation of the Jewish populace [τὸ πλῆθος] showed itself in various forms. The feebler folk, congregating round the temple, indulged in transports of frenzy [ἐδαιμονία, 'experienced spirit or divine possession'] and fabricated oracular utterances [θειωδέστερον] to fit the crisis [*War* 1.347].

Evidently Josephus (or his source) considers these people who engaged in making prophetic utterances to be of the lower class. They may have been peasants from the countryside who had fled into Jerusalem as Herod and his army advanced upon the city. Some who congregated in the temple experienced or expressed some form of prophetic gift. We are not told what were the contents of these prophetic oracles, but we can reasonably assume that they were probably oracles of deliverance in the face of their crisis, because no opposition is recorded as having been expressed against them. Their method of prophecy according to Josephus was possession by a spirit—possibly evil—though those who participated would not take this view. We can describe it simply as the experience of some form of an ecstatic state.

A clearer example of this type of popular prophet is Joshua ben Hananiah. Josephus describes him as the final in a list of portents to which the Jews of Jerusalem failed to pay heed prior to the first Jewish War. Josephus states concerning him that

> four years before the war, when the city was enjoying profound peace and prosperity, there came to the feast at which it is the custom of all Jews to erect tabernacles to God, one Jesus, son of Ananias [or in Hebrew: Joshua ben Hananiah], a rude peasant [τῶν ἰδιωτῶν ἄγροικος], who, standing in the temple, suddenly began to cry out, 'A voice from the east, a voice from the west, a voice from the four winds; a voice against Jerusalem and the sanctuary, a voice against the bridegroom and the bride, a voice against the people'. Day and night he went about all the alleys with this cry upon his lips. Some of the leading citizens, incensed at these ill-omened words, arrested the fellow and severely chastised him. But he, without a word on his own behalf or for the private ear of those who smote him, only continued his cries as before. Thereupon, the magistrates, supposing, as was

> indeed the case, that the man was under some supernatural impulse [δαιμονιώτερον τὸ κίνημα], brought him before the Roman governor . . . [*War* 6.300-303].

Josephus' account continues (*War* 6.304-309) by describing his flogging by the Romans and his perseverence in proclaiming his message for seven years and five months (62–69 CE). Joshua died when, during the seige of Jerusalem, he uttered his final oracle to the people: 'Woe once more to the city and to the people and to the temple . . . and to me also' (*War* 6.309). He was then struck by a stone hurled over the wall by the Romans and died.

Joshua ben Hananiah is described by Josephus as a 'rustic peasant', thus clearly indicating his social class. He evidently arrived from the country for the Feast of Tabernacles and began to pronounce his oracle in the temple, though he probably pronounced it elsewhere in the city as well. He faced opposition primarily from the Jewish aristocracy, but from the Romans as well.

Both Joshua's oracles are clearly poetic in form, though, according to David Aune's analysis, neither conform to the woe oracles in the OT or apocalyptic literature.[71] The term 'voice' is a clearly recognized idiom referring to the voice of God, and its use here in a negative context would be understood by the people as the voice of God pronouncing judgment.[72] It is an oracle of doom announcing that some calamity was going to fall upon the temple, the city of Jerusalem and its inhabitants.

Another example is that of an unnamed prophet during the final days of the seige of Jerusalem (70 CE). Josephus explains that the Roman soldiers in the process of pillaging and razing Jerusalem and the temple proceeded to the final remaining portico of the outer court. Here 6,000 people had taken refuge. The soldiers set fire to it with the result that all 6,000 were killed. In *War* 6.285 Josephus explains that

> they owed their destruction to a false prophet [ψευδοπροφήτης], who had on that day proclaimed to the people in the city that God commanded them to go up to the temple court, to receive there the tokens of their deliverance [τὰ σημεῖα τῆς σωτηρίας].

It is not entirely clear whether this prophet should be classified as a leadership prophet or a solitary prophet. The action taken by this multitude is not that of an extended movement as in the examples of leadership prophets. Yet his oracle did specifically call them to action (in which no doubt the prophet participated). A prophet could pronounce an oracle which might call upon people to take a particular action without it being considered a movement. In this case the action would only take a very

---

71 For an analysis of its oracular form, see Aune, *Prophecy*, 135-37.
72 Aune, *Prophecy*, 137.

short time, and there is no evidence that the group would continue any sustained activity afterward. Furthermore, there is no evidence that this prophet was functioning in a leadership role. So I have included him among the solitary popular prophets. This decision is strengthened by observing that the context indicates that Josephus has selected this prophet to serve as an example of several other solitary prophets who were functioning at the same time (discussed below).

In this example it is clear that the prophet expected some form of divine intervention by which the people would somehow be delivered from the ever-tightening noose of the Roman army which encircled them. Because the prophetic oracle commanded them to go to the temple courts, this expectation of divine deliverance may be based upon a belief that God would protect his temple (cf. Jer. 7.4), but this is somewhat speculative.

The final example of solitary popular prophets immediately follows Josephus' description of the above unnamed prophet who serves as an example for other solitary prophets of the time. Josephus explains that

> numerous prophets [προφῆται], indeed, were at this period suborned by the tyrants to delude the people, by bidding them await help from God [τὴν ἀπὸ τοῦ θεοῦ βοήθειαν], in order that desertions might be checked and that those who were above fear and precaution might be encouraged by hope...
>
> Thus it was that the wretched people [δῆμον] were deluded at that time by charlatans and pretended messengers of the deity; while they neither heeded nor believed in the manifest portents that foretold the coming desolation ... [*War* 6.286, 288].

Josephus then proceeds to describe a number of these portents which included a star and a comet over the city, lights shining in the temple, a cow giving birth to a lamb in the midst of the temple courts, the opening of the temple gates in the middle of the night, the appearance of celestial armies, a divine voice being heard in the temple, and the announcement of doom by Joshua ben Hananiah (*War* 6.289-309). Josephus explains twice that these portents were interpreted by the common people (with the help of these prophets) as portents of salvation, but the scribes and the learned (including Josephus) interpreted them correctly as indicating the coming desolation of the city and temple (*War* 6.291, 295-96).

We are not told to which class these prophets belonged, but they are considered here to be popular prophets because their prophetic ministry was oriented toward the common people. Their oracles evidently announced the imminent deliverance which God would perform on their behalf, in contrast to the oracles by Joshua ben Hananiah which announced God's judgment and their doom. Richard A. Horsley's analysis of the portents, especially the visions of celestial armies, indicates the apocalyptic mood of the people at that time.[73] Thus, the evidence indicates the eschatological orientation of these prophets.

### 9.5.3 *Summary*

To summarize the preceding discussion, we have observed that popular prophets had one of two possible social functions, depending upon whether they led movements or remained alone. The leadership popular prophets may be characterized by a number of common elements. First of all, they led large peasant movements in Judea (and one in Samaria). Secondly, they faced opposition and suffered death at the hands of the Romans, and were sometimes opposed by the Jerusalem aristocracy as well. Thirdly, the entire orientation of the strategy and ideology of these prophetic movements indicates that their primary goal was deliverance. The large response by the people to these prophets indicates the widespread sense of oppression and dissatisfaction among the peasantry, thus leading to felt needs for deliverance which these prophets were able to touch. The limited data concerning these prophetic movements do not make explicit the precise causes for this widespread sense of oppression and dissatisfaction among the peasants. However, a general recognition of the political and socio-economic realities of this period of Palestinian history suggest two probable causes: (1) political domination by the imperialist power of Rome, combined with a sense of frustration with the Jewish ruling aristocracy who were perceived by the peasants as supporting that domination, and (2) economic deprivation resulting from over-taxation and exploitation by rich landowners. These two probable causes do not signify that conditions were terrible in an absolute sense, but rather a condition of *relative deprivation* which leads to a *sense* of oppression and dissatisfaction.[74] Among the prophetic movements we have examined, the most explicit evidence for such causes may be perceived in the Egyptian's evident intent to replace the ruling authorities in Jerusalem. The support given to the Roman opposition by the Jewish aristocracy suggests that the Egyptian was critical of both.[75]

73  Horsley, 'Popular Prophets', 453; Horsley and Hanson, *Bandits*, 182-83.
74  Talmon ('Pursuit of the Millenium', 137, emphasis removed) comments concerning relative deprivation in the context of the development of millenarism: 'The predisposing factor was often not so much any particular hardship but a markedly uneven relation between expectations and the means of their satisfaction'. In many cases this may be traced to 'the inability to satisfy traditional expectations'. Cf. Gager's discussion (*Kingdom and Community*, 27-28) of relative deprivation with respect to early Christianity.
75  Cf. §10.3 for discussion of such political and socio-economic problems as background for the responses by these prophetic movements; cf. also Borg, *Conflict*, 27-49; Applebaum, 'Economic Life', 631-77; Horsley, 'Prophetic Movements', 17-20; Horsley and Hanson, *Bandits*, 1-87; Horsley, *Spiral of Violence*, 3-145.

A fourth common element among these prophetic movements is that their basic tactic for achieving deliverance was to gather their groups together and lead them in a symbolic event at which point they evidently believed God would intervene to perform the expected deliverance. The use of violence by the groups was evidently not part of their strategy (except possibly for the Samaritan); they were trusting rather in supernatural intervention on their behalf. They were pacifist, but they still gathered and were taking an active role in the execution of their expectations. While Josephus seems to downplay this aspect, these prophetic movements were probably eschatologically oriented. Fifthly, the symbolic events employed important images and themes from the past history of the people. For the Samaritans, it was Mt Gerizim and the sacred vessels hidden there. For the Jewish peasants, symbols were derived from the most important time in their past when God had intervened on their behalf to deliver them—the Exodus and the Conquest. Sixthly, we are given little indication of the methods by which the prophets were able to make their prophecies, except that a couple of times Josephus comments about them being under (or claiming to be) 'divine inspiration'. The prophecies themselves were evidently some form of oracle by which the people were called to participate in a symbolic event which they were assured would take place by God's help and lead to their deliverance.[76]

The solitary popular prophets had a number of characteristics in common with the leadership prophets. Either they were peasants themselves or else their prophecies were oriented to a peasant audience.[77] Some emphasized a promise of deliverance, which may also have had an eschatological orientation. We have also one example of a prophet of doom. But in a number of features, these solitary prophets are different from the leadership prophets. The solitary prophets of which we have a record are all associated with sieges of Jerusalem, and thus are more closely identified geographically with this city in particular. Further-

---

76  Barnett ('Jewish Sign Prophets', 679-97) identifies these prophets as 'sign prophets' because some of them promise 'signs of deliverance'. But this nomenclature is inadequate for two reasons. First of all, not all prophets promised signs. Secondly, the sign was not the most important idea, but rather the deliverance to which the sign pointed. A better title from Barnett's point of view would have been 'deliverance prophets'. I have decided, however, to identify the prophets by their social role and function instead of the content of their prophecies; cf. the discussion of my typology in §9.2.2.

77  Horsley ('Popular Prophets', 445) states that 'if a concrete social phenomenon did not identifiably belong to the distinctive literary groups (or, highly unlikely, to the ruling class), then it would almost certainly have been a movement among the common people, the overwhelming majority of whom would have been peasants in an agrarian society'.

more, in some cases, they were identified as prophesying in the temple itself. A second point of difference is that they did not seem to face the opposition which was faced by the leadership prophets. In the case of the leadership prophets, either they or their followers were killed and scattered, in contrast to the solitary prophets who were at least tolerated. This difference in opposition faced by these two different types of prophets may be explained by observing that the felt needs of the people to whom they addressed themselves were quite different. With respect to the solitary prophets, it was not political domination or economic deprivation in general which they faced (as with the leadership prophets), but the more immediate problem of fear of military defeat and death. Thus, neither of the groups of solitary prophets who prophesied deliverance faced any real opposition, though Joshua ben Hananiah, who raised those fears instead, was opposed, though even he was allowed to continue prophesying. The results of this discussion may now be tabulated.

Table 3: *Social Description of Popular Prophets*

|  | Samaritan | Theudas | Several Not Named (under Felix) |
|---|---|---|---|
| *Social Factors* | | | |
| Prophet's Class, Status | Samaritan | | |
| Group Class, Status | peasants | peasants | peasants |
| Group Size | large | large | large |
| Geographic Location | Samaria | Judea | Judea |
| Support, Alliances | Samaritan Council | | |
| Opposition | Pilate, Roman army | Fadus, Roman army | Felix, Roman army |
| *Strategy and Ideology* | | | |
| Interests, Goals | restoration of sacred items, deliverance? | deliverance? | deliverance |
| Tactics | weapons, climb mountain | possessions, go to Jordan, divine help | go to wilderness, divine help |
| Symbols | Mt Gerizim, sacred vessels | Jordan River, part and cross river, (Exodus/Conquest) | wilderness, 'signs of deliverance', (Exodus/Conquest) |
| Beliefs | eschatological prophet | divine help, eschatological? | 'God's design', eschatological |
| Nature of Prophecy | call together, promise events | call together, promise events | call together, promise events |
| Subjects of Prophecy | eschatological restoration | deliverance | deliverance, |
| Methods of Prophecy | | | 'divine inspiration' |

| | Egyptian | One Not Named (under Festus) | Several Not Named (Herod's Seige) |
|---|---|---|---|
| *Social Factors* | | | |
| Prophet's Class, Status | Egyptian | | |
| Group Class, Status | peasants | peasants | peasants |
| Group Size | large (30,000/4,000) | | |
| Geographic Location | Judea | Judea | Jerusalem, temple |
| Support, Alliances | | | |
| Opposition | Felix, Roman army, Jerusalem aristocracy | Festus, Roman army | |
| *Strategy and Ideology* | | | |
| Interests, Goals | deliverance of Jerusalem | deliverance, 'salvation and rest' | deliverance? |
| Tactics | group march, divine help | go to wilderness, divine help? | |
| Symbols | wilderness, Mt of Olives, walls fall down (Exodus/Conquest) | wilderness (Exodus/Conquest) | temple? |
| Beliefs | divine help, eschatological | divine help?, eschatological? | |
| Nature of Prophecy | call together, promise events | call together, promise events | oracles |
| Subjects of Prophecy | deliverance of Jerusalem | deliverance | deliverance? |
| Methods of Prophecy | | | ecstatic state |

| | Joshua ben (Hananiah) | One Not Named (during Jewish War) | Several Not Named (during Jewish War) |
|---|---|---|---|
| *Social Factors* | | | |
| Prophet's Class, Status | peasant | | |
| Group Class, Status | | peasants | peasants |
| Group Size | | | |
| Geographic Location | Jerusalem, temple | Jerusalem, temple | Jerusalem |
| Support, Alliances | | | Jewish aristocracy |
| Opposition | Romans, Jewish aristocracy | | |
| *Strategy and Ideology* | | | |
| Interests, Goals | | deliverance | deliverance |
| Tactics | | go to temple, divine help | wait, divine help |
| Symbols | temple? | temple | |

| Beliefs | | divine help, 'signs of deliverance', eschatological? | divine help |
| Nature of Prophecy | oracle | | oracles |
| Subjects of Prophecy | judgment | deliverance | deliverance |
| Methods of Prophecy | divine inspiration | | |

## 9.6  Conclusion

John the Baptist appears to have been perceived by many of his contemporaries as either functioning, or claiming to function, in a prophetic role, depending upon whether or not they agreed with his ministry. We have, therefore, pursued in this chapter a socio-historical analysis of the various types of prophetic figures who appeared during the late Second Temple period in Palestine, in order to provide a framework in which John the Baptist may be interpreted. The typology used for this analysis is based upon the social roles of the various prophets and, therefore, consists of three main types: clerical prophet, sapiential prophet and popular prophet.

The clerical prophet's exercise of the prophetic gift was associated with his priestly status, and those known to us were in the upper or ruling class. Their prophecies involved primarily predictions of future or distant events of a political or military nature, based upon hearing a heavenly voice or interpreting dreams or scripture.

The sapiential prophet was a person whose exercise of the prophetic gift was associated with functioning as a wise person. As wise persons they functioned in advisory or teaching roles, and thus may be considered as part of the Jewish intellectual elite. The known examples of this type were associated with one of two Jewish sects: the Essenes and the Pharisees. However, while such a prophetic gift was evidently integral to the Essene movement, its association with the Pharisees may have been merely a chance occurrence. The prophecies involved prediction, primarily with respect to the political future of certain figures, by means of the interpretation of scripture or dreams, or the reception of visions. These prophetic skills were taught by the Essene sapiential prophets. One example from a Pharisaic prophet was political, but may have had eschatological or messianic overtones.

Our analysis of popular prophets—prophets whose milieu was among the common populace—was further classified according to whether they functioned with respect to the common people as leaders of a movement or remained solitary figures. The prophetic ministry of the leadership popular prophets was characterized not only by leading large peasant movements, but by the severe opposition and ruthless suppression they received. These movements were oriented toward the deliverance of those peasants from the oppression and dissatisfaction they felt toward their lot. These prophetic figures called the people to gather together and participate in a symbolic action reminiscent of their past religious heritage, especially the events associated with the Exodus and Conquest. The prophetic figures evidently promised the people that the deliverance would take place by divine intervention. These prophetic movements appear to have had an eschatological orientation.

Most of the solitary popular prophets also appear to have had a similar eschatological orientation accentuating deliverance (though one was a prophet of doom). But the ministry of these prophets is associated with seiges of Jerusalem, and, thus, the type of deliverance is military rather than the more diffuse social/political/economic orientation of the eschatological deliverance conceived of by the leaders of the prophetic movements. Because the solitary prophets remained solitary and did not begin large movements, and because the type of deliverance they prophesied did not challenge the *status quo* as did that of the leadership prophets, these prophets did not face the same measure of opposition and oppression that the leadership prophets did.

We should observe at this point that, while the social roles of clerical and sapiential prophets were different, the understanding of the nature, subjects and methods of the prophetic gift is quite similar: they heard voices as well as interpreted dreams and scripture to predict the future. Josephus used in his accounts of clerical and sapiential prophets a number of different words to identify this notion of prediction.[78] However, except for the προφητ- word group, he never used any of these words to describe popular prophets. Rather, he described the popular prophets as 'commanding' (κελεύω), 'persuading' (πείθω) and 'promising' (ἐπαγγέλλομαι). Josephus' description provides very little information concerning the methods by which these popular prophets made their prophecies; what little description he gives suggests that they announced prophetic oracles under the claim of divine inspiration.[79] This distinction

---

78 These include μαντεία (*War* 4.625), μάντευμα (*War* 1.79; *Ant.* 13.312), μάντις (*War* 1.80; 2.112; *Ant.* 13.313; 17.345), προαγορεύω (*War* 2.159), προαπάγγελμα (*War* 1.78), προγιγνώσκω (*War* 2.159), πρόγνωσις (*Ant.* 13.300; 15.373; 17.43), προδείκνυμι (*War* 3.404), προεῖδον (*War* 1.69), προεῖπον (*War* 3.406; *Ant.* 13.300, 311, 312 [2x]; 15.4), προερέω (*War* 1.79; 4.629), προθεσπίζω (*War* 4.626), προλέγω (*Ant.* 13.300, 311; 17.43), προμαντεύομαι (*War* 3.305), πρόρρησις (*Ant.* 17.45), προῦπτος (*Ant.* 17.41), προφητεία (*War* 1.68; *Ant.* 13.299), and προφητεύω (*War* 1.69).

79 With respect to solitary popular prophets, Joshua ben Hananiah's proclamations clearly have an oracular form (*War* 6.301), and Josephus states that 'as was indeed the case, that the man was under some supernatural impulse' (*War* 6.304); 'supernatural impulse' (δαιμονιώτερον τὸ κίνημα) could be translated more expansively as 'a divinely empowered/given impression/emotion'. Similarly, the prophets in the temple during Herod's seige were said to have 'indulged in transports of frenzy

between clerical and sapiential prophets on the one hand and popular prophets on the other hand with respect to the nature, subjects and methods of prophecy suggests that we are dealing with two quite different forms of prophecy. The clerical and sapiential prophets could be identified by the term 'seer' (μάντις),[80] while the popular prophets appear to fit more closely the classical OT forms of prophecy and prophets.[81] We are in agreement, then, with Richard A. Horsley who has argued that those whom we are calling the *leadership popular prophets* and their movements 'are clearly informed by the memory of the great acts of deliverance accomplished through the agency of Moses or Joshua', while the *solitary popular prophets* 'appear to stand in the tradition of Israelite oracular prophets'.[82]

[ἐδαιμονία, experienced spirit/divine-possession] and fabricated oracular utterances [θειωδέστερον]' (*War* 1.347). This latter example suggests some form of ecstatic state.

With respect to leadership popular prophets, Josephus is even less descriptive, perhaps because he has a more sustained negative opinion of them than of the solitary prophets (he was positive in his portrayal of Joshua ben Hananiah). However, concerning the several unnamed prophets during Felix's procuratorship, Josephus states that they operated 'under the pretence of divine inspiration [προσχήματι θειασμοῦ]', with which they evidently led their movements to believe that in the wilderness 'God would give them tokens [better: 'signs'] of deliverance [σημεῖα ἐλευθερίας]' (*War* 2.259-60; cf. 6.285). This description by Josephus may imply that these leadership prophets used prophetic oracles.

80   The μαντ- word group is used by Josephus twice with respect to himself (*War* 3.405; 4.625), four times with respect to Judas the Essene (*War* 1.79, 80; *Ant.* 13.312, 313), and twice in the context of his narration concerning Simon the Essene (*War* 1.80; *Ant.* 17.345). He never uses the word with respect to either type of popular prophet.

81   Horsley ('Popular Prophets', 443-46) makes the same distinction between seers and prophets, though he discusses seers only with respect to the Essene sapiential prophets. But I have shown here that the category of 'seer' extends beyond the sapiential prophets to include the clerical prophets as well.

82   Horsley, 'Popular Prophets', 462; cf. the more extended discussion in Horsley and Hanson, *Bandits*, 136-46. While I agree with tracing these influences back to the Exodus/Conquest traditions of Moses and Joshua and to the oracular traditions of the OT prophets, I argued in §9.2.2 that, with respect to the popular prophets of the late Second Temple period, it is incorrect to distinguish solitary popular prophets as oracular from leadership popular prophets as non-oracular. I do not think Horsley *states* the distinction in this way, but his perspective *implies* it.

Chapter 10

# THE SOCIO-POLITICAL ORIENTATION
# OF JOHN'S PROPHETIC MINISTRY

## 10.1 *Introduction*

A complete discussion of John the Baptist would analyse all aspects of his life and ministry as revealed in our sources. This work is more limited, however, since it focuses on John's prophetic ministry within his social, cultural and historical context. Therefore, while this chapter discusses John's prophetic ministry, it is concerned only with those aspects which assist us in appreciating it within its socio-political context.[1] To accomplish this we consider first of all what type of prophet John most closely approximates according to the typology constructed in the preceding chapter. Then, using several of the elements from the social description of that type, we compare John's prophetic ministry with other prophets similar to him in order to elucidate the socio-political orientation of John and his movement. The elements considered include John's interests, tactics, symbolic event, opposition, and finally his arrest and execution.

The title for this chapter may appear strange if one thinks that John was a prophet and, therefore, that his interests were only 'religious' because he emphasized repentance, forgiveness of sins, baptism, as well as imminent judgment and restoration. Such a view is inadequate on at least two counts. First of all, it represents an inadequate view of what a prophet is. The classic OT prophets, such as Elijah, Isaiah or Jeremiah, had a 'religious' viewpoint, but it was a viewpoint applied to the *social* injustices of the day and the *political* problems facing those in authority. Secondly, this view is inadequate because it separates the realm of religion from social and political issues. While such a dichotomy is possible (sadly) in the modern, Western world, it was not possible in the context of Second Temple Judaism, for Judaism's religious orientation was inextricably linked with its social and political situation. The Torah, both written and oral, was understood to regulate most aspects of Jewish daily life (regardless of the extent to which individuals and groups practised such regulation).[2] The Jewish socio-political organizations and struc-

---

1   For example, aspects of John's prophetic ministry which are not discussed here include John's dress and diet (cf. note in §10.6.2) and the prophetic forms of John's

tures were bound up with the Jewish religious framework, so that any discussion of either the socio-political or the religious structures and organizations of Palestinian culture would include the high priesthood, Sanhedrin, temple, synagogue, Pharisees, scribes, Sadducees, Herodians and the Herodian dynasty, and even the Roman/Gentile presence. All of these had both a socio-political and a religious orientation. In fact, within the context of first-century Palestine, it is difficult to conceive how an organization or structure could be religious without having social and/or political ramifications. Furthermore, at that time the Jewish religious faith was bound up with socio-political concepts of Israel as the people of God and as a nation, the covenantal responsibilities of the Torah for social relationships, the possession of the promised land, etc. Thus, when we appreciate the socio-political elements in the Jewish faith combined with the socio-political context of first-century Palestine an examination of the socio-political orientation of John's ministry becomes essential.[3]

## 10.2 *John's Identity as a Leadership Popular Prophet*

In the preceding chapter we concluded that John was perceived as a prophet by at least some segments of the Jewish populace in Palestine. We therefore analysed the known examples of prophets in Palestine during the late Second Temple period in order to provide a socially-descriptive grid against which to appreciate John. Our first task is to determine into which of the prophetic types John best fits. We may then make certain observations concerning John by comparing elements of his ministry with the features characteristic of that particular type.

It could be argued that John should be classified as a clerical prophet because he comes from a priestly family (Lk. 1.5-23). But there is no evidence that John's prophetic ministry was associated with the temple or his functioning in a priestly *role*. That he came from a priestly *background* assists us in appreciating the function of his baptism, but this is different from a clerical role shaping the expression of his prophetic role.

---

speech (cf. Aune, *Prophecy*, 129-32).

2  Cf. Safrai, 'Religion in Everyday Life', 2.793-833.

3  Schürer (*History*, 1.346) states that John's ministry 'was certainly not without a political impact. For at that time the mass of the people were unable to differentiate between their religious and political hopes.' The unity of the social and political elements with the religious in Judaism is widely recognized, but unfortunately, not always are its inferences appreciated. For example, cf. the recent comments to this effect by Saldarini (*Pharisees*, 5-7) on the study of Jewish groups, and by Horsley (*Spiral of Violence*, 149-55) on the study of the historical Jesus.

The situation in the Middle East today continues to demonstrate the inextricable union between religion and socio-political realities. This is manifested by both Judaism in Israel and Islamic fundamentalism in the Arab world.

This is substantiated by observing that the nature of his ministry is quite different from that of a clerical prophet. Therefore, this alternative for identifying John's prophetic type is not plausible.

It might be possible to argue that John should be understood as a sapiential prophet. It has been argued that John was a member of the Essene community at Qumran. Therefore, if John was an Essene, or had been an Essene but broke away from the sect, his prophetic ministry could be interpreted as that of an Essene sapiential prophet. However, John's membership of the Qumran community is at best conjectural, and most of those who support such a conjecture admit that John must have broken from the community prior to undertaking his prophetic ministry as we now know it.[4] Furthermore, the character of John's prophetic ministry is quite different from that of an Essene sapiential prophet.

John the Baptist's prophetic identity and ministry is much closer to that of the popular prophet. Josephus' description of John as 'commanding the Jews to practise virtue' (*Ant.* 18.117) provides no specific social identity for his audience. But Josephus' description adds a further com-

---

4    Examples of those who support a connection between John and the Qumran community: Brownlee, 'John the Baptist', 33-53; Robinson, 'Baptism of John', 11-27; Geyser, 'Youth of John', 70-75; Steinmann, *John the Baptist*, 5-61. Examples of those who deny such a connection: Rowley, 'Baptism of John', 218-29; Sutcliffe, 'Baptism', 179-88. While there are similarities between John's ministry and the teaching and practices of the Qumran community, such similarities do not establish a connection. It is better to trace these similarities to the common milieu of sectarian Judaism in the late Second Temple period and to the common location of the wilderness and Jordan Valley. That John knew about the Qumran community is highly plausible, for at least part of his ministry was located just a few miles away. But common milieu is not the same as connection or dependence. Such a position enables us to appreciate the similarities without 'explaining' them by requiring dependence, as well as appreciating the differences without removing them by requiring uniformity. Cross (*Library of Qumran*, 152 n. 9) states: 'at best we can affirm that there are contacts between the preaching of John and the teaching of the Essenes of Palestine (and Qumran)'. Similarly, Scobie ('John the Baptist', 69, cf. 58-69) states: 'the Scrolls support the view which sees John in the context of a number of roughly similar groups active in the Jordan valley area and making up a non-conformist, baptist, sectarian movement within the Judaism of the period. This movement forms the background of John's ministry, and undoubtedly influenced his thought at many points.' Cf. Cullmann, 'Significance of the Qumran Texts', 18-25; Wink, 'John the Baptist', 75-103; Vermes, *Qumran in Perspective*, 219.
         Thiering (*Teacher of Righteousness*; *Gospels and Qumran*, esp. 71-77, 108-10) has proposed a theory in which John the Baptist is the leader of the Qumran community and is to be identified with the Teacher of Righteousness. Jesus began his ministry within the Qumran community as the Messiah of Israel, the Davidic Messiah, but led a rebellion against the priestly hierarchy of the Qumran community and established a new, lay community promoting equality. This rebellion and betrayal of Qumran teaching led the Qumran community to name Jesus 'the Man of the Lie'. Thiering's theory is highly speculative and quite implausible. It has not found acceptance with other scholars. Cf. critiques of Thiering's work by Wacholder, 'Review of *Teacher of Righteousness*', 147-48; VanderKam, 'Review of *Gospel* [sic] *and Qumran*', 512-14.

ment concerning John's audience: 'And when others gathered together [around John] (for they were also excited to the utmost by listening to [his] teachings), Herod . . . feared his great persuasiveness with the people might lead to some kind of strife . . .' (*Ant.* 18.118). Josephus is implying that John's audience grew larger to include 'the people' in general. This suggests an audience largely made up of common people. Such an audience is also implied by the evidence of the NT. For example Mk 1.5 states: 'And there went out to him all the country of Judea, and all the people of Jerusalem'. The emphatic 'all' in the description may be hyperbolic, yet it indicates that John's audience was drawn from the Judean rural peasantry as well as the urban poor from Jerusalem. The Jewish aristocracy also expressed an interest in John (Q 3.7; cf. Jn 1.24), but primarily because they were critical of his ministry. John addressed all Israel with his prophetic call, but those who expressed a positive interest in him (those baptized as well as interested observers)[5] and considered him to be a prophet were drawn primarily from the common people, composed of the rural peasantry and the urban poor.[6]

But should we view John as a leadership or a solitary popular prophet? The discussion by Richard A. Horsley and John S. Hanson concerning these prophets (using the terms 'oracular' and 'action' prophets) classifies John the Baptist as an oracular prophet, or in our terms, a solitary prophet. Their decision is based primarily on two points. First of all, in their analysis, oracular prophets were of two types: 'There were prophets who, like most of their classical predecessors, preached repentance and pronounced judgment; and there were those who announced God's impending deliverance, like Second Isaiah and Zechariah'.[7] Horsley and Hanson classify two oracular prophets as prophets of judgment: Joshua ben Hananiah and John the Baptist. Thus, their first reason for including John as an oracular or solitary prophet is because his message is one of judgment. Secondly, they state that 'nothing in our texts indicates that John intended to found a sect or lead a mass movement in a decisive eschatological event of deliverance'.

Both these arguments used by Horsley and Hanson for their classification suffer from a number of weaknesses. With respect to their first argument, I have already criticized above their use of the terms 'oracular' and 'action' prophet for its implication that an action prophet does not pronounce oracles (§9.2.2). Consequently, just because we have evi-

---

5    Cf. Q 7.29-30; Mt. 3.5 = Mk 1.5; Lk. 3.10-14; Lk. 3.15, 18; Mt. 21.26 = Mk 11.32 = Lk. 20.6.

6    On the social structure of Palestine in John's day see Horsley, *Spiral of Violence*, 90-99; Jeremias, *Jerusalem*, 87-267.

7    Horsley and Hanson, *Bandits*, 172-73; cf. Horsley, 'Popular Prophets', 450-54.

dence that John announced prophetic oracles does not mean he is an oracular prophet rather than an action prophet. As well, the content of a prophetic message cannot distinguish between oracular and action prophets because one type of oracular prophet pronounced oracles of deliverance, and the action prophets in promising deliverance would probably have used a similar type of oracle. Therefore, if both types of prophets, oracular and action, could focus on deliverance, then the content of their message cannot distinguish between them.

With respect to Horsley and Hanson's second argument, contrary to their contention, there is evidence that John was the leader of a movement. In the discussion above of John's baptism functioning as an initiatory rite into the true, remnant Israel, we examined Josephus' statement in *Ant.* 18.117 that part of John's message was 'to gather together by baptism' (βαπτισμῷ συνιέναι). We concluded that John was calling his audience to 'gather together' into some form of a group and that baptism is the means whereby the group is gathered. This is explicit evidence of group formation. This group evidently considered themselves to be the repentant and thus the true, remnant Israel (cf. §6.4.5). It is interesting that Horsley and Hanson recognize the initiatory function of John's baptism and that it was the means by which persons entered the true Israel. They state: 'Baptism in the Jordan was the rite . . . by which persons passed into the eschatologically reconstituted community of Israel which would survive God's judgment'. They go on to say that 'the requirement for membership in the eschatological people is, very concretely, social and economic, and not vaguely "spiritual" '.[8] Yet, surprisingly, Horsley and Hanson have not considered the implications of this for appreciating John's prophetic role as a leader: it was John who made the proclamation which called the people to repentance and baptized those who responded. It was John whose ministry and leadership called into existence this 'eschatologically reconstituted community of Israel'.

Another piece of evidence is suggested in Josephus' account by his statement that

> when others gathered together [around John] (for they were also excited to the utmost by listening to [his] teachings), Herod . . . feared that his great persuasiveness with the people might lead to some kind of strife (for they seemed as if they would do everything which he counselled) [*Ant.* 18.118].

The picture here is not simply that of a large crowd gathered to hear John, but of a large crowd gathered together who were excited by his preaching and were evidently committed to doing anything John said. The excitement combined with the existence of a committed crowd suggests the followers of John were in some sense functioning as a move-

8    Horsley and Hanson, *Bandits*, 178.

ment. The NT paints a similar picture: large crowds going out to hear John and be baptized by him (Mt. 3.5-6 = Mk 1.5; Lk. 3.7, 10, 15, 18).

Our discussion of John's perception of imminent judgment and restoration also suggested that his ministry must be perceived as effecting the formation of a movement.[9] This evidence of the formation of a group with John as its leader does not necessitate that the movement be organized in a specific way, or that they engage in a separatist, communal lifestyle (cf. the Jesus movement). Rather, they constituted a group of people who perceived themselves to be distinct from others, manifesting an insider/outsider perspective (cf. §6.4.5). As the prophet whose ideology and ministry created the distinctives which constituted this group, John would have been perceived as the leader of this movement. Therefore, in terms of our typology of prophets, John is a leadership popular prophet.

The socially descriptive analysis of Palestinian prophets in the preceding chapter, as with all social analyses, creates ideals, for the typology is generated from that which is common between them rather than that which is distinctive. But specific historical figures do not necessarily conform to these ideals in all respects, for while they all have some of those elements in common, they also have elements which are different or distinctive. With respect to John's ministry, it is interesting to observe that there are similarities as well as differences with respect to the strategy and ideology of his movement in comparison with the other prophetic movements. But we are faced with a major problem when we attempt to compare his movement with the others: when we include the evidence of Josephus as well as the NT, the quantity and specificity of the data we have for John is so much greater than that for the other leadership prophets. As a consequence, by comparing all elements of this data, John could be made to appear more distinct than he actually was. For example, both Josephus and the NT indicate that John's message included cer-

---

9   §8.5. Other lines of evidence could include the fact that John had a group of disciples who remained with him (Q 7.18-19; Mt. 9.14 = Mk 2.18 = Lk. 5.33; Lk. 11.1). Quite evidently, this group was not coextensive with those who had been baptized by him, for most returned to their homes. Neither was the character of this group like that of rabbinic disciples. They appear to be gathered around John not so much to be taught Torah, but rather to participate fully in John's program. A closer parallel to the composition and structure of John's movement would be that of Jesus. Jesus also had a group of disciples who remained with him, but the Jesus movement also included a larger following who were identified with him, spent short periods of time with him, but did not follow him from place to place. Even long after John was dead, and far away from the location where he ministered, individuals still identified themselves as John's disciples (Acts 19.1-7). It could also be argued that, because the response of the authorities to solitary prophets (opposed but tolerated) was different to that of leadership prophets (opposed and executed; cf. §9.5), the response of Antipas to John's ministry suggests that he was a leadership prophet.

tain ethical instructions. But there is no evidence that the other leadership prophets provided ethical instructions for their followers. One might conclude that John's movement was ethically oriented while the others were not. But, such a conclusion is an illegitimate argument from silence. This silence is to be expected because Josephus does not wish to portray these leadership prophets in a positive light. In fact, there is very little we know of the messages proclaimed by these prophets. The only indications we have from Josephus are brief phrases such as 'promising signs of deliverance' or 'calling the people to follow them into the wilderness'. Whereas, if these other movements were responding to perceived social injustices, it is quite implausible to think that they would not provide instruction concerning social justice. Therefore, we can legitimately compare and contrast John only with the other leadership prophets in those areas where we actually have data for both. Since this chapter concentrates upon the socio-political orientation of John's ministry, the most profitable aspects for comparison with the social description developed in the preceding chapter include the interests, tactics, symbolic event, opposition to and death of John (and his movement).

### 10.3 *The Interests of John and his Movement*

We have seen that the primary emphasis of the leadership prophets lay consistently upon deliverance of the common people, and that deliverance was from the socio-economic and political oppression they were experiencing at the hands of the Jewish aristocracy and the Roman occupying forces. When we turn to John, Josephus' description of his preaching as commanding 'the Jews to practise virtue and act with justice toward one another and with piety toward God' shows little awareness of this specific concept of deliverance, though the principles of virtue, justice and piety are consistent with such a concept. In the NT, John the Baptist does proclaim deliverance, but it is a deliverance from the imminent judgment carried out by the expected figure who will 'baptize with fire', and whose 'winnowing shovel is in his hand to clean the threshing floor' (Q 3.16-17). Viewed superficially, this type of deliverance would appear quite different from the other leadership prophets. But this is not necessarily the case. If these other prophets proclaimed deliverance from oppression, especially with an eschatological perspective which they appeared to have, it would have been natural for them to have pronounced God's judgment upon those who oppressed, and to do so in theological and eschatological terms, as did John the Baptist. That they did so is suggested by Josephus' statement that they believed 'God would give them signs of deliverance' (*War* 2.259).[10] Therefore, other leadership prophets were probably more similar to John in this respect than might appear at first.

But the question to pursue is, did John's movement have implications for the issues of socio-economic deprivation and political oppression in the way evidenced by the other leadership prophets (cf. §9.5)? The precise terminology Josephus used to describe John's ethical imperative reflects categories which would have been more understandable to his Roman audience than those which would have actually been used by John (cf. §2.2, 6.2.1). But if the ideas reflected by those terms are placed within a Jewish context, where especially the ideas of justice and piety are conceived of as having social, communal, and even national overtones, then this ethical imperative would naturally be understood as focusing on those social, communal and political aspects of life in which there was injustice and impiety. This socio-political orientation was an integral part of the Jewish people's deep religious and ethical heritage as God's covenant people and nation. This heritage with its socio-political orientation stands in stark contrast with the socio-political realities the people faced. No doubt many aspects of Jewish life in Palestine during the late Second Temple period would have been viewed as unjust, but two general aspects were frequently experienced by the common people which would naturally come to mind if they heard a call such as the one John proclaimed.

The first aspect is the socio-political struggle of a people subjugated to foreign domination, whether directly, as in Judea, where a Roman governor ruled, or indirectly, as in Galilee and Perea, where a client ruler ruled on behalf of Rome. In either case, a proud and independent people were being subjugated to rule by a foreign imperial power.[11] The issue is not as straightforward as 'Romans vs. Jews', because some Jewish people supported the domination of Rome, and benefited thereby. These would have included wealthy landowners as well as the temple establishment and some of the leading Jewish families.[12] But the ignominy experienced by the majority of Jews under Rome's subjugation was compounded by the actions of the occupying forces which offended Jewish sensibilities, such as Pilate bringing images into Jerusalem, or Pilate appropriating temple funds to build an aqueduct, or Herod Antipas building a Hellenistic city on a graveyard.[13]

---

10  Cf. *War* 6.285; *Ant.* 20.167-68, 188.
11  For further discussion see Horsley, *Spiral of Violence*, 1-145.
12  Cf. Horsley, *Spiral of Violence*, 6-31; Applebaum, 'Economic Life', 2.656-664, 691-92; Hoehner, *Herod Antipas*, 70-72; Goodman, *Ruling Class*, 51-75.
13  *War* 2.167-77 = *Ant.* 18.55-62; *Ant.* 18.36-38. Cf. Borg, *Conflict*, 27-72; Horsley, *Spiral of Violence*, 59-120. Cf. Kraeling ('Roman Standards', 284-85) who states: 'Since the days of Pompey there had, of course, existed in Jewish life a broad contradiction between the ideal of national integrity and the hope of the nation's lead-

Closely linked to this first aspect, and partially derived from it, is a second aspect of Jewish life in which injustice was rampant: the socio-economic issues of debt, taxes and landowner oppression. For the common person in Palestine during this period, whether urban poor or rural peasant, the socio-economic oppression was bad and getting worse. Horsley and Hanson point out that the socio-economic pressures on the peasantry included the tithe and other dues for the temple, tribute to Rome, special levies of Roman taxes, and the support of Jewish refugees. They state that

> the effect of any one of these pressures on the productivity and subsistence of the Jewish peasantry would have been to drive the peasants into debt. If a peasant family, after rendering up 40 percent or more of its harvest, then had too little left to survive until the next harvest, it would have to borrow grain for food, or for seed for the next sowing. . . Continued borrowing would increase a family's debt significantly, with a great risk of complete loss of land. One would then sink into the ranks of the rural proletariat, the landless day laborers, or one could become a sharecropping tenant, perhaps on one's own former parcel of land. . . Large landed estates administered by stewards and farmed by tenants had become familiar.[14]

Thus, Josephus' description of John's message as a call to virtue, justice and piety might appear quite harmless to a Roman reader (which Josephus probably intended), but when placed within the context of first-century Palestine with its social, economic and political problems, that message was a threat to those who supported the *status quo*. But to those who experienced oppression under that very *status quo*, John's message pointed to the possibility of deliverance which in turn raised the hopes and expectations of the common people.

That John's ethical imperative was in fact interpreted this way by his audience is suggested by Josephus' account in *Ant.* 18.118 of the people's response to John's teaching: 'they were also excited to the utmost by listening to [his] teachings'. As well, his account of Herod's fear also suggests the same thing: John's 'great persuasiveness with the people might

ership in world affairs on the one side, and Roman or Herodian domination and the secularization of even higher religious circles on the other'. He goes on to observe 'that this basic contradiction may have played its part in heightening the sense of tension reflected in the Baptist's proclamation is quite probable, especially in view of the fact that the appearance of Roman procurators in Judea and the gradual degeneration of the high-priesthood had served to accentuate it'. But Kraeling observes that Pilate's action of bringing Roman standards into Jerusalem may have been the specific event 'to ignite the fire of prophetic intuition'.

14 Horsley and Hanson, *Bandits*, 58-59, cf. 52-63. Cf. Brunt, 'Josephus on Social Conflicts', 149-153; Rhoads, *Israel in Revolution*, 80-82; Applebaum, 'Economic Life', 2.631-700; Horsley, *Spiral of Violence*, 20-58; Rajak, *Josephus*, 119-28; Goodman, *Ruling Class*, 51-75.

lead to some kind of strife (for they seemed as if they would do every-thing which he counselled)'.

When this evidence from Josephus is placed alongside John's eschato-logical proclamation of imminent judgment and restoration reported in the NT, such a message would be explosive in terms of the socio-political implications of deliverance. We considered above how John's percep-tion of the new situation involved the removal of the unrepentant wicked as well as the purifying and blessing of John's righteous ones and their restoration to a new situation of social justice for the true, remnant Israel.[15] All this points to a radical change in the social order—a rever-sal of the *status quo*.

Similarly, John's ethical concerns reflected in NT texts emphasize the implications of repentance: 'Bear fruit that befits repentance' (Q 3.8). Those trees which are not bearing good fruit are about to be chopped down and burned (Q 3.9). That these ethical concerns stressed espe-cially the issues of socio-economic oppression is suggested by Luke's account of John answering queries concerning what people should do to 'bear fruit'. He instructs those who possess sufficient to share with the deprived. Tax collectors must not abuse the people through over-taxation. Soldiers must not abuse their authority for selfish gain (Lk. 3.10-14).[16] That John addressed these concerns suggests that they were also the concerns of those who responded to his ministry.

---

15   §8.5; cf. Farmer, 'John the Baptist', 2.959-61.

16   To what extent Lk 3.10-14 reflects authentic Baptist material is problematic. It is found only in Luke. Bultmann (*Synoptic Tradition*, 145) rejected its authenticity, asserting that it had been 'naïvely put into the Baptist's mouth as though soldiers had gone on a pilgrimage to John' and that the language demonstrates it is a 'late Hel-lenistic product' designed for catechetical purposes. This function is plausible, but a later function does not prejudge authenticity; it is implausible that catechetical material would be created and then placed *in the mouth of John*, when it is Jesus who is the prime authority for the early Christian communities. Soldiers 'on a pilgrimage' is a caricature; there is no reason why soldiers, especially Jewish soldiers, could not express an interest in John's teaching. Bammel ('The Baptist', 105) also rejects the authenticity of this passage. Concerning the language of the passage (cf. Bultmann) he cites Wellhausen's claim (*Lucae*, 5) that the passage contains 'eigentümlich griechischen Ausdrücke' and thus was probably composed by Luke. Unfortunately, none of these authors support this contention with specific linguistic data. The terms for tax-collectors and soldiers (τελώνης, στρατευόμενος, lit. 'one who serves as a soldier', from στρατιά, 'army', or στρατιώτης, 'soldier') are hardly Lukan (e.g. τελώνης: Q 7.29; 7.34; Mk 2.15-16, etc.; cf. 1 Macc. 13.39; στρατ-: Q 7.8; Mt. 22.7; Mk 15.16, etc.; cf. LXX: Isa. 29.7, etc.). The verbs used to describe the actions of the tax-collectors and soldiers are more probable candidates. The verb πράσσω ('to do, practise') is used frequently in the NT, but only Luke uses it with the more technical sense of collecting money (taxes, interest; Lk. 3.13; 19.23). The verb διασείω ('to extort') is used only here in the NT, and συκοφαντέω ('to accuse falsely, extort') is used twice in the NT, both in Luke: 3.14; 19.8. These are quite specialized verbs, but they are all used in the LXX with the same sense they have in this pericope (e.g. πράσσω: 1 Macc. 10.35; 2 Macc. 12.43; διασείω: 3 Macc. 7.21; συκοφαντέω: Gen.

One might be tempted to draw a distinction between John and the other prophetic movements in that John called for his followers to manifest social justice in their current situation and at the same time expected a radically new situation in which justice and righteousness would reign, while the other prophetic movements only demonstrate the expectation of a radically new situation. However, as noted above, our sources are silent concerning whether or not other leadership prophets gave ethical instruction for the current situation. To draw this type of distinction would be invalid. Consequently, in that area where we have data from both to compare, John and his movement demonstrate similar interests to other prophetic movements among the common people: they all looked for a radically new situation in which social justice would be demonstrated.

## 10.4 *The Tactics of John and his Movement*

The preceding survey of leadership prophets observed that their basic tactic for achieving deliverance was to gather their movements together and lead them in a symbolic event, at which point they evidently believed God would intervene to perform the expected deliverance. The use of violence by the groups was not part of their strategy (except possibly the Samaritan, but even here it is questionable; cf. §9.5.2); they trusted rather in supernatural intervention. Thus, their tactics were corporate (they acted *together* in one group), activist (as a group together they took a positive *action*), and yet pacifist.

43.18; Lev. 19.11). The most that can be said from this evidence that they were used in Jewish circles prior to their use here in Luke is that the composer, or equally *the translator*, knew these terms and employed them here. In contrast, Schürmann (*Lukasevangelium*, 1.169 n. 53) notes the presence of non-Lukan vocabulary which he argues is evidence of Luke's use of a source, though he recognizes Lukan reformulation. Bammel's theory (105-106) as to why this pericope is inserted here in Luke is highly implausible.

This pericope might have been originally in Q because Luke's special material contains no other traditions concerning John (cf. Marshall, *Luke*, 142), and repentant followers of John are identified in Q as tax-collectors in contrast with unrepentant leaders (Q 7.29-30; cf. Schürmann, 1.169); cf. also Sato, *Q*, 61-62. But this evidence only renders its presence in Q a possibility and no more.

It is sometimes asserted that the ethics expressed here are rather weak and bourgeois (e.g. Bammel, 105), and so hardly represent the ethics of John. But this fails to appreciate the covenantal and social implications of what is stated; cf. Sahlin, 'Früchte der Umkehr', 54-68; Nolland, *Luke*, 1.149; Marshall, 142.

I would suggest that a reasonably balanced position with respect to this pericope is that it probably reflects genuine Baptist material with respect to the ethical positions espoused for various groups, but that its form and terminology are due to translation and subsequent shaping of the tradition. Cf. Fitzmyer, *Luke*, 1.465, 469-71; Nolland, 1.147, 149-50; Marshall, 141-44; Schürmann, 166-69.

John's tactics are similar in one respect. There is no evidence that he or his movement planned to use violence to bring about their new situation. He also trusted in divine intervention: God will execute judgment and restoration (through his agent). We considered the possibility that this expected figure might have been conceived as employing military power (§8.5), in a manner similar to the Egyptian who led his group to the Mount of Olives probably expecting the fulfilment of Zech. 14.1-4 in which Yahweh fights against the foreign powers who occupy Jerusalem.[17] As were the other prophetic movements, John's movement was also pacifist.[18]

But in other respects John's tactics differed from the approach taken by the other leadership prophets. He summoned the people to the Jordan to receive repentance-baptism. By means of this baptism he 'gathered together' his group (*Ant.* 18.117), which became the true, remnant Israel. However, his movement did not undertake an action all together in one location at one time as did the other movements. While John had disciples who perhaps remained with him, the majority of the members of his movement returned to their various walks of life. There they evidently were expected to demonstrate the 'fruits of repentance', or in Josephus' terms, to demonstrate justice and piety. But John's movement did not engage in a corporate activity at which time they expected supernatural intervention. Thus, while other prophetic movements were corporate and activist, John's movement was dispersed and passivist.

### 10.5  *The Symbolic Event of John and his Movement*

We also observed that other prophetic movements engaged in symbolic events at which time they expected supernatural intervention. These events derived their symbolism from important events in the past history of the people,[19] especially the Exodus and Conquest—events in which God had spectacularly intervened on their behalf, and which they still celebrated annually. John's tactics differed due to being a dispersed and passivist movement, but that does not mean he did not use similar symbolism to create a symbolic event which would express the expectations

---

17  *War* 2.261-63 = *Ant.* 20.169-72; cf. §9.5.2.
18  Cf. Rivkin, 'Locating John the Baptizer', 79.
19  Hanson (*Dawn of Apocalyptic*, 212, my emphasis) points out that 'the ruling classes, because of their vested interest in the institutional structures of the immediate past, construct a program for restoration on the basis of those recently disrupted structures so as to preserve their position of supremacy. The alienated and oppressed classes *look to the more distant past for models* which call into question the position of power claimed by the ruling classes, and readily adhere to prophetic figures calling for revolutionary changes on the basis of such archaic models.' Hanson cites Weber, *Sociology of Religion*, 80ff, 106-107.

of his followers. The obvious suggestion for a symbolic event is John's baptism which functioned to foreshadow the expected figure's ministry (cf. §6.4.4). But it is unclear how this could be a symbol from the people's past history, especially the Exodus and Conquest. However, observing the symbolic actions of the other leadership prophets is illuminating.[20] In *all cases* the symbolic events performed by the movements involved a journey through the wilderness. For example, Josephus describes in *War* 2.261-62 the Egyptian who 'collected a following of about thirty thousand dupes, and led them by a circuitous route from the desert [ἐκ τῆς ἐρημίας] to the mount called the mount of Olives'. Similarly, in the case of Theudas, he 'persuaded the majority of the masses to take up their possessions and to follow him to the Jordan river. He stated that he was a prophet and that at his command the river would be parted and would provide them an easy passage' (*Ant.* 20.97). In this case the word 'wilderness' is not mentioned, but it is implied because the trip to the Jordan would take them through the wilderness. For Theudas though, the Jordan river itself functions as an important part of the symbolic event. That the wilderness was a regular and prominent feature in these prophetic movements is indicated by Josephus himself in his summarizing description of several such leadership prophets in *War* 2.259: 'they persuaded the multitude to act like madmen, and led them out into the desert [εἰς τὴν ἐρημίαν] under the belief that God would give them tokens [or 'signs'] of deliverance'. The parallel passage in *Ant.* 20.168 also mentions the wilderness, but adds: 'For they said that they would show them unmistakable marvels and signs that would be wrought in harmony with God's design [ἐναργῆ τέρατα καὶ σημεῖα κατὰ τὴν τοῦ θεοῦ πρόνοιαν γινόμενα]'. Horsley explains that

> the 'tokens of deliverance' and 'signs and wonders' are clearly allusions to the great historical acts of deliverance wrought by God in the exodus from slavery in Egypt, the way through the wilderness, and perhaps entry into the promised holy land. Thus, remembering God's gracious acts of salvation in the past, the prophets and their followers were proceeding out into the wilderness, the symbolic place of purification and preparation, eager to experience new acts of deliverance like those of old.

With respect to Theudas' use of the Jordan river, Horsley observes that

> although Josephus' account is insufficient to permit determination of the precise historical analogy that informed Theudas' movement, two alternatives appear probable: (1) a reverse 'conquest': as Joshua had parted the waters of the Jordan River for the original 'conquest' of the promised land, so Theudas was planning to part the waters in a reverse conquest, a retreat

---

20  I disregard the Samaritan at this point because his use of a symbolic event employed traditions which were specifically Samaritan. In the use of specific traditions, it is more helpful to compare John with *Jewish* leadership prophets.

> into the wilderness in order to be purified and to prepare the way of the
> Lord, perhaps indeed then to enact a new 'conquest'; (2) a new exodus
> and/or entry: as Moses parted the waters for the liberation from Egypt
> and/or as Joshua had parted the waters of the Jordan for entry into the
> promised land, so Theudas was acting as God's agent in the new liberation
> from oppression under the Romans and/or in the reentry into the land of
> promise. Exodus from Egypt and entry into the land had long been jux-
> taposed in Israelite-Jewish traditions...[21]

As with these other prophetic movements the NT closely associates
John also with the wilderness, but we must examine the evidence to
ascertain its reliability. Matthew specifies the wilderness 'of Judea' and
evidently understood the Jordan river to be included in this wilderness
(3.1). Mark leaves the wilderness unspecified, but also understood it to
include the Jordan river (1.4). Luke also does not further identify the
wilderness, but indicates a movement on the part of John from the
wilderness (cf. 1.80) as the location of his prophetic call to 'the region
about the Jordan' where he went afterwards in order to preach (3.2-3).[22]
The question of the precise identification of these locations is complicated by the fact that in each of these Gospels 'wilderness' is the closest
point of contact between John the Baptist and the quotation of Isa. 40.3
which each Evangelist uses to interpret John's ministry. Willi Marxsen
argues that Mark combines the two traditions of wilderness preacher and
Jordan baptizer, but the baptizing tradition is the only authentic one.
Mark has combined the two by adding 'in the wilderness' in order that
his portrayal of John could fulfil the Isa. 40.3 prophecy. Thus, Marxsen
understands Mark to be using the wilderness with theological intent (he
fulfils OT prophecy) rather than as an actual geographical location.
Marxsen's fundamental reason for distinguishing these two traditions is
the assumption that 'the wilderness' and 'the region about the Jordan'
are incompatible as references to the same locality because the first indicates lack of water, while the latter includes a river.[23]  However, ἔρημος

---

21  Horsley, 'Popular Prophets', 457. On the 'wilderness' tradition, cf. Kittel, 'ἔρημος',
    2.657-59; Hengel, *Zealots*, 249-53; Mauser, *Christ in the Wilderness*, 15-61; Talmon,
    'Desert Motif', 31-63; Davies, *Gospel and the Land*, 75-90.

22  It is sometimes suggested that Luke separates the wilderness from the area around
    the Jordan (e.g. Schürmann, *Lukasevangelium*, 1.155) in distinction to Matthew and
    Mark, and thus betrays a lack of understanding of the region's geography. However,
    it should be noted carefully that, while Luke indicates a movement of John's part, he
    is not necessarily implying that the two are distinct from one another. The region
    identified as wilderness is more extensive than that portion of the wilderness
    identified as 'the region about the Jordan'. Cf. Fitzmyer, *Luke*, 1.459; Marshall,
    *Luke*, 135.

23  Marxsen, *Mark the Evangelist*, 34-38. Marxsen has two other secondary arguments
    for separating the wilderness-preacher tradition from the Jordan-baptizer tradition:
    (1) neither the fourth Gospel nor the *Gospel of the Ebionites* is aware of a wilderness
    tradition; (2) the difficulty of the wilderness tradition may be removed from 1.4 and
    the thought flows smoothly through 1.4-5. However, in the fourth Gospel, John is

('wilderness') does not necessarily indicate a desert without water, but rather an uninhabited, uncultivated area, often used for grazing. Josephus (*War* 3.515) describes the Jordan river 'meandering through a long wilderness area' before reaching the Dead Sea. Both C.C. McCown and R.W. Funk have demonstrated that 'the wilderness' and 'the region about the Jordan' refer to the southern portion of the Jordan valley extending as far north as Wadi Far'ah and including both the western and eastern slopes.[24] Therefore, Marxsen's objection to the authenticity of the wilderness tradition must be rejected. Walter Wink concludes:

> It would be more accurate to say, then, that Mark *preserved* the wilderness tradition which he found in his sources because it suited his theological purpose, or better, that his theological purpose was itself *created* by this element in the tradition. Because John *was* 'in the wilderness' the Isaiah citation becomes relevant.[25]

While John preached and baptized in the wilderness/Jordan area, it is unlikely that he preached *only* there. If he needed to address people, it is quite possible that he preached where people were—in towns and villages.[26] If so, he called them to the wilderness and to the Jordan. This may be one reason why the Evangelists state that John was '*preaching* a baptism' rather than just administering it.

John's location in the wilderness and use of the Jordan river has been subject to a variety of interpretations, which need not be discussed here.[27] The fact that the movements led by the other leadership proph-

identified with the wilderness by his citation of Isa. 40.3 in 1.23, and located in the region beyond the Jordan (1.28; 3.26; 10.40). There is no need to remove the difficulty of the wilderness tradition if no such difficulty in fact exists, as is shown here. Bultmann (*Synoptic Tradition*, 246, following Schmidt, *Rahmen*, 18ff, as did Marxsen) also understood the link between John and the wilderness to be a Christian invention, but as a part of the documentary tradition rather than a Markan addition.

24   McCown, 'Scene of John's Ministry', 113-31; McCown, 'Gospel Geography', 1-25; Funk, 'Wilderness', 205-14. McCown ('Scene of John's Ministry') concludes that Matthew's specification of 'the wilderness *of Judea*' is incorrect because in the OT the term 'the wilderness of Judah' never includes the Jordan valley. However, Funk (208) has shown McCown to be incorrect at this point. Matthew's specification of the wilderness as 'of Judea' may have clarified the approximate area in which John ministered, but this clarification may also have artificially limited John to the west bank of the Jordan. However, Funk (214) concludes that the wilderness of Judea included 'the lower Jordan valley and possibly the eastern slopes of the valley'. Gundry (*Matthew*, 42, 375-76) suggests that for Matthew Judea included the Transjordan, which is confirmed by Mt. 19.1.

25   Wink, *John the Baptist*, 5, his emphasis.

26   Cf. the geographical locations for John's ministry mentioned in Jn 1.28; 3.23; Dodd, *Historical Tradition*, 236, 279. Hollenbach ('Social Aspects', 859) considers it probable 'that John went to preach his message in populated places, in the villages and cities, even in Jerusalem itself'. Cf. Kraeling, *John the Baptist*, 64.

27   For examples and discussion cf. Davies and Allison, *Matthew*, 1.290-91; Scobie, *John the Baptist*, 41-48; Steinmann, *John the Baptist*; Ernst, *Johannes der Täufer*, 278-84. The concern here is only with the socio-political implications.

ets employed the wilderness for Exodus/Conquest symbolism indicates that these were important symbols for the common people of Judea in John's day. We need to be sensitive, therefore, to how John's audience would have perceived his choice of the wilderness and Jordan river as the location for his ministry. We must credit John with being aware of this perception and, therefore, his choice of this location suggests his approval of their perception and the symbolism involved.

But what might that symbolism be? Unfortunately, our evidence does not provide us with an explicit answer. But, if the use made by the other prophetic movements of the wilderness tradition and Exodus/Conquest symbolism is associated with the preceding examination of John's baptism and his proclamation of an expected figure, then it is possible to arrive at a plausible suggestion. We observed above that John administered his baptism in association with the Jordan river, and that he also appears to have spent a considerable amount of his time on the eastern side of the Jordan, in Perea. If we imagine what a member of John's movement did and combine it with the John's understanding of what his group constituted and the expectations they had for the future, then we can perhaps appreciate John's symbolic event. People would leave their homes in Jerusalem/Judea, where they experienced a sense of oppression and deprivation, perhaps reminiscent of what their ancestors experienced in Egypt. They would travel through the wilderness to the Jordan river following the call of the prophet John, again reminiscent of the people of Israel travelling through the wilderness under the leadership of a great prophetic figure, Moses. They would come to the Jordan river and enter it (possibly crossing to the other side), reminding them of other 'crossings': the Red Sea and the Jordan river in the Exodus and Conquest. Here they were baptized by John with a repentance-baptism which functioned to initiate them into the group of prepared people, the true Israel. As such, they expected imminently the restoring ministry of God's agent who would make them a holy group and remove the wicked from within their midst, possibly also creating a 'holy land' in which they could live in righteousness and experience social justice (cf. §6.4). The people would come up out of the Jordan (or possibly recross from Perea into Judea), reminiscent of the people under Joshua's leadership entering the land, and possibly associated with the imagery of a return from exile. The people, now constituting the true, remnant Israel, were reentering their land in a symbolic act of 'possessing it', anticipating its imminent fulfilment when the expected figure would arrive.[28]

---

28  Drury's structural analysis ('Mark 1.1-15', 29-32) interprets the use of wilderness and baptism in Mk 1.1-15 in a way similar to what I have here. The wilderness here in Mk 1 'is the wilderness of the exodus where Israel was for forty years before entering the land by crossing the Jordan'. The reference to 'all' Judea going to John leaves

Our evidence does not explicitly state that John utilized the wilderness and the Jordan in this fashion. But the symbolic use made of these by other prophetic movements to enact 'Exodus/Conquest' events indicates that this symbolism was significant for the common people of John's day.[29] It is plausible that the actions performed by the people in coming through the wilderness, being baptized in the Jordan and returning to their homes in Palestine, functioned as a symbolic event in the ministry of John. That John or his audience conceived it in precisely the way I have suggested here is plausible but not possible to confirm.

It could be objected that John baptized elsewhere and that, therefore, the Jordan river is not essential.[30] But I am not suggesting that the Jordan river was essential; only that John appears to have concentrated his ministry in the wilderness and at the Jordan, and that *when* he did so, which was evidently most of the time, it could have had the significance of a symbolic event. If John baptized elsewhere, the functions of his baptism would remain the same and his eschatological proclamation would not need to change. Such a change in location would only mean that his ministry at that point was not employing all elements of this symbolism.

We should observe two differences between John's movement and the other prophetic movements in this regard. The other prophetic movements evidently engaged in the symbolic event as a group gathered all together at one time. But with John, the symbolic event would have been an ongoing symbolism throughout the duration of his ministry at the Jordan. Also, the other prophetic movements, as they engaged in their symbolic event, evidently thought they were participating in the deliverance and that the supernatural intervention would take place at that time. However, in John's symbolic event, re-entering the land may have symbolized possessing it, but the followers of John were not

the land empty; 'Mark is running the nation's history backwards'. Then the people receive John's baptism; 'it is a Jordan baptism, a going through water to get the promise' (31). Drury's interpretation, however, is at the level of early Christian understanding, so that Mark is portraying 'corporately . . . the emergence of their faith, individually . . . [their] conversion and baptism' (34). If this was 'vivid to the early Christians' (34), how much more for the Jews who actually participated in the symbolism! Cf. Badcock, 'Baptism of Christ', 155-60; as cited by Marsh, *Baptism*, 38 n. 1; Hengel, *Zealots*, 253.

29  Cf. the organization of the army and the plan for the war portrayed in 1QM 2–9 which is patterned after a similar structure for Israel in the wilderness in Num. 1.1–10.10. Davies (*1QM*, 28) observes that 'it is probable that the war which cols. II–IX describes is seen as a new "entry into a promised land" which, like the original entry, involves a period of forty years'.

30  Cf. Scobie (*John the Baptist*, 116) who makes such an argument, but he does so in the context of examining whether the waters of the Jordan were an essential element of the baptism of John.

actualizing the possession in any way; they were only anticipating its imminent fulfilment.

## 10.6  *The Opposition to John and his Movement*

### 10.6.1  *Herod Antipas*

The data concerning John the Baptist demonstrate quite clearly that he was in conflict with Herod Antipas, tetrarch of Galilee and Perea. It is beyond the limits of this work to examine all aspects of their relationship in detail;[31] we must limit ourselves to simply elucidating those elements which shed light on the socio-political orientation of John's ministry.

The synoptic Gospels state that Herod Antipas had imprisoned John because John had rebuked him for his marriage to Herodias, for she had formerly been married to Antipas' brother, Philip:[32] 'It is not lawful for you to have your brother's wife' (Mk 6.17b). Josephus, on the other hand, states that John was imprisoned because Herod Antipas had perceived John as a political threat: 'he feared his [i.e. John's] great persuasiveness with the people might lead to some kind of strife . . .' (*Ant.* 18.118). These two accounts of Antipas' motives for arresting John are quite different—the one personal and moral, and the other public and political—but they are not incompatible with each other; rather, they reflect the differing viewpoints of the authors.[33] We shall examine below Josephus' account of John's arrest (§10.7), but, at this point, we should observe the socio-political implications of John's rebuke of Antipas for marrying his brother's wife.

Lev. 18.16 prohibits marrying the wife of one's brother. Consequently, John's rebuke that Antipas' marriage to Herodias is not lawful accuses Antipas of breaking the Torah. But Lev. 20.21 clarifies the prohibition by placing an evaluation upon such a relationship: 'If a man marries his brother's wife, it is impurity (נִדָּה). He has uncovered his brother's nakedness; they shall be childless.'[34] In light of John's concern for

---

31  For a complete discussion of their relationship see Hoehner, *Herod Antipas*, 110-71 and the literature cited there.

32  Both Mt. 14.3 and Mk 6.17 identify this brother as Philip, while Lk. 3.19 does not name the brother. Josephus, in *Ant.* 18.109, identifies Herodias' former husband as Herod, not Philip. Many scholars understand Matthew and Mark to be incorrect at this point (e.g. Scobie, *John the Baptist*, 181; Schürer, *History*, 1.344 n. 19), but it is quite plausible that the Herod identified by Josephus may have also had the name Philip. For defence of this position see especially Hoehner, *Herod Antipas*, 131-36; also Lane, *Mark*, 215-16; Guelich, *Mark*, 1.331.

33  Schürer, *History*, 1.346; Hoehner, *Herod Antipas*, 140-41; Scobie, *John the Baptist*, 178-86.

34  The synoptic Gospels are consistent in recording that John's objection to Antipas' marriage was that he was married to a woman who had formerly been married to his brother. This contravenes the Torah (cf. Lev. 18.16; 20.21). Evidently the issue was

purity, his rebuke of Antipas most probably had a second implication: as a result of his marriage, Antipas was in a condition of impurity. Such a rebuke might also apply to many other persons in Palestine at that time, but the recipient of John's rebuke was the person who ruled a significant portion of Palestine. Thus, John was charging a ruler, a major portion of whose subjects were Jews,[35] with being both a Torah-breaker and impure.

There is no evidence that John actually approached Antipas personally with this criticism, at least while John was free and preaching publicly.[36] Rather, John's criticisms were probably made publicly to the crowds who gathered about him, and Antipas received a report about it.[37] Such charges would not have greatly concerned Antipas, whose personal religious orientation toward Judaism was, at best, superficial and minimal.[38] The criticism, while having socio-political overtones, does not appear to have serious implications when taken by itself. It might

not Antipas' divorce of his first wife, nor was it the fact that he was now married to his niece. For further discussion see Hoehner, *Herod Antipas*, 137-39 n. 4.

35 Hoehner, *Herod Antipas*, 53-56.

36 If Antipas conversed with John after his arrest (cf. Mk 6.20) or engaged in any type of examination or trial, then it may be reasonably presumed that John addressed Antipas directly on this matter.

37 This appears the most probable case when Josephus' account is taken together with those of the synoptic Gospels. The use of the dative in Mt. 14.4 (αὐτῷ) and Mk 6.18 (τῷ 'Ηρῴδη) to designate Herod as the object of John's rebuke (Lk. 3.19 places the entire clause in the passive) is commonly translated as a dative of indirect object (i.e. 'John said to Antipas'), but it could equally be understood as a dative of reference (i.e. 'John said about Antipas').

38 Herod the Great was probably an Idumaean, a half-Jew, though his friend and historian, Nicolaus of Damascus, presented Herod as a full-blooded Jew whose family belonged to the leading Jews returning from the exile (*Ant.* 14.8-9; cf. *War* 1.124). Apparently,'Herod's Judaism was, by all accounts, very superficial' (Schürer, *History*, 1.311), but he did attempt to avoid giving offence in certain matters, such as avoiding images on coins and permitting only priests to build the temple. However, his cultural commitments were Hellenistic, and his political commitments were to Rome (Schürer, 1.308-15). Antipas probably was educated as a normal Jewish boy would have been in Palestine, but was later sent to Rome to complete his education in Hellenism and Roman policies (*Ant.* 17.20), though here he resided with Pollio (probably Asinius Pollio) and remained under Jewish influence (*Ant.* 17.20; 15.342-43; cf. Hoehner, *Herod Antipas*, 12-17). Antipas was, however, similar to his father, in not only his ambition, but also his cultural and political commitments. He was sensitive in some respects to Jewish concerns, as evidenced by his coins bearing no image, his attendance at Jewish feasts (Lk. 23.7), and his apparent involvement in bringing a complaint against Pilate's public display of a votive shield in Jerusalem (Philo, *Leg. Gai.* 299-300). But he built his capital city, Tiberias, on a graveyard, which offended Jewish sensibilities by contravening Jewish tradition (*Ant.* 18.39), and he erected images in public places (*Life* 65). His imprisonment and execution of John the Baptist, a popular figure among his subjects (*Ant.* 18.118-19), further demonstrates his commitment to a policy of ruthless loyalty to Rome. For further discussion of Herod Antipas' life see Schürer, 1.340-53; Hoehner.

lessen any political allegiance which his Jewish subjects had towards him and possibly foster political discontent as well.[39] But when an accusation that a ruler of Jews is a Torah-breaker and impure is placed within the same context as John's proclamation of the imminent removal and destruction of the wicked (which would include Antipas, from John's point of view and those who followed him) by an expected figure of judgment and restoration (possibly perceived as a new ruler figure), then his rebuke of Antipas takes on new, indeed serious, implications for Antipas' continued political control of his subjects.[40]

John's accusation could also be perceived as a political threat from another direction as well. John's ministry was located primarily in the wilderness regions at the southern end of the Jordan river, and a considerable amount of this time was spent on the eastern side, in Perea. This would place John in contact with the Nabateans, not only because their border was less that 20 km to the east, but because goods from the east passed along a major trade route through Nabatea and then Perea. As a trading people, Nabatean nationals would travel this route and so come in contact with John the Baptist. Antipas' marriage with the daughter of the Aretas IV, king of the Nabateans, had been part of a treaty with the Nabateans promoting the peace and stability of the region, but this divorce of Aretas' daughter was taken as a personal insult against the Nabatean royal family. It later led to a war between Antipas and Aretas in which Antipas was defeated; only Roman assistance saved him (*Ant.* 18.109-25). Thus, Carl H. Kraeling correctly observes that John's rebuke

> was not only embarrassing, it was politically explosive. It meant aligning the pious Jewish inhabitants of Peraea with those of Arabic stock against their sovereign and thus fomenting sedition and encouraging insurrection.[41]

When these factors are placed within the context of John's view of the current situation (illuminated by his pronouncement of the sinfulness of his generation and his call to repentance) in contrast to the expected situation (the removal and destruction of the wicked and the purifying and blessing of the righteous), John's decision to rebuke Antipas may have been deliberately selected by him to highlight the contrast between

---

39   That this was a real possibility may be seen from the outbreak of discontent against actions instituted by Herod the Great towards the end of his life and after his death; cf. *War* 1.648-55 = *Ant.* 17.149-67; *War* 2.39-79 = *Ant.* 17.250-98; Schürer, *History*, 1.325-35; Smallwood, *Jews under Roman Rule*, 96-113.

40   Hoehner (*Herod Antipas*, 142) observes that John's 'denunciation is significant, for at the climax of Messianic expectation the laws of God are heightened, and believers [are] far less tolerant towards those who oppose the Law'.

41   Kraeling, *John the Baptist*, 90-91, cf. 87-91; Hoehner, *Herod Antipas*, 142-45; on Aretas IV see Wright, 'Nabataean Neighbor', 3-4; Schürer, *History*, 1.582-83.

the current and expected situations and the practical socio-political changes which the expected situation implied.

Luke states in 3.19 that John not only rebuked Antipas for his marriage to Herodias, but he also rebuked him 'for all the evil things that Herod had done'. We are not told what these were, and the limited historical knowledge we have concerning Antipas makes it difficult to identify other specific actions for which he could be rebuked. However, it is most probable that there were other items for which Antipas could be rebuked, especially when perceived from the point of view of Jewish piety.[42] The fact that he was both a member of the infamous Herodian family, and a pro-Roman client ruler would provide more than enough ammunition from that point of view. Antipas' arrest and execution of John was just one more evil thing, and that is not only the opinion of Luke (3.20), but also a popular Jewish opinion according to Josephus, who explains that 'to some of the Jews it seemed that Herod's army had been destroyed by God, who was exacting vengeance (indeed justly) as satisfaction for John who was called Baptist' (*Ant.* 18.116; cf. 18.119).[43]

Clearly then, John stood in opposition to Herod Antipas and condemned him, the context of which demonstrates the socio-political orientation of John's prophetic ministry. Evidence for the socio-political implications of John's ministry may be gleaned from a closer examination of Josephus' description of John's audience and his effect upon them, as well as the consequence which this had upon Herod Antipas. This examines the conflict from the opposite point of view: Herod stood in opposition to John. Josephus explains in *Ant.* 18.118 that John's ministry had a tremendous impact on his audience;[44] he uses statements such as: 'they were excited even to the utmost . . . his great persuasiveness with the people . . . they seemed as if they would do everything which he counselled. . .' What produced such a powerful response is mentioned simply as '[his] teachings'. John's teachings, that is his ethical demand for virtue, justice and piety as described in 18.117, if understood from the point of view of personal piety, would not by themselves be a great threat to Antipas. But I demonstrated above that John's teachings

42 E.g. his construction of his capital city, Tiberias, on a graveyard; *Ant.* 18.38.
43 It is possible that the Jewish people recalled John the Baptist when Antipas was defeated because John was memorable for his denunciation of Antipas' marriage.
44 I suggested in §2.2.2 that the 'others' referred to a wider audience of Jews, but that nothing in the context suggests that they could not have included Gentiles. We observed above that the close proximity of John's location to both Nabatea and the trade routes from the east suggest that there is every likelihood that these 'others' included not only Jews, but foreigners and Gentiles as well, especially Nabateans. Lachs ('John the Baptist', 28-32) argues that in Mt. 3.5-6 (also Mk 1.5 and Lk. 3.7) John's audience is described as 'Jerusalem and all Judea and all the countryside surrounding the river Jordan', and thus included Gentiles.

as described by Josephus (and confirmed by the NT) demonstrate a concern for social justice (§10.3). When understood from this point of view and associated with the announcement of imminent, eschatological judgment and restoration, these supposedly innocent 'teachings' are explosive when addressed to the common people who were experiencing a sense of oppression and deprivation. When the complete import of these teachings is appreciated, then Josephus' description of John attracting large crowds who are excited and will do anything John says is easily understood, as is Antipas' fear that this would lead to civil strife. John was a threat to the socio-policical *status quo*, and it was Antipas who was at the top of that socio-political ladder.

John's ministry becomes a greater and more real threat when another element of John's message is considered: he called his audience 'to gather together by means of baptism' (*Ant.* 18.117; cf. §6.4.5). The gathering together of discontented, excited people is usually perceived by governments as a threat,[45] but when combined with the implication that the gathering together is to form a new movement it would certainly become a threat to this *status quo*.

Thus, the combination of the implications of John's message with the excited response of large crowds was a threat to Antipas. He did not fear John, but the possibility that a popular movement might attempt to put into practice the implications of John's message.[46] Thus Josephus explains that Antipas feared στάσις ('strife') caused by the radically innovative (νεώτερος) message John announced (cf. §2.2.2). He therefore stood in opposition to John and decided to remove this potential threat by having John executed.

### 10.6.2 *The Temple Establishment*

We observed in discussing John's baptism that it functioned to mediate divine forgiveness and that John appeared to function as a mediator of that forgiveness. By thus offering an alternative to the temple, John's ministry was encroaching upon the exclusive domain of the temple priesthood. As John's popularity grew, he would probably have been perceived as a real threat to those whose authority was based upon the temple. I suggested that there were most probably two foci for criticism

---

45  Cf. *Ant.* 15.366. This is equally true in the twentieth century as it was in the first.
46  Rivkin ('Locating John the Baptizer', 83-84, his emphasis) states that Antipas 'had good reason to fear the *political* implications of John's religious teachings once it became evident that he was attracting crowds who might in a surge of religious exaltation and zeal act out the political implications of John's call for repentance and let loose a torrent of revolutionary violence. . . Crowds were dangerous even if not a political word was being uttered. Religious teachings become political teachings *ipso facto* the moment that a scattering of individuals had clustered into a crowd.'

of the temple. First of all, the temple establishment, in order to remain in power, accommodated and capitulated to the foreign occupying power of Rome. Secondly, they were frequently perceived as wealthy and corrupt, and sometimes as greedy and violent. Which of these common perceptions of the temple establishment John was criticizing is not known, though the two are closely related so that choosing between them is perhaps not necessary. For common people who were experiencing feelings of oppression and deprivation, the wealth of the temple establishment may have been a real affront, especially as their contribution to that wealth was increasing their own economic hardship (cf. §6.4.6).

The idea that John was critical of the temple establishment is also supported by the possibility that Q 3.7b, 8b was originally addressed to the Sadducees, who formed a group closely associated with the temple establishment. In calling them to repentance and warning them of imminent wrath, he was challenging their position at the top of the Jewish social, economic and political ladder. He was threatening the *status quo* they worked to maintain.[47]

John's opposition to the temple establishment is a reasonable probability. The foci for that opposition which I have suggested are quite possible. However, it is interesting that John, a member of a rural priestly family (cf. §6.4.2), has so radically repudiated his priestly heritage and social position. We might ask what initially caused John to take such a radical position.[48] A possible answer is suggested by the historical context of first-century Palestine: the alienation between the aristocratic, urban priests and the lower, rural priests. The Qumran community is an example of such alienation, expressed by a separatist, wilderness existence.[49] Josephus reports that prior to the first Jewish War the priestly

47  Cf. Jn 1.19, 24. It is possible that John may have been influenced especially by the prophet Malachi in his critique of the temple establishment. We considered above (§7.7, 8.3) the possibility that John's expected figure in the role of Yahweh's agent was the figure of Elijah-*redivivus*, but the evidence was not conclusive. However, if John conceived of a purification of the priesthood, then he may have been thinking in terms of this figure. On the other hand, if Q 3.7-9 was addressed originally to the Sadducees, the emphasis is not so much upon their purification, but upon their destruction! Whether or not this is the case, Mal. 3.3-5 would provide support for John's criticism of the temple establishment, especially in light of other criticisms levelled by this same prophet elsewhere in his prophecy.

48  John's wilderness habitat and his diet (Mt. 3.1, 4 = Mk 1.4, 6 = Lk. 3.2; cf. Lk. 1.15, 80) might be an ascetic lifestyle which expressed his alienation. His asceticism became identified closely with him in proverbial form: 'For John came neither eating nor drinking . . .' (Q 7.33). Hollenbach, 'Social Aspects', 853; Brownlee, 'John the Baptist', 33; Kraeling, *John the Baptist*, 10-15; Andersen, 'Diet of John', 60-74; Böcher, 'Kein Brot', 90-92; Brock, 'Baptist's Diet', 113-24; Davies, 'Essene Kashruth', 569-71.

49  For example, 1QpHab cites Hab. 2.8 and then interprets it: 'Because thou hast plundered many nations all the remnant of the peoples will plunder thee, the explan-

aristocracy abused the rural priests and common people by forcibly collecting from the threshing floors the tithes due the rural priests.[50]  If John's alienation is to be explained, it 'must', in the words of Carl H. Kraeling, 'have its roots in some bitter experience. . .'[51]  The most plausible explanation is that John experienced alienation, oppression and deprivation as a lower, rural priest, the causes of which may be traced to the policies of the temple establishment: accommodation to the Roman occupying forces and the strengthening of their own base of wealth and power.[52]  With his message of imminent judgment and restoration John addressed the needs of the common people who perceived themselves as oppressed and deprived; John also perceived himself in similar terms.

### 10.6.3 *The Romans*

There is no evidence of conflict *directly* between John the Baptist and the Romans.  However, if the socio-political observations made thus far concerning John's opposition to Herod Antipas and the temple establishment are valid, then a factor common to both of these opponents is that they represented the imperialist power of Rome.  Herod Antipas was Rome's client ruler in Galilee and Perea—Rome legitimated his authority and ultimately removed him from power and exiled him.  During the period of John's ministry Judea was ruled directly by a Roman governor (Rome had dismissed Herod Archelaus from office and banished him), and he was responsible for setting up and deposing the high priests, who, by directing the temple establishment, were responsible for controlling most of the internal affairs of Judea within the confines of Roman policy.[53]  If their control over the affairs of their respec-

---

ation of this concerns the last Priests of Jerusalem who heap up riches and gain by plundering the peoples' (1QpHab 9.3-5). Cf. Cross, *Library of Qumran*, 95-119. Hanson (*Dawn of Apocalyptic*, e.g. 209-28) traces opposition and alienation among priestly groups to a much earlier period.

50  *Ant.* 20.180-81; cf. 18.205-207; *b. Pes.* 57a; *t. Men.* 13.21; Horsley, *Spiral of Violence*, 46-48; Applebaum, 'Economic Life', 2.691-92; Horsley, *Liberation*, 96-99; cf. Ford's discussion ('Zealotism', 280-92) which suggests that 'the sources for Luke's Infancy Narrative present a climate of Zealot enthusiasm'.

51  Kraeling, *John the Baptist*, 16. Cf. Hollenbach, 'Social Aspects', 855. While this is plausible, I do not think we can say it was *one particular* bitter experience. It might be better to express this idea more generally: John's alienation may be traced to his bitter experience as a member of a rural priestly family.

52  Cf. Kraeling, *John the Baptist*, 16-27; Hollenbach, 'Social Aspects', 852-56; Ernst, *Johannes der Täufer*, 271-72; Horsley, *Liberation*, 91-100. A far less plausible explanation is offered by Goldsmith (*John the Baptist*), whose psychological analysis traces John's asceticism to his childhood experiences of being repressed by puritanically minded parents; cf. the summary and critique by Scobie, *John the Baptist*, 204-206.

53  For example, Smallwood (*Jews under Roman Rule*, 82) explains that the function of a client ruler 'was to prepare his subjects for assimilation into the Roman empire as a province by introducing features of Greco-Roman culture. . .' On the Roman policy of using client rulers in colonial situations, see Smallwood, 82-83; Schürer, *History*,

tive domains was not satisfactory to the Romans, they were removed and replaced by others who would be more responsive to Roman policies; this happened to the high priests, Herod Archelaus, and ultimately to Herod Antipas as well. Therefore, these authorities ruled by having to glance constantly over their shoulders at the Romans as they strove to maintain the *status quo* as defined by them. So, while the evidence in our sources indicates that John was only in direct conflict with Herod Antipas and the temple establishment, *indirectly* he probably stood in opposition to Rome as well, for Rome was at least partially responsible for his conflict with Antipas and the temple establishment.[54]

Since no evidence exists which explicitly indicates John's opposition to Rome, we cannot know whether John perceived himself in opposition to Rome or not. However, the examination above of John's perception of the coming situation arising out of the expected figure's judgment and restoration suggests that all those responsible for the social injustice experienced by John and those who responded to him would be judged and removed (§8.5). The Romans, at least those present within Palestine, would fall within John's category of the unrepentant and would be subject to such judgment. Furthermore, if John thought of Palestine being restored to the state of a 'holy land', this too would suggest that he stood opposed to Rome's imperial rule and expected its removal by the expected figure.[55]

### 10.7 *The Arrest and Execution of John*

Each of the prophetic movements examined in the preceding chapter was the object of swift and brutal extermination by the authorities. Pilate killed many of the followers of the Samaritan, though others escaped, and he executed the leaders (*Ant.* 18.85-87). Fadus killed many of the followers of Theudas, took others prisoner, and beheaded

---

1.316-17, 373-74; Horsley, *Spiral of Violence*, 7-15, and the literature they cite.

54  Jewish resistance to Rome is sometimes considered to be limited to the 'Zealots', but recent research has demonstrated that the Zealot movement did not actually begin until shortly before the first Jewish Revolt (cf. comments on 'Zealot prophets' in §9.2.2). Rather, resistance to Rome from the period of Herod the Great's reign to the Jewish Revolt primarily consisted of mass movements by the common people and sometimes involved certain of the intellectual elite (e.g. Pharisees). Borg (*Conflict*, 39) states: 'that which united the protestors was sorrow and anger at the loss of autonomy, loyalty to the practices enjoined by Torah, and concern for the holiness of the land and Temple, all of which were threatened by the penetration of Gentile power. . .' On Jewish attitudes to Roman rule and their resistance against it, see §10.2; Borg, 27-49; Horsley and Hanson, *Bandits*; Horsley, *Spiral of Violence*, 1-120.

55  Cf. Farmer ('John the Baptist', 2.959) who indicates that John's message must be viewed against a background of expecting 'deliverance from the clutches of the Gentiles'.

*John the Baptizer and Prophet*

Theudas himself (*Ant.* 20.97-98). The Egyptian met the same response from Felix, though in this case the Egyptian managed to escape (*War* 2.261-63 = *Ant.* 20.169-72). A similar fate met all the leaders of these prophetic movements and their followers (cf. §9.5.2). In each of these cases what led to the military strike against the prophetic movement and the execution of its leader appears to have been the need to eliminate a potential or actual threat to the social and political stability of the region.[56]

Similarly, John the Baptist was arrested by Herod Antipas, held prisoner in Machaerus[57] and finally executed. The synoptic Gospels explain John's arrest as the response by Herod and his new wife to John's condemnation of their marriage (Mt. 14.3-12 = Mk 6.17-29; cf. Lk. 3.19-20).[58] In this case, the motive is primarily a personal one of seeking

---

56  E.g. *War* 2.260, 264; *Ant.* 18.85, 88.

57  The record in Mk 6 begins with Jesus teaching in Nazareth in Galilee (6.1-2) as well as the surrounding villages (6.6b). Herod Antipas hears of Jesus' ministry and thinks he is John risen from the dead (6.14-16). For Antipas to hear such rumours of Jesus' Galilean ministry implies that he was probably living in his Galilean home in Tiberias at the time. The narrative continues by recording Antipas' banquet and execution of John (6.17-29). This could imply that the banquet was also held in Tiberias and thus this is where John was imprisoned and executed. On the other hand, Josephus explains that 'because of the suspicion of Herod, he [i.e. John], after being sent bound to Machaerus (the fortress mentioned before) was executed there' (*Ant.* 18.119). It is best to accept Josephus' statement that the location was Machaerus because it is an unequivocal identification, and there is no reason for Josephus to alter any information he would have on this subject. On the other hand, it is only a superficial reading of the Markan account which concludes that John was imprisoned and executed in Tiberias (Mt. 14.1-12 and Lk. 2.18-20 leave the location unspecified). The narrative links Jesus' Galilean ministry with Antipas, in Tiberias, hearing of Jesus and equating him with John. The record of John's execution is a flashback, explaining why Antipas thought Jesus was John risen from the dead. We are not told how much time had elapsed between John's execution and Antipas hearing of Jesus, but the text implies that it was at least a short time. Antipas could easily have moved his entourage from Machaerus to Tiberias in the meantime.

This view is supported by other evidence. Machaerus was part of Antipas' territory and was an excellent fortification with a beautiful palace and excellent provisions for food and water. It would be cooler in the summer than Tiberias because it was some 3,000 feet higher in altitude (cf. *War* 7.164-77, 186-89; Hoehner, *Herod Antipas*, 147). It would, therefore, be natural for Antipas to live at least part of the time there, and could equally have been the location of a banquet such as recorded in Mk 6. Furthermore, John's ministry seemed to have been located in the region of Perea and the Dead Sea rather than Galilee (Mt. 3.1, 6; Mk 1.4-5; Lk. 3.2-3; Jn 1.28). There is no record of John going to Galilee, though it is possible that Jn 3.23 is a reference to a ministry by John in Samaria. On the Samaritan ministry see Scobie, *John the Baptist*, 163-77; Albright, 'Recent Discoveries', 159-160. On 4.38 as a possible reference to John, see Robinson, 'The "Others" ', 61-66, but against, see Cullmann, 'Samaria', 185-92.

58  The historical reliability of the NT account concerning Antipas' banquet and John's beheading is a complex issue. It is not necessary to examine the issues involved because I am concerned here only with the fact that John was executed by Herod Antipas—a fact concerning which the independent witnesses of Josephus and the NT

revenge. On the other hand, Josephus explains that Herod had John arrested because he feared some form of socio-political unrest arising from a popular movement created by the common people putting into practice the implications of John's teachings. These two motives for John's arrest appear contrary to one another. However, as we observed above, John's condemnation of Antipas' marriage was fraught with socio-political danger for Antipas (cf. §10.6.1), and so the Evangelists' moral and theological emphasis is consistent with Josephus' political one. Similarly, in Josephus' account the immediately preceding narrative explains the conflict between Aretas and Antipas because of his marriage to Herodias (*Ant.* 18.109-13) which led ultimately to Antipas' downfall (*Ant.* 18.113-15). This order of events in Josephus' narrative might suggest that the problems associated with Antipas' marriage caused him to fear strife among the people.[59] If this is the case, then Josephus' political perspective is open to the Gospels' emphasis upon John's moral condemnation.

Therefore, the socio-political explanation provided by Josephus and the personal and moral explanation provided by the NT are probably presenting two sides of the complex set of factors which motivated Antipas' arrest of John. These factors evidently included: (1) John's ministry was causing excitement among the common people which appeared to be in danger of spilling over into civil unrest; (2) John's preaching had socio-political implications which were an implied threat to the *status quo* and so to Antipas' position; (3) John's condemnation of Antipas' marriage could exacerbate the already politically unstable relationship with the Nabateans just a few miles to the east of where John was preaching; and (4) the effrontery of John's condemnation probably aggravated and even angered Antipas and/or Herodias. This last factor is probably insufficient by itself, but in conjunction with the others, John's arrest and execution by Antipas was a quite 'reasonable' action for a client ruler of Rome to take. Thus, the fate of John is the same as that of the other leadership prophets,[60] and the socio-political motivations for their execution appear quite similar.

In comparing the response to John and his movement with the response to the other prophetic movements, there are two ways in which John and his movement were dealt with differently from the other prophetic movements. In the first case, it was the Roman authorities who dealt

---

agree. For discussion see Hoehner, *Herod Antipas*, 149-71; Gnilka, 'Martyrium', 78-92; Guelich, *Mark*, 1.324-34.

59  Sollertinsky, 'Death of St John', 512; Hoehner, *Herod Antipas*, 145.
60  The fate of the leadership prophets stands in contrast to that of the solitary prophets. While the latter faced opposition, they were not executed.

with the other movements, while it was Herod Antipas who dealt with John. In the other examples, the Roman governor dealt with the problems directly because they were ruling Judea and Samaria directly, and the other movements were located there. In the case of John, while his ministry drew crowds from Judea and may have been based at times on the western bank of the Jordan, he spent at least a portion of his time in Perea. Rome did not rule here directly, but through its client ruler, Herod Antipas, who was nevertheless responsible to Rome for maintaining the peace and stability of the region. This is, therefore, a superficial difference.

The second difference is more substantial. In each of the other examples, the wrath of the Roman authorities fell upon the leader as well as his followers, with the result that not only was the leader executed, but many of those involved in the movement as well were executed or imprisoned and the rest dispersed. Antipas' response to John's movement, however, appears to have been to arrest and execute only John. It is possible that a few of John's closer disciples might have been arrested along with him, but our sources are silent; they only record John's arrest and execution. In any case, John's movement did not face the wholesale slaughter experienced by the other movements. There are at least three factors in John's case which might explain this difference. First of all, as I indicated above, John's tactics differed somewhat from those of the other movements. John did not call his followers together to engage in a corporate activity at which time they expected supernatural intervention as did the other groups. While other prophetic movements were corporate and activist, John's movement was dispersed and passivist (cf. §10.4). With the other movements, the threat was what the prophets were *actually leading* the people to do, while the threat in John's case was the *potential* of what the people might do. Thus, in John's case the threat from the movement was only potential; John himself was more the focus of the threat than were the other leadership prophets. Josephus' account indicates that Antipas' strategy appears to have been that to remove the actual threat caused by John would dispel the potential problem caused by the movement (*Ant.* 18.118). Secondly, as I suggested earlier, one of the factors motivating Antipas was personal: anger at John casting aspersion on his marriage (cf. §10.6.1). This would also serve to concentrate attention upon John alone. Thirdly, being a client ruler responsible to Rome, Antipas may have been politically astute enough to think that a wholesale slaughter would cause an outcry from his Jewish subjects great enough to reach the ears of Rome. If this had happened, he might have been deposed in a scenario similar to that which had earlier surrounded his brother Archelaus.[61]

## 10.8 *Conclusion*

In the preceding chapters we saw that aspects of John's baptismal practice and his proclamation of an expected figure suggested that John's
ministry was more than just a 'religious' phenomenon. Consequently, a
full appreciation of his ministry necessitates that it be perceived of as
having a socio-political orientation as well. What was suggested in these
preceding chapters has been highlighted and clarified in this chapter by
placing John's ministry within the context of similar prophetic movements and observing the similarities as well as the differences between
John's ministry and those of other leadership prophets.

John's activity of baptizing and his proclamation of judgment and restoration produced a movement drawn primarily from among the common people. Similar to the response made to other leadership prophets,
the perception by these people of oppression and deprivation contributed to their positive and excited response to John's ministry. But
John's tactics were somewhat different in realizing deliverance from
those of the other leadership prophets. The tactics of both John and the
other prophets were pacifist, but, while the others were corporate and
activist in their approach, John's movement was dispersed and passivist.
The other prophetic movements engaged in symbolic events employing
the wilderness (and in one case the Jordan river) to typologically enact
deliverance, recalling motifs of the Exodus/Conquest. Similarly, John's
ministry was associated with the wilderness and the Jordan, and it is possible that the people coming to the wilderness to be baptized by John in
the Jordan were also enacting a symbolic event in which they anticipated
the repossession and cleansing of the land by the expected figure. In the
case of this symbolic event, however, John's followers did not participate
in it as a corporate body all at the same time.

Just as the other leadership prophets faced conflict and opposition
from the ruling authorities, so did John. With respect to the others, the

---

61 Archelaus was appointed ethnarch of Judea, Samaria and Idumea by the Roman
emperor in 4 BCE following the death of his father, Herod the Great. His rule (to 6
CE), which was tyrannical and brutal, came to an end when a delegation of his subjects brought charges against him before Caesar (*War* 2.111 = *Ant.* 17.342-44). On
Archelaus' rule, see Schürer, *History*, 1.353-57; Smallwood, *Jews under Roman Rule*,
102-17.

Antipas' rule of his Jewish subjects appears to have been characterized in most
cases by astuteness. He maintained, at least superficially, the public appearance of
practising Judaism, while pursuing a policy of Hellenization. His downfall was not
due to his internal rule but to a disastrous mistake in foreign policy. For a description of his rule, see Schürer, 1.340-44; Smallwood, 183-87; Hoehner, *Herod Antipas*,
83-109.

source of that conflict was chiefly the Roman authorities in Judea. With John on the other hand, the greater amount of data allows us to trace that conflict to animosity between John and Herod Antipas, and probably between John and the temple establishment as well. But behind both these sources of conflict stood the imperialist power of Rome. This conflict between John and the other leadership prophets on the one hand and the authorities on the other led to them all being executed by those authorities. That those who followed John were largely spared, in contrast to those who followed the other leadership prophets, may be explained by the difference in John's tactics as well as the difference between the ruling style of Roman governors and Herod Antipas.

Chapter 11

## CONCLUSION

### 11.1 *Contributions to Research*

A survey of the individual chapters of this book would be needlessly repetitive at this point, for a review may be found in the conclusion to each one. Rather, it may be more helpful at this point to summarize those areas in which these investigations make a contribution to research. Many of these contributions are not startlingly new (as in any well-worked area of research), for they build upon and extend the work of many scholars. But this work does contribute new arguments and new appreciations of the data to support a particular understanding of John.

### 11.1.1 *Methodological Contributions*

The major methodological contribution of this book is the extensive presentation and analysis of the contextual data in order to appreciate the social, cultural and historical milieu in which John functioned. I did not perform this contextual analysis for all areas, but rather focused on John's public roles: he was a baptizer and a prophet. This contextual analysis unfortunately contributes to the length of the work, but it does allow us to appreciate the range of understanding being expressed in Second Temple Judaism in the areas considered. For example, I did not argue deductively that John's baptism 'originated from proselyte baptism' or 'is the same as immersions at Qumran'. Instead, by showing similarities and differences between them, we inductively considered the range of ablutory practices and functions in John's milieu. Then we examined the data concerning the practice and functions of John's baptism, after which we could profitably compare John's baptism with his milieu. This approach, whether with respect to John's baptism, prophetic announcement or prophetic role, allows us to appreciate both John's similarities and his distinctive features within his social, cultural and historical context.

Secondly, a corollary to the preceding methodological approach is the attempt to be sensitive to the social and historical realities in Palestine during the late Second Temple period. For example, an awareness of the socio-economic difficulties facing the urban poor and rural peasants during this period enables us to appreciate the social and political implications of John's proclamation.

Thirdly, it is widely recognized that with respect to John we are fortunate to have, in addition to the Christian sources, the account of his ministry provided by Josephus. Unfortunately, all too often this historical source is not given the necessary attention and weight due to an independent historical source. I have attempted to rectify this weakness by incorporating into this work a careful exegesis of Josephus' account in *Ant.* 18.116-19 and by giving equal weight to this source.

### 11.1.2 *Contextual Contributions*

By contextual contributions I refer to those areas in which this work has made a contribution to the social, cultural and historical context of Second Temple Judaism, apart from any implication it might have had for understanding John. Chapters 4, 5 and 7 gather together in one place surveys and analyses of an extensive body of material concerning ablutions and expected figures respectively. While the survey conducted in Chapter 9 has been done before,[1] nevertheless, I believe that my analysis contributes a more adequate typology of prophets in Second Temple Palestine as well as a descriptive analysis of the social context, the strategy and the ideology of these prophets.

There are also several, more specific contributions made in this book which assist in appreciating the Second Temple context, of which the following are examples. In assessing the function of immersions in Second Temple Judaism we concluded after careful consideration that the tradition contained in the extensive addition to *T. Levi* 2.3 (cited as 2.3B and supported by 4QTLevi ar[a]) should be considered as evidence in the examination of immersions during the Second Temple period, and that it supports the use of an immersion to symbolize cleansing from sin and conversion to God (§4.3.4). Also with respect to immersions, 1QS 2.25–3.9 is frequently cited in the secondary literature, but often without adequate support for the conclusions drawn from the passage. The analysis here has contributed an extensive exegesis of this text and its context to support the conclusions drawn from it (§5.3).

In examining expected figures of judgment and restoration we concluded that, while Yahweh was certainly a figure who was expected to judge and restore, he was not merely one expected figure among the others. Rather, Jewish thinking perceived a relationship between God and the other figures whereby those expected figures were conceived of as agents carrying out God's judgment and restoration. Thus, a person in that period could expect God to be coming to judge and restore in theological/celestial terms and at the same time expect an agent to execute the judgment and restoration in historical/terrestrial terms (§7.8).

### 11.1.3 *Historical Contributions*

A work of this nature produces a multitude of historical conclusions concerning John the Baptist, each having a greater or lesser degree of probability. Many of these conclusions are not unique to this work, but the investigations provided here contribute a more extensive and reasoned analysis to support particular conclusions and to reject others than is often found in other studies of John the Baptist.

Our historical investigations have led to one historical conclusion concerning John which is of major and overarching significance: John's ministry produced a Jewish sectarian movement (esp. §6.4.5, 8.4, 8.5, 10.2). Arising out of the analysis of John both as a baptizer and as a prophet, this conclusion has, in turn, illuminated our appreciation of John in those roles. Furthermore, it places John's ministry more concretely within its social, cultural and historical context.

As well as concluding that John was a leader of a prophetic movement, we also reached several other historical conclusions in this work which present a useful development of positions which may have originally been suggested by others. For example, my analysis indicated that John's baptism functioned in several ways depending on the perspective from which it is viewed. But these functions work together to form the ideological matrix for John's baptism (§6.4). Each of these functions has similarities in John's Jewish milieu, but John's particular matrix of those functions is distinctive (§6.5).

Again, the argument that John's expected figure is to be identified as God is not unique, but we observed that Jewish expectations concerning these figures functioned at two levels, with God being understood as the prime initiator of judgment and restoration at a theological/celestial level, but that other agents functioned on his behalf to execute the judgment and restoration at a historical/terrestrial level. John's proclamation had a theological emphasis, focusing on the theological/celestial level. But other evidence indicates that he perceived that the judgment and restoration would be carried out at the historical/terrestrial level by one of God's agents, though it is not possible to determine with any probability which of these agents he expected (§8.3).

The examination of John's perception of the judgment and restoration is helpful in placing John's expectations (and those of his audience) more concretely within the historical tensions being experienced in first-century Palestine. John did not expect the 'end of the world' but a radical reorientation of the concrete, socio-historical situation in which the Jewish people in Palestine found themselves (§8.5).[1]

---

1    Cf. Horsley, 'Popular Prophets', 435-63; Horsley and Hanson, *Bandits*, 135-89; Aune, *Prophecy*, 103-52.

My analysis of John's socio-political orientation in light of other prophetic movements illuminated similarities and differences between John's movement and these other movements. While John's interest in deliverance is similar, of particular significance are the differences in John's tactics when compared with those of the other prophetic movements (§10.4). That John's movement was dispersed and passivist may have contributed to the fact that John alone was executed rather than large portions of his movement being slaughtered (§10.7). The use made by the other prophetic movements of the wilderness (and Jordan river) to re-enact a symbolic event employing Exodus/Conquest traditions suggests that John may have been using the wilderness and Jordan to create for his movement a similar form of symbolic event (§10.5). Furthermore, John appears to have been in conflict not only with Herod Antipas, but also with the temple establishment and, at least indirectly, the Roman occupying forces (§10.6).

### 11.1.4 *Exegetical Contributions*
With respect to the passages about John the Baptist, it has been the intention throughout this book to illuminate the texts by placing them within a thorough and realistic analysis of John's milieu in Second Temple Judaism. Consequently, the exegesis of these texts has usually been limited to determining what historical information could be gleaned from them. Nevertheless, some insights emerged concerning these pericopae which were specifically exegetical in nature. For example, several arguments were advanced to indicate that Q 3.17 does not picture the farmer winnowing but rather cleaning the threshing floor by gathering the wheat into the granary and burning the chaff. This interpretation affects how one interprets the function of John's ministry, its relationship to that of the expected figure, and John's perception of the new situation (§8.4.2).

We also concluded that the most probable audience for Q 3.7-9, and especially 3.7b, 8b, was the Sadducees, representing the interests of the temple establishment. This provides additional support for the view that John was critical of the temple establishment (§6.2.2.2).

The exegesis of Josephus' description of John in *Ant.* 18.116-19 made several contributions to a clearer understanding of the passage (primarily because this passage has not been the object of commentaries, etc.). For example, additional support was provided for the interpretation that Josephus is indicating the formation of a group in the clause 'to gather together by baptism' (§6.4.5). We also concluded that, while Josephus' description of John's message had been Hellenized, his portrayal of John's baptism is more Jewish in orientation except for the distinction made between the body and the soul (§6.2.1). Josephus' description of John's baptism does contribute to our appreciation of the functions of John's baptism, especially as a purification from uncleanness caused by moral contagion and as an initiatory rite into the true, remnant Israel (§6.4.3, 6.4.5).

## 11.2 *Areas for Further Research*

All research builds on the work of others. In this book I have been indebted to many scholars as I have stood on their shoulders to make my contributions. But I realize that there are areas where others could do the same with my work. Two areas could be suggested.

First of all, the major and overarching conclusion to this work is that John's ministry created a Jewish sectarian movement. This has been established on the basis of an exegesis of the relevant passages and a sensitivity to John's social and historical context. One could now apply models derived from the social sciences to John's movement in order to further illuminate how John's movement fits within his milieu. Especially relevant in this regard would be a comparison of John's movement to various forms of millenarian movements.[2]

Secondly, I refer back to my own interest, expressed in the Introduction, concerning the historical Jesus (§1.1). In light of this work, it would be profitable to investigate how appreciating John the Baptist in his social, cultural and historical context might contribute to understanding Jesus within his context which was quite similar to John's. For example, one might consider the possibility that, having been baptized by John, Jesus' own ministry began as a baptizer (Jn 3.26; 4.1). What implications does this have for understanding the origins of Jesus' ministry? To what extent was Jesus' teaching shaped by John, and to what extent does Jesus distinguish himself from him? Another approach one might take is to compare John's movement with the early Jesus movement. What similarities and differences can be observed? What possible ways did the form of John's movement contribute to the form and function of the early Jesus movement? Investigations of this kind would take us back to the earliest Christian theological interpretation of John the Baptist as the one who 'prepared the way' for the Messiah, and it may well be that this interpretation has historical validity after all: John the Baptist may indeed have been the forerunner of Jesus.

---

2   Cf. Wallace, 'Revitalization Movements', 264-81; Wilson, *Magic and the Millenium*, 16-30; with application to movements in Second Temple Judaism, cf. Gager, *Kingdom and Community*, 19-37; Aune, *Prophecy*, 126-29.

# BIBLIOGRAPHY

## 1. *Primary Sources: Texts and Translations*

Allegro, J.M., ed. and trans. *Qumran Cave 4: I (4Q158–4Q186)*. Vol. 5 of *Discoveries in the Judaean Desert*. Oxford: Oxford University Press, 1968.

*The Apostolic Fathers*. LCL. 2 vols. Trans. K. Lake. Cambridge, MA: Harvard University Press; London: Heinemann, 1912–13.

Baillet, M., ed. and trans. *Qumran Grotte 4 III (4Q482–4Q520)*. Vol. 7 of *Discoveries in the Judaean Desert*. Oxford: Oxford University Press, 1982.

Barthélemy, D., and J.T. Milik, ed. and trans. *Qumran Cave 1*. Vol. 1 of *Discoveries in the Judaean Desert*. Oxford: Oxford University Press, 1955.

Berendts, A., and K. Grass, trans. *Flavius Josephus: Vom Jüdischen Kriege Buch I-IV, nach der slavischen Übersetzung deutsch herausgegeben und mit dem griechischen Text verglichen*. 2 vols. Dorpat: n.p., 1924–27.

Beyer, K., ed. *Die aramäischen Texte vom Toten Meer*. Göttingen: Vandenhoeck und Ruprecht, 1984.

Black, M., ed. *Apocalypsis Henochi Graece*. PVTG 3. Leiden: Brill, 1970.

———— trans. *The Book of Enoch or 1 Enoch*. SVTP 7. Leiden: Brill, 1985.

Blackman, P., trans. *Mishnayoth*. 7 vols. 2nd edn. New York: Judaica, 1983.

Bowman, J., trans. *Samaritan Documents Relating to their History, Religion, and Life*. Pittsburgh Original Texts and Translations Series 2. Pittsburgh: Pickwick, 1977.

Brenton, L.C.L., trans. *The Septuagint with Apocrypha: Greek and English*. London: Samuel Bagster and Sons, 1851; repr. Grand Rapids: Zondervan, n.d.

Brownlee, W.H., trans. *The Dead Sea Manual of Discipline: Translation and Notes*. BASORSup 10–12. New Haven: American Schools of Oriental Research, 1951.

———— *The Midrash Pesher of Habakkuk*. SBLMS 24. Missoula, MT: Scholars, 1979.

Burrows, M., ed. *The Dead Sea Scrolls of St Mark's Monastery*. Vol 2.2. New Haven: American Schools of Oriental Research, 1951.

Cameron, R., ed. *The Other Gospels: Non-Canonical Gospel Texts*. Cambridge: Lutterworth, 1982.

Chadwick, H., trans. *Origen: Contra Celsum*. Cambridge: Cambridge University Press, 1953.

Charles, R.H., trans. *The Apocrypha and Pseudepigrapha of the Old Testament in English*. 2 vols. Oxford: Oxford University Press, 1913.

———— trans. *The Greek Versions of the Testaments of the Twelve Patriarchs*. Oxford: Oxford University Press, 1908; repr. Hildescheim: Georg Olms, 1966.

Charlesworth, J.H., ed. *The Old Testament Pseudepigrapha*. 2 vols. Garden City: Doubleday, 1983–85.

Cohen, A., trans. *The Minor Tractates of the Talmud*. 2 vols. London: Soncino, 1965.

Danby, H., trans. *The Mishnah*. Oxford: Oxford University Press, 1933.

de Jonge, M., ed. *Testament XII Patriarchum: Edited according to Cambridge University Library MS Ff 1.24 fol. 203a-261b*. PVTG 1. 2nd edn. Leiden: Brill, 1970.

———— ed. *The Testaments of the Twelve Patriarchs: A Critical Edition of the Greek Text*. PVTG 1.2. Leiden: Brill, 1978.

Denis, A. -M., ed. *Fragmenta Pseudepigraphorum Quae Supersunt Graece una cum Historicum et Auctorum Judaeorum Hellenistarum Fragmentis*. PVTG 3. Leiden: Brill, 1970.

———— *Concordance Grecque des Pseudépigraphes d'Ancien Testament*. Louvain-la-Neuve: Institⁿᵗ Orientaliste Université Catholique de Louvain; Leiden: Brill,

1987, 813-925.

*Dio Cassius: Roman History*. LCL. 9 vols. Trans. E. Cary. Cambridge, MA: Harvard University Press; London: Heinemann, 1914–27.

Dupont-Sommer, A., trans. *The Essene Writings from Qumran*. Trans. G. Vermes. Oxford: Blackwell, 1961; repr. Gloucester: Peter Smith, 1973.

Elliger, K., and W. Rudolph, ed. *Biblia Hebraica Stuttgartensia*. Rev. edn. Stuttgart: Deutsche Bibelgesellschaft, 1977.

Epstein, I., trans. *The Babylonian Talmud*. 35 vols. London: Soncino, 1935–52.

——— trans. *The Babylonian Talmud: Hebrew-English Edition*. 30 vols. London: Soncino, 1972–84.

*Eusebius: The Ecclesiastical History*. LCL. 2 vols. Trans. K. Lake (vol. 1), J.E.L. Oulton (vol. 2). Cambridge, MA: Harvard University Press; London: Heinemann, 1926–32.

Fitzmyer, J.A., and D.J. Harrington, ed. and trans. *A Manual of Palestinian Aramaic Texts*. BibOr 34. Rome: Biblical Institute, 1978.

Freedman, H., and M. Simon, trans. *Midrash Rabbah*. 10 vols. London: Soncino, 1939.

Gaster, T.H., trans. *The Dead Sea Scriptures*. 3rd edn. Garden City: Doubleday, 1976.

*The Greek New Testament*. UBS. 3rd edn. Ed. K. Aland *et al*. New York: American Bible Society, 1975.

Guillaumont, A. *et al.*, trans. *The Gospel according to Thomas*. Leiden: Brill; London: Collins, 1959.

Hennecke, E., W. Schneemelcher, and R. McL. Wilson, ed. and trans. *New Testament Apocrypha*. 2 vols. Philadelphia: Westminster, 1963–65.

Holm-Nielsen, S. *Hodayot: Psalms from Qumran*. Aarhus: Universitetsforlaget, 1960.

Horgan, M.P. *Pesharim: Qumran Interpretations of Biblical Books*. CBQMS 8. Washington, DC: Catholic Biblical Association, 1979.

Istrin, V.M., ed. *La prise de Jérusalem de Josèphe le Juif*. 2 vols. Trans. P. Pascal. Paris: n.p., 1934–38.

James, M.R., trans. *The Lost Apocrypha of the Old Testament*. London: SPCK, 1920.

*St Jerome: Select Letters*. LCL. Trans. F.A. Wright. Cambridge, MA: Harvard University Press; London: Heinemann, 1933.

*Josephus*. LCL. 10 vols. Trans. H.St.J. Thackeray (vols. 1–4), H.St.J. Thackeray and R. Marcus (vol. 5), R. Marcus (vols 6–7), R. Marcus and A. Wikgren (vol. 8), L.H. Feldman (vols. 9–10). Cambridge, MA: Harvard University Press; London: Heinemann, 1926–65.

Kittel, B.P. *The Hymns of Qumran: Translation and Commentary*. SBLDS 50. Chico, CA: Scholars, 1981.

Klijn, A.F.J., and G.J. Reinink. *Patristic Evidence for Jewish-Christian Sects*. NovTSup 36. Leiden: Brill, 1973.

Knibb, M.A., trans. *The Ethiopic Book of Enoch: A New Edition in the Light of the Aramaic Dead Sea Fragments*. 2 vols. Oxford: Oxford University Press, 1978.

——— *The Qumran Community*. CCWJCW 2. Cambridge: Cambridge University Press, 1987.

Kobelski, P.J. *Melchizedek and Melchiresa*. CBQMS 10. Washington, DC: Catholic Biblical Association, 1981.

Lauterbach, J.Z., trans. *Mekilta de-Rabbi Ishmael*. 3 vols. Philadelphia: Jewish Publication Society of America, 1933–35.

Lohse, E., ed. and trans. *Die Texte aus Qumran: Hebräisch und Deutsch*. 4th edn. Darmstadt: Wissenschaftliche Buchgesellschaft, 1986.

Maier, J., trans. *The Temple Scroll*. JSOTSup 34. Trans. R.T. White. Sheffield: JSOT Press, 1985.

Mansoor, M. *The Thanksgiving Hymns*. STDJ 3. Leiden: Brill, 1961.

Mead, G.R.S., trans. *The Gnostic John the Baptizer*. London: John M. Watkins, 1924.

——— trans. *Pistis Sophia*. 2nd edn. London, n.p., 1921.

Mescerskij, N.A., ed. *Istorija iudeskoij vojny Josifa Flavija* [= *History of the War of the*

*Jews of Flavius Josephus in Old Russian*, in Russian]. Moscow: n.p., 1958.

Metzger, B.M., trans. *The Apocrypha of the Old Testament: Revised Standard Version.* Rev. edn. Oxford: Oxford University Press, 1977.

Milik, J.T., trans. *The Books of Enoch: Aramaic Fragments of Cave 4.* Oxford: Oxford University Press, 1976.

———— 'Le Testament de Lévi en Araméen'. *RB* 62 (1955): 398-406.

Neusner, J., trans. *The Tosefta.* 6 vols. New York: Ktav, 1977–83.

*New American Standard Bible.* Chicago: Moody, 1975.

*New Revised Standard Version.* Oxford: Oxford University Press, 1989.

Niese, B., ed. *Flavii Iosephi Opera.* 2nd edn. 4 vols. Berlin: Weidmannsche, 1955.

*Novum Testamentum Graece.* NA. 26th edn. Ed. E. Nestle *et al.* Stuttgart: Deutsche Bibelstiftung, 1979.

*Philo.* LCL. 12 vols. Trans. F.H. Colson (vols. 2, 6–9), F.H. Colson and G.H. Whitaker (vols. 1, 3–5), F.H. Colson and J.W. Earp (vol. 10), R. Marcus (supp. 1–2). Cambridge, MA: Harvard University Press; London: Heinemann, 1929–53.

Pietersma, A., S.T. Comstock, and H.W. Attridge., trans. *The Apocalypse of Elijah.* SBLTT 19. Chico, CA: Scholars, 1981.

*Pliny: Natural History.* LCL. 10 vols. Trans. H. Rackham (vols. 1–5, 9) and W.H.S. Jones (vols. 6–8). Cambridge, MA: Harvard University Press; London: Heinemann, 1938–52.

Rahlfs, A., ed. *Septuaginta.* 2 vols. Stuttgart: Deutsche Bibelstiftung, 1935.

*Revised Standard Version.* Oxford: Oxford University Press, 1977.

Robinson, J.M., ed. *The Nag Hammadi Library in English.* 3rd edn. San Francisco: Harper and Row, 1988.

Schmidt, C., and V. MacDermot, trans. *Pistis Sophia.* NHS 9. Leiden: Brill, 1978.

*Suetonius: The Lives of the Caesars.* LCL. 2 vols. Trans. J.C. Rolfe. Cambridge, MA: Harvard University Press; London: Heinemann, 1913–14.

*Tacitus: The Histories.* LCL. 2 vols. Trans. C.H. Moore. Cambridge, MA: Harvard University Press; London: Heinemann, 1925–31.

Thackeray, H.St.J. 'Appendix: The Principal Additional Passages in the Slavonic Version'. In *Josephus.* LCL. Cambridge, MA: Harvard University, 1928, 9.635-660.

Vermes, G., trans. *The Dead Sea Scrolls in English.* 3rd edn. London: Penguin, 1987.

Wernberg-Møller, P. *The Manual of Discipline: Translated and Annotated with an Introduction.* STDJ 1. Leiden: Brill, 1957.

Whiston, W., trans. *The Works of Josephus.* 4 vols. London: Lackington, Allen and Co., 1806.

Zuckermandel, M.S., ed. *Tosephta: Based on the Erfurt and Vienna Codices.* Rev. edn. Jerusalem: Wahrmann Books, 1970.

## 2. *Reference Works: Concordances, Lexica and Grammars*

[Abbey of Maredsous], ed. *A Concordance to the Apocrypha/Deuterocanonical Books of the Revised Standard Version.* Grand Rapids: Eerdmans, 1983.

Aland, K., ed. *Synopsis of the Four Gospels: Greek-English Edition.* 7th edn. Stuttgart: German Bible Society, 1984.

Bachmann, H., and W.A. Slaby, ed. *Computer-Konkordanz zum Novum Testamentum Graece.* Berlin: Walter de Gruyter, 1980.

Bauer, W. *A Greek-English Lexicon of the New Testament and Other Early Christian Literature.* Trans. and rev. by W.F. Arndt, F.W. Gingrich, and F.W. Danker. 2nd edn. Chicago: University of Chicago Press, 1979.

Blass, F., and A. Debrunner. *A Greek Grammar of the New Testament and Other Early Christian Literature.* Trans. and rev. by R.W. Funk. Chicago: University of Chicago Press, 1961.

Brooks, J.A., and C.W. Winbury. *Syntax of New Testament Greek.* Washington, DC: University Press of America, 1979.

Brown, F., S.R. Driver, and C.A. Briggs. *A Hebrew and English Lexicon of the Old Testament*. Oxford: Oxford University Press, 1906.

Burton, E.D. *Syntax of the Moods and Tenses in New Testament Greek*. 3rd edn. Edinburgh: T. and T. Clark, 1898.

Davidson, A.B. *Hebrew Syntax*. 3rd edn. Edinburgh: T. and T. Clark, 1901.

Denis, A.-M., ed. *Concordance Grecque des Pseudépigraphes d'Ancien Testament*. Louvain-la-Neuve: Institut Orientaliste Université Catholique de Louvain; Leiden: Brill, 1987.

Edwards, R.A., ed. *A Concordance to Q*. SBLSBS 7. Chico, CA: Scholars, 1975.

Even-Shoshan, A., ed. *A New Concordance of the Bible*. 2nd edn. Jerusalem: 'Kiryat-Sefer' Publishing House, 1989.

Funk, R.W. *A Beginning-Intermediate Grammar of Hellenistic Greek*. SBLSBS 2. 3 vols. 2nd edn. Missoula, MT: Scholars, 1973.

——— ed. *New Gospel Parallels*. FFNT. 2 vols. Philadelphia: Fortress, 1985.

Hatch, E., and H.A. Redpath, ed. *Concordance to the Septuagint and Other Greek Versions of the Old Testament*. 3 vols. in 2. Oxford: Oxford University Press, 1897; repr. Grand Rapids: Baker Book House, 1983.

Holladay, W.L. *A Concise Hebrew and Aramaic Lexicon of the Old Testament*. Grand Rapids: Eerdmans, 1971.

Horsley, G.H.R., ed. *New Documents Illustrating Early Christianity*. 4 vols. North Ryde, NSW: Macquarie University, 1981–87.

Jastrow, M. *A Dictionary of the Targumim, The Talmud Babli and Yerushalami, and the Midrashic Literature*. 1903; repr. New York: Judaica, 1971.

Kautzsch, E., ed. *Gesenius' Hebrew Grammar*. 2nd edn. Rev. by A.E. Cowley. Oxford: Oxford University Press, 1910.

Kloppenborg, J.S., ed. *Q Parallels*. FFNT. Sonoma, CA: Polebridge, 1988.

Kuhn, K.G., ed. *Konkordanz zu den Qumrantexten*. Göttingen: Vandenhoeck und Ruprecht, 1960.

——— 'Nachträge zur "Konkordanz zu den Qumrantexten" '. *RevQ* 4 (1963–64): 163-234.

Liddell, H.G., and R. Scott. *A Greek-English Lexicon*. 9th edn (with a supplement). Rev. by H.S. Jones. Oxford: Oxford University Press, 1968.

Metzger, B.M. *A Textual Commentary on the Greek New Testament*. Rev. edn. London, New York: United Bible Societies, 1975.

Moule, C.F.D. *An Idiom Book of New Testament Greek*. 2nd edn. Cambridge: Cambridge University Press, 1959.

Moulton, J.H., and G. Milligan., ed. *The Vocabulary of the Greek Testament Illustrated from the Papyri and Other Non-Literary Sources*. 1930; repr. Grand Rapids: Eerdmans, 1982.

Moulton, J.H., W.F. Howard, and N. Turner. *A Grammar of New Testament Greek*. 4 vols. Edinburgh: T. and T. Clark, 1908–76.

Rengstorf, K.H., ed. *A Complete Concordance to Flavius Josephus*. 4 vols. Leiden: Brill, 1973–83.

Robertson, A.T. *A Grammar of the Greek New Testament in the Light of Historical Research*. 4th edn. Nashville: Broadman, 1934.

Smyth, H.W. *Greek Grammar*. 1920; Cambridge, MA: Harvard University Press, 1984.

Thomas, R.L., ed. *New American Standard Exhaustive Concordance of the Bible*. Nashville: Holman, 1981.

Waltke, B.K., and M. O'Connor. *An Introduction to Biblical Hebrew Syntax*. Winona Lake, IN: Eisenbrauns, 1990.

Wigram, G.V., ed. *The Englishman's Hebrew and Chaldee Concordance of the Old Testament*. 5th edn. 1860; repr. Grand Rapids: Zondervan, 1970.

Williams, R.J. *Hebrew Syntax: An Outline*. 2nd edn. Toronto: University of Toronto Press, 1976.

Zerwick, M. *Biblical Greek*. 4th edn. Trans. and ed. J. Smith. Rome: Biblical Institute, 1963.


3. *Secondary Literature*


Abrahams, I. *Studies in Pharisaism and the Gospels*. First Series. Cambridge: Cambridge University Press, 1917.
————— *Studies in Pharisaism and the Gospels*. Second Series. Cambridge: Cambridge University Press, 1924.
————— 'How Did the Jews Baptize?'. *JTS* 12 (1911): 609-12.
Ackroyd, P.R. *Exile and Restoration*. OTL. Philadelphia: Westminster, 1968.
Albright, W.F. 'Some Observations Favoring the Palestinian Origin of the Gospel of John'. *HTR* 17 (1924): 189-95.
————— 'Recent Discoveries in Palestine and the Gospel of St John'. In *The Background of the New Testament and Its Eschatology: In Honour of Charles Harold Dodd*. Ed. W.D. Davies and D. Daube. Cambridge: Cambridge University Press, 1956, 153-71.
Albright, W.F., and C.S. Mann. 'Qumran and the Essenes: Geography, Chronology, and Identification of the Sect'. In *The Scrolls and Christianity*. Theological Collections 11. Ed. M. Black. London: SPCK, 1969, 11-25.
Allegro, J.M. 'Further Messianic References in Qumran Literature'. *JBL* 75 (1956): 174-87.
————— 'Fragments of a Qumran Scroll of Eschatological *Midrashim*'. *JBL* 77 (1958): 350-54.
Allen, L.C. *The Books of Joel, Obadiah, Johan and Micah*. NICOT. Grand Rapids: Eerdmans, 1976.
Allen, W.C. *A Critical and Exegetical Commentary on the Gospel according to S. Matthew*. ICC. 2nd edn. Edinburgh: T. and T. Clark, 1907.
Allison, D.C. 'Elijah Must Come First'. *JBL* 103 (1984): 256-58.
Andersen, F.I. 'The Diet of John the Baptist'. *AbrN* 3 (1961–62): 60-74.
Anderson, B.W. 'Exodus Typology in Second Isaiah'. In *Israel's Prophetic Heritage: Essays in Honor of James Muilenburg*. Ed. G.W. Anderson and W. Harrelson. London: SCM, 1962, 177-95.
Anderson, H. 'The Old Testament in Mark's Gospel'. In *The Use of the Old Testament in the New and Other Essays: Studies in Honor of William Franklin Stinespring*. Ed. J.M. Efird. Durham: Duke University Press, 1972, 280-306.
————— *The Gospel of Mark*. NCB. Grand Rapids: Eerdmans, 1976.
Applebaum, S. 'Economic Life in Palestine'. In *The Jewish People in the First Century*. CRINT 1.2. Ed. S. Safrai and M. Stern. Assen: Van Gorcum; Philadelphia: Fortress, 1976, 631-700.
Argyle, A.W. 'An Alleged Semiticism [Part 1]'. *ExpTim* 66 (1954–55): 177.
————— 'An Alleged Semiticism [Part 2]'. *ExpTim* 67 (1955–56): 247.
Attridge, H.W. *The Interpretation of Biblical History in the Antiquitates Judaicae of Flavius Josephus*. HDR 7. Missoula, MT: Scholars, 1976.
————— 'Historiography'. In *Jewish Writings of the Second Temple Period*. CRINT 2.2. Ed. M.E. Stone. Assen: Van Gorcum; Philadelphia: Fortress, 1984, 157-84.
————— 'Josephus and His Works'. In *Jewish Writings of the Second Temple Period*. CRINT 2.2. Ed. M.E. Stone. Assen: Van Gorcum; Philadelphia: Fortress, 1984, 185-232.
————— 'Jewish Historiography'. In *Early Judaism and Its Modern Interpreters*. T ⌐ Bible and Its Modern Interpreters 2. Ed. R.A. Kraft and G.W.E. Nickelsburg. Philadelphia: Fortress, 1986, 311-43.
Aune, D.E. 'The Use of προφήτης in Josephus'. *JBL* 101 (1982): 419-21.
————— *Prophecy in Early Christianity and the Ancient Mediterranean World*. Grand

Rapids: Eerdmans, 1983.

Averbeck, R.E. 'The Focus of Baptism in the New Testament'. *GTJ* 2 (1981): 265-301.

Avigad, N. *Discovering Jerusalem*. Oxford: Blackwell, 1984.

Bachmann, M. 'Johannes der Täufer bei Lukas: Nachzügler oder Vorläufer?'. In *Wort in der Zeit: neutestamentliche Studien: Festgabe für Karl Heinrich Rengstorf zum 75. Geburtstag*. Ed. W. Haubeck and M. Bachmann. Leiden: Brill, 1980, 123-55.

Badcock, F.J. 'The Significance of the Baptism of Christ'. *Interpreter* 13 (1916–17): 155-60.

Badia, L.F. *The Qumran Baptism and John the Baptist's Baptism*. Lanham, MD: University Press of America, 1980.

Baillet, M. *et al*. 'Le travail d'édition des fragments manuscrits de Qumran'. *RB* 63 (1956): 49-67.

Baldensperger, W. *Der Prolog des vierten Evangeliums: sein polemisch-apologetischer Zweck*. Tübingen: Mohr, 1898.

Bamberger, B.J. *Proselytism in the Talmudic Period*. 2nd edn. New York: Ktav, 1968.

Bammel, E. 'The Baptist in Early Christian Tradition'. *NTS* 18 (1971–72): 95-128.

Bampfylde, G. 'The Prince of the Host in the Book of Daniel and the Dead Sea Scrolls'. *JSJ* 14 (1983): 129-34.

——— 'The Similitudes of Enoch: Historical Allusions'. *JSJ* 15 (1984): 9-31.

Bardtke, H. 'Literaturbericht über Qumran VII. Teil: Die Sektenrolle 1QS'. *TRu* 38 (1974): 257-91.

Barnard, L.W. 'Matt 3.11//Lk 3.16'. *JTS* 8 (1957): 107.

Barnett, P.W. 'The Jewish Sign Prophets—A.D. 40–70: Their Intentions and Origin'. *NTS* 27 (1980–81): 681-97.

Barrett, C.K. *The Holy Spirit and the Gospel Tradition*. London: SPCK, 1947.

——— 'The Lamb of God'. *NTS* 1 (1954–55): 210-18.

——— *The Gospel According to St John*. 2nd edn. London: SPCK, 1978.

——— 'Apollos and the Twelve Disciples of Ephesus'. In *The New Testament Age: Essays in Honor of Bo Reicke*. Ed. W.C. Weinrich. Macon, GA: Mercer University Press, 1984, 1.29-39.

Barton, J. *Oracles of God: Perceptions of Ancient Prophecy in Israel after the Exile*. London: Darton, Longman and Todd, 1986.

Baumgarten, J.M. 'Sacrifice and Worship among the Jewish Sectarians of the Dead Sea (Qumran) Scrolls'. In J.M. Baumgarten. *Studies in Qumran Law*. SJLA 24. Leiden: Brill, 1977, 39-56 [repr. from *HTR* 46 (1953): 141-59].

——— 'Essenes and the Temple: A Reappraisal'. In J.M. Baumgarten. *Studies in Qumran Law*. SJLA 24. Leiden: Brill, 1977, 57-74.

——— 'The Essene Avoidance of Oil and the Laws of Purity'. In J.M. Baumgarten. *Studies in Qumran Law*. SJLA 24. Leiden: Brill, 1977, 88-97 [repr. from *RevQ* 6 (1967): 183-93].

——— 'Exclusions from the Temple: Proselytes and Agrippa I'. *JJS* 33 (1982): 215-25.

Beall, T.S. *Josephus' Description of the Essenes Illustrated by the Dead Sea Scrolls*. SNTSMS 58. Cambridge: Cambridge University Press, 1988.

Beare, F.W. *The Gospel According to Matthew*. San Francisco: Harper and Row, 1981.

Beasley-Murray, G.R. *Baptism in the New Testament*. Grand Rapids: Eerdmans, 1962.

——— 'Baptism, Wash: βαπτίζω'. *NIDNTT* 1.143-50.

——— 'Baptism, Wash: λούω'. *NIDNTT* 1.150-53.

——— 'Baptism, Wash: νίπτω'. *NIDNTT* 1.153-54.

——— *Jesus and the Kingdom of God*. Grand Rapids: Eerdmans, 1986.

——— *John*. WBC 36. Waco, TX: Word Books, 1987.

Becker, J. *Johannes der Täufer und Jesus von Nazareth*. BSt 63. Zürich: Neukirchener, 1972.

——— *Messianic Expectation in the Old Testament*. Trans. D.E. Green. Edinburgh: T. and T. Clark, 1980.

Becker, U. 'Gospel, Evangelize, Evangelist: εὐαγγέλιον, κτλ.'. *NIDNTT* 2.107-15.

Behm, J., and E. Würthwein. 'νοέω, κτλ.'. *TDNT* 4.948-1022.

Bellinzoni, A.J., J.B. Tyson, and W.O. Walker, ed. *The Two-Source Hypothesis: A Critical Appraisal*. Macon, GA: Mercer University Press, 1985.

Bénétreau, S. 'Baptêmes et ablutions dans le Judaism l'originalité de Jean-Baptiste'. *FoiVie* 80 (1981): 96-108.

Benoit, P. 'Qumran and the New Testament'. In *Paul and Qumran*. Ed. J. Murphy-O'Connor. London: Chapman, 1968, 1-30 [repr. from *NTS* 7 (1960–61): 276-96].

Bentzen, A. *King and Messiah*. London: Lutterworth, 1955.

Bernard, J.H. *A Critical and Exegetical Commentary on the Gospel according to St John*. ICC. 2 vols. Ed. A.H. McNeile. Edinburgh: T. and T. Clark, 1928.

Best, E. 'Spirit-Baptism'. *NovT* 4 (1960): 236-43.

Betz, O. 'Die Proselytentaufe der Qumransekte und die Taufe im Neuen Testament'. *RevQ* 1 (1958–59): 213-34.

Bickerman, E. 'Jean-Baptiste au Désert'. In *Studies in Jewish and Christian History*. AGJU 9. Ed. M. Hengel, M. Stern, and P. Schäfer. Leiden: Brill, 1986, 3.7-21 [repr. from *Byzantion* 16 (1942–43)].

Bilde, P. *Flavius Josephus, between Jerusalem and Rome: His Life, His Works, and their Importance*. JSPSup 2. Sheffield: JSOT Press, 1988.

Black, M. 'The Eschatology of the Similitudes of Enoch'. *JTS* 3 (1952): 1-10.

——— 'The Account of the Essenes In Hippolytus and Josephus'. In *The Background of the New Testament and Its Eschatology: In Honour of Charles Harold Dodd*. Ed. W.D. Davies and D. Daube. Cambridge: Cambridge University Press, 1956, 172-75.

——— *An Aramaic Approach to the Gospels and Acts*. 3rd edn. Oxford: Oxford University Press, 1967.

——— 'The Dead Dea Scrolls and Christian Origins'. In *The Scrolls and Christianity*. Theological Collections 11. Ed. M. Black. London: SPCK, 1969, 97-106.

——— 'Judas of Galilee and Josephus's "Fourth Philosophy"'. In *Josephus-Studien: Untersuchungen zu Josephus, dem antiken Judentum und dem Neuen Testament: Otto Michel zum 70. Geburtstag gewidmet*. Ed. O. Betz, K. Haacker, and M. Hengel. Göttingen: Vandenhoeck und Ruprecht, 1974, 45-54.

——— 'The "Parables" of Enoch (1 En. 37–71) and the "Son of Man"'. *ExpTim* 88 (1976–77): 5-8.

——— *The Scrolls and Christian Origins: Studies in the Jewish Background of the New Testament*. Brown Judaic Studies 48. New York: Charles Scribner's Sons, 1961; repr. Chico, CA: Scholars, 1983.

——— 'Aramaic Barnāshā and the Son of Man'. *ExpTim* 95 (1983–84): 200-206.

——— *The Book of Enoch or 1 Enoch*. SVTP 7. Leiden: Brill, 1985.

Bleeker, C.J. 'Some Introductory Remarks on the Significance of Initiation'. In *Initiation*. NumenSup 10. Ed. C.J. Bleeker. Leiden: Brill, 1965, 15-20.

——— ed. *Initiation*. NumenSup 10. Leiden: Brill, 1965.

Blenkinsopp, J. 'Prophecy and Priesthood in Josephus'. *JJS* 25 (1974): 239-62.

——— *A History of Prophecy in Israel*. London: SPCK, 1984.

Böcher, O. 'Ass Johannes der Täufer kein Brot (Luk. vii.33)?'. *NTS* 18 (1971–72): 90-92.

——— 'Johannes der Täufer in der neutestamentlichen Überlieferung'. In *Rechtfertigung—Realismus—Universalismus in biblischer Sicht: Festschrift für A. Köberle*. Ed. G. Müller. Darmstadt: Wissenschiftliche Buchgesellschaft, 1978, 45-68.

——— 'Lukas und Johannes der Täufer'. *SNTU* 4 (1979): 27-44.

Boismard, M.-É. *St John's Prologue*. Trans. C. Dominicans. London: Blackfriars, 1957.

——— 'Les traditions johanniques concernant le Baptiste'. *RB* 70 (1963): 5-42.

Boman, T. *Die Jesus Überlieferung im Lichte der neueren Volkskunde*. Göttingen: Vandenhoeck und Ruprecht, 1967.

Bonnard, P. *L'Évangile selon Saint Matthieu*. 2nd edn. CNT 1. Neuchatel: Delachaux et Niestlé, 1970.

Booth, R.P. *Jesus and the Laws of Purity: Tradition History and Legal History in Mark 7*. JSNTSup 13. Sheffield: JSOT Press, 1986.

Borg, M.J. 'The Currency of the Term "Zealot" '. *JTS* 22 (1971): 504-12.

—— *Conflict, Holiness and Politics in the Teachings of Jesus*. Studies in the Bible and Early Christianity 5. Lewiston, NY: Edwin Mellen, 1984.

—— *Jesus: A New Vision*. San Francisco: Harper and Row, 1987.

—— 'An Orthodoxy Reconsidered: The "End-of-the-World-Jesus" '. In *The Glory of Christ in the New Testament: Studies in Christology in Memory of George Bradford Caird*. Ed. L.D. Hurst and N.T. Wright. Oxford: Oxford University Press, 1987, 207-17.

Borgen, P. 'John and the Synoptics: Can Paul Offer Help?'. In *Tradition and Interpretation in the New Testament: Essays in Honor of E. Earle Ellis for His 60th Birthday*. Ed. G.F. Hawthorne and O. Betz. Grand Rapids: Eerdmans, 1987, 80-94.

Bornkamm, G. *Jesus of Nazareth*. Trans. I. McLuskey and F. McLuskey. London: Hodder and Stoughton, 1960.

Bowen, C.R. 'John the Baptist in the New Testament'. *AJT* 16 (1912): 90-106.

Bowman, J. 'Prophets and Prophecy in Talmud and Midrash'. *EvQ* 22 (1950): 107-14, 202-20, 255-75.

—— 'Did the Qumran Sect Burn the Red Heifer?'. *RevQ* 1 (1958–59): 73-84.

—— *Samaritan Documents Relating to their History, Religion, and Life*. Pittsburgh Original Texts and Translations Series 2. Pittsburgh: Pickwick, 1977.

Brandon, S.G.F. *The Fall of Jerusalem and the Christian Church*. 2nd edn. London: SPCK, 1957.

—— *Jesus and the Zealots*. New York: Charles Scribner's Sons, 1967.

Brandt, W. *Die jüdischen Baptismen*. BZAW 18. Giessen: Töpelmann, 1910.

Braun, H. *Qumran und das Neue Testament*. 2 vols. Tübingen: Mohr, 1966.

—— 'Der Täufertaufe und die qumranischen Waschungen'. *ThVia* 9 (1963): 1-4.

Brekelmans, C.H.W. 'The Saints of the Most High and Their Kingdom'. *OTS* 14 (1965): 305-29.

Bretscher, P.G. ' "Whose Sandals?" (Matt 3.11)'. *JBL* 86 (1967): 81-87.

Brett, M.G. 'Four or Five Things to Do with Texts: A Taxonomy of Interpretive Interests'. In *The Bible in Three Dimensions*. JSOTSup 87. Ed. D.J.A. Clines, S.E. Fowl, and S.E. Porter. Sheffield: JSOT Press, 1990, 357-77.

Brock, S. 'The Baptist's Diet in Syriac Sources'. *OrChr* 54 (1970): 113-24.

Brooke, G.J. *Exegesis at Qumran: 4QFlorilegium in Its Jewish Context*. JSOTSup 29. Sheffield: JSOT Press, 1985.

Broshi, M. 'The Credibility of Josephus'. *JJS* 33 (1982): 379-84.

Brower, K. 'Elijah in the Markan Passion Narrative'. *JSNT* 18 (1983): 85-101.

Brown, C. 'Prophet: προφήτης, κτλ.'. *NIDNTT* 3.74-92.

Brown, P. 'The Rise and Function of the Holy Man in Late Antiquity'. *Journal of Roman Studies* 61 (1971): 80-101.

Brown, R.E. 'The Messianism of Qumran'. *CBQ* 19 (1957): 53-82.

—— 'John the Baptist in the Gospel of John'. In R.E. Brown. *New Testament Essays*. London: Geoffrey Chapman, 1965, 132-40 [repr. from *CBQ* 22 (1960): 292-98].

—— *The Gospel According to John*. 2 vols. AB 29. Garden City: Doubleday, 1966–70.

—— 'The Teacher of Righteousness and the Messiah(s)'. In *The Scrolls and Christianity*. Theological Collections 11. Ed. M. Black. London: SPCK, 1969, 37-44.

—— *The Birth of the Messiah*. Garden City: Doubleday, 1977.

—— 'Gospel Infancy Narrative Research from 1976 to 1986: Part II (Luke)'. *CBQ* 48 (1986): 660-80.

Brownlee, W.H. 'A Comparison of the Covenanters of the Dead Sea Scrolls with Pre-Christian Jewish Sects'. *BA* 13 (1950): 50-72.

—— 'The Servant of the Lord in the Qumran Scrolls, [Part] I'. *BASOR* 132 (1953): 8-15.

—— 'The Servant of the Lord in the Qumran Scrolls, [Part] II'. *BASOR* 135 (1954): 33-38.

—— 'Messianic Motifs of Qumran and the New Testament'. *NTS* 3 (1956–57): 12-30,

195-210.
—— 'John the Baptist in the New Light of Ancient Scrolls'. In *The Scrolls and the New Testament*. Ed. K. Stendahl. London: SCM, 1958, 33-53, 252-56 [repr. from *Int* 9 (1955): 71-90].
—— *The Midrash Pesher of Habakkuk*. SBLMS 24. Missoula, MT: Scholars, 1979.
Bruce, F.F. *The Acts of the Apostles*. 2nd edn. Grand Rapids: Eerdmans, 1952.
—— 'John the Forerunner'. *FT* 94 (1965): 182-90.
—— *The Book of the Acts*. Rev. edn. NICNT. Grand Rapids: Eerdmans, 1988.
Brunt, P.A. 'Josephus on Social Conflicts in Roman Judaea'. *Klio* 59 (1977): 149-53.
Buber, M. *Kingship of God*. 3rd edn. Trans. R. Scheinmann. London: Allen and Unwin, 1967.
Buchanan, G. *Tyrannicall-Government Anatomized: Or, A Discourse Concerning Evil Councellors; Being the Life and Death of John the Baptist*. London: John Field, 1642.
Buchanan, G.W. 'The Role of Purity in the Structure of the Essene Sect'. *RevQ* 4 (1963–64): 397-406.
Büchler, A. *Studies in Sin and Atonement in the Rabbinic Literature of the First Century*. 1928; repr. New York: Ktav, 1967.
—— *Types of Jewish-Palestinian Piety From 70 BCE to 70 CE: The Ancient Pious Men*. 1922; repr. Farnborough: Jew's College Publications, 1969.
Budd, P.J. *Numbers*. WBC 5. Waco, TX: Word Books, 1984.
Bultmann, R. *Jesus and the Word*. Trans. L.P. Smith and E.H. Lantero. New York: Charles Scribner's Sons, 1934.
—— *Theology of the New Testament*. 2 vols. Trans. K. Grobel. New York: Charles Scribner's Sons, 1951–55.
—— *The History of the Synoptic Tradition*. Rev. edn. Trans. J. Marsh. New York: Harper and Row, 1963.
—— *The Gospel of John*. Trans. G.R. Beasley-Murray. Oxford: Blackwell, 1971.
Burrows, E.W. 'Did John the Baptist Call Jesus "The Lamb of God"?'. *ExpTim* 85 (1974): 245-49.
Burrows, M. 'The Discipline Manual of the Judaean Covenanters'. *OTS* 8 (1950): 156-92.
—— 'The Messiahs of Aaron and Israel (DSD IX, 11)'. *ATR* 34 (1952): 202-206.
—— 'Prophecy and the Prophets at Qumran'. In *Israel's Prophetic Heritage: Essays in Honor of James Muilenburg*. Ed. G.W. Anderson and W. Harrelson. London: SCM, 1962, 223-32.
Cadbury, H.J., F.J. Foakes-Jackson, and K. Lake. 'The Greek and Jewish Traditions of Writing History'. In *The Beginnings of Christianity*. Ed. F.J. Foakes-Jackson and K. Lake. London: Macmillan, 1922, 2.7-29.
Cadoux, C.J. *The Historic Mission of Jesus*. London: Lutterworth, 1941.
Cameron, P.S. *Violence and the Kingdom: The Interpretation of Matthew 11.12*. 2nd edn. ANTJ 5. Frankfurt am Main: Peter Lang, 1988.
Caragounis, C.C. *The Son of Man: Vision and Interpretation*. WUNT 38. Tübingen: Mohr, 1986.
Carey, G.L. 'The Lamb of God and Atonement Theories'. *TynBul* 32 (1981): 97-122.
Carmignac, J. 'Le document de Qumran sur Melkisédeq'. *RevQ* 7 (1969-71): 343-78.
Carmignac, J., and P. Guilbert. *Les Textes de Qumran*. 2 vols. Paris: Letouzey et Ané, 1961.
Carroll, R.P. *When Prophecy Failed: Reactions and Responses to Failure in the Old Testament Prophetic Traditions*. London: SCM, 1979.
Carson, D.A. *Exegetical Fallacies*. Grand Rapids: Baker Book House, 1984.
Casey, M. *The Son of Man: The Interpretation and Influence of Daniel 7*. London: SPCK, 1979.
Cassuto, U. *A Commentary on the Book of Exodus*. Trans. I. Abrahams. Jerusalem: Magnes, 1967.
Chamblin, K. 'Gospel and Judgment in the Preaching of John the Baptist'. *TynBul* 13

(1963): 7-15.

———— 'John the Baptist and the Kingdom of God'. *TynBul* 15 (1964): 10-16.

Charlesworth, J.H. 'The SNTS Pseudepigrapha Seminars at Tübingen and Paris on the Books of Enoch'. *NTS* 25 (1978–79): 315-23.

———— 'The Concept of the Messiah in the Pseudepigrapha'. In *ANRW* 2.19.1. Ed. H. Temporini and W. Haase. Berlin: Walter de Gruyter, 1979, 188-218.

———— 'The Origin and Subsequent History of the Authors of the Dead Sea Scrolls: Four Transitional Phases among the Qumran Essenes'. *RevQ* 10 (1979–81): 213-33.

———— *The Pseudepigrapha and Modern Research: With a Supplement*. SBLSCS 7S. Chico, CA: Scholars, 1981.

———— *The Old Testament Pseudepigrapha and the New Testament*. SNTSMS 54. Cambridge: Cambridge University Press, 1985.

———— *Jesus Within Judaism*. New York: Doubleday, 1988.

Childs, B.S. *Exodus: A Commentary*. OTL. London: SCM, 1974.

———— *Introduction to the Old Testament as Scripture*. Philadelphia: Fortress, 1979.

———— *Old Testament Theology in a Canonical Context*. Philadelphia: Fortress, 1985.

Christiansen, E.J. 'Taufe als Initiation in der Apostelgeschichte'. *ST* 40 (1986): 55-79.

Cohen, S.J.D. *Josephus in Galilee and Rome: His Vita and Development as a Historian*. CSCT 8. Leiden: Brill, 1979.

———— 'Masada: Literary Tradition, Archaeological Remains, and the Credibility of Josephus'. *JJS* 33 (1982): 385-405.

Collins, J.J. 'The Son of Man and the Saints of the Most High in the Book of Daniel'. *JBL* 93 (1974): 50-66.

———— 'The Place of the Fourth Sibyl in the Development of Jewish Sibyllina'. *JJS* 25 (1974): 365-80.

———— *The Apocalyptic Vision of the Book of Daniel*. HSM 16. Missoula, MT: Scholars, 1977.

———— 'The Heavenly Representative: The "Son of Man" in the Similitudes of Enoch'. In *Ideal Figures in Ancient Judaism: Profiles and Paradigms*. SBLSCS 12. Ed. G.W.E. Nickelsburg and J.J. Collins. Chico, CA: Scholars, 1980, 111-33.

———— 'Testaments'. In *Jewish Writings of the Second Temple Period*. CRINT 2.2. Ed. M.E. Stone. Assen: Van Gorcum; Philadelphia: Fortress, 1984, 325-55.

———— *Daniel with an Introduction to Apocalyptic Literature*. FOTL 20. Grand Rapids: Eerdmans, 1984.

———— *The Apocalyptic Imagination*. New York: Crossroad, 1984.

———— 'The Sibylline Oracles'. In *Jewish Writings of the Second Temple Period*. CRINT 2.2. Ed. M.E. Stone. Assen: Van Gorcum; Philadelphia: Fortress, 1984, 357-83.

———— *Between Athens and Jerusalem*. New York: Crossroad, 1986.

———— 'The Testamentary Literature in Recent Scholarship'. In *Early Judaism and Its Modern Interpreters*. The Bible and Its Modern Interpreters 2. Ed. R.A. Kraft and G.W.E. Nickelsburg. Atlanta: Scholars, 1986, 268-85.

———— 'Messianism in the Maccabean Period'. In *Judaisms and Their Messiahs at the Turn of the Christian Era*. Ed. J. Neusner, W.S. Green, and E. Frerichs. Cambridge: Cambridge University Press, 1987, 97-109.

Collins, M.F. 'The Hidden Vessels in Samaritan Traditions'. *JSJ* 3 (1972): 97-116.

Colpe, C. 'ὁ υἱὸς τοῦ ἀνθρώπου'. *TDNT* 8.400-77.

Conzelmann, H. *The Theology of St Luke*. Trans. G. Buswell. New York: Harper and Row, 1960; repr. Philadelphia: Fortress, 1982.

Cothenet, É. 'Qumran et le Nouveau Testament: A. Jean-Baptiste'. *DBSup* 9.980-96.

Craigie, P.C. *The Book of Deuteronomy*. NICOT. Grand Rapids: Eerdmans, 1976.

———— *Psalms 1–50*. WBC 19. Waco, TX: Word Books, 1983.

Cranfield, C.E.B. *The Gospel According to Saint Mark*. 5th edn. CGTC. Cambridge: Cambridge University Press, 1977.

Creed, J.M. 'Josephus on John the Baptist'. *JTS* 23 (1922): 59-60.

———— *The Gospel According to St Luke*. London: Macmillan, 1930.

———— 'The Slavonic Version of Josephus' History of the Jewish War'. *HTR* 25 (1932): 277-319.

Cross, F.M. *The Ancient Library of Qumran and Modern Biblical Studies*. London: Duckworth, 1958.

Crossan, J.D. *The Cross that Spoke: The Origins of the Passion Narrative*. San Francisco: Harper and Row, 1988.

Cullmann, O ''Ο ὀπίσω μου ἐρχόμενος'. In *The Early Church*. Ed. A.J.B. Higgins. London: SCM, 1956, 177-82 [repr. from *ConNT* 11 (1947): 26-32].

———— 'Samaria and the Origins of the Christian Mission'. In *The Early Church*. Ed. A.J.B. Higgins. London: SCM, 1956, 185-92.

———— 'The Significance of the Qumran Texts for Research into the Beginnings of Christianity'. In *The Scrolls and the New Testament*. Ed. K. Stendahl. London: SCM, 1958, 18-32, 251-52 [repr. from *JBL* 74 (1955): 213-26].

———— *The Christology of the New Testament*. Rev. edn. Trans. S.C. Guthrie and C.A.M. Hall. Philadelphia: Westminster, 1963.

Culpepper, R.A. 'The Pivot of John's Prologue'. *NTS* 27 (1980): 1-31.

Dahl, N.A. 'The Origin of Baptism'. *NorTT* 56 (1955): 36-52.

Dalman, G. *Arbeit und Sitte in Palästina*. 7 vols. 1928–42; repr. Hildescheim: Georg Olms, 1964.

Daniélou, J. *The Work of John the Baptist*. Baltimore: Helicon, 1966.

Darton, G.C. *St John the Baptist and the Kingdom of Heaven*. London: Darton, Longman and Todd, 1961.

Daube, D. *The New Testament and Rabbinic Judaism*. London: Athlone, 1956.

Davenport, G.L. 'The "Anointed of the Lord" in Psalms of Solomon 17'. In *Ideal Figures in Ancient Judaism: Profiles and Paradigms*. SBLSCS 12. Ed. G.W.E. Nickelsburg and J.J. Collins. Chico, CA: Scholars, 1980, 67-92.

Davids, P.H. 'The Gospels and Jewish Tradition: Twenty Years after Gerhardsson'. In *Gospel Perspectives*. Ed. R.T. France and D. Wenham, Sheffield: JSOT Press, 1980, 1.75-99.

Davies, D. 'An Interpretation of Sacrifice in Leviticus'. *ZAW* 89 (1977): 387-99.

Davies, P.R. *1QM, the War Scroll from Qumran*. BibOr 32. Rome: Biblical Institute, 1977.

———— 'Eschatology in the Book of Daniel'. *JSOT* 17 (1980): 33-53.

———— *The Damascus Covenant*. JSOTSup 25. Sheffield: JSOT Press, 1982.

———— 'The Ideology of the Temple in the Damascus Document'. *JJS* 33 (1982): 287-301.

———— *Daniel*. OTG. Sheffield: JSOT Press, 1985.

Davies, S.L. 'John the Baptist and Essene Kashruth'. *NTS* 29 (1983): 569-71.

Davies, W.D. *The Gospel and the Land*. Berkeley: University of California Press, 1974.

———— *Paul and Rabbinic Judaism*. 4th edn. Philadelphia: Fortress, 1980.

Davies, W.D., and D.C. Allison. *A Critical and Exegetical Commentary on the Gospel According to Saint Matthew*. ICC. Vol. 1. Edinburgh: T. and T. Clark, 1988.

de Jonge, M. *The Testaments of the Twelve Patriarchs: A Study of Their Text, Composition, and Origin*. Van Gorcum's Theologische Bibliotheek 25. Assen: Van Gorcum, 1953.

———— 'The Use of the Word "Anointed" in the Time of Jesus'. *NovT* 8 (1966): 132-48.

———— 'Notes on Testament of Levi II-VII'. In *Studies on the Testaments of the Twelve Patriarchs: Text and Interpretation*. SVTP 3. Ed. M. de Jonge. Leiden: Brill, 1975, 247-60.

———— 'The Testaments of the Twelve Patriarchs: Central Problems and Essential Viewpoints'. In *ANRW* 2.20.1. Ed. H. Temporini and W. Haase. Berlin: Walter de Gruyter, 1987, 359-420.

de Jonge, M., and A.S. van der Woude. '11QMelchizedek and the New Testament'. *NTS* 12 (1965–66): 301-26.

de Vaux, R. *Ancient Israel*. Trans. J. McHugh. London: Darton, Longman and Todd.

1961.

——— *Archaeology and the Dead Sea Scrolls*. Rev. edn. London: Oxford University Press, 1973.

de Villiers, P.G.R. 'The Messiah and Messiahs in Jewish Apocalyptic'. *Neot* 12 (1981): 75-110.

de Vries, S.J. 'Sin, Sinners'. *IDB* 4.361-76.

Deissmann, A. *Light from the Ancient East*. Trans. L.R.M. Strachan. London: Hodder and Stoughton, 1910.

del Medico, E.H. 'Les Esséniens dans l'oeuvre de Flavius Josèphe'. *Byzantinoslavica* 13 (1952–53): 193-202.

Delcor, M. 'Le vocabulaire juridique, cultuel et mystique de l' "initiation" dans la secte de Qumran'. In *Qumran-Probleme*. Ed. H. Bardtke. Berlin: Akademie, 1963, 109-34.

——— 'Melchizedek from Genesis to the Qumran Texts and the Epistle to the Hebrews'. *JSJ* 2 (1971): 115-35.

Dequeker, L. 'The "Saints of the Most High" in Qumran and Daniel'. *OTS* 18 (1973): 108-87.

Derrett, J.D.M. 'Herod's Oath and the Baptist's Head (Mk 6.17-29)'. *BZ* 9 (1965): 49-59, 233-46.

Dibelius, M. *Die urchristliche Überlieferung von Johannes dem Täufer*. Göttingen: Vandenhoeck und Ruprecht, 1911.

——— *From Tradition to Gospel*. Trans. B.L. Woolf., 1971; repr. Cambridge: James Clark, 1982.

Dimant, D. 'Qumran Sectarian Literature'. In *Jewish Writings of the Second Temple Period*. CRINT 2.2. Ed. M.E. Stone. Assen: Van Gorcum; Philadelphia: Fortress, 1984, 483-550.

Dodd, C.H. *The Interpretation of the Fourth Gospel*. Cambridge: Cambridge University Press, 1953.

——— *Historical Tradition in the Fourth Gospel*. Cambridge: Cambridge University Press, 1963.

Douglas, M. *Purity and Danger: An Analysis of the Concepts of Pollution and Taboo*. 1966; repr. London: ARK, 1984.

Downing, F.G. 'Redaction Criticism: Josephus' Antiquities and the Synoptic Gospels [Part] 1'. *JSNT* 8 (1980): 46-65.

——— 'Redaction Criticism: Josephus' Antiquities and the Synoptic Gospels [Part] 2'. *JSNT* 9 (1980): 29-48.

Draper, J.A. 'A Targum of Isaiah in 1QS III, 2-3'. *RevQ* 11 (1982–84): 265-69.

Driver, G.R. *The Judaean Scrolls: The Problem and a Solution*. Oxford: Blackwell, 1965.

Driver, S.R. *A Critical and Exegetical Commentary on Deuteronomy*. ICC. 3rd edn. Edinburgh: T. and T. Clark, 1902.

Drury, J. 'Mark 1.1-15: An Interpretation'. In *Alternative Approaches to New Testament Study*. Ed. A.E. Harvey. London: SPCK, 1985, 25-36.

Dulière, W.L. 'Les adaptations de Jean le Baptiste à la structuration du Nouveau Testament'. *ZRGG* 19 (1967): 308-20.

Dunkerley, R. 'The Riddles of Josephus'. *HibJ* 53 (1954–55): 127-34.

Dunn, J.D.G. *Baptism in the Holy Spirit*. Philadelphia: Westminster, 1970.

——— 'Spirit-and-Fire Baptism'. *NovT* 14 (1972): 81-92.

——— 'Let John be John: A Gospel for Its Time'. In *Das Evangelium und die Evangelien: Vorträge vom Tübinger Symposium 1982*. WUNT 28. Ed. P. Stuhlmacher. Tübingen: Mohr, 1983, 309-39.

——— *The Evidence for Jesus*. London: SCM, 1985.

Dupont-Sommer, A. *The Jewish Sect of Qumran and the Essenes*. Vallentie: Mitchell, 1954.

——— 'Culpabilité et rites de purification dans la secte juive de Qoumran'. *Sem* 15 (1965): 61-70.

——— *The Essene Writings from Qumran*. Trans. G. Vermes. 1961; repr. Gloucester: Peter Smith, 1973.

Durham, J.I. *Exodus*. WBC 3. Waco, TX: Word Books, 1987.

Eaton, J.H. *Kingship and the Psalms*. Biblical Seminar 3. 2nd edn. Sheffield: JSOT Press, 1986.

[Editorial Staff]. 'Proselytes'. *EncJud* 13.1182-93.

[Editorial Staff]. 'Purity and Impurity, Ritual'. *EncJud* 13.1405-14.

Edwards, R.A. *A Theology of Q*. Philadelphia: Fortress, 1976.

Eichrodt, W. *Theology of the Old Testament*. OTL. 2 vols. Trans. J.A. Baker. Philadelphia: Westminster, 1961–67.

Eisler, R. *The Messiah Jesus and John the Baptist according to Flavius Josephus' Recently Discovered 'Capture of Jerusalem' and Other Jewish and Christian Sources*. Trans. A.H. Krappe. London: Methuen, 1931.

Elgvin, T. 'The Qumran Covenant Festival and the Temple Scroll'. *JJS* 36 (1985): 103-106.

Elliott, J.H. 'Social-Scientific Criticism of the New Testament and Its Social World: More on Method and Models'. *Semeia* 35 (1986): 1-33.

Ellis, E.E. *The Gospel of Luke*. Rev. edn. NCB. Grand Rapids: Eerdmans, 1974.

Endres, J.C. *Biblical Interpretation in the Book of Jubilees*. CBQMS 18. Washington, DC: Catholic Biblical Association, 1987.

Enslin, M.S. 'Once Again: John the Baptist'. *RL* 27 (1957–58): 557-66.

——— 'Ebionites'. *IDB* 2.5-6.

——— 'John and Jesus'. *ZNW* 66 (1975): 1-18.

——— 'Once More, The Messiah'. In *Essays on the Occasion of the Seventieth Anniversary of the Dropsie University*. Ed. A.I. Katsh and L. Nemoy. Philadelphia: Dropsie University, 1979, 49-61.

Ernst, J. *Johannes der Täufer: Interpretation—Geschichte—Wirkungsgeschichte*. BZNW 53. Berlin: Walter de Gruyter, 1989.

Evans, C.A. *Life of Jesus Research: An Annotated Bibliography*. NTTS 13. Leiden: Brill, 1989.

——— 'Jesus' Action in the Temple: Cleansing or Portent of Destruction?'. *CBQ* 51 (1989): 237-70.

——— 'Jesus' Action in the Temple and Evidence of Corruption in the First-Century Temple'. In *Society of Biblical Literature 1989 Seminar Papers*. SBLSP 28. Ed. D.J. Lull. Atlanta: Scholars, 1989, 522-39.

Fahy, T. 'St John and Elias'. *ITQ* 23 (1956): 285-86.

Faierstein, M.M. 'Why Do the Scribes Say that Elijah Must Come First?'. *JBL* 100 (1981): 75-86.

Farmer, W.R. 'John the Baptist'. *IDB* 2.955-62.

——— *The Synoptic Problem: A Critical Analysis*. Macon, GA: Mercer University Press, 1976.

——— *Jesus and the Gospel: Tradition, Scripture, and Canon*. Philadelphia: Fortress, 1982.

Farris, S. *The Hymns of Luke's Infancy Narratives: Their Origin, Meaning, and Significance*. JSNTSup 9. Sheffield: JSOT Press, 1985.

Feldman, L.H. *Scholarship on Philo and Josephus (1937–1962)*. Studies in Judaica 1. New York: Yeshiva University, 1963.

——— *Josephus and Modern Scholarship (1937–1980)*. Berlin: Walter de Gruyter, 1984.

——— 'Flavius Josephus Revisited: The Man, His Writings, and His Significance'. In *ANRW* 2.21.2. Ed. H. Temporini and W. Haase. Berlin: Walter de Gruyter, 1984, 763-862.

Ferch, A.J. *The Son of Man in Daniel 7*. Andrews University Seminary Doctoral Dissertation Series 6. Berrien Springs: Andrews University Press, 1983.

Filson, F.V. *A Commentary on the Gospel according to St Matthew*. BNTC. London: A. and C. Black, 1960.

———— 'John the Baptist'. *ISBE* 2.1108-11.
Finegan, J. *Handbook of Biblical Chronology*. Princeton: Princeton University Press, 1964.
Finkelstein, L. 'The Institution of Baptism for Proselytes'. *JBL* 52 (1933): 203-11.
Fitzmyer, J.A. 'The Priority of Mark and the "Q" Source in Luke'. In *Jesus and Man's Hope*. Ed. D.G. Buttrick. Pittsburg: Perspective, 1970, 1.131-70.
———— ' "4QTestimonia" and the New Testament'. In J.A. Fitzmyer. *Essays on the Semitic Background of the New Testament*. London: Geoffrey Chapman, 1971, 59-89 [repr. from *TS* 18 (1957): 513-37].
———— 'The Aramaic "Elect of God" and the New Testament'. In J.A. Fitzmyer. *Essays on the Semitic Background of the New Testament*. London: Geoffrey Chapman, 1971, 127-60 [repr. from *CBQ* 27 (1965): 348-72].
———— 'Further Light on Melchizedek from Qumran Cave 11'. In J.A. Fitzmyer. *Essays on the Semitic Background of the New Testament*. London: Geoffrey Chapman, 1971, 245-67 [repr. from *JBL* 86 (1967): 25-41].
———— *The Dead Sea Scrolls: Major Publications and Tools for Study*. SBLSBS 8. Rev. edn. Missoula, MT: Scholars, 1977.
———— *The Gospel According to Luke*. 2 vols. AB 28. Garden City: Doubleday, 1981–85.
———— 'More about Elijah Coming First'. *JBL* 104 (1985): 295-96.
———— *Luke the Theologian*. London: Geoffrey Chapman, 1989.
Fleddermann, H. 'John and the Coming One (Matt 3.11-12//Lk 3.16-17)'. In *Society of Biblical Literature 1984 Seminar Papers*. SBLSP 23. Ed. K.H. Richards. Chico, CA: Scholars, 1984, 377-84.
Flemington, W.F. *The New Testament Doctrine of Baptism*. London: SPCK, 1948.
———— 'Baptism'. *IDB* 1.348-53.
Flusser, D. 'The Dead Sea Sect and Pre-Pauline Christianity'. In *Scripta Hierosolymitana*. Jerusalem: Magnes, 1958, 4.215-66.
———— 'The Baptism of John and the Dead Sea Sect'. In *Essays on the Dead Sea Scrolls: In Memory of E.L. Sukenik*. Ed. C. Rabin and Y. Yadin. Jerusalem: Hekhal Ha-Sefer, 1961, 209-38 (Hebrew).
Foakes-Jackson, F.J., and K. Lake, ed. *The Beginnings of Christianity*. 5 vols. London: Macmillan, 1920–33.
Ford, J.M. 'Zealotism and the Lukan Infancy Narratives'. *NovT* 18 (1976): 280-92.
Fornara, C.W. *The Nature of History in Ancient Greece and Rome*. Berkeley: University of California Press, 1983.
Fowl, S. 'Reconstructing and Deconstructing the Quest of the Historical Jesus'. *SJT* 42 (1989): 319-33.
France, R.T. *Jesus and the Old Testament*. 1971; repr. Grand Rapids: Baker Book House, 1982.
Freyne, S. 'The Charismatic'. In *Ideal Figures in Ancient Judaism: Profiles and Paradigms*. SBLSCS 12. Ed. G.W.E. Nickelsburg and J.J. Collins. Chico, CA: Scholars, 223-58.
Friedrich, G. 'εὐαγγελίζομαι, κτλ.'. *TDNT* 2.707-37.
Frymer-Kensky, T. 'Pollution, Purification, and Purgation in Biblical Israel'. In *The Word of the Lord Shall Go Forth: Essays in Honor of David Noel Freedman in Celebration of His Sixtieth Birthday*. Ed. C.L. Meyers and M. O'Connor. Winona Lake, IN: Eisenbrauns, 1983, 399-414.
Fuchs, A. 'Intention und Adressaten der Busspredigt des Täufers bei Mt 3,7-10'. In *Jesus in der Verkündigung der Kirche*. SNTU A1. Ed. A. Fuchs. Freistadt: Plöchl, 1976, 62-75.
Fuller, R.H. *The Foundations of New Testament Christology*. New York: Charles Scribner's Sons, 1965.
Funk, R.W. 'The Wilderness'. *JBL* 78 (1959): 205-14.
Gabba, E. 'Literature'. In *Sources for Ancient History*. Ed. M. Crawford. Cambridge: Cambridge University Press, 1983, 1-79.

Gager, J.G. *Kingdom and Community: The Social World of Early Christianity*. Englewood Cliffs, NJ: Prentice-Hall, 1975.

Garnet, P. *Salvation and Atonement in the Qumran Scrolls*. WUNT 2.3. Tübingen: Mohr, 1977.

Gärtner, B. *The Theology of the Gospel of Thomas*. Trans. E.J. Sharpe. London: Collins, 1961.

——— *The Temple and the Community in Qumran and the New Testament*. SNTSMS 1. Cambridge: Cambridge University Press, 1965.

Gaster, M. *The Samaritans*. Oxford: Oxford University Press, 1925.

——— *Samaritan Eschatology*. Vol. 1 of *Samaritan Oral Law and Ancient Traditions*. New York: The Search Publishing House, 1932.

Gavin, F. *The Jewish Antecedents of the Christian Sacraments*. London: SPCK, 1928.

Gerhardsson, B. *The Gospel Tradition*. ConBNT 15. Lund: Gleerup, 1986.

Geyser, A.S. 'The Youth of John the Baptist: A Deduction from the Break in the Parallel Account of the Lucan Infancy Story'. *NovT* 1 (1956): 70-75.

Giblin, C.H. 'Two Complementary Literary Structures in John 1.1-18'. *JBL* 104 (1985): 87-103.

Ginzberg, L. *An Unknown Jewish Sect*. 1922; repr. New York: Jewish Theological Seminary, 1976.

Glasson, T.F. 'John the Baptist in the Fourth Gospel'. *ExpTim* 67 (1955–56): 245-46.

Glazier-McDonald, B. *Malachi: The Divine Messenger*. SBLDS 98. Atlanta: Scholars, 1987.

Gnilka, J. 'Die Essenischen Tauchbäder und die Johannestaufe'. *RevQ* 3 (1961–62): 185-207.

——— 'Der Täufer Johannes und der Ursprung der christlichen Taufe'. *Bibel und Leben* 4 (1963): 39-49.

——— 'Das Martyrium Johannes' des Täufers (Mk 6,17-29)'. In *Orientierung an Jesus: Zur Theologie der Synoptiker für Josef Schmid*. Ed. P. Hoffmann. Freiburg: Herder, 1973, 78-92.

——— *Das Evangelium nach Markus*. EKKNT 2. 2 vols. Zürich: Benziger; Neukirchen-Vluyn: Neukirchener, 1978–79.

——— *Das Matthäusevangelium*. HTKNT 1. Freiburg: Herder, 1986.

Goguel, M. *Au Seuil de L'Évangile: Jean-Baptiste*. Paris: Payot, 1928.

——— *Jesus*. 2nd edn. Trans. O. Wyon. London: Allen and Unwin, 1958.

Goldingay, J.E. *Daniel*. WBC 30. Dallas: Word Books, 1989.

Goldsmith, M. *John the Baptist: A Modern Interpretation*. London: Arthur Barker, 1935.

Goldstein, J.A. *I Maccabees*. AB 41. New York: Doubleday, 1976.

——— *II Maccabees*. AB 41A. New York: Doubleday, 1983.

Goodman, M. *The Ruling Class of Judaea*. Cambridge: Cambridge University Press, 1987.

Goppelt, L. *Theology of the New Testament*. 2 vols. Trans. J.E. Alsup. Ed. J. Roloff. Grand Rapids: Eerdmans, 1981.

Gould, E.P. *A Critical and Exegetical Commentary on the Gospel according to St Mark*. ICC. Edinburgh: T. and T. Clark, 1896.

Gowan, D.E. *Eschatology in the Old Testament*. Edinburgh: T. and T. Clark, 1986.

Grant, F.C. 'The Economic Background of the New Testament'. In *The Background of the New Testament and Its Eschatology: In Honour of Charles Harold Dodd*. Ed. W.D. Davies and D. Daube. Cambridge: Cambridge University Press, 1956, 96-114.

Grant, R.M., and D.N. Freedman. *The Secret Sayings of Jesus according to the Gospel of Thomas*. London: Collins, 1960.

Green, W.S. 'Palestinian Holy Men: Charismatic Leadership and Rabbinic Tradition'. In *ANRW* 2.19.2. Ed. H. Temporini and W. Haase. Berlin: Walter de Gruyter, 1979, 619-47.

——— 'Introduction: Messiah in Judaism: Rethinking the Question'. In *Judaisms and Their Messiahs at the Turn of the Christian Era*. Ed. J. Neusner, W.S. Green, and

E. Frerichs. Cambridge: Cambridge University Press, 1987, 1-14.

Greenfield, J.C., and M.E. Stone, 'The Enochic Pentateuch and the Date of the Similitudes'. *HTR* 70 (1977): 51-65.

Greenspahn, F.E. 'Why Prophecy Ceased'. *JBL* 108 (1989): 37-49.

Grelot, P. 'Notes sur le Testament Araméen de Lévi'. *RB* 63 (1956): 391-406.

Grobel, K. 'He that Cometh after Me'. *JBL* 60 (1941): 397-401.

Guelich, R.A. ' "The Beginning of the Gospel": Mark 1.1-15'. *BR* 27 (1982): 5-15.

——— *Mark 1–8.26.* WBC 34A. Dallas: Word Books, 1989.

Guignebert, C. *The Jewish World in the Time of Jesus.* Trans. S.H. Hooke. London: Routledge and Kegan Paul, 1939.

Guilbert, P. 'La Règle de la Communauté'. In *Les Textes de Qumran.* Ed. J. Carmignac and P. Guilbert. Paris: Letouzey et Ané, 1.9-80.

Gundry, R.H. *The Use of the Old Testament in St Matthew's Gospel with Special Reference to the Messianic Hope.* NovTSup 18. Leiden: Brill, 1967.

——— *Matthew.* Grand Rapids: Eerdmans, 1982.

Haenchen, E. *The Acts of the Apostles.* Trans. B. Noble and G. Shinn. Oxford: Blackwell, 1971.

——— *A Commentary on the Gospel of John.* Hermeneia. 2 vols. Trans. R.W. Funk. Philadelphia: Fortress, 1984.

Hahn, F. *The Titles of Jesus in Christology: Their History in Early Christianity.* Trans. H. Knight and G. Ogg. London: Lutterworth, 1969.

Hanson, P.D. *The Dawn of Apocalyptic.* Rev. edn. Philadelphia: Fortress, 1979.

Harrelson, W. 'Nonroyal Motifs in the Royal Eschatology'. In *Israel's Prophetic Heritage: Essays in Honor of James Muilenburg.* Ed. B.W. Anderson and W. Harrelson. London: SCM, 1962, 147-65.

Harris, M.J. 'Appendix: Prepositions and Theology in the Greek New Testament'. *NIDNTT* 3.1171-215.

Harrison, R.K. 'The Rites and Customs of the Qumran Sect'. In *The Scrolls and Christianity.* Theological Collections 11. Ed. M. Black. London: SPCK, 1969, 26-36.

Hartman, L. *Prophecy Interpreted: The Formation of Some Jewish Apocalyptic Texts and of the Eschatological Discourse Mark 13 par.* Trans. N. Tomkinson and J. Gray. Lund: Gleerup, 1966.

Hartman, L.F., and A.A. di Lella. *The Book of Daniel.* AB 23. Garden City: Doubleday, 1978.

Harvey, A.E. *Jesus and the Constraints of History.* Philadelphia: Westminster, 1982.

Harvey, V.A., and S.M. Ogden. 'How New Is the "New Quest of the Historical Jesus"?'. In *The Historical Jesus and the Kerygmatic Christ.* Ed. C.E. Braaten and R.A. Harrisville. New York: Abingdon, 1964, 197-242.

Hasel, G.F. 'The Identity of "The Saints of the Most High" in Daniel 7'. *Bib* 56 (1975): 173-92.

Havener, I. *Q: The Sayings of Jesus.* GNS 19. Wilmington, DE: Michael Glazier, 1987.

Heichelheim, F.M. 'Roman Syria'. In *An Economic Survey of Ancient Rome.* Ed. T. Frank. 1938; repr. Paterson: Pageant Books, 1959, 4.121-257.

Hemer, C.J. *The Book of Acts in the Setting of Hellenistic History.* WUNT 49. Ed. C.H. Gempf. Tübingen: Mohr, 1989.

Hengel, M. *Judaism and Hellenism.* 2 vols. Trans. J. Bowden. Philadelphia: Fortress, 1974.

——— *Studies in the Gospel of Mark.* Trans. J. Bowden. Philadelphia: Fortress, 1985.

——— *The Zealots.* Trans. D. Smith. Edinburgh: T. and T. Clark, 1989.

Heron, J. 'The Theology of Baptism'. *SJT* 8 (1955): 36-52.

Higgins, A.J.B. 'The Priestly Messiah'. *NTS* 13 (1966–67): 211-39.

Hill, D. *The Gospel of Matthew.* NCB. Grand Rapids: Eerdmans, 1972.

——— 'Jesus and Josephus' "Messianic Prophets" '. In *Text and Interpretation: Studies in the New Testament Presented to Matthew Black.* Ed. E. Best and R. McL. Wilson. Cambridge: Cambridge University, 1979, 143-54.

———— *New Testament Prophecy*. New Foundations Theological Library. Atlanta: John Knox, 1979.

Hindley, J.C. 'Towards a Date for the Similitudes of Enoch: An Historical Approach'. *NTS* 14 (1967–68): 551-65.

Hirsch, E.G. 'Proselyte'. *JewEnc* 10.220-24.

Hobbs, T.R. *2 Kings*. WBC 13. Waco, TX: Word Books, 1985.

Hoehner, H.W. *Chronological Aspects of the Life of Christ*. Grand Rapids: Zondervan, 1977.

———— *Herod Antipas*. Cambridge: Cambridge University Press, 1972; repr. Grand Rapids: Zondervan, 1980.

Hoffman, P. *Studien zur Theologie der Logienquelle*. NTAbh 8. Münster: Aschendorff, 1972.

Holladay, W.L. *The Root Subh in the Old Testament*. Leiden: Brill, 1958.

Hollenbach, P.W. 'Social Aspects of John the Baptizer's Preaching Mission in the Context of Palestinian Judaism'. In *ANRW* 2.19.1. Ed. H. Temporini and W. Haase. Berlin: Walter de Gruyter, 1979, 850-75.

———— 'The Conversion of Jesus: From Jesus the Baptizer to Jesus the Healer'. In *ANRW* 2.25.1. Ed. H. Temporini and W. Haase. Berlin: Walter de Gruyter, 1982, 196-219.

———— 'Recent Historical Jesus Studies and the Social Sciences'. In *Society of Biblical Literature 1983 Seminar Papers*. SBLSP 22. Ed. K.H. Richards. Chico, CA: Scholars, 1983, 61-78.

Holm-Nielsen, S. *Hodayot: Psalms from Qumran*. Aarhus: Universitetsforlaget, 1960.

Holtz, T. 'Die Standespredigt Johannes des Täufers'. In *Ruf und Antwort: Festschrift Ernst Fuchs*. Leipzig: n.p., 1964, 461-74.

Hooker, M.D. *The Son of Man in Mark*. London: SPCK, 1967.

———— 'John the Baptist and the Johannine Prologue'. *NTS* 16 (1969–70): 354-58.

Hookey, J.R. 'John the Baptist in the Context of Contemporary Religious Movements within Judaism'. PhD Thesis: University of Edinburgh, 1963–64.

Horbury, W. 'The Messianic Associations of "The Son of Man" '. *JTS* 36 (1985): 4-55.

Horgan, M.P. *Pesharim: Qumran Interpretations of Biblical Books*. CBQMS 8. Washington, DC: Catholic Biblical Association, 1979.

Horsley, R.A. 'The Sicarii: Ancient Jewish "Terrorists" '. *JR* 59 (1979): 435-58.

———— 'Josephus and the Bandits'. *JSJ* 10 (1979): 37-63.

———— 'Ancient Jewish Banditry and the Revolt against Rome, A.D. 66–70'. *CBQ* 43 (1981): 409-32.

———— 'Popular Messianic Movements around the Time of Jesus'. *CBQ* 46 (1984): 471-95.

———— ' "Like One of the Prophets of Old": Two Types of Popular Prophets at the Time of Jesus'. *CBQ* 47 (1985): 435-63.

———— 'High Priests and the Politics of Roman Palestine'. *JSJ* 17 (1986): 23-55.

———— 'Popular Prophetic Movements at the Time of Jesus: Their Principal Features and Social Origins'. *JSNT* 26 (1986): 3-27.

———— 'The Zealots: Their Origin, Relationships and Importance in the Jewish Revolt'. *NovT* 28 (1986): 159-92.

———— *Jesus and the Spiral of Violence*. San Francisco: Harper and Row, 1987.

———— *Sociology and the Jesus Movement*. New York: Crossroad, 1989.

———— *The Liberation of Christmas: The Infancy Narratives in Social Context*. New York: Crossroad, 1989.

Horsley, R.A., and J.S. Hanson. *Bandits, Prophets, and Messiahs: Popular Movements in the Time of Jesus*. New Voices in Biblical Studies. Minneapolis, MN: Winston, 1985.

Horton, F.L. *The Melchizedek Tradition: A Critical Examination of the Sources to the Fifth Century A.D. and in the Epistle to the Hebrews*. SNTSMS 30. Cambridge: Cambridge University Press, 1976.

Huffmon, H.B. 'The Origins of Prophecy'. In *Magnalia Dei: The Mighty Acts of God: Essays on the Bible and Archaeology in Memory of G. Ernest Wright*. Ed. F.M. Cross, W.E. Lemke, and P.D. Miller. Garden City: Doubleday, 1976, 171-86.

Hughes, J.H. 'John the Baptist: The Forerunner of God Himself'. *NovT* 14 (1972): 191-218.

Hughes, P.E. 'The Value of Josephus as a Historical Source'. *EvQ* 15 (1943): 179-83.

Huppenbauer, H. 'טהר und טהרה in der Sektenregel von Qumran'. *TZ* 13 (1957): 350-351.

Isenberg, S.R. 'Millenarism in Greco-Roman Palestine'. *Rel* 4 (1974): 26-46.

———— 'Power through Temple and Torah in Greco-Roman Palestine'. In *Christianity, Judaism and Other Greco-Roman Cults: Studies for Morton Smith at Sixty*. Ed. J. Neusner. Leiden: Brill, 1975, 2.24-52.

Jack, J.W. *The Historic Christ*. London: James Clark, 1933.

Jacobson, A.D. 'The Literary Unity of Q'. *JBL* 101 (1982): 365-89.

Jenni, E. ' "Kommen" im theologischen Sprachgebrauch des Alten Testaments'. In *Wort—Gebot— Glaube: Beiträge zur Theologie des Alten Testaments: Walther Eichrodt zum 80. Geburtstag*. Ed. J.J. Stam *et al.* Zürich: Zwingli, 1970, 251-61.

Jeremias, Joachim. 'Der Ursprung der Johannestaufe'. *ZNW* 28 (1929): 312-20.

———— 'Proselytentaufe und des Neues Testament'. *TZ* 5 (1949): 418-28.

———— *Infant Baptism in the First Four Centuries*. Trans. D. Cairns. London: SCM, 1960.

———— ''Ηλ(ε)ίας'. *TDNT* 2.928-41.

———— *Jerusalem in the Time of Jesus*. Trans. F.H. Cave and C.H. Cave. London: SCM, 1969.

Jeremias, Jörg. *Theophanie: Die Geschichte einer alttestamentlichen Gattung*. Neukirchen-Vluyn: Neukirchener, 1965.

———— 'Theophany in the OT'. *IDBSup* 896-98.

Johnson, S.E. *A Commentary on the Gospel according to St Mark*. BNTC. 2nd edn. London: A. and C. Black, 1977.

Judge, E.A. 'The Decrees of Caesar at Thessalonica'. *RTR* 30 (1971): 1-7.

Kaiser, O. *Isaiah 13–39*. OTL. Trans. R.A. Wilson. Philadelphia: Westminster, 1974.

———— *Isaiah 1–12*. OTL. 2nd edn. Trans. J. Bowden. Philadelphia: Westminster, 1983.

Kaiser, W.C. 'The Promise of the Arrival of Elijah in Malachi and the Gospels'. *GTJ* 3 (1982): 221-33.

Käsemann, E. 'Das Problem des historischen Jesus'. *ZTK* 51 (1954): 125-53.

———— 'The Problem of the Historical Jesus'. In E. Käsemann. *Essays on New Testament Themes*. Trans. W.J. Montague. London: SCM, 1964; Philadelphia: Fortress, 1964, 15-47 [repr. from *ZTK* 51 (1954): 125-53].

———— 'The Disciples of John the Baptist in Ephesus'. In E. Käsemann. *Essays on New Testament Themes*. Trans. W.J. Montague. London: SCM, 1964; repr. Philadelphia: Fortress, 1982, 136-48.

Kazmierski, C.R. 'The Stones of Abraham: John the Baptist and the End of Torah (Matt 3,7-10 par. Luke 3,7-9)'. *Bib* 68 (1987): 22-40.

Keck, L.E. 'John the Baptist in Christianized Gnosticism'. In *Initiation*. NumenSup 10. Ed. C.J. Bleeker. Leiden: Brill, 1965, 184-94.

———— 'The Introduction to Mark's Gospel'. *NTS* 12 (1965–66): 352-70.

Kee, H.C. 'Synoptic Studies'. In *The New Testament and Its Modern Interpreters*. The Bible and Its Modern Interpreters 3. Ed. E.J. Epp and G.W. MacRae. Philadelphia: Fortress; Atlanta, Georgia, 1989, 245-69.

Kelber, W.H. *The Oral and the Written Gospel*. Philadelphia: Fortress, 1983.

Kennard, J.S. 'Gleanings from the Slavonic Josephus Controversy'. *JQR* 39 (1948–49): 161-70.

Kilgallen, J.J. 'John the Baptist, the Sinful Woman, and the Pharisee'. *JBL* 104 (1985): 675-79.

Kirkpatrick, P.G. *The Old Testament and Folklore Study*. JSOTSup 62. Sheffield: JSOT Press, 1988.

Kirschner, R. 'The Vocation of Holiness in Late Antiquity'. *VC* 38 (1984): 105-24.

Kittel, B.P. *The Hymns of Qumran: Translation and Commentary*. SBLDS 50. Chico, CA: Scholars, 1981.

Kittel, G. 'ἔρημος, κτλ.'. *TDNT* 2.657-60.

Klausner, J. *Jesus of Nazareth: His Life, Times, and Teaching*. Trans. H. Danby. New York: Macmillan, 1925.

───── *The Messianic Idea in Israel*. Trans. W.F. Stinespring. London: Allen and Unwin, 1956.

Kleinknecht, H. *et al.* 'πνεῦμα, κτλ.'. *TDNT* 6.332-455.

Klijn, A.F.J., and G.J. Reinink. *Patristic Evidence for Jewish Christian Sects*. NovTSup 36. Leiden: Brill, 1973.

Kloppenborg, J.S. *The Formation of Q*. Philadelphia: Fortress, 1987.

Knibb, M.A. *The Ethiopic Book of Enoch: A New Edition in the Light of the Aramaic Dead Sea Fragments*. 2 vols. Oxford: Oxford University Press, 1978.

───── 'The Date of the Parables of Enoch: A Critical Review'. *NTS* 25 (1978–79): 345-59.

───── *The Qumran Community*. CCWJCW 2. Cambridge: Cambridge University Press, 1987.

Knox, J. 'The "Prophet" in New Testament Christology'. In *Lux in Lumine: Essays to Honor W. Norman Pittenger*. Ed. R.A. Norris. New York: Seabury, 1966, 23-34, 171-74.

Kobelski, P.J. *Milchizedek and Melchiresa*. CBQMS 10. Washington, DC: Catholic Biblical Association, 1981.

Koch, K. 'אטא'. *TDOT* 4.309-19.

Koester, H. 'One Jesus and Four Primitive Gospels'. In J.M. Robinson and H. Koester. *Trajectories through Early Christianity*. Philadelphia: Fortress, 1971, 158-204.

───── *Introduction to the New Testament*. 2 vols. FFNT. Philadelphia: Fortress, 1982.

Kraeling, C.H. 'The Episode of the Roman Standards at Jerusalem'. *HTR* 35 (1942): 263-89.

───── *John the Baptist*. New York: Charles Scribner's Sons, 1951.

Krauss, S. 'Baptism'. *JewEnc* 2.499-500.

Krentz, E. ' "None Greater Among Those Born from Women": John the Baptist in the Gospel of Matthew'. *CurTM* 10 (1983): 333-38.

Krieger, N. 'Barfuß Buße tun'. *NovT* 1 (1956): 227-28.

───── 'Ein Mensch in weichen Kleidern'. *NovT* 1 (1956): 228-30.

Kuhn, K.G. 'The Lord's Supper and the Communal Meal at Qumran'. In *The Scrolls and the New Testament*. Ed. K. Stendahl. London: SCM, 1958, 65-93.

───── 'The Two Messiahs of Aaron and Israel'. In *The Scrolls and the New Testament*. Ed. K. Stendahl. London: SCM, 1958, 54-64.

───── 'προσήλυτος'. *TDNT* 6.727-44.

Kümmel, W.G. *Promise and Fulfilment: The Eschatological Message of Jesus*. Trans. D.M. Barton. London: SCM, 1957.

Kysar, R. *The Fourth Evangelist and His Gospel*. Minneapolis, MN: Augsburg, 1975.

───── *John, the Maverick Gospel*. Atlanta: John Knox, 1976.

Lachs, S.T. 'John the Baptist and His Audience'. *Gratz College Annual of Jewish Studies* 4 (1975): 28-32.

Lacocque, A. *The Book of Daniel*. Trans. D. Pellauer. London: SPCK, 1979.

Ladouceur, D.J. 'Josephus and Masada'. In *Josephus, Judaism, and Christianity*. Ed. L.H. Feldman and G. Hata. Leiden: Brill 1987, 95-113.

Lagrange, M. -J. 'Jean-Baptiste et Jésus d'après le texte slave'. *RB* 39 (1930): 29-46.

Lampe, G.W.H. *The Seal of the Spirit*. London: Longmans, Green, 1951.

Lane, W.L. *The Gospel According to Mark*. NICNT. Grand Rapids: Eerdmans, 1974.

Lang, F. 'Erwägungen zur eschatologischen Verkündigung Johannes des Täufers'. In *Jesus Christus in Historie und Theologie: Neutestamentliche Festschrift für Hans Conzelmann zum 60. Geburtstag*. Ed. G. Strecker. Tübingen: Mohr, 1975, 459-73.

LaSor, W.S. 'The Messianic Idea in Qumran'. In *Studies and Essays in Honor of Abraham A. Neuman*. Ed. M. Ben-Horin, B.D. Weinryb, and S. Zeitlin. Leiden: Brill, 1962, 343-64.

Laubach, F., and J. Goetzmann. 'Conversion: ἐπιστρέφω, μεταμέλομαι, μετάνοια, κτλ.'. *NIDNTT* 1.353-59.

Laubscher, F.D.T. 'God's Angel of Truth and Melchizedek'. *JSJ* 3 (1972): 46-51.

Laufen, R. *Die Doppelüberlieferungen der Logienquelle und des Markusevangeliums*. BBB 54. Bonn: Hanstein, 1980.

Laurin, R.B. 'The Problem of Two Messiahs in the Qumran Scrolls'. *RevQ* 4 (1963–64): 39-52.

Leaney, A.R.C. *A Commentary on the Gospel according to St Luke*. BNTC. A. and C. Black, 1958.

———— *The Rule of Qumran and Its Meaning*. NTL. Philadelphia: Westminster, 1966.

Lehmann, M.R. ' "Yom Kippur" in Qumran'. *RevQ* 3 (1961–62): 117-24.

Leipoldt, J. *Die urchristliche Taufe im Lichte der Religionsgeschichte*. Leipzig: Dörffling und Franke, 1928.

Lentzen-Deis, F. *Die Taufe Jesu nach den Synoptikern: Literarkritische und gattungsgeschichtliche Untersuchungen*. Frankfurter Theologische Studien 4. Frankfurt-am-Main: Knecht, 1970.

Léon-Dufour, X. ' "Et là, Jésus baptisait" (Jn 3,22)'. In *Mélanges Eugène Tisserant*. Studi E Testi 231. Vatican: Biblioteca Apostolica Vaticana, 1964, 1.295-309.

Levison, N. 'The Proselyte in Biblical and Early Post-Biblical Times'. *SJT* 10 (1957): 45-56.

Licht, J. 'An Analysis of the Treatise of the Two Spirits in DSD'. In *Scripta Hierosolymitana*. Ed. C. Rabin and Y. Yadin. Jerusalem: Magnes, 1958, 4.88-100.

Lichtenberger, H. 'Atonement and Sacrifice in the Qumran Community'. In *Approaches to Ancient Judaism*. BJS 9. Ed. W.S. Green. Chico, CA: Scholars, 1980, 159-71.

———— 'Täufergemeinden und früchristliche Täuferpolemik im letzten Drittel des 1. Jahr-hunderts'. *ZTK* 84 (1987): 36-57.

———— 'Reflections on the History of John the Baptist's Communities'. In *Folia Orientalia* 25 (1988): 45-49.

———— 'The Dead Sea Scrolls and John the Baptist: Reflexions on Josephus' Account of John the Baptist'. Unpublished paper read at the Dead Sea Scrolls Symposium in Jerusalem, April 1988.

Lieberman, S. 'The Discipline in the So-Called Dead Sea Manual of Discipline'. *JBL* 71 (1952): 199-206.

Lindars, B. *The Gospel of John*. NCB. Grand Rapids: Eerdmans, 1972.

———— 'John and the Synoptic Gospels: A Test Case'. *NTS* 27 (1980–81): 287-94.

———— *Jesus Son of Man: A Fresh Examination of the Son of Man Sayings in the Gospels in the Light of Recent Research*. London: SPCK, 1983.

Lindeskog, G. 'Johannes der Täufer'. *ASTI* 12 (1983): 55-83.

Lindner, H. *Die Geschichtsauffassung des Flavius Josephus im Bellum Judaicm*. Leiden: Brill, 1972.

Livingstone, G.H. 'טמא'. *TWOT* 1.277-79.

Lohmeyer, E. *Johannes der Täufer*. Vol. 1 of *Das Urchristentum*. Göttingen: Vandenhoeck und Ruprecht, 1932.

———— 'Zur evangelischen Überlieferung von Johannes dem Täufer'. *JBL* 51 (1932): 300-19.

———— *Das Evangelium des Markus*. MeyerK 2. Göttingen: Vandenhoeck und Ruprecht, 1953.

———— *Das Evangelium des Matthäus*. MeyerK 1. Göttingen: Vandenhoeck und Ruprecht, 1956.

Lord, A.B. 'The Gospels as Oral Traditional Literature'. In *The Relationships Among the Gospels: An Interdisciplinary Dialogue*. Ed. W.O. Walker. San Antonio, TX: Trinity University Press, 1978, 33-91.

Lübbe, J. 'A Reinterpretation of 4QTestimonia'. *RevQ* 12 (1985–87): 187-97.
Lupieri, E.F. 'John the Baptist: The First Monk: A Contribution to the History of the Figure of John the Baptist in the Early Monastic World'. In *Monasticism: A Historical Overview*. Word and Spirit 6. Still River: St Bede's Publications, 1984, 11-23.
——— *Giovanni Battista nelle tradizioni sinottiche*. SB 82. Brescia: Paideia Editrice, 1988.
Luz, U. 'Q 3-4'. In *Society of Biblical Literature 1984 Seminar Papers*. SBLSP 23. Ed. K.H. Richards. Chico, CA: Scholars, 1984, 375-76.
——— *Das Evangelium nach Matthäus*. EKKNT 1. Zürich: Benziger; Neukirchen-Vluyn: Neukirchener, 1985.
——— *Matthew 1–7*. Trans. W.C. Linss. Minneapolis, MN: Augsburg, 1989.
MacDonald, J. *The Theology of the Samaritans*. London: SCM, 1964.
MacGregor, G.H.C. 'John the Baptist and the Origins of Christianity'. *ExpTim* 46 (1934–35): 355-62.
Mackie, G.M. *Bible Manners and Customs*. London: A. and C. Black, 1898.
MacLeod, J. 'John the Baptist's Question'. *EvQ* 1 (1929): 166-80.
Makrides, V.N. 'Considerations on Mark 11.27-33 par'. *Deltion Biblikon Meleton* 14 (1985): 43-55.
Malchow, B.V. 'The Messenger of the Covenant in Mal. 3.1'. *JBL* 103 (1984): 252-55.
Maloney, E.C. *Semitic Interference in Marcan Syntax*. SBLDS 51. Chico, CA: Scholars, 1981.
Mann, C.S. *Mark*. AB 27. New York: Doubleday, 1986.
Manson, T.W. *The Sayings of Jesus*. London: SCM, 1949.
——— 'John the Baptist'. *BJRL* 36 (1953–54): 395-412.
Manson, W. *Jesus the Messiah*. London: Hodder and Stoughton, 1943.
Mansoor, M. *The Thanksgiving Hymns*. STDJ 3. Leiden: Brill, 1961.
Mantey, J.R. 'Baptism in the Dead Sea Manual of Discipline'. *RevExp* 51 (1954): 522-27.
Marcus, R. 'Pharisees, Essenes, and Gnostics'. *JBL* 73 (1954): 157-61.
Marriott, G.L. 'Locusts and Wild Honey'. *ExpTim* 30 (1918–19): 280-81.
Marsh, H.G. *The Origin and Significance of New Testament Baptism*. Publications of the University of Manchester 225; Theological Series 5. Manchester: Manchester University Press, 1941.
Marshall, I.H. *The Gospel of Luke*. NIGTC. Grand Rapids: Eerdmans, 1978.
Martyn, J.L. 'We Have Found Elijah'. In *Jews, Greeks and Christians: Religious Cultures in Late Antiquity: Essays in Honor of W.D. Davies*. SJLA 21. Ed. R. Hamerton-Kelly and R. Scroggs. Leiden: Brill, 1976, 181-219.
Marxsen, W. *Mark the Evangelist*. 2nd edn. Trans. J. Boyce *et al.* 1959; Nashville: Abingdon, 1969.
Mason, R.A. *The Books of Haggai, Zechariah and Malachi*. CBC. Cambridge: Cambridge University Press, 1977.
Mattill, A.J. *Luke and Last Things*. Dillsboro, NC: Western North Carolina Press, 1979.
Mauser, U.W. *Christ in the Wilderness*. SBT 39. London: SCM, 1963.
Mayes, A.D.H. *Deuteronomy*. NCB. London: Marshall, Morgan and Scott, 1979.
Mays, J.L. *Hosea: A Commentary*. OTL. Philadelphia: Fortress, 1969.
McArthur, H.K., ed. *In Search of the Historical Jesus*. London: SPCK, 1970.
McCasland, S.V. 'The Way'. *JBL* 77 (1958): 222-30.
McCown, C.C. 'The Scene of John's Ministry and Its Relation to the Purpose and Outcome of His Mission'. *JBL* 59 (1940): 113-31.
——— 'Gospel Geography: Fiction, Fact and Truth'. *JBL* 60 (1941): 1-25.
McNeile, A.H. *The Gospel According to St Matthew*. London: Macmillan, 1915.
Mearns, C.L. 'The Parables of Enoch—Origin and Date'. *ExpTim* 89 (1977–78): 118-19.
——— 'Dating the Similitudes Of Enoch'. *NTS* 25 (1978–79): 360-69.
——— 'The Son of Man Trajectory and Eschatological Development'. *ExpTim* 97 (1985): 8-12.

Meeks, W.A. _The Moral World of the First Christians_. Library of Early Christianity 6. Philadelphia: Westminster, 1986.

Meier, J.P. 'John the Baptist in Matthew's Gospel'. _JBL_ 99 (1980): 383-405.

Merklein, H. 'Die Umkehrpredigt bei Johannes dem Täufer und Jesus von Nazaret'. _BZ_ 25 (1981): 29-46.

Meyer, B.F. _The Aims of Jesus_. London: SCM, 1979.

Meyer, F.B. _John the Baptist_. London: Morgan and Scott, n.d.

Meyer, R. 'προφήτης, κτλ.'. C. Prophecy and Prophets in the Judaism of the Hellenistic-Roman Period'. _TDNT_ 6.812-28.

Meyers, C.L., and E. Meyers. _Haggai, Zechariah 1-8_. AB 25B. Garden City: Doubleday, 1987.

Michaelis, J.D. _Einleitung in die göttlichen Schriften des Neuen Bundes_. N.p.: n.p., 1788.

Michel, O. 'Spät-jüdisches Prophetentum'. In _Neutestamentliche Studien für Rudolf Bultmann_. Ed. W. Eltester. Berlin: Töpelmann, 1954, 60-66.

Mihelic, J.L. 'Shovel'. _IDB_ 4.340.

Milgrom, J. 'Sin-Offering or Purification-Offering?'. _VT_ 21 (1971): 237-39.

——— 'Two Kinds of HATTA'T'. _VT_ 26 (1976): 333-37.

——— 'Studies in the Temple Scroll'. _JBL_ 97 (1978): 501-23.

——— 'The Paradox of the Red Cow (Num 19)'. _VT_ 31 (1981): 62-72.

Milik, J.T. 'Le Testament de Lévi en Araméen'. _RB_ 62 (1955): 398-406.

——— 'Milkî-ṣedek et Milkî-reša͏ᶜ dans les anciens écrits juifs et chrétiens'. _JJS_ 23 (1972): 95-144.

Miller, M.P. 'The Function of Isa 61.1-2 in 11Q Melchizedek'. _JBL_ 88 (1969): 467-69.

Minear, P.S. 'Luke's Use of the Birth Stories'. In _Studies in Luke-Acts_. Ed. L.E. Keck and J.L. Martyn, 1966; repr. Philadelphia: Fortress, 1980, 111-30.

Miner, D.F. 'A Suggested Reading for 11Q Melchizedek 17'. _JSJ_ 2 (1971): 144-48.

Moehring, H.R. 'Josephus on Marriage Customs of the Essenes'. In _Early Christian Origins: Studies in Honor of H.R. Willoughby_. Ed. A. Wikgren. Chicago: Quadrangle Books, 1961, 120-27.

——— 'Josephus ben Matthai and Flavius Josephus: The Jewish Prophet and Roman Historian'. In _ANRW_ 2.21.2. Ed. H. Temporini and W. Haase. Berlin: Walter de Gruyter, 1984, 864-944.

Momigliano, A. 'Josephus as a Source for the History of Judaea'. In _Cambridge Ancient History_. Ed. S.A. Cook _et al_. Cambridge: Cambridge University Press, 1952, 10.884-87.

Montefiore, C.G. _The Synoptic Gospels_. 2 vols. 2nd edn. London: Macmillan, 1927.

Montefiore, H. 'Josephus and the New Testament'. _NovT_ 4 (1960): 139-60, 307-18.

Montgomery, J.A. _A Critical and Exegetical Commentary on the Book of Daniel_. ICC. Edinburgh: T. and T. Clark, 1927.

——— 'Ascetic Strains in Early Judaism'. _JBL_ 51 (1932): 183-213.

——— _The Samaritans: The Earliest Jewish Sect_. 1907; repr. New York: Ktav, 1968.

Moore, G.F. _Judaism in the First Centuries of the Christian Era_. 3 vols. Cambridge, MA: Harvard University Press, 1946-48.

Morris, L. _Studies in the Fourth Gospel_. Grand Rapids: Eerdmans, 1969.

Mosley, A.W. 'Historical Reporting in the Ancient World'. _NTS_ 12 (1965-66): 10-26.

Mowinckel, S. _He that Cometh_. Trans. G.W. Anderson. Oxford: Blackwell, 1956.

Mowry, L. 'The Dead Sea Scrolls and the Background for the Gospel of John'. _BA_ 17 (1954): 78-97.

Muddiman, J.B. 'Jesus and Fasting: Mark 2.18-22'. In _Jésus aux origines de la Christologie_. BETL 40. Ed. J. Dupont. Gembloux: J. Duculot, 1975, 271-81.

Muilenburg, J. 'The Beginning of the Gospels and the Qumran Manual of Discipline'. _USQR_ 10 (1955): 23-29.

Murphy-O'Connor, J. 'La genèse littéraire de la Règle de la Communauté'. _RB_ 76 (1969): 528-49.

——— 'The Judean Desert'. In _Early Judaism and Its Modern Interpreters_. The Bible and

Its Modern Interpreters 2. Ed. R.A. Kraft and G.W.E. Nickelsburg. Philadelphia: Fortress, 1986, 119-56.

Myers, J.M. *I and II Esdras*. AB 42. Garden City: Doubleday, 1974.

Napier, B.D. 'Prophet, Prophetism'. *IDB* 3.896-919.

Neill, S., and N.T. Wright, *The Interpretation of the New Testament: 1861–1986*. 2nd edn. Oxford: Oxford University Press, 1988.

Nepper-Christensen, P. 'Die Taufe im Matthäusevangelium im Lichte der Traditionen über Johannes der Täufer'. *NTS* 31 (1985): 189-207.

Neuman, A.A. 'A Note on John the Baptist and Jesus in Josippon'. *HUCA* 23 (1950–51): 137-49.

Neusner, J. 'The Fellowship (חבורה) in the Second Jewish Commonwealth'. *HTR* 53 (1960): 125-42.

—————— *From Politics to Piety: The Emergence of Pharisaic Judaism*. Englewood Cliffs, NJ: Prentice-Hall, 1973.

—————— *The Idea of Purity In Ancient Judaism*. SJLA 1. Leiden: Brill, 1973.

—————— *Judaism: The Evidence of the Mishnah*. Chicago: University of Chicago Press, 1981.

—————— *Judaism in the Beginning of Christianity*. Philadelphia: Fortress, 1984.

—————— *The Mishnah before 70*. BJS 51. Atlanta: Scholars, 1987.

Newing, E.G. 'Religions of Pre-Literary Societies'. In *The World's Religions*. Ed. N. Anderson. 4th edn. Grand Rapids: Eerdmans, 1975, 11-48.

Newton, M. *The Concept of Purity at Qumran and in the Letters of Paul*. SNTSMS 53. Cambridge: Cambridge University Press, 1985.

Nickelsburg, G.W.E. *Resurrection, Immortality, and Eternal Life in Intertestamental Judaism*. Cambridge, MA: Harvard University Press, 1972.

—————— 'Eschatology in the Testament of Abraham: A Study of the Judgment Scene in the Two Recensions'. In *Studies on the Testament of Abraham*. SBLSCS 6. Ed. G.W.E. Nickelsburg. Missoula, MT: Scholars, 1976, 23-64.

—————— *Jewish Literature between the Bible and the Mishnah*. Philadelphia: Fortress, 1981.

—————— 'Salvation without and with a Messiah: Developing Beliefs in Writings Ascribed to Enoch'. In *Judaisms and Their Messiahs at the Turn of the Christian Era*. Ed. J. Neusner, W.S. Green, and E. Frerichs. Cambridge: Cambridge University Press, 1987, 49-68.

Niese, B. 'Josephus'. *ERE* 7.569-79 [repr. from *HZ* 76 (1896): 193-237].

Nineham, D.E. *Saint Mark*. Philadelphia: Westminster, 1963.

Nodet, E. 'Jésus et Jean-Baptiste selon Josèphe'. *RB* 92 (1985): 321-48, 497-524.

Nolland, J. 'A Misleading Statement of the Essene Attitude to the Temple'. *RevQ* 9 (1977–78): 555-62.

—————— *Luke 1–9.20*. WBC 35A. Dallas: Word Books, 1989.

North, C.R. *The Second Isaiah*. Oxford: Oxford University Press, 1964.

Noth, M. *Exodus: A Commentary*. OTL. Trans. J.S. Bowden. London: SCM, 1962.

—————— *Numbers: A Commentary*. OTL. Trans. J.D. Martin. London: SCM, 1968.

—————— 'The Holy Ones of the Most High'. In M. Noth. *The Laws in the Pentateuch and Other Studies*. London: SCM, 1984, 215-28.

Oakman, D.E. 'Jesus and Agrarian Palestine: The Factor of Debt'. In *Society of Biblical Literature 1985 Seminar Papers*. SBLSP 24. Ed. K.H. Richards. Atlanta: Scholars, 1985, 57-73.

—————— *Jesus and the Economic Questions of His Day*. Studies in the Bible and Early Christianity 8. Lewiston, NY: Edwin Mellen, 1986.

Oepke, A. 'βάπτω, κτλ.'. *TDNT* 1.529-46.

Oliver, H.H. 'The Lucan Birth Stories and the Purpose of Luke-Acts'. *NTS* 10 (1963–64): 202-26.

Orton, D.E. *The Understanding Scribe: Matthew and the Apocalyptic Ideal*. JSNTSup 25. Sheffield: JSOT Press, 1989.

Overholt, T.W. 'Seeing Is Believing: The Social Setting of Prophetic Acts of Power'.

    *JSOT* 23 (1982): 3-31.
Parker, P. 'Bethany beyond Jordan'. *JBL* 74 (1955): 257-61.
Patzia, A.G. 'Did John the Baptist Preach a Baptism of Fire and the Holy Spirit?'. *EvQ*
    40 (1968): 21-27.
Payot, C. 'Jean Baptiste censuré'. *ETR* 45 (1970): 273-83.
Peli, P.H., F.F. Bruce, and J. Haberman. 'Asceticism'. *EncJud* 3.677-84.
Pesch, R. *Das Markusevangelium.* HTKNT 2.1–2. 2 vols. Freiburg: Herder, 1976.
Petersen, D.L. *Late Israelite Prophecy: Studies in Deutero-Prophetic Literature and in*
    *Chronicles.* SBLMS 23. Missoula, MT: Scholars, 1977.
——— *The Roles of Israel's Prophets.* JSOTSup 17. Sheffield: JSOT Press, 1981.
Plummer, A. 'Baptism'. *HDB* 1.238-45.
——— *A Critical and Exegetical Commentary on the Gospel according to S. Luke.* ICC.
    5th edn. Edinburgh: T. and T. Clark, 1922.
Polag, A. 'The Text of Q'. In I. Havener. *Q: The Sayings of Jesus.* Wilmington, DE:
    Michael Glazier, 1987, 109-65.
Pooler, L.A. 'The Baptism of John (Matt 3.5,6)'. *ExpTim* 27 (1915): 382-83.
Porteous, N. *Daniel.* OTL. 2nd edn. London: SCM, 1979.
Porter, J.R. 'The Origins of Prophecy in Israel'. In *Israel's Prophetic Tradition: Essays in*
    *Honor of Peter R. Ackroyd.* Ed. R. Coggins, A. Philips, and M. Knibb. Cam-
    bridge: Cambridge University Press, 1982, 12-31.
Porter, S.E. 'Thucydides 1.22.1 and Speeches in Acts: Is There a Thucydidean View?'.
    *NovT* 32 (1990): 121-42.
Posner, R. 'Ablution'. *EncJud* 2.81-86.
Poythress, V.S. 'The Holy Ones of the Most High in Daniel VII'. *VT* 26 (1976): 208-13.
Puech, É. 'Notes sur le manuscrit de XIQMilkîsédeq'. *RevQ* 12 (1985–87): 483-513.
Pusey, K. 'Jewish Proselyte Baptism'. *ExpTim* 95 (1983–84): 141-45.
Pyrke, E.J. 'Some Aspects of Eschatology in the Dead Sea Scrolls'. In *Studia Evangelica.*
    TU 103. Ed. F.L. Cross. Berlin: Akademie, 1968, 5.296-302.
Pyrke, J. 'Eschatology in the Dead Sea Scrolls'. In *The Scrolls and Christianity.* Theolo-
    gical Collections 11. Ed. M. Black. London: SPCK, 1969, 45-57.
——— 'John the Baptist and the Qumran Community'. *RevQ* 4 (1964): 483-96.
——— 'The Sacraments of Holy Baptism and Holy Communion in the Light of the
    Ritual Washings and Sacred Meals at Qumran'. *RevQ* 5 (1964–66): 543-52.
Quell, G. *et al.* 'ἁμαρτάνω, κτλ.'. *TDNT* 1.267-316.
Raabe, P.R. 'Daniel 7: Its Structure and Role in the Book'. *HAR* 9 (1985): 267-75.
Rabin, C. *Qumran Studies.* SJ 2. Oxford: Oxford University Press, 1957.
Rajak, T. *Josephus: The Historian and His Society.* London: Duckworth, 1983.
Reicke, B. 'Die Verkündigung des Täufers nach Lukas'. In *Jesus in der Verkündigung der*
    *Kirche.* SNTU A1. Ed. A. Fuchs. Freistadt: Plöchl, 1976, 50-61.
——— 'Die jüdischen Baptisten und Johannes der Täufer'. In *Jesus in der Verkündigung*
    *der Kirche.* SNTU A1. Ed. A. Fuchs. Freistadt: Plöchl, 1976, 76-88.
——— 'John's Baptism'. In *Jesus, the Gospels, and the Church: Essays in honor of Wil-*
    *liam R. Farmer.* Ed. E.P. Sanders. Macon, GA: Mercer University Press, 1987,
    209-24.
Reid, S.B. 'The End of Prophecy in the Light of Contemporary Social Theory: A Draft'.
    In *Society of Biblical Literature 1985 Seminar Papers.* SBLSP 24. Ed. K.H.
    Richards. Atlanta: Scholars, 1985, 515-23.
Reiling, J. 'The Use of ΨΕΥΔΟΠΡΟΦΗΤΗΣ in the Septuagint, Philo and Josephus'.
    *NovT* 13 (1971): 147-56.
Reimarus, H.S. *Fragments.* Ed. C.H. Talbert; trans. R.S. Fraser. London: SCM, 1971.
Reinach, S. 'Jean-Baptiste et Jésus suivant Josèphe'. *REJ* 87 (1929): 113-36.
Rendtorff, R. *et al.* 'προφήτης, κτλ.'. *TDNT* 6.781-861.
Reumann, J. 'The Quest for the Historical Baptist'. In *Understanding the Sacred Text:*
    *Essays in Honor of Morton S. Enslin on the Hebrew Bible and Christian*
    *Beginnings.* Ed. J. Reumann. Valley Forge: Judson, 1972, 181-99.

Rhoads, D.M. *Israel in Revolution: 6–74 CE: A Political History Based on the Writings of Josephus*. Philadelphia: Fortress, 1976.

Richardson, H.N. 'Chaff'. *IDB* 1.549.

———— 'Threshing'. *IDB* 4.636.

———— 'Winnowing'. *IDB* 4.854.

Riches, J. *Jesus and the Transformation of Judaism*. London: Darton, Longman and Todd, 1980.

Richter, G. 'Bist du Elias? (Joh. 1,21) [Parts 1, 2]'. *BZ* 6 (1962): 79-92, 238-56.

———— 'Bist du Elias? (Joh. 1,21) [Part 3]'. *BZ* 7 (1963): 63-80.

Riesenfeld, H. 'The Gospel Tradition and Its Beginnings'. In H. Riesenfeld. *The Gospel Tradition*. Philadelphia: Fortress, 1970, 1-29 [repr. from *SE* 1 (1959): 43-65].

Rife, J.M. 'The Standing of John the Baptist'. In *Festschrift to Honor F. Wilbur Gingrich*. Ed. E.H. Barth and R.E. Cocroft. Leiden: Brill, 1972, 205-208.

Ringgren, H. *The Faith of Qumran*. Trans. E.T. Sander. Philadelphia: Fortress, 1963.

Rivkin, E. 'Messiah, Jewish'. *IDBSup* 588-91.

———— 'Locating John the Baptizer in Palestinian Judaism: The Political Dimension'. In *Society of Biblical Literature 1983 Seminar Papers*. SBLSP 22. Ed. K.H. Richards. Chico, CA: Scholars, 1983, 79-85.

Roberts, J.J.M. 'The Davidic Origin Of the Zion Tradition'. *JBL* 92 (1973): 329-44.

———— 'Zion in the Theology of the Davidic-Solomonic Empire'. In *Studies in the Period of David and Solomon and Other Essays*. Ed. T. Ishida. Winona Lake, IN: Eisenbrauns, 1982, 93-108.

———— 'The Divine King and the Human Community in Isaiah's Vision of the Future'. In *Quest for the Kingdom of God: Essays in Honor of George E. Mendenhall*. Winona Lake, IN: Eisenbrauns, 1987, 127-36.

Robinson, A. 'God, the Refiner of Silver'. *CBQ* 11 (1949): 188-90.

Robinson, H.W. 'Hebrew Sacrifice and Prophetic Symbolism'. *JTS* 43 (1942): 129-39.

Robinson, J.A.T. 'The Baptism of John and the Qumran Community'. In J.A.T. Robinson. *Twelve New Testament Studies*. London: SCM, 1962, 11-27 [repr. from *HTR* 50 (1957): 175-91].

———— 'Elijah, John and Jesus'. In J.A.T. Robinson. *Twelve New Testament Studies*. London: SCM, 1962, 28-52 [repr. from *NTS* 4 (1958): 263-81].

———— 'The "Others" of John 4.38'. In J.A.T. Robinson. *Twelve New Testament Studies*. London: SCM, 1962, 61-66 [repr. from *SE* 1 (1959): 510-15].

———— 'The Relation of the Prologue of John to the Gospel of St John'. In J.A.T. Robinson. *Twelve More New Testament Studies*. London: SCM, 1984, 65-76 [repr. from *NTS* 9 (1962–63): 120-29].

———— *The Priority of John*. London: SCM, 1985.

Robinson, J.M. '*LOGOI SOPHON*: On the Gattung of Q'. In J.M. Robinson and H. Koester. *Trajectories through Early Christianity*. Philadelphia: Fortress, 1971, 71-113.

———— 'The Johannine Trajectory'. In J.M. Robinson and H. Koester. *Trajectories through Early Christianity*. Philadelphia: Fortress, 1971, 232-68.

———— 'The Problem of History in Mark'. In *The Problem of History in Mark and Other Marcan Studies*. London: SCM, 1957; repr. Philadelphia: Fortress, 1982, 55-143.

———— 'A New Quest of the Historical Jesus'. In J.M. Robinson. *A New Quest of the Historical Jesus and Other Essays*. Philadelphia: Fortress, 1983, 9-125.

———— 'The Preaching of John: Work Sheets for the Reconstruction of Q'. In *Society of Biblical Literature 1984 Seminar Papers*. SBLSP 23. Ed. K.H. Richards. Atlanta: Scholars, 1984, 305-46.

———— 'On Bridging the Gulf from Q to the Gospel of Thomas (or Vice Versa)'. In *Nag Hammadi, Gnosticism, and Early Christianity*. Ed. C.W. Hedrick and R. Hodgson. Peabody, MA: Hendrickson, 1986, 127-75.

Rogers, C.F. 'How Did the Jews Baptize? [Part 1]'. *JTS* 12 (1911): 437-45.

———— 'How Did the Jews Baptize? [Part 2]'. *JTS* 13 (1912): 411-14.

Rogerson, J.W. 'The Use of Sociology In Old Testament Studies'. In *Congress Volume 1983*. VTSup 36. Ed. J.A. Emerton. Leiden: Brill, 1985, 245-56.

Rowley, H.H. 'Jewish Proselyte Baptism and the Baptism of John'. *HUCA* 15 (1940): 313-34.

—— 'The Baptism of John and the Qumran Sect'. In *New Testament Essays: Studies in Memory of T.W. Manson*. Ed. A.J.B. Higgins. Manchester: Manchester University Press, 1959, 218-29.

Rubinstein, A. 'Observations on the Old Russian Version of Josephus' Wars'. *JSS* 2 (1957): 329-48.

Rudolph, W. *Haggai—Sacharja 1–8—Sacharja 9–14—Maleachi*. KAT 13.3–4. 2 vols. Gütersloh: Gütersloher Verlagshaus Mohn, 1975–76.

Runciman, W.G. *The Methodology of Social Theory*. Vol. 1 of *A Treatise on Social Theory*. Cambridge: Cambridge University Press, 1983.

Safrai, S. 'Religion in Everyday Life'. In *The Jewish People in the First Century*. CRINT 1.2. Ed. S. Safrai and M. Stern. Assen: Van Gorcum; Philadelphia: Fortress, 1976, 793-833.

—— 'The Temple'. In *The Jewish People in the First Century*. CRINT 1.2. Ed. S. Safrai and M. Stern. Assen: Van Gorcum; Philadelphia: Fortress, 1976, 865-907.

—— 'The Synagogue'. In *The Jewish People in the First Century*. CRINT 1.2. Ed. S. Safrai and M. Stern. Assen: Van Gorcum; Philadelphia: Fortress, 1976, 908-44.

Sahlin, H. 'Die Früchte der Umkehr: Die ethische Verkündigung Johannes des Täufers nach Lk 3.10-14'. *ST* 1 (1947): 54-68.

Saldarini, A.J. *Pharisees, Scribes and Sadducees in Palestinian Society*. Wilmington, DE: Michael Glazier, 1988.

Sanders, E.P. *Jesus and Judaism*. Philadelphia: Fortress, 1985.

Sato, M. *Q und Prophetie*. WUNT 2.29. Tübingen: Mohr, 1988.

Schadewaldt, W. 'The Reliability of the Synoptic Tradition'. In M. Hengel. *Studies in the Gospel of Mark*. Trans. J. Bowden. Philadelphia: Fortress, 1985, 89-113.

Schalit, A. 'Josephus Flavius'. *EncJud* 10.251-65.

Schenk, W. 'Gefangenschaft und Tod des Täufers: Erwägungen zur Chronologie und ihren Konsequenzen'. *NTS* 29 (1983): 453-83.

Schiffman, L.H. *The Halakhah at Qumran*. SJLA 16. Leiden: Brill, 1975.

—— 'Communal Meals at Qumran'. *RevQ* 10 (1979–81): 45-56.

—— *The Eschatological Community of the Dead Sea Scrolls: A Study of the Rule of the Congregation*. SBLMS 38. Atlanta: Scholars, 1989.

Schmidt, K.L. *Der Rahmen der Geschichte Jesu*. Berlin: Trowitzsch und Sohn, 1919.

Schmitt, J. 'Le Milieu Baptiste de Jean le Précurseur'. In *Exegese Biblique et Judaisme*. Ed. J.E. Ménard. Strasbourg: Palais Universitaire, 1973, 237-53.

Schnackenburg, R. *The Gospel According to St John*. 3 vols. Trans. K. Smyth *et al.* New York: Crossroad, 1980–82.

Schnutenhaus, F. 'Das Kommen und Erscheinen Gottes im Alten Testament'. *ZAW* 76 (1964): 1-22.

Schreckenberg, H. *Bibliographie zu Flavius Josephus*. ALGHJ 1. Leiden: Brill, 1968.

—— *Bibliographie zu Flavius Josephus: Supplementband mit Gesamtregister*. ALGHJ 14. Leiden: Brill, 1979.

Schulz, S. *Q: Die Spruchquelle der Evangelisten*. Zürich: Theologischer, 1972.

Schürer, E. *The History of the Jewish People in the Age of Jesus Christ*. 3 vols. Rev. and ed. G. Vermes *et al.* Edinburgh: T. and T. Clark, 1973–87.

Schürmann, H. *Das Lukasevangelium*. HTKNT 3.1–2. 2 vols. Freiburg: Herder, 1969.

Schüssler Fiorenza, E. 'Cultic Language in Qumran and the NT'. *CBQ* 38 (1976): 159-77.

Schütz, R. *Johannes der Täufer*. ATANT 50. Zürich: Zwingli, 1967.

Schweitzer, A. *The Quest of the Historical Jesus: A Critical Study of its Progress from Reimarus to Wrede*. 2nd edn. Trans. W. Montgomery. London: A. and C. Black, 1911.

Scobie, C.H.H. *John the Baptist*. London: SCM, 1964.

—————— 'John the Baptist'. In *The Scrolls and Christianity*. Theological Collections 11. Ed. M. Black. London: SPCK, 1969, 58-69.

Sekki, A.E. *The Meaning of RUAH at Qumran*. SBLDS 110. Atlanta: Scholars, 1989.

Sherwin-White, A.N. *Roman Society and Roman Law in the New Testament*. 1963; repr. Grand Rapids: Baker Book House, 1978.

Shutt, R.J.H. *Studies in Josephus*. London: SPCK, 1961.

Sigal, P. 'Manifestations of Hellenistic Historiography in Select Judaic Literature'. In *Society of Biblical Literature 1984 Seminar Papers*. SBLSP 23. Ed. K.H. Richards. Chico, CA: Scholars, 1984, 161-85.

Silva, M. *Biblical Words and Their Meaning*. Grand Rapids: Zondervan, 1983.

Sint, J.A. 'Die Eschatologie des Täufers, Die Täufergruppen und die Polemik der Evangelien'. In *Vom Messias zum Christus*. Ed. K. Schubert. Vienna: Herder, 1964, 55-163.

Skehan, P.W., and A.A. di Lella. *The Wisdom of Ben Sira*. AB 39. New York: Doubleday, 1987.

Slingerland, H.D. *The Testaments of the Twelve Patriarchs: A Critical History of Research*. SBLMS 21. Missoula, MT: Scholars, 1977.

Smalley, S.S. *John: Evangelist and Interpreter*. Exeter: Paternoster, 1978.

Smallwood, E.M. 'High Priests and Politics in Roman Palestine'. *JTS* 13 (1962): 14-34.

—————— *The Jews under Roman Rule*. SJLA 20. 2nd edn. Leiden: Brill, 1981.

—————— 'Philo and Josephus as Historians of the Same Events'. In *Josephus, Judaism, and Christianity*. Ed. L.H. Feldman and G. Hata. Leiden: Brill 1987, 114-29.

Smith, D. 'Jewish Proselyte Baptism and the Baptism of John'. *ResQ* 25 (1982): 13-32.

Smith, D.M. 'The Use of the Old Testament in the New'. In *The Use of the Old Testament in the New and Other Essays: Studies in Honor of William Franklin Stinespring*. Ed. J.M. Efird. Durham: Duke University Press, 1972, 3-65.

—————— 'John and the Synoptics: Some Dimensions of the Problem'. *NTS* 26 (1979–80): 425-44.

Smith, J.M.P. *A Critical and Exegetical Commentary on the Book of Malachi*. ICC. Edinburgh: T. and T. Clark, 1912.

Smith, M. 'Zealots and Sicarii: Their Origins and Relation'. *HTR* 64 (1971): 1-19.

—————— 'Palestinian Judaism in the First Century'. In *Israel: Its Role in Civilization*. Ed. M. Davis. New York: Harper and Row, 1956; repr. New York: Arno, 1977, 67-81.

Smith, R.L. *Micah–Malachi*. WBC 32. Waco, TX: Word Books, 1984.

Sollertinsky, S. 'The Death of St John the Baptist'. *JTS* 1 (1900): 507-28.

Staley, J. 'The Structure of John's Prologue: Its Implications for the Gospel's Narrative Structure'. *CBQ* 48 (1986): 241-64.

Starcky, J. 'Les quatre étapes du messianisme a Qumran'. *RB* 70 (1963): 481-505.

—————— 'Qumran et le Nouveau Testament: B. Quelques thèmes majeurs'. *DBSup* 9.996-1006.

Starr, J. 'The Unjewish Character of the Markan Account of John the Baptist'. *JBL* 51 (1932): 227-37.

Stauffer, E. *New Testament Theology*. Trans. J. Marsh. London: SCM, 1955.

Stein, R.H. *The Synoptic Problem*. Grand Rapids: Baker Book House, 1987.

Steinmann, J. *Saint John the Baptist and the Desert Tradition*. Trans. M. Boyes. New York: Harper and Brothers; London: Longmans, 1958.

Stendahl, K 'The Scrolls and the New Testament: An Introduction and a Perspective'. In *The Scrolls and the New Testament*. Ed. K. Stendahl. London: SCM, 1958, 1-17, 249-51.

Stern, M. 'The Reign of Herod and the Herodian Dynasty'. In *The Jewish People in the First Century*. CRINT 1.1. Ed. S. Safrai and M. Stern. Assen: Van Gorcum; Philadelphia: Fortress, 1974, 216-307.

—————— 'The Province of Judaea'. In *The Jewish People in the First Century*. CRINT 1.1. Ed. S. Safrai and M. Stern. Assen: Van Gorcum; Philadelphia: Fortress, 1974,

308-76.

——— 'Aspects of Jewish Society: The Priesthood and other Classes'. In *The Jewish People in the First Century*. CRINT 1.2. Ed. S. Safrai and M. Stern. Assen: Van Gorcum; Philadelphia: Fortress, 1976, 561-630.

Stone, M.E. *Scriptures, Sects and Visions: A Profile of Judaism from Ezra to the Jewish Revolts*. Philadelphia: Fortress, 1980.

——— 'Apocalyptic Literature'. In *Jewish Writings of the Second Temple Period*. CRINT 2.2. Ed. M.E. Stone. Assen: Van Gorcum; Philadelphia: Fortress, 1984, 383-441.

Strack, H.L., and P. Billerbeck. *Kommentar zum Neuen Testament aus Talmud und Midrasch*. 6 vols. München: C.H. Beck, 1922–61.

Strauss, D.F. *The Life of Jesus Critically Examined*. 4th edn. Trans. G. Eliot. London: Swan Sonnenschein, 1902.

Streeter, B.H. 'Was the Baptist's Preaching Apocalyptic?'. *JTS* 14 (1913): 549-52.

Strugnell, J. 'Flavius Josephus and the Essenes: *Antiquities* XVIII.18–22'. *JBL* 77 (1958): 106-15.

Stuhlmacher, P. *Das paulinische Evangelium*. Vol. 1. FRLANT 95. Göttingen: Vandenhoeck und Ruprecht, 1968.

Styler, G.M. 'The Priority of Mark'. In C.F.D. Moule. *The Birth of the New Testament*. BNTC. 2nd edn. London: A. and C. Black, 1962, 223-32.

Sukenik, E.L. *Ancient Synagogues in Palestine and Greece*. London: Oxford University Press, 1934.

Sutcliffe, E.F. 'Sacred Meals at Qumran?'. *HeyJ* 1 (1960): 48-65.

——— 'Baptism and Baptismal Rites at Qumran?'. *HeyJ* 1 (1960): 179-88.

Suter, D.W. *Tradition and Composition in the Parables of Enoch*. SBLDS 47. Missoula, MT: Scholars, 1979.

Talmon, S. 'The Calendar Reckoning of the Sect from the Judaean Desert'. In *Scripta Hierosolymitana*. Jerusalem: Magnes, 1958, 4.162-199.

——— 'The Sectarian גחי—A Biblical Noun'. *VT* 3 (1953): 133-40.

——— 'The "Desert Motif" in the Bible and in Qumran Literature'. In *Biblical Motifs: Origins and Transformations*. Ed. A. Altmann. Cambridge, MA: Harvard University Press, 1966, 31-63.

——— 'Waiting for the Messiah: The Spiritual Universe of the Qumran Covenanters'. In *Judaisms and Their Messiahs at the Turn of the Christian Era*. Ed. J. Neusner, W.S. Green, and E. Frerichs. Cambridge: Cambridge University Press, 1987, 111-37.

——— 'Pursuit of the Millenium: The Relation Between Religious and Social Change'. *Archives Européennes de Sociologie* 3 (1962): 125-48.

Taylor, J.E. 'A Graffito Depicting John the Baptist in Nazareth?'. *PEQ* 119 (1987): 142-48.

Taylor, T.M. 'The Beginnings of Jewish Proselyte Baptism'. *NTS* 2 (1955–56): 193-98.

Taylor, V. *The Gospel According to St Mark*. 2nd edn. 1966; repr. Grand Rapids: Baker, 1981.

Teeple, H.M. *The Mosaic Eschatological Prophet*. JBLMS 10. Philadelphia: Society of Biblical Literature, 1957.

Thackeray, H.St.J. *Josephus: The Man and the Historian*. 1929; repr. New York: Ktav, 1967.

Theissen, G. *Sociology of Early Palestinian Christianity*. Trans. J. Bowden. Philadelphia: Fortress, 1978.

Thiering, B.E. *Redating the Teacher of Righteousness*. Australian and New Zealand Studies in Theology and Religion. Sydney: Theological Explorations, 1979.

——— 'Inner and Outer Cleansing at Qumran as a Background for New Testament Baptism'. *NTS* 26 (1979–80): 266-77.

——— 'Qumran Initiation and New Testament Baptism'. *NTS* 27 (1980–81): 615-31.

——— *The Gospels and Qumran: A New Hypothesis*. Australian and New Zealand Studies in Theology and Religion. Sydney: Theological Explorations, 1981.

Thomas, J. *Le mouvement baptiste en Palestine et Syrie (150 av. J.C. - 300 ap. J.C.)*. Gembloux: Duculot, 1935.

Thyen, H. 'ΒΑΠΤΙΣΜΑ ΜΕΤΑΝΟΙΑΣ ΕΙΣ ΑΦΕΣΙΝ ΑΜΑΡΤΙΩΝ'. In *The Future of Our Religious Past: Essays in Honour of Rudolf Bultmann*. Ed. J.M. Robinson; trans. C.E. Carlston and R.P. Scharlemann. London: SCM, 1971, 131-68.

Toombs, L.E. 'Clean and Unclean'. *IDB* 1.641-48.

Torrance, T.F. 'Proselyte Baptism'. *NTS* 1 (1954–55): 150-54.

—— 'The Origins of Baptism'. *SJT* 11 (1958): 158-71.

Trilling, W. 'Die Täufertradition bei Matthaeus'. *BZ* 3 (1959): 271-89.

Tucker, G.M. 'Prophecy and the Prophetic Literature'. In *The Hebrew Bible and Its Modern Interpreters*. The Bible and Its Modern Interpreters 1. Ed. D.A. Knight and G.M. Tucker. Chico, CA: Scholars, 1985.

Tuckett, C.M. *The Revival of the Griesbach Hypothesis*. SNTSMS 44. Cambridge: Cambridge University Press, 1983.

—— *Nag Hammadi and the Gospel Tradition*. Edinburgh: T. and T. Clark, 1986.

Turner, N. 'An Alleged Semiticism'. *ExpTim* 66 (1954–55): 252-54.

Urbach, E.E. *The Sages: Their Concepts and Beliefs*. 2 vols. 2nd edn. Trans. I. Abrahams. Jerusalem: Magnes, 1979.

VanderKam, J.C. *Textual and Historical Studies in the Book of Jubilees*. HSM 14. Missoula, MT: Scholars, 1977.

—— 'Review of *Gospel* [sic] *and Qumran*'. *CBQ* 45 (1983): 512-14.

—— *Enoch and the Growth of an Apocalyptic Tradition*. CBQMS 16. Washington, DC: Catholic Biblical Association of America, 1984.

van der Woude, A.S. 'Melchisedek als himmlische Erlösergestalt in den neugefundenen eschatologischen Midraschim aus Qumran Höhle XI'. *OTS* 14 (1965): 354-73.

van Unnik, W.C. *Flavius Josephus als historischer Schriftsteller*. Franz Delitzsch Volesungen 1972. Ed. Institutum Judaicum Delitzschianum. Heidelburg: Lambert Schneider, 1978.

Varneda, P.V.I. *The Historical Method of Josephus*. ALGHJ 19. Leiden: Brill, 1986.

Verhoff, P.A. *The Books of Haggai and Malachi*. NICOT. Grand Rapids: Eerdmans, 1987.

Vermes, G. 'Baptism and Jewish Exegesis: New Light from Ancient Sources'. *NTS* 4 (1957–58): 308-19.

—— 'Essenes—Therapeutai—Qumran'. *Durham University Journal* 52 (1960): 97-115.

—— 'The Use of בר נש/בר נשא in Jewish Aramaic'. In M. Black. *An Aramaic Approach to the Gospels and Acts*. 3rd edn. Oxford: Oxford University Press, 1967, 311-30.

—— *Jesus the Jew*. Philadelphia: Fortress, 1973.

—— *The Dead Sea Scrolls: Qumran in Perspective*. London: Collins, 1977.

Vielhauer, P. 'Tracht und Speise Johannes des Täufers'. In *Aufsätze zum Neuen Testament*. TBü 31. München: n.p., 1965.

—— 'Johannes der Täufer'. 3rd edn. *RGG* 3.803-807.

Virgulin, S. 'Recent Discussion of the Title "Lamb of God" '. *Scr* 13 (1961): 74-80.

von Dobbeler, S. *Das Gericht und das Erbarmen Gottes*. BBB 70. Frankfurt am Main: Athenäum, 1988.

von Rad, G. *Old Testament Theology*. 2 vols. Trans. D.M.G. Stalker. New York: Harper and Row, 1962–65.

—— *Deuteronomy: A Commentary*. OTL. Trans. D. Barton. London: SCM, 1966.

Wacholder, B.Z. 'Review of *Teacher of Righteousness*'. *JBL* 101 (1982): 47-48.

Wallace, A.F.C. 'Revitalization Movements'. *AmerAnth* 58 (1950): 264-81.

Wallace, D.H. 'The Essenes and Temple Sacrifice'. *TZ* 13 (1957): 335-38.

Watts, J.D.W. *Isaiah 1–33*. WBC 24. Waco, TX: Word Books, 1985.

—— *Isaiah 34–66*. WBC 25. Waco, TX: Word Books, 1987.

Wcela, E.A. 'The Messiah(s) of Qumran'. *CBQ* 26 (1964): 340-49.

Webb, R.L. ' "Apocalyptic": Observations on a Slippery Term'. *JNES* 49 (1990): 115-26.

Weber, M. *The Sociology of Religion*. Trans. E. Fischoff. London: Methuen, 1963.

Weiß, K. 'Messianismus in Qumran und im Neuen Testament'. In *Qumran-Probleme*. Ed. H. Bardtke. Berlin: Akademie, 1963, 353-68.

Wellhausen, J. *Das Evangelium Lucae*. Berlin: Georg Reimer, 1904.

Wenham, G.J. *The Book of Leviticus*. NICOT. Grand Rapids: Eerdmans, 1979.

Wentling, J.L. 'A Comparison of the Elijan Motifs in the Gospels of Matthew and Mark'. In *Proceedings: Eastern Great Lakes Biblical Society*. Ed. P. Sigal. Grand Rapids: Eastern Great Lakes Biblical Society, 1982, 2.104-25.

Werblowsky, R.J.Z. 'A Note on Purification and Proselyte Baptism'. In *Christianity, Judaism and Other Greco-Roman Cults: Studies for Morton Smith at Sixty*. Ed. J. Neusner. Leiden: Brill, 1975, 3.200-205.

Wernberg-Møller, P. *The Manual of Discipline: Translated and Annotated with an Introduction*. STDJ 1. Leiden: Brill, 1957.

Westermann, C. *Isaiah 40–66: A Commentary*. OTL. Trans. D.M.G. Stalker. Philadelphia: Westminster, 1969.

—— *Praise and Lament in the Psalms*. Trans. K.R. Crim and R.N. Soulen. Atlanta: John Knox, 1981.

Whiston, W. 'Dissertation 1: The Testimonies of Josephus Concerning Jesus Christ, John the Baptist, and James the Just Vindicated'. In *The Works of Flavius Josephus*. Trans. W. Whiston. London: Allen, 1806, 4.363-80.

Whybray, R.N. *Isaiah 40–66*. NCB. London: Marshall, Morgan and Scott, 1975.

Widmer, G. 'Jean-Baptiste censuré'. *ETR* 45 (1970): 273-83.

Wieder, N. 'The Doctrine of the Two Messiahs among the Karaites'. *JJS* 6 (1955): 14-23.

Wilcox, M. 'Qumran Eschatology: Some Observations on 1QS'. *AusBR* 9 (1961): 37-42.

Williamson, G.A. *The World of Josephus*. London: Secker and Warburg, 1964.

Williamson, H.G.M. 'The Sure Mercies of David: Subjective or Objective Genitive?'. *JSS* 23 (1978): 31-49.

Wilson, B.R. *Magic and the Millenium*. London: Heinemann, 1973.

Wilson, F.M. 'The Son of Man in Jewish Apocalyptic Literature'. *StBibTh* 8 (1978): 28-51.

Wilson, R. McL. *Studies in The Gospel of Thomas*. London: Mowbray, 1960.

—— 'The Gospel of Thomas'. In *Studia Evangelica*. TU 88. Ed. F.L. Cross. Berlin: Academie, 1964, 447-59.

Wink, W. 'John the Baptist and the Gospel'. ThD dissertation, Union Theological Seminary, 1963.

—— *John the Baptist in the Gospel Tradition*. SNTSMS 7. Cambridge: Cambridge University Press, 1968.

Witherington, B. 'Jesus and the Baptist—Two of a Kind?'. In *Society of Biblical Literature 1988 Seminar Papers*. SBLSP 27. Ed. D.J. Lull. Atlanta: Scholars, 225-48.

Wolff, C. 'Zur Bedeutung Johannes des Täufers im Markusevangelium'. *TLZ* 102 (1977): 857-65.

Wolff, H.W. 'Herrschaft Jahwes und Messiasgestalt im Alten Testament'. *ZAW* 54 (1936): 168-202.

Wood, B.G. 'To Dip or Sprinkle? The Qumran Cisterns in Perspective'. *BASOR* 256 (1984): 45-60.

Wright, A. 'The Baptist's Advice to the Several Classes: Luke 3.10-14'. *ExpTim* 27 (1915–16): 408-10.

Wright, D.P. *The Disposal of Impurity: Elimination Rites in the Bible and in Hittite and Mesopotamian Literature*. SBLDS 101. Atlanta: Scholars, 1987.

Wright, G.E. 'Herod's Nabataean Neighbor'. *BA* 1 (1938): 3-4.

—— *Biblical Archaeology*. Rev. edn. Philadelphia: Westminster, 1962.

Yadin, Y. *The Temple Scroll: The Hidden Law of the Dead Sea Sect*. London: Wiedenfeld and Nicolson, 1985.

Yamauchi, E.M. 'Mandaeism'. *IDBSup* 563.

—— *Pre-Christian Gnosticism*. 2nd edn. Grand Rapids: Eerdmans, 1983.

Yates, J.E. 'The Form of Mark 1.8b'. *NTS* 4 (1957–58): 334-38.

Yoder, J.H. *The Politics of Jesus*. Grand Rapids: Eerdmans, 1972.

Ysebaert, J. *Greek Baptismal Terminology: Its Origin and Early Development*. Nijmegen: Dekker and Van de Vegt, 1962.

Zeitlin, S. 'The Halaka in the Gospels and Its Relation to the Jewish Law at the Time of Jesus'. *HUCA* 1 (1924): 357-73.

—— 'The Slavonic Josephus and Its Relation to Josippon and Hegesippus'. *JQR* 20 (1929–30): 1-50.

—— *Josephus on Jesus with Particular Reference to the Slavonic Josephus and the Hebrew Josippon*. Philadelphia: Dropsie College, 1931.

—— 'A Note on Baptism for Proselytes'. *JBL* 52 (1933): 78-79.

—— 'The Hoax of the "Slavonic Josephus" '. *JQR* 39 (1948–49): 171-80.

—— 'A Survey of Jewish Historiography: From the Biblical Period to the Sefer ha-Kabbalah with Special Emphasis on Josephus [Part 1]'. *JQR* 59 (1968–69): 171-214.

—— 'A Survey of Jewish Historiography: From the Biblical Period to the Sefer ha-Kabbalah with Special Emphasis on Josephus [Parts 2, 3]'. *JQR* 60 (1969–70): 37-68, 375-406.

Zeller, D. 'Elija und Elischa im Frühjudentum'. *BK* 41 (1986): 154-60.

Ziesler, J.A. 'The Removal of the Bridegroom: A Note on Mark 2.18-22 and Parallels'. *NTS* 19 (1972–73): 190-94.

## INDEX OF ANCIENT LITERATURE

### OLD TESTAMENT

## APOCRYPHA

NEW TESTAMENT

QUMRAN

## RABBINIC LITERATURE

## NAG HAMMADI

## NEW TESTAMENT APOCRYPHA

## OTHER CHRISTIAN AUTHORS

## OTHER ANCIENT AUTHORS

# INDEX OF MODERN AUTHORS

James, M.R. 117
Jastrow, M. 311
Jenni, E. 222
Jeremias, Joachim 53, 123-25, 127-28,
    204, 254, 307, 352
Jeremias, Jörg 222
Johnson, M.D. 121-22
Judge, E.A. 308
Kaiser, O. 256
Kaiser, W.C. 251
Käsemann, E. 20, 69, 273
Kautzsch, E. 290
Kazmierski, C.R. 176
Keck, L.E. 78
Kee, H.C. 87, 125, 234
Kelber, W.H. 88
Kirkpatrick, P.G. 88
Kittel, G. 362
Klausner, J. 229, 232-33, 254
Kleinknecht, H. 273
Klijn, A.F.J. 81, 83
Kloppenborg, J.S. 48, 50, 63, 169, 280-81
Knibb, M.A. 134, 138, 142, 147-48, 154,
    157, 237-38, 246, 249
Kobelski, P.J. 240-42
Koch, K. 99
Koester, H. 78, 81
Kraeling, C.H. 24, 131, 167, 178-80, 182,
    186, 193-94, 201, 203, 205, 215,
    270, 282, 285, 287, 304, 356-57,
    363, 368, 371-72
Krentz, E. 56
Kuhn, K.G. 138, 151, 236
Kümmel, W.G. 281-82
Kysar, R. 77, 90

Lachs, S.T. 369
Lacocque, A. 229, 240, 245
Lake, K. 187-88
Lambdin, T.O. 78
Lane, W.L. 52-53, 55, 366
Laubach, F. 184-85
Laufen, R. 48, 264-66, 270-71
Laurin, R.B. 236
Leaney, A.R.C. 64, 134, 141-43, 145,
    147-48, 156-58
Leipoldt, J. 123, 201
Lessing, G.E. 24
Levison, N. 123
Licht, J. 156
Lichtenberger, H. 36
Lieberman, S. 213

Lindars, B. 90, 267
Lindner, H. 320
Livingstone, G.H. 99
Lohmeyer, E. 48, 51, 60, 64, 70, 186-87,
    201, 205, 287
Lohse, E. 134, 147
Lord, A.B. 88
Lupieri, E.F. 24-25, 51, 54, 56, 60, 78
Luz, U. 57-58, 82, 176

MacDermot, V. 78
MacDonald, J. 334
Mackie, G.M. 295, 297
Maier, J. 134
Malchow, B.V. 251-52
Maloney, E.C. 187
Manson, T.W. 48, 272-73, 287
Manson, W. 282
Mansoor, M. 235
Marcus, R. 109, 115-16, 322
Marsh, H.G. 123, 170, 180, 183, 186,
    201, 203, 282, 365
Marshall, I.H. 63-64, 67, 174, 176-77,
    193, 264-65, 269-70, 272, 275,
    280, 282, 289, 296, 359, 362
Martyn, J.L. 287
Marxsen, W. 25, 51, 170, 362-63
Mason, R.A. 252
Mattill, A.J. 60, 64, 70
Mauser, U.W. 362
Mayes, A.D.H. 100
McArthur, H.K. 87, 90
McCown, C.C. 363
McNeile, A.H. 272, 288, 300
Mead, G.R.S. 44-45, 78
Mearns, C.L. 246
Meeks, W.A. 35
Meier, J.P. 56, 58, 60
Merklein, H. 186
Mescerskij, N.A. 43
Metzger, B.M. 74, 175
Meyer, B.F. 20, 87
Meyer, F.B. 24
Meyer, R. 313-14
Michaelis, J.D. 76
Mihelic, J.L. 295
Milgrom, J. 99, 135, 137
Milik, J.T. 117-18, 227, 241, 245-46
Miller, M.P. 241
Minear, P.S. 67
Moehring, H.R. 42, 115
Momigliano, A. 42